Laura Prisament's

Meryl Streep

Personality	Important Events	Personal life
• After her husband died she relied on work to creat a "divertion" for the grief she was in		• her first husband Cazel was a small time actress like her • he died in March of 1978 of cancer • She then got re-maried september 1978

Contents

Articles

References

Article Licenses

Meryl Streep

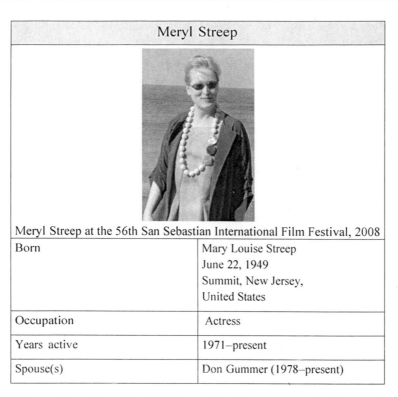

Meryl Streep	
Meryl Streep at the 56th San Sebastian International Film Festival, 2008	
Born	Mary Louise Streep June 22, 1949 Summit, New Jersey, United States
Occupation	Actress
Years active	1971–present
Spouse(s)	Don Gummer (1978–present)

Mary Louise "Meryl" Streep (born June 22, 1949) is an American actress who has worked in theatre, television and film. She is widely regarded as one of the most talented and respected movie actors both of her generation and of the present time.[1] [2] [3]

Streep made her professional stage debut in 1971's *The Playboy of Seville*, before her screen debut in the television movie *The Deadliest Season* in 1977. In that same year, she made her film debut with *Julia*. Both critical and commercial success came quickly with roles in *The Deer Hunter* (1978) and *Kramer vs. Kramer* (1979), the former giving Streep her first Oscar nomination and the latter her first win. She later won an Academy Award for Best Actress for her performance in *Sophie's Choice* (1982).

Streep has received 16 Academy Award nominations, winning two, and 25 Golden Globe nominations, winning seven, more nominations than any other actor in the history of either award. Her work has also earned her two Emmy Awards, two Screen Actors Guild Awards, a Cannes Film Festival award, four New York Film Critics Circle Awards, five Grammy Award nominations, a BAFTA award, an Australian Film Institute Award and a Tony Award nomination, amongst others. She was awarded the American Film Institute's Lifetime Achievement Award in 2004.

Early life and background

Streep was born Mary Louise Streep in Summit, New Jersey, the daughter of Mary Wolf (née Wilkinson), a commercial artist and former art editor, and Harry William Streep, Jr., a pharmaceutical executive.[4] [5] [6] She has two brothers, Dana and Harry.[7] Streep is of German, Swiss and English ancestry.[8] [9] Her heritage can be traced back ten generations to Loffenau, from where her second great-grandfather, Gottfried Streeb, emigrated to the United States, and where one of her ancestors served as mayor. Another line of the Streep family was from Giswil, a small town in Switzerland. Her maternal ancestry can be traced to Pennsylvania and Rhode Island. Her eighth great-grandfather, Lawrence Wilkinson, was one of the first Europeans to settle Rhode Island. Streep is also a distant relative of William Penn, the founder of Pennsylvania, and records show her family were among the first purchasers of land in Pennsylvania.[8] [10]

She was raised a Presbyterian,[11] [12] [13] and grew up in Bernardsville, New Jersey, where she attended Bernards High School.[14] She received her B.A., *cum laude* in Drama at Vassar College in 1971 (where she briefly received instruction from Jean Arthur), but also enrolled as an exchange student at Dartmouth College for a semester before it became coeducational. She subsequently earned an M.F.A. from Yale School of Drama. While at Yale, she played a variety of roles onstage,[15] from the glamorous Helena in A Midsummer Night's Dream to an eighty-year old woman in a wheelchair in a comedy written by then-unknown playwrights Christopher Durang and Albert Innaurato.[16] [17] "It was immediately apparent," said then-dean Robert Brustein, "that she was destined for greatness."[18]

Early career

Streep performed in several theater productions in New York after graduating from Yale School of Drama, including the New York Shakespeare Festival productions of *Henry V*, *The Taming of the Shrew* with Raúl Juliá, and *Measure for Measure* opposite Sam Waterston and John Cazale, who became her fiancé. She starred on Broadway in the Brecht/Weill musical *Happy End*, and won an Obie for her performance in the all-sung off-Broadway production of *Alice at the Palace*.

Streep began auditioning for film roles, and later recalled an unsuccessful audition for Dino De Laurentiis for the leading role in *King Kong*. De Laurentiis commented to his son in Italian, "She's ugly. Why did you bring me this thing?" and was shocked when Streep replied in fluent Italian.[19] Streep's first feature film was *Julia* (1977), in which she played a small but pivotal role during a flashback scene. Streep was living in New York City with her fiancé, Cazale, who had been diagnosed with bone cancer. He was cast in *The Deer Hunter* (1978), and Streep was delighted to secure a small role because it allowed her to remain with Cazale for the duration of filming. She was not specifically interested in the part, commenting, "They needed a girl between the two guys and I was it."[20]

She played a leading role in the television miniseries *Holocaust* (1978) as an Aryan woman married to a Jewish artist in Nazi era Germany. She later explained that she had considered the material to be "unrelentingly noble",[20] and had taken the role only because she had needed money.[21] Streep travelled to Germany and Austria for filming while Cazale remained in New York. Upon her return, Streep found that Cazale's illness had progressed, and she nursed him until his death on March 12, 1978. She spoke of her grief and her hope that work would provide a diversion; she accepted a role in *The Seduction of Joe Tynan* (1979) with Alan Alda, later commenting that she played it on "automatic pilot",[20] and performed the role of Kate in *The Taming of the Shrew* for Shakespeare in the Park.[22] With an estimated audience of 109 million, *Holocaust* brought a degree of public recognition to Streep, who was described in August 1978 as "on the verge of national visibility".[21] She won the Primetime Emmy Award for Outstanding Lead Actress – Miniseries or a Movie for her performance.

The Deer Hunter (1978) was released a month later, and Streep was nominated for the Academy Award for Best Supporting Actress for her performance.

Streep played a supporting role in *Manhattan* (1979) for Woody Allen, later stating that she had not seen a complete script and was given only the six pages of her own scenes,[23] and that she had not been permitted to improvise a word of her dialogue.[24] Asked to comment on the script for *Kramer vs. Kramer* (1979), in a meeting with the producer Stan Jaffee, director Robert Benton and star Dustin Hoffman, Streep insisted that the female character was not representative of many real women who faced marriage breakdown and child custody battles, and was written as "too evil".[20] Jaffee, Benton and Hoffman agreed with Streep, and the script was revised.[20] In preparing for the part, Streep spoke to her own mother about her life as a mother and housewife with a career,[25] and frequented the Upper East Side neighborhood in which the film was set.[20] Benton allowed Streep to write her dialogue in two of her key scenes, despite some objection from Hoffman.[26] Jaffee and Hoffman later spoke of Streep's tirelessness, with Hoffman commenting, "She's extraordinarily hardworking, to the extent that she's obsessive. I think that she thinks about nothing else but what she's doing."[27]

Streep drew critical acclaim for her performance in each of her three films released in 1979: the romantic comedy *Manhattan*, the political drama, *The Seduction of Joe Tynan* and the family drama, *Kramer vs. Kramer*. She was awarded the Los Angeles Film Critics Association Award for Best Supporting Actress, National Board of Review Award for Best Supporting Actress and National Society of Film Critics Award for Best Supporting Actress for her collective work in the three films. Among the awards won for *Kramer vs. Kramer* were the Academy Award and Golden Globe Award for Best Supporting Actress.

1980s

After prominent supporting roles in two of the 1970s most successful films, the consecutive winners of the Academy Award for Best Picture, *The Deer Hunter* and *Kramer vs. Kramer*, and praise for her versatility in several supporting roles, Streep progressed to leading roles. Her first was *The French Lieutenant's Woman* (1981). A story within a story drama, the film paired Streep with Jeremy Irons as contemporary actors, telling their modern story as well as the Victorian era drama they were performing. A *New York Magazine* article commented that while many female stars of the past had cultivated a singular identity in their films, Streep was a "chameleon", willing to play any type of role.[28] Streep was awarded a BAFTA Award for Best Actress in a Leading Role for her work.

Streep at the Academy Awards, 1988

Her next film, the psychological thriller, *Still of the Night* (1982) reunited her with Robert Benton, the director of *Kramer vs. Kramer*, and co-starred Roy Scheider and Jessica Tandy. Vincent Canby, writing for the *New York Times* noted that the film was an homage to the works of Alfred Hitchcock, but that one of its main weaknesses was a lack of chemistry between Streep and Scheider, concluding that Streep "is stunning, but she's not on screen anywhere near long enough".[29]

As the Polish holocaust survivor in *Sophie's Choice* (1982), Streep's emotional dramatic performance and her apparent mastery of a Polish accent drew praise. William Styron wrote the novel with Ursula Andress in mind for the part of Sophie, but Streep was very determined to get the role. After she obtained a pirated copy of the script, she went to Alan J. Pakula and threw herself on the ground begging him to give her the part. Streep filmed the "choice" scene in one take and refused to do it again, as she found shooting the scene extremely painful and emotionally draining.[30] Among several notable acting awards, Streep won the Academy Award for Best Actress for her performance.

She followed this success with a biographical film, *Silkwood* (1983), in which she played her first real-life character, the union activist Karen Silkwood. She discussed her preparation for the role in an interview with Roger Ebert and said that she had met with people close to Silkwood to learn more about her, and in doing so realized that each person saw a different aspect of Silkwood.[31] Streep concentrated on the events of Silkwood's life and concluded, "I didn't try to turn myself into Karen. I just tried to look at what she did. I put together every piece of information I could find about her... What I finally did was look at the events in her life, and try to understand her from the inside."[31]

Her next films were a romantic comedy, *Falling in Love* (1984) opposite Robert De Niro, and a British drama, *Plenty* (1985). Roger Ebert said of Streep's performance in *Plenty* that she conveyed "great subtlety; it is hard to play an unbalanced, neurotic, self-destructive woman, and do it with such gentleness and charm... Streep creates a whole character around a woman who could have simply been a catalogue of symptoms."[32]

Out of Africa (1985) starred Streep as the Danish writer Karen Blixen and co-starred Robert Redford. A significant critical success, the film received a 63% "fresh" rating from Rotten Tomatoes.[33] Streep co-starred with Jack Nicholson in her next two films, the dramas *Heartburn* (1986) and *Ironweed* (1987), in which she sang onscreen for the first time since the television movie, *Secret Service*, in 1977. In *A Cry in the Dark* (1988), she played the biographical role of Lindy Chamberlain, an Australian woman who had been convicted of the murder of her infant daughter in which Chamberlain claimed her baby had been taken by a dingo. Filmed in Australia, Streep won the Australian Film Institute Award for Best Actress in a Leading Role, a Best Actress at the Cannes Film Festival, the New York Film Critics Circle Award for Best Actress and was nominated for several other awards for her portrayal of Chamberlain.

In *She-Devil* (1989), Streep played her first comedic film role, opposite Roseanne Barr. Richard Corliss, writing for *Time*, commented that Streep was the "one reason" to see the film and observed that it marked a departure from the type of role for which she had been known, saying, "Surprise! Inside the Greer Garson roles Streep usually plays, a vixenish Carole Lombard is screaming to be cut loose."[34]

1990s and 2000s

From 1984 to 1990, Streep won six People's Choice Awards for Favorite Motion Picture Actress and, in 1990, was named World Favorite.

In the 1990s, Streep took a greater variety of roles, including a drug addicted movie actress in a screen adaptation of Carrie Fisher's novel *Postcards from the Edge*, with Dennis Quaid and Shirley MacLaine. Streep and Goldie Hawn had established a friendship and were interested in making a film together. After considering various projects, they decided upon *Thelma and Louise*, until Streep's pregnancy coincided with the filming schedule, and the producers decided to proceed with Susan Sarandon and Geena Davis.[19] They subsequently filmed the farcical black comedy, *Death Becomes Her*, with Bruce Willis as their co-star. *Time*'s Richard Corliss wrote approvingly of Streep's "wicked-witch routine" but dismissed the film as "*She-Devil* with a make-over".[35]

Biographer Karen Hollinger describes this period as a downturn in the popularity of Streep's films, which reached its nadir with the failure of *Death Becomes Her*, attributing this partly to a critical perception that her comedies had been an attempt to convey a lighter image following several serious but commercially unsuccessful dramas, and more significantly to the lack of options available to an actress in her forties.[36] Streep commented that she had limited her options by her preference to work in Los Angeles, close to her family,[36] a situation that she had anticipated in a 1981 interview when she commented, "By the time an actress hits her mid-forties, no one's interested in her anymore. And if you want to fit a couple of babies into that schedule as well, you've got to pick your parts with great care."[28]

Streep appeared with Glenn Close in the movie version of Isabel Allende's *The House of the Spirits*, the screen adaptation of *The Bridges of Madison County* with Clint Eastwood, *The River Wild*, *Marvin's Room* (with Diane Keaton and Leonardo DiCaprio), *One True Thing*, and *Music of the Heart*, in a role that required her to learn to play the violin.

Streep is adept with foreign accents and some of her best known roles have called for them. In *The Bridges of Madison County*, she played a woman from Bari, Italy, in *Sophie's Choice* she adopted a Polish accent, and in *Out of Africa* she spoke in a Danish accent.

In 2001, Streep voiced the Blue Fairy in Steven Spielberg's *A.I. Artificial Intelligence*. In 2002, Meryl Streep costarred with Nicolas Cage in Spike Jonze's *Adaptation.* as real-life author Susan Orlean, for which she won the Golden Globe Award for Best Supporting Actress, and with Nicole Kidman and Julianne Moore in *The Hours*. She also appeared with Al Pacino and Emma Thompson in the HBO adaptation of Tony Kushner's six-hour play, *Angels in America*, in which she had four roles. She received her second Emmy Award for *Angels in America*, which reunited her with director Mike Nichols (who had previously directed her in Silkwood, Heartburn, and Postcards from the Edge). Meryl Streep also played Aunt Josephine in *Lemony Snicket's A Series of Unfortunate Events* with Jim Carrey.

In addition, she appeared in Jonathan Demme's remake of *The Manchurian Candidate*, costarring Denzel Washington, in which she played a role first performed by Angela Lansbury. Since 2002, Streep has hosted the annual event Poetry & the Creative Mind, a benefit in support of National Poetry Month and a program of the Academy of American Poets. Streep co-hosted the annual Nobel Peace Prize Concert with Liam Neeson in Oslo, Norway, in 2001.

Streep in 2004

In 2004, Streep was awarded the AFI Life Achievement Award by the Board of Directors of the American Film Institute, which honors an individual for a lifetime contribution to enriching American culture through motion pictures and television.

Streep's more recent film releases are *Prime* (2005); the Robert Altman film *A Prairie Home Companion*, with Lindsay Lohan and Lily Tomlin; and the box office success *The Devil Wears Prada*, with Anne Hathaway, which earned Streep the 2007 Golden Globe Award for Best Actress in a Musical or Comedy and an Academy Award nomination.

In 2008, she appeared as Donna in the film version of the ABBA musical *Mamma Mia!*, For this role she won the award of Best Female Performance at the National Movie Awards (UK), and received a Golden Globe nomination for Best Actress in a Comedy/Musical. She played Sister Aloysius in the 2008 film adaptation of John Patrick Shanley's *Doubt*. She received both an Academy Award nomination for Best Actress and a Golden Globe nomination for Best Actress in a Drama for that film. She also shared the Broadcast Film Critics Association Award for Best Actress with Anne Hathaway for the role, and won a Screen Actors Guild Award for Outstanding Performance by a Female Actor in a Leading Role.[37]

In 2009, she starred in *Julie & Julia*, in which she played the late Julia Child. For this role she won the Golden Globe Award for Best Actress – Motion Picture Musical or Comedy and also shared the Broadcast Film Critics Association Award for Best Actress with Sandra Bullock. Streep also received a nomination for the Academy Award for Best Actress for this performance. She then starred in Nancy Meyers' romantic comedy *It's Complicated*, with Alec Baldwin and Steve Martin.[38] She also received nomination for the Golden Globe Award for Best Actress – Motion Picture Musical or Comedy for this film.[39] Streep also lent her voice to Mrs. Felicity Fox in the stop-motion film *Fantastic Mr. Fox*.

In July 2010, it was announced that Streep will star in an upcoming comedy entitle *Mommy & Me* alongside Tina Fey who will play her daughter. The film is being directed by Stanley Tucci.[40]

Theatre

In New York City, she appeared in the 1976 Broadway double bill of Tennessee Williams' *27 Wagons Full of Cotton* and Arthur Miller's *A Memory of Two Mondays*. For the former, she received a Tony Award nomination for Best Featured Actress in a Play. Her other early Broadway credits include Anton Chekhov's *The Cherry Orchard* and the Bertolt Brecht-Kurt Weill musical *Happy End* in which she originally appeared off-Broadway at the Chelsea Theater Center. She received Drama Desk Award nominations for both productions. Once Streep's film career flourished, she took a long break from stage acting.

In July 2001, Streep returned to the stage for the first time in more than twenty years, playing Arkadina in the Public Theater's revival of Anton Chekhov's *The Seagull*. The staging, directed by Mike Nichols, also featured Kevin Kline, Natalie Portman, Philip Seymour Hoffman, Christopher Walken, Marcia Gay Harden, and John Goodman.

In August and September 2006, she starred onstage at The Public Theater's production of *Mother Courage and Her Children* at the Delacorte Theatre in Central Park.[41] The Public Theater production was a new translation by playwright Tony Kushner (*Angels in America*), with songs in the Weill/Brecht style written by composer Jeanine

Tesori (*Caroline, or Change*); veteran director George C. Wolfe was at the helm. Streep starred alongside Kevin Kline and Austin Pendleton in this three-and-a-half-hour play in which she sang and appeared in almost every scene.

Music

After appearing in *Mamma Mia!*, Streep's rendition of the song "*Mamma Mia*" rose to popularity in the Portuguese music charts, where it has so far peaked at #8.[42]

At the 35th People's Choice Awards, her version of *Mamma Mia* won an award for "Favorite Song From A Soundtrack".[43] In 2008, Streep was nominated for a Grammy Award (her fifth nomination) for her work on the *Mamma Mia!* soundtrack.

Streep (fourth from left) at the premiere of *Mamma Mia!*

Personal life

Meryl Streep was in a relationship with actor John Cazale until his death in March of 1978.[44] Streep then married sculptor Don Gummer on September 30, 1978.[45] They have four children: Louisa Jacobson Gummer (born June 1991), Grace Jane, Henry Wolfe, and Mamie Gummer. Both Grace and Mamie are actresses.[5]

When asked if religion plays a part in her life in an interview in 2009, Meryl Streep replied, "I follow no doctrine. I don't belong to a church or a temple or a synagogue or an ashram."[46]

Awards

Streep holds the record for the most Academy Award nominations of any actor, having been nominated 16 times since her first nomination in 1979 for *The Deer Hunter* (13 for Best Actress and 3 for Best Supporting Actress).

Meryl Streep is the most nominated performer for a Golden Globe Award (she has 25 nominations as of 2009) and has won the most Golden Globes overall since her win for *Julie & Julia* in 2010. Streep received a star on the Hollywood Walk of Fame in 1998.

In 2003, she was awarded an honorary César Award by the French *Académie des Arts et Techniques du Cinéma*. In 2004 at the Moscow International Film Festival, Meryl Streep was honored with the Stanislavsky Award for the outstanding achievement in the career of acting and devotion to the principles of Stanislavsky's school.

In 2004, Streep received the AFI Life Achievement Award.

May 27, 2004 was proclaimed "Meryl Streep Day" by Manhattan Borough President C. Virginia Fields.

Streep receiving her honorary degree from Harvard University on May 27, 2010

In 2009, she was awarded an honorary Doctorate of Fine Arts by Princeton University.[47]

In 2010, she was elected to the American Academy of Arts and Letters,[48] and awarded an honorary Doctor of Arts degree by Harvard University.[49]

Work

Filmography

Year	Film	Role	Notes
1977	*Julia*	Anne Marie	
1978	*The Deer Hunter*	Linda	National Society of Film Critics Award for Best Supporting Actress Nominated—Academy Award for Best Supporting Actress Nominated—BAFTA Award for Best Actress in a Leading Role Nominated—Golden Globe Award for Best Supporting Actress - Motion Picture
1979	*Manhattan*	Jill	Los Angeles Film Critics Association Award for Best Supporting Actress (also for *The Seduction of Joe Tynan* and *Kramer vs. Kramer*) National Board of Review Award for Best Supporting Actress (also for *The Seduction of Joe Tynan* and *Kramer vs. Kramer*) National Society of Film Critics Award for Best Supporting Actress (also for *The Seduction of Joe Tynan* and *Kramer vs. Kramer*) Nominated—BAFTA Award for Best Actress in a Supporting Role
	The Seduction of Joe Tynan	Karen Traynor	Los Angeles Film Critics Association Award for Best Supporting Actress (also for *Manhattan* and *Kramer vs. Kramer*) National Board of Review Award for Best Supporting Actress (also for *Manhattan* and *Kramer vs. Kramer*) National Society of Film Critics Award for Best Supporting Actress (also for *Manhattan* and *Kramer vs. Kramer*) New York Film Critics Circle Award for Best Supporting Actress (also for *Kramer vs. Kramer*)
	Kramer vs. Kramer	Joanna Kramer	Academy Award for Best Supporting Actress Golden Globe Award for Best Supporting Actress - Motion Picture Kansas City Film Critics Award for Best Supporting Actress Los Angeles Film Critics Association Award for Best Supporting Actress (also for *The Seduction of Joe Tynan* and *Manhattan*) National Board of Review Award for Best Supporting Actress (also for *The Seduction of Joe Tynan* and *Manhattan*) National Society of Film Critics Award for Best Supporting Actress (also for *The Seduction of Joe Tynan* and *Manhattan*) New York Film Critics Circle Award for Best Supporting Actress (also for *The Seduction of Joe Tynan*) Nominated—BAFTA Award for Best Actress in a Leading Role
1981	*The French Lieutenant's Woman*	Sarah/Anna	BAFTA Award for Best Actress in a Leading Role Golden Globe Award for Best Actress - Motion Picture Drama Los Angeles Film Critics Association Award for Best Actress Nominated—Academy Award for Best Actress
1982	*Still of the Night*	Brooke Reynolds	
	Sophie's Choice	Sophie Zawistowski	Academy Award for Best Actress Boston Society of Film Critics Award for Best Actress Golden Globe Award for Best Actress - Motion Picture Drama Kansas City Film Critics Award for Best Actress (shared with Julie Andrews for *Victor Victoria*) Los Angeles Film Critics Association Award for Best Actress National Board of Review Award for Best Actress National Society of Film Critics Award for Best Actress New York Film Critics Circle Award for Best Actress Nominated—BAFTA Award for Best Actress in a Leading Role

1983	Silkwood	Karen Silkwood	Kansas City Film Critics Award for Best Actress Nominated—Academy Award for Best Actress Nominated—BAFTA Award for Best Actress in a Leading Role Nominated—Golden Globe Award for Best Actress - Motion Picture Drama
1984	Falling in Love	Molly Gilmore	David di Donatello Award for Best Foreign Actress
1985	Plenty	Susan Traherne	
	Out of Africa	Karen Blixen	David di Donatello Award for Best Foreign Actress Kansas City Film Critics Award for Best Actress Los Angeles Film Critics Association Award for Best Actress Nominated—Academy Award for Best Actress Nominated—BAFTA Award for Best Actress in a Leading Role Nominated—Golden Globe Award for Best Actress - Motion Picture Drama
1986	Heartburn	Rachel Samstat	Valladolid International Film Festival Best Actress
1987	Ironweed	Helen Archer	Nominated—Academy Award for Best Actress
1988	A Cry in the Dark	Lindy Chamberlain	Australian Film Institute Award for Best Actress in a Leading Role Best Actress Award (Cannes Film Festival) New York Film Critics Circle Award for Best Actress Nominated—Academy Award for Best Actress Nominated—Golden Globe Award for Best Actress - Motion Picture Drama
1989	She-Devil	Mary Fisher	Nominated—Golden Globe Award for Best Actress - Motion Picture Musical or Comedy
1990	Postcards from the Edge	Suzanne Vale	American Comedy Award for Funniest Lead Actress in a Motion Picture NominatedAcademy Award for Best Actress Nominated—Golden Globe Award for Best Actress - Motion Picture Musical or Comedy
1991	Defending Your Life	Julia	Nominated—Saturn Award for Best Actress
1992	Death Becomes Her	Madeline Ashton	Nominated—Golden Globe Award for Best Actress - Motion Picture Musical or Comedy
1993	The House of the Spirits	Clara del Valle Trueba	
1994	The River Wild	Gail Hartman	Nominated—Golden Globe Award for Best Actress - Motion Picture Drama Nominated—Screen Actors Guild Award for Outstanding Performance by a Female Actor in a Leading Role
1995	The Bridges of Madison County	Francesca Johnson	Nominated—Academy Award for Best Actress Nominated—Chicago Film Critics Association Award for Best Actress Nominated—Golden Globe Award for Best Actress - Motion Picture Drama Nominated—Screen Actors Guild Award for Outstanding Performance by a Female Actor in a Leading Role
1996	Before and After	Dr. Carolyn Ryan	
	Marvin's Room	Lee	Nominated—Chlotrudis Award for Best Supporting Actress Nominated—Golden Globe Award for Best Actress - Motion Picture Drama Nominated—Screen Actors Guild Award for Outstanding Performance by a Cast in a Motion Picture
1998	Dancing at Lughnasa	Kate 'Kit' Mundy	Nominated—Irish Film and Television Awards — Best Actor in a Female Role
	One True Thing	Kate Gulden	Nominated—Academy Award for Best Actress Nominated—Golden Globe Award for Best Actress - Motion Picture Drama Nominated—Satellite Award for Best Actress - Motion Picture Drama Nominated—Screen Actors Guild Award for Outstanding Performance by a Female Actor in a Leading Role

1999	*Chrysanthemum*	Narrator	
	Music of the Heart	Roberta Guaspari	Nominated—Academy Award for Best Actress Nominated—Golden Globe Award for Best Actress - Motion Picture Drama Nominated—Screen Actors Guild Award for Outstanding Performance by a Female Actor in a Leading Role
2001	*A.I. Artificial Intelligence*	Blue Fairy	(voice cameo)
2002	*Adaptation.*	Susan Orlean	Chicago Film Critics Association Award for Best Supporting Actress Florida Film Critics Circle Award for Best Supporting Actress Golden Globe Award for Best Supporting Actress - Motion Picture Southeastern Film Critics Association Award for Best Supporting Actress Nominated—Academy Award for Best Supporting Actress Nominated— BAFTA Award for Best Actress in a Supporting Role Nominated— Broadcast Film Critics Association Award for Best Supporting Actress Nominated—London Film Critics Circle Film Award for Actress of the Year Nominated—Online Film Critics Society Award for Best Supporting Actress Nominated—Phoenix Film Critics Society Award for Best Supporting Actress Nominated—Phoenix Film Critics Society Award for Best Cast Nominated— Satellite Award for Best Supporting Actress - Motion Picture Nominated— Screen Actors Guild Award for Outstanding Performance by a Cast in a Motion Picture
	The Hours	Clarissa Vaughan	Silver Bear for Best Actress (shared with Julianne Moore and Nicole Kidman) Nominated—BAFTA Award for Best Actress in a Leading Role Nominated— Golden Globe Award for Best Actress - Motion Picture Drama Nominated—Las Vegas Film Critics Society Award for Best Supporting Actress Nominated— Phoenix Film Critics Society Award for Best Cast Nominated—Satellite Award for Best Actress - Motion Picture Drama Nominated—Screen Actors Guild Award for Outstanding Performance by a Cast in a Motion Picture
2003	*Stuck on You*	Herself	
2004	*The Manchurian Candidate*	Eleanor Shaw	Nominated—BAFTA Award for Best Actress in a Supporting Role Nominated—Golden Globe Award for Best Supporting Actress - Motion Picture Nominated—Saturn Award for Best Actress
	Lemony Snicket's A Series of Unfortunate Events	Aunt Josephine	
2005	*Prime*	Lisa Metzger, therapist	

2006	*A Prairie Home Companion*	Yolanda Johnson	National Society of Film Critics Award for Best Supporting Actress (also for *The Devil Wears Prada*) Nominated—Gotham Awards – Best Ensemble Cast
	"The Music of Regret"	The Woman	(short musical)
	The Devil Wears Prada	Miranda Priestly, editor-in-chief	Golden Globe Award for Best Actress - Motion Picture Musical or Comedy North Texas Film Critics Award for Best Actress London Film Critics Circle Film Award for Actress of the Year National Society of Film Critics Award for Best Supporting Actress (also for *A Prairie Home Companion*) Satellite Award for Best Actress - Motion Picture Musical or Comedy Nominated—Academy Award for Best Actress Nominated—BAFTA Award for Best Actress in a Leading Role Nominated—Broadcast Film Critics Association Award for Best Actress Nominated—Chicago Film Critics Association Award for Best Actress Nominated—Online Film Critics Society Award for Best Actress Nominated—Screen Actors Guild Award for Outstanding Performance by a Female Actor in a Leading Role Nominated—MTV Movie Award for Best Villain
	The Ant Bully	Queen Ant	(voice)
2007	*Dark Matter*	Joanna Silver	
	Evening	Lila Wittenborn Ross	
	Rendition	Corrine Whitman, CIA official	
	Lions for Lambs	Janine Roth	
2008	*Mamma Mia!*	Donna Sheridan	Irish Film and Television Award for Best International Actress – People's Choice Rembrandt Award (NL) – Best International Actress National Movie Award (UK) — Best Female Performance Nominated—Golden Globe Award for Best Actress - Motion Picture Musical or Comedy Nominated—Satellite Award for Best Actress - Motion Picture Musical or Comedy
	Doubt	Sister Aloysius Beauvier	Broadcast Film Critics Association Award for Best Actress(tied with Anne Hathway for *Rachel Getting Married*) Iowa Film Critics Award for Best Actress Kansas City Film Critics Circle Award for Best Actress North Texas Film Critics Award for Best Actress Phoenix Film Critics Society Award for Best Actress Screen Actors Guild Award for Outstanding Performance by a Female Actor in a Leading Role Washington D.C. Area Film Critics Association Award for Best Actress Nominated—Academy Award for Best Actress Nominated—BAFTA Award for Best Actress in a Leading Role Nominated—Chicago Film Critics Association Award for Best Actress Nominated—Golden Globe Award for Best Actress - Motion Picture Drama Nominated—London Film Critics Circle Film Award for Actress of the Year Nominated—Satellite Award for Best Actress - Motion Picture Drama Nominated—Screen Actors Guild Award for Outstanding Performance by a Cast in a Motion Picture

2009	*Julie & Julia*	Julia Child	Boston Society of Film Critics Award for Best Actress
			North Texas Film Critics Award for Best Actress
			Golden Globe Award for Best Actress - Motion Picture Musical or Comedy
			New York Film Critics Online
			New York Film Critics Circle Award for Best Actress(also for *The Fantastic Mr. Fox*)
			Phoenix Film Critics Society Award for Best Actress
			San Francisco Film Critics Circle Award for Best Actress
			Southeastern Film Critics Association Award for Best Actress
			Oklahoma Film Critics Circle Award for Best Actress
			Satellite Award for Best Actress - Motion Picture Musical or Comedy
			Kansas City Film Critics Circle Award for Best Actress
			Broadcast Film Critics Association Award for Best Actress ((tied with Sandra Bullock))
			Nominated—Academy Award for Best Actress Nominated—Alliance of Woman Journalists Award for Best Actress Nominated—BAFTA Award for Best Actress in a Leading Role Nominated—Detroit Film Critics Society Award for Best Actress Nominated—Screen Actors Guild Award for Outstanding Performance by a Female Actor in a Leading Role Nominated—San Diego Film Critics Society Award for Best Actress Nominated—Houston Film Critics Society Award for Best Actress Nominated—St Louis Gateway Film Critics Association Award for Best Actress Nominated—Toronto Film Critics Association Award for Best Actress Nominated—Washington D.C. Area Film Critics Association for Best Actress
	Fantastic Mr. Fox	Mrs. Fox[50]	(voice) New York Film Critics Circle Award for Best Actress (also for *Julie & Julia*)
	It's Complicated	Jane Adler	Irish Film and Television Award for Best International Actress – People's Choice National Board of Review Award for Best Cast Nominated—Golden Globe Award for Best Actress - Motion Picture Musical or Comedy
2010	*Mommy and Me*		
2011	*The Iron Lady*	Margaret Thatcher	
	Great Hope Springs		

Television

Year	Title	Role	Notes		Year	Title	Role	Notes
			1976 (Uncommon Women and Others) (Leilah)		1978	*Holocaust*	Inga Helms Weiss	Primetime Emmy Award for Outstanding Lead Actress - Miniseries or a Movie
			1977 (The Deadliest Season) (Sharon Miller)					
1994	*The Simpsons*	Jessica Lovejoy	Episode: "Bart's Girlfriend"					
1999	*King of the Hill*	Aunt Esme Dauterive	Episode: "A Beer Can Named Desire"					

1997	...First Do No Harm	Lori Reimuller	Nominated—Emmy Award for Outstanding Lead Actress in a Television Movie Nominated—Golden Globe Award for Best Actress in a Television Film Nominated—Satellite Award for Best Actress in a Television Film				
2003	Angels in America	Ethel Rosenberg The Rabbi Hannah Pitt Angel Australia	Emmy Award for Outstanding Lead Actress in a Miniseries Golden Globe Award for Best Actress in a Miniseries Gracie Allen Award for Outstanding Female Lead in a Drama Special Satellite Award for Best Actress in a Miniseries Screen Actors Guild Award for Outstanding Female Actor in a Miniseries				

Stage

Year	Production	Role	Notes
1975	Trelawny of the Wells	Miss Imogen Parrott	
1976	27 Wagons Full of Cotton	Flora Meighan	Theatre World Award – Debut performance, Broadway/Off-Broadway Nominated—Drama Desk Award for Outstanding Actress in a Play Nominated—Tony Award for Best Performance by a Featured Actress in a Play
	A Memory of Two Mondays	Patricia	
	Secret Service	Edith Varney	
	Henry V	Katherine	
	Measure for Measure	Isabella	
1977	Happy End	Lieutenant Lillian Holiday	
	The Cherry Orchard	Dunyasha	
1978	Alice at the Palace	Alice	
	The Taming of the Shrew	Kate	
1979	Taken in Marriage	Andrea	
1980–81	Alice at the Palace	Alice	
2001	The Seagull	Irina Nikolayevna	Nominated—Drama Desk Award for Outstanding Actress in a Play
2006	Mother Courage and Her Children	Mother Courage	Drama League Award — Distinguished Performance Award Nominated—Drama Desk Award for Outstanding Actress in a Play

Bibliography

- Napoleon, Davi. *Chelsea on the Edge: The Adventures of an American Theater.* Includes discussion of Streep's performance in Robert Kalfin's production of *Happy End* at the Chelsea Theater and on Broadway. Iowa State University Press. ISBN-0-8138-1713-7, 1991.
- *Finding Herself: The Prime of Meryl Streep* [51] by Molly Haskell, *Film Comment*, May/June 2008.
- Hollinger, Karen (2006). *The Actress: Hollywood Acting and the Female Star* [52]. Routledge. ISBN 0415977924.

External links

- Meryl Streep [53] at the Internet Movie Database
- Meryl Streep [54] at the Internet Broadway Database
- Meryl Streep [55] at the Internet Off-Broadway Database
- Meryl Streep [56] at the TCM Movie Database
- Merylstreeponline.net [57]- official website
- www.streepinstyle.info [58] - Polish website
- Meryl Streep at BAFTA [59] 40 minute webcast, January 2009

References

[1] Santas, Constantine (2002). *Responding to Film*. Rowman & Littlefield. p. 187. ISBN 0830415807.

[2] Hollinger, Karen (2006). *The Actress: Hollywood Acting and the Female Star*. CRS Press. pp. 94–95. ISBN 0415977924.

[3] *The Middle East*. Library Information and Research Service. 2005. p. 204.

[4] Robert Battle. "Meryl Streep" (http://freepages.genealogy.rootsweb.ancestry.com/~battle/celeb/streep.htm).Ancestry.com. . Retrieved 2009-01-16.

[5] "Meryl Streep Biography (1949–)" (http://www.filmreference.com/film/65/Meryl-Streep.html). Film Reference.com. . Retrieved 2009-01-16.

[6] ASSOCIATED PRESS (2001-10-03). "Artist Mary W. Streep , mother of actress Meryl, dies at 86" (http://pqasb.pqarchiver.com/ newsday/access/82788043.html?dids=82788043:82788043&FMT=ABS&FMTS=ABS:FT&type=current&date=Oct+03,+2001& author=THE+ASSOCIATED+PRESS&pub=Newsday+(Combined+editions)&desc=OBITUARIES+/+Mary+Wilkinson+Streep,+ Mother+of+the+Actress&pqatl=google). The Star-Ledger. . Retrieved 2009-12-16.

[7] "Meryl Streep Biography" (http://movies.yahoo.com/movie/contributor/1800018835/bio). Yahoo! Movies. .

[8] "Meryl Streep" (http://www.pbs.org/wnet/facesofamerica/profiles/meryl-streep/70/). Faces of America. 2010. . Retrieved 2010-02-05.

[9] McKenzie, Joi-Marie (2010-02-04). "Henry Louis Gates Says He Broke Meryl Streep's Heart" (http://www.nbcwashington.com/blogs/ niteside/Henry-Louis-Gates-Explores-Immigrant-Origins-of-Famous-Americans-83509992.html). Niteside. . Retrieved 2010-02-04.

[10] "Faces of America: Meryl Streep" (http://www.pbs.org/wnet/facesofamerica/profiles/meryl-streep/70/),PBS, *Faces of America* series, with Professor Henry Louis Gates, Jr., 2010.

[11] " Meryl Streep (http://www.imdb.com/title/tt0611276/)". *Inside the Actors Studio*. Bravo. 1998-11-22. No. 1, season 5.

[12] Horowitz, Joy (1991-03-17). "That Madcap Meryl. Really!" (http://query.nytimes.com/gst/fullpage. html?res=9D0CE7DA133BF934A25750C0A967958260). *New York Times*. . Retrieved 2009-01-13.

[13] "Press Archive" (http://web.archive.org/web/20070929141718/http://simplystreep.com/press/press1992movieline.htm). *Simply Streep.com*. Archived from the original (http://simplystreep.com/press/press1992movieline.htm) on 2007-09-29. .

[14] "N.J. Teachers Honor 6 Graduates" (http://nl.newsbank.com/nl-search/we/Archives?p_product=PI&s_site=philly&p_multi=PI& p_theme=realcities&p_action=search&p_maxdocs=200&p_topdoc=1&p_text_direct-0=0EB29697FA2C7F62& p_field_direct-0=document_id&p_perpage=10&p_sort=YMD_date:D&s_trackval=GooglePM). *The Philadelphia Inquirer*. 1983-11-12. . Retrieved 2007-07-20. "Streep is a graduate of Bernards High School in Bernardsville..."

[15] "Yale library's list of all roles played at Yale by Meryl Streep" (http://www.library.yale.edu/humanities/theater/Meryl_Streep's_roles. doc). . Retrieved 2010-03-07.

[16] 1974 *New York Times* review (http://books.google.com/books?id=bkNrqBbGfTgC&pg=PA365&lpg=PA365&ots=38AriP8tb3& dq="the+idiots+Karamazov"+gussow&ie=ISO-8859-1&output=html), reprinted in Mel Gussow, *Theatre on the Edge*, p.365

[17] Gussow, Mel (1991-01-07). "1991 *New York Times* article" (http://www.nytimes.com/1991/01/07/movies/ critic-s-notebook-luring-actors-back-to-the-stage-they-left-behind.html?pagewanted=1). Nytimes.com. . Retrieved 2010-03-07.

[18] Robert S. Brustein, *Letters to a Young Actor*, p.61 (http://books.google.com/books?id=3ejEl3_jNtUC&pg=PA61&lpg=PA60& dq="Meryl+Streep"+Yale&ie=ISO-8859-1&output=html) This book also contains details of her performances at Yale.

[19] "Information, Considered & Delayed Projects" (http://www.simplystreep.com/site/career/considered/).SimplyStreep.com. . Retrieved 2009-06-07.

[20] "Magazines Archive" (http://www.simplystreep.com/magazines/197902msmagazine.php).SimplyStreep.com. . Retrieved 2009-08-14. citing "Meryl Streep to the Rescue". *Ms. Magazine*. February 1979.

[21] "Magazines Archive" (http://www.www.simplystreep.com/magazines/197808horizon.htm).SimplyStreep.com. . Retrieved 2009-06-07. citing "Star Treks". *Horizon Magazine*. August 1978.

[22] "Magazines Archive" (http://www.simplystreep.com/site/career/stage/). SimplyStreep.com. . Retrieved 2009-06-07. citing "From Homecoming Queen to Holocaust". *TV Guide*. June 1978.

[23] "Magazines Archive" (http://www.simplystreep.com/magazines/197903lookmagazine.htm). SimplyStreep.com. . Retrieved 2009-06-07. citing "Streep Year". *Look Magazine*. March 1979.

[24] Hollinger, Karen (2006). *The Actress: Hollywood Acting and the Female Star* (http://books.google.com/?id=89W0QMDjA7gC& pg=PA71&dq=Meryl+Streep#PPA76,M1). Routledge. p. 76. ISBN 0415977924. .

[25] Hollinger, p. 75

[26] Hollinger, p. 77

[27] "Magazines Archive" (http://www.www.simplystreep.com/magazines/197911playgirl.htm). SimplyStreep.com. . Retrieved 2009-06-07. citing "The Freshest Face in Hollywood". *Playgirl Magazine*. November 1979.

[28] Denby, David (1981-09-21). "Meryl Streep is Madonna and siren in *The French Lieutenant's Woman*" (http://books.google.com/ books?id=-OUCAAAAMBAJ&pg=PA26&dq=Meryl+Streep&lr=#PPA26,M1). *New York Magazine*: p. 27. . Retrieved 2009-06-15.

[29] Canby, Vincent (1985-09-20). "'Still of the Night,' in Hitchcock Manner" (http://movies.nytimes.com/movie/ review?res=9C02E2D8123BF93AA25752C1A964948260). *New York Times*. . Retrieved 2009-06-06.

[30] "What Makes Meryl Magic" (http://www.time.com/time/magazine/article/0,9171,924815-8,00.html). *Time*.1981-09-07. . Retrieved 2009-06-15.

[31] Ebert, Roger; David Bordwell (2006). *Awake in the dark: the best of Roger Ebert: forty years of reviews, essays, and interviews* (http:// books.google.com/?id=YIU1jlgPjr8C&pg=PA64&dq=Meryl+Streep#PPA64,M1). University of Chicago Press. p. 64. ISBN 0226182002.
.

[32] Ebert, Roger (1982-11-19). "'Plenty' review" (http://rogerebert.suntimes.com/apps/pbcs.dll/article?AID=/19850920/REVIEWS/ 509200303/1023). *Chicago Sun Times*. . Retrieved 2009-06-06.

[33] "Out of Africa (1985)" (http://www.rottentomatoes.com/m/out_of_africa/). Rotten Tomatoes. . Retrieved 2009-06-06.

[34] Corliss, Richard (1989-12-11). "Warty Worm, "She-Devil" review" (http://www.time.com/time/magazine/article/0,9171,959340,00. html). *Time magazine*. . Retrieved 2009-06-07.

[35] Corliss, Richard (1992-08-03). "Beverly Hills Corpse, "Death Becomes Her" review" (http://www.time.com/time/magazine/article/ 0,9171,976129,00.html). *Time magazine*. . Retrieved 2009-06-07.

[36] , p. 78

[37] Hetrick, Adam (2009-01-09). "Winners of the 2009 Critics' Choice Awards, announced" (http://www.playbill.com/news/article/125025. html). *Playbill*. . Retrieved 2009-01-14.

[38] "Alec Baldwin and Meryl Streep Eying Romantic Comedy" (http://popcritics.com/2008/08/ alec-baldwin-and-meryl-streep-eying-romantic-comedy). Pop Critics. 2008-08-18. . Retrieved 2008-09-29.

[39] 08:30 AM ET. "Golden Globe nominations announced" (http://news-briefs.ew.com/2009/12/15/golden-globes-nominations/). News-briefs.ew.com. . Retrieved 2010-03-07.

[40] "Fey and Streep to Play Daughter and Mother in Tucci-Directed Movie" (http://www.tvguide.com/News/Fey-Streep-Play-1021148. aspx). TVGuide.com. .

[41] Brantley, Ben (2006-08-22). "Mother Courage and Her Children" (http://theater2.nytimes.com/2006/08/22/theater/reviews/22moth. html). *New York Times*. . Retrieved 2009-01-15.

[42] "Portuguese Music Charts" (http://acharts.us/portugal_singles_top_50/2009/04). .}

[43] "People Choice Awards Results" (http://www.peopleschoice.com/pca/awards/nominees/index.jsp?year=2009). .

[44] http://theplaylist.blogspot.com/2010/06/richard-shepard-talks-john-cazale-doc.html

[45] http://news.google.com/newspapers?id=Hw4gAAAAIBAJ&sjid=pmUFAAAAIBAJ&pg=1223,438388&dq=meryl+streep+don+ gummer&hl=en

[46] "Movies, marriage, and turning sixty," The Independent (UK), Jan. 24, 2009.

[47] Eric Quiñones (2009-06-02). "Princeton awards five honorary degrees" (http://www.princeton.edu/main/news/archive/S24/39/63E27/ index.xml?section=topstories). Princeton. . Retrieved 2009-06-03.

[48] "Meryl Streep elected to elite arts academy" (http://news.bbc.co.uk/2/hi/entertainment/8617016.stm). BBC News. 2010-04-13. . Retrieved 2010-04-13.

[49] "Honorary degrees awarded" (http://news.harvard.edu/gazette/story/2010/05/honorary-degrees/). Harvard University. 2010-05-27. . Retrieved 2010-05-27.

[50] "Meryl Streep voicing a role in Wes Anderson's 'Fantastic Mr. Fox'" (http://news-briefs.ew.com/2009/05/meryl-streep-vo.html). *Entertainment Weekly*. 2009-05-06. . Retrieved 2009-05-06.

[51] http://www.filmlinc.com/fcm/mj08/streep.htm

[52] http://books.google.com/?id=89W0QMDjA7gC&pg=PA71&dq=Meryl+Streep#PPA76,M1

[53] http://www.imdb.com/name/nm0000658/

[54] http://www.ibdb.com/person.asp?ID=01321

[55] http://www.lortel.org/LLA_archive/index.cfm?search_by=people&first=Meryl&last=Streep&middle=

[56] http://tcmdb.com/participant/participant.jsp?participantId=185873

[57] http://www.merylstreeponline.net/

[58] http://www.streepinstyle.info

[59] http://www.bafta.org/learning/webcasts/meryl-streep,681,BA.html

List of awards and nominations received by Meryl Streep

List of Meryl Streep's awards

Meryl Streep at the 61st Academy Awards

Award	Wins	Nominations
Academy Awards	2	16
BAFTA Awards	1	13
Emmy Awards	2	3
Golden Globe Awards	7	25
Grammy Awards	0	4
SAG Awards	2	12
Tony Awards	0	1

This is a list of awards and nominations for Meryl Streep, whose acting career in motion pictures, television, and on stage spans over 30 years. As of 2009, Streep holds the record for the most acting Academy Award nominations received by any actor with 16; she has won twice (Best Supporting Actress for *Kramer vs. Kramer* in 1979 and Best Actress for *Sophie's Choice* in 1982). She also holds the record for the most Golden Globe Award nominations with 25, and the record for the most Golden Globe wins with seven. She is the most critically acclaimed actress of the modern era.

Film and television awards

Academy Awards

(Reference:[1])

Year	Nominated work	Category	Result
1978	*The Deer Hunter*	Best Supporting Actress	Nominated
1979	*Kramer vs. Kramer*		Won
1981	*The French Lieutenant's Woman*	Best Actress	Nominated
1982	*Sophie's Choice*		Won
1983	*Silkwood*		Nominated
1985	*Out of Africa*		Nominated
1987	*Ironweed*		Nominated
1988	*A Cry in the Dark*		Nominated
1990	*Postcards from the Edge*		Nominated
1995	*The Bridges of Madison County*		Nominated
1998	*One True Thing*		Nominated
1999	*Music of the Heart*		Nominated
2002	*Adaptation*	Best Supporting Actress	Nominated
2006	*The Devil Wears Prada*	Best Actress	Nominated
2008	*Doubt*		Nominated
2009	*Julie & Julia*		Nominated

BAFTA Awards

(Reference:[2])

Year	Nominated work	Category	Result
1979	The Deer Hunter	Best Actress in a Leading Role	Nominated
	Manhattan	Best Actress in a Supporting Role	Nominated
1980	Kramer vs. Kramer	Best Actress in a Leading Role	Nominated
1981	The French Lieutenant's Woman	Best Actress in a Leading Role	Won
1983	Sophie's Choice	Best Actress in a Leading Role	Nominated
1984	Silkwood	Best Actress in a Leading Role	Nominated
1986	Out of Africa	Best Actress in a Leading Role	Nominated
2002	The Hours	Best Actress in a Leading Role	Nominated
	Adaptation.	Best Actress in a Supporting Role	Nominated
2004	The Manchurian Candidate	Best Actress in a Supporting Role	Nominated
2006	The Devil Wears Prada	Best Actress in a Leading Role	Nominated
2008	Doubt	Best Actress in a Leading Role	Nominated
2009	Julie & Julia	Best Actress in a Leading Role	Nominated

Golden Globe Awards

(Reference:[3])

Year	Nominated work	Category	Result
1978	The Deer Hunter	Best Supporting Actress - Motion Picture	Nominated
1979	Kramer vs. Kramer		Won
1981	The French Lieutenant's Woman	Best Actress - Motion Picture Drama	Won
1982	Sophie's Choice		Won
1983	Silkwood		Nominated
1985	Out of Africa		Nominated
1988	A Cry in the Dark		Nominated

Year	Film	Category	Result
1989	*She-Devil*	Best Actress - Motion Picture Musical or Comedy	Nominated
1990	*Postcards from the Edge*		Nominated
1992	*Death Becomes Her*		Nominated
1994	*The River Wild*	Best Actress - Motion Picture Drama	Nominated
1995	*The Bridges of Madison County*		Nominated
1996	*Marvin's Room*		Nominated
1997	*...First Do No Harm*	Best Actress - Miniseries or Television Film	Nominated
1998	*One True Thing*	Best Actress - Motion Picture Drama	Nominated
1999	*Music of the Heart*		Nominated
2002	*The Hours*		Nominated
	Adaptation.	Best Supporting Actress - Motion Picture	Won
2003	*Angels in America*	Best Actress - Miniseries or Television Film	Won
2004	*The Manchurian Candidate*	Best Supporting Actress - Motion Picture	Nominated
2006	*The Devil Wears Prada*	Best Actress - Motion Picture Musical or Comedy	Won
2008	*Doubt*	Best Actress - Motion Picture Drama	Nominated
	Mamma Mia!	Best Actress - Motion Picture Musical or Comedy	Nominated
2009	*It's Complicated*		Nominated
	Julie & Julia		Won

Primetime Emmy Awards

(Reference:[4])

Year	Nominated work	Category	Result
1978	*Holocaust*	Outstanding Lead Actress - Miniseries or a Movie	Won
1997	*...First Do No Harm*	Outstanding Lead Actress - Miniseries or a Movie	Nominated
2004	*Angels in America*	Outstanding Lead Actress - Miniseries or a Movie	Won

Screen Actors Guild Awards

Year	Nominated work	Category	Result
1994[5]	*The River Wild*	Outstanding Performance by a Female Actor in a Leading Role - Motion Picture	Nominated
1995[6]	*The Bridges of Madison County*	Outstanding Performance by a Female Actor in a Leading Role - Motion Picture	Nominated
1996[7]	*Marvin's Room*	Outstanding Performance by a Cast in a Motion Picture	Nominated[I]
1998[8]	*One True Thing*	Outstanding Performance by a Female Actor in a Leading Role - Motion Picture	Nominated
1999[9]	*Music of the Heart*	Outstanding Performance by a Female Actor in a Leading Role - Motion Picture	Nominated
2002[10]	*The Hours*	Outstanding Performance by a Cast in a Motion Picture	Nominated[II]
	Adaptation.	Outstanding Performance by a Cast in a Motion Picture	Nominated[III]
2003[11]	*Angels in America*	Outstanding Performance by a Female Actor in a Miniseries or Television Movie	Won
2006[12]	*The Devil Wears Prada*	Outstanding Performance by a Female Actor in a Leading Role - Motion Picture	Nominated
2008	*Doubt*	Outstanding Performance by a Female Actor in a Leading Role - Motion Picture[13]	Won
		Outstanding Performance by a Cast in a Motion Picture[14]	Nominated[IV]
2009	*Julie & Julia*	Outstanding Performance by a Female Actor in a Leading Role - Motion Picture	Nominated

Other industry awards

American Comedy Awards			
Year	Nominated work	Category	Result
1990	*Postcards from the Edge*	Funniest Actress in a Motion Picture (Leading Role)	Won

American Movie Awards			
Year	Nominated work	Category	Result
1980	*The Deer Hunter*	Best Supporting Actress	Won

Australian Film Institute Awards			
Year	Nominated work	Category	Result
1988	*Evil Angels (A Cry in the Dark)*	Best Actress in a Leading Role	Won

Chlotrudis Awards			
Year	Nominated work	Category	Result
1996	*Marvin's Room*	Best Supporting Actress	Nominated

David di Donatello			
Year	Nominated work	Category	Result
1984	*Falling in Love*	Best Foreign Actress (Migliore Attrice Straniero)	Won
1985	*Out of Africa*	Best Foreign Actress (Migliore Attrice Straniero)	Won

Gotham Awards			
Year	Nominated work	Category	Result
1999	-	Lifetime Achievement Award	Won
2006	*A Prairie Home Companion*	Best Ensemble Cast	Nominated[V]

Gracie Allen Awards			
Year	Nominated work	Category	Result
2003	*Angels in America*	Outstanding Female Lead in a Drama Special	Won

Irish Film and Television Awards			
Year	Nominated work	Category	Result
1998	*Dancing at Lughnasa*	Best Actor in a Female Role	Nominated
2009	*It's Complicated*	Best International Actress - People's Choice	Won

National Board of Review Awards			
Year	Nominated work	Category	Result
1979[15]	*Kramer vs. Kramer*	Best Supporting Actress	Won
	Manhattan		
	The Seduction of Joe Tynan		
1982[15]	*Sophie's Choice*	Best Actress	Won
2008[16]	*Doubt*	Best Ensemble Cast	Won[IV]

Satellite Awards			
Year	Nominated work	Category	Result
1998	...First Do No Harm	Best Performance by an Actress in a Mini-Series or Motion Picture Made for Television	Nominated
1999	One True Thing	Best Performance by an Actress in a Motion Picture - Drama	Nominated
2003	The Hours	Best Performance by an Actress in a Motion Picture, Drama	Nominated
	Adaptation.	Best Performance by an Actress in a Supporting Role, Comedy or Musical	Nominated
2004	Angels in America	Best Performance by an Actress in a Miniseries or a Motion Picture Made for Television	Won
2006	The Devil Wears Prada	Best Actress in a Motion Picture, Comedy or Musical	Won
2008	Mamma Mia!	Best Actress in a Motion Picture, Comedy or Musical	Nominated
	Doubt	Best Actress in a Motion Picture, Drama	Nominated
2009	Julie & Julia	Best Actress in a Motion Picture, Comedy or Musical	Won

Saturn Awards			
Year	Nominated work	Category	Result
1991	Defending Your Life	Best Actress	Nominated
1992	Death Becomes Her	Best Actress	Nominated
2005	The Manchurian Candidate	Best Supporting Actress	Nominated

Critics' awards

Boston Society of Film Critics Awards			
Year	Nominated work	Category	Result
1982	Sophie's Choice	Best Actress	Won
2009	Julie & Julia	Best Actress	Won

Broadcast Film Critics Association Awards			
Year	Nominated work	Category	Result
2002	*Adaptation.*	Best Supporting Actress	Nominated
2006	*The Devil Wears Prada*	Best Actress	Nominated
2008	*Doubt*	Best Actress	Won[VI]
		Best Acting Ensemble	Nominated[IV]
2009	*Julie & Julia*	Best Actress	Won

Chicago Film Critics Association Awards			
Year	Nominated work	Category	Result
2002	*Adaptation.*	Best Supporting Actress	Won
2006	*The Devil Wears Prada*	Best Actress	Nominated
2008	*Doubt*	Best Actress	Nominated
2009	*Julie & Julia*	Best Actress	Nominated

Florida Film Critics Circle Awards			
Year	Nominated work	Category	Result
2002	*Adaptation.*	Best Supporting Actress	Won

Kansas City Film Critics Circle Awards			
Year	Nominated work	Category	Result
1979	*Kramer vs. Kramer*	Best Actress	Won
1982	*Sophie's Choice*	Best Actress	Won[VII]
1983	*Silkwood*	Best Actress	Won
1985	*Out of Africa*	Best Actress	Won
2008	*Doubt*	Best Actress	Won
2009	*Julie & Julia*	Best Actress	Won

Las Vegas Film Critics Society Awards			
Year	Nominated work	Category	Result
2002	*The Hours*	Best Supporting Actress	Nominated

London Critics' Circle Film Awards			
Year	Nominated work	Category	Result
2004	*Adaptation.*	Actress of the Year	Nominated
2007	*The Devil Wears Prada*	Actress of the Year	Won
2009	*Doubt*	Actress of the Year	Nominated
2010	*Julie & Julia*	Actress of the Year	Nominated

Los Angeles Film Critics Association Awards			
Year	Nominated work	Category	Result
1979[17]	*Kramer vs. Kramer*	Best Supporting Actress	Won
	Manhattan		
	The Seduction of Joe Tynan		
1981[18]	*The French Lieutenant's Woman*	Best Actress	Won
1982[19]	*Sophie's Choice*	Best Actress	Won
1985[20]	*Out of Africa*	Best Actress	Won

National Society of Film Critics Awards			
Year	Nominated work	Category	Result
1979[16]	*The Deer Hunter*	Best Supporting Actress	Won
1980[16]	*Kramer vs. Kramer*	Best Supporting Actress	Won
	Manhattan		
	The Seduction of Joe Tynan		
1983[16]	*Sophie's Choice*	Best Actress	Won
2007[16]	*The Devil Wears Prada*	Best Supporting Actress	Won
	A Prairie Home Companion		

New York Film Critics Circle Awards			
Year	Nominated work	Category	Result
1979	*Kramer vs. Kramer*	Best Supporting Actress	Won
	The Seduction of Joe Tynan		
1982	*Sophie's Choice*	Best Actress	Won
1988	*A Cry in the Dark*	Best Actress	Won
2009	*Julie & Julia*	Best Actress	Won

Online Film Critics Society Awards			
Year	Nominated work	Category	Result
2003	*Adaptation.*	Best Supporting Actress	Nominated
2007	*The Devil Wears Prada*	Best Actress	Nominated

Phoenix Film Critics Society Awards			
Year	Nominated work	Category	Result
2003	*Adaptation.*	Best Supporting Actress	Nominated
		Best Acting Ensemble	Nominated[III]
	The Hours	Best Acting Ensemble	Nominated[II]
2008	*Doubt*	Best Actress	Won
2009	*Julie & Julia*	Best Actress	Won

Southeastern Film Critics Association Awards			
Year	Nominated work	Category	Result
2002	*Adaptation.*	Best Supporting Actress	Won
2009	*Julie & Julia*	Best Actress	Won

Washington DC Area Film Critics Association Awards			
Year	Nominated work	Category	Result
2008	*Doubt*	Best Actress	Won

Festival awards

Berlin International Film Festival			
Year	Nominated work	Category	Result
1999	-	Berlinale Camera	Won
2003[1]	*The Hours*	Silver Bear for Best Actress	Won[VIII]

Cannes Film Festival			
Year	Nominated work	Category	Result
1989[1]	*A Cry in the Dark*	Best Actress	Won

Outfest			
Year	Nominated work	Category	Result
2002	*The Hours*	Best Performance by an Actress in a Leading Role	Won

Moscow International Film Festival			
Year	Nominated work	Category	Result
2004	-	Stanislavsky Prize	Won

San Sebastián International Film Festival			
Year	Nominated work	Category	Result
2008	-	Donostia Lifetime Achievement Award	Won

Valladolid International Film Festival			
Year	Nominated work	Category	Result
1986	*Heartburn*	Best Actress	Won

Audience awards

MTV Movie Awards			
Year	Nominated work	Category	Result
2007	*The Devil Wears Prada*	Best Villain	Nominated

National Movie Awards			
Year	Nominated work	Category	Result
2008	*Mamma Mia!*	Best Female Performance	Won

People's Choice Awards		
Year	Category	Result
1984[21]	Favorite Motion Picture Actress	Won
1985[22]	Favorite Motion Picture Actress	Won
1986[23]	Favorite All-Around Female Entertainer	Won
	Favorite Motion Picture Actress	Won
1987[24]	Favorite Motion Picture Actress	Won
1989[25]	Favorite Actress in a Dramatic Motion Picture	Won
1990[26]	Favorite Motion Picture Actress	Won
	World-Favorite Motion Picture Actress	Won

Teen Choice Awards			
Year	Nominated work	Category	Result
2006	*The Devil Wears Prada*	Movies - Choice Chemistry	Nominated[IX]
		Movies - Choice Sleazebag	Nominated

Goldene Kamera		
Year	Category	Result
2009	Best Actress - International	Won

Theatre awards

Drama Desk Awards

Year	Nominated work	Category	Result
1975-76[27]	*Secret Service*	Outstanding Actress in a Play	Nominated
	A Memory of Two Mondays		
	27 Wagons Full of Cotton		
	Trelawny of the "Wells"		
1976-77[28]	*The Cherry Orchard*	Outstanding Featured Actress in a Play	Nominated
	Happy End	Outstanding Actress in a Musical	Nominated
2001-02[29]	*The Seagull*	Outstanding Actress in a Play	Nominated
2006-07[30]	*Mother Courage and Her Children*	Outstanding Actress in a Play	Nominated

Obie Awards

Year	Nominated work	Category	Result
1981[16]	*Alice in Concert*	Performance	Won

Theatre World Awards

Year	Work	Category	Result
1976[31]	*27 Wagons Full of Cotton*	-	Won

Tony Awards

Year	Work	Category	Result
1976[32]	*27 Wagons Full of Cotton*	Best Featured Actress in a Play	Nominated

Music awards

Grammy Awards

Year	Work	Category	Result
2009[33]	*Mamma Mia!*	Best Compilation Soundtrack Album for Motion Picture, Television or Other Visual Media	Nominated[x]

Other honors

Meryl Streep received an Honorary César at the 2003 César Awards and a Life Achievement Award from the American Film Institute in 2004.[34] In addition to her acting awards, Streep was named Woman of the Year by the Hasty Pudding Theatricals in 1980 and was the recipient of the Crystal Award from Women in Film in 1998. She was given a Gala Tribute by the Film Society of Lincoln Center in 2008.[35]

Streep has a star on the Hollywood Walk of Fame located at 7020 Hollywood Boulevard.

Meryl also received an Honorary Degree from Princeton University in 2009.

She was inducted into the New Jersey Hall of Fame in 2008.

Notes

I Shared with Robert De Niro, Leonardo DiCaprio and Diane Keaton.

II Shared with Toni Collette, Claire Danes, Jeff Daniels, Stephen Dillane, Ed Harris, Allison Janney, Nicole Kidman, Julianne Moore, John C. Reilly and Miranda Richardson.

III Shared with Nicolas Cage, Chris Cooper, Brian Cox, Cara Seymour and Tilda Swinton.

IV Shared with Amy Adams, Viola Davis and Philip Seymour Hoffman.

V Shared with Woody Harrelson, Tommy Lee Jones, Garrison Keillor, Kevin Kline, Lindsay Lohan, Virginia Madsen, John C. Reilly, Maya Rudolph, Lily Tomlin, L.Q. Jones, Sue Scott and Tim Russell.

VI Tied with Anne Hathaway for *Rachel Getting Married*.

VII Tied with Julie Andrews for *Victor Victoria*.

VIII Shared with Nicole Kidman and Julianne Moore.

IX Shared with Anne Hathaway.

X Shared with various artists.

References

[1] "Meryl Streep: Awards & Nominations" (http://movies.yahoo.com/movie/contributor/1800018835/awards). *Yahoo! Movies.*. Retrieved 22 January 2009.

[2] "Searchable Awards Database: Meryl Streep" (http://www.bafta.org/awards-database.html?sq=meryl+streep). *British Academy of Film and Television Arts.*. Retrieved 21 January 2009.

[3] "Meryl Streep" (http://www.goldenglobes.org/browse/member/29717). *Hollywood Foreign Press Association.*. Retrieved 21 January 2009.

[4] "Meryl Streep: Biography" (http://www.tvguide.com/celebrities/meryl-streep/bio/165859). *TV Guide.*. Retrieved 23 January 2009.

[5] "1st Annual SAG Awards Nominees" (http://www.sagawards.org/1_award_nom). *Screen Actors Guild.* 25 February 1995.. Retrieved 22 January 2009.

[6] "2nd Annual SAG Awards Nominees" (http://www.sagawards.org/2_award_nom). *Screen Actors Guild.* 24 February 1996.. Retrieved 22 January 2009.

[7] "3rd Annual SAG Awards Nominees" (http://www.sagawards.org/3_award_nom). *Screen Actors Guild.* 22 February 1997.. Retrieved 22 January 2009.

[8] "5th Annual SAG Awards Nominees" (http://www.sagawards.org/5_award_nom). *Screen Actors Guild.*. Retrieved 22 January 2009.

[9] "6th Annual SAG Awards Nominees" (http://www.sagawards.org/6_award_nom). *Screen Actors Guild.*. Retrieved 22 January 2009.

[10] "9th Annual SAG Awards Nominees" (http://www.sagawards.org/9_award_nom). *Screen Actors Guild.*. Retrieved 22 January 2009.

[11] "10th Annual Screen Actors Guild Award Recipients" (http://www.sagawards.org/10_award_nom). *Screen Actors Guild.*. Retrieved 22 January 2009.

[12] Screen Actors Guild (4 January 2007). "13th Annual Screen Actors Guild Awards Nominations" (http://www.sagawards.org/PR_070104). Press release.. Retrieved 22 January 2009.

[13] Screen Actors Guild (25 January 2009). "Final 15th Annual SAG Awards Recipient Press Release" (http://www.sagawards.org/PR_090125). Press release.. Retrieved 26 January 2009.

[14] Screen Actors Guild (18 December 2008). "Nominations Announced for the 15th Annual Screen Actors Guild Awards" (http://www.sagawards.org/PR_081218). Press release.. Retrieved 22 January 2009.

[15] "Search: Meryl Streep" (http://www.nbrmp.org/search/?search=meryl+streep). *National Board of Review of Motion Pictures.*. Retrieved 31 January 2009.

[16] "Meryl Streep: Awards" (http://www.variety.com/profiles/people/Awards/31440/Meryl+Streep.html?dataSet=1). *Variety.* . Retrieved 23 January 2009.

[17] "5th Annual Los Angeles Film Critics Association Awards" (http://www.lafca.net/years/1979.html).*Los Angeles Film Critics Association.* . Retrieved 21 January 2009.

[18] "7th Annual Los Angeles Film Critics Association Awards" (http://www.lafca.net/years/1981.html).*Los Angeles Film Critics Association.* . Retrieved 21 January 2009.

[19] "8th Annual Los Angeles Film Critics Association Awards" (http://www.lafca.net/years/1982.html).*Los Angeles Film Critics Association.* . Retrieved 21 January 2009.

[20] "11th Annual Los Angeles Film Critics Association Awards" (http://www.lafca.net/years/1985.html).*Los Angeles Film Critics Association.* . Retrieved 21 January 2009.

[21] "People's Choice Awards 1984" (http://www.pcavote.com/pca/show/nominees/index.jsp?year=1984).*PCAvote.com.* . Retrieved 24 January 2009.

[22] "People's Choice Awards 1985" (http://www.pcavote.com/pca/show/nominees/index.jsp?year=1985).*PCAvote.com.* . Retrieved 24 January 2009.

[23] "People's Choice Awards 1986" (http://www.pcavote.com/pca/show/nominees/index.jsp?year=1986).*PCAvote.com.* . Retrieved 24 January 2009.

[24] "People's Choice Awards 1987" (http://www.pcavote.com/pca/show/nominees/index.jsp?year=1987).*PCAvote.com.* . Retrieved 24 January 2009.

[25] "People's Choice Awards 1989" (http://www.pcavote.com/pca/show/nominees/index.jsp?year=1989).*PCAvote.com.* . Retrieved 24 January 2009.

[26] "People's Choice Awards 1990" (http://www.pcavote.com/pca/show/nominees/index.jsp?year=1990).*PCAvote.com.* . Retrieved 24 January 2009.

[27] "1975-1976 22nd Drama Desk Awards" (http://www.dramadesk.com/1975_1976dd.html). *Drama Desk.* . Retrieved 21 January 2009.

[28] "1976-1977 23rd Drama Desk Awards" (http://www.dramadesk.com/1976_1977dd.html). *Drama Desk.* . Retrieved 21 January 2009.

[29] "2001-2002 48th Drama Desk Awards" (http://www.dramadesk.com/2001_2002dd.html). *Drama Desk.* . Retrieved 21 January 2009.

[30] Drama Desk (26 April 2007). "52nd Annual Drama Desk Awards Nominations Announced" (http://www.dramadesk.com/press047. html). Press release. . Retrieved 21 January 2009.

[31] "Our Most Recent Award Recipients" (http://www.theatreworldawards.org/award.html). *Theatre World Awards.* . Retrieved 21 January 2009.

[32] "Search Results: Meryl Streep" (http://www.tonyawards.com/p/tonys_search?start=0&year=&award=&lname=Meryl+Streep& fname=&show=). *TonyAwards.com.* . Retrieved 21 January 2009.

[33] "The 51st Grammy Awards Nominations List" (http://content.grammy.com/grammy_awards/51st_show/list.aspx). *National Academy of Recording Arts and Sciences.* . Retrieved 21 January 2009.

[34] Levy, Rochelle L.. "2004: Meryl Streep" (http://www.afi.com/tvevents/laa/laa04.aspx). *American Film Institute.* . Retrieved 22 January 2009.

[35] "Gala Tribute to Meryl Streep" (http://www.filmlinc.com/special/gala/pastkeep/merylstreep.html). *Film Society of Lincoln Center.* . Retrieved 21 January 2009.

Julia (1977 film)

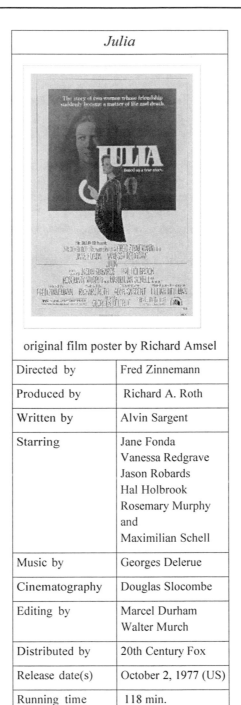

Julia	
original film poster by Richard Amsel	
Directed by	Fred Zinnemann
Produced by	Richard A. Roth
Written by	Alvin Sargent
Starring	Jane Fonda Vanessa Redgrave Jason Robards Hal Holbrook Rosemary Murphy and Maximilian Schell
Music by	Georges Delerue
Cinematography	Douglas Slocombe
Editing by	Marcel Durham Walter Murch
Distributed by	20th Century Fox
Release date(s)	October 2, 1977 (US)
Running time	118 min.
Country	United States
Language	English

Julia is a 1977 film made by 20th Century Fox. It is based on Lillian Hellman's book *Pentimento*, a portion of which purports to tell the story of her relationship with her lifelong friend, "Julia," who fought against the Nazis in the years prior to World War II. The film was directed by Fred Zinnemann and produced by Richard Roth, with Julien Derode as executive producer and Tom Pevsner as associate producer, from a screenplay adapted by Alvin Sargent.

Synopsis

The young Lillian and the young Julia, daughter of a wealthy family being brought up by her grandparents in the U.S., enjoy a childhood together and an extremely close relationship in late adolescence. Later, while medical-student/physician Julia (Vanessa Redgrave) attends Oxford and the University of Vienna and studies with such luminaries as Sigmund Freud, Lillian (Jane Fonda) suffers through revisions of her play with her mentor and sometime lover, Dashiell Hammett (Jason Robards) at a New England beachhouse.

After becoming a celebrated playwright, Lillian is invited to a writers' conference in Russia. Julia, having taken on the battle against Nazism, enlists Lillian *en route* to smuggle money through Nazi Germany which will assist in the anti-Nazi cause. It is a dangerous mission, especially for a Jewish intellectual on her way to Russia.

During a brief meeting with Julia on this trip, Lillian learns that her friend has a child named Lily, living with a baker in Alsace. Shortly after her return to the United States, Lillian is informed of Julia's murder. The details of her death are shrouded in secrecy. Lillian unsuccessfully looks for Julia's child in Alsace and also discovers that Julia's family wants nothing to do with the child, if she exists, probably for financial reasons.

Production

The film was shot on location in England and France.

Principal cast

- Jane Fonda - Lillian Hellman
- Vanessa Redgrave - Julia
- Jason Robards - Dashiell Hammett
- Maximilian Schell - Johann
- Hal Holbrook - Alan Campbell
- Rosemary Murphy - Dorothy Parker
- Meryl Streep - Anne Marie
- John Glover - Sammy
- Lisa Pelikan - Julia (younger)

Julia features the first film performances of Meryl Streep and Lisa Pelikan.

Awards

Julia won Academy Awards for:

- Best Actor in a Supporting Role (Jason Robards);
- Best Actress in a Supporting Role (Vanessa Redgrave);
- Best Writing, Screenplay Based on Material from Another Medium (Alvin Sargent)

It was nominated for an Academy Award for:

- Best Actor in a Supporting Role (Maximilian Schell);
- Best Actress in a Leading Role (Jane Fonda);
- Best Cinematography;
- Best Costume Design;
- Best Director;
- Best Film Editing;
- Best Music, Original Score;
- Best Picture.

It also won the BAFTA Award for Best Film.

External links

- *Julia* [1] at the Internet Movie Database
- *Julia* [2] at Rotten Tomatoes

References

[1] http://www.imdb.com/title/tt0076245/
[2] http://www.rottentomatoes.com/m/1011324-julia/

The Deer Hunter

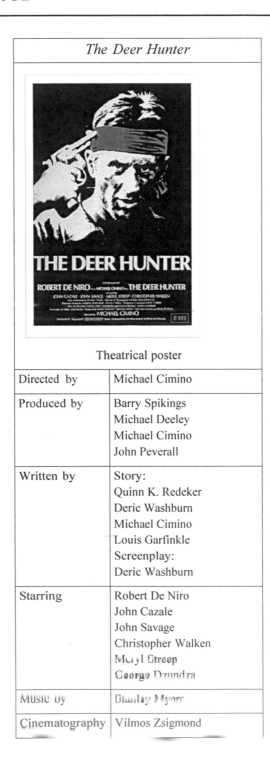

The Deer Hunter	
Theatrical poster	
Directed by	Michael Cimino
Produced by	Barry Spikings Michael Deeley Michael Cimino John Peverall
Written by	Story: Quinn K. Redeker Deric Washburn Michael Cimino Louis Garfinkle Screenplay: Deric Washburn
Starring	Robert De Niro John Cazale John Savage Christopher Walken Meryl Streep George Dzundza
Music by	Stanley Myers
Cinematography	Vilmos Zsigmond

Editing by	Peter Zinner
Studio	EMI Films
Distributed by	Universal Pictures (US) EMI Films (Worldwide Sales)
Release date(s)	December 8, 1978 (Limited) February 23, 1979 (Wide)
Running time	182 minutes
Country	United States
Language	English, Vietnamese
Budget	US$15,000,000[1]
Gross revenue	US$48,979,328[1]

The Deer Hunter is an epic 1978 American war drama film co-written and directed by Michael Cimino about a trio of Rusyn American steel worker friends and their infantry service in the Vietnam War. The film stars Robert De Niro, Christopher Walken, Meryl Streep, John Savage, John Cazale, and George Dzundza. The story takes place in Clairton, a small working class town on the Monongahela River south of Pittsburgh and then in Vietnam, somewhere in woodland and in Saigon, during the Vietnam War.

The Deer Hunter meditates on the moral and mental consequences of battle as well as the effects of politically-manipulated patriotism upon common values (friendship, honor, family) in a tightly-knit community. It deals with such controversial issues as suicide, post-traumatic stress disorder, infidelity and mental illness. The scenes of Russian roulette, while highly controversial on release, have been viewed as a metaphor for the Vietnam War itself. The film won five Academy Awards, including Best Picture and Best Director and was named by the American Film Institute as the 53rd Greatest Movie of All Time on the 10th Anniversary Edition of the AFI's 100 Years...100 Movies list.

Plot

Critics and film historians have often noted how the film is divided into three equal thirds or acts. Likewise the plot synopsis is also divided into three acts, spanning the years of 1966-1974.[2]

Act I

In Clairton, a small working class town in Western Pennsylvania, in early 1968, Rusyn American steel workers Michael (De Niro), Steven (Savage), and Nick (Walken), with the support of their friends Stanley (Cazale), John (Dzundza) and Axel (Aspegren), are preparing for two rites of passage: marriage and military service.

The opening scenes set the character traits of the three main characters. Michael is the no-nonsense, serious but unassuming leader of the three, Steven the loving, near-groom, pecked at by his mother for not wearing a scarf with his tuxedo and Nick is the quiet, introspective man who loves hunting because, "I like the trees...you know...the way the trees are..." The recurring theme of "one shot," which is how Michael prefers to take down a deer, is introduced.

Before the trio ships out, Steven and his girlfriend, Angela (who is pregnant by another man but loved by Steven nonetheless) get married in an elaborate Russian Orthodox wedding. In the meantime, Michael must contain his own feelings for Nick's lovely but pensive girlfriend Linda (Streep), who has just moved out of her abusive father's house.

At the wedding reception held at the local VFW, the guys all get drunk, dance, sing and have a good time, but then notice an Army Green Beret in full dress uniform sitting at the end of the bar. Michael buys the soldier a drink and tries to strike up a conversation with him to find out what Vietnam is like, but the soldier ignores Michael. After Michael confronts him to explain that he, Steven and Nick are going to Vietnam, the Green Beret raises his glass and says "fuck it" to everyone's shock and amazement. Obviously disturbed and under mental anguish, the Green Beret again toasts them with "fuck it." After being restrained by the others from starting a fight with the Green Beret, Michael goes back to the bar with the others and in a mocking jest to the Green Beret, raises his glass and toasts him with "fuck it." The Green Beret then glances over at Michael and grins smugly, knowing exactly what Michael and the others will face.

Later, during the wedding toast to Steven and Angela, a toast with a tradition of good luck for the couple who drinks from conjoined goblets without spilling a drop, a drop of blood-red wine unknowingly spills on her wedding gown, again foreshadowing the coming events. Near the end of the reception, Nick asks Linda to marry him, and she agrees. Later that night, after a drunk and naked Michael runs through the streets of town, Nick chases him down and begs Michael not to leave him "over there" if anything happens. The next day, Michael and the remaining friends go deer hunting one last time, and Michael again scores a deer with "one shot."

Act II

The film then jumps abruptly to a war-torn village, where U.S. helicopters attack a communist occupied Vietnamese village with napalm. A North Vietnamese soldier throws a stick grenade into a hiding place full of civilians. An unconscious Mike (now a staff sergeant in the Army Special Forces) wakes up to see the NVA soldier shoot a woman carrying a baby. In revenge Mike burns the NVA with a flame thrower and then shoots him numerous times with an M16. Meanwhile a unit of UH-1 helicopters drops off several US infantrymen, Nick and Steven among them. Michael, Steven, and Nick unexpectedly find each other just before they are captured and held together in a riverside prisoner of war camp with other US Army and ARVN prisoners. For entertainment, the sadistic guards force their prisoners to play Russian roulette and gamble on the outcome.

All three friends are forced to play. Steven aims the gun above his head, grazing himself with the bullet and is punished by incarceration to an underwater cage, full of rats and the bodies of others who earlier faced the same fate. Michael and Nick manage to kill their captors and escape. Mike had earlier argued with Nick about whether Steven could be saved but after killing their captors he rescues Steven.

The three float downriver on a tree branch. An American helicopter accidentally finds them, but only Nick is able to climb aboard. The weakened Steven falls back into water and Mike plunges in the water to rescue him. Unluckily, Steven breaks both legs in the fall. Mike helps him to reach the river bank, and then carries him through the jungle to friendly lines. Nick is psychologically damaged and recuperating in a military hospital in Saigon with no knowledge on the status of his friends. At night, he aimlessly stumbles through the red-light district. At one point, he encounters Julien Grinda (Pierre Segui), a champagne-drinking friendly Frenchman outside a gambling den where men play Russian roulette for money. Grinda entices the reluctant Nick to participate, and leads him into the den. Mike is present in the den, watching the game, but the two friends do not notice each other at first. When Mike does see Nick, he is unable to get his attention. Mike cannot catch up with Nick and Grinda as they speed away.

Act III

Back in the U.S., Mike returns home but maintains a low profile. He tells the cab driver to pass by the house where all his friends are assembled, as he is embarrassed by the fuss made over him by Linda and the others. Mike goes to a hotel and struggles with his feelings, as he thinks both Nick and Steven are dead or missing. He eventually visits Linda and grows close to her, but only because of the friend they both think they have lost. Mike goes hunting with Axel, John and Stanley one more time, and after tracking a beautiful deer across the woods, takes his "one shot" but pulls the rifle up and fires into the air, unable to take another life. He then sits on a rock escarpment and yells out, "OK?", which echoes back at him from the opposing rock faces leading down to the river, signifying his fight with his mental demons over losing Steven and Nick. He also berates Stanley for carrying around a small revolver and waving it around, not realizing it is still loaded. He knows the horror of war and wants no part of it anymore.

Mike is eventually told about Angela, whom he goes to visit at the home of Steven's mother. She is lethargic and barely responsive. She writes a phone number on a scrap of paper, which leads Mike to the local veterans' hospital where Steven has been for several months. He has lost both his legs and is partially paralyzed. Mike visits Steven, who reveals that someone in Saigon has been mailing large amounts of cash to him, and Mike is convinced that it is Nick. Mike brings Steven home to Angela and then travels to Saigon just before its fall in 1975. He tracks down the Frenchman Grinda, who has made a lot of money from the Russian-roulette-playing American.

He finds Nick in a crowded roulette club, but Nick appears to have no recollection of his friends or his home in Pennsylvania. Mike sees the needle tracks on his arm, a sign of drug abuse. He realizes that Nick thinks he (Michael) and Steven are dead, since he is the only one who made it back on the helicopter. Mike enters himself in a game of Russian roulette against Nick, attempting to persuade him to come home, but Nick's mind is gone. In the last moment, after Mike's attempts to remind him of their trips hunting together, he finally breaks through, and Nick recognizes Mike and smiles. Nick then tells Mike, "one shot" and raises the gun to his temple and pulls the trigger. The bullet is in the gun chamber and Nick kills himself. Horrified, Michael tries to revive him to no avail.

Epilogue

Back in America in 1974, there is a funeral for Nick, whom Michael brings home, good to his promise. The film ends with the whole cast at their friends bar, singing "God Bless America" and toasting in Nick's honor.

Production

Pre-production

When the movie was being planned during the mid-1970s, Vietnam was still a taboo subject with all major Hollywood studios. English Company EMI Films (headed by Sir Bernard Delfont) initially arranged financing.[3] Universal got involved with the picture at a much later stage. Scouts for the film traveled over 100,000 miles by plane, bus, and car to find locations for filming. The initial budget of the film was $8.5 million.[4]

The picture reunited producers Barry Spikings and Michael Deeley; the two had previously collaborated on the cult classic *The Man Who Fell to Earth*.

Screenplay

The film began with a spec script called "The Man Who Came To Play", written by Louis Garfinkle and Quinn K. Redeker. Producer Michael Deeley purchased the first draft script from Garfinkle–Redeker for $19,000.[5] Deeley hired writer-director Michael Cimino, confident that he could further develop the principal characters without losing the essence of the original script.[5] While Garfinkle and Redeker had nothing to do with the writing or filming of *The Deer Hunter*, they ultimately shared a "Story By" writer's credit with Cimino and Washburn due to a Writers Guild arbitration process.[6]

Cimino worked for six weeks with Deric Washburn on the script before firing him.[7] Cimino and Washburn had previously collaborated with Stephen Bochco on the screenplay for *Silent Running*. According to Cimino, he would call Washburn while on the road scouting for locations and feed him notes on dialogue and story. Upon reviewing Washburn's draft, Cimino said, "I came back, and read it and I just could not believe what I read. It was like it was written by some body who was... mentally deranged."[7] Cimino confronted Washburn at the Studio Marquis in LA about the draft and Washburn supposedly replied that he couldn't take the pressure and had to go home.[7]

Cimino would later claim to have written the entire screenplay himself,[7] although a WGA arbitration awarded Washburn sole "Screenplay By" credit. All four writers, Garfinkle, Redeker, Cimino, and Washburn, received an Oscar nomination for Best Original Screenplay for this film.

In the original script, the roles of Mike and Nick were reversed in the last half of the film. Nick returns home to Linda, while Mike remains in Vietnam, sends money home to help Steven, and meets his tragic fate at the Russian roulette table.[8]

Casting

- Robert De Niro as S/Sgt. Michael "Mike" Vronsky. Roy Scheider was originally cast in this role. De Niro prepared by socializing with steelworkers in local bars and by visiting their homes. Cimino would introduce De Niro as his agent, Harry Ufland. No one recognized him.[7] De Niro claims this was his most physically-exhausting film. He explained that the scene where Michael visits Steve in the hospital for the first time was the most emotional scene that he was ever involved with.[9]
- Christopher Walken as Cpl. Nikanor "Nick" Chevotarevich. Walken achieved the withdrawn, hollow look of his character by eating nothing but rice and bananas. His performance garnered his first Academy Award, for Best Supporting Actor.
- John Savage as Steven Pushkov. Cimino originally wanted Brad Dourif for the role.
- Meryl Streep as Linda. Streep improvised many of her lines.
- John Cazale as Stanley aka "Stosh". All scenes involving Cazale, who had end-stage bone cancer, had to be filmed first. Because of his illness, the studio initially wanted to get rid of him, but his fiancee, Meryl Streep, and Cimino threatened to walk away if they did. He was also uninsurable, and according to Streep, De Niro paid for his insurance because he wanted him in the film. This was his last film, as he died shortly after filming wrapped.
- George Dzundza as John Welsh
- Chuck Aspegren as Peter "Axel" Axelrod. Aspegren was not an actor, he was the foreman at an East Chicago steel works visited early in pre-production by De Niro and Cimino. They were so impressed with him that they offered him the role.[7] He was the second person to be cast in the film, after De Niro.
- Shirley Stoler as Steven's mother
- Rutanya Alda as Angela Ludhjduravic-Pushkov
- Amy Wright as Bridesmaid
- Joe Grifasi as Bandleader

Shooting

This was the first feature film depicting the Vietnam War to be filmed on location in Thailand. All scenes were shot on location (no sound stages). The cast and crew viewed large amounts of news footage from the war to ensure authenticity. The film was shot over a period of six months.

Each of the six principal male characters in the movie carried a photo in their back pocket of them all together as children so as to enhance the sense of camaraderie amongst them. As well as this, director Cimino had the props department fashion complete Pennsylvania IDs for each of them, complete with driver's licenses, medical cards and various other pieces of paraphernalia, so as to enhance each actor's sense of their character.[3]

The Wedding Scenes

The wedding scenes were filmed in the summer, but were set in the fall.[3] To accomplish a look of fall, leaves were removed from trees and painted orange. They were then reattached to the trees.[10] It took five days to film. An actual priest was cast as the priest at the wedding.[3] The choir featured in the film was the actual choir at the church. They had to sing the hymns more than 50 times. During filming, director Cimino encouraged the many extras to treat the festivities as a real wedding, so as to increase the authenticity of the scenes. Prior to filming the wedding reception, Cimino instructed the extras to take empty boxes from home and wrap them as if they were wrapping real wedding gifts and bring them to the set the next day. The false gifts would then be used as props for the wedding reception. The extras did as they were told, however, when Cimino inspected the "props" he noticed that the "gifts" were a lot heavier than empty boxes otherwise would be. Cimino tore the wrapping paper off a few of the packages, only to find that the extras had in fact wrapped real gifts for the "wedding". Rutanya Alda actually struck her head quite hard on the doorway during the first take while being carried out of the reception hall; this is why the scene includes John Savage warning her in the take which was used.

The Bar

The bar was specially constructed in an empty storefront in Mingo Junction, Ohio for $25,000; it later became an actual saloon for local steel mill workers.[3] U.S. Steel allowed filming inside its Cleveland mill, including placing the actors around the furnace floor, only after securing a $5 million insurance policy.[3] When the guys are leaving the factory and heading to Welsh's Lounge, Nick (Walken) encourages Michael (De Niro) to drive faster. In real life, Walken has a phobia of going too fast in cars.

Hunting the Deer

Dzundza completely blows the toast line when the group arrives in the mountains the first time. His reaction is legitimate, and a few of the other actors can be seen laughing in response. According to the film's cinematographer Vilmos Zsigmond, the scene where the deer is shot by Michael (De Niro) was filmed by giving the trained deer a sedative; it took half an hour for the drug to take effect; they had fenced off an area limiting the deer's range and two cameras were used. The deer which Michael allows to get away was actually an elk - the same one often used on commercials for Hartford Insurance.[11] The crew had a very difficult time trying to get the elk to look at them, as it was apparently used to various noises; it finally looked at them when someone in the crew yawned.

Vietnam

De Niro and Savage performed their own stunts in the fall into the river, filming the 30ft drop 15 times in two days. During the helicopter stunt, the runners caught on the ropes and as the helicopter rose, it threatened to seriously injure De Niro and Savage. The actors gestured and yelled furiously to the crew in the helicopter to warn them. Footage of this is included in the film.[12]

According to Cimino, De Niro requested a live bullet in the revolver for the scene in which he subjects John Cazale's character to an impromptu game of Russian roulette, to heighten the intensity of the situation. Cazale agreed without protest,[7] but obsessively rechecked the gun before each take to make sure that the live round wasn't next in the chamber.[3] Director Cimino convinced Walken to spit in De Niro's face. When Walken actually did it, De Niro was completely shocked, as evidenced by his reaction in the film. In fact, De Niro was so furious about it he nearly left the set. Cimino later said of Walken, "He's got courage!" The cast and crew slept on the floor of the warehouse where the Saigon Russian roulette sequences were shot. The scene where Savage is yelling, "Michael, there's rats in here, Michael" as he is stuck in the river is actually Savage yelling at the director because of his fear of rats which were infesting the river area. He was yelling for the director to pull him out of the water because of the rats. The slapping in the Russian roulette sequences was 100% authentic. The actors grew very agitated by the constant slapping, which, naturally, added to the realism of the scenes.

Filming Locations

- St. Theodosius Russian Orthodox Cathedral, Cleveland, Ohio. The name plaque is clearly visible in one scene.
- Lemko Hall, Cleveland, Ohio. The wedding banquet. The name is clearly visible in one scene.
- Patpong, Bangkok, Thailand, the area used to represent Saigon's red light district.
- Sai Yok, Kanchanaburi Province, Thailand
- North Cascades National Park, Washington State, US.
- Steubenville, Ohio, for some mill and neighborhood shots.
- Struthers, Ohio, for external house and long-range road shots.
- Weirton, West Virginia, for mill and trailer shots.

Music

- The theme song of *The Deer Hunter*, Stanley Myers's "Cavatina" (also known as "He Was Beautiful"), performed by classical guitarist John Williams, is commonly known as "The Theme from The Deer Hunter".
- The sub-theme music is "Can't Take My Eyes Off Of You", a 1967 hit song, sung by Frankie Valli. It is played a few times in this movie.
- During the wedding ceremonies and party, the Eastern Orthodox Church songs such as "Slava" and Russian folk songs such as "Korobushka" and "Katyusha" are played.
- Russian Orthodox funeral music is also employed during Nick's funeral scene, mainly "Vechnaya pamyat", which means "memory eternal".[13]

Post production

Director Cimino spent five months mixing the soundtrack. Since this was his first Dolby film, he was eager to exploit the technology to its fullest potential. A short battle sequence, for example, (200 feet of film) took five days to dub. For the re-creation of the American evacuation of Saigon, he accompanied composer Stanley Myers to the location and had him listen to the sounds of vehicles, tanks, and jeep horns as the sequence was being filmed. Myers then composed music for the sequence in the same key as the horns, so that it would blend with the images creating one truly bleak experience.

Release

Deer Hunter was released for a one week engagement in New York and Los Angeles for Oscar consideration on December 8, 1978.[14] [15] The film was given a wide release on February 23, 1979[14] and eventually grossed $48,979,328 at the box office.[1]

CBS paid $3.5 million for three runs of the film. The network later cancelled the acquisition on the contractually permitted grounds of the film containing too much violence for US network transmission.[16]

During screenings of the short version of the film, director Cimino bribed the projectionist to interrupt it, in order to obtain better reviews of the long version.[7]

Analysis

Controversy over Russian Roulette

One of the most talked-about sequences in the film, the Vietcong's use of Russian Roulette with POWs was criticized as being contrived and unrealistic since there were no documented cases of Russian Roulette in the Vietnam War.[17] [18] Director Cimino was also criticized for one-sidedly portraying all the North Vietnamese as despicable, sadistic racists and killers. Cimino countered that his film was not political, polemical, literally accurate, or posturing for any particular point of view.[18] He further defended his position by saying that he had news clippings from Singapore that confirm Russian Roulette was used during the war (without specifying which article).[7]

During the Berlin International Film Festival in 1979, the Soviet delegation expressed its indignation with the film which, in their opinion, insulted the Vietnamese people in numerous scenes. The socialist states felt obliged to voice their solidarity with the "heroic people of Vietnam". They protested against the screening of the film and insisted that it violated the statutes of the festival, since it in no way contributed to the "improvement of mutual understanding between the peoples of the world".[19] The ensuing domino effect led to the walk-outs of the Cubans, East Germans, Bulgarians, Poles and Czechoslovakians, and two members of the jury resigned in sympathy.

In his review, Roger Ebert defended the artistic license of Russian Roulette, arguing "it is the organizing symbol of the film: Anything you can believe about the game, about its deliberately random violence, about how it touches the sanity of men trapped in play, it will apply to the war as a whole. It is a brilliant symbol because, in the context of this story, it makes any ideological statement about the war superfluous."[20]

Film critic & biographer David Thomson also agrees that the film works despite the controversy: "There were complaints that the North Vietnamese had not employed Russian roulette. It was said that the scenes in Saigon were fanciful or imagined. And it was suggested that De Niro, Christoher Walken, and John Savage were too old to have enlisted for Vietnam (Savage, the youngest of the three, was thirty). Three decades later, 'imagination' seems to have stilled those worries... and *The Deer Hunter* is one of the great American films."[21]

Director's trademarks

In only his second film as a director, Cimino continued to develop the trademarks that would come to define his directorial career[22] :

- Abrupt flashforwards (The cut from the bar to Vietnam)
- Casting of non-professional actors in supporting roles (Chuck Aspegren as Axel)
- Characters who become disillusioned with the American Dream (Mike, Steve, and Nick all come back psychologically and/or physically damaged from the war).
- Controversial subject matter (the aforementioned Russian Roulette sequences).
- Sudden bursts of violence in seemingly tranquil or naturalistic settings (the war fighting in the Vietnam jungle).
- Striking visual style: Painterly compositions, jittery tracking shots, and wide vista establishing shots that emphasize the earth/nature (The wide establishing shots of the steel town, the jungles of Vietnam and Saigon).

Reception

Critical reaction

The film's initial reviews were largely enthusiastic. Roger Ebert of the *Chicago Sun-Times* gave the film four stars and called it "one of the most emotionally shattering films ever made."[20] Gene Siskel from the *Chicago Tribune* praised the film, saying, "This is a big film, dealing with big issues, made on a grand scale. Much of it, including some casting decisions, suggest inspiration by *The Godfather*."[23] Leonard Maltin also gave the film four stars, calling it a "sensitive, painful, evocative work".[24] Vincent Canby of the *New York Times* called *The Deer Hunter* "a big, awkward, crazily ambitious motion picture that comes as close to being a popular epic as any movie about this country since *The Godfather*. It's vision is that of an original, major new filmmaker."[25] David Denby of *New York* called it "an epic" with "qualities that we almost never see any more - range and power and breadth of experience."[26] Jack Kroll of *Time* asserted it put director Cimino "right at the center of film culture."[27] Stephen Farber pronounced the film in *New West* magazine as "the greatest anti-war movie since *La Grande Illusion*."[27]

Pauline Kael of *The New Yorker* wrote a praise-worthy review with some reservations: "[It is] a small minded film with greatness in it... with an enraptured view of common life... [but] enraging, because, despite its ambitiousness and scale, it has no more moral intelligence than the Eastwood action pictures."[27]

The film holds a metascore of 73 on Metacritic, based on 7 reviews,[23] and 91% on Rotten Tomatoes, based on 43 reviews.[28] The RT consensus is:

> Its greatness is blunted by its length and one-sided point of view, but the film's weaknesses are overpowered by Michael Cimino's sympathetic direction and a series of heartbreaking performances from Robert De Niro, Meryl Streep, and Christopher Walken.[28]

Top Ten Lists

- 3rd - Roger Ebert, *Chicago Sun-Times*[29]
- 3rd - Gene Siskel, *Chicago Tribune*[30]

Academy Award-winning film director Milos Forman considers *The Deer Hunter* to be one of the ten greatest films of all time.[31]

Revisionism following *Heaven's Gate*

After Cimino's next film, *Heaven's Gate*, debuted to lacerating reviews, several critics revised their positions on *The Deer Hunter*. In his book *Final Cut: Dreams and Disaster in the Making of Heaven's Gate*, Steven Bach wrote, "critics seemed to feel obliged to go on the record about *The Deer Hunter*, to demonstrate that their critical credentials were un-besmirched by having been, as Sarris put it, 'taken in.'"[32]

More recently, BBC film critic Mark Kermode challenged the film's status among generally-praised film classics: "There is an unwritten rule in film criticism that certain films are beyond rebuke. *Citizen Kane, Some Like It Hot, 2001, The Godfather Part II...* all these are considered to be classics of such universally accepted stature... At the risk of being thrown out of the 'respectable film critics' circle, may I take this opportunity to declare officially that in my opinion *The Deer Hunter* is one of the worst films ever made, a rambling self indulgent, self aggrandising barf-fest steeped in manipulatively racist emotion, and notable primarily for its farcically melodramatic tone which is pitched somewhere between shrieking hysteria and somnambulist somberness."[33]

Awards

Academy Awards record
1. Best Supporting Actor, Christopher Walken
2. Best Director, Michael Cimino
3. Best Editing, Peter Zinner
4. Best Picture, Barry Spikings, Michael Deeley, Michael Cimino, John Peverall
5. Best Sound, Richard Portman, William L. McCaughey, Aaron Rochin, C. Darin Knight
Golden Globe Awards record
1. Best Director, Michael Cimino
BAFTA Awards record
1. Best Cinematography, Vilmos Zsigmond
2. Best Editing, Peter Zinner

The Deer Hunter won Academy Awards in 1978 for Best Picture, Best Director (Michael Cimino), Best Actor in a Supporting Role (Christopher Walken), Best Film Editing, and Best Sound.[18] [34] In addition, it was nominated for Best Actor in a Leading Role (Robert De Niro), Best Actress in a Supporting Role (Meryl Streep), Best Cinematography (Vilmos Zsigmond) and Best Writing, Screenplay Written Directly for the Screen (Michael Cimino, Deric Washburn, Louis Garfinkle and Quinn Redeker).[18] [34] John Wayne's final public appearance was to present the Best Picture Oscar to *The Deer Hunter*.[34] It was not a film he was fond of, since it presented a very different view of the Vietnam War than his own movie, *The Green Berets*, had a decade earlier.[8]

Cimino won the only Golden Globe for *The Deer Hunter*, for Best Director. Other nominations the film included Best Motion Picture - Drama, De Niro for Best Motion Picture Actor - Drama, Walken for Best Motion Picture Actor in a Supporting Role, Streep for Best Motion Picture Actress in a Supporting Role, and Washburn for Best Screenplay - Motion Picture.[35]

In total, the film garnered 21 awards and 19 nominations.[35]

Legacy

In 1996, *The Deer Hunter* was selected for preservation in the United States National Film Registry by the Library of Congress as being "culturally, historically, or aesthetically significant".[35][36]

The film ranks 467th in *Empire*'s 2008 list of the 500 greatest movies of all time,[37] noting:

> Cimino's bold, powerful 'Nam epic goes from blue-collar macho rituals to a fiery, South East Asian hell and back to a ragged singalong of America The Beautiful. De Niro holds it together, but Christopher Walken, Meryl Streep and John Savage are unforgettable.[37]

As of May 27, 2010, *The Deer Hunter* is #130 on IMDb's List of Top 250 movies as voted by its users.[38]

Jan Scruggs, a Vietnam veteran who became a counselor with the U.S. Department of Labor, thought of the idea of building a National Memorial for Vietnam Veterans after seeing a screening of the film in March 1979, and he established and operated the memorial fund which paid for it.[39] Director Cimino was invited to the memorial's opening.[7]

The deaths of approximately twenty-five people who died playing Russian roulette were reported as having been influenced by scenes in the movie.[40] Actor Jacques Segui, who plays Julien, lost a friend in real life to a game of Russian Roulette during the Indo-China War.[8]

American Film Institute recognition

- AFI's 100 Years... 100 Movies #79[41]
- AFI's 100 Years... 100 Thrills #30[42]
- AFI's 100 Years... 100 Movies (10th Anniversary Edition) #53[43]

Home media release

The Deer Hunter has twice been released on DVD in America. The first 1998 issue was by Universal, with no extra features and a non-anamorphic transfer, has since been discontinued.[44] A second version, part of the "Legacy Series", was released as a two-disc set on September 6, 2005, with an anamorphic transfer of the film. The set features a cinematographer's commentary by Vilmos Zsigmond, deleted and extended scenes, and production notes.[45] The Region 2 version of *The Deer Hunter*, released in the UK and Japan, features a commentary track from director Michael Cimino. The film was released on HD DVD on December 26, 2006.[46] StudioCanal released the film on the Blu-Ray format in countries other than the United States on March 11, 2009.[47]

See also

- *The Deer Hunter* (novel)
- *The Last Hunter* – An Italian film originally made as an unofficial sequel

References

Bibliography

- Auster, Albert; Quart, Leonard (2002). "The seventies". *American film and society since 1945*. Greenwood Publishing Group. ISBN 9780275967420.
- Bach, Steven (1999). *Final Cut: Art, Money, and Ego in the Making of Heaven's Gate, the Film That Sank United Artists (Updated Edition)*. Newmarket Press. ISBN 1-55704-374-4.
- Deeley, Michael (April 7, 2009). *Blade Runners, Deer Hunters, & Blowing the Bloody Doors Off: My Life in Cult Movies*. New York, NY: Pegasus Books LLC. ISBN 978-1605980386.

- Maltin, Leonard. (August 2008). *Leonard Maltin's 2009 Movie Guide*. Penguin Group Inc. ISBN 978-0-452-28978-9.
- Scruggs, Jan C., and Swerdlow, Joel L. (April 1985). *To Heal a Nation: The Vietnam Veterans Memorial*. New York: Harpercollins. ISBN 978-0060154042

External links

- *The Deer Hunter* [48] at the Internet Movie Database
- *The Deer Hunter* [49] at Allmovie
- *The Deer Hunter* [50] at Box Office Mojo
- *The Deer Hunter* [51] at Rotten Tomatoes
- Trailer [52] for *The Deer Hunter* on YouTube.
- Critics' Picks: 'The Deer Hunter' [53] by New York Times film critic A.O. Scott on YouTube.

References

[1] The Deer Hunter (1978) (http://www.boxofficemojo.com/movies/?id=deerhunter.htm). Box Office Mojo. Retrieved May 26th, 2010.

[2] Roger Ebert: "Michael Cimino's 'The Deer Hunter' is a three-hour movie in three major movements."; Tim Dirks: "The overlong film is roughly divided into equal thirds or acts, spanning the time period 1968-1975"

[3] Director's commentary by Michael Cimino. Included on *The Deer Hunter* UK region 2 DVD release and the StudioCanal Blu-Ray.

[4] Deeley, Pg. 171

[5] Deeley, Pg. 163

[6] Deeley, Pg. 164

[7] *Realizing The Deer Hunter: An Interview with Michael Cimino*. Blue Underground. Interview on the *The Deer Hunter* UK Region 2 DVD and the StudioCanal Blu-Ray. First half of video on YouTube (http://www.youtube.com/watch?v=3Fy2ukXfVVY)

[8] The Deer Hunter (1978) - Trivia (http://www.imdb.com/title/tt0077416/trivia). IMDb. Retrieved 2010-07-25.

[9] Robert De Niro AFI Life Achievement Award Tribute (2003)

[10] *Shooting The Deer Hunter: An interview with Vilmos Zsigmond*. Blue Underground. Interview with the cinematographer, located on *The Deer Hunter* UK Region 2 DVD and StudioCanal Blu-Ray. First half of video on YouTube (http://www.youtube.com/watch?v=XUdifNdwO1g).

[11] Deeley, Pg. 174

[12] *Playing The Deer Hunter: An interview with John Savage*. Blue Underground. Interview with the actor Savage, located on the UK Region 2 DVD and StudioCanal Blu-Ray. First half of video on YouTube (http://www.youtube.com/watch?v=l1ovPVUa5HA)

[13] Researching the Brothers Karamazov - Guest lectures/ Sheehan (http://www.dartmouth.edu/~karamazo/sheehan.html).Retrieved May 17, 2010.

[14] The Deer Hunter (1978) - Release dates (http://www.imdb.com/title/tt0077416/releaseinfo).IMDb. Retrieved 2010-07-25.

[15] Bach, Pg. 166

[16] Deeley, Pg. 181

[17] Auster & Quart, Pg. 120-1

[18] Dirks, Tim. The Deer Hunter (http://www.filmsite.org/deer.html). Greatest Films. Retrieved May 26, 2010.

[19] "1979 Yearbook" (http://www.berlinale.de/en/archiv/jahresarchive/1979/01_jahresblatt_1979/01_Jahresblatt_1979.html). Berlin International Film Festival. . Retrieved 2010-07-28.

[20] Ebert, Roger (March 9, 1979). The Deer Hunter (http://rogerebert.suntimes.com/apps/pbcs.dll/article?AID=/19790309/REVIEWS/903090301/1023). *Chicago Sun-Times*. Retrieved April 30th, 2010.

[21] Thomson, David (October 14, 2008). *"Have You Seen . . . ?": A Personal Introduction to 1,000 Films*. Knopf. p. 209. ISBN 978-0307264619.

[22] Michael Cimino (I) - Biography (http://www.imdb.com/name/nm0001047/bio). IMDb. Retrieved 2010-08-23.

[23] *The Deer Hunter* Reviews (http://www.metacritic.com/video/titles/deerhunter). Metacritic. Retrieved April 30th, 2010.

[24] Maltin, Pg. 338

[25] Bach, Pg. 167

[26] Bach, Pg. 167-8

[27] Bach, Pg. 168

[28] "The Deer Hunter (1978)" (http://www.rottentomatoes.com/m/deer_hunter). *Rotten Tomatoes*. . Retrieved 2009-09-23.

[29] Ebert, Roger (December 15, 2004). "Ebert's 10 Best Lists 1967-present" (http://rogerebert.suntimes.com/apps/pbcs.dll/article?AID=/20041215/COMMENTARY/41215001/1023). *Chicago Sun-Times*. . Retrieved 2010-10-20.

[30] Siskel and Ebert Top Ten Lists (1969-1998) (http://www.innermind.com/misc/s_e_top.htm). Retrieved April 30th, 2010.

[31] Top Ten Lists by Critics and Filmmakers (http://www.combustiblecelluloid.com/faves.shtml). Combustible Celluloid. Retrieved June 12, 2010.

[32] Bach, Pg. 370

[33] Kermode, Mark. "Oh deer, oh deer, oh deer" (http://www.film4.com/features/article/oh-deer-oh-deer-oh-deer). *Film4.*. Retrieved 2010-05-27.

[34] All the Oscars: 1978 - 51st Annual Academy Awards (http://theoscarsite.com/1978.htm).Retrieved May 26th, 2010.

[35] The Deer Hunter (1978) - Awards (http://www.imdb.com/title/tt0077416/awards). IMDb. Retrieved May 27, 2010.

[36] Films Selected to The National Film Registry 1989-2008 (http://www.loc.gov/film/nfrchron.html). Library of Congress. Retrieved June 11, 2010.

[37] "The 500 Greatest Movies Of All Time" (http://www.empireonline.com/500/7.asp). *Empire.*. Retrieved 06-02-2010.

[38] IMDb Top 250 - *The Deer Hunter* (http://www.imdb.com/chart/top?tt0077416). IMDb. Retrieved May 27, 2010.

[39] Scruggs & Swerdlow, Pg. 7

[40] The Deer Hunter and Suicides (http://www.snopes.com/movies/films/deerhunter.asp). Snopes.com. Retrieved June 12, 2010.

[41] AFI's 100 YEARS...100 MOVIES (1998) (http://connect.afi.com/site/DocServer/movies100.pdf?docID=264).American Film Institute. Retrieved May 6th, 2010.

[42] AFI's 100 Years... 100 Thrills (http://connect.afi.com/site/DocServer/thrills100.pdf?docID=250). American Film Institute. Retrieved April 30th, 2010.

[43] "AFI's 100 Years... 100 Movies" (http://www.afi.com/tvevents/100years/movies.aspx). American Film Institute. .

[44] "The Deer Hunter (1978) - DVD details" (http://www.imdb.com/title/tt0077416/dvd). IMDb. . Retrieved 2010-08-12.

[45] "The Deer Hunter (Universal Legacy Series)" (http://www.amazon.com/Deer-Hunter-Universal-Legacy/dp/B000AABCU2/ ref=sr_1_2?ie=UTF8&s=dvd&qid=1281672115&sr=8-2). Amazon.com. . Retrieved 2010-08-12.

[46] The Deer Hunter HD-DVD (http://www.amazon.com/Deer-Hunter-HD-DVD/dp/B000K7VHUA/ref=ed_oe_hdd).Amazon.com. Retrieved May 18, 2010.

[47] "Achetez le Blu-Ray Voyage au bout de l'enfer à 19.99 € sur StudioCanal" (http://www.studiocanaldvd.com/fr/ produit_6_scv_53855_acheter_Blu-Ray_Voyage_au_bout_de_l'enfer_en_stock.php) (in French). StudioCanal.com. . Retrieved 2010-05-19.

[48] http://www.imdb.com/title/tt0077416/

[49] http://www.allmovie.com/work/13060

[50] http://www.boxofficemojo.com/movies/?id=deerhunter.htm

[51] http://www.rottentomatoes.com/m/deer_hunter//

[52] http://www.youtube.com/watch?v=3Gqit3zVmyc

[53] http://www.youtube.com/watch?v=jonkduDdc5k

Manhattan (film)

Manhattan	
Theatrical release poster	
Directed by	Woody Allen
Produced by	Charles H. Joffe
Written by	Woody Allen Marshall Brickman
Starring	Woody Allen Diane Keaton Michael Murphy Mariel Hemingway Meryl Streep
Music by	George Gershwin
Cinematography	Gordon Willis
Editing by	Susan E. Morse
Distributed by	United Artists
Release date(s)	April 25, 1979
Running time	96 minutes
Country	United States
Language	English
Gross revenue	$39,946,780[1]

Manhattan is a 1979 American romantic comedy film about Isaac Davis, a twice-divorced 42-year-old comedy writer dating a 17-year-old high school girl. Isaac eventually falls in love with his best friend's mistress. The movie was written by Allen and Marshall Brickman, who had also successfully collaborated on *Annie Hall*, and directed by Allen. *Manhattan* was filmed in black and white and 2.35:1 widescreen.

The film was nominated for two Academy Awards for Best Actress in a Supporting Role (Mariel Hemingway) and Best Writing, Screenplay Written Directly for the Screen. It also won the BAFTA Award for Best Film. The film was won on American Film Institute's "100 Years... 100 Laughs". This film is number 63 on Bravo's "100 Funniest

Movies". In 2001, the United States Library of Congress deemed the film "culturally significant" and selected it for preservation in the National Film Registry.

Plot

The film opens with a montage of images of Manhattan accompanied by George Gershwin's *Rhapsody in Blue*. TV writer Isaac Davis (Woody Allen), is introduced as a man writing a book about his love for New York City. He is a twice-divorced 42-year-old dealing with the women in his life who gives up his unfulfilling job as a comedy writer. He is dating Tracy (Mariel Hemingway), a 17-year old high school girl. His best friend, Yale (Michael Murphy), married to Emily (Anne Byrne), is having an affair with Mary Wilkie (Diane Keaton); her ex-husband and former teacher Jeremiah (Wallace Shawn) also appears. Isaac's lesbian ex-wife, Jill (Meryl Streep), is writing a confessional book about their marriage.

When Isaac meets Mary, her cultural snobbery rubs him the wrong way. Isaac runs into her again at an Equal Rights Amendment fund raising event at the Museum of Modern Art and accompanies her for the cab ride home. They chat until sunrise, a sequence that culminates in the iconic shot of the Queensboro Bridge. In spite of a growing attraction to Mary, Isaac continues his relationship with Tracy. But he emphasizes that theirs can't be a serious affair and encourages the girl to go to London to study acting. In another iconic scene, at Tracy's request, they go on a carriage ride through Central Park.

After Yale breaks up with Mary, he suggests Isaac ask her out. Isaac does, always having felt Tracy is too young for him. Isaac breaks up with Tracy, much to her dismay, and before long Mary has virtually moved into his apartment. Emily is curious about Isaac's new girlfriend, and after several meetings between the two couples, including one where Emily reads out portions of Jill's new book about her marriage with Isaac, Yale leaves Emily to resume his relationship with Mary. A betrayed Isaac confronts Yale at the college where he teaches, but he says he found Mary first. Isaac responds by discussing Yale's extramarital affairs with Emily, but she thinks Isaac introduced Mary to Yale. In the denouement, Isaac lies on his sofa, musing into a tape recorder about the things that make "life worth living"—the final item, after which he sets down the microphone, is "Tracy's face."

He leaves his apartment and sets out on foot for Tracy's. He arrives at her family's doorman apartment just as she is leaving for England. He says that she doesn't have to go and that he doesn't want "that special thing" about her to change. She replies that the plans have already been made and reassures him that "not everyone gets corrupted": "You've got to have faith in people". He gives her a slight smile segueing into final shots of the skyline with *Rhapsody in Blue* playing again.

Cast

- Woody Allen as Isaac Davis
- Diane Keaton as Mary Wilkie
- Michael Murphy as Yale Pollack
- Mariel Hemingway as Tracy
- Meryl Streep as Jill
- Anne Byrne as Emily
- Michael O'Donoghue as Dennis
- Wallace Shawn as Jeremiah
- Karen Ludwig as Connie
- Charles Levin, Karen Allen, and David Rasche as Television actors
- Mary Linn Baker and Frances Conroy as Shakespearean actors

Production

According to Allen, the idea for *Manhattan* originated from his love of George Gershwin's music. He was listening to one of the composer's albums of overtures and thought, "this would be a beautiful thing to make ... a movie in black and white ... a romantic movie".[2] Allen has said that *Manhattan* was "like a mixture of what I was trying to do with *Annie Hall* and *Interiors*".[3] He also said that his film deals with the problem of people trying to live a decent existence in an essential junk-obsessed contemporary culture without selling out, admitting that he himself could conceive of giving away all of "[his] possessions to

The iconic bridge shot

charity and living in much more modest circumstances", continuing, "I've rationalized my way out of it so far, but I could conceive of doing it".[4]

Allen talked to cinematographer Gordon Willis about how fun it would be to shoot the film in black and white, Panavision aspect ratio (2.35:1) because it would give "a great look at New York City, which is sort of one of the characters in the film".[5] Allen decided to shoot his film in black and white "because that's how I remember it from when I was small. Maybe it's a reminiscence from old photographs, films, books and all that. But that's how I remember New York. I always heard Gershwin music with it, too. In *Manhattan* I really think that we — that's me and cinematographer Gordon Willis — succeeded in showing the city. When you see it there on that big screen it's really decadent".[6] The picture was shot on location with the exception of some of the scenes in the planetarium which were filmed on a set..[7]

The iconic bridge shot was done at 5 am.[8] The bridge had two sets of necklace lights on a timer controlled by the city. When the sun comes up, the bridge lights go off. Willis made arrangements with the city to leave the lights on and he would let them know when they got the shot. Afterwards, they could be turned off. As they started to shoot the scene, one string of bridge lights went out and Allen was forced to use that take.[8]

After finishing the film, Allen was very unhappy with it and asked United Artists not to release it. He offered to make a film for free instead.[9] Allen has never said why he disliked the movie in any interview which has puzzled many of his fans who consider it to be one of his best.

Reaction

Manhattan opened in 29 North American theaters on April 25, 1979. It grossed $485,734 ($16,749 per screen) in its opening weekend, and earned $39.9 million in its entire run.[10]

The film was shown out of competition at the 1979 Cannes Film Festival in May.[11]

The film received largely positive reviews and currently has a rating of 98% on Rotten Tomatoes[12] . Gary Arnold, in the *Washington Post*, wrote, "*Manhattan* has comic integrity in part because Allen is now making jokes at the expense of his own parochialism. There's no opportunity to heap condescending abuse on the phonies and sellouts decorating the Hollywood landscape. The result appears to be a more authentic and magnanimous comic perception of human vanity and foolhardiness".[13] In his review for *Newsweek* magazine, Jack Kroll wrote, "Allen's growth in every department is lovely to behold. He gets excellent performances from his cast. The increasing visual beauty of his films is part of their grace and sweetness, their balance between Allen's yearning romanticism and his tough eye for the fatuous and sentimental - a balance also expressed in his best screen play yet".[14] In his review for the *Chicago Sun Times*, Roger Ebert wrote, "Diane Keaton gives us a fresh and nicely edged New York intellectual. And Mariel Hemingway deserves some kind of special award for what's in some ways the most difficult role in the film".[15]

Alexander Walker of the *London Evening Standard* wrote, "So precisely nuanced is the speech, so subtle the behaviour of a group of friends, lovers, mistresses and cuckolds who keep splitting up and pairing off like unstable molecules".[16] *Time* film critic Frank Rich wrote at the time that Allen's film is "tightly constructed, clearly focused intellectually, it is a prismatic portrait of a time and place that may be studied decades hence to see what kind of people we were". Recently, J. Hoberman wrote in the *Village Voice*, "The New York City that Woody so tediously defended in *Annie Hall* was in crisis. And so he imagined an improved version. More than that, he cast this shining city in the form of those movies that he might have seen as a child in Coney Island—freeing the visions that he sensed to be locked up in the silver screen".[17]

Allen was named best director for *Manhattan* by the New York Film Critics Circle.[18] The National Society of Film Critics also named Allen best director along with Robert Benton who directed *Kramer vs. Kramer*.[19] The film was nominated for Academy Awards for Best Actress in a Supporting Role (Mariel Hemingway) and Best Writing, Screenplay Written Directly for the Screen.[20] It also won the BAFTA Award for Best Film.

The film was #46 on American Film Institute's "100 Years... 100 Laughs". This film is number 63 on Bravo's "100 Funniest Movies." In 2001, the United States Library of Congress deemed the film "culturally significant" and selected it for preservation in the National Film Registry. It is also ranked #4 on Rotten Tomatoes' 25 Best Romantic Comedies.[21]

American Film Institute recognition

- 2000: AFI's 100 Years... 100 Laughs #46
- 2002: AFI's 100 Years... 100 Passions #66

Manhattan also inspired the song "Remember Manhattan" written by Richard Marx and Fee Waybill from Marx's debut album.

Home release

Allen wanted to preserve Willis's compositions and insisted that the aspect ratio be preserved when the film was released on video (an unusual request in a time when widescreen films were normally panned and scanned for TV and video release). As a result, all copies of the film on video (and most television broadcasts) were letterboxed, originally with a gray border.[2]

External links

- *Manhattan* [22] at the Internet Movie Database
- *Manhattan* [23] at Allmovie
- *Manhattan* [24] at Box Office Mojo
- *Manhattan* [25] at Rotten Tomatoes
- *The Film Journal*: Woody's *Manhattan* at 25 [26]
- *The Reeler* interview with Gordon Willis [27]

References

[1] http://www.boxofficemojo.com/movies/?id=manhattan.htm

[2] Fox, Julian (September 1, 1996). "Woody: Movies from Manhattan". Overlook Hardcover.

[3] Brode, Douglas (1987). "Woody Allen: His Films and Career". Citadel Press.

[4] Rich, Frank (April 30, 1979). "An Interview with Woody". Time.

[5] Bjorkman, Stig (1993). "Woody Allen on Woody Allen". Grove Press. pp. 108.

[6] Palmer, Myles (1980). "Woody Allen". Proteus. pp. 112.

[7] Bjorkman 1993, p. 112.

[8] Willis, Gordon (April 6, 2004). "Made in *Manhattan*" (http://www.moviemaker.com/directing/article/made_in_manhattan_2930/). *Moviemaker*. . Retrieved 2009-02-13.

[9] Bjorkman 1993, p. 116.

[10] "*Manhattan*" (http://www.boxofficemojo.com/movies/?id=manhattan.htm). Box Office Mojo. May 2, 1979. . Retrieved 2007-01-11.

[11] "Festival de Cannes: Manhattan" (http://www.festival-cannes.com/en/archives/ficheFilm/id/1894/year/1979.html). *festival-cannes.com.* . Retrieved 2009-05-25.

[12] "*Manhattan*" (http://www.rottentomatoes.com/m/manhattan/). Rotten Tomatoes. May 2, 1979. . Retrieved 2009-05-27.

[13] Arnold, Gary (May 2, 1979). "Woody Allen's Comic High: A Delightful and Deluxe Rhapsody of Wry Romance". Washington Post.

[14] Kroll, Jack (April 30, 1979). "Woody's Big Apple". Newsweek.

[15] Ebert, Roger (January 1, 1979). "*Manhattan*" (http://rogerebert.suntimes.com/apps/pbcs.dll/article?AID=/19790101/REVIEWS/901010322/1023). Chicago Sun-Times. . Retrieved 2008-01-11.

[16] Palmer 1980, p. 114.

[17] Hoberman, J (July 10, 2007). "Defending *Manhattan*" (http://www.villagevoice.com/film/0728,hoberman,77195,20.html). *Village Voice.* . Retrieved 2007-07-11.

[18] "*Kramer vs. Kramer* selected best film". *Globe and Mail.* December 21, 1979.

[19] Arnold, Gary (January 3, 1980). "Film Critics' Pick of the Year". *Washington Post.*

[20] Arnold, Gary (February 26, 1980). "*Kramer, Jazz* Lead Nominees". *Washington Post.*

[21] "25 Best Romantic Comedies" (http://www.rottentomatoes.com/guides/best_romantic_comedies/manhattan/). *Rotten Tomatoes.* 2009. . Retrieved 2009-02-12.

[22] http://www.imdb.com/title/tt0079522/

[23] http://www.allmovie.com/work/31285

[24] http://www.boxofficemojo.com/movies/?id=manhattan.htm

[25] http://www.rottentomatoes.com/m/manhattan/

[26] http://www.thefilmjournal.com/issue8/manhattan.html

[27] http://www.thereeler.com/features/letters_from_gordon.php

The Seduction of Joe Tynan

The Seduction of Joe Tynan	
 Theatrical release poster	
Directed by	Jerry Schatzberg
Produced by	Martin Bregman
Written by	Alan Alda
Starring	Alan Alda Barbara Harris Meryl Streep Rip Torn Melvyn Douglas
Music by	Bill Conti
Cinematography	Adam Holender
Editing by	Evan A. Lottman
Distributed by	Universal Pictures
Release date(s)	August 17, 1979
Running time	107 minutes
Country	United States
Language	English

The Seduction of Joe Tynan is a 1979 American political film drama directed by Jerry Schatzberg and produced by Martin Bregman.[1] The screenplay was written by Alan Alda, who also played the title role.[2]

The film stars Alda, Barbara Harris, and Meryl Streep, with Rip Torn, Melvyn Douglas, Charles Kimbrough, and Carrie Nye.[3]

Plot

A respected liberal Senator Joe Tynan is asked to to lead the opposition to a Supreme Court appointment.

Cast

- Alan Alda as Joe Tynan
- Barbara Harris as Ellie Tynan
- Meryl Streep as Karen Traynor
- Rip Torn as Senator Kittner
- Melvyn Douglas as Senator Birney
- Charles Kimbrough as Francis
- Carrie Nye as Aldena Kittner
- Michael Higgins as Senator Pardew
- Blanche Baker as Janet
- Chris Arnold as Jerry
- Maureen Anderman as Joe's Secretary
- John Badila as Reporter on TV Screen
- Robert Christian as Arthur Briggs
- Maurice Copeland as Edward Anderson
- Lu Elrod as Congresswoman at Party

Awards

Wins

- Los Angeles Film Critics Association Awards: LAFCA Award, Best Supporting Actor, Melvyn Douglas; Best Supporting Actress, Meryl Streep; 1979.
- National Board of Review of Motion Pictures: NBR Award, Best Supporting Actress, Meryl Streep; 1979.
- National Society of Film Critics: NSFC Award, 0Best Supporting Actress, Meryl Streep; 1979.
- New York Film Critics Circle Awards: NYFCC Award, Best Supporting Actress, Meryl Streep; 1979.
- American Movie Awards: Marquee, Best Actor, Alan Alda; 1980.

External links

- *The Seduction of Joe Tynan* [4] at the Internet Movie Database

References

[1]   Rich, Frank (1979-08-20). "Split Ticket" (http://www.time.com/time/magazine/article/0,9171,947366,00.html). *TIME.* .

[2]   Maslin (1979-08-17). "Screen: Alan Alda Writes and Stars in 'Joe Tynan'; Coping With Fame" (http://select.nytimes.com/gst/abstract. html?res=FA0F13FC385D12728DDDAE0994D0405B898BF1D3). *The New York Times*: p. C6. .

[3]   "The Seduction of Joe Tynan" (http://www.variety.com/review/VE1117794735.html?categoryid=31&cs=1). *Variety*. 1979-01-01. .

[4]   http://www.imdb.com/title/tt0079875/

Kramer vs. Kramer

Kramer vs. Kramer	
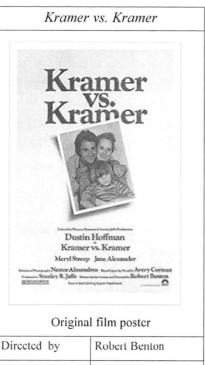 Original film poster	
Directed by	Robert Benton
Produced by	Richard Fischoff Stanley R. Jaffe
Written by	Avery Corman (novel) Robert Benton
Starring	Dustin Hoffman Meryl Streep Justin Henry Jane Alexander
Music by	Paul Gemignani Herb Harris John Kander Erma E. Levin Roy B. Yokelson Antonio Vivaldi
Cinematography	Néstor Almendros
Editing by	Gerald B. Greenberg Ray Hubley Bill Pankow
Distributed by	Columbia Pictures
Release date(s)	December 17, 1979
Running time	105 minutes
Country	United States
Language	English
Gross revenue	$104,986,000[1]

→ Person she always fought with

Kramer vs. Kramer is a 1979 American drama film adapted by Robert Benton from the novel by Avery Corman, and directed by Benton. The film tells the story of a married couple's divorce and its impact on everyone involved, including the couple's young son. It received the Academy Award for Best Picture in 1979.

Plot

Ted Kramer (Dustin Hoffman), a workaholic advertising executive, is just given his agency's biggest new account. After spending the evening chatting with his boss about handling a new and very large account, he returns home to find his wife Joanna (Meryl Streep) in the process of leaving him.

Ted is left to raise their son Billy (Justin Henry) by himself. Ted and Billy begin to resent each other as Ted no longer has time to carry his increased workload, and Billy misses the love and attention he received from his mother. After many months of unrest, Ted and Billy begin to cope with the situation and eventually grow to love and care for one another.

Ted befriends his neighbor Margaret (Jane Alexander), who initially had counseled Joanna to leave Ted. Margaret is a fellow single parent and the two become kindred spirits. One day as the two sit in the park watching their children play, Billy falls off the jungle gym and severely cuts his face. Picking him up, Ted sprints several blocks through oncoming traffic to the hospital, where he comforts his son tenderly, representing his increased emotional connection and sense of responsibility for the child since his wife left.

Fifteen months after she walked out, Joanna returns to New York in order to claim Billy, and a custody battle ensues. During the custody hearing, both Ted and Joanna are unprepared for the brutal character assassinations that their lawyers unleash on the other. For instance, Margaret is forced to confess that she advised Joanna to leave Ted if she was as unhappy as she professed, although she also attempts to tell Joanna on the stand that her husband has profoundly changed. Eventually, the damaging facts that Ted was fired because of his conflicting responsibilities with his son, forcing him to take a lower-paid job, come out in court, as do the details of Billy's accident.

Finally, the court awards custody to Joanna, not so much due to the evidence on both sides but due to the assumption that a child is best raised by their mother. Ted discusses appealing the case, but his lawyer warns that Billy himself would have to take the stand in the resulting trial and Ted cannot bear the thought of submitting his child to such an ordeal. He therefore decides not to contest custody.

On the morning that Billy is to move in with Joanna, Ted and Billy make breakfast together, mirroring the meal that Ted tried to cook the first morning after Joanna left. They hug in a very tender moment as they both know this is their last breakfast together. Joanna calls from the ground floor, asking Ted to come down to talk. She tells Ted that, while she loves Billy and wants him with her, she knows that he is already home, and that his true home is with Ted. She will therefore not take him. As she enters the elevator, she asks her ex-husband "How do I look?". The movie ends with the elevator doors closing on the emotional Joanna, right after Ted answers, "You look terrific," as she heads upstairs to talk to Billy.

Cast

- Dustin Hoffman as Ted Kramer
- Meryl Streep as Joanna Kramer
- Justin Henry as Billy Kramer
- Jane Alexander as Margaret Phelps
- Petra King as Petie Phelps
- Melissa Morell as Kim Phelps
- Howard Duff as John Shaunessy
- George Coe as Jim O'Connor
- JoBeth Williams as Phyllis Bernard

- Howland Chamberlain as Judge Atkins
- Dan Tyra as Court Clerk

Production

Kate Jackson was originally offered the role played by Meryl Streep but was forced to turn it down. At the time, Jackson was appearing in the TV series *Charlie's Angels*, and producer Aaron Spelling told her that they were unable to rearrange the shooting schedule to give her time off to do the film.[2] At the time, Streep was cast as Phyllis (the one-night stand Ted has); this role was eventually given to JoBeth Williams when Streep was cast as Joanna.

Legal inaccuracies

The film review book *Reel Justice* notes that it is unlikely Billy would have been called to the stand during an appeal. An appeal is based on the records of the previous trial, which means no new evidence is to be submitted, so no one is called to testify. Billy is also too young for his opinions to be considered a determinant in a custody case. Furthermore, if Billy had to be questioned, a private discussion with the judge in his chambers or with a social worker and/or child psychologist would have sufficed by most legal opinions.

The book also notes that the judge ruled for the mother solely on the "Tender Years Doctrine", that a child is better off with his mother by default, a legal assumption that was already losing credibility by 1979. An equivalent ruling today would be considered an abuse of judicial discretion.

In one trial scene, Ted Kramer's lawyer was harshly grilling Joanna Kramer for answers, at one point actually shouting at her. This, under any real circumstances, would have undoubtedly ended up in an objection from the prosecution for badgering the witness.

Both lawyers were being improper in demanding "yes or no" responses from witnesses in a non-juried custody case, without allowing the witnesses to fully explain their answers. The judge should have allowed the witness to explain, or the opposing lawyers could have requested redirecting testimony to supply that explanation. To modern eyes, even lay ones, these scenes stand out as stretching credibility.

Reception

The film received positive impact from critics, receiving 88% positive reviews on Rotten Tomatoes. [3] Roger Ebert of the Chicago Sun Times gave the film four stars, giving praise to the screenplay by Robert Benton, "His characters aren't just talking to each other, they're revealing things about themselves and can sometimes be seen in the act of learning about their own motives. That's what makes "Kramer vs. Kramer" such a touching film: We get the feeling at times that personalities are changing and decisions are being made even as we watch them."[4]

Cultural impact

Kramer vs. Kramer reflected a cultural shift which occurred during the 1970s and the period of second-wave feminism, when ideas about motherhood and fatherhood were changing. The film was widely praised for the way in which it gave equal weight and importance to both Joanna and Ted's points of view.[5]

Awards and nominations

The film won 5 Oscars, another 31 wins and 15 nominations.

Wins

- Academy Award for Best Picture
- Academy Award for Best Director
- Academy Award for Best Writing, Screenplay Based on Material from Another Medium
- Academy Award for Best Actor in a Leading Role - Dustin Hoffman
- Academy Award for Best Actress in a Supporting Role - Meryl Streep
- Golden Globe Award for Best Motion Picture – Drama
- Golden Globe Award for Best Motion Picture Actor - Drama, Dustin Hoffman
- Golden Globe Award for Best Motion Picture Actress in a Supporting Role, Meryl Streep
- Golden Globe Award for Best Screenplay - Motion Picture
- David di Donatello for Best Foreign Film
- David di Donatello for Best Foreign Actor (1980) - Dustin Hoffman

Nominations

- Academy Award for Best Actress in a Supporting Role - Jane Alexander
- Academy Award for Best Cinematography
- Academy Award for Best Film Editing
- Academy Award for Best Actor in a Supporting Role - Justin Henry. To date, Henry is the youngest person ever nominated for an Academy Award.
- Golden Globe Award for Best Director - Robert Benton
- Golden Globe Award for Best Supporting Actor - Justin Henry
- Golden Globe Award for Best Supporting Actress - Jane Alexander
- Golden Globe Award for New Star of the Year in a Motion Picture – Male - Justin Henry
- BAFTA Award for Best Film - Stanley R. Jaffe
- BAFTA Award for Best Actor in a Leading Role - Dustin Hoffman
- BAFTA Award for Best Actress in a Leading Role - Meryl Streep
- BAFTA Award for Best Direction - Robert Benton
- BAFTA Award for Best Editing - Gerald B. Greenberg
- BAFTA Award for Best Screenplay - Robert Benton
- César Award for Best Foreign Film

See also

- "Kramer vs. Kramer: Kenny to Cosmo"

External links

- *Kramer vs. Kramer* [6] at the Internet Movie Database
- *Kramer vs. Kramer* [7] at Allmovie
- *Kramer vs. Kramer* [8] at the TCM Movie Database
- *Kramer vs. Kramer* [9] at Rotten Tomatoes

References

[1] "Kramer vs Kramer (1979)" (http://www.boxofficemojo.com/movies/?id=kramervskramer.htm). Box Office Mojo. . Retrieved 2008-11-17.

[2] Spelling, Aaron; Graham, Jefferson (1996). *A Prime-Time Life: An Autobiography*. New York: St. Martin's Press. p. 112. ISBN 0-312-14268-4.

[3] "Kramer vs. Kramer (1979)" (http://www.rottentomatoes.com/m/kramer_vs_kramer/). . Retrieved April 29,2010.

[4] "Kramer vs. Kramer (1979)" (http://rogerebert.suntimes.com/apps/pbcs.dll/article?AID=/19791201/REVIEWS/41004001/1023). . Retrieved April 29,2010.

[5] :: rogerebert.com :: Reviews :: Kramer vs. Kramer (xhtml) (http://rogerebert.suntimes.com/apps/pbcs.dll/article?AID=/19791201/REVIEWS/41004001/1023)

[6] http://www.imdb.com/title/tt0079417/

[7] http://www.allmovie.com/work/27688

[8] http://tcmdb.com/title/title.jsp?stid=4665

[9] http://www.rottentomatoes.com/m/kramer_vs_kramer/

The French Lieutenant's Woman (film)

The French Lieutenant's Woman	
Original film poster	
Directed by	Karel Reisz
Produced by	Leon Clore
Written by	Harold Pinter John Fowles(novel)
Starring	Meryl Streep Jeremy Irons Hilton McRae David Warner Penelope Wilton Lynsey Baxter Leo McKern
Music by	Carl Davis
Cinematography	Freddie Francis
Editing by	John Bloom
Distributed by	United Artists
Release date(s)	United States: 18 September 1981
Running time	129 min.
Country	UK
Language	English

The French Lieutenant's Woman is a 1981 film directed by Karel Reisz and adapted by playwright Harold Pinter. It is based on the novel of the same title by John Fowles. The music score is by Carl Davis and the cinematography by Freddie Francis.

The film stars Meryl Streep and Jeremy Irons with Hilton McRae, Jean Faulds, Peter Vaughan, Colin Jeavons, Liz Smith, Patience Collier, Richard Griffiths, David Warner, Alun Armstrong, Penelope Wilton and Leo McKern.

Streep was nominated for Academy Award for Best Actress, as well as the film was nominated for Academy Award for Best Writing (Adapted Screenplay), but both lost to *On Golden Pond*. The film also nominated for three more Academy Awards.

Background and production

The plot concerns the love affair between a Victorian gentleman and a woman who has been jilted by a French officer, scandalizing the "polite society" of Lyme Regis.

In the original book, the author is very much present - constantly addressing the reader directly and commenting on his characters, and on Victorian society in general, from his Twentieth-century perspective. A direct adaptation would have required a continual voice over.

Instead, the film creates the effect of the 19th Century society looked at from a 20th Century perspective by having a story within a story, the Victorian story being a film being shot in the present and the actors portraying the two Victorian characters having a love affair in their actual life, with the film shifting constantly between the two centuries. And though the actors are not bound by Victorian mores in their actual present-day lives, their affair still presents hard dilemmas since each is in a relationship to somebody else.

Also, instead of trying to create a literal translation of the novel's alternate endings, Pinter's screenplay adopted a more cinematic approach by having the characters' story end one way and the actors' another.

The book was published in 1969 and unlike his previous novels the transfer to the big screen was a protracted process with the film rights changing hands a number of times before a treatment, funding and cast were eventually finalized. In 1977 Malcolm Bradbury and Christopher Bigsby approached Fowles to suggest they work on a television adaptation which Fowles was amenable to, but then producer Saul Zaentz came in and the film version was finally greenlit.

A number of names were attached to the project, directors mooted included Sidney Lumet, Robert Bolt, Fred Zinnemann and Milos Forman. The script went through a number of treatments including one by Dennis Potter in 1975 and James Costigan in 1976 before Pinter's final draft was used. Actors considered for the role of Charles Smithson/Mike included Robert Redford and Richard Chamberlain and Sarah/Anna included Francesca Annis, Gemma Jones and Fowles's choice Helen Mirren.[1]

Carl Davis' award-winning music performed by an unidentified orchestra and Viola soloist Kenneth Essex, who in earlier years had appeared as one of the four string soloists on several Beatles singles including Eleanor Rigby.

Awards and nominations

Academy Awards

Nominations [2]

- Best Actress in a Leading Role: Meryl Streep
- Best Art Direction-Set Decoration: Assheton Gorton, Ann Mollo
- Best Costume Design
- Best Film Editing
- Best Writing, Screenplay Based on Material from Another Medium.

BAFTA Awards

Wins

- Anthony Asquith Award for Film Music: Carl Davis
- Best Actress: Meryl Streep
- Best Sound: Don Sharp, Ivan Sharrock, Bill Rowe

Nominations

- Best Film
- Best Actor: Jeremy Irons
- Best Cinematography: Freddie Francis
- Best Costume Design: Tom Rand
- Best Direction: Karel Reisz
- Best Editing: John Bloom
- Best Production Design/Art Direction: Assheton Gorton
- Best Screenplay: Harold Pinter

Golden Globe Awards

Win

- Best Actress: Meryl Streep

Nominations

- Best Motion Picture - Drama
- Best Screenplay: Harold Pinter

Other awards

- Evening Standard British Film Award Best Film: Karel Reisz
- David di Donatello Awards: Best Screenplay - Foreign Film: Harold Pinter
- Los Angeles Film Critics Association Awards: Best Actress: Meryl Streep

External links

- *The French Lieutenant's Woman* [3] at the Internet Movie Database

References

[1] John Fowles, The French Lieutenant's Diary, Granta #86, 2004, ISBN 0 90 314169 8

[2] "NY Times: The French Lieutenant's Woman" (http://movies.nytimes.com/movie/18627/The-French-Lieutenant-s-Woman/awards). *NY Times*. . Retrieved 2008-12-31.

[3] http://www.imdb.com/title/tt0082416/

Still of the Night (film)

Still of the Night	
Theatrical poster	
Directed by	Robert Benton
Produced by	Arlene Donovan
Written by	Robert Benton David Newman (story)
Starring	Roy Scheider Meryl Streep Jessica Tandy Josef Sommer
Music by	John Kander
Cinematography	Néstor Almendros
Editing by	Gerald B. Greenberg Bill Pankow
Distributed by	MGM
Release date(s)	November 19, 1982
Running time	93 minutes
Country	United States
Language	English
Gross revenue	$5,979,947 (USA)

Still of the Night is a 1982 American psychological thriller film, directed by Robert Benton and written by Benton and David Newman. It features Roy Scheider, Meryl Streep, and Jessica Tandy. Scheider plays a psychiatrist who falls in love with a woman (Streep) who may be the psychopathic killer of one of his clients. The film has been compared to the works of Alfred Hitchcock.

Plot

Manhattan psychiatrist Dr. Sam Rice (Roy Scheider) is visited by glamorous, enigmatic Brooke Reynolds (Meryl Streep). Brooke was having an affair with one of Rice's patients, George Bynum (Josef Sommer). Bynum was just killed and Brooke asks Rice to return a watch to Bynum's wife and not reveal the affair.

Rice is visited by Det. Vitucci (Joe Grifasi) but refuses to give any information on Bynum who has been seeing him twice a week for two years. After the police warn him that he may be a target because the killer may believe he knows something of the murder, Rice reviews Bynum's case files detailing his affairs with women at the office and his unusual relationship and affair with Brooke, also a co-worker at Christie's Auction House. Bynum reveals that one of his girlfriends has killed before and may kill again and he is afraid.

The police believe the killer is a woman and may strike again. Rice gradually falls for Brooke but is disturbed by thoughts that he is being followed, possibly by a woman. After Rice is mugged, the mugger wearing his coat is killed in the same manner as Bynum. Rice also tries to follow clues from the case file with his psychiatrist mother, Grace (Jessica Tandy), including a strange dream of Bynum's where he is chased by a child in mysterious mansion.

After more suspicious behavior by Brooke, Rice tails her to her family's estate on Long Island. She relates a tale of her guilt in the accidental death of her father, and that Bynum would create a scandal if she broke up with him. Rice realizes through clues in the dream that Bynum's previous girlfriend was Gail Peters (Sara Botsford) who blames Brooke for the breakup of her affair. She is trying to frame Brooke (and has meanwhile killed Vitucci), and since that hasn't worked, she arrives at the estate to kill Brooke and Rice. As they are about to leave the house, Brooke forgets something in the house and goes back. While shes in the house, Gail appears out of no where and stabs Sam in the car with a knife appering to be dead. Brooke sees Gail and makes a run to the house. In a tense climax, Brooke recreates Bynum's dream but narrowly escapes as Gail falls to her death over a bluff. Sam eventually appears not dead and the both of them hug.

Cast

- Roy Scheider as Dr. Sam Rice
- Meryl Streep as Brooke Reynolds
- Jessica Tandy as Dr. Grace Rice
- Joe Grifasi as Joseph Vitucci
- Sara Botsford as Gail Phillips
- Josef Sommer as George Bynum
- Rikke Borge as Heather Wilson
- Irving Metzman as Murray Gordon

Reception

Still of the Night received an aggrigate score of 67% fresh from rottentomatos.com website. Variety stated "It comes as almost a shock to see a modern suspense picture that's as literate, well acted and beautifully made as Still Of The Night. Despite its many virtues, however, Robert Benton's film has its share of serious flaws, mainly in the area of plotting."

External links

- *Still of the Night* [1] at the Internet Movie Database
- *Still of the Night* [2] at Allmovie
- *Still of the Night* [3] at Rotten Tomatoes
- *New York Times* review [4]

References

[1] http://www.imdb.com/title/tt0084732/

[2] http://www.allmovie.com/work/46914

[3] http://www.rottentomatoes.com/m/still_of_the_night/

[4] http://movies2.nytimes.com/mem/movies/review.html?_r=1&title1=&title2=Still%20of%20the%20Night%20%28Movie%29&
reviewer=VINCENT%20CANBY&v_id=46914&pdate=19821119&

Sophie's Choice (film)

Sophie's Choice	
 Theatrical release poster	
Directed by	Alan J. Pakula
Produced by	Alan J. Pakula Keith Barish William C.Gerrity Martin Starger
Written by	Alan J. Pakula William Styron (novel)
Narrated by	Peter MacNicol
Starring	Meryl Streep Kevin Kline Peter MacNicol
Music by	Marvin Hamlisch
Cinematography	Nestor Almendros
Editing by	Evan Lottman
Studio	ITC Entertainment
Distributed by	Universal Pictures
Release date(s)	December 8, 1982
Running time	150 minutes
Country	United States
Language	English Polish German
Budget	$12 million
Gross revenue	$30,036,000

Sophie's Choice is a 1982 American drama romance film that tells the story of a Polish immigrant, Sophie, and her tempestuous lover who share a boarding house with a young writer in Brooklyn.

The film stars Meryl Streep, Kevin Kline, and Peter MacNicol. Alan J. Pakula directed the movie and wrote the script from a novel by William Styron, also called *Sophie's Choice*.

This is widely regarded as Meryl Streep's finest performance, and it won her the Academy Award for Best Actress. The film was nominated for Best Cinematography (Néstor Almendros), Costume Design (Albert Wolsky), Best Music (Marvin Hamlisch), and Best Writing, Screenplay Based on Material from Another Medium (Alan J. Pakula).

Plot

In 1947, the movie's narrator, Stingo (Peter MacNicol), relocates to Brooklyn in order to write a novel and is befriended by Sophie Zawistowski (Meryl Streep), a Polish immigrant, and her lover, Nathan Landau (Kevin Kline).

One evening, Stingo learns from Sophie that she was married but her husband and her father were killed in a German work camp and that she was interned in the Auschwitz Nazi concentration camp.

Nathan is constantly jealous, and when he is in one of his violent mood swings he convinces himself that Sophie is unfaithful to him and abuses and harasses her. There is a flashback showing Nathan rescuing Sophie from near death from starvation shortly after her immigration to the U.S.

Sophie eventually reveals that her father was a Nazi sympathizer. Sophie had a lover, Józef (Neddim Prohic), who lived with his half-sister, Wanda (Katharina Thalbach), a leader in the Resistance. Wanda tried to convince Sophie to translate some stolen Gestapo documents, but fearing she may endanger her children, she declined. Two weeks later Józef was murdered by the Gestapo, and Sophie was arrested and sent to Auschwitz with her children. Upon arrival, Jan (Adrian Kaltika), Sophie's son, was sent to the children's camp, and her daughter, Eva (Jennifer Lawn), was sent to her death in Crematorium Two.

Nathan tells Sophie and Stingo that the research that he is doing at the pharmaceutical company is so groundbreaking that he will win the Nobel Prize.

At a meeting with Nathan's physician brother, Stingo learns that Nathan is mentally ill (Paranoid Schizophrenic) and that all of the "research facilities" that Nathan has worked at have been "expensive funny farms." (He has a job in the library of a pharmaceutical firm, which his brother got for him, and occasionally helps researchers with their research, but otherwise, is not one at all.)

After Nathan discharges a firearm over the telephone in a violent rage, Sophie and Stingo flee to a hotel, where Sophie describes the incident giving rise to the film's title. While being unloaded in Auschwitz, Sophie was asked to choose which of her children would live and which would die. When she was unable to choose, a Nazi officer said both would be sent to die, so she chose Jan to survive.

Sophie and Stingo make love, but while Stingo is sleeping, Sophie, tormented by her memory, returns to Nathan, where both Sophie and Nathan commit suicide by taking cyanide.

Stingo moves away from Brooklyn and into a small farm his father recently inherited in southern Virginia to finish writing his novel.

Cast

- Meryl Streep as Zofia "Sophie" Zawistowski
- Kevin Kline as Nathan Landau
- Peter MacNicol as Stingo
- Rita Karin as Yetta Zimmerman
- Stephen D. Newman as Larry Landau
- Josh Mostel as Morris Fink
- Marcell Rosenblatt as Astrid Weinstein
- Moishe Rosenfeld as Moishe Rosenblum
- Robin Bartlett as Lillian Grossman
- Eugene Lipinski as Polish professor
- John Rothman as Librarian
- Neddim Prohic as Jòzef
- Katharina Thalbach as Wanda
- Jennifer Lawn as Eva Zawistowski
- Adrian Kalitka as Jan Zawistowski
- Joseph Leon as Dr. Blackstock
- David Wohl as English teacher

Casting notes

William Styron wrote the novel with Ursula Andress in mind for the part of Sophie, but Meryl Streep was very determined to get the role. After she obtained a bootlegged copy of the script, she went after Alan J. Pakula and threw herself on the ground begging him to give her the part. Streep filmed the "choice" scene in one take. Being a mother herself, she found shooting the scene extremely painful and emotionally draining and refused to do it again.[1] Streep's characterization was voted the third greatest movie performance of all time by *Premiere Magazine*.[2]

Reception

Sophie's Choice won the Academy Award for Best Actress (Meryl Streep) and was nominated for Best Cinematography (Néstor Almendros), Costume Design (Albert Wolsky), Best Music (Marvin Hamlisch), and Best Writing, Screenplay Based on Material from Another Medium (Alan J. Pakula). The film was also ranked #1 in the Roger Ebert's Top Ten List for 1982 and was listed on AFI's 100 Years... 100 Movies (10th Anniversary Edition).

In popular culture

In an episode of Friends, Phoebe had grown attached to a puppy her mom had lent her and when Rachel saw Phoebe struggling with whether to give it back or not, she said, "Oh, I can't watch this. It's like Sophie's Choice." Monica mentioned she'd never seen it, to which Rachel responded, "Oh, it was only okay."

In another episode of Friends when Ross is asked to choose between dinosaurs and sex (after he instantly chooses sex over food), he replies, "My God, it's like Sophie's Choice."[3]

In an episode of That 70's show, Jackie had to choose between money or Kelso, which prompted Eric to say, "It's like Sophie's Choice for morons." (One of the few anachronisms in the show, as neither the book nor film had been released during the timeframe of the episode.)

It has been mentioned in a few episodes of the Big Bang Theory and in the second episode of Modern Family when Cameron becomes emotional when thinking about the movie and having to choose between his baby Lily or partner Mitchell.[4]

In the episode "Showmance" of the series *Glee,* when faced with the decision of either paying for the sun nook or the grand foyer in their new house, Terri Schuester whimpers, "It's my very own Sophie's choice."

In an episode of The Cleveland Show, Cleveland sings a freestyle rap with the closing line "My rhymes are even harder than sophie's choice, peace"

In the 5th season of the Office, avid Meryl Streep fan, Michael Scott, refers to the dilemma of choosing between renting the Devil Wears Prada again or finally viewing Sophie's Choice.

Awards and nominations

Academy Awards

- Best Actress - Meryl Streep (won)
- Best Cinematography - Nestor Almendros (nominated)
- Best Costume Design - Albert Wolsky (nominated)
- Best Original Score - Marvin Hamlisch (nominated)
- Best Screenplay: Adapted - Pakula (nominated)

BAFTA Awards

- Best Actress - Streep (nominated)
- Most Outstanding Newcomer to Film - Kevin Kline (nominated)

Golden Globe Awards

- Best Actress: Drama - Streep (won)
- Best Film: Drama (nominated)
- New Star of the Year in a Motion Picture: Male - Kline (nominated)

Writers Guild of America

- Best Drama Adapted from Another Medium - Pakula (nominated)

See also

- 1982 in film
- List of Holocaust films

External links

- *Sophie's Choice* [5] at the Internet Movie Database
- *Sophie's Choice* [6] at Allmovie
- *Sophie's Choice* [7] at Box Office Mojo
- *Sophie's Choice* [8] at Rotten Tomatoes

References

[1] "What Makes Meryl Magic" (http://www.time.com/time/magazine/article/0,9171,924815-8,00.html). *Time*.1981-09-07. . Retrieved 2007-03-28.

[2] The 100 Greatest Performances of All Time (http://www.premiere.com/List/The-100-Greatest-Performances-of-All-Time/ The-100-Greatest-Performances-of-All-Time-24-1). Retrieved on 2009-02-14.

[3] Friends (1994) - Memorable quotes (http://www.imdb.com/title/tt0108778/quotes). Retrieved on 23 May 2010.

[4] Modern Family – "The Bicycle Thief" (Cultural Learnings) (http://cultural-learnings.com/2009/09/30/modern-family-the-bicycle-thief/). Retrieved on 23 May 2010.

[5] http://www.imdb.com/title/tt0084707/

[6] http://www.allmovie.com/work/45699

[7] http://www.boxofficemojo.com/movies/?id=sophieschoice.htm

[8] http://www.rottentomatoes.com/m/sophies_choice/

Silkwood

Silkwood	
Original poster	
Directed by	Mike Nichols
Produced by	Michael Hausman Mike Nichols
Written by	Nora Ephron Alice Arlen
Starring	Meryl StreepKurt Russell Cher Craig T. Nelson
Music by	Georges Delerue
Cinematography	Miroslav Ondricek
Editing by	Sam O'Steen
Distributed by	20th Century Fox
Release date(s)	December 14, 1983
Running time	131 minutes
Country	United States
Language	English
Gross revenue	$35,615,609 (US)[1]

Silkwood is a 1983 American drama film directed by Mike Nichols. The screenplay by Nora Ephron and Alice Arlen was inspired by the true-life story of Karen Silkwood, who died in a suspicious car accident while investigating alleged wrongdoing at the Kerr-McGee plutonium plant where she worked.

Plot

Karen Silkwood, a hard-living metallurgy worker at the Kerr-McGee plant in Cimarron, Oklahoma, shares a ramshackle house with two co-workers, her boyfriend Drew Stephens and her lesbian friend Dolly Pelliker. In addition to working tedious hours making plutonium fuel rods for nuclear reactors and dealing with the constant threat of exposure to radiation, her time is consumed by an ongoing battle waged against her former common law husband in an effort to have more time with their three children. In the little leisure time she has, she enjoys drinking and indulging in recreational drug use.

Because the plant has fallen behind on a major contract, employees are required to work long hours of overtime and managers are falsifying safety reports and cutting corners wherever possible, risking the welfare of the personnel. Karen approaches the union with her concerns and becomes active in lobbying for safeguards. She travels to Washington, D.C. where she interacts with union officials who appear to be more interested in the publicity she is generating than her welfare and that of her co-workers.

When Karen and several others become contaminated by radiation, plant officials try to minimize the incident. When she discovers the negatives of photographs of the faulty fuel rods that caused her illness have been retouched and records of inadequate safety measures have been altered, Karen decides to conduct an investigation of her own. Complications arise in her personal life when Drew, unable to deal with her obsession with gathering evidence, moves out and funeral parlor beautician Angela joins the household as Dolly's lover.

Once she feels she has gathered all the proof of wrongdoing she needs, Karen contacts a reporter from the *New York Times* and arranges a meeting. In the film's final moments, the scene fades out as Karen sees headlights in her rear-view mirror, then fades in on the aftermath of her fatal one-car crash, and the viewer is left to decide whether the crash was truly an accident or deliberately caused.

Production

The film was shot on location in Albuquerque and Los Alamos in New Mexico and Dallas, Howe, Texas City, and Tom Bean in Texas.

Cast

- Meryl Streep ..... Karen Silkwood
- Kurt Russell ..... Drew Stephens
- Cher ..... Dolly Pelliker
- Craig T. Nelson ..... Winston
- Fred Ward ..... Morgan
- Diana Scarwid ..... Angela
- Ron Silver ..... Paul Stone
- Josef Sommer ..... Max Richter
- Charles Hallahan ..... Earl Lapin
- Sudie Bond ..... Thelma Rice
- Henderson Forsythe ..... Quincy Bissell
- Bruce McGill ..... Mace Hurley
- David Strathairn ..... Wesley
- M. Emmet Walsh ..... Walt Yarborough

Critical reception

Vincent Canby of the *New York Times* called the film "a precisely visualized, highly emotional melodrama that's going to raise a lot of hackles" and "a very moving work." He added, "There are, however, problems, not unlike those faced by Costa-Gavras in his *State of Siege* and *Missing*, and they are major. Mr. Nichols and his writers . . . have attempted to impose a shape on a real-life story that, even as they present it, has no easily verifiable shape. We are drawn into the story of Karen Silkwood by the absolute accuracy and unexpected sweetness of its Middle American details and then, near the end, abandoned by a film whose images say one thing and whose final credit card another. The muddle of fact, fiction and speculation almost, though not quite, denies the artistry of all that's gone before." He concluded, "I realize that films shouldn't be judged in bits and pieces, but it's difficult not to see *Silkwood* in that way. For most of its running time it is so convincing - and so sure of itself - that it seems a particular waste when it goes dangerously wrong. It's like watching a skydiver execute all sorts of graceful, breathtaking turns, as he appears to ignore gravity and fly on his own, only to have him smash to earth when the chute doesn't open."[2]

Roger Ebert of the *Chicago Sun-Times* rated the film four stars and commented, "It's a little amazing that established movie stars like Streep, Russell and Cher could disappear so completely into the everyday lives of these characters."[3]

David Sterritt of the *Christian Science Monitor* called the film "a fine example of Hollywood's love-hate attitude toward timely and controversial subject matter." He continued, "The movie sides with Silkwood as a character, playing up her spunk and courage while casting wry, sidelong glances at her failings. When it comes to the issues connected with her, though, the filmmakers slip and slide around, providing an escape hatch . . . for every position and opinion they offer. This makes the movie less polemical than it might have been, and a lot more wishy-washy . . . This is too bad, because on other levels *Silkwood* is a strong and imaginative film. Meryl Streep gives the year's most astounding performance by an actress, adding vigor and complexity to almost every scene with her endlessly inventive portrayal of the eccentric heroine. The supporting players skillfully follow her lead."[4]

Box office

The film opened in 257 theaters in the United States on December 14, 1983 and grossed $1,218,322 on its opening weekend, ranking #12 at the box office. By its seventh week of release it had expanded to 816 screens and reached #1. It eventually earned $35,615,609 in the US.[1]

Awards and nominations

- Academy Award for Best Actress (Meryl Streep, nominee)
- Academy Award for Best Supporting Actress (Cher, nominee)
- Academy Award for Best Director (Mike Nichols, nominee)
- Academy Award for Best Original Screenplay (Nora Ephron and Alice Arlen, nominees)
- Academy Award for Best Film Editing (Sam O'Steen, nominee)
- BAFTA Award for Best Actress in a Leading Role (Meryl Streep, nominee)
- BAFTA Award for Best Actress in a Supporting Role (Cher, nominee)
- Golden Globe Award for Best Supporting Actress – Motion Picture (Cher, winner)
- Golden Globe Award for Best Motion Picture – Drama (nominee)
- Golden Globe Award for Best Actress – Motion Picture Drama (Meryl Streep, nominee)
- Golden Globe Award for Best Supporting Actor – Motion Picture (Kurt Russell, nominee)
- Golden Globe Award for Best Director (Mike Nichols, nominee)
- Kansas City Film Critics Circle Award for Best Actress (Meryl Streep, winner)
- Writers Guild of America Award for Best Original Screenplay (Nora Ephron and Alice Arlen, nominees)

DVD releases

Anchor Bay Entertainment released the film on DVD in Region 1 on June 15, 1999. Viewers had the option of anamorphic widescreen or fullscreen formats.

A Region 2 DVD was released by PT Video on April 8, 2002.

A second Region 1 DVD was released by MGM Home Entertainment on October 7, 2003. It is in anamorphic widescreen format with subtitles in English, Spanish, and French.

External links

- *Silkwood* [5] at the Internet Movie Database
- *Silkwood* [6] at Allmovie

References

[1] BoxOfficeMojo.com (http://www.boxofficemojo.com/movies/?id=silkwood.htm)

[2] *New York Times* review (http://movies.nytimes.com/movie/review?res=9C07EFD61638F937A25751C1A965948260)

[3] *Chicago Sun-Times* review (http://rogerebert.suntimes.com/apps/pbcs.dll/article?AID=/19831214/REVIEWS/312140302/1023)

[4] *Christian Science Monitor* review (http://www.csmonitor.com/1984/0105/010506.html)

[5] http://www.imdb.com/title/tt0086312/

[6] http://www.allmovie.com/work/44734

Falling in Love (film)

Falling in Love	
The film poster.	
Directed by	Ulu Grosbard
Produced by	Marvin Worth
Written by	Michael Cristofer
Starring	Robert De Niro Meryl Streep Harvey Keitel
Music by	Dave Grusin
Cinematography	Peter Suschitzky
Editing by	Michael Kahn
Distributed by	Paramount Pictures
Release date(s)	November 21, 1984
Running time	106 minutes
Country	United States
Language	English

Falling in Love is a 1984 American romantic-drama film starring Meryl Streep and Robert De Niro and directed by Ulu Grosbard. Its plot is based on (or inspired by) the 1945 British film Brief Encounter.

Cast

- Robert De Niro as Frank Raftis
- Meryl Streep as Molly Gilmore
- Harvey Keitel as Ed Lasky
- Jane Kaczmarek as Ann Raftis
- George Martin as John Trainer
- David Clennon as Brian Gilmore
- Dianne Wiest as Isabelle
- Victor Argo as Victor Rawlins
- Wiley Earl as Mike Raftis
- Jesse Bradford as Joe Raftis
- Chevi Colton as Elevator Woman
- Frances Conroy as Waitress
- James Ryan as Cashier
- Kenneth Welsh as Doctor

Plot synopsis

Two married strangers meet randomly, become friends, and fall in love. They spend time together, riding the train into the city of New York, and begin meeting for coffee or lunch. They enjoy their time together and this enjoyment eventually blossoms into love.

Trivia

The Hindi movie Kabhi Alvida Na Kehna is partly inspired by this movie.

External links

- *Falling in Love* [1] at the Internet Movie Database

References

[1] http://www.imdb.com/title/tt0087233/

Plenty (film)

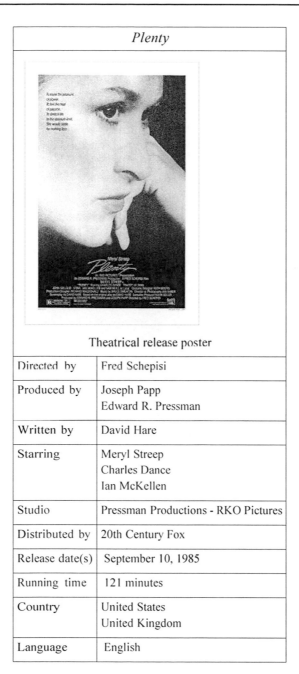

Plenty	
Theatrical release poster	
Directed by	Fred Schepisi
Produced by	Joseph Papp Edward R. Pressman
Written by	David Hare
Starring	Meryl Streep Charles Dance Ian McKellen
Studio	Pressman Productions - RKO Pictures
Distributed by	20th Century Fox
Release date(s)	September 10, 1985
Running time	121 minutes
Country	United States United Kingdom
Language	English

Plenty is a 1985 British drama film directed by Fred Schepisi and starring Meryl Streep . It was adapted from David Hare's play of the same name.

Plot

The plot focuses on Susan Traherne, irreparably changed by her experiences as a fighter for the French Resistance during World War II. She is determined to achieve what she wishes in the post-war world which, after her time away, she finds trivial and inadequate, while acting with complete disregard for everybody around her.

Cast

- Meryl Streep as Susan Traherne
- Charles Dance as Raymond Brock
- Tracey Ullman as Alice Park
- John Gielgud as Sir Leonard Darwin
- Sting as Mick
- Ian McKellen as Sir Andrew Charleson
- Sam Neill as Lazar

Awards

Ullman and Gielgud were nominated for BAFTA Awards, and Gielgud was named Best Supporting Actor by both the Los Angeles Film Critics Association and the National Society of Film Critics.

Critical reception

Movie critic Roger Ebert gave the film three-and-a-half stars out of four [1] . He said about Ms. Streep's performance that "it is a performance of great subtlety; it is hard to play an unbalanced, neurotic, self-destructive woman, and do it with such gentleness and charm... Streep creates a whole character around a woman who could have simply been a catalogue of symptoms."

External links

- *Plenty* [2] at the Internet Movie Database

References

[1] Ebert, Rogert. 1985. Movie Review of Plenty, The Chicago Sun Times (http://rogerebert.suntimes.com/apps/pbcs.dll/article?AID=/ 19850920/REVIEWS/509200303/1023)
[2] http://www.imdb.com/title/tt0089816/

Out of Africa (film)

Out of Africa	
theatrical poster	
Directed by	Sydney Pollack
Produced by	Sydney Pollack
Written by	Source books: Judith Thurman Errol Trzebinski Karen Blixen Screenplay: Kurt Luedtke
Starring	Robert Redford Meryl Streep Klaus Maria Brandauer
Music by	John Barry
Cinematography	David Watkin
Editing by	Fredric Steinkamp William Steinkamp Pembroke Herring Sheldon Kahn
Distributed by	Universal Pictures
Release date(s)	18 December 1985 *(US)*
Running time	160 mins.
Country	United States
Language	English
Budget	$31,000,000 *(est.)*
Gross revenue	$87,071,205[1]

Out of Africa is a film released in 1985.[1] The story based loosely on the autobiographical book *Out of Africa* written by Isak Dinesen (the pseudonym of the author Karen Blixen), which was published in 1937, with additional material from Dinesen's book *Shadows on the Grass* and other sources. This film received 28 film awards, including seven Academy Awards.

The book and the film

The book describes events during the period from 1914 to 1931 concerning the European settlers and the native people in the bush country of Kenya (in British East Africa). Its setting spans from seaside at Mombasa up to Nairobi, and from Mount Kenya to Kilimanjaro, as told from the lyrical, poetic viewpoint of Danish Baroness Karen von Blixen-Finecke. The book was continually in print during the 20th century, and it has been reprinted by many publishers, and in several different languages.

The film was adapted into a screenplay by the writer Kurt Luedtke, and it was directed by the American director Sydney Pollack. Its stars were Meryl Streep as the Baroness Karen von Blixen-Finecke; Robert Redford as Denys Finch Hatton; and Klaus Maria Brandauer (as Baron Bror von Blixen-Finecke). Other actors and actresses in this film included Michael Kitchen as Berkeley Cole; Malick Bowens as Farah; Stephen Kinyanjui as the Chief; Michael Gough as Baron Delamere; Suzanna Hamilton as Felicity, who is based on the noted aviatrix Beryl Markham); and the model Iman as Mariammo.

Plot

The film opens in Denmark as an older Karen Blixen (Streep) briefly remembers hunting in Denmark, then the years she spent mostly residing in Africa (1914 through 1931, with the exception of a period when she had to return to Denmark for special medical treatment). Looming large in her memories is the figure of Denys Finch Hatton (Redford), a local big-game hunter whom she met when she arrived in Africa to start what she thought would be a dairy farm in partnership with her husband, the Baron Bror von Blixen-Finecke (Brandauer).

Things turn out differently for her than anticipated, since the blue-blooded but poor financially Baron has used her money to purchase a coffee plantation - rather than a dairy farm. He also shows little inclination to put any real work into it, preferring to hunt wild animals, instead. While from the beginning, their marriage is depicted as mostly symbiotic (her family has money, while the Baron has a title), Karen does eventually develop feelings for him, and she is distressed when she learns of his extramarital affairs.

To make matters worse, Karen contracts syphilis from her philandering husband, which at the time was a very dangerous disease. This became the necessity for her to return to Denmark for a possible cure using expert treatment with the new and experimental medicine Salvarsan, invented in 1910. This was before the discovery and development of penicillin or any other antibiotic usable against syphilis.

After she has recovered and returned to Africa, a relationship between her and Denys begins to develop. However, after many unsuccessful attempts at turning their affair into a lasting relationship, she realizes that Denys is as impossible to own or tame as Africa itself.

Karen lives in a large house equipped with fine European furniture. She also decides that she needs to open a school to teach reading, writing, and arithmetic, and also some European customs, to the African people of her area. On the other hand, Denys prefers adventures in the outdoors, and he leaves the natives to their own devices. Denys's upcoming death in a plane crash is foreshadowed in this film by the tale of Maasai people who reportedly would always perish in captivity. At his funeral in the Ngong Hills, as Karen prepares to toss a handful of soil into the grave in a European ceremony, she hesitates, and then she turns away from the other Europeans, and she brushes her hand through her hair instead, as is the African custom.

In this film, Karen finds it necessary to return to Denmark permanently, following a catastrophic fire that destroys her entire farm of coffee plants. After being away for more than 20 years, Karen became an author and a storyteller, writing about her experiences and letters from Africa, and remembering.

Cast

- Robert Redford - Denys Finch Hatton
- Meryl Streep - Karen Blixen
- Klaus Maria Brandauer - Bror Blixen/Hans Blixen
- Michael Kitchen - Berkeley Cole
- Malick Bowens - Farah
- Joseph Thiaka - Kamante
- Stephen Kinyanjui - Kinanjui
- Michael Gough - Baron Delamere
- Suzanna Hamilton - Felicity
- Rachel Kempson - Lady Belfield
- Graham Crowden - Lord Belfield
- Benny Young - Minister
- Leslie Phillips - Sir Joseph (this was presumably meant to be Sir Joseph Aloysius Byrne, who took office as the Governor in early 1931)
- Dr. Steven Kee - Extra
- Iman - Mariammo

Production

This film tells the story as a series of six loosely coupled episodes from Karen's life, intercut with her narration. The final two narrations, the first a reflection on Karen's experiences in Kenya and the second a description of Denys's grave, were taken from her book *Out of Africa*, while the others have been written for the film in imitation of her very lyrical writing style. The pace of this film is often rather slow, reflecting Blixen's book, "Natives dislike speed, as we dislike noise..."[2]

Out of Africa was filmed using descendants of several people of the Kikuyu tribe who are named in the book, near the actual Ngong Hills outside Nairobi, but not inside of Karen's (second) three-bedroom house "Mbagathi" (now the Karen Blixen Museum). The filming took place in her first house "Mbogani", close to the museum, which is a dairy today. The scenes set in Denmark were actually filmed in Surrey, England.

Differences between the film and real life events

This film quotes the start of the book, "I had a farm in Africa, at the foot of the Ngong Hills" [p. 3], and Denys recites, "He prayeth well that loveth well both man and bird and beast" from *The Rime of the Ancient Mariner*, which becomes the epitaph inscribed on Finch-Hatton's grave marker [p. 370].

This film differs significantly from the book, leaving out the devastating locust swarm, some local shootings, Karen's writings with the German army, and the down-scaling the size of her 4,000 acre (16 km²) farm, with 800 Kikuyu workers and 18-oxen wagon.

The film also takes liberties with Karen's and Denys's romance. They met at a hunting club, not in the plains. Denys was away from Kenya for two years on military assignment in Egypt, which is not mentioned. Denys took up flying and began to lead safaris after he moved in with Karen. The film also ignores the fact that Karen was pregnant at least once with Denys's child, but she suffered from miscarriages. Furthermore, Denys was decidedly English, but this fact was down-played by the hiring of the actor Robert Redford, an inarguably All-American actor who had previously worked with Pollack. When Redford accepted the contract to play Finch Hatton, he did so fully intending to play him as an Englishman. This conception was later nixed by the director Sydney Pollack. Pollack thought that this would become too distracting for the audiences, with hearing Redford speak in an English accent. In fact, Redford reportedly had to re-record some of his lines from early takes in the filming, in which he still spoke with a trace of English accent.

Soundtrack

The music for *Out of Africa*, including Mozart's *Clarinet Concerto* and African traditional songs, also has many second-generation compositions by the Englishman John Barry, based on his earlier movie music, "temp-tracked" in the editing of the film by the director Sydney Pollack, such as *Born Free* (1966), *Robin and Marian* (1976), and *The Last Valley* (1970 - 71), which inspired the music *Flying over Africa*, over Lake Nakuru's flamingos. Barry's score for *Out of Africa* was listed in fifteenth place in the American Film Institute's list of *100 Years of Film Scores*.

Technical notes on the film

In the Director's Notes on the DVD[3] for *The Interpreter*, Sydney Pollack stated that he filmed *Out of Africa* and his later films of that decade in "4 to 3"; and that it "...probably was one I should have had in widescreen". The aspect ratio of 4:3 conflicts with that reported in www.ImdB.com, which states that the film's aspect ratio is 1.85:1, the decimal equivalent of 16:9.[4] In his director's notes, Pollack stated that prior to the filming of *Out of Africa*, he made motion pictures exclusively in the widescreen format and style, and that he did not resume the widescreen format until his movie, *The Interpreter*, in 2005.

In 1985, there were no steam locomotives still operational in Kenya. Therefore, the producers and their advisors decided to assemble a simulated steam train that was instead pushed from the rear by an available diesel locomotive. The simulated steam locomotive burned rubber tires in its simulated boiler, and liquid oxygen was used as an oxidizer to give the appearance of a coal-fired boiler. This replica of a steam locomotive - and also the passengers cars used during the filming - have been put on display in the Nairobi Railway Museum.

Awards and honors

Academy Awards

The film won seven Academy Awards and was nominated in a further four categories.[5]

Won

- Best Picture
- Best Director (Sydney Pollack)
- Best Art Direction (Stephen Grimes, Josie MacAvin)
- Best Cinematography (David Watkin)
- Writing Adapted Screenplay (Kurt Luedtke)
- Original Music Score
- Sound

Nominated

- Best Actress (Meryl Streep)
- Best Supporting Actor (Klaus Maria Brandauer)
- Costume Design (Milena Canonero)
- Film Editing (Fredric Steinkamp, William Steinkamp, Pembroke Herring, and Sheldon Kahn)

Golden Globes

The film won three Golden Globes (Best Picture, Supporting Actor, Original Score).

AFI

American Film Institute recognition

- 2002 AFI's 100 Years... 100 Passions #13
- 2005 AFI's 100 Years of Film Scores #15

External links

- *Out of Africa* [6] at the Internet Movie Database
- *Out of Africa* [7] at the TCM Movie Database
- *Out of Africa* [8] at Allmovie
- *Out of Africa* [9] at Rotten Tomatoes

References

[1] "Out of Africa - Overview" (cast/gross/plot), allmovie, 2007, webpage: amovie36787 (http://allmovie.com/cg/avg.dll?p=avg& sql=1:36787).

[2] *Out of Africa*, p. 252

[3] The Interpreter, DVD#25835, Universal Studios

[4] IMDB: Technical specifications for Out of Africa (1985) (http://www.imdb.com/title/tt0089755/technical)

[5] "NY Times: Out of Africa" (http://movies.nytimes.com/movie/36787/Out-of-Africa/awards). *NY Times*. . Retrieved 2009-01-01.

[6] http://www.imdb.com/title/tt0089755/

[7] http://tcmdb.com/title/title.jsp?stid=19122

[8] http://www.allmovie.com/work/36787

[9] http://www.rottentomatoes.com/m/out_of_africa/

Heartburn (film)

Heartburn	
Original poster	
Directed by	Mike Nichols
Produced by	Robert Greenhut Mike Nichols
Written by	Nora Ephron
Starring	Meryl Streep Jack Nicholson
Music by	Carly Simon
Cinematography	Néstor Almendros
Editing by	Sam O'Steen
Distributed by	Paramount Pictures
Release date(s)	July 25, 1986
Running time	108 minutes
Country	United States
Language	English
Gross revenue	$25,314,189 (US) [1] .

Heartburn is a 1986 American drama film directed by Mike Nichols. The screenplay by Nora Ephron is based on her semi-autobiographical novel of the same name, which was inspired by her tempestuous second marriage to Carl Bernstein and his affair with Margaret Jay.

Plot

New York City food writer Rachel Samstat and Washington, D.C. political columnist Mark Forman meet at a mutual friend's wedding and, after a whirlwind courtship, they marry, despite Rachel's reservations. They purchase a dilapidated Georgetown townhouse in Washington and the ongoing and seemingly never-ending renovations create some stress in their relationship. Rachel, overjoyed to discover she is pregnant, is determined to make her marriage work and becomes a stay-at-home mom. When she discovers evidence of Mark's extramarital affair with socialite Thelma Rice during her pregnancy with her second child, she leaves him and takes their daughter Annie to New York, where she moves in with her father and tries to jump start her career. Mark eventually convinces her to return home, but when it's obvious his philandering will never end, Rachel leaves him for good.

Production

The film was shot on location in Manhattan, Washington, D.C., and Alexandria, Virginia.

Mandy Patinkin originally was cast as Mark Forman but was replaced after filming began. [2]

The film's score was composed by Carly Simon. The main theme, "Coming Around Again," as well as the end credits song, "Itsy Bitsy Spider," are included in Simon's 1987 album *Coming Around Again*.

Cast

- Mcryl Streep ..... Rachel Samstat
- Jack Nicholson ..... Mark Forman
- Stockard Channing ..... Julie Siegel
- Jeff Daniels ..... Richard
- Miloš Forman ..... Dmitri
- Steven Hill ..... Harry Samstat
- Catherine O'Hara ..... Betty
- Mamie Gummer ..... Annie
- Joanna Gleason ..... Diana
- Anna Maria Horsford ..... Della
- Richard Masur ..... Arthur Siegel
- Maureen Stapleton ..... Vera
- Mercedes Ruehl ..... Eve
- Kevin Spacey ..... Subway Thief

Critical reception

Roger Ebert of the *Chicago Sun-Times* called it "a bitter, sour movie about two people who are only marginally interesting" and placed much of the blame on screenwriter Nora Ephron, who "should have based her story on somebody else's marriage. That way, she could have provided the distance and perspective that good comedy needs." He felt "she apparently had too much anger to transform the facts into entertaining fiction." [3]

Variety thought it was "a beautifully crafted film with flawless performances and many splendid moments, yet the overall effect is a bit disappointing" and added, "While the day-to-day details are drawn with a striking clarity, Ephron's script never goes much beyond the mannerisms of middle-class life. Even with the sketchy background information, it's hard to tell what these people are feeling or what they want." [4]

Pauline Kael of *The New Yorker* wrote: "The movie is full of talented people, who [...] are fun to watch, but after a while the scenes that don't point anywhere begin to add up, and you start asking yourself: 'What is this movie about?' You are still asking when it's over, and by then a flatness, a disappointment, is likely to have settled ovet the fillips you'd enjoyed," noting that "[t]hough Ephron is a gifted and a witty light essayist, her novel is no more than a variant of a princess fantasy: Rachel, the wife, is blameless; Mark, the husband, is simply a bad egg—an adulterer. And, reading the book, you don't have to take Rachel the bratty narrator very seriously; her self-pity is so thinly masked by humor and unabashed mean-spiritedness that you feel that the author is exploiting her life—trashing it by presenting it as a juicy, fast-action comic strip about a marriage of celebrities." [5]

Box office

The film opened in 843 theaters in the United States on July 25, 1986 and earned $5,783,079 on its opening weekend, ranking #2 at the box office behind *Aliens*. It eventually grossed a total of $25,314,189 in the US. [1]

Awards and nominations

Meryl Streep was named Best Actress at the Valladolid International Film Festival for her performance.

External links

- *Heartburn* [6] at the Internet Movie Database

References

[1] BoxOffice Mojo.com (http://www.boxofficemojo.com/movies/?id=heartburn.htm)

[2] *Heartburn* at Turner Classic Movies (http://www.tcm.com/tcmdb/title.jsp?stid=4630&category=Misc Notes)

[3] *Chicago Sun-Times* review (http://rogerebert.suntimes.com/apps/pbcs.dll/article?AID=/19860725/REVIEWS/607250301/1023)

[4] *Variety* review (http://www.variety.com/review/VE1117791547.html?categoryid=31&cs=1&p=0)

[5] Pauline Kael, "Pairs", The Current Cinema, The New Yorker, August 11, 1986, page 77

[6] http://www.imdb.com/title/tt0091188/

Ironweed (film)

Ironweed	
Theatrical poster.	
Directed by	Hector Babenco
Produced by	Keith Barish Marcia Nasatir
Written by	William Kennedy
Starring	Jack Nicholson Meryl Streep Carroll Baker Tom Waits
Music by	John Morris
Cinematography	Lauro Escorel
Editing by	Anne Goursaud
Distributed by	TriStar Pictures
Release date(s)	December 18, 1987
Running time	143 minutes
Country	United States
Language	English

Ironweed is a 1987 film directed by Argentine-born Brazilian Hector Babenco.[1]

The picture is based on the Pulitzer Prize-winning novel of the same title by William Kennedy and concerns the relationship of a homeless couple: Francis, an alcoholic, and Helen, a terminally ill woman during the Great Depression. Kennedy also wrote the screenplay.

It stars Jack Nicholson, Meryl Streep, Carroll Baker, Michael O'Keefe, Diane Venora, Fred Gwynne, Tom Waits, and Nathan Lane. The film was nominated for Academy Awards for Best Actor in a Leading Role (Nicholson) and Best Actress in a Leading Role (Streep).

Major portions of the film were shot on location in Albany, New York, including Jay Street at Lark Street, Albany Rural Cemetery and the Miss Albany Diner on North Pearl Street.

Plot

The film is set in the later years of the Great Depression.

Francis Phelan (Jack Nicholson) is a washed-up baseball player who deserted his family back in the 1920s when he accidentally and drunkenly dropped his son and killed him. Since then, Phelan has been a bum, punishing himself.

Wandering into Albany, New York, Phelan seeks out his lover and drinking companion, Helen Archer (Meryl Streep). The two meet up in a mission managed by Reverend Chester (James Gammon), and later in Oscar Reo's (Fred Gwynne) gin mill. Over the next few days, Phelan takes a few minor jobs to support his habit, while he ponders the past and present.

A chance for a reconciliation with his wife Annie Phelan (Carroll Baker) is abandoned when a group of local vigilantes with baseball bats take it upon themselves to drive the homeless out of Albany.

Cast

- Jack Nicholson as Francis Phelan
- Meryl Streep as Helen Archer
- Carroll Baker as Annie Phelan
- Michael O'Keefe as Billy Phelan
- Diane Venora as Margaret "Peg" Phelan
- Fred Gwynne as Oscar Reo
- Margaret Whitton as Katrina Dougherty
- Tom Waits as Rudy
- Jake Dengel as Pee Wee
- Nathan Lane as Harold Allen
- James Gammon as Reverend Chester
- Will Zahrn as Rowdy Dick
- Laura Esterman as Nora Lawlor
- Joe Grifasi as Jackson
- Black-Eyed Susan as Clara
- Hy Anzell as Rosskam
- Ted Levine as Pocono Pete
- William H Cassidy as Homeless Man
- Robert H. Fickies as Gravedigger

Critical reception

The film was received with enthusiasm because of the presence of stars Jack Nicholson and Meryl Streep. Movie critic Roger Ebert wrote, "Nicholson and Streep play drunks in *Ironweed*, and actors are said to like to play drunks, because it gives them an excuse for overacting. But there is not much visible 'acting' in this movie; the actors are too good for that." Ebert gave the film three stars out of four.[2] The film has an 90% rating in the film website Rotten Tomatoes.[3] Ms. Streep received raves from most critics; Janet Maslin of *The New York Times* wrote that "Meryl Streep, as ever, is uncanny. Miss Streep uses the role of Helen as an opportunity to deliver a stunning impersonation of a darty-eyed, fast-talking woman of the streets, an angry, obdurate woman with great memories and no future. There isn't much more to the film's Helen than this, and indeed the character may go no deeper, but she's a marvel all the same. Behind the runny, red-rimmed eyes, the nervous chatter and the haunted expression, Miss Streep is even more utterly changed than her costar, and she even sings well. The sequence in which Helen entertains the real and imagined patrons of a bar room with a rendition of 'He's Me Pal' is a standout."[4]

External links

- *Ironweed* [5] at Rotten Tomatoes.
- *Ironweed* [6] at the Internet Movie Database
- *Ironweed* [7] at Allmovie
- The Gravedigger on location with IRONWEED [8]

References

[1] *Ironweed* (http://www.imdb.com/title/tt0093277/) at the Internet Movie Database.

[2] Roger Ebert (February, 1988) "Ironweed" (http://rogerebert.suntimes.com/apps/pbcs.dll/article?AID=/19880212/REVIEWS/802120302/1023,)

[3] Rotten Tomatoes "Ironweed (1987): Movie Reviews" (http://www.rottentomatoes.com/m/ironweed/)

[4] Maslin, Janet. The New York Times (December, 1987) "Ironweed (1987) Film: 'Ironweed,' From Hector Babenco" (http://movies.nytimes.com/movie/review?res=9B0DE5DB163BF93BA25751C1A961948260,)

[5] http://www.rottentomatoes.com/m/ironweed/

[6] http://www.imdb.com/title/tt0093277/

[7] http://www.allmovie.com/work/25409

[8] http://hphotos-snc1.fbcdn.net/hs212.snc1/7931_100997543253912_100000310018134_23761_2111316_n.jpg

A Cry in the Dark

A Cry in the Dark	
International poster	
Directed by	Fred Schepisi
Produced by	Menahem Golan Yoram Globus Verity Lambert
Written by	Robert Caswell Fred Schepisi Based on a book by John Bryson
Starring	Meryl Streep Sam Neill
Music by	Bruce Smeaton
Cinematography	Ian Baker
Editing by	Jill Bilcock
Distributed by	Warner Bros. (US) Cannon Films (International)
Release date(s)	4 November 1988 Australia 11 November 1988 USA 17 May 1989 France 19 May 1989, South Africa 26 May 1989 UK
Running time	121 minutes
Country	Australia/United States
Language	English

A Cry in the Dark (Initially released in Australia as *Evil Angels*) is a 1988 Australian docudrama film directed by Fred Schepisi. The screenplay by Schepisi and Robert Caswell is based on John Bryson's 1985 book *Evil Angels*, the title under which the film was released in Australia. It chronicles the case of Azaria Chamberlain, a nine-week-old baby girl who disappeared from a campground near Uluru (known as Ayers Rock at the time) in August 1980 and the struggle of her parents, Michael and Lindy, to prove their innocence to a public convinced that they were complicit in her death.

The film was released less than two months after the Chamberlains finally were exonerated by the Northern Territory Court of Appeals of all charges filed against them.[1]

Plot

Seventh-day Adventist Church pastor Michael Chamberlain, his wife Lindy, their two sons, and their nine-week-old daughter Azaria are on a camping holiday in the Outback. With the baby sleeping in their tent, the family is enjoying a barbecue with their fellow campers when a cry is heard. Lindy returns to the tent to check on Azaria and is certain she sees a dingo with something in its mouth running off as she approaches. When she discovers the infant is missing, everyone joins forces to search for her, without success. It is assumed what Lindy saw was the animal carrying off the child, and a subsequent inquest rules her account of events is true.

The tide of public opinion soon turns against the Chamberlains. For many, Lindy seems too stoic, too coldhearted, and too accepting of the disaster that has befallen her. Gossip about her begins to swell and soon is accepted as statements of fact. The couple's beliefs are not widely practiced in the country, and when the media reports a rumor that the name Azaria means "sacrifice in the wilderness" (when in fact it means "blessed of God"), the public is quick to believe they decapitated their baby with a pair of scissors as part of a bizarre religious rite. Law-enforcement officials find new witnesses, forensics experts, and a lot of circumstantial evidence - including a small wooden coffin Michael uses as a receptacle for his parishioners' packs of unsmoked cigarettes - and reopen the investigation, and eventually Lindy is charged with murder. Seven months pregnant, she ignores her attorneys' advice to play on the jury's sympathy and appears emotionless on the stand, convincing onlookers she's guilty of the crime of which she's accused. As the trial progresses, Michael's faith in his religion and his belief in his wife disintegrate, and he stumbles through his testimony, suggesting he's concealing the truth. In October 1982, Lindy is found guilty and sentenced to life imprisonment with hard labor, while Michael is found guilty as an accessory and given an 18-month suspended sentence.

More than three years later, while searching for the body of an English tourist who fell from Uluru, police discover a small item of clothing that is identified as the jacket Lindy had insisted Azaria was wearing over her jumpsuit, which had been recovered early in the investigation. She immediately is released from prison, the case is reopened, and all convictions against Lindy and Michael are overturned.

Cast

- Meryl Streep as Lindy Chamberlain
- Sam Neill as Michael Chamberlain
- Bruce Myles as Ian Barker, Q.C.
- Neil Fitzpatrick as John Phillips, Q.C.
- Charles Tingwell as Justice James Muirhead
- Maurie Fields as Justice Denis Barritt
- Nick Tate as Det. Graeme Charlwood
- Lewis Fitz-Gerald as Stuart Tipple

Reception

In his review in *The New York Times*, Vincent Canby said the film "has much of the manner of a television docudrama, ultimately being a rather comforting celebration of personal triumph over travails so dread and so particular that they have no truly disturbing, larger application. Yet *A Cry in the Dark* is better than that, mostly because of another stunning performance by Meryl Streep, who plays Lindy Chamberlain with the kind of virtuosity that seems to redefine the possibilities of screen acting . . . Though Sam Neill is very good as Lindy Chamberlain's tormented husband, Miss Streep supplies the guts of the melodrama that are missing from the screenplay. Mr. Schepisi has chosen to present the terrible events in the outback in such a way that there's never any doubt in the audience's mind about what happened. The audience doesn't worry about the fate of the Chamberlains as much as it worries about the unconvincing ease with which justice is miscarried. Mr. Schepisi may have followed the facts of the case, but he has not made them comprehensible in terms of the film. The manner by which justice miscarries is the real subject of the movie. In this screenplay, however, it serves only as a pretext for a personal drama that remains chilly and distant . . . As a result, the courtroom confrontations are so weakened that *A Cry in the Dark* becomes virtually a one-character movie. It's Mr. Schepisi's great good fortune that that one character is portrayed by the incomparable Meryl Streep."[2]

Roger Ebert of the *Chicago Sun-Times* observed, "Schepisi is successful in indicting the court of public opinion, and his methodical (but absorbing) examination of the evidence helps us understand the state's circumstantial case. In the lead role, Streep is given a thankless assignment: to show us a woman who deliberately refused to allow insights into herself. She succeeds, and so, of course, there are times when we feel frustrated because we do not know what Lindy is thinking or feeling. We begin to dislike the character, and then we know how the Australian public felt. Streep's performance is risky, and masterful."[3]

In the *Washington Post*, Rita Kempley said, "Streep - yes, with another perfect accent - brings her customary skillfulness to the part. It's not a showy performance, but the heroine's internal struggle seems to come from the actress' pores. Neill, who costarred with Streep in *Plenty*, is quite good as a humble, bewildered sort who finally breaks under cross-examination."[4]

Variety made note of the "intimate, incredible detail in the classy, disturbing drama."[5]

In June 2008, the American Film Institute revealed its "Ten top Ten"—the best ten films in ten "classic" American film genres—after polling over 1,500 people from the creative community. *A Cry in the Dark* was acknowledged as the ninth best film in the courtroom drama genre.[6]

In the "The Stranded" episode of Seinfeld, it gives a satirical homage to the film when Elaine does an impression of the film and exclaims "Maybe the dingo ate your baby?"

Awards and nominations

- Academy Award for Best Actress (Meryl Streep, nominee)
- Australian Film Institute Award for Best Film (winner)
- Australian Film Institute Award for Best Actress in a Leading Role (Streep, winner)
- Australian Film Institute Award for Best Actor in a Leading Role (Sam Neill, winner)
- Australian Film Institute Award for Best Direction (winner)
- Australian Film Institute Award for Best Adapted Screenplay (winner)
- Australian Film Institute Award for Best Original Music Score (nominee)
- Australian Film Institute Award for Best Achievement in Editing (nominee)
- Golden Globe Award for Best Motion Picture - Drama (nominee)
- Golden Globe Award for Best Actress - Motion Picture Drama (nominee)
- Golden Globe Award for Best Director - Motion Picture (nominee)
- Golden Globe Award for Best Screenplay (nominee)

- New York Film Critics Circle Award for Best Actress (Streep, winner)
- 1989 Cannes Film Festival - Best Actress (Streep, winner)[7]
- 1989 Cannes Film Festival - Palme D'Or (nominee)[7]

See also

- Cinema of Australia

References

[1] Harper, Dan (March 2001). "*A Cry in the Dark* Review" (http://www.sensesofcinema.com/contents/01/13/cry.html). SensesOfCinema.com. . Retrieved 25 April 2008.

[2] Canby, Vincent (11 November 1988). "Reviews/Film; Meryl Streep in 'A Cry in the Dark'" (http://movies.nytimes.com/movie/review?res=940DE1DF1039F932A25752C1A96E948260). *New York Times*. . Retrieved 25 April 2008.

[3] Ebert, Roger (11 November 1988). "*A Cry in the Dark* Review" (http://rogerebert.suntimes.com/apps/pbcs.dll/article?AID=/19881111/REVIEWS/811110301/1023).*Chicago Sun-Times*. . Retrieved 25 April 2008.

[4] Kempley, Rita (11 November 1988). "*A Cry in the Dark* (PG-13) Review" (http://www.washingtonpost.com/wp-srv/style/longterm/movies/videos/acryinthedark.htm). *Washington Post*. . Retrieved 25 April 2008.

[5] Variety Staff (1988). "*A Cry in the Dark, Australia: Evil Angels* Review." (http://www.variety.com/review/VE1117790171.html?categoryid=31&cs=1&p=0). *Variety*. . Retrieved 25 April 2008.

[6] "AFI's 10 Top 10" (http://www.afi.com/10top10/crdrama.html). American Film Institute. 2008-06-17. . Retrieved 2008-06-18.

[7] "Festival de Cannes: A Cry in the Dark" (http://www.festival-cannes.com/en/archives/ficheFilm/id/232/year/1989.html). *festival-cannes.com*. . Retrieved 2009-08-01.

Bibliography

- Bryson, John. *Evil Angels*. Ringwood, Australia: Penguin Books, 1985 (first edition). ISBN 0-67080-993-4.
- Chamberlain, Lindy. *Through My Eyes: Lindy Chamberlain, An Autobiography*. Melbourne, Australia: William Heinemann, 1990. ISBN 0-85561-331-9.

External links

- Official site (http://www.acryinthedarkmovie.com/)
- *Evil Angels* (http://www.imdb.com/title/tt0094924/) at the Internet Movie Database
- *A Cry in the Dark* (http://www.allmovie.com/work/11693) at Allmovie
- *A Cry in the Dark* (http://www.rottentomatoes.com/m/cry_in_the_dark/) at Rotten Tomatoes

She-Devil (film)

She-Devil	
Film poster	
Directed by	Susan Seidelman
Produced by	Jonathan Brett Susan Seidelman
Written by	Screenplay: Barry Strugatz Mark R. Burns Novel: Fay Weldon
Starring	Meryl Streep Roseanne Barr
Music by	Howard Shore
Cinematography	Oliver Stapleton
Editing by	Craig McKay
Distributed by	Orion Pictures
Release date(s)	December 8, 1989
Running time	99 minutes
Country	United States
Language	English

She-Devil is a 1989 American film starring Meryl Streep and Roseanne Barr. It was directed by Susan Seidelman. It is the second adaptation of the novel *The Life and Loves of a She-Devil* by British writer Fay Weldon, after a BBC TV adaptation was first broadcast in 1986.

Plot

Ruth is a frumpy, overweight housewife and mother, who desperately tries to please her accountant husband Bob. After Bob meets romance novelist Mary Fisher at a dinner party, they begin having an affair; Mary also hires him as her accountant. Though aware of the affair, Ruth initially lives in denial (believing it to be a fling which Bob will leave) and continues to take care of her two children, Nicolette and Andrew, and doing other household chores. However, Ruth soon begins to feel ragged after trying to get things prepared for Bob's parents' visit, culminating with Ruth finding Andrew's dead gerbil in a casserole pot. After Ruth confronts him about his affair in front of his parents, Bob decides to pack up his things and leave Ruth with the kids, calling her a liability and telling her she is a bad mother, a lousy wife, a terrible cook, and has the appearance of a "she-devil." Now at her breaking point, Ruth vows to get revenge on both Bob and Mary. Ruth writes a list of Bob's four assets: his home, his family, his career, and his freedom, crossing off each one as it is destroyed.

With Bob away at Mary's mansion by the sea and the kids at school, she sets the house on fire by various means including lighting two cigarettes and tossing in a waste basket, placing aerosol cans in the microwave to set off an explosion, and overloading an electrical outlet, causing it to burn to the ground. Every possession is destroyed except for the dog, a framed photo of the family, and, significantly for Ruth's plan of revenge, Bob's file on Mary's finances.

Having destroyed Bob's first asset - his house - she drops the children off at Mary's mansion to live with their father. After seeing in Mary's file that Mary pays for her mother to live in an expensive nursing home, Ruth takes a job there under the pseudonym Vesta Rose. Ruth forms friendships with Mary's estranged mother and with her co-worker Nurse Hooper, a diminutive 22-year veteran at the home. As part of her plan, Ruth gets Mary's mother thrown out of the home and she moves in with her daughter, much to Mary's chagrin.

Ruth later partners with Hooper to start the Vesta Rose Employment Agency, which helps downtrodden, socially rejected women find good jobs in exchange for them (unwittingly) helping Ruth in her quest for vengeance against Bob, such as Olivia Honey, who is hired at Bob's firm as his secretary. Though Bob falls for Olivia at first sight, he fires her after she confesses her love for him; a heartbroken Olivia reveals to Ruth that Bob wires interest from his clients' accounts into an offshore Swiss bank account. Both women break into Bob's firm to wire larger amounts of money from Bob's clients' accounts into Bob's Swiss account, making his embezzlement more visible to his clients. Ruth then reports Bob's crimes to the IRS.

Meanwhile, the second of Bob's assets - his family - crumbles; Mary's relationship with Bob grows distant as he continues to sleep with other women; Mary has a hard time keeping Bob's children under control (since Bob is unwilling to lay down the law with them) and is forced to do various chores, as her staff's attentions are occupied elsewhere; and her mother, Mrs. Fisher, reveals her daughter's life-long secrets to a reporter for People magazine while Mary is on the phone. Compounding matters is the poor reception of Mary's new novel titled "Love in the Rinse Cycle," to the point that not even one person appears at her book signing, and Mary learning of Bob's affairs when she recognizes Bob's ring in photocopied pictures of a man's hands grabbing a woman's behind. However, she finally develops the courage to regain control of her life; upon seeing the maid Ute walk off the job and everyone partying around, she fires the butler Garcia and lays down the law with Bob, the children, and Mrs. Fisher.

Mary throws a party to cheer herself up and also spend time with her friends. Although the party has so far gone well (her laying down the law more or less successful), the atmosphere soon shatters when police officers interrupt the party with a warrant for Bob's arrest. While discussing Bob's defense, Bob's lawyer unknowingly reveals Bob's embezzlement from Mary. This proves the final straw for Mary, who promptly dumps Bob and fires him as her accountant. In addition, Bob and his lawyer's attempts to make a secret deal with a judge are rendered moot when another judge is put in his place (courtesy of another of Ruth's "private army" of Vesta Rose employees). Bob is convicted and sentenced to 18 months in prison; thus, his remaining assets - his career and his freedom - are destroyed.

The film then cuts to 18 months later. While Bob has greatly reformed while serving his sentence in prison, looking forward to spending his time with his family upon his release, Mary has barely changed at all. After the events with

Bob, Mary sells her mansion. Her new book is called "Trust and Betrayal: A Docu-novel of Love, Money and Skepticism," proves to be a critical and commercial success; however, she is soon back to her old ways, flirts with a Frenchman at her book signing.

The film ends with Ruth walking down a city street, followed by dozens of women, seemingly satisfied with the comeuppance she devilishly dished out on Bob and Mary.

Cast

- Roseanne Barr as Ruth Patchett
- Meryl Streep as Mary Fisher
- Ed Begley, Jr. as Bob
- Linda Hunt as Hooper
- Sylvia Miles as Mrs. Fisher
- Elisebeth Peters as Nicolette Patchett
- Bryan Larkin as Andy Patchett
- A Martinez as Garcia
- Maria Pitillo as Olivia Honey
- Mary Louise Wilson as Mrs. Trumper
- Susan Willis as Ute
- Jack Gilpin as Larry
- Robin Leach as Himself
- Nitchie Barrett as Bob's Secretary
- June Gable as Realtor

Soundtrack

The soundtrack for *She-Devil* was released on CD and audio cassette by Mercury Records on December 5, 1989.

1. "I Will Survive" - Safire

2. "You Can Have Him - Carmel

3. "C'mon And Get My Love" - D-Mob

4. "Always" - Tom Kimmel

5. "You're The Devil In Disguise - Elvis Presley

6. "Party Up" - Chubby Checker

7. "Tren D'Amour" - Jermaine Stewart

8. "That's What I Call Love" - Kate Ceberano

9. "Tied Up" - Yello

10. "It's Getting Hot" - The Fat Boys

Reception

Reception to *She-Devil* was mixed, with a 41% "Rotten" score at Rotten Tomatoes,

Roger Ebert gave the film three stars out of four and wrote, "The proof of it is that, on the basis of this movie, Streep didn't have to retire to her own dressing room to ask herself what she was doing in a movie with Barr".

Awards

Meryl Streep was nominated for the "Best Actress for a Musical or Comedy" Golden Globe in 1990.

In popular culture

A 1989 issue of *Mad* magazine spoofed several movie reviews including one called "She-Devil." The commentary said that "the producers went out of their way for uglification. Roseanne has a huge black mole on her cheek, as if the film was trying to convince the audience she was unattractive next to Meryl". The drawing shows an exploded house and a shocked Ed Begley Jr. and Meryl Streep demanding an explanation from Roseanne: Meryl: "You have blown up your husband's house, estranged his kids, and worked to ruin him! Why are you doing this?"

Roseanne: "Well, two women in my group therapy suggested it to me."

Meryl: "Who?!"

Roseanne: "Kathleen Turner and Glenn Close!"

The mention of Close and Turner were references to *Fatal Attraction* and *War of the Roses*. The spoof was also a crossover with Roseanne's sitcom husband John Goodman and their girths, where he is shown holding hands with Roseanne and saying to the reader "We have to hold hands. Otherwise one of these panels will fall right off your page", and showing Goodman looking at Al Pacino and Ellen Barkin in bed, a reference to Sea of Love, which premiered the same time as She-Devil.

The BBC TV version was somewhat different than the film. In the British version Ruth was also unattractive and overweight, but she began her revenge only after extensive efforts to keep her husband to herself; such as intensive exercise and plastic surgery in an effort to make herself more attractive like Mary. The American film had more subtle changes to Ruth's appearance, as it shows her going from a frumpy housewife to a self-confident business owner. Ruth trades in her glasses for contacts, has minor plastic surgery to remove her mole, and gets a trendier hairstyle and starts to wear more fashionable clothes.

External links

- *She-Devil* [1] at the Internet Movie Database
- *She-Devil* [2] at Rotten Tomatoes

References

[1] http://www.imdb.com/title/tt098309/
[2] http://www.rottentomatoes.com/m/shedevil/

Postcards from the Edge (film)

Postcards from the Edge	
Original poster	
Directed by	Mike Nichols
Produced by	John Calley Mike Nichols
Written by	Carrie Fisher
Starring	Meryl Streep Shirley MacLaine Dennis Quaid Gene Hackman Rob Reiner
Music by	Carly Simon
Cinematography	Michael Ballhaus
Editing by	Sam O'Steen
Distributed by	Columbia Pictures
Release date(s)	September 14, 1990
Running time	101 minutes
Country	United States
Language	English
Gross revenue	$39,071,603 (US) [1]

Postcards from the Edge is a 1990 American dramedy film directed by Mike Nichols. The screenplay by Carrie Fisher is based on her 1987 semi-autobiographical novel of the same title.

Plot

Actress Suzanne Vale (Meryl Streep) is a recovering drug addict trying to pick up the pieces of her career and get on with her life after being discharged from a rehab center she entered to kick a cocaine-acid-Percodan habit. When she is ready to return to work her agent advises her the studio's insurance policy will cover her only if she lives with a "responsible" individual such as her mother Doris Mann (Shirley MacLaine) who was the reigning musical comedy star of the 1950s and '60s. Suzanne is loath to return to the woman she struggled to escape from for years after growing up in her shadow. The situation is not helped by the fact Doris is loud, competitive, manipulative, self-absorbed and given to offering her daughter unsolicited advice with insinuating value judgments while treating her like a child.

Unaware producer Jack Faulkner (Dennis Quaid) is the one who drove her to the hospital during her last overdose Suzanne agrees to go out with him. During the course of a passionate first date he professes intense and eternal love for her and she believes every word is true. She learns from Evelyn Ames (Annette Benning), a bit player in her latest film, that Jack is sleeping with her as well. Still dressed in the costume she wears as a uniformed cop in the schlock movie she drives to Jack's house and confronts him. As their argument escalates he implies she was much more interesting when she was trying to function while under the influence.

At home Suzanne learns from Doris that her sleazy business manager Marty Wiener has absconded with all her money. This leads to a verbal brawl between the two women and Suzanne storms out to go to a looping session. There the paternalistic director Lowell Korshack (Gene Hackman) tells her he has more work for her as long as she remains clean and sober.

Suzanne arrives home and discovers Doris has crashed her car into a tree after drinking too much wine. She rushes to her hospital bedside where the two have a heart-to-heart talk while Suzanne fixes her mother's makeup and arranges a scarf on her head to conceal the fact she misplaced her wig in the accident. Looking and feeling better Doris musters her courage and faces the media waiting for her. Suzanne runs into Dr. Frankenthal (Richard Dreyfus), who had pumped her stomach after her last overdose, and he invites her to see a movie with him but she declines telling him she's not ready to date yet. Dr. Frankenthal tells her he's willing to wait until she is.

In the film's closing moments Suzanne performs "I'm Checkin' Out", a foot-stomping Country Western number, for a scene in Lowell Korshack's new film.

Production

In discussing adapting the book for the screen director Mike Nichols commented "For quite a long time we pushed pieces around, but then we went with the central story of a mother passing the baton to her daughter." [2] He added "Carrie doesn't draw on her life any more than Flaubert did. It's just that his life wasn't so well known." [2]

Responding to questions about how closely the film's Suzanne/Doris relationship parallels her relationship with her mother Debbie Reynolds Carrie Fisher stated "I wrote about a mother actress and a daughter actress. I'm not shocked that people think it's about me and my mother. It's easier for them to think I have no imagination for language, just a tape recorder with endless batteries." [2] In the DVD commentary she notes that her mother wanted to portray Doris but Nichols cast Shirley MacLaine instead.

Blue Rodeo accompanied Meryl Streep on "I'm Checkin' Out" which was written by Shel Silverstein. Other songs performed in the film include "I'm Still Here" by Stephen Sondheim and "You Don't Know Me" by Cindy Walker and Eddy Arnold.

Cast

- Meryl Streep ..... Suzanne Vale
- Shirley MacLaine ..... Doris Mann
- Dennis Quaid ..... Jack Faulkner
- Gene Hackman ..... Lowell Kolchek
- Richard Dreyfuss ..... Dr. Frankenthal
- Rob Reiner ..... Joe Pierce
- Mary Wickes ..... Grandma
- Conrad Bain ..... Grandpa
- Annette Bening ..... Evelyn Ames
- Simon Callow ..... Simon Asquith
- Gary Morton ..... Marty Wiener
- C. C. H. Pounder ..... Julie Marsden

- Barbara Garrick ..... Carol
- Anthony Heald ..... George Lazan
- Dana Ivey ..... Wardrobe Mistress
- Oliver Platt ..... Neil Bleene

Jerry Orbach filmed a scene as Suzanne's father, as divulged by writer Carrie Fisher in the DVD commentary, however it was cut.

Critical reception

Vincent Canby of the *New York Times* said the film "seems to have been a terrifically genial collaboration between the writer and the director, Miss Fisher's tale of odd-ball woe being perfect material for Mr. Nichols's particular ability to discover the humane sensibility within the absurd." [3]

Roger Ebert of the *Chicago Sun-Times* observed, "What's disappointing about the movie is that it never really delivers on the subject of recovery from addiction. There are some incomplete, dimly seen, unrealized scenes in the rehab center, and then desultory talk about offscreen AA meetings. But the film is preoccupied with gossip; we're encouraged to wonder how many parallels there are between the Streep and MacLaine characters and their originals, Fisher and Debbie Reynolds . . . *Postcards from the Edge* contains too much good writing and too many good performances to be a failure, but its heart is not in the right place." [4]

Hal Hinson of the *Washington Post* said, "Meryl Streep gives the most fully articulated comic performance of her career, the one she's always hinted at and made us hope for." He felt the film's earlier section was "the movie's best, primarily because Nichols is so focused on Streep. In fact, almost nothing else seems to matter to him . . . But while Nichols is servicing his star, he lets the other areas of the film go slack . . . [He] is finely attuned to the natural surreality of a movie set, but when he moves away from the show-biz satire and concentrates on the mother-daughter relationship, the movie falters." [5]

Box office

The film opened in 1,013 theaters in the United States on September 14, 1990 and grossed $7,871,856 on its opening weekend, ranking #1 at the box office. It eventually earned $39,071,603 in the US. [1]

Awards and nominations

- Academy Award for Best Actress (Meryl Streep, nominee)
- Academy Award for Best Song (Shel Silverstein, nominee)
- BAFTA Award for Best Actress in a Leading Role (Shirley MacLaine, nominee)
- BAFTA Award for Best Adapted Screenplay (Carrie Fisher, nominee)
- BAFTA Award for Best Film Music (Carly Simon, nominee)
- Golden Globe Award for Best Actress – Motion Picture Musical or Comedy (Meryl Streep, nominee)
- Golden Globe Award for Best Supporting Actress – Motion Picture (Shirley MacLaine, nominee)
- Golden Globe Award for Best Original Song (Shel Silverstein, nominee)
- American Comedy Award for Funniest Lead Actress in a Motion Picture (Meryl Streep, winner)
- London Critics Circle Film Award for Newcomer of the Year (Annette Bening, winner)

External links

- *Postcards from the Edge* [6] at the Internet Movie Database

References

[1] BoxOfficeMojo.com (http://www.boxofficemojo.com/movies/?id=postcardsfromtheedge.htm)

[2] *Entertainment Weekly*, September 28, 1990 (http://www.ew.com/ew/article/0,,318238,00.html)

[3] *New York Times* review (http://movies.nytimes.com/movie/review?res=9C0CEFD8173FF931A2575AC0A966958260)

[4] *Chicago Sun-Times* review (http://rogerebert.suntimes.com/apps/pbcs.dll/article?AID=/19900912/REVIEWS/9120301/1023)

[5] *Washington Post* review (http://www.washingtonpost.com/wp-srv/style/longterm/movies/videos/postcardsfromtheedgerhinson_a0a998.htm)

[6] http://www.imdb.com/title/tt0100395/

Defending Your Life

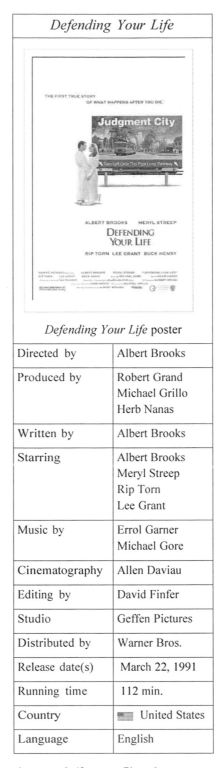

Defending Your Life	
Defending Your Life poster	
Directed by	Albert Brooks
Produced by	Robert Grand Michael Grillo Herb Nanas
Written by	Albert Brooks
Starring	Albert Brooks Meryl Streep Rip Torn Lee Grant
Music by	Errol Garner Michael Gore
Cinematography	Allen Daviau
Editing by	David Finfer
Studio	Geffen Pictures
Distributed by	Warner Bros.
Release date(s)	March 22, 1991
Running time	112 min.
Country	United States
Language	English

Defending Your Life is a 1991 romantic comedy/fantasy film about a man who must justify his life-long lack of assertiveness after he dies and arrives in the afterlife. The film was written, directed by, and stars Albert Brooks. It also stars Meryl Streep, Rip Torn and Lee Grant. Shirley MacLaine has a cameo appearance as herself, acting as the holographic host of the "Past Lives Pavilion", a reference to her publicly known belief in reincarnation. The movie was filmed entirely in and around Los Angeles, California. Despite its comedic overtones, *Defending Your Life* contains elements of drama and allegory.

Plot

Daniel Miller (Albert Brooks) dies in a car accident on his birthday and is sent to the afterlife. He arrives in Judgment City, a purgatory-like waiting area populated by the recently-deceased of the western half of the United States, where he is to undergo the process of having his life on earth judged. Daniel and the rest of the recently-deceased are offered many Earth-like amenities in the city while they undergo their judgment processes, from all-you-can-eat restaurants (which cause no weight gain) to bowling alleys and comedy clubs.

As explained to Daniel, people from Earth use so little of their brains (3-5%) that they spend most of their lives functioning on the basis of their fears. "When you use more than 5% of your brain, you don't want to be on Earth, believe me," explains Bob Diamond (Rip Torn), Daniel's defense attorney. If the Judgement court determines that Daniel has conquered his fears, he will be sent on to the next phase of existence, where he will be able to use more of his brain and thus be able to experience more of what the universe has to offer. Otherwise, his soul will be reincarnated on Earth to live another life in another attempt at moving past fear. In the process, he may advance up the universe's proverbial food chain.

Daniel's judgment process is presided over by two judges (played by Lillian Lehman and George D. Wallace). Diamond argues that Daniel should move onto the next phase, against Diamond's formidable opponent, Lena Foster (Lee Grant), who Diamond informs Daniel is known as "the Dragon Lady". Each utilizes video-like footage from selected days in the defendant's life, which Diamond and his opponent show during the proceedings to illustrate their case.

During the procedure, Daniel meets and falls in love with Julia (Meryl Streep), a woman who lived a seemingly perfect life of courage and generosity, especially compared to his. The proceedings do not go well for Daniel. Foster shows a series of episodes in which Daniel did not overcome his fears, as well as various other bad decisions. The final nail in his coffin, it seems, is when Foster, on the last day of arguments, plays footage of his previous night with Julia, in which he declines to sleep with her, for what Foster believes is his same lack of courage. It is ruled that Daniel will return to Earth. Meanwhile, Julia is judged worthy to move on.

Daniel finds himself strapped in on a tram to return to Earth, when he spots Julia on a different tram across the tram lanes. On a seemingly spur-of-the-moment impulse, he unstraps himself, escapes from the moving tram, and risks injury to stow away on Julia's. Although he cannot enter it at first, the entire event is being monitored by both Bob Diamond and Lena Foster, who convince the judges that this display of courage has earned Daniel the right to move on. They open the doors on Julia's tram, allowing Daniel in, reuniting him with Julia and allowing them both to move on to their next phases of existence together.

Video releases

Defending Your Life was released on VHS and Laserdisc in early 1992. Both of these editions have since gone out of print. Warner Bros. Home Video released a DVD on April 3, 2001, in a cardboard snap case. It features 1.85:1 anamorphic widescreen formatting, and subtitles in English, French, Spanish, and Portuguese. Apart from cast and crew information and the film's theatrical trailer, the DVD contains no extras. Warners also rereleased the film in 2001 in a two-pack DVD set with Brooks' *Looking for Comedy in the Muslim World*.

Reception

Variety called it an "inventive and mild bit of whimsy" in which Brooks has a "little fun with the Liliom idea of being judged in a fanciful afterlife, but he doesn't carry his conceit nearly far enough."[1] Roger Ebert called it "funny in a warm, fuzzy way" and a film with a "splendidly satisfactory ending, which is unusual for an Albert Brooks film."[2] *The New York Times* called it "the most perceptive and convincing among a recent spate of *carpe diem* movies"— a reference to films such as *Dead Poets Society* (1989), *Field of Dreams* (1989), and *Ghost* (1990).[3] Richard Schickel wrote:[4]

Defending Your Life is better developed as a situation than it is as a comedy (though there are some nice bits, like a hotel lobby sign that reads, WELCOME KIWANIS DEAD). But Brooks has always been more of a muser than a *tummler*, and perhaps more depressive than he is manic. He asks us to banish the cha-cha-cha beat of conventional comedy from mind and bend to a slower rhythm. His pace is not that of a comic standing up at a microphone barking one-liners, but of an intelligent man sitting down by the fire mulling things over. And in this case offering us a large slice of angel food for thought.

The film received mostly positive reviews from critics and holds a 96% rating on review aggregator Rotten Tomatoes (based on 26 reviews).[5]

The film was not a box office success, grossing about $16 million in the United States. It received three Saturn Award nominations for Best Actress (Meryl Streep), Best Fantasy Film, and Best Writing (Albert Brooks).[6]

See also

*   *What Dreams May Come*, a novel by Richard Matheson published in 1978. It was adapted into a film in 1998 starring Robin Williams, and its plot explores similar themes.

External links

*   *Defending Your Life* [7] at the Internet Movie Database
*   *Defending Your Life* [8] at Allmovie
*   *Defending Your Life* [9] at Rotten Tomatoes
*   *Defending Your Life (DVD)* [10] at Warner Bros.

References

[1]   "Defending Your Life" (http://www.variety.com/review/VE1117790339.htm). Variety. 1991. . Retrieved 2009-10-18.

[2]   Roger Ebert (April 5, 1991). "Defending Your Life" (http://rogerebert.suntimes.com/apps/pbcs.dll/article?AID=/19910405/REVIEWS/ 104050301/1023). Chicago Sun-Times. . Retrieved 2009-10-18.

[3]   Caryn James (April 21, 1991). "Carpe Diem Becomes Hot Advice" (http://movies.nytimes.com/movie/ review?res=9D0CE7DA1339F932A15757C0A967958260). The New York Times. . Retrieved 2009-10-18.

[4]   Richard Schickel (March 25, 1991). "Defending Your Life" (http://www.time.com/time/magazine/article/0,9171,972587,00.html). Time. . Retrieved 2009-10-18.

[5]   *Defending Your Life* (http://www.rottentomatoes.com/m/defending_your_life/) at Rotten Tomatoes. Retrieved 2009-10-18.

[6]   Awards for *Defending Your Life* (http://www.imdb.com/title/tt0101698/awards) from the Internet Movie Database

[7]   http://www.imdb.com/title/tt0101698/

[8]   http://www.allmovie.com/work/13087

[9]   http://www.rottentomatoes.com/m/defending_your_life/

[10]   http://whv.warnerbros.com/WHVPORTAL/Portal/product.jsp?OID=7938

Death Becomes Her

Death Becomes Her	
 Theatrical release poster	
Directed by	Robert Zemeckis
Produced by	Steve Starkey Robert Zemeckis
Written by	Martin Donovan David Koepp
Starring	Meryl Streep Bruce Willis Goldie Hawn
Music by	Alan Silvestri
Editing by	Arthur Schmidt
Distributed by	Universal Pictures
Release date(s)	July 31, 1992
Running time	104 min.
Language	English
Budget	$55,000,000
Gross revenue	$149,000,000

Death Becomes Her is a 1992 dark comedy film directed by Robert Zemeckis and starring Goldie Hawn, Meryl Streep, and Bruce Willis. The film focuses on two rivaling women (Streep and Hawn) who drink a magic potion that promises eternal youth. However, after they both are killed in their fight for the love of a mortician (Willis), the potion revives them as the undead and they are forced to maintain their deteriorating bodies forever.

Death Becomes Her won an Academy Award for Best Visual Effects. Despite mixed reviews, the film was a commercial success.

Plot

Actress Madeline Ashton (Meryl Streep) and writer Helen Sharp (Goldie Hawn) are longtime romantic rivals. Helen's life falls apart when glamorous Madeline steals her fiancé, plastic surgeon Ernest Menville (Bruce Willis), and marries him. Helen becomes an obese, depressed woman and is arrested and placed in a mental institution, where she is consumed by thoughts of revenge against Madeline. Madeline's career on Broadway ends in 1978, and 14 years later she is still struggling with her fading looks and by-gone acting career. Ernest, now an alcoholic and miserable in his marriage, has been reduced to working as a high-end mortician, restoring the looks of celebrities for their funerals. By this time, Helen has been rehabilitated, and is the successful author of "Forever Young". When Madeline and Helen meet again at Helen's book-signing party, Helen appears miraculously rejuvenated, thin, and youthful.

Madeline, jealous and dumbfounded by Helen, seeks the aid of mysterious Lisle von Rhoman (Isabella Rossellini), who claims she has discovered the secret of eternal youth. She offers Madeline a magical potion to reverse the process of aging. Madeline buys the potion for an undisclosed (but presumably very high) sum of money and drinks it, reverting to her youthful and shapely form. Lisle then warns Madeline to take perfect care of her new body.

In the meantime, Helen has seduced Ernest and conspired with him to kill Madeline. However, before their elaborate plan can be carried out, Ernest and Madeline have a heated argument and Ernest pushes Madeline down their grand staircase; Madeline breaks her neck and lands motionless at the bottom. Believing her dead, Ernest rushes to phone Helen for advice, not noticing Madeline begin to sit up and approach him, her head twisted backwards. After a trip to the ER, and finding out she has no pulse, a body temperature below 80 degrees, and two shattered vertebrae, they put her in the morgue after she faints in the doctor's office. Amazed, Ernest thinks that her resurrection is a miracle and a sign that they are meant to be together, and uses his mortician skills to repair the damage done to Madeline's body.

Helen, thinking that Madeline is dead, arrives at the house to bury her, but Madeline, very much alive and having overheard their plot against her life, shoots Helen with a double-barreled shotgun. When Helen revives, despite the basketball-size hole gaping through her stomach, Madeline guesses correctly that Helen was also a customer of Lisle's. The two undead rivals fight, but fail to do any real damage or even inflict pain upon each other. They then reconcile their differences and beg Ernest to repair their incredibly damaged bodies. Ernest agrees on the condition that he never see them again after the work is done. However, Madeline and Helen discover that his repairs are only temporary; they will need Ernest to perform routine maintenance to their bodies forever. They conspire to make Ernest drink the potion as well, knocking him unconscious and taking him to Lisle. Although Lisle makes an impassioned argument for immortality, Ernest refuses the potion, stating that a life lived forever is worthless. Ernest now knows that immortality is not a dream, but a nightmare.

In trying to escape, Ernest climbs across the roof of Lisle's mansion to get to an exit door, but slips after being startled by Madeline and Helen (who followed him upstairs) and his suspenders get caught on the rain gutter, dangling him several stories about the ground. Madeline and Helen implore one last time that he drink the potion so he will survive his inevitable fall. Ernest refuses again, drops the potion, then falls after it when his suspenders break. He lands in Lisle's swimming pool and escapes. With Ernest gone and Lisle shunning them after their incompetence, Helen and Madeline realize, much to their chagrin, that they will now have to take care of each other forever.

Thirty-seven years later (2029), Ernest has died. Madeline and Helen attend his funeral, using veils to cover their horribly deteriorated forms. Ernest is eulogized as having lived a good and adventurous life, accomplishing much more in his mortal lifespan than Helen and Madeline are ever likely to do in their self-centered immortality. Helen weeps and in attempt to wipe her eyes she tears out her eyelid. She asks Madeline for a can of spray paint and the two bicker over it. They look up at the priest when he describes Ernest as having attained eternal life and youth through his accomplishments, his good works, and his descendants, who carry on his name. Faced with an alternative concept of immortality, Madeline and Helen mock the priest and leave.

Outside the church, Helen slips on the missing can – dropped on the steps – and begins to lose her balance, just as Madeline did in her earlier confrontation with Ernest. When Madeline hesitates in helping her back up, Helen pulls her down and the two women tumble to the bottom of the steps, shattering to pieces as they land. The film ends with Helen's tottering, decapitated head asking Madeline's head, "Do you remember where you parked the car?"

Cast

- Goldie Hawn as Helen Sharp
- Meryl Streep as Madeline Ashton
- Bruce Willis as Dr. Ernest Menville
- Isabella Rossellini as Lisle von Rhoman
- Ian Ogilvy as Chagall
- Adam Storke as Dakota
- Nancy Fish as Rose, Madeleine's Maid
- Alaina Reed Hall as Psychologist
- Michelle Johnson as Anna, Chagall's Aide
- Mary Ellen Trainor as Vivian Adams
- William Frankfather as Mr. Franklin
- John Ingle as Eulogist

Awards and nominations

Award	Role	Result
Academy Award	Best Visual Effects	Won
Golden Globe	Best Performance by an Actress in a Motion Picture - Comedy/Musical (Meryl Streep)	Nominated
Saturn Award	Best Actor (Bruce Willis)	Nominated
Saturn Award	Best Actress (Meryl Streep)	Nominated
Saturn Award	Best Supporting Actress (Isabella Rosellini)	Won

Special effects

Like most of director Robert Zemeckis' films, *Death Becomes Her* was a technically complex movie to make, and the production had its fair share of mishaps. For example, in a scene where Helen Sharp and Madeline Ashton are battling with shovels, Meryl Streep accidentally scarred Goldie Hawn's face. Despite the film's winning for an Academy Award for its effects, Streep admitted that she disliked working on a project that focused so heavily on special effects, saying:

> My first, my last, my only. I think it's tedious. Whatever concentration you can apply to that kind of comedy is just shredded. You stand there like a piece of machinery — they should get machinery to do it. I loved how it turned out. But it's not fun to act to a lampstand. "Pretend this is Goldie, right here! Uh, no, I'm sorry, Bob, she went off the mark by five centimeters, and now her head won't match her neck!" It was like being at the dentist.[1]

Reception

The film received mixed reviews. It currently holds a 53% approval rating at Rotten Tomatoes based on 19 reviews (10 positive, 9 negative).[2] Gene Siskel and Roger Ebert both gave the film a 'thumbs down', commenting that while the film had great special effects, it lacked any real substance or character depth.[3]

Despite the lackluster reception, it won an Academy Award, Meryl Streep was nominated for a Golden Globe for her performance and the film was number 1 at the box office.

Soundtrack

The score was composed by Italo-American film composer Alan Silvestri.[4]

External links

- *Death Becomes Her* [5] at the Internet Movie Database
- *Death Becomes Her* [6] at the TCM Movie Database
- Movie stills [7]

References

[1] "Depth Becomes Her" (http://www.ew.com/ew/article/0,,275733_4,00.html). *Entertainment Weekly.*. 2000-03-24. . Retrieved 2007-01-25.

[2] Death Becomes Her (http://www.rottentomatoes.com/m/death_becomes_her/)Rotten Tomatoes profile

[3] *Death Becomes Her* review (http://bventertainment.go.com/tv/buenavista/atm/reviews.html?sec=1&subsec=759) Atthemoviestv.com

[4] 10 of the Most Underrated Horror Scores! (http://www.bloody-disgusting.com/news/20063)

[5] http://www.imdb.com/title/tt0104070/

[6] http://tcmdb.com/title/title.jsp?stid=19219

[7] http://film.virtual-history.com/film.php?filmid=821

The House of the Spirits (film)

The House of the Spirits	
Theatrical release poster	
Directed by	Bille August
Produced by	Bernd Eichinger
Written by	Isabel Allende (novel) Bille August
Starring	Jeremy Irons Meryl Streep Glenn Close Winona Ryder Antonio Banderas
Music by	Hans Zimmer
Cinematography	Jörgen Persson
Distributed by	Miramax Films
Release date(s)	1993
Running time	140 min.
Country	Portugal Germany Denmark United States
Language	English
Budget	$40 000 000

The House of the Spirits is a 1993 dramatic movie starring Jeremy Irons, Meryl Streep, Glenn Close, Winona Ryder, and Antonio Banderas. The supporting cast includes Vanessa Redgrave, Maria Conchita Alonso, Armin Mueller-Stahl and Jan Niklas. It was directed by Bille August, and based on the Isabel Allende novel *La Casa de los Espíritus*.

Principal photography took place in Denmark, but some scenes were filmed in Lisbon and Alentejo, Portugal. It won awards at the Bavarian Film Awards, German Film Awards, Golden Screen (Germany), Havana Film Festival, and Robert Festival (Denmark), as well as from the German Phono Academy and the Guild of German Art House Cinemas.

Plot

Prologue

At the beginning of the movie, we see a young woman arrive at a house with an old man. She leads him in the house and sits him on a chair, where he asks to be alone. The young woman sits down on the stairs, close to where a little girl is playing. The young woman starts pondering about life, and soon begins to narrate a story.

Clara and Esteban

The woman states her mother, Clara Del Valle, knew that she was in love with Esteban Trueba the first time she saw him, even though she was still a child. However, Esteban Trueba (Jeremy Irons), had come to propose to Rosa the Beautiful, Clara's sister. As he is rather poor, Esteban leaves his fiancée with her family to earn some money for the wedding first.

Clara has special telekinetic powers and can sometimes foresee the future. One day, she has a vision and tells her sister Rosa that there will be a death in the family. The next day, Rosa dies from poisoning. It is figured out that Rosa drank a poisoned drink meant for her father Severo. Clara is blaming herself for her sister's death and decides never to speak again.

Esteban arrives heartbroken at the funeral. At home, his sister Férula (Glenn Close) confronts him saying that he has to work to support her and their sick mother. Esteban leaves for his newly bought hacienda Tres Marias. He finds many natives living on his land and tells them to work for him for food and shelter. For the next twenty years, Esteban makes Tres Marias an example of a successful hacienda. However, he also rapes the peasant girl Pancha Garcia (Sarita Choudhury) who is working for him. Meanwhile, Clara lives in her own world of fantasy with her family.

One day, twenty years later, Esteban receives a letter stating his mother has died. After her funeral, Esteban decides to ask for Clara's hand, despite Férula telling him Clara is too sickly and won't take care of him. When he shows up at the Del Valle family's house, Clara (Meryl Streep) asks him right away if he has come to ask her to marry him, thus speaking again for the first time in twenty years. Esteban confirms he is there to marry Clara, and the two go out for a walk.

Férula meets Clara at a coffee shop to talk to her about her own future, and Clara, already knowing about Férula's worries where to live, promises her that she can live with her and Esteban in Tres Marias after the wedding. Férula is overwhelmed with happiness realising that she has found a friend in her new sister-in-law.

Some time later, Férula goes to church to confess that she has strange feelings for Clara. She reports uneasiness when Clara sleeps with Esteban, and also fierce dedication to her sister-in-law. She realises that she is feeling much more for Clara than she should. Esteban senses this and is resentful of Férula's interference in his family.

Clara's parents are killed in a terrible accident on the way to visit their pregnant daughter. Clara soon after gives birth to a girl, named Blanca, as she predicted. Some years later, Pancha Garcia appears at the family house with her and Esteban's bastard teenage son, Esteban Garcia. She asks for money and tells Esteban Trueba the he cannot get rid of her and his son. Esteban Trueba is very annoyed and goes back to play with Blanca. Esteban Garcia comes back to the house later when no one is looking. He finds the child Blanca and begins to molest her. Férula calls Blanca's name and Esteban García leaves running.

Clara has been giving classes to the peasant children and Blanca. Pedro Tercero, the little son of the peasant Segundo at Tres Marias befriends Blanca, and after school she goes out to play with him. The two are gone for hours, and Esteban Trueba, Férula and Clara start worrying. The two children are eventually found playing in the lagoon. Esteban Trueba doesn't like that his daughter playing with a peasant boy, and decides to send Blanca to a boarding school.

Blanca and Pedro Tercero

The next scene has Blanca, who is now the same woman from the prologue, talking. She says that she had been split from Pedro Tercero a long time, but now she had graduated, they can finally be together. The grown up Blanca (Winona Ryder) is coming home to Três Marias in a car, with graduation vests on. At night, Blanca goes out to the lagoon where she meets the grown up Pedro Tercero (Antonio Banderas). They kiss, talk and Blanca leaves. That night while Esteban goes to a political party, there is an earthquake, and Férula climbs into bed with Clara. When Esteban sees this, he is so angry that he throws Férula out of the house telling her never to step close to his family again. Clara overhears him threatening his sister and feels sad and disappointed about it.

Some time later, Esteban brings the French count de Satigny to his home whom he wants to marry Blanca. While Satigny is still visiting, Esteban catches Pedro preaching revolutionary ideas to the peasant people. He punishes him with a fierce whipping and banishing him from Tres Marias.

At dinner, Férula suddenly appears. She walks into the house, kisses Clara on the forehead and leaves again. Clara tells them that Férula is dead. Clara and Esteban drive into town and are brought to Férula's poor house by a priest. There they find Férula dead on the bed.

Pedro has returned to Tres Marias talking to the peasants about their rights and nearly gets shot by Esteban. That night, the count de Satigny, who is visiting again, watches Blanca and Pedro meeting secretly at the lagoon. He reveals Blanca's lover to her father who immediately drags Blanca back to the house. He promises to kill Pedro; when Clara argues with him about it, he hits his wife and she falls. When Clara rises, she coldly tells him that she will never speak to him again. Clara moves with Blanca to her parents' house in the capital.

Meanwhile, Esteban is alone in Três Marias. He blames Pedro for everything, and is offering a reward for whoever can take him to Pedro's hiding place. Esteban Garcia (Vincent Gallo), Esteban Trueba's bastard son, states he can take him to Pedro's hiding place. Garcia takes Esteban to Pedro, and Esteban tries to kill Pedro, unsuccessfully. When Garcia asks for his reward, Esteban Trueba replies that traitors don't get rewards. Garcia walks away angrily.

Blanca eventually finds out she is pregnant. Esteban then tries to force a wedding between the count de Satigny and Blanca, so as to not have any bastards in the family. He tries to convince his daughter by telling her that Pedro Tercero is dead. Blanca angrily refuses, but her mother eventually comforts her by telling her that Pedro is still alive.

Revolution

Some years later, Esteban who has become an old man is busy with his political career but seems to be rather lonely. He comes to Clara's and Blanca's house to apologise. He asks Clara to let him stay with her and to show his granddaughter Alba who he has never seen before.

He moves in with them but Clara still does not talk to him and he constantly keeps feuding with Blanca. While the family is celebrating Alba's birthday, Esteban Garcia knocks on the door. Blanca answers, not recognizing the man who abused her as a child. Garcia asks to talk to Esteban Trueba. Esteban Trueba is asked by his bastard son to help him get into the military academy. He reminds Trueba of the reward he never got and Trueba gives him a cheque.

The election is on, and Esteban still believes that his Conservative Party will win as usual. Later on, the People's Front wins the election. While Esteban grieves, Blanca goes out on the street to celebrate and to meet Pedro. The two kiss and celebrate together for the rest of the night. A few days later, Pedro is able to meet his daughter Alba for the first time with her mother at an ice-cream parlour. Blanca and Pedro are able to meet regularly now, and things seem to be perfect.

While Alba and her grandmother Clara are setting up a Christmas tree, Clara feels she is leaving this world, and decides to prepare for death. She gives Alba notebooks and jewelry to give to Blanca. Kissing Alba goodbye, Clara dies. When Blanca and Esteban arrive in a car, Alba goes out to tell them grandma is dead. The three hug and cry together.

However, conspiracy on part of the Conservative Party eventually leads up to the coup d'état. Although Esteban seems happy, believing it is for the good of the country and that the military will hand the power back to the Conservative Party, he proves himself wrong. The military does not hand the power back, and a Military Dictatorship is started. People related to the People's Party are captured or even killed. Blanca is highly involved, and eventually the Political Police comes to arrest her for being with Pedro Tercero. Blanca asks her father to hide Pedro in their house and to help him getting out of the country.

Blanca is tortured and abused by her half-brother Esteban Garcia, now an important member of the military. She nevertheless refuses to reveal where Pedro is. She is put in a cell, where Clara's spirit appears to tell her not to wish for death.

Esteban attends to his daughter's wishes and helps Pedro Tercero to find exile in Canada. Esteban then tries to get Blanca out of prison and desperately asks an old prostitute friend of his, now an influential lady, to help get Blanca out. She succeeds and one morning a beaten and dirty Blanca arrives at the house. Esteban is shocked to see his daughter in such a state and realises what he has done.

Epilogue

The movie ends with the opening scene, Blanca and Esteban returning to Tres Marias with Alba. There Esteban is finally visited by Clara's spirit who comes to help him die.

Blanca sits outside and ponders on her life. To her, life now is Pedro and Alba, and while Alba plays in the front door with the leaves swirling in the wind, the movie ends.

Differences Between the Movie and the Novel

- Clara did not fall in love with Esteban the first time she saw him. In the book, in fact, she says she never loved him at all.
- In the novel, it is stated Clara was the fifteenth child of her parents, of which eleven were alive. However, in the film, Clara's only mentioned sister is Rosa.
- Nana, Clara's nanny as a child and later nanny to her children, is not named or mentioned in the movie. The Del Valle's unnamed Indian servant plays some of her roles in the book.
- Clara's idol Uncle Marcos is also not mentioned at all in the movie.
- Esteban's hacienda was a family heritage.
- In the book, Esteban stays at Tres Marías 9 years, rather than 20.
- Pancha Garcia, the woman Esteban raped, was sister to Segundo in the book. This is not mentioned in the movie. Esteban also raped many other women during his stay in Las Tres Marías, and even after his marriage. This is not mentioned either.
- Clara's powers in the movie differ from the book, where she can also talk to ghosts.
- In the book, Esteban and Clara go on a honeymoon after marrying, and move into a house in the capital, not Las Tres Marías. Later, when going to spend a summer at Tres Marías, Clara likes it and decides to stay.
- Clara is not supposed to know about her parent's death in the book, as Esteban believes it will threaten her pregnancy, but she find out in a dream, whereas in the movie she is quickly told.
- Clara also has two twin sons in the book, Jaime and Nicolas.

- Nicolás had a lover in the book named Amanda, with whom Jaime was also in love. Amanda was absent from the movie.
- Esteban García, Esteban's bastard son, hardly has a role in the novel. It is Esteban's bastard grandson (also named Esteban García) who has the important role.
- Pedro Tercero plays the guitar in the book, and sings a song about the Chickens and the Fox. In the movie, the song is transformed into a story he tells at Clara's school, and he does not play the guitar.
- Blanca is not sent to a boarding school in the book: instead, Esteban and Clara move back to the capital, where Blanca spends the year, going to Las Tres Marías for summer. During her teenage years, after an earthquake which causes her parents to stay in Las Tres Marías, Blanca, now in a boarding school, fakes an illness so she can go live in Las Tres Marías too.
- The tremendous earthquake that happens in Las Tres Marías and cause some 10000 casualties in the whole country is absent from the movie.
- In the book, Clara and Blanca move to the capital house after Esteban hits Clara, not Clara's parents' house.
- Esteban's revenge towards Pedro Tercero in the book is partially successful: he manages to cut off three of Pedro's fingers.
- Blanca actually does marry the Count Jean de Satigny in the book, but leaves his house still pregnant when she discovers his love towards pornography, especially using the Indian servants.
- Alba is born in Clara's capital house, and Clara predicts good luck and happiness in her future.
- It is Alba and not Blanca who is pampered by Esteban.
- Esteban García's abuses of Blanca as a child happen to Alba in the actual novel. He also kisses her forcefully in the mouth at her fourteenth birthday, when coming to ask for Esteban to give him a reference to get into the military.
- Blanca and Pedro manage to meet before the People's Party win in the book.
- In the book, Alba is introduced to her father earlier, but knows him only as her mother's lover and a good friend, believing the count to be her father.
- In the novel, Alba is a teenager during the Coup, and is going to university, while in the movie she is a child.
- Miguel, Amanda's brother and later Alba's lover, who is a revolutionist, is absent in the movie.
- Alba participates in various revolutionist manifestations before and after the Coup, due to her link with Miguel. Blanca, in the novel, has little interest in these.
- Alba is arrested by the Political Police for dating Miguel, and is tortured and abused by Esteban Garcia in the novel. She then wishes for death, and Clara's spirit comes to tell her not to. She is later released with the help of an old prostitute. This whole sequence happens to Blanca in the movie, with the difference that she is arrested for dating Pedro Tercero.
- In the novel, Blanca and Pedro Tercero leave for Canada alone, Alba does not come with them. In the movie Pedro Tercero goes to Canada alone: Blanca will reach him only after Esteban's death, and Alba will go with her mother.
- In the novel, Esteban dies in the capital house, with Alba by his side, confusing her with Clara and Rosa, instead of alone in Las Tres Marías with Clara's spirit.
- Alba is pregnant at the end of the novel, but she doesn't know if the child is Miguel's or Esteban Garcia's. Blanca's character in the movie, who takes over most of Alba's role, is not pregnant and decides to leave the nation, whereas Alba, in the novel, wants to remain until she can.

The main difference is that Alba's role is minimized, and Blanca takes over most of that role:

- Being pampered by Esteban Trueba as a child.
- Being abused by Esteban Garcia as a child.
- Being involved in the rebel and revolutionist demonstrations due to a romantic link.
- Being arrested because of said romantic link.
- Being tortured and abused by Esteban Garcia, to be later released with the help of the old prostitute.

However, Blanca also plays her novel role in the movie such as:

- Her involvement with Pedro.
- The fight she has with her father and that makes him slap Clara.
- The bastard child she has.
- Meeting Pedro as a lover.
- Hiding Pedro during the Coup, and later going into exile with him.

This combination of two roles into Blanca was probably done to shorten the movie in length.

Soundtrack

Two songs appear in the film: "La Paloma", a Spanish–Cuban–Mexican tune sung by popular Chilean singer Rosita Serrano; and "La Cumparsita", a classic Uruguayan tango tune performed by German bandleader Adalbert Lutter and his orchestra.[1]

External links

- *The House of the Spirits* [2] at the Internet Movie Database

References

[1] "Soundtracks for The House of the Spirits" (http://www.imdb.com/title/tt0107151/soundtrack). *Internet Movie Database*. . Retrieved 22 March 2010.
[2] http://www.imdb.com/title/tt0107151/

The River Wild

Not to be confused with Wild River.

The River Wild	
Original theatrical poster	
Directed by	Curtis Hanson
Produced by	David Foster Lawrence Turman
Written by	Denis O'Neill
Starring	Meryl Streep Kevin Bacon David Strathairn John C. Reilly Joseph Mazzello
Music by	Jerry Goldsmith Maurice Jarre (rejected theme)
Cinematography	Robert Elswit
Editing by	David Brenner Joe Hutshing
Distributed by	Universal Pictures
Release date(s)	30 September 1994 (USA) 24 February 1995 (UK)
Running time	108 minutes
Language	English American Sign Language
Budget	$45,000,000

The River Wild is a 1994 American thriller film directed by Curtis Hanson and starring Meryl Streep, Kevin Bacon, David Strathairn, John C. Reilly, and Joseph Mazzello. The story involves a family on a whitewater rafting trip who encounter two violent criminals in the wilderness.

Plot

A Boston couple, Gail (Meryl Streep) and Tom (David Strathairn) are having marital problems. Gail, a rafting expert, decides to take their child Roarke (Joseph Mazzello) on a holiday rafting down the Salmon River in Idaho, along with their pet dog. At the last minute Tom joins them. As they are setting off they meet a couple of other rafters, Wade (Kevin Bacon) and Terry (John C. Reilly), who appear to be friendly.

After a day's rafting the family make camp for the night, but Tom continues to work on his laptop computer rather than enter fully into the experience. The family are joined by Wade and Terry who help to celebrate Roarke's birthday. Gail flirts with Wade. However, after a while Wade begins acting suspiciously and Gail decides it would be best to part ways. During the morning's rafting Wade reveals to Roarke that they have a gun with them. As they raft down the river the parents discuss an exit strategy that will allow them to leave the two men behind, and at lunch they attempt to leave on their raft and get away before Wade and Terry realize what is going on.

Their attempt fails and Wade pulls the gun on them and assaults Tom. Gail then realizes that an armed robbery she had heard about was actually carried out by Wade and Terry, and their rafting trip is actually a way for them to get away. The family are forced to raft at gunpoint down the rest of the river before they all set up camp for the night. During the night Tom attempts to steal the gun off the sleeping Terry but is heard and has to run into the bushes and to the river. Wade gives chase and believes he has shot him when he hears a loud splash into the water.

It's revealed that Wade and Terry, in order to aid their escape, want to go on down the river to a set of rapids where in recent years one person was killed and another was left paralyzed. Consequently, rafting is no longer allowed. Wade and Terry force the rafters down through the rapids despite Gail's repeated attempts to flip the raft and so force Wade and Terry out of the river.

Meanwhile a park ranger (Benjamin Bratt), who knows Gail, is white water canoeing down the river. He bumps into the group; but Wade holds the gun to Gail's back and pretends that everything is OK. Later, he appears again but this time Wade shoots him and he falls dying into the river.

Tom reappears and manages to flip the raft. Gail and Roarke, who have been tied to the raft by Wade, remain in the raft and to get hold of the gun, which had fallen into the water. whilst Tom is fighting Terry. The struggle ends when Gail throws the bag of money into the water and shoots Wade whose dead body floats off down river. The film ends with the family and Terry (who has been arrested) being helicoptered out.

Cast

(in order of appearance)

- Meryl Streep as Gail
- Joseph Mazzello as Roarke
- Stephanie Sawyer as Willa
- David Strathairn as Tom
- Elizabeth Hoffman as Gail's Mother
- Victor H. Galloway as Gail's Father
- Diane Delano as Ranger
- Thomas F. Duffy as Ranger
- Kevin Bacon as Wade
- John C. Reilly as Terry
- William Lucking as Frank
- Benjamin Bratt as Ranger Johnny
- Paul Cantelon as Violinist
- Glenn Morshower as Policeman

Production

Many of the film's whitewater scenes were filmed on the Kootenai River in Montana. Additional scenes were filmed on the Rogue River, in Southern Oregon and the Middle Fork of the Flathead River. Meryl Streep did most of her own stunts in the film. Streep had a scare at the end of one day of filming when Hanson asked her to shoot one more scene, which she protested against because of exhaustion. Streep, however decided to attempt the scene and with a lack of strength from fatigue was swept off the raft into the river and was in danger of drowning, before she was rescued. On being rescued Streep said to Hanson "In the future, when I say I can't do something, I think we should believe me," to which Hanson agreed.

The Kootenay River valley used in the film

Release

The film premiered on September 30, 1994 in the United States but release was delayed in the United Kingdom until February 24, 1995. The film grossed a total of $94,216,343 worldwide, earning $46,816,343 domestically in the United States and $47,400,000 abroad.

Reception

The River Wild generally received a mixed reaction by critics although the scenery and cinematography of the film was widely praised. Film critic James Berardinelli praised the production of the film in its cinematography and score and the pace of the rafting experience to the audience. He praised Curtis Hanson's directing in that like *The Hand That Rocks the Cradle*, Hanson, "could manipulate characters and situations within the comfortable confines of a formula plot", describing it as a "level of excitement designed to submerge implausibilities and minor gaffes, and a film which "braves the rapids while keeping the viewer afloat amidst its churning waters".[1] He also praised Streep's powerful performance as a female action hero but described the film overall as "a cut below a white-knuckler".[1]

Roger Ebert of the *Chicago Sun Times* also highlighted the best elements of the film as the cinematography, which he described as "great looking" and the performances by Bacon and Streep, who he described as "putting a lot humor and intelligence into her character".[2] However, Ebert identified serious flaws in the strength of the plot, remarking that, "movies like this are so predictable in their overall stories that they win or lose with their details...*The River Wild* was constructed from so many ideas, characters and situations recycled from other movies that all the way down the river I kept thinking: Been there".[2] He emphasised the lack of credibility in the storyline and sheer impossibility of some scenes, particularly involving David Strathairn as he outruns the pace of the river and his scenes with the cliff and his Swiss Army knife.[2]

Streep received Golden Globe and Screen Actors Guild (SAG) nomination for best actress for her portrayal of a former river guide turned wife and mother. Bacon received a Golden Globe nomination for Best Performance by an Actor in a Supporting Role in a Featured Film. Neither of them won the Golden Globe, with the awards going to Jessica Lange in *Blue Sky* and Martin Landau in *Ed Wood* respectively.

External links

- *The River Wild* [3] at the Internet Movie Database

References

[1] Beradinelli, James (1994). "The River Wild" (http://www.reelviews.net/movies/r/river_wild.html). Reelviews.net. . Retrieved March 18, 2009.

[2] Ebert, Roger (1994). "The River Wild" (http://rogerebert.suntimes.com/apps/pbcs.dll/articleAID=/19940930/REVIEWS/409300302/1023). Chicago Sun Times. . Retrieved March 18, 2009.

[3] http://www.imdb.com/title/tt0110997/

The Bridges of Madison County (film)

The Bridges of Madison County	
Original poster designed by Bill Gold.	
Directed by	Clint Eastwood
Produced by	Clint Eastwood Kathleen Kennedy
Written by	Richard LaGravenese Robert James Waller (novel)
Starring	Clint Eastwood Meryl Streep
Music by	Lennie Niehaus
Cinematography	Jack N. Green
Editing by	Joel Cox
Studio	Malpaso Productions Amblin Entertainment
Distributed by	Warner Bros.
Release date(s)	June 2, 1995
Running time	135 minutes
Country	United States
Language	English
Budget	$22 million
Gross revenue	$182,016,617

The Bridges of Madison County is a 1995 American romantic drama film based on the best-selling novel by Robert James Waller. It was produced by Amblin Entertainment and Malpaso Productions, and distributed by Warner Bros.. The film was produced and directed by Clint Eastwood with Kathleen Kennedy as co-producer and the screenplay was adapted by Richard LaGravenese. The film stars Eastwood and Meryl Streep, who was nominated for the Academy Award for Best Actress in 1996 for her performance in the film.

Plot

The film is set in the summer of 1965. It tells the story of Francesca (Meryl Streep), a lonely, insightful Italian housewife in Iowa. While her husband and children are away at the Illinois State Fair, she meets and falls in love with a photographer (Clint Eastwood) who has come to Madison County, Iowa to shoot a photographic essay for National Geographic on the covered bridges in the area. The four days they spend together are a turning point in her life and she writes of her experience in a diary which is discovered by her children after her death and they are stunned by it.

Differences between the book and the film include where Francesca is from Naples in the book andBari in the film. The children look through her effects after her death at the start of the film and towards the back of the book. Note that also in the film as Francesca and Robert are driving toward Roseman Bridge on the first day, they pass the same farm twice on their right in the pick up.

Cast

- Clint Eastwood ... Robert Kincaid
- Meryl Streep ... Francesca Johnson
- Annie Corley ... Carolyn Johnson
- Victor Slezak ... Michael Johnson
- Jim Haynie ... Richard Johnson
- Sarah Kathryn Schmitt ... Young Carolyn
- Christopher Kroon ... Young Michael
- Phyllis Lyons ... Betty
- Debra Monk ... Madge
- Richard Lage ... Lawyer Peterson
- Michelle Benes ... Lucy Redfield

Reception

The Bridges of Madison County received critical acclaim on its initial release. It currently has a score of 90% on Rotten Tomatoes. The film ranked 90 in the AFI's 100 Years... 100 Passions and tied with *Goodbye South, Goodbye* and *Carlito's Way* to be dubbed the best film of the 1990s in a poll by Cahiers du Cinema[1] .

Awards

Won

- ASCAP Film and Television Music Awards:
  - Top Box Office Films
- Blue Ribbon Awards (Japan):
  - Best Foreign Language Film
- BMI Film & TV Awards:
  - BMI Film Music Award (Lennie Niehaus)
- Kinema Junpo Awards (Japan):
  - Best Foreign Language Film Director (Clint Eastwood)
- Mainichi Film Concours (Japan):
  - Best Foreign Language Film

Nominated

- Academy Awards:
  - Best Actress in a Leading Role (Meryl Streep)
- American Society of Cinematographers:
  - Outstanding Achievement in Theatrical Releases (Jack N. Green)
- Awards of the Japanese Academy (Japan):
  - Best Foreign Film
- César Awards (France):
  - Best Foreign Film
- Golden Globe Awards:
  - Best Actress in a Motion Picture - Drama (Meryl Streep)
  - Best Motion Picture - Drama
- Screen Actors Guild Awards (SAG):
  - Outstanding Performance by a Female Actor in a Leading Role (Meryl Streep)

See also

- Madison County, Iowa

External links

- *The Bridges of Madison County* [2] at the Internet Movie Database
- *The Bridges of Madison County* [3] at Allmovie
- Bridges of Madison County Photos [4]
- *The Bridges of Madison County* [5] at Rotten Tomatoes

References

[1] http://alumnus.caltech.edu/~ejohnson/critics/cahiers.html#y2005
[2] http://www.imdb.com/title/tt0112579/
[3] http://www.allmovie.com/work/134725
[4] http://www.roundamerica.com/tours/tourDetail.cfm?tour_id=9067
[5] http://www.rottentomatoes.com/m/bridges_of_madison_county/

Before and After (film)

Before and After	
 Theatrical release poster	
Directed by	Barbet Schroeder
Produced by	Barbet Schroeder Susan Hoffman
Written by	Rosellen Brown (novel) Ted Tally
Narrated by	Julia Weldon
Starring	Meryl Streep Liam Neeson Edward Furlong Julia Weldon Alfred Molina
Music by	Howard Shore
Cinematography	Luciano Tovoli
Editing by	Lee Percy
Studio	Caravan Pictures
Distributed by	Hollywood Pictures
Release date(s)	February 23, 1996
Running time	108 min.
Country	▀▀▀ United States
Language	English
Budget	$35 million

Before and After is a 1996 film, based on the 1992 novel of the same title by American writer Rosellen Brown. The movie was directed by Barbet Schroeder and starred Meryl Streep as Dr. Carolyn Ryan, Liam Neeson as Ben Ryan, Edward Furlong as Jacob Ryan, and Julia Weldon as Judith Ryan (who also narrated the movie).

Plot

In a small Massachusetts town, Dr. Carolyn Ryan (Meryl Streep) and her sculptor husband Ben (Liam Neeson) seem to live an idyllic life with their two children Jacob (Edward Furlong) and Judith (Julia Weldon). Their world is shattered one evening when Sheriff Fran Conklin (Daniel von Bargen) arrives to tell them that Martha Taverner has been killed and witnesses saw Jacob with her just before she died. When he asks to speak with Jacob, the family realize that he's not in his room as they thought. Conklin asks to look at Jacob's car, but Ben refuses to allow it. When Conklin tries to ask Judith where Jacob is, Ben becomes openly hostile, demanding the sheriff get a warrant.

When Conklin leaves to get the warrant, Ben inspects Jacob's car, finding clothes and a car jack with blood on them. He burns the clothes and cleans the jack before the police return. When he tells Carolyn what he has done, she is afraid that Ben may have destroyed evidence that could help them find Jacob, as she is fearful that a maniac may have killed both Martha and her son. The Ryans plaster the town with signs trying to find Jacob, but the town ostracizes them, assuming Jacob is a murderer.

Postcards start to arrive from Jacob. The first is from Boston. Over the course of five weeks, he sends postcards from all over the country. Carolyn is convinced that he's been kidnapped and wants to alert the police. Ben remains wary of disclosing anything, insisting they must keep the postcards a secret. Eventually Jacob is caught and brought back home to stand trial. For the first several days, he is catatonic, only speaking aloud to enter his plea at the arraignment.

He first speaks to Judith in their treehouse when she asks him if he really traveled all over the country. He explained that he would take the train to the Boston airport once a week and press the postcards on people who were headed to the cities on the cards. He would explain that he had just returned from a vacation there but forgotten to mail the postcards to his parents, and he did not want them to think he'd forgotten them. The travelers would mail the cards for him when they arrived at their destination.

During dinner one evening, the family receives another harassing phone call from one of the townspeople. Ben playfully toys with the caller, but offers an impassioned defense of his son. Touched by his father's sincerity, Jacob finally opens up and explains what happened.

He had been fighting with Martha when she revealed that she was pregnant, in addition to the fact that she had been sleeping with several other boys. They made up, but while they made love in Jacob's car, they got snowed in. Unable to free the car through a variety of methods, they decided to try and jack one end of the car up while they packed snow under the other end. Their fight reignited and got violent. Martha swung a crowbar at Jacob and missed him by an inch. Furious, he charged at her, knocking her to the ground. She landed on the jack, which drove through her head, killing her.

Ben decides that it is best to not reveal the truth. He coaches Jacob on a different version of the story, which they tell to their lawyer (Alfred Molina), but the plan goes awry when Ben is deposed by the grand jury and realizes that there is no father-son privilege which exempts him from testifying. As the grand jury continues, the pressure on the family builds to a breaking point. When Carolyn is called to testify, she reveals the truth. Jacob's lawyer is incensed, but he explains that he will simply treat Carolyn as a hostile witness and her testimony will amount to hearsay, since it conflicts with Jacob's account of the events.

When Ben discovers what Carolyn has done, he is furious. A family argument ensues and in the morning, Jacob is missing again. He turns up at the police station, where he has given a full confession. As a minor, he needs his parents to sign his confession. Ben refuses, explaining that he could never sign anything that took Jacob away from him.

Jacob is sentenced to five years for involuntary manslaughter, and Ben is sentenced to one year for his cover up. The family relocates to Miami, and the final shot is of all four paddling together in a canoe.

External links

- *Before and After* [1] at the Internet Movie Database
- *Before and After* [2] at Allmovie

References

[1] http://www.imdb.com/title/tt0115645/
[2] http://www.allmovie.com/work/136116

Marvin's Room (film)

Marvin's Room's	
Theatrical poster	
Directed by	Jerry Zaks
Written by	Scott McPherson John Guare[1]
Starring	Meryl Streep Leonardo DiCaprio Diane Keaton Robert De Niro
Music by	Rachel Portman
Cinematography	Piotr Sobociński
Editing by	Jim Clark
Distributed by	Miramax Films
Release date(s)	December 18, 1996
Running time	98 minutes
Country	United States
Language	English

Marvin's Room is a 1996 film based on the play of the same name by Scott McPherson[2] . The play, which was directed by David Petrarca, was adapted for the screen by McPherson and directed by Jerry Zaks. Mcpherson died in 1992 of AIDS at age 33[3]

It stars Meryl Streep, Leonardo DiCaprio, Diane Keaton, Robert De Niro, Hume Cronyn, Gwen Verdon, Hal Scardino and Dan Hedaya. Original music for the film was provided by Rachel Portman and has Carly Simon singing the theme song "Two Little Sisters" with Meryl Streep adding background vocals.

Plot

A man who had a stroke 17 years ago is left incapacitated and bed-ridden. He has been cared for by his daughter Bessie (Diane Keaton), and totally ignored by his other daughter, Lee (Meryl Streep), who moved to Ohio with her husband 20 years ago and has never contacted her family. Now, however, Bessie's doctor has informed her that she has leukemia and needs a bone marrow transplant[4] and she turns to her sister for help. Lee, in turn, turns to her son Hank (Leonardo DiCaprio), who has been committed to a mental asylum for setting fire to his mother's house. When Lee finds that she may have to take over her father's care, she at first begins shopping around for nursing homes. Eventually, the sisters grow close to one another, their father Marvin, and Lee's son.[5] [6]

Cast

- Meryl Streep - Lee
- Leonardo DiCaprio - Hank
- Diane Keaton - Bessie
- Robert De Niro - Dr. Wally
- Hume Cronyn - Marvin
- Gwen Verdon - Ruth
- Hal Scardino - Charlie
- Dan Hedaya - Bob

Awards

Nominations:

- Academy Award for Best Actress: Diane Keaton
- 1997: Golden Globe: Best Actress, Drama: Meryl Streep[7]
- 1997: Screen Actors Guild: Best Cast[8]
- 1997: Screen Actors Guild: Diane Keaton
- 1997: Screen Actors Guild: Gwen Verdon

Further reading

- Marvin's Room [9] *Screen Adaptation: A Scriptwriting Handbook*, by Kenneth Portnoy. Published by Focal Press, 1998. ISBN 0240803493.
- McPherson, Scott (1992). *Marvin's Room* (First edition ed.). New York: Plume drama. ISBN 0452269229.
- Grace in Suffering: *Marvin's Room* [10] *Praying the Movies: Daily Meditations from Classic Films*, by Edward McNulty, McNulty. Geneva Press, 2001. ISBN 0664501559.

External links

- *Marvin's Room* [11] at the Internet Movie Database
- *Marvin's Room* [12] at Allmovie
- *Marvin's Room* [13] at Rottentomatoes.
- *Marvin's Room* [14] at San Francisco Chronicle.

Video links

- Marvin's Room Clippings [15]

References

[1]   Credits - *Marvin's Room* (http://www.tcm.com/tcmdb/title.jsp?stid=443540&category=Full Credits) *Turner Classic Movies.*

[2]   Two Wrenching Dramas Find Unexpected New Lives (http://query.nytimes.com/gst/fullpage. html?res=9B01E5D9113CF93BA35751C1A960958260) *New York Times, December 8, 1996.*

[3]   A Door Left Ajar in 'Marvin's Room' (http://www.washingtonpost.com/wp-srv/style/longterm/movies/review97/fmarvinsroom.htm) by David Richards, *Washington Post Staff Writer, January 5, 1997.*

[4]   Review - Marvin's Room Explores the Ties That Bind (http://www.imagesjournal.com/issue02/reviews/marvin.htm) by Gary Johnson, *imagesjournal.com*, Issue 2.

[5]   Overview (http://movies.nytimes.com/movie/136646/Marvin-s-Room/overview) *New York Times.*

[6]   'Marvin's Room': No Emote Control (http://www.washingtonpost.com/wp-srv/style/longterm/movies/review97/marvinsroomhowe. htm) by Desson Howe, *Washington Post Staff Writer, January 10, 1997.*

[7]   List of Awards and Nominations for Meryl Streep

[8]   *Marvin's Room* Awards (http://www.imdb.com/title/tt0116999/awards) *Internet Movie Database*

[9]   http://books.google.com/books?id=fRDi4q77fUsC&pg=PA108&dq=%22Marvin%27s+Room%22&as_brr=0

[10] http://books.google.com/books?id=QS_xkphVR28C&pg=PA23&dq=%22Marvin%27s+Room%22&lr=&as_brr=0#PPA24,M1

[11] http://www.imdb.com/title/tt116999/

[12] http://www.allmovie.com/work/136646

[13] http://www.rottentomatoes.com/m/marvins_room/

[14] http://www.sfgate.com/cgi-bin/article.cgi?f=/c/a/1997/01/10/DD55989.DTL&type=printable

[15] http://video.google.com/videosearch?q=Marvin%27s+Room+1996&sourceid=navclient-ff&ie=UTF-8& rlz=1B3GGGL_enIN297IN297&um=1&sa=X&oi=video_result_group&resnum=4&ct=title#

Dancing at Lughnasa (film)

Dancing at Lughnasa	
 Theatrical release poster	
Directed by	Pat O'Connor
Produced by	Gerrit Folsom (line producer) Jane Barclay (executive producer) Sharon Harel Noel Pearson (producer) Rod Stoneman (executive producer - Bórd Scannán na hÉireann/The Irish Film Board)
Written by	Brian Friel (play) Frank McGuinness (screenplay)
Narrated by	Gerard McSorley
Starring	Meryl Streep Michael Gambon Catherine McCormack Kathy Burke Sophie Thompson Brid Brennan Rhys Ifans Lorcan Cranitch John Kavanagh Marie Mullen
Distributed by	Sony Pictures Classics
Release date(s)	November 13, 1998
Running time	95 minutes
Country	Ireland United Kingdom United States
Language	English

Dancing at Lughnasa is a 1998 film adapted from the Brian Friel play of the same title, directed by Pat O'Connor.

The movie competed in the Venice Film Festival of 1998. It won an Irish Film and Television Award for Best Actor in a Female Role by Brid Brennan. It was also nominated for 6 other awards, including the Irish Film and Television Award for Best Feature Film and the Best Actress Award for Meryl Streep.

Cast and characters

- Meryl Streep – Kate Mundy
- Michael Gambon – Father Jack Mundy
- Catherine McCormack – Christina Mundy
- Kathy Burke – Maggie Mundy
- Sophie Thompson – Rose Mundy
- Brid Brennan – Agnes Mundy
- Rhys Ifans – Gerry Evans
- Darrell Johnston – Michael Mundy
- Lorcan Cranitch – Danny Bradley
- Peter Gowen – Austin Morgan
- Dawn Bradfield – Sophie McLoughlin
- Marie Mullen – Vera McLoughlin
- John Kavanagh – Father Carlin
- Kate O'Toole – Chemist

Reception and Awards

Although the film received average reviews (67% 'Fresh' rating on Rotten Tomatoes), most critics praised the performance of the entire cast. Janet Maslin, critic of the New York Times said that "Meryl Streep has made many a grand acting gesture in her career, but the way she simply peers out a window in *Dancing at Lughnasa* ranks with the best. Everything the viewer need know about Kate Mundy, the woman she plays here, is written on that prim, lonely face and its flabbergasted gaze."[1] Peter Travis of Rolling Stone magazine wrote that "a luminous cast reveals long-buried feelings. Meryl Streep finds the expansive soul behind prim schoolteacher Kate. And she is matched by Kathy Burke's bawdy Maggie, Brid Brennan's secretive Agnes, Sophie Thompson's slow-witted Rose and Catherine McCormack's bold Christina, who never married the father of her son."[2]

Kathy Burke received a nomination for Best Supporting Actress - Drama from the International Press Academy (Satellite Awards).

A display of mementos from the filming is on display at the St. Connell's Museum in Glenties.

External links

- *Dancing at Lughnasa* [3] at the Internet Movie Database
- *Dancing at Lughnasa* [4] at Allmovie
- *Dancing at Lughnasa* [5] at the Internet Broadway Database

References

[1] Maslin, Janet, 1998. The New York Times, Movie Review of Dancing at Lughnasa, Nov 13, 1998 (http://movies.nytimes.com/movie/review?res=9B04E3DA1431F930A25752C1A96E958260)

[2] Travis, Peter. 1998. Rolling Stone Magazine, Movie Review of Dancing at Lughnasa (http://www.rollingstone.com/reviews/movie/5948007/review/5948008/dancing_at_lughnasa)

[3] http://www.imdb.com/title/tt0120643/

[4] http://www.allmovie.com/work/173467

[5] http://www.ibdb.com/production.asp?id=4647

One True Thing

One True Thing	
Theatrical release poster	
Directed by	Carl Franklin
Written by	Karen Croner
Starring	Renée Zellweger
	William Hurt
	Meryl Streep
	Tom Everett Scott
	Lauren Graham
	Nicky Katt
	Diana Canova
Music by	Cliff Eidelman
Distributed by	Universal Studios
Release date(s)	September 18, 1998
Country	United States
Language	English

One True Thing is a 1998 American drama film directed by Carl Franklin. It tells the story of a woman who is forced to put her life on hold in order to care for her mother who is dying of cancer. It was adapted by Karen Croner from the novel by Anna Quindlen. It was directed by Carl Franklin. The movie stars Meryl Streep, Renée Zellweger, William Hurt, Tom Everett Scott, Lauren Graham and Nicky Katt. Bette Midler sings the lead song, "My One True Friend", over the end credits. The track was first released on Midler's 1998 album *Bathhouse Betty*.

Storyline

Ellen Gulden, has a high pressure job writing for New York magazine. As the movie begins, she is visiting her family home for her father's surprise birthday party. It becomes obvious that she deeply admires her father, George, a once-celebrated novelist and college professor, but has barely restrained disdain for her mother, Kate, and the domestic life she lives. When it is discovered that Kate has cancer, George pressures Ellen to come home and take care of her mother. Ellen is taken aback by this request, knowing it could jeopardize her career and love interest, but finally agrees, caving in to her father's appeals and inducements.

As Ellen helps her mother with domestic chores while her father goes about his usual business without helping much, Ellen begins to reassess her views of her parents. She realizes she always brushed her mother aside and idealized her father, despite his self-centered focus on his career and - she discovers - longtime habit of having flings with his female students.

Ellen attempts to find a place for herself in her parents' life, while struggling to continue writing on a freelance basis and maintain her relationship with her boyfriend in New York. Over time, Ellen grows closer to her mother and learns more about her parents' marriage -- including realizing that Kate has known about George's affairs all along. Ellen also learns that her father's philandering days have become lonely nights of drinking at a local bar to numb the pain of never again achieving success with, nor even being able to complete, further novels. George admits to Ellen that the reason he loved Kate was that she was full of light shining through everything, and he couldn't bear the thought of her light slipping away.

As her mother is dying, Ellen tells her she loves her and Kate said she knew it, she'd always known it.

After Kate's death, the autopsy reveals that Kate actually died of a morphine overdose, and a District Attorney questions Ellen about her mother's death. Scenes from this interview are interspersed throughout the movie and point to Ellen being suspected of having assisted her mother's suicide. In the closing scene, by Kate's grave, Ellen has returned from a new job she found in New York with the Village Voice. She is planting daffodils when she sees her father approaching, their first encounter since the funeral. George tells Ellen she was very brave to do what she did, and she looks puzzled until she realizes George thinks she had given her mother the fatal overdose. Ellen replies that she had thought the accomplice was the father. They both realize Kate must have taken her own life.

George speaks to Ellen of how much he loved Kate, considering her his muse, his "one true thing." As the movie ends, Ellen is explaining to her father how to plant the daffodil bulbs and he is helping, foreshadowing, it seems, their reconciliation based on mutual long overdue appreciation of Kate.

Cast

- Meryl Streep as Kate Gulden
- Renée Zellweger as Ellen Gulden
- William Hurt as George Gulden
- Tom Everett Scott as Brian Gulden
- Lauren Graham as Jules
- Nicky Katt as Jordan Belzer
- James Eckhouse as District Attorney

Accolades

Streep was nominated for the Academy Award for Best Actress for her performance in the film, and her performance drew praise from numerous critics, notably Mick LaSalle in the *San Francisco Chronicle*, who declared, "After 'One True Thing', critics who persist in the fiction that Streep is a cold and technical actress will need to get their heads examined. She is so instinctive and natural - so thoroughly in the moment and operating on flights on inspiration - that she's able to give us a woman who's at once wildly idiosyncratic and utterly believable." *Los Angeles Times* film critic Kenneth Turan noted that Streep's role "is one of the least self-consciously dramatic and surface showy of her career, but Streep adds a level of honesty and reality that makes [her performance] one of her most moving."

Film Location

Morristown, NJ

External links

- *One True Thing* [1] at the Internet Movie Database
- *One True Thing* [2] at Allmovie

References

[1] http://www.imdb.com/title/tt0120776/
[2] http://www.allmovie.com/work/173495

Music of the Heart

Music of the Heart	
Directed by	Wes Craven
Produced by	Susan Kaplan
Written by	Pamela Gray
Starring	Meryl Streep Angela Bassett Aidan Quinn Gloria Estefan Cloris Leachman Jane Leeves Kieran Culkin Charlie Hofheimer
Music by	Mason Daring
Cinematography	Peter Deming
Editing by	Gregg Featherman Patrick Lussier
Release date(s)	October 29, 1999
Running time	124 min
Country	United States
Language	English
Budget	$27 Million
Gross revenue	$74,859,394

Music of the Heart is a 1999 dramatic film. This film was produced by Craven-Maddalena Films and Miramax Films, and distributed by Buena Vista Distribution.

The film stars Meryl Streep, Aidan Quinn, Gloria Estefan, and Angela Bassett. It was director Wes Craven's only foray outside of the horror/thriller genre aside from his contribution to the multifacted and directorially diverse *Paris, je t'aime*. It was also his only film to get nominated at the Academy Awards. Wes Craven is known for directing the horror films *A Nightmare on Elm Street*, *The Hills Have Eyes* and the *Scream* trilogy.

Background

Madonna was originally signed to play the role of Roberta Guaspari Demetras, but left the project before filming began, citing "creative differences" with Wes Craven. She had already studied for many months to play the violin. Streep learned to play a Bach violin concerto for the film.

Storyline

Inspired by the true story of the Opus 118 Harlem School of Music and 'Small Wonders', a 1996 documentary about the school, the film opens with Roberta having been deserted by her US Navy husband and feeling devastated, almost suicidal. Encouraged by her mother, she attempts to rebuild her life and a friend from student days recommends her to the head teacher of a school in the tough New York area of East Harlem. Despite a degree in music education, she has little experience in actual music teaching, but she's taken on as a substitute violin teacher. With a combination of toughness and determination, she inspires a group of kids, and their initially skeptical parents. The program slowly develops and attracts publicity.

Ten years later, the string program is still running successfully at three schools, but suddenly the school budget is cut and Roberta is out of a job. Determined to fight the cuts, she enlists the support of former pupils, parents and teachers and plans a grand fund-raising concert, 'Fiddlefest', to raise money so that the program can continue. But with a few weeks to go and all participants furiously rehearsing, they lose the venue. Fortunately, the husband of a publicist friend is a violinist in the Guarneri String Quartet, and he enlists the support of other well-known musicians, including Isaac Stern and Itzhak Perlman. They arrange for the concert to be mounted at Carnegie Hall.

Other famous musicians join in the performance, which is a resounding success.

The film's end credits declare that the Opus 118 program is still running successfully. They also report that the school's funding was restored during the making of the film.

"Review: 'Music of the Heart' hits all the right notes" [1] CNN, October 29, 1999. Accessed January 28, 2007.]</ref> The children of Opus 118 - Harlem School of Music, led by Roberta Guaspari, performed with Madonna twice in 1998: "Frozen" at the Annual Rain Forest Benefit at Carnegie Hall, New York and at the 1998 VH1 Fashion Awards performing "The Power of Good-Bye".[2]

Awards and nominations

Streep received nominations for an Academy Award, a Golden Globe and a Screen Actors Guild Award for her lead performance.[3]

The film's theme song, "Music Of My Heart", scored songwriter Diane Warren a nomination for an Academy Award for Best Original Song, and a Grammy Award nomination for Best Song Written for a Motion Picture, Television or Other Visual Media.[3]

The film marked the screen debut of singer Gloria Estefan.[4]

- This is the second collaboration between Craven and Angela Bassett, she previously appared on the comedy horror film *Vampire In Brooklyn*.

Critical reception

The film got mixed reviews but with a positive trend. Most critics applauded Meryl Streep's portrayal of Roberta Guaspari. The film had a 68% approval rating at Rotten Tomatoes.[5] Critic Eleanor Ringel Gillespie of the *Atlanta Journal-Constitution* concluded that "There are more challenging movies around. More original ones, too. But "Music of the Heart gets the job done, efficiently and entertainingly."[6] Roger Ebert gave the film three stars out of four and wrote that "Meryl Streep is known for her mastery of accents; she may be the most versatile speaker in the movies. Here you might think she has no accent, unless you've heard her real speaking voice, then you realize that

Guaspari's speaking style is no less a particular achievement than Streep's other accents. This is not Streep's voice, but someone else's - with a certain flat quality, as if later education and refinement came after a somewhat unsophisticated childhood."[7] Steve Rosen said that "The key to Meryl Streep's fine performance is that she makes Guaspari unheroically ordinary. Ultimately that makes her even more extraordinary." [8]

Soundtrack album track listing

1. "Music Of My Heart" - Gloria Estefan and *NSYNC (4:32)
2. "Baila" - Jennifer Lopez (3:54)
3. "Turn the Page" - Aaliyah (4:16)
4. "Groove With Me Tonight (Pablo Flores English Radio Version)" - Menudo (4:37)
5. "Seventeen" - Tre O (3:48)
6. "One Night With You" - C Note (5:04)
7. "Do Something (Organized Noize Mix)" - Macy Gray (3:53)
8. "Revancha de Amor" - Gizelle d'Cole (4:06)
9. "Nothing Else" - Julio Iglesias, Jr. (4:23)
10. "Love Will Find You" - Jaci Velasquez (4:34)
11. "Music Of My Heart" (Pablo Flores Remix) - Gloria Estefan and *NSYNC (4:23)
12. "Concerto in D Minor for Two Violins" - Itzhak Perlman and Joshua Bell (3:56)

Box office

The film opened at #5 at the North American box office making $3.6 million USD in its opening weekend.

External links

- *Music of the Heart* [9] at the Internet Movie Database
- Movie stills [10]
- Opus 118 Harlem School of Music [11]

References

[1] http://www.cnn.com/SHOWBIZ/Movies/9910/28/review.musicofheart/
[2] The Official Opus 118 Harlem School of Music Website (http://www.opus118.org)
[3] Awards for "Music of the Heart" (1999) (http://www.imdb.com/title/tt0166943/awards) IMDb. Accessed January 28, 2007.
[4] "Review: 'Music of the Heart' hits all the right notes" (http://www.cnn.com/SHOWBIZ/Movies/9910/28/review.musicofheart/) CNN, October 29, 1999. Accessed January 28, 2007.
[5] Rotten Tomatoes, Music of the Heart Movie Reviews (http://www.rottentomatoes.com/m/music_of_the_heart/?name_order=asc)
[6] Ringel Gillespie, Eleanor, The Atlanta Journal-Constituional, 1998, Music of the Heart Movie Review (http://www.accessatlanta.com/movies/content/shared/movies/reviews/M/musicoftheheart.html)
[7] Ebert, Roger, 1998, Music of the Heart Movie Review (http://rogerebert.suntimes.com/apps/pbcs.dll/article?AID=/19991029/REVIEWS/910290302/1023)
[8] Rosen, Steve, 1998, Music of the Heart Movie Review (http://www.denverpost.com/movie/heart1029.htm)
[9] http://www.imdb.com/title/tt0166943/
[10] http://film.virtual-history.com/film.php?filmid=20954
[11] http://www.opus118.org/

A.I. Artificial Intelligence

A.I. Artificial Intelligence	
Directed by	Steven Spielberg
Produced by	Steven Spielberg Stanley Kubrick Jan Harlan Kathleen Kennedy Walter F. Parkes Bonnie Curtis
Written by	Short story Brian Aldiss Screen story: Ian Watson Screenplay: Steven Spielberg
Narrated by	Ben Kingsley
Starring	Haley Joel Osment Frances O'Connor Jude Law Sam Robards Jake Thomas William Hurt
Music by	John Williams
Cinematography	Janusz Kamiński
Editing by	Michael Kahn
Studio	Amblin Entertainment
Distributed by	DreamWorks Warner Bros.
Release date(s)	June 29, 2001
Running time	146 minutes
Country	United States

Language	English
Budget	$100 million
Gross revenue	$235,926,552

A.I. Artificial Intelligence, also known as *Artificial Intelligence: A.I.* or simply *A.I.*, is a 2001 Academy Award nominated science fiction film directed, co-produced and co-written by Steven Spielberg. Based on Brian Aldiss' short story "Super-Toys Last All Summer Long", the film stars Haley Joel Osment, Frances O'Connor, Jude Law, Sam Robards, Jake Thomas and William Hurt. Set sometime in the future, *A.I.* tells the story of David, a child-like android programmed with the unique ability to love.

Development of *A.I.* originally began with Stanley Kubrick in the early 1970s. Kubrick hired a series of writers up until the mid-1990s, including Brian Aldiss, Bob Shaw, Ian Watson and Sara Maitland. The film languished in development hell for years because Kubrick felt computer-generated imagery was not advanced enough to create the David character, whom he believed no child actor would believably portray. In 1995 Kubrick handed *A.I.* to Steven Spielberg, but the film did not gain momentum until Kubrick's death in 1999. Spielberg remained close to Watson's film treatment for the screenplay, and replicated Kubrick's secretive style of filmmaking. *A.I.* was greeted with mostly positive reviews from critics and became a moderate financial success. This film was dedicated to Kubrick's memory with a small credit after the credits, saying "For Stanley Kubrick"

Plot

Global warming has led to ecological disasters all over the world, along with occluding humanity itself. Humanity's best efforts to maintain civilization have led to the creation of new robots known as "mechas"; advanced humanoid robots which are capable of emulating thoughts and emotions. David (Haley Joel Osment), is an advanced prototype model created by Cybertronics, a manufacturer of mechas, which is designed to resemble a human child and to virtually feel love for its human owners. Cybertronics test this newest creation on one of their employees, Henry Swinton (Sam Robards), and his wife Monica, (Frances O'Connor). The Swintons have a son named Martin (Jake Thomas), who has been placed in suspended animation until a cure can be found for his rare disease. Although Monica is initially frightened of David, she eventually warms to him after activating his imprinting protocol, which irreversibly causes David to feel love for her as a child loves a mother. As David continues to live with the Swintons, he is befriended by Teddy (voiced by Jack Angel); a wise, robotic teddy bear (Supertoy) who takes upon himself the responsibility of David's well-being.

Martin is suddenly cured and brought home; a sibling rivalry ensues between Martin and David. Martin's cruel and scheming behavior backfires when he and his friends activate David's self-protection programming at a pool party; David gets frightened and clings to Martin, inadvertently pulling him into the pool. Alarmed, Henry decides to destroy David at the factory where he was built, but Monica instead leaves him (alongside Teddy) in a forest to live as unregistered mechas. David is captured for an anti-mecha Flesh Fair, an event where obsolete or damaged mechas are destroyed before cheering crowds. David almost ends up getting destroyed by a barrel of acid, but the crowd is swayed by David's pleas for mercy, and he escapes along with Gigolo Joe (Jude Law), a male prostitute mecha who is on the run after being framed for murder by the husband (Enrico Colantoni) of one of his clients.

The two set out to find the Blue Fairy, whom David remembers from the story *The Adventures of Pinocchio*. As in the story, he believes that she will transform him into a real boy, so Monica will love him and take him back. Joe and David make their way to the decadent metropolis of Rouge City. Information from a holographic volumetric display answer engine called "Dr. Know" (voiced by Robin Williams) eventually leads them to the top of the Rockefeller Center in the flooded ruins of New York City, using a submersible vehicle they have stolen from the authorities, still hot on Joe's tail. When they arrive at New York, David's creator Professor Hobby (William Hurt) enters, after David destroys an android that looks exactly like him, and excitedly tells David that finding him was a test, which has demonstrated the reality of his love and desire, something no other robot could do until now. In Professor Hobby's office, David finds a room full of Davids and Darlenes (David's female counter-parts), packaged and ready to sell to anyone looking for "A love of their own." A disheartened David attempts to commit suicide by falling from a ledge into the ocean, but Joe rescues him. A little while later, Joe is captured by the authorities, but David escapes.

David and Teddy take the submersible to the fairy, which turns out to be a statue from a submerged attraction at Coney Island. Teddy and David are trapped when the Wonder Wheel falls on their vehicle. Believing the Blue Fairy to be real, he asks to be turned into a real boy, repeating his wish without end, until the ocean freezes.

The film switches to the 5th millennium. Humanity has become extinct and New York is buried under several hundred feet of glacial ice.[1] Earth is now being excavated and studied by the descendants of the mechas, now silicon-based supermechas possessing some form of telekinesis and telepathy.[2] They find David and Teddy, the only two functional mechas who knew living humans. David wakes up, finds the frozen stiff Blue Fairy, and tries to touch her. However, because of the time passed and the damage to the statue, it cracks and collapses immediately. David realizes that the fairy was fake. Using David's memories, the supermechas reconstruct the Swinton home, and explain to him via a mecha of the Blue Fairy (voiced by Meryl Streep) that he cannot become human. However, they create a clone of Monica from a lock of her hair which has been faithfully saved by Teddy, and restore her memories from the space-time continuum. However, one of the supermechas (voiced by Ben Kingsley) explains that she will live for only one day and that the process cannot be repeated. David spends the happiest day of his life playing with Monica and Teddy. The ephemeral Monica tells David that she loves him as she drifts slowly away from the world. This was the "everlasting moment" David had been looking for; he closes his eyes, and goes "to that place where dreams are born".

Cast

- Haley Joel Osment as David: An android, known as a mecha, created by Cybertronics programmed with the ability to love. He is adopted by Henry and Monica Swinton, but a sibling rivalry ensues once their son Martin comes out of suspended animation. Osment was Spielberg's first and only choice for the role. The two had met before Spielberg finished the screenplay. Osment decided it was best not to blink his eyes to perfectly portray a robot. He also set himself to have good posture.[3]
- Frances O'Connor as Monica Swinton: David's adopted mother who reads him *The Adventures of Pinocchio*. She is first displeased to have David at her house but soon falls in love with him. Monica is devastated when it is decided to abandon David.
- Jude Law as Gigolo Joe: A male prostitute mecha programmed with the ability to love, like David, but in a different sense. Gigolo Joe uses songs such as "I Only Have Eyes for You" and "Bobbie, Walter" to seduce women. He meets David at a Flesh Fair and takes him to Rouge City. Law took inspirations from Fred Astaire and Gene Kelly for the portrayal of Gigolo Joe.[4]
- Sam Robards as Henry Swinton: An employee at Cybertronics and husband of Monica. Henry is reluctant to have David home and soon feels David is becoming a danger to the family.
- Jake Thomas as Martin Swinton: Henry and Monica's first son who was placed in suspended animation. When Martin comes back, he convinces David to cut off a lock of Monica's hair.
- William Hurt as Professor Allen Hobby: He is responsible for commissioning the creation of David. He resides in the ruined city Manhattan. It is revealed that David is modeled after Hobby's own son named David, who seems to have died at a young age.

Jack Angel provides the voice of Teddy, while Brendan Gleeson cameos as Lord Johnson-Johnson, the owner and master of ceremonies of the Flesh Fair. Robin Williams voices Dr. Know, Meryl Streep voices Blue Fairy, Ben Kingsley narrates the film as the leader of the futuristic mechas, and appears briefly as one of the technicians who repairs David after he eats spinach; Chris Rock plays/voices a mecha killed at the Flesh Fair, and Adrian Grenier plays a teen in van.

Production

Stanley Kubrick began development on an adaptation of "Super-Toys Last All Summer Long" (which he eventually retitled *A.I*) in the early 1970s, hiring the short story's author, Brian Aldiss to write a film treatment. In 1985 Kubrick brought longtime friend Steven Spielberg to produce the film,[5] along with Jan Harlan. Warner Bros. agreed to co-finance the film and cover distribution duties.[6] *A.I.* labored in development hell, with Aldiss being fired over creative differences in the late 1980s.[7] Bob Shaw served as writer very briefly, leaving after six weeks because of Kubrick's demanding work schedule. Kubrick then hired Ian Watson to write the film in March 1990. Aldiss later remarked, "Not only did the bastard fire me, he hired my enemy [Watson] instead." Kubrick handed Watson *The Adventures of Pinocchio* for inspiration, calling *A.I.* "a picaresque robot version of *Pinocchio*".[6] [8]

Three weeks later Watson gave Kubrick his first story treatment, and concluded his work on *A.I.* in May 1991 with another treatment, at 90-pages. Gigolo Joe was originally conceived as a GI character, but Watson suggested changing him to a gigolo. Kubrick joked "I guess we lost the kiddie market."[6] In the meantime, Kubrick dropped *A.I.* to work on a film adaptation of *Wartime Lies*, feeling computer animation was not advanced enough to create the David character. However, after the release of *Jurassic Park* (with its innovative use of computer-generated imagery), it was announced in November 1993 that production would begin in 1994.[9] Dennis Muren and Ned Gorman, who worked on *Jurassic Park*, became visual effects supervisors,[7] but Kubrick was displeased with their previsualization, and the expense of hiring Industrial Light & Magic.[2]

Stanley [Kubrick] showed Steven [Spielberg] 650 drawings which he had, and the script and the story, everything. Stanley said, "Look, why don't you direct it and I'll produce it." Steven was almost in shock.

Producer Jan Harlan, on Spielberg's first meeting with Kubrick about *A.I.*[10]

In early 1994 the film was in pre-production with Christopher "Fangorn" Baker as concept artist, and Sara Maitland assisted on the story, which gave it "a feminist fairy-tale focus".[6] Maitland said that Kubrick never referred to the film as *A.I.*, but as *Pinocchio*.[2] Chris Cunningham became the new visual effects supervisor. Some of his unproduced work for *A.I.* can be seen on the DVD *The Work of Director Chris Cunningham*.[11] Aside from considering computer animation, Kubrick also had Joseph Mazzello do a screen test for the lead role.[2]

Cunningham helped assemble a series of "little robot-type humans" for the David character. Harlan said "We tried to construct a little boy with a movable rubber face to see whether we could make it look appealing. But it was a total failure, it looked awful." Hans Moravec served as a technical consultant.[2] Meanwhile, Kubrick and Harlan thought *A.I.* would be closer to Steven Spielberg's sensibilities as director.[12] [13] Kubrick handed the director's position to Spielberg in 1995, but Spielberg chose to direct other projects, and convinced Kubrick to remain as director.[10] [14] Kubrick then put the film on hold due to his commitment to *Eyes Wide Shut* (1999).[15] After the filmmaker's death in May 1999, Harlan and Christiane Kubrick approached Spielberg to take over the director's position.[16] [17] By November 1999 Spielberg was writing the screenplay based on Watson's 90-page story treatment. It was his first solo screenplay credit since *Close Encounters of the Third Kind* (1977).[18] Spielberg remained close to Watson's treatment, but removed various sex scenes with Gigolo Joe, which Kubrick had in mind.[13]

Pre-production was briefly halted during February 2000, because Spielberg pondered directing four other projects, which were *Harry Potter and the Philosopher's Stone*, *Minority Report*, *Memoirs of a Geisha*, and a Charles Lindbergh biopic.[15] [19] When he decided to fast track, Spielberg brought Chris Baker back as concept artist.[14] The original start date was July 10, 2000[13] but filming was delayed until August.[20] The Swinton house was constructed on Stage 16 at Warner Bros. Studios, while Stage 20 was used for other sets. *A.I.* was mostly shot on sound stages, except for a couple of scenes in Oregon.[21] [22] Spielberg copied Kubrick's obsessively secretive approach to filmmaking by refusing to give the complete script to cast and crew, banning press from the set, and making actors sign confidentiality agreements. Scientist Cynthia Breazeal served as technical consultant during production.[13] [23] Haley Joel Osment and Jude Law applied prosthetic makeup daily in an attempt to look "shinier, very robotic-like".[3] Bob Ringwood (*Batman*, *Troy*) served as the costume designer. For the citizens of Rouge City, Ringwood studied people on the Las Vegas Strip.[24] Spielberg also found post production on *A.I.* difficult because he was simultaneously preparing to shoot *Minority Report*.[25]

Warner Bros. used an alternate reality game titled *The Beast* to promote the film. Over forty websites were created. There were to be a series of video games for the Xbox video game console that followed the storyline of *The Beast*, but they went undeveloped. To avoid audiences mistaking *A.I.* for a family film, no action figures were created, although Hasbro released a talking Teddy following the film's release in October 2001.[13] *A.I.* had its premiere at the Venice Film Festival in 2001.[26] The film opened in 3,242 theaters in the United States on June 29, 2001, earning $29,352,630 during its opening weekend. *A.I* went on to gross $78.62 million in US totals as well as $157.31 million in foreign countries, coming to a worldwide total of $235.93 million.[27] *A.I.* earned twice as much money overseas than it did in North America, which is a rare occurrence. The film was a modest financial success since it recouped more than twice the amount of its $100 million budget.

Reception

The film received generally positive reviews. Based on 181 reviews collected by *Rotten Tomatoes*, 73% of the critics gave the film positive notices. The website described the critical consensus perceiving the film as "a curious, not always seamless, amalgamation of Kubrick's chilly bleakness and Spielberg's warm-hearted optimism. [The film] is, in a word, fascinating."[28] By comparison *Metacritic* collected an average score of 65, based on 32 reviews.[29]

Producer Jan Harlan stated that Kubrick "would have applauded" the final film, while Kubrick's widow Christiane also enjoyed *A.I.*[30] However, Brian Aldiss was vocally displeased with the film stating, "It's crap. Science fiction has to be logical, and it's full of lapses in logic."[31] Richard Corliss heavily praised Spielberg's direction, as well as the cast and visual effects.[32] Roger Ebert wrote that it was "Audacious, technically masterful, challenging, sometimes moving [and] ceaselessly watchable. [But] the movie's conclusion is too facile and sentimental, given what has gone before. It has mastered the artificial, but not the intelligence."[33] Jonathan Rosenbaum compared *A.I.* to *Solaris* (1972), and praised both "Kubrick for proposing that Spielberg direct the project and Spielberg for doing his utmost to respect Kubrick's intentions while making it a profoundly personal work."[34] Film critic Armond White, of the *New York Press*, praised the film noting that "each part of David's journey through carnal and sexual universes into the final eschatological devastation becomes as profoundly philosophical and contemplative as anything by cinema's most thoughtful, speculative artists–Borzage, Ozu, Demy, Tarkovsky."[35]

James Berardinelli found the film "consistently involving, with moments of near-brilliance, but far from a masterpiece. In fact, as the long-awaited 'collaboration' of Kubrick and Spielberg, it ranks as something of a disappointment." He particularly criticized the ending: 'The film's final half-hour is a curiosity, and not a successful one — a prolonged, needless epilogue which force-feeds us a catharsis that feels as false as it is extraneous to an otherwise fine story.'[36] Mick LaSalle gave a largely negative review. "*A.I.* exhibits all its creators' bad traits and none of the good. So we end up with the structureless, meandering, slow-motion endlessness of Kubrick combined with the fuzzy, cuddly mindlessness of Spielberg." Dubbing it Spielberg's "first boring movie", LaSalle also believed the robots at the end of the film were aliens, and compared Gigolo Joe to the "useless" Jar Jar Binks, yet praised Robin Williams for his portrayal of a futuristic Albert Einstein.[37] Peter Travers gave a mixed review, concluding "Spielberg cannot live up to Kubrick's darker side of the future."[38] Spielberg responded to some of the criticisms of the film, stating that many of the "so called sentimental" elements of *A.I.*, including the ending, were in fact Kubrick's and vice-versa the darker elements were his own.[39] However, Sara Maitland, who worked on the project with Kubrick in the 1990s, claimed that one of the reasons Kubrick never started production on *AI* was because he had a hard time making the ending work.[40]

"People pretend to think they know Stanley Kubrick, and think they know me, when most of them don't know either of us," Spielberg told film critic Joe Leydon in 2002. "And what's really funny about that is, all the parts of *A.I.* that people assume were Stanley's were mine. And all the parts of *A.I.* that people accuse me of sweetening and softening and sentimentalizing were all Stanley's. The teddy bear was Stanley's. The whole last 20 minutes of the movie was completely Stanley's. The whole first 11, 40 minutes of the film — all the stuff in the house — was word for word, from Stanley's screenplay. This was Stanley's vision."

"Eighty percent of the critics got it all mixed up. But I could see why. Because, obviously, I've done a lot of movies where people have cried and have been sentimental. And I've been accused of sentimentalizing hard-core material. But in fact it was Stanley who did the sweetest parts of *A.I.*, not me. I'm the guy who did the dark center of the movie, with the Flesh Fair and everything else. That's why he wanted me to make the movie in the first place. He said, 'This is much closer to your sensibilities than my own.'"[41]

Visual effects supervisors Dennis Muren, Stan Winston, Michael Lantieri and Scott Farrar were nominated the Academy Award for Visual Effects, while John Williams was nominated for Original Music Score.[42] Steven Spielberg, Jude Law and Williams received nominations at the 59th Golden Globe Awards.[43] The visual effects department was once again nominated at the 55th British Academy Film Awards.[44] *A.I.* was successful at the Saturn Awards. Spielberg (for his screenplay), the visual effects department, Williams and Haley Joel Osment (Performance by a Younger Actor) won in their respective categories. The film also won Best Science Fiction Film and for its DVD release. Frances O'Connor and Spielberg (as director) were also nominated.[45]

In late 2009, film critic A.O. Scott named *A.I.* the second best film of the 2000s, calling it "the most misunderstood movie of the past ten years" and Spielberg's "unsung masterpiece".[46]

The film appeared on several 'Best of the 2000s' film lists. In the Film Comment poll, it was ranked as 30th.[47] *Slant* magazine ranked it 23rd.[48] Finally, *Indie Wire* rated it 10th in their Best of the Decade Critics Survey 2000s.[49]

External links

- Official website [50]
- *A.I. Artificial Intelligence* [51] at Allmovie
- *A.I. Artificial Intelligence* [52] at the Internet Movie Database
- *A.I. Artificial Intelligence* [53] at Rotten Tomatoes
- *A.I. Artificial Intelligence* [54] at Box Office Mojo
- *Super-Toys Last All Summer Long* [55]
- Jude Law Interview [56] by Charlie Rose
- Spielberg's AI: Another Cuddly No-Brainer [57] by Stevan Harnad
- Jon Bastian (2001-07-13). "*A.I.* in Depth" [58]. Filmmonthly.com.
- AI by Timothy Kreider [59] originally printed in Film Quarterly.

References

[1] Jim Windolf (2007-12-02). "Q&A: Steven Spielberg" (http://www.vanityfair.com/culture/features/2008/02/ spielberg_qanda200802?currentPage=4). *Vanity Fair*. . Retrieved 2007-12-02.

[2] "The Kubrick FAQ Part 2: *A.I.*" (http://www.visual-memory.co.uk/faq/index2.html#slot14). *The Kubrick Site*. . Retrieved 2008-08-05.

[3] Haley Joel Osment, A Portrait of David, 2001, Warner Home Video; DreamWorks

[4] Jude Law, A Portrait of Gigolo Joe, 2001, Warner Home Video; DreamWorks

[5] Scott Brake (2001-05-10). "Spielberg Talks About the Genesis of *A.I.*" (http://movies.ign.com/articles/200/200038p1.html). *IGN*. . Retrieved 2008-08-04.

[6] "Plumbing Stanley Kubrick" (http://www.ianwatson.info/kubrick.htm). Ian Watson. . Retrieved 2008-07-07.

[7] Steven Gaydos (2000-03-15). "The Kubrick Connection" (http://www.variety.com/article/VR1117779484). *Variety*. . Retrieved 2008-07-19.

[8] Dana Haris (2000-03-15). "Spielberg lines up *A.I.*, Report" (http://www.variety.com/article/VR1117779498). *Variety*. . Retrieved 2008-07-16.

[9] Christian Moerk (1993-11-02). "*A.I.* next for Kubrick at Warners" (http://www.variety.com/article/VR115550). *Variety*. . Retrieved 2008-07-07.

[10] Kenneth Plume (2001-06-28). "Interview with Producer Jan Harlan" (http://movies.ign.com/articles/300/300920p1.html). *IGN*. . Retrieved 2008-08-05.

[11] "The Work of Director Chris Cunningham" (http://www.notcoming.com/features/cunningham/).NotComing.com. . Retrieved 2008-07-19.

[12] "A.I. Artificial Intelligence" (http://www.variety.com/article/VR1117799373). *Variety*. 2001-05-15. . Retrieved 2008-07-19.

[13] Liane Bonin (2001-06-28). "Boy Wonder" (http://www.ew.com/ew/article/0,,165660,00.html). *Entertainment Weekly*.. Retrieved 2008-07-15.

[14] Steven Spielberg, Jan Harlan, Kathleen Kennedy, Bonnie Curtis, Creating *A.I.*, 2001, Warner Home Video; DreamWorks

[15] Christian Moerk (1999-12-23). "Spielberg encounters close choices to direct" (http://www.variety.com/article/VR1117760260). *Variety*. . Retrieved 2008-07-15.

[16] Scott Brake (2001-06-29). "Producing *A.I.*" (http://movies.ign.com/articles/300/300984p1.html). *IGN*. . Retrieved 2008-08-04.

[17] Army Archerd (1999-07-15). "*Annie* Tv'er nab tops talent" (http://www.variety.com/article/VR1117742990). *Variety*. . Retrieved 2008-07-14.

[18] Michael Fleming (1999-11-16). "West pursues *Prisoner*; Spielberg scribbles" (http://www.variety.com/article/VR1117758075). *Variety*. . Retrieved 2008-07-16.

[19] Peter Bart (2000-01-24). "It's scary up there" (http://www.variety.com/article/VR1117761198). *Variety*. . Retrieved 2008-07-15.

[20] Brian Zoromski (2000-06-30). "*A.I.* Moves Full Speed Ahead" (http://movies.ign.com/articles/034/034162p1.html).*IGN*. . Retrieved 2008-08-04.

[21] Scott Brake (2000-08-03). "*A.I.* Set Reports!" (http://movies.ign.com/articles/034/034165p1.html).*IGN*. . Retrieved 2008-08-04.

[22] Christopher "Fangorn" Baker, Rick Carter, *A.I.* From Drawings to Sets, 2001, Warner Home Video; DreamWorks

[23] Bill Higgins (2000-11-06). "BAFTA hails Spielberg" (http://www.variety.com/article/VR1117788785).*Variety*. . Retrieved 2008-08-06.

[24] Bob Ringwood (http://www.imdb.com/name/nm0727674/), Dressing *A.I.*, 2001, Warner Home Video; DreamWorks

[25] Charles Lyons (2001-01-18). "Inside Move: Cruise staying busy" (http://www.variety.com/article/VR1117792198).*Variety*. . Retrieved 2008-07-18.

[26] David Rooney (2001-04-16). "'Dust' in the wind for Venice fest" (http://www.variety.com/index.asp?layout=festivals&jump=story&id=1061&articleid=VR1117797100&cs=1). *Variety*. . Retrieved 2008-07-19.

[27] "A.I. Artificial Intelligence" (http://www.boxofficemojo.com/movies/?id=ai.htm). Box Office Mojo. . Retrieved 2008-07-08.

[28] "A.I. Artificial Intelligence" (http://www.rottentomatoes.com/m/ai_artificial_intelligence/). Rotten Tomatoes. . Retrieved 2008-07-08.

[29] "A.I. Artificial Intelligence (2001): Reviews" (http://www.metacritic.com/video/titles/ai?q=A.I.). Metacritic. . Retrieved 2008-07-08.

[30] Army Archerd (2000-06-20). "*A.I.* A Spielberg/Kubrick prod'n" (http://www.variety.com/article/VR1117801772). *Variety*. . Retrieved 2008-08-06.

[31] Bryan Appleyard (2007-12-012). "Why don't we love science fiction?" (http://entertainment.timesonline.co.uk/tol/arts_and_entertainment/books/article2961480.ece). *Times Online*. . Retrieved 2009-09-05.

[32] Richard Corliss (2001-06-17). "*A.I.* – Spielberg's Strange Love" (http://www.time.com/time/sampler/article/0,8599,130942,00.html). *Time*. . Retrieved 2008-08-06.

[33] "A.I. Artificial Intelligence" (http://rogerebert.suntimes.com/apps/pbcs.dll/article?AID=/20010629/REVIEWS/106290301/1023). Roger Ebert. . Retrieved 2008-08-06.

[34] Jonathan Rosenbaum (2001-06-29). "The Best of Both Worlds" (http://www.chicagoreader.com/movies/archives/2001/0107/010713.html). *Chicago Reader*. . Retrieved 2008-08-06.

[35] White, Armond (2001-07-04). "Spielberg's A.I. Dares Viewers to Remember and Accept the Part of Themselves that Is Capable of Feeling" (http://www.nypress.com/article-4331-spielbergs-ai-dares-viewers-to-remember-and-accept-the-part-of-themselves-that-is-capable-of-feeling.html). *The New York Press*. Retrieved 2010-04-26.

[36] James Berardinelli (2001-06-29). "A.I." (http://www.reelviews.net/movies/a/ai.html). ReelViews (http://www.reelviews.net). . Retrieved 2008-08-06.

[37] Mick LaSalle (2001-06-29). "Artificial foolishness" (http://www.sfgate.com/cgi-bin/article.cgi?f=/c/a/2001/06/29/DD239232.DTL). *San Francisco Chronicle*. . Retrieved 2008-08-06.

[38] Peter Travers (2001-06-21). "A.I. Artificial Intelligence" (http://www.rollingstone.com/reviews/movie/5949345/review/5949346/ai_artificial_intelligence). *Rolling Stone*. . Retrieved 2008-08-06.

[39] "Steven Spielberg". Mark Kermode. *The Culture Show*. 2006-11-04.

[40] http://www.visual-memory.co.uk/faq/index2.html#slot14 The Kubrick FAQ Part 2

[41] Joe Leydon (2002-06-20). "'Minority Report' looks at the day after tomorrow -- and is relevant to today" (http://www.movingpictureshow.com/dialogues/mpsSpielbergCruise.html). *MovingPictureShow.com*. . Retrieved 2009-04-29.

[42] "Academy Awards: 2002" (http://www.imdb.com/Sections/Awards/Academy_Awards_USA/2002). Internet Movie Database. . Retrieved 2008-07-14.

[43] "59th Golden Globe Awards" (http://www.imdb.com/Sections/Awards/Golden_Globes_USA/2002). Internet Movie Database. . Retrieved 2008-07-14.

[44] "55th British Academy Film Awards" (http://www.imdb.com/Sections/Awards/BAFTA_Awards/2002). Internet Movie Database. . Retrieved 2008-07-14.

[45] "Saturn Awards: 2002" (http://www.imdb.com/Sections/Awards/Academy_of_Science_Fiction_Fantasy_And_Horror_Films_USA/2002). Internet Movie Database. . Retrieved 2008-07-14.

[46] Disney (date unknown). Retrieved from http://bventertainment.go.com/tv/buenavista/atm/specials/bestofthedecade/index.html.

[47] http://www.filmlinc.com/b/?p=1490

[48] http://www.slantmagazine.com/film/feature/best-of-the-aughts-film/216/page_8

[49] http://www.indiewire.com/survey/best_of_the_decade_critics_survey_2000s/best_of_the_decade

[50] http://aimovie.warnerbros.com/

[51] http://www.allmovie.com/work/246161

[52] http://www.imdb.com/title/tt0212720/

[53] http://www.rottentomatoes.com/m/ai_artificial_intelligence/

[54] http://www.boxofficemojo.com/movies/?id=ai.htm

[55] http://www.visual-memory.co.uk/amk/doc/0068.html

[56] http://video.google.com/videoplay?docid=-7897356503742745317&q=jude+law&pl=true

[57] http://eprints.ecs.soton.ac.uk/6469/1/ai.html

[58] http://www.filmmonthly.com/Behind/Articles/AIinDepth/AIinDepth.html

[59] http://www.thepaincomics.com/A.I.pdf

Adaptation (film)

Adaptation.	
Theatrical release poster	
Directed by	Spike Jonze
Produced by	Jonathan Demme Vincent Landay Edward Saxon
Written by	Screenplay: Charlie Kaufman Book: Susan Orlean
Starring	Nicolas Cage Meryl Streep Chris Cooper Cara Seymour Tilda Swinton Brian Cox
Music by	Carter Burwell
Cinematography	Lance Acord
Editing by	Eric Zumbrunnen
Studio	Beverly Detroit Clinica Estetico Good Machine Intermedia Magnet Productions Propaganda Films
Distributed by	Columbia Pictures
Release date(s)	December 6, 2002
Running time	114 min.
Country	United States
Language	English

Budget	$19 million
Gross revenue	$32,801,173

Adaptation (rendered as Adaptation.) is a 2002 American comedy-drama film directed by Spike Jonze and written by Charlie Kaufman. The film is based on Susan Orlean's non-fiction book *The Orchid Thief* through self-referential events. The film stars Nicolas Cage as Charlie and Donald Kaufman, Meryl Streep as Susan, with Chris Cooper, Cara Seymour, Brian Cox, Tilda Swinton, Ron Livingston and Maggie Gyllenhaal. The film tells the story of Charlie Kaufman's difficult struggle to adapt *The Orchid Thief* into a film. In addition, Orlean romances with John Laroche while Charlie enlists the help of his twin brother Donald.

The film had been in development as far back as 1994. Jonathan Demme brought the project to Columbia Pictures with Kaufman writing the script. Kaufman went through writer's block and did not know what to think of *The Orchid Thief*. In turn Kaufman wrote a script about his experience adapting *The Orchid Thief* into a screenplay. Tom Hanks was at one point set for the role of Charlie Kaufman while John Turturro was approached to portray Laroche. Jonze signed to direct and filming finished in June 2001. *Adaptation.* received positive reviews and critical acclaim, as well as outstanding success at the 75th Academy Awards, 60th Golden Globe Awards and 56th British Academy Film Awards. It has since developed a strong cult following, which almost all of Spike Jonze and Charlie Kaufman's works have developed.

Plot

In 1992, John Laroche and his wife run a successful Florida nursery, but tragedy strikes and Laroche's wife, mother and uncle are involved in a car accident. Laroche's mother and uncle are killed immediately, but his wife goes into a coma, divorcing Laroche and suing him once she regains consciousness. One month later, Laroche's home and everything he owns is destroyed by Hurricane Andrew. Meanwhile, local Seminoles hire Laroche due to his vast knowledge of flowers and orchid poaching. However, the Seminoles are using the extract of the Ghost Orchid as an illicit drug, and not for tribal ceremonials as Laroche thought.

Two years later, Laroche is caught at the Fakahatchee Strand Preserve State Park and the ensuing trial captures the attention of *New Yorker* journalist Susan Orlean. Laroche and Susan become great friends, with Susan writing *The Orchid Thief*. Laroche and Susan then become romantically involved, while Susan is still married, albeit unhappily, in New York. *The Orchid Thief* is then optioned by Columbia Pictures.

During the filming of *Being John Malkovich*, the self-loathing and agoraphobic Charlie Kaufman is hired to write the screenplay. At the same time Charlie is going through melancholic depression and his twin brother Donald moves into his house in Los Angeles, mooching off Charlie. Donald decides to become a screenwriter like Charlie, and visits the seminars of Robert McKee. Charlie wants to adapt the script into a faithful adaptation of *The Orchid Thief*, hoping to impress Valerie Thomas. However, he realizes that there is no narrative involved and finds it impossible to turn the book into a film, going through a serious case of writer's block.

Meanwhile, Donald's spec script for a clichéd psychological thriller, called *The Thr3e*, sells for over one million dollars, while Charlie accidentally starts writing his script with self-reference. Already well over his deadline with Columbia Pictures, Charlie visits Susan in New York for advice on the screenplay. In New York, Charlie finds that he is not courageous enough to meet Susan, leaving without consulting with her. Charlie visits a McKee seminar in New York, gaining advice from McKee, and bringing Donald to assist with the story structure. Donald even agrees to go on an interview with Susan, posing as Charlie and remains wary of Susan's answers. With Donald convinced that Susan is lying, he and Charlie follow Susan to Florida where she meets Laroche. Charlie finds Susan and Laroche taking the Ghost Orchid drug and having sex.

This is followed by a sequence of events which include a car chase, Donald being shot and then killed in a car crash, Laroche being killed by an alligator and Susan being arrested by the police. His writer's block broken, Charlie finally summons up the courage to tell his former love interest, Amelia, that he is still in love with her. He finishes his script, with Gérard Depardieu in mind to portray him in the film.

Cast

- Nicolas Cage as Charlie Kaufman / Donald Kaufman
- Meryl Streep as Susan Orlean
- Chris Cooper as John Laroche
- Cara Seymour as Amelia Kavan
- Brian Cox as Robert McKee
- Tilda Swinton as Valerie Thomas
- Ron Livingston as Marty Bowen
- Maggie Gyllenhaal as Caroline Cunningham
- Judy Greer as Alice
- Stephen Tobolowsky (deleted scenes) as Ranger Steve Neely
- Bob Yerkes as Charles Darwin
- Curtis Hanson as Susan's husband
- Doug Jones as Augustus Margary
- Susan Orlean (uncredited) as Woman in supermarket
- Lance Acord (uncredited) as Himself
- John Cusack (uncredited) as Himself
- Spike Jonze (uncredited) as Himself
- Catherine Keener (uncredited) as Herself
- John Malkovich (uncredited) as Himself

Tom Hanks was originally set for the double role of Charlie and Donald Kaufman, while *Variety* was convinced Donald was a real person.[1] Cage took the role for a $5 million salary,[2] and wore a fatsuit during filming.[3] Streep expressed dire interest in the role before being cast,[2] and took a salary cut in recognition of the film's budget.[4] John Turturro was approached to portray John Laroche.[5] Cooper heavily considered turning down Laroche, but accepted it after his wife's persistence.[6] Albert Finney, Christopher Plummer, Terence Stamp and Michael Caine were considered for the role of Robert McKee, but McKee personally suggested Brian Cox to filmmakers.[7]

Nicolas Cage portrays Charlie and Donald Kaufman through split screen photography.

Litefoot and Jay Tavare have small roles as Seminole Indians. John Cusack, Catherine Keener, John Malkovich, Lance Acord and Spike Jonze have uncredited cameos as themselves in scenes where Charlie Kaufman is on the set of *Being John Malkovich*. More cameos include Doug Jones as Augustus Margary for a small scene when Susan fantasizes about the history of orchid poaching, Jim Beaver as Ranger Tony, director Curtis Hanson as Orlean's husband, and David O. Russell as a *New Yorker* journalist.

Production

"The emotions that Charlie is going through [in the film] are real and they reflect what I was going through when I was trying to write the script. Of course there are specific things that have been exaggerated or changed for cinematic purposes. Part of the experience of watching this movie is the experience of seeing that Donald Kaufman is credited as the co-screenwriter. It's part of the movie, it's part of the story."

—Charlie Kaufman on writing the script[8]

The idea to do a film adaptation of Susan Orlean's *The Orchid Thief* dates back to 1994.[9] Fox 2000 purchased the film rights in 1997,[10] eventually selling them to Jonathan Demme, who set the project at Columbia Pictures. Charlie Kaufman was hired to write the script, but went through writer's block and did not know what to think of *The Orchid Thief*.[11] In turn, Kaufman wrote about his experience adapting the script through exaggerated events, and created a fictional "brother" named Donald Kaufman. Charlie even went as far as putting Donald's name on the script and dedicated the film to the fictional character.[12] By September 1999, Kaufman had written two drafts of the script,[13] and turned in another draft in November 2000.[14]

Kaufman explained, "The idea of how to write the film didn't come to me until quite late. It was the only idea I had, I liked it, and I knew there was no way it would be approved if I pitched it. So I just wrote it and never told the people I was writing it for. I only told Spike Jonze, as we were making *John Malkovich* and he saw how frustrated I was. Had he said I was crazy, I don't know what I would have done."[15] In addition Kaufman stated, "I really thought I was ending my career by turning that in!"[16] *Adaptation.* went on fast track in April 2000, with Kaufman mildly rewriting the script.[1] Scott Brake of *IGN* leaked the script on the Internet in June 2000,[17] as did Drew "Moriarty" McWeeny of *Ain't It Cool News* in October.[18] Columbia Pictures committed to North America distribution only after Intermedia came aboard to finance the film in exchange for international distribution rights.[19] Filming started in late March 2001 in Los Angeles, California, and finished by June.[5] The "evolution" fantasy sequence was created by Digital Domain, while Skywalker Sound was responsible for the audio mixing of *Adaptation*.

Reception

Columbia Pictures had at one point announced a late 2001 theatrical release date.[5] *Adaptation.* opened on December 6, 2002 in the United States for a limited release. The film then was released nationwide on February 14, 2003, earning $1,130,480 in its opening weekend in 672 theaters. *Adaptation.* went on to gross $22.5 million in North America and $10.3 million in foreign countries, coming at a total of $32.8 million.[20] Based on 193 reviews collected by *Rotten Tomatoes*, *Adaptation.* received an average 91% overall approval rating;[21] the film was more balanced with the 34 critics in Rotten Tomatoes' "Top Critics", receiving a 85% approval rating.[22] By comparison, Metacritic calculated an average score of 83 from 40 reviews.[23]

Roger Ebert of the *Chicago Sun-Times* believed the film was something "That leaves you breathless with curiosity, as it teases itself with the directions it might take. To watch the film is to be actively involved in the challenge of its creation."[24] He later added the film to his "Great Movies" collection.[25] At the end of 2009, Ebert named the film one of the best of the decade. Wesley Morris of *The Boston Globe* thought "This is epic, funny, tragic, demanding, strange, original, boldly sincere filmmaking. And the climax, the portion that either sinks the entire movie or self-critically explains how so many others derail, is bananas."[26] David Ansen of *Newsweek* felt Meryl Streep had not "been this much fun to watch in years",[27] while Mike Clark of *USA Today* gave a largely negative review, mainly criticizing the ending: "Too smart to ignore but a little too smugly superior to like, this could be a movie that ends up slapping its target audience in the face by shooting itself in the foot."[28]

Chris Cooper won the Academy Award for Best Supporting Actor, while Nicolas Cage (Actor in a Leading Role) and Streep (Supporting Actress) were nominated. Charlie and Donald Kaufman were nominated for Best Adapted Screenplay. Donald became the first truly fictitious person nominated for an Oscar.[29] Cooper and Streep won their respective categories at the 60th Golden Globe Awards. Spike Jonze, Cage and Kaufman were nominated for awards while *Adaptation.* was nominated for Best Motion Picture – Musical or Comedy.[30] Cage, Cooper and Streep received nominations at the 56th British Academy Film Awards, with Kaufman winning Best Adapted Screenplay.[31]

References

[1] Michael Fleming (6 April 2000). "Brothers in a Conundrum; Rat Pack lives" (http://www.variety.com/article/VR1117780287). Variety. . Retrieved 5 April 2008.

[2] Claude Brodesser; Charles Lyons; Dana Harris (23 August 2000). "Cage has *Adaptation.* inclination" (http://www.variety.com/article/ VR1117785470). Variety. . Retrieved 5 April 2008.

[3] Stax (3 May 2001). ""Hey, Fatboy!"" (http://movies.ign.com/articles/057/057663p1.html). IGN. . Retrieved 5 April 2008.

[4] Claude Brodesser (6 September 2000). "Streep eyes *Adaptation.*" (http://www.variety.com/article/VR1117786034). Variety. . Retrieved 5 April 2008.

[5] Greg Dean Schmitz. "Greg's Preview — Adaptation." (http://web.archive.org/web/20070518021750/http://movies.yahoo.com/movie/ preview/1808402845). Yahoo!. . Retrieved 13 April 2008.

[6] Claude Brodesser; Jill Tiernan; Geoffrey Berkshire (23 March 2003). "Backstage notes" (http://www.variety.com/article/VR1117883243. html?categoryid=1043&cs=1). Variety. . Retrieved 8 April 2008.

[7] Lynn Smith (3 November 2002). "Being Robert McKee, both on screen and off". Los Angeles Times.

[8] Spence D (5 December 2002). "Spike Jonze and Charlie Kaufman Discuss *Adaptation*" (http://movies.ign.com/articles/379/379456p1. html). IGN. . Retrieved 5 April 2008.

[9] Bill Desowittz (18 August 2002). "Development players make personal choices" (http://www.variety.com/article/VR1117871334). Variety. . Retrieved 5 April 2008.

[10] Oliver Jones (17 December 1999). "Cruise in tune with *Shaggs* project" (http://www.variety.com/article/VR1117760122). Variety. . Retrieved 5 April 2008.

[11] Jonathan Bing (26 February 2001). "Lit properties are still hottest tickets" (http://www.variety.com/article/VR1117794235). Variety. . Retrieved 5 April 2008.

[12] Claude Brodesser (10 November 1999). "Scribe revisiting reality" (http://www.variety.com/article/VR1117757917). Variety. . Retrieved 5 April 2008.

[13] Charlie Kaufman (24 September 1999). "*Adaptation.*: Second Draft" (http://www.beingcharliekaufman.com/adaptation.pdf). BeingCharlieKaufman.com. . Retrieved 16 April 2008.

[14] Charlie Kaufman (21 November 2000). "*Adaptation.*: Revised Draft" (http://www.beingcharliekaufman.com/adaptationnov2000.pdf). BeingCharlieKaufman.com. . Retrieved 16 April 2008.

[15] Michael Fleming (14 November 2002). "What will follow film success for Eminem?" (http://www.variety.com/article/VR1117876083). Variety. . Retrieved 5 April 2008.

[16] Stax (13 March 2002). "Charles Kaufman Talks Shop" (http://movies.ign.com/articles/355/355413p1.html). IGN. . Retrieved 5 April 2008.

[17] Scott Brake (8 June 2000). "Script Review of Charlie Kaufman's *Adaptation*" (http://movies.ign.com/articles/035/035453p1.html). IGN. . Retrieved 8 April 2008.

[18] Drew "Moriarty" McWeeny (10 October 2000). "Moriarty Rumbles About *Adaptation, The Royal Tenenbaums,* and *Catch Me If You Can!*" (http://www.aintitcool.com/display.cgi?id=7162). Ain't It Cool News. . Retrieved 17 April 2008.

[19] Charles Lyons (18 June 2001). "Helmers let out a rebel yell" (http://www.variety.com/article/VR1117801603). Variety. . Retrieved 5 April 2008.

[20] "Adaptation. (2002)" (http://boxofficemojo.com/movies/?id=adaptation.htm). Box Office Mojo. . Retrieved 8 April 2008.

[21] "Adaptation (2002)" (http://www.rottentomatoes.com/m/adaptation/).Rotten Tomatoes. . Retrieved 8 April 2008.

[22] "Adaptation.: Rotten Tomatoes' Top Critics" (http://www.rottentomatoes.com/m/adaptation/?critic=creamcrop). Rotten Tomatoes. . Retrieved 8 April 2008.

[23] "Adaptation. (2002): Reviews" (http://www.metacritic.com/video/titles/adaptation?q=Adaptation).Metacritic. . Retrieved 8 April 2008.

[24] Roger Ebert (20 December 2002). "Adaptation" (http://rogerebert.suntimes.com/apps/pbcs.dll/article?AID=/20021220/REVIEWS/ 212200302/1023). Chicago Sun-Times. . Retrieved 11 April 2008.

[25] Roger Ebert's "Great Movies" essay about Adaptation. (http://rogerebert.suntimes.com/apps/pbcs.dll/article?AID=/20080918/ REVIEWS08/809180300/1004)

[26] Wesley Morris (20 December 2002). "A revolutionary look at the evolution of creativity" (http://www.boston.com/movies/ display?display=movie&id=1810). The Boston Globe. . Retrieved 11 April 2008.

[27] David Ansen (9 December 2002). "Meta-Movie Madness" (http://www.newsweek.com/id/66762).Newsweek. . Retrieved 12 April 2008.

[28] Mike Clark (5 December 2002). "Cage's *Adaptation?* Durr, Charlie" (http://www.usatoday.com/life/movies/reviews/ 2002-12-05-adaptation_x.htm). USA Today. . Retrieved 12 April 2008.

[29] "Academy Awards: 2003" (http://imdb.com/Sections/Awards/Academy_Awards_USA/2003). Internet Movie Database. . Retrieved 11 April 2008.

[30] "Golden Globes: 2003" (http://www.imdb.com/Sections/Awards/Golden_Globes_USA/2003). Internet Movie Database. . Retrieved 12 April 2008.

[31] "BAFTA Awards: 2003" (http://www.imdb.com/Sections/Awards/BAFTA_Awards/2003). Internet Movie Database. . Retrieved 12 April 2008.

- *Adaptation*, Shooting Script (http://books.google.co.in/books?id=M2VX6twRp9gC&printsec=frontcover& dq=adaptation&source=bl&ots=nGgWJ9_5at&sig=AhSG-PFC5nAKaanUChj-cQaU0F0&hl=en& ei=ylfxS7PmMdCzrAer5_iTBw&sa=X&oi=book_result&ct=result&resnum=6& ved=0CDoQ6AEwBQ#v=onepage&q&f=false), by Charlie Kaufman, Spike Jonze. Nick Hern Books, 2002. ISBN 1854597086.

External links

- Official website (http://www.sonypictures.com/homevideo/adaptation-superbit/index.html)
- *Adaptation.* (http://www.allmovie.com/work/260395) at Allmovie
- *Adaptation.* (http://www.imdb.com/title/tt0268126/) at the Internet Movie Database
- *Adaptation.* (http://www.beingcharliekaufman.com/movies/adaptation.htm) at BeingCharlieKaufman.com
- *Adaptation.* (http://www.rottentomatoes.com/m/adaptation/) at Rotten Tomatoes
- *Adaptation.* (http://boxofficemojo.com/movies/?id=adaptation.htm) at Box Office Mojo
- Susan Orlean's original article for *The New Yorker* (http://www.susanorlean.com/articles/orchid_fever.html)

The Hours (film)

The Hours	
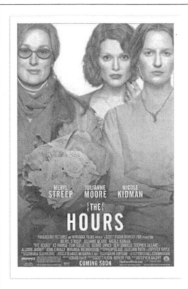 Theatrical release poster	
Directed by	Stephen Daldry
Produced by	Robert Fox Scott Rudin
Written by	David Hare Based on the novel by Michael Cunningham
Starring	Nicole Kidman Julianne Moore Meryl Streep
Music by	Philip Glass
Cinematography	Seamus McGarvey
Editing by	Peter Boyle
Studio	Scott Rudin Productions
Distributed by	Paramount Pictures (US) Miramax Films (worldwide)
Release date(s)	December 25, 2002 (New York & L.A.) December 27, 2002 (United States) February 14, 2003 (United Kingdom)
Running time	114 minutes
Country	United States United Kingdom
Language	English
Budget	$25 million
Gross revenue	$108,846,072

The Hours is a 2002 drama film directed by Stephen Daldry, and starring Nicole Kidman, Meryl Streep, Julianne Moore and Ed Harris. The screenplay by David Hare is based on the 1999 Pulitzer Prize-winning novel of the same title by Michael Cunningham.

The plot focuses on three women of different generations whose lives are interconnected by the novel *Mrs. Dalloway* by Virginia Woolf. Among them are Clarissa Vaughan (Streep), a New Yorker preparing an award party for her AIDS-stricken long-time friend and poet, Richard (Harris) in 2001; Laura Brown (Moore), a pregnant 1950s California housewife with a young boy and an unhappy marriage; and Virginia Woolf herself (Kidman) in 1920s England, who is struggling with depression and mental illness whilst trying to write her novel.

The film was released in Los Angeles and New York City on Christmas Day 2002, and was given a limited release in the US and Canada two days later on December 27, 2002. It did not receive a wide release in the US until January 2003, and was then released in UK cinemas on Valentine's Day that year. Critical reaction to the film was mostly positive, and Nicole Kidman won an Oscar at the 2003 Academy Awards for her portrayal of Virginia Woolf.

Plot

With the exception of the opening and final scenes, which depict the 1941 suicide by drowning of Virginia Woolf (Nicole Kidman) in the River Ouse, the action takes place within the span of a single day in three different years, and alternates among them throughout the film. In 1923, renowned author Woolf has begun writing the book *Mrs. Dalloway* in her home in the town of Richmond in suburban London. In 1951, troubled Los Angeles housewife Laura Brown (Julianne Moore) tries to find escape from her dreary existence by reading the same book. In 2001, New Yorker Clarissa Vaughan (Meryl Streep) is the embodiment of the title character of Woolf's work as she spends the day preparing for a party she is hosting in honor of her friend Richard, a poet and author living with AIDS who is to receive an award for career achievement.

Virginia, who has experienced several nervous breakdowns and suffers from recurring bouts of severe depression, feels trapped in her home. Intimidated by her servants, Nelly and Lottie, and constantly monitored by her husband Leonard, who operates the Hogarth Press at home in order to be close to her at all times, Woolf both welcomes and dreads an afternoon visit from her sister Vanessa and her children. After their departure, Virginia flees to the railway station where she is awaiting a train to central London when Leonard arrives to bring her home. He expresses his distress at living in constant fear of her making a further attempt on her life; she replies that she also lives under the permanent threat of a return to mental illness, but argues that she has to live as she is and not seek a refuge from the reality of her identity.

Pregnant with her second child, Laura spends her days in her tract home with her quiet young son Richie. She married her husband, Dan, soon after World War II and on the surface they are living the American Dream; she is nevertheless, deeply unhappy. She and Richie prepare a birthday cake for Dan's birthday, but the end result is a disaster. Her neighbor Kitty unexpectedly drops in to ask her if she can feed her dog while she's in the hospital undergoing a medical procedure. Kitty is pretending to be upbeat. Laura senses her fear and boldly kisses her on the lips, a gesture Kitty accepts, although she ignores any hidden meaning it may have had. With renewed determination, Laura bakes another cake, which she is happier with, cleans the kitchen, and then takes Richie to stay with Mrs. Latch while she supposedly runs some errands before dinner. Instead she checks into a luxury hotel, where she intends to commit suicide. Before taking the pills she has brought with her, she begins to read *Mrs. Dalloway* and drifts off to sleep. Awakening from a dream in which the hotel room was flooded, she has a change of heart, picks up Richie, and returns home, where the family celebrates Dan's birthday.

Clarissa, stressed in particular about the celebration dinner she's planning for her close friend Richard, particularly by his increasingly debilitating illness, is a bundle of nerves as she tries to accomplish all she needs to do before Richard's award ceremony. The two were romantic during their college days, but he has spent the better part of his life engaging in gay relationships, including one with Louis Waters, who left him years ago but is returning to Manhattan from his home in San Francisco for the festivities. Clarissa herself is a lesbian who has been living with

Sally Lester for 10 years, and the mother of university student Julia, both of whom are trying to help her prepare. Eventually we discover Richard is in fact young Richie Brown, Laura's son. When Clarissa arrives at his apartment to help him dress for the ceremony, she finds him in a manic state. Perched on the window ledge, he confesses he has struggled to stay alive for Clarissa's sake but, no longer willing to live with his illness, he throws himself out a window. Later that night Laura, having been notified of her son's suicide by Clarissa, arrives at her apartment. Laura reveals her decision to abandon her family after the birth of her daughter was one she felt she needed to make in order to maintain her sanity.

Cast

1923

- Nicole Kidman as Virginia Woolf
- Stephen Dillane as Leonard Woolf
- Miranda Richardson as Vanessa Bell
- Lyndsey Marshal as Lottie Hope
- Linda Bassett as Nelly Boxall

1951

- Julianne Moore as Laura Brown
- John C. Reilly as Dan Brown
- Jack Rovello as Richie Brown
- Toni Collette as Kitty
- Margo Martindale as Mrs. Latch

2001

- Meryl Streep as Clarissa Vaughan
- Ed Harris as Richard "Richie" Brown
- Allison Janney as Sally Lester
- Claire Danes as Julia Vaughan
- Jeff Daniels as Louis Waters

Critical reception

Stephen Holden of the *New York Times* called the film "deeply moving" and "an amazingly faithful screen adaptation" and added, "Although suicide eventually tempts three of the film's characters, *The Hours* is not an unduly morbid film. Clear eyed and austerely balanced would be a more accurate description, along with magnificently written and acted. Mr. Glass's surging minimalist score, with its air of cosmic abstraction, serves as ideal connective tissue for a film that breaks down temporal barriers."[1]

Mick LaSalle of the *San Francisco Chronicle* observed, "Director Stephen Daldry employs the wonderful things cinema can do in order to realize aspects of *The Hours* that Cunningham could only hint at or approximate on the page. The result is something rare, especially considering how fine the novel is, a film that's fuller and deeper than the book ... It's marvelous to watch the ways in which [David Hare] consistently dramatizes the original material without compromising its integrity or distorting its intent ... Cunningham's [novel] touched on notes of longing, middle-aged angst and the sense of being a small consciousness in the midst of a grand mystery. But Daldry and Hare's [film] sounds those notes and sends audiences out reverberating with them, exalted."[2]

Richard Schickel of *Time* criticized its simplistic characterization, saying that: "Watching The Hours, one finds oneself focusing excessively on the unfortunate prosthetic nose Kidman affects in order to look more like the novelist. And wondering why the screenwriter, David Hare, and the director, Stephen Daldry, turn Woolf, a woman of incisive mind, into a hopeless ditherer ... He also criticized its overt politicization: "But this movie is in love with female victimization. Moore's Laura is trapped in the suburban flatlands of the '50s, while Streep's Clarissa is moored in a hopeless love for Laura's homosexual son (Ed Harris, in a truly ugly performance), an AIDS sufferer whose relentless anger is directly traceable to Mom's long-ago desertion of him. Somehow, despite the complexity of the film's structure, this all seems too simple-minded. Or should we perhaps say agenda driven? The same criticisms might apply to the fact that both these fictional characters (and, it is hinted, Woolf herself) find what consolation they can in a rather dispassionate lesbianism. This ultimately proves insufficient to lend meaning to their lives or profundity to a grim and uninvolved film, for which Philip Glass unwittingly provides the perfect score — tuneless, oppressive, droning, painfully self-important."[3]

Peter Travers of *Rolling Stone* awarded the film, which he thought "sometimes stumbles on literary pretensions," two out of four stars. He praised the performances, commenting, "Kidman's acting is superlative, full of passion and feeling ... Moore is wrenching in her scenes with Laura's son (Jack Rovello, an exceptional child actor). And Streep is a miracle worker, building a character in the space between words and worlds. These three unimprovable actresses make *The Hours* a thing of beauty."[4]

Steve Persall of the *St. Petersburg Times* said it "is the most finely crafted film of the past year that I never want to sit through again. The performances are flawless, the screenplay is intelligently crafted, and the overall mood is relentlessly bleak. It is a film to be admired, not embraced, and certainly not to be enjoyed for any reason other than its expertise ... Glacially paced and somberly presented, *The Hours* demands that viewers be as impressed with the production as the filmmakers are with themselves ... Whatever the reason - too gloomy, too slow, too slanted - [it] is too highbrow and admirably dull for most moviegoers. It's the kind of film that makes critics feel smarter by recommending it, even at the risk of damaging credibility with mainstream audiences who automatically think any movie starring Kidman, Streep and Moore is worth viewing. *The Hours* will feel like days for them."[5]

Phillip French of *The Observer* called it "a moving, somewhat depressing film that demands and rewards attention." He thought "the performances are remarkable" but found the Philip Glass score to be "relentless" and "over-amplified."[6]

Peter Bradshaw of *The Guardian* rated the film three out of five stars and commented, "It is a daring act of extrapolation, and a real departure from most movie-making, which can handle only one universe at a time . . . The performances that Daldry elicits . . . are all strong: tightly managed, smoothly and dashingly juxtaposed under a plangent score. I have to confess I am agnostic about Nicole Kidman, who as Woolf murmurs her lines through an absurd prosthetic nose. It's almost a Hollywood Disability. You've heard of Daniel Day-Lewis and *My Left Foot*. This is Nicole and her Big Fake Schnoz. It doesn't look anything like the real Virginia's sharp, fastidious features . . . Julianne Moore gives [a] superbly controlled, humane performance . . . Streep's performance is probably the most fully realised of the three: a return to the kind of mature and demanding role on which she had a freehold in yesterday's Hollywood . . . Part of the bracing experimental impact of the film was the absence of narrative connection between the three women. Supplying one in the final reel undermines its formal daring, but certainly packs an emotional punch. It makes for an elegant and poignant chamber music of the soul."[7]

The Hours currently has 81% positive reviews on the movie review aggregator site Rotten Tomatoes, with 150 of 186 counted reviews giving it a "fresh" rating and an average rating of 7.4 out of 10 — with the consensus that "the movie may be a downer, but it packs an emotional wallop. Some fine acting on display here."[8] On Metacritic, the film holds an average score of 81 out of 100, based on 39 reviews.[9]

Box office

The Hours opened in New York City and Los Angeles on Christmas Day 2002 and went into limited release in the United States and Canada two days later. It grossed $1,070,856 on eleven screens in its first two weeks of release. On January 10, 2003, it expanded to 45 screens, and the following week it expanded to 402. On February 14 it went into wide release, playing in 1,003 theaters in the US and Canada.[10] With an estimated budget of $25 million, the film eventually earned $41,675,994 in the US and Canada and $67,170,078 in foreign markets for a total worldwide box office of $108,846,072. It was the 56th highest grossing film of 2002.[11]

Soundtrack

The film's score by Philip Glass won the BAFTA Award for Best Film Music and was nominated for the Academy Award for Best Original Score and the Golden Globe Award for Best Original Score. The soundtrack album was nominated for the Grammy Award for Best Score Soundtrack Album for a Motion Picture, Television or Other Visual Media.

External links

- *The Hours* [12] at the Internet Movie Database
- *The Hours* [13] at Allmovie
- *The Hours* [14] at Rotten Tomatoes
- *The Hours* [15] at Metacritic
- *The Hours* - filming the railway sequences [16]

References

[1] Holden, Stephen (2002-12-27). ""New York Times" review" (http://www.nytimes.com/2002/12/27/movies/27HOUR.html). Nytimes.com. . Retrieved 2010-07-19.

[2] Mick LaSalle, Chronicle Movie Critic (2002-12-27). ""San Francisco Chronicle" review" (http://www.sfgate.com/cgi-bin/article.cgi?f=/ c/a/2002/12/27/DD114138.DTL). Sfgate.com. . Retrieved 2010-07-19.

[3] By RICHARD SCHICKEL Monday, Dec. 23, 2002 (2002-12-23). ""Time" review" (http://www.time.com/time/magazine/article/ 0,9171,1003931,00.html). Time.com. . Retrieved 2010-07-19.

[4] *Rolling Stone* review (http://www.rollingstone.com/reviews/movie/5947733/review/5947734/the_hours)

[5] ""St. Petersburg Times" review" (http://www.sptimes.com/2003/01/16/Weekend/_The_Hours__drags_on_.shtml).Sptimes.com. . Retrieved 2010-07-19.

[6] Phillip French. ""The Observer" review" (http://www.guardian.co.uk/theobserver/2003/feb/16/7).Guardian. . Retrieved 2010-07-19.

[7] Peter Bradshaw (2003-02-14). ""The Guardian" review" (http://www.guardian.co.uk/culture/2003/feb/14/artsfeatures). Guardian. . Retrieved 2010-07-19.

[8] "*The Hours*" (http://www.rottentomatoes.com/m/hours/). Rotten Tomatoes. . Retrieved 2010-07-01.

[9] "*The Hours*" (http://www.metacritic.com/video/titles/hours). Metacritic. . Retrieved 2010-07-01.

[10] "BoxOfficeMojo.com" (http://www.boxofficemojo.com/movies/?page=weekend&id=hours.htm).BoxOfficeMojo.com. 2002-12-27. . Retrieved 2010-07-19.

[11] "BoxOfficeMojo.com" (http://www.boxofficemojo.com/movies/?id=hours.htm).BoxOfficeMojo.com. . Retrieved 2010-07-19.

[12] http://www.imdb.com/title/tt0274558/

[13] http://www.allmovie.com/work/272631

[14] http://www.rottentomatoes.com/m/hours/

[15] http://www.metacritic.com/film/titles/hours

[16] http://www.vintagecarriagestrust.org/filmlist.htm

Stuck on You (film)

Stuck on You	
Brothers Stick Together	
Directed by	Farrelly Brothers
Produced by	Farrelly Brothers Mark Charpentier Marc S. Fischer Garrett Grant Kris Meyer Hal Olofsson Bradley Thomas Charles B. Wessler Endrick Lekay (uncredited)
Written by	Screenplay: Farrelly Brothers Bennett Yellin Charles B. Wessler
Starring	Matt Damon Greg Kinnear Eva Mendes Wen Yann Shih Pat Crawford Brown Cher
Cinematography	Daniel Mindel
Editing by	Christopher Greenbury Dave Terman
Distributed by	20th Century Fox
Release date(s)	December 12, 2003 *(US)*
Running time	118 minutes
Country	United States
Language	English
Budget	$55,000,000
Gross revenue	$64,000,000 (worldwide)

Stuck On You is a 2003 comedy film directed by the Farrelly brothers and starring Matt Damon and Greg Kinnear.

Matt Damon and Greg Kinnear would team up again in the 2010 feature Green Zone.

Plot

Stuck On You is a Farrelly Brothers comedy about a pair of conjoined twins. They use their unique deformity as a means to gain acceptance and live as normally as possible within everyday life. Everything is going great until Walt (Greg Kinnear) follows his dreams of making it as a Hollywood actor, and persuades his hesitant brother Bob (Matt Damon) to go along for the ride.

The brothers also have to deal with the complications of dating as Bob meets and falls in love with May (Wen Yann Shih), a woman he met online, who is unaware that Bob has a conjoined twin.

Cast

- Matt Damon as Bob Tenor
- Greg Kinnear as Walt Tenor
- Eva Mendes as April Mercedes
- Wen Yann Shih as May Fong
- Pat Crawford Brown as Mimmy
- Ray Valliere as Rocket
- Tommy Songin as Tommy
- Terence Bernie Hines as Moe Neary
- Cher as Herself
- Jackie Flynn as Howard
- Seymour Cassel as Morty O'Reilly
- Griffin Dunne as Himself
- Bridget Tobin as Vineyard Cutie
- Danny Murphy as Dicky
- Malcolm G. Chace Jr. as Vineyard Buddie
- Meryl Streep as herself
- Steve Tyler as Detective Reudy
- Dane Cook as Officer Fraioli
- Fernanda Lima as Susie

Reception

Critics

On the review website Rotten Tomatoes, 60% of critics gave the film positive reviews, based on 152 reviews, and an average rating of 6/10, with the consensus: "An unusually sweet and charming comedy by the Farrelly brothers. Fans may miss the distinct lack of bodily fluids though." [1]

Box office

Although the movie was able to make back its production budget by grossing $34 million domestically and $32 internationally,[2] its box office draw considerably underperformed the Farrelly Brothers previous hits. It only managed third place in its opening weekend box office (US) despite having the largest theater count of any movie that weekend (Dec 12-14 2003).

Music

The song "Human" recorded by Cher, who appears in the film, and produced by David Foster was included in the soundtrack. There was no official release, but in Germany the song was released on a promotional CD of the soundtrack called "Unzertrennlich" and that version clocks 3:49. The song can be heard during the end credits of the film and is played during a scene in a club. This is the first Farrelly Brothers film not to have an Official Soundtrack.

Pete Yorn recorded a cover of the Albert Hammond classic "It Never Rains in Southern California" for the film, and like the aforementioned Cher song, remains unreleased. The Kings of Leon songs "California Waiting", "Molly Chambers" and "Holy Roller Novocaine" are all featured in the film as well, from the bands first EP *Holy Roller Novacaine*. Greg Kinnear's version of "Summertime" is an almost note-for-note cover of the Billy Stewart version. Eight minutes out in the movie, while at a bar, Morten Abel's song "Welcome Home" is played.

External links

- *Stuck On You* [3] at the Internet Movie Database
- *Stuck on You* [4] at Rotten Tomatoes

References

[1] "Stuck on You" (http://www.rottentomatoes.com/m/stuck_on_you/). Rotten Tomatoes. . Retrieved 2010-03-23.

[2] http://www.boxofficemojo.com/movies/?id=stuckonyou.htm

[3] http://www.imdb.com/title/tt0338466/

[4] http://www.rottentomatoes.com/m/stuck_on_you/

The Manchurian Candidate (2004 film)

The Manchurian Candidate	
Theatrical release poster	
Directed by	Jonathan Demme
Produced by	Jonathan Demme Ilona Herzberg Scott Rudin Tina Sinatra
Written by	Screenplay: Daniel Pyne Dean Georgaris Novel: Richard Condon
Starring	Denzel Washington Meryl Streep Liev Schreiber Jon Voight Jeffrey Wright Bruno Ganz Ted Levine Vera Farmiga
Music by	Rachel Portman
Cinematography	Tak Fujimoto
Editing by	Carol Littleton Craig McKay
Distributed by	Paramount Pictures
Release date(s)	July 30, 2004
Running time	129 minutes
Country	United States
Language	English
Budget	$80 million (estimated)

Gross revenue	$96,105,964 (worldwide)

The Manchurian Candidate is a 2004 American thriller film based on the 1959 novel of the same name by Richard Condon, and a reimagining of the previous 1962 film.

The film stars Denzel Washington as Bennett Marco, a tenacious, virtuous soldier, Liev Schreiber as Raymond Shaw, a U.S. Representative from New York, manipulated into becoming a vice-presidential candidate, Jon Voight as Tom Jordan, a U.S. Senator and challenger for vice president and Meryl Streep as Eleanor Shaw, also a senator and the manipulative, ruthless mother of Raymond Shaw.

Plot

Major Bennett "Ben" Marco (Denzel Washington) is a war veteran who begins to doubt what is commonly known about his famous army unit. During Operation Desert Storm, Sergeant First Class Raymond Shaw (Liev Schreiber) supposedly rescued all but two members in his unit, of which Marco was the commanding officer. While this made Shaw a war hero, gained him the Medal of Honor, and launched him into a career in politics, Marco and other members of the troop feel that while they remember that Shaw *did* rescue them, they do not actually remember him doing it.

The members begin to come together in a dystopian near-future America defined by jingoism, islamophobia, and increasing corporate influence. Shaw, now a United States Congressman, becomes his party's candidate for Vice-President. He is an unexpected candidate, as Connecticut Senator Tom Jordan (Jon Voight) was the leading choice for some time. Jordan is pushed aside by Shaw's mother, Virginia Senator Eleanor Shaw (Meryl Streep), who blackmails the party leaders into nominating her son. An obvious rivalry exists between Eleanor Shaw and Tom Jordan, partly due to a past relationship between Raymond Shaw and Jordan's daughter Jocelyne (Vera Farmiga).

After Shaw is nominated, Marco begins investigating what really happened during the war. Allied with an FBI agent named Rosie (Kimberly Elise) he links the mystery of his lost platoon to Manchurian Global, an international weapons manufacturer with major political connections, including the Shaw family. Soon Marco discovers Manchurian Global's brainwashing of his "lost" platoon, and their plans to take over the White House with Shaw, under the power of the company and Eleanor Shaw, who is even more power hungry than she appears.

Soon Eleanor Shaw begins to take matters into her own hands, trusting Manchurian Global less and less. Her ruthlessness is shown when she uses her own brainwashed son to assassinate Senator Jordan, who had been contacted by Marco and had begun to support his investigation in an attempt to expose her plan. As she becomes more and more controlling, it is soon revealed that the Vice-Presidential spot is not what she has in mind for her son, but the presidency. On election night, the newly elected president will be assassinated, and the planned assassin of Shaw's running mate is none other than Marco himself, who was also brainwashed in the war. With the help of the FBI, Marco arranges a private meeting with Shaw in a school which he was to cast his vote in. Marco tries once again to convince Shaw of what is happening to him. Shaw seems to agree, and gives Marco his Medal of Honor, which he says he does not deserve. Marco takes it, and Shaw receives a phone call from his mother, who wants to talk to Marco. Marco answers it, and is soon "activated" by her.

After Eleanor Shaw activates her son, he becomes helpless and weak. Shaw washes down her son, kissing him repeatedly on the lips and stroking the back of his neck. They then get ready to go to the election party.

Shaw and Marco begin to regain a conscious state even while under Manchurian Global's control. At the election night celebration party, the newly elected Shaw and Major Marco realize what must be done. Shaw leads his mother onto the stage with him, moving them into the spot where the President should be and blocking Marco's shot. Marco then fires one shot, killing both of them as they hug. Just before Marco can kill himself (which had been part of Eleanor Shaw's plan), Rosie stops him by shooting him in the shoulder. The FBI seemingly covers up Marco's involvement, pinning a Manchurian Global conspirator with the shooting. In the last scene, Rosie takes Marco to the compound he was brainwashed in, apparently in conjunction with the FBI investigating. Marco realizes what has happened, and lets the sea take away a picture of the "lost platoon" along with Shaw's Medal of Honor as if erasing what happened in that compound.

Cast

- Denzel Washington as Major Bennett Marco
- Meryl Streep as Senator Eleanor Prentiss Shaw
- Liev Schreiber as Congressman Raymond Prentiss Shaw
- Kimberly Elise as Eugenie Rose
- Jon Voight as Senator Thomas Jordan
- Vera Farmiga as Jocelyne Jordan
- Jeffrey Wright as CPL Al Melvin
- Simon McBurney as Dr. Atticus Noyle
- Bruno Ganz as Delp
- David Keeley as Agent Evan Anderson
- Ted Levine as Colonel Howard
- Miguel Ferrer as Colonel Garret
- Dean Stockwell as Mark Whiting
- Jude Ciccolella as David Donovan
- Tom Stechschulte as Governor Robert "Bob" Arthur
- Pablo Schreiber as PFC Eddie Ingram
- Anthony Mackie as PFC Robert Baker III
- Robyn Hitchcock as Laurent Tokar
- Obba Babatunde as Senator Wells
- Zeljko Ivanek as Vaughn Utly

Because the film takes place during a presidential campaign, Al Franken makes a cameo appearance as himself, while Sidney Lumet, Anna Deavere Smith, Roy Blount, Jr. and Fab Five Freddy make short appearances as political pundits. Roger Corman also cameos as the Secretary of State. Beau Sia can be seen briefly on a TV-screen, as the presenter of a late-night comedy show while Gayle King can be seen on TV-screens several times as the presenter of a political chat show.

Box office

The film grossed $65,955,630 in North America and $30,150,334 in other territories, totaling $96,105,964 worldwide.[1]

Critical reception

The film received mostly positive reviews. Based on 199 reviews collected by Rotten Tomatoes, the film has an overall approval rating from critics of 81%, with an average score of 7.1/10.[2] Among Rotten Tomatoes' Cream of the Crop, which consists of popular and notable critics from the top newspapers, websites, television, and radio programs, the film holds an overall approval rating of 77%.[3] By comparison, Metacritic, which assigns a normalized rating out of 100 top reviews from mainstream critics, calculated an average score of 76, based on 41 reviews.[4]

Mick LaSalle of the *San Francisco Chronicle* wrote about Mrs. Streep that "no one can talk about the acting in 'The Manchurian Candidate' without rhapsodizing about Streep (in the role originated by Angela Lansbury). She has the Hillary hair and the Karen Hughes attack-dog energy, but the charm, the inspiration and the constant invention are her own. She gives us a senator who's a monomaniac, a mad mommy and master politician rolled into one, a woman firing on so many levels that no one can keep up—someone who loves being evil as much as Streep loves acting. She's a pleasure to watch—and to marvel at—every second she's onscreen."[5]

Awards and nominations

2005 Academy of Science Fiction, Fantasy & Horror Films (Saturn Awards)

- Nominated - Best Action/Adventure/Thriller Film
- Nominated - Best Supporting Actor (Film) — Liev Schreiber
- Nominated - Best Supporting Actress (Film) — Meryl Streep

2005 BAFTA Film Awards

- Nominated - Best Actress in a Supporting Role — Meryl Streep

2005 Black Reel Awards

- Nominated - Best Supporting Actor — Jeffrey Wright
- Nominated - Best Supporting Actress — Kimberly Elise

2005 Golden Globe Awards

- Nominated - Best Supporting Actress - Motion Picture — Meryl Streep

See also

- 2004 in film
- Cinema of the United States
- List of American films of 2004

External links

- *The Manchurian Candidate* [6] at the Internet Movie Database
- *The Manchurian Candidate* [7] at Rotten Tomatoes
- *The Manchurian Candidate* [8] at Box Office Mojo

References

[1] "The Manchurian Candidate (2004)" (http://www.boxofficemojo.com/movies/?id=manchuriancandidate.htm). *Box Office Mojo*. . Retrieved May 30, 2010.

[2] "The Manchurian Candidate (2004)" (http://www.rottentomatoes.com/m/manchurian_candidate/). *Rotten Tomatoes*. . Retrieved May 30, 2010.

[3] "The Manchurian Candidate (2004): Cream of the Crop" (http://www.rottentomatoes.com/m/manchurian_candidate/?critic=creamcrop). *Rotten Tomatoes*. . Retrieved May 30, 2010.

[4] "The Manchurian Candidate reviews" (http://www.metacritic.com/video/titles/manchuriancandidate2004). *Metacritic*. . Retrieved May 30, 2010.

[5] LaSalle, Mick (July 30, 2004). "Terrorist attacks, corporate control, election controversy: Sound familiar? 'The Manchurian Candidate' has it all." (http://www.webcitation.org/5q7FcZ2d6). *San Francisco Chronicle*. Archived from the original (http://www.sfgate.com/cgi-bin/article.cgi?f=/c/a/2004/07/30/DDGFD7V6NG1.DTL) on May 30, 2010. . Retrieved May 30, 2010.

[6] http://www.imdb.com/title/tt0368008/

[7] http://www.rottentomatoes.com/m/manchurian_candidate/

[8] http://www.boxofficemojo.com/movies/?id=manchuriancandidate.htm

Lemony Snicket's A Series of Unfortunate Events

Lemony Snicket's A Series of Unfortunate Events	

Theatrical poster	
Directed by	Brad Silberling
Produced by	Laurie MacDonald Walter F. Parkes Jim Van Wyck
Written by	Robert Gordon Daniel Handler (books)
Narrated by	Jude Law
Starring	Jim Carrey Emily Browning Liam Aiken Kara Hoffman Shelby Hoffman Timothy Spall Meryl Streep Catherine O'Hara
Music by	Thomas Newman
Cinematography	Emmanuel Lubezki
Editing by	Michael Kahn
Studio	Nickelodeon Movies Scott Rudin Productions
Distributed by	Paramount Pictures DreamWorks
Release date(s)	December 16, 2004 *United States.* December 17, 2004
Running time	107 minutes
Country	United States

Language	English
Budget	$140 million[1]
Gross revenue	$209,073,645

Lemony Snicket's A Series of Unfortunate Events is a 2004 black comedy film directed by Brad Silberling based on the first three novels in *A Series of Unfortunate Events*: *The Bad Beginning*, *The Reptile Room*, and *The Wide Window* by Lemony Snicket. The film stars Jim Carrey as Count Olaf, a mysterious theatre troupe actor who attempts to steal the inheritance of the three wealthy Baudelaire orphans played by Emily Browning, Liam Aiken, and Kara and Shelby Hoffman. The film is narrated by Jude Law as Lemony Snicket and features many celebrity guest stars including Timothy Spall, Billy Connolly, Meryl Streep and Catherine O'Hara.

Nickelodeon Movies purchased the film rights to Daniel Handler's book series in May 2000 and soon began development of a film. Barry Sonnenfeld signed on to direct in June 2002. He hired Handler to adapt the screenplay and courted Jim Carrey for Count Olaf. Sonnenfeld eventually left over budget concerns in January 2003 and Brad Silberling took over. Robert Gordon rewrote Handler's script, and principal photography started in November 2003. *A Series of Unfortunate Events* was entirely shot using sound stages and backlots at Paramount Pictures and Downey Studios. The film received generally favorable reviews from critics, grossed approximately $209 million worldwide, and won the Academy Award for Best Makeup.

Plot

The film starts with a deceiving opening featuring "The Littlest Elf" , a fake programme, after a few seconds, a record scratching sound plays, with the author Lemony Snicket announcing that "The Littlest Elf will not be the movie seen in the cinema. Inventor Violet Baudelaire, her intelligent younger brother Klaus, and their sharp-toothed, precocious baby sister Sunny are orphaned when a mysterious fire destroys their parents' mansion. Mr. Poe, the banker in charge of the Baudelaire estate, entrusts them to their "closest relative" like their parents' will says (Poe mistakenly interprets it as the relative that lives closest to them) the obnoxious Count Olaf, who is only interested in the money the children will inherit, and loses custody of the children after attempting to kill them in a staged train accident.

Poe then sends the Baudelaires to live with their uncle, Dr. Montgomery Montgomery, a cheerfully eccentric herpetologist. Planning a trip with the children to Peru, their stay with Uncle Monty is cut short when Olaf appears in disguise as a man named Stephano, who murders Monty and frames a large and poisonous viper for the killing. As the disguised Olaf prepares to spirit the children away, Sunny reveals the snake's true gentle nature, and Olaf's plot is exposed. Poe accepts Olaf's guilt, though not his true identity. Olaf abandons his disguise and escapes.

The orphans are then sent to live at Lake Lachrymose, where their Aunt Josephine resides in a house perched precariously on the edge of a cliff overlooking the waters of the vast lake. She has numerous irrational fears, and yet lives in a house filled with many things of which she is afraid, as her fear of realtors prevents her from moving. A room of photographs and documents apparently contains clues to the cause of the fire that killed the orphans' parents. However, Olaf arrives once again, disguised as a sailor named Captain Sham, and quickly gains Josephine's confidence. A hurricane comes to Lake Lachrymose, and Olaf regains custody of the children after rescuing them and leaving Josephine to be eaten alive by deadly leeches.

Olaf concocts his final plan involving a play starring himself and Violet. In the play, his character marries Violet's character, but in such a way that the staged marriage is legal, gaining him access to her inheritance. This move is accomplished by Olaf's casting of Justice Strauss, as the supposed judge in the play; with her in this role, the marriage is technically legal. To ensure Violet's co-operation, he holds Sunny hostage. However, Klaus climbs the tower of Olaf's house, rescues Sunny, and uses a light-focusing apparatus to incinerate Olaf's marriage certificate. Klaus also discovers that it was Olaf who set fire to the Baudelaire mansion, using that same aparatus. Olaf is arrested, sentenced but subsequently has his sentence quashed on appeal and disappears. At the ruins of the Baudelaire mansion, the three orphans find a letter left to them by their parents. The envelope also contains a spyglass, one of several that Klaus signifies to imply the presence of a secret society to which his parents and relatives belonged. The orphans are then sent to new "fortunate" guardians.

Cast

- Jim Carrey as Count Olaf
- Jude Law as Lemony Snicket (narrator)
- Liam Aiken as Klaus Baudelaire
- Emily Browning as Violet Baudelaire
- Kara and Shelby Hoffman as Sunny Baudelaire
- Timothy Spall as Mr. Poe
- Billy Connolly as Uncle Monty
- Meryl Streep as Aunt Josephine
- Catherine O'Hara as Justice Strauss
- Cedric the Entertainer as the constable
- Luis Guzmán as bald man
- Jamie Harris as the hook-handed man
- Craig Ferguson as the person of indeterminate gender
- Jennifer Coolidge as a white-faced woman
- Jane Adams as a white-faced woman
- Dustin Hoffman (uncredited) as the critic
- John Dexter as Gustav
- Deborah Theaker as Mrs. Poe
- Jane Lynch (uncredited) as the realtor

Author Daniel Handler initially viewed Count Olaf as being a James Mason-type.[2] Carrey was not familiar with the book series when he was cast, but he became a fan of the series. "Handler's books are just a bold and original way to tell a children's story," the actor explained. Carrey was also attracted to the role despite self-parody concerns.[3] Director Brad Silberling was open to Carrey's idea of improvisation for various scenes, especially the Stephano and Captain Sham alter egos.[4] To make his prosthetic makeup more comfortable and easier to apply, Carrey shaved his head bald for the part.[3] The actor's inspiration for Olaf's voice was a combining the voices of Orson Welles and Béla Lugosi.[5]

Emily Browning was cast as Violet Baudelaire when she auditioned at a casting call in Australia. She was sent Handler's original script when Barry Sonnenfeld was planning to direct, and she screentested for the part using a British accent. The actress was not cast until Silberling took over; her character's accent was then changed to American. Browning became a fan of the books after reading Handler's original script.[6]

Production

Development

Nickelodeon Movies purchased the film rights of the *A Series of Unfortunate Events* book series in May 2000.[7] Paramount Pictures, owner of Nickelodeon Movies, agreed to co-finance, along with Scott Rudin.[8] Various directors, including Terry Gilliam and Roman Polanski, were interested in making the film. One of author Daniel Handler's favorite candidates was Guy Maddin.[2] In June 2002, Barry Sonnenfeld was hired to direct. He was chosen because he previously collaborated with Rudin and because of his black comedy directing style from *The Addams Family, Addams Family Values* and *Get Shorty*.[9] Sonnenfeld referred to the *Lemony Snicket* books as his favorite children's stories.[10] The director hired Handler to write the script[11] with the intention of making *Lemony Snicket* as a musical,[6] and cast Jim Carrey as Count Olaf in September 2002.[11]

The film suffered setbacks in development in December 2002. Rudin left *Unfortunate Events* over budget concerns. While Sonnenfeld and Carrey remained, Sonnenfeld admitted he was skeptical of Paramount's $100 million budget. The studio decided that changing the shoot from Hollywood to Wilmington, North Carolina would be less expensive.[10] The April 2003 start date was also pushed back.[12] Paramount eventually settled the situation in January 2003 by enlisting help from DreamWorks to co-finance the film, but Sonnenfeld vacated the director's position. Rudin and Sonnenfeld had no involvement with the film afterward, but were credited as executive producers. Carrey remained with approval over the hiring of the next director.[13]

> "Very little of what I wrote is in the film, which I actually think is appropriate being as that I was writing it for Barry Sonnenfeld. It's a director's medium and Brad Siberling makes entirely different films from Barry Sonnenfeld. I wasn't filled with resentment because they didn't use it [my script], I was just disappointed because I'd worked a long time [on it] and Scott Rudin, Barry Sonnenfeld and I were all sort of ready to go, along with Jim Carrey, with the film that we had. So it was sort of a long, rocky, journey. But that's all [in the past]."
>
> — Series author Daniel Handler[2]

Brad Silberling signed on to direct in February 2003.[14] He was not familiar with the book series when he was first approached. He quickly read the first three books and was excited that "Hollywood was taking a chance to put over $100 million to adapt these inventive children's books onto screen".[15] Handler, who wrote eight drafts of the script for Sonnenfeld,[2] was replaced by Robert Gordon in May 2003.[16] Handler approved of the changes that were made to his original screenplay.[17] "I was offered credit on the film for screenwriting by the Writers Guild of America," Handler continued, "but I didn't take it because I didn't write it. I felt like it would be an insult to the guy who did."[2]

Filming

Filming was set to begin in October 2003, but it was pushed back.[14] Principal photography for *Lemony Snicket's A Series of Unfortunate Events* began on November 10, 2003,[18] using the sound stages and backlot at Paramount Studios in Hollywood. Director Brad Silberling avoided using too many digital or chroma key effects because he wanted the younger actors to feel as if they were working in a realistic environment. Olaf's mansion occupied two sound stages, while the graveyard and the ruins of the Baudelaire mansion were constructed on the Paramount backlot. After 21 weeks of shooting at Paramount,[19] production then moved to Downey Studios, a former NASA facility,[20] for eight more weeks. Downey housed the circular railroad crossing set complete with forced perspective scenery, as well as a newly-constructed water tank complete with over one million gallons of water. The water tank was instrumental in filming scenes at Briny Beach, Lake Lachrymose, Domocles Dock and Curdled Cave.[19] Filming for *A Series of Unfortunate Events* ended on May 29, 2004.[21]

Design

Some scenery was designed to accustom forced perspective techniques, combined with matte paintings.

Silberling, production designer Rick Heinrichs and costume designer Colleen Atwood all aimed for the film's setting to be ambiguous, giving it a "timeless" feel. Heinrichs also added steampunk designs to the period.[19] To contribute to the setting, Silberling hired Emmanuel Lubezki as the cinematographer because he was impressed with the trio's work on *Sleepy Hollow*.[22]

Lubezki compared the cinematic similarities to *Sleepy Hollow*, notably the monochromatic look of both films. He also choose a specific color palette backdrop for *A Series of Unfortunate Events*. "The story is very episodic, so we picked a different color scheme for each section. For example," Lubezki continued, "Count Olaf's house has a lot of greens, blacks and grays; the house of Uncle Monty has a lot of greens and browns and a bit of yellow; and the house of Aunt Josephine has blues and blacks."[22] The railroad crossing set was constructed on a cyclorama, which was the most ambitious setpiece for the art department on using elements of "in house" special effects and matte paintings.[19]

Robert D. Yeoman replaced Lubezski as cinematographer when Lubezski had to leave the production to commit to *The New World*. Yeoman mostly worked on the expansive harbor set at Downey.[22] The art direction was inspired by *The Night of the Hunter*, which also influenced Handler for the writing of his books.[15] Atwood commented that the Mr. Poe character was based on Edward Gorey paintings.[23]

Visual effects

Industrial Light & Magic (ILM), supervised by Stefen Fangmeier,[22] created the film's 505 visual effects-shots.[24] The filmmakers used as few digital effects as possible,[22] though the train and smoke for the railroad crossing scene was entirely created using computer animation. ILM also used color grading techniques for the Lake Lachrymose scene, which required complete animation for the leeches. The digital animators studied footage of the 2003 Atlantic hurricane season to accurately depict Hurricane Herman, which was ILM's most ambitious use of computer-generated imagery (CGI) for the film.[24]

Nexus Productions designed the opening "Littlest Elf" animated sequence by modeling it after stop motion animation and completing it with computer animation.[18] The snakes at Uncle Monty's house were a combination of real snakes and animatronics. The animatronics, primarily the Incredibly Deadly Viper, were used as reference models that ILM later enhanced using CGI.[19]

Because working with infants was sometimes risky in producing a film, four scenes involving Sunny Baudelaire required CGI with motion capture technology.[25] Among these are the shot of Sunny hanging on to a table by her teeth, catching a spindle with her mouth and the scene where she is entangled with the Incredibly Deadly Viper. Animation supervisor Colin Brady used his baby daughter for motion capture recording.[25] A remote controlled animatronic of Sunny was also designed by Kevin Yagher.[26]

Costumes

Colleen Atwood designed the films' costumes. According to Emily Browning regarding the costumes[27] :

> The costumes were brilliant, Colleen Atwood is a genius. She is an evil genius because the clothes were so uncomfortable (laughs). They weren't uncomfortable like a full corset but it was sort of a bodice. I needed heels because Liam was so much taller than me. It didn't help much because he is so tall. I was so excited when I saw the dress and I thought "I can't wait to wear it" and then after a week I couldn't wait to get it off. This was the black dress. The wedding dress I wasn't allowed to sit in because the material was so fine that it got creased and you couldn't un-crease it and also the train was so long that it would always get caught on things.

Reception

Marketing

In October 2002, Nickelodeon Movies hired Activision to create the film's tie-in video game. The agreement also included options for sequels.[28] Director Brad Silberling delivered his first cut of the film to the studio in August 2004. Fearing his original version was "too dark", Paramount and Dreamworks conducted test screenings. The film was then re-edited over family-friendliness concerns. Given its December release, the film's marketing campaign was criticized for being a deliberately anti-holiday comedy with taglines like, "Taking the cheer out of Christmas" and "Mishaps. Misadventures. Mayhem. Oh Joy."[29] The premiere for *Lemony Snicket's A Series of Unfortunate Events* was held at the Cinerama Dome on December 13, 2004. A 20,000-square-foot tent display on Vine Street was decorated with pieces from the film's sets.[17]

Release

The film was released in the United States and Canada on December 17, 2004 in 3,620 theaters, earning $30,061,756 in its opening weekend.[30] In its run, *A Series of Unfortunate Events* managed to stay in the number one position for its first week, before facing competition from *Meet the Fockers*, *The Aviator* and *Coach Carter*.[31] The film eventually grossed $118,634,549 in US totals and $90,439,096 elsewhere, coming to a worldwide total of $209,073,645.[30] It is the highest grossing film under the Nickelodeon Movies banner.[32] Paramount Home Video released the film on DVD on April 26, 2005 in both single-disc and two-disc special edition format.[33] [34]

Critical analysis

Based on 151 reviews collected by *Rotten Tomatoes*, 71% of the critics enjoyed *A Series of Unfortunate Events* with an average score of 6.6 out of 10.[35] The film was more balanced with 31 critics in *Rotten Tomatoes*' "Top Critics" poll, receiving a 58% approval rating on a 6.5 score.[36] By comparison, *Metacritic* calculated that the film received generally favorable reviews from critics with an average score of 62 out of 100, based on 37 reviews.[37]

Robert K. Elder of the *Chicago Tribune* praised Rick Heinrichs's production design and Jim Carrey for having a balanced performance as a scene stealer. Elder called the film "exceptionally clever, hilariously gloomy and bitingly subversive."[38] Desson Thomson from *The Washington Post* reasoned over the characterization of Count Olaf, "Olaf is a humorless villain in the book. He's not amusing like Carrey at all. To which I would counter: If you can't let Carrey be Carrey, put someone boring and less expensive in the role. In his various disguises he's rubbery, inventive and improvisationally inspired. I particularly liked his passing imitation of a dinosaur."[39]

Ty Burr, writing in *The Boston Globe*, observed, "Director Brad Silberling has essentially made a Tim Burton movie without the weird shafts of adolescent pain. At the same time, Silberling's not a hack like Chris Columbus, and *Snicket* has more zip and inspired filmcraft than the first two *Harry Potter* films. The film's no masterpiece, but at least you're in the hands of people who know what they're doing. The movie, like the books, flatters children's innate sense that the world is *not* a perfect place and that anyone who insists otherwise is trying to sell you something. How you deal with the cognitive dissonance of a $125 million Hollywood picture telling you this is up to you. At least there are no Lemony Snicket Happy Meals. Yet."[40]

Internet reviewer James Berardinelli felt that "the film is first and foremost a fantasy, but there are dark currents running just beneath the surface. I give Silberling credit for not allowing them to swallow the film. *Lemony Snicket's A Series of Unfortunate Events* manages to remain witty throughout."[41] Roger Ebert gave a mixed review: "Jim Carrey is over the top as Count Olaf, but I suppose a character named Count Olaf is over the top by definition. I liked the film, but I'll tell you what. I think this one is a tune-up for the series, a trial run in which they figure out what works and what needs to be tweaked. The original *Spider-Man* was a disappointment, but the same team came back and made *Spider-Man 2*, the best superhero movie ever made."[42] Scott Foundas of *Variety* gave a negative review, criticizing the filmmakers for sacrificing the storyline in favor of visual elements such as set design and cinematography. He wrote, "*A Series of Unfortunate Events* suggests what *Mary Poppins* might have looked like had Tim Burton directed it. Not surprisingly, Burton's longtime production designer Rick Heinrichs was responsible for the sets, while ace Emmanuel Lubezki (Burton's *Sleepy Hollow*) contributed the expressionistic lighting schemes."[43]

Awards

Makeup designer Valli O'Reilly and Bill Corso won the Academy Award for Best Makeup, making it the only Nickelodeon Movie to win an Academy Award. Production designer Rick Heinrichs and set decorator Cheryl Carasik (Art Direction), Colleen Atwood (Costume Design) and composer Thomas Newman (Original Music Score) were also nominated for their work at 77th Academy Awards.[44] The film lost the Saturn Award for Best Fantasy Film to *Spider-Man 2*, but was honored for its DVD special edition release. O'Reilly and Corso were also nominated the Saturn Award for Best Make-up, but lost to *Hellboy*.[45]

Planned franchise

Paramount Pictures and Nickelodeon Movies hoped the film would become a franchise like the *Harry Potter* film series.[9] Jim Carrey was attracted to the film because he found it to be a good recurring franchise character that would still allow him each time to dive into a new role.[15] "I don't have a deal [for a sequel], but it's one that I wouldn't mind doing again because there are so many characters," the actor explained in December 2004. "I mean, it's just so much fun. It's so much fun being a bad actor playing a character..."[5] In May 2005, producer Laurie MacDonald said "*Lemony Snicket* is still something Paramount is interested in pursuing and we're going to be talking with them more."[46] In an October 2008 interview, Daniel Handler said that "a sequel does seem to be in the works. Paramount has had quite a few corporate shakeups. Of course many, many plans in Hollywood come to naught, but I'm assured that another film will be made. Someday. Perhaps."[47] In June 2009, Silberling confirmed he still talked about the project with Handler, and suggested the sequel be a stop motion film because the lead actors have grown too old. "In an odd way, the best thing you could do is actually have Lemony Snicket say to the audience, 'Okay, we pawned the first film off as a mere dramatization with actors. Now I'm afraid I'm going to have to show you the real thing.'"[48]

External links

- Official website [49]
- *Lemony Snicket's A Series of Unfortunate Events* [50] at the Internet Movie Database
- *Lemony Snicket's A Series of Unfortunate Events* [51] at Allmovie
- *Lemony Snicket's A Series of Unfortunate Events* [52] at Rotten Tomatoes
- *Lemony Snicket's A Series of Unfortunate Events* [53] at Metacritic
- *Lemony Snicket's A Series of Unfortunate Events* [54] at Box Office Mojo

References

[1] Elder, Sean (December 5, 2004). "A Victory for Terror (the Good Kind)" (http://www.nytimes.com/2004/12/05/movies/05lemo.htm). *The New York Times*. . Retrieved April 7, 2009.

[2] Spence D. (December 16, 2004). "Interview: Lemony Snicket" (http://movies.ign.com/articles/574/574000p1.html).*IGN*. . Retrieved April 7, 2009.

[3] Otto, Jeff (March 12, 2004). "An Interview with Jim Carrey" (http://movies.ign.com/articles/498/498545p1.html). *IGN*.. Retrieved April 7, 2009.

[4] Jim Carrey, Brad Silberling. (2005) (DVD). *Building a Bad Actor*. Paramount.

[5] Otto, Jeff (December 15, 2004). "Interview: Jim Carrey" (http://movies.ign.com/articles/573/573820p1.html). *IGN*. . Retrieved April 7, 2009.

[6] Paul Fischer (December 14, 2004). "Interview: Emily Browning" (http://web.archive.org/web/20071216050330/http://www.darkhorizons.com/news04/lemony2.php).*Dark Horizons*. . Retrieved July 16, 2009.

[7] Hayes, Dade (May 10, 2000). "Nickelodeon Movies nabs Snicket series" (http://www.variety.com/article/VR1117781435). *Variety*. . Retrieved April 5, 2009.

[8] Bing, Jonathan (February 26, 2002). "H'w'd stalks crime scribe" (http://www.variety.com/article/VR1117861500).*Variety*. . Retrieved April 5, 2009.

[9] Fleming, Michael (June 11, 2002). "Par on *Snicket* ticket" (http://www.variety.com/article/VR1117868357). *Variety*. . Retrieved April 5, 2009.

[10] Fleming, Michael (December 12, 2002). "*Snicket* in thicket" (http://www.variety.com/article/VR1117877394).*Variety*.. Retrieved April 5, 2009.

[11] Fleming, Michael (September 18, 2002). "Jim's juiced for *Lemony*" (http://www.variety.com/article/VR1117873013).*Variety*. . Retrieved April 5, 2009.

[12] Fleming, Michael (July 13, 2003). "Diaz sings *Jane* refrain" (http://www.variety.com/article/VR1117889255).*Variety*.. Retrieved April 5, 2009.

[13] Fleming, Michael (January 12, 2003). "Helmer leaves *Snicket* post" (http://www.variety.com/article/VR1117878598).*Variety*. . Retrieved April 5, 2009.

[14] Fleming, Michael (February 19, 2003). "Silberling joining *Snicket* ticket" (http://www.variety.com/article/VR1117880840). *Variety*. . Retrieved April 5, 2009.

[15] Otto, Jeff (November 22, 2004). "Set Visit: Lemony Snicket's A Series of Unfortunate Events" (http://movies.ign.com/articles/567/567650p1.html). *IGN*. . Retrieved April 7, 2009.

[16] Fleming, Michael (May 7, 2003). "Scribe brings new map to *Snicket* thicket" (http://www.variety.com/article/VR1117885786). *Variety*. . Retrieved April 5, 2009.

[17] Archerd, Army (December 13, 2004). "Crystal king on B'way" (http://www.variety.com/article/VR1117914932).*Variety*. . Retrieved April 5, 2009.

[18] "Movie Preview: Lemony Snicket's A Series of Unfortunate Events" (http://www.ew.com/ew/article/0,,679412,00.html). *Entertainment Weekly*. August 10, 2004. . Retrieved April 7, 2009.

[19] *A Woeful World*, 2005, Paramount DVD

[20] Graser, Marc (July 25, 2004). "'Burbs blossom on H'w'd backlots" (http://www.variety.com/article/VR1117908190).*Variety*. . Retrieved April 5, 2009.

[21] Fleming, Michael (September 13, 2003). "Just ticket for *Snicket*" (http://www.variety.com/article/VR1117892463).*Variety*. . Retrieved April 5, 2009.

[22] Williams, David E. (December 2004). "A Darker Side of Fantasy" (http://www.theasc.com/magazine/dec04/lemony/index.html). *American Cinematographer*. . Retrieved June 20, 2009.

[23] Colleen Atwood, Timothy Spall. (2005) (DVD). *Costumes and Other Suspicious Disguises*. Paramount.

[24] (DVD) *Trains, Leeches & Hurricanes*. Paramount. 2005.

[25] (DVD) *An Even More Alarming Conspiracy Involving Sunny*. Paramount. 2005.

[26] (DVD) *An Alarming Conspiracy Involving Sunny*. Paramount. 2005.

[27] http://www.google.com.my/url?sa=t&source=web&ct=res&cd=2&url=http%3A%2F%2Fwww.agirlsworld. com%2Frachel%2Fhangin-with%2Femilybrowning.html&ei=GsOvSo32HNalkQXF2YCWBg& usg=AFQjCNF5qyMe_GNZ6mQfF8y_zDaebYJMgA

[28] Bloom, David (October 29, 2002). "A fortunate event for Handler" (http://www.variety.com/article/VR1117875116).*Variety.* . Retrieved April 5, 2009.

[29] McNary, Dave (December 12, 2004). "*Lemony*-fresh?" (http://www.variety.com/article/VR1117914812). *Variety.* . Retrieved April 10, 2009.

[30] "Lemony Snicket's A Series of Unfortunate Events" (http://www.boxofficemojo.com/movies/?id=lemonysnicket.htm).*Box Office Mojo.* . Retrieved April 8, 2009.

[31] "The Top Movies, Weekend of January 14, 2005" (http://www.the-numbers.com/charts/weekly/2005/20050114.php).*The Numbers.* . Retrieved April 8, 2009.

[32] "Nickelodeon Movies" (http://www.boxofficemojo.com/franchises/chart/?id=nickelodeon.htm). *Box Office Mojo.* . Retrieved April 8, 2009.

[33] "Lemony Snicket's A Series of Unfortunate Events (Widescreen Edition) (2004)" (http://www.amazon.com/exec/obidos/ASIN/ B0007PICAS). *Amazon.com.* . Retrieved April 8, 2009.

[34] "Lemony Snicket's A Series of Unfortunate Events (2-Disc Special Collector's Edition) (2004)" (http://www.amazon.com/exec/obidos/ ASIN/B0007TKGQW). *Amazon.com.* . Retrieved April 8, 2009.

[35] "Lemony Snicket's A Series of Unfortunate Events" (http://www.rottentomatoes.com/m/lemony_snicket/). *Rotten Tomatoes.* . Retrieved April 8, 2009.

[36] "Lemony Snicket's A Series of Unfortunate Events: Top Critics" (http://www.rottentomatoes.com/m/lemony_snicket/ ?critic=creamcrop). *Rotten Tomatoes.* . Retrieved April 8, 2009.

[37] "Lemony Snicket's A Series of Unfortunate Events (2004): Reviews" (http://www.metacritic.com/film/titles/lemonysnicket). *Metacritic.* . Retrieved April 8, 2009.

[38] Elder, Robert K. (December 15, 2004). "Movie review: *Lemony Snicket's A Series of Unfortunate Events*" (http://chicago.metromix.com/ movies/review/movie-review-lemony-snickets/159406/content). *Chicago Tribune.* . Retrieved April 10, 2009.

[39] Thomson, Deeson (April 17, 2004). "A Fortunate Series of Scenes" (http://www.washingtonpost.com/wp-dyn/articles/ A4634-2004Dec16.html). *The Washington Post.* . Retrieved April 10, 2009.

[40] Burr, Ty (April 17, 2004). "Artful direction makes *Snicket* a most fortunate event" (http://www.boston.com/movies/ display?display=movie&id=6976). *The Boston Globe.* . Retrieved April 10, 2009.

[41] Berardinelli, James. "Lemony Snicket's A Series of Unfortunate Events" (http://www.reelviews.net/movies/l/lemony_snicket.html). *ReelViews.* . Retrieved April 11, 2009.

[42] Ebert, Roger (April 17, 2004). "Lemony Snicket's A Series of Unfortunate Events" (http://rogerebert.suntimes.com/apps/pbcs.dll/ article?AID=/20041216/REVIEWS/41130004/1023). *Chicago Sun-Times.* . Retrieved April 11, 2009.

[43] Foundas, Scott (December 10, 2004). "Lemony Snicket's A Series of Unfortunate Events" (http://www.variety.com/review/ VE1117925724.html?categoryid=31&cs=1). *Variety.* . Retrieved April 11, 2009.

[44] "1994 (77) Academy Awards" (http://awardsdatabase.oscars.org/ampas_awards/DisplayMain.jsp?curTime=1239426524794). *Academy of Motion Picture Arts and Sciences.* . Retrieved April 10, 2009.

[45] "Past Saturn Awards" (http://www.saturnawards.org/past.html). *Academy of Science Fiction, Fantasy & Horror Films.* . Retrieved April 10, 2009.

[46] Otto, Jeff (May 25, 2005). "Producers Talk Ring 3 and Snicket Sequel" (http://movies.ign.com/articles/618/618877p1.html). *IGN.* . Retrieved April 7, 2009.

[47] Scott, Ronnie (October 2008). "An Interview With Daniel Handler" (http://bookslut.com/features/2008_10_013548.php). *BookSlut.com.* . Retrieved April 7, 2009.

[48] Ditzian, Eric (June 3, 2009). "*Lemony Snicket* Director Brad Silberling Plans To Do Each Film In Different Medium" (http://moviesblog. mtv.com/2009/06/03/lemony-snicket-director-brad-silberling-plans-to-do-each-film-in-different-medium/).*MTV News.* . Retrieved June 4, 2009.

[49] http://www.unfortunateeventsmovie.com/

[50] http://www.imdb.com/title/tt00339291/

[51] http://www.allmovie.com/work/286685

[52] http://www.rottentomatoes.com/m/lemony_snicket/

[53] http://www.metacritic.com/film/titles/lemonysnicket

[54] http://www.boxofficemojo.com/movies/?id=lemonysnicket.htm

Prime (film)

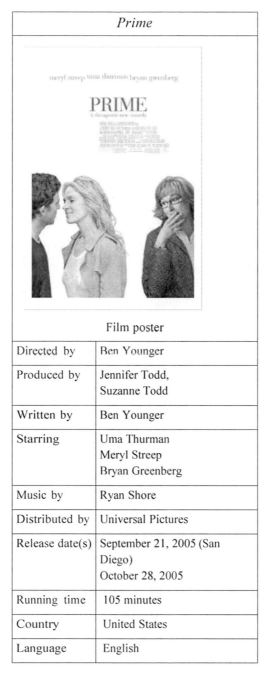

Prime	
Film poster	
Directed by	Ben Younger
Produced by	Jennifer Todd, Suzanne Todd
Written by	Ben Younger
Starring	Uma Thurman Meryl Streep Bryan Greenberg
Music by	Ryan Shore
Distributed by	Universal Pictures
Release date(s)	September 21, 2005 (San Diego) October 28, 2005
Running time	105 minutes
Country	United States
Language	English

Prime is a 2005 American romantic comedy film starring Uma Thurman, Meryl Streep and Bryan Greenberg. It was written and directed by Ben Younger. The film has grossed $67,937,503 worldwide.

Plot

Rafi (Uma Thurman) is a recently divorced, 37-year-old career woman from Manhattan who becomes romantically involved with David (Bryan Greenberg), a talented 23-year-old Jewish painter from the Upper West Side. Rafi shares all her secrets with her therapist Lisa (Meryl Streep) who, unbeknownst to Rafi, is David's mother. Lisa, supportive of Rafi's relationship with a younger man, discovers the connection and finds herself not only faced with the ethical and moral dilemma of counseling David's girlfriend, but also the reality that she feels differently about the relationship now that she knows her son is involved. Lisa consults her own therapist, and they decide that it is in the best interest of her patient Rafi for Lisa to continue treatment, as long as the relationship remains the "fling" it appears to be.

However, Lisa soon realizes that the relationship is serious, and tells Rafi that she is David's mother. Feeling embarrassed and feeling betrayed, Rafi ends her treatment with Lisa. Their differences causing problems between them, Rafi and David break up. A couple of weeks later, David is enjoying a night on the town with his best friend; he gets drunk and ends up sleeping with Sue, Rafi's friend from work. The same day, after bumping into each other at the supermarket and going back to David's place, David and Rafi start seeing each other again. They also try to make the relationship stronger by going to a Friday night dinner at Lisa's apartment. The rift between Rafi and David's mother is patched up, although Rafi brings up the possibility of her and David having children, to which Lisa reacts strongly. A few days later, Rafi discovers that David had slept with Sue, and David and Rafi fight. After sulking for some time, David goes to seek Lisa's help as both his mother and as a therapist. She advises him to do what he can to keep the relationship, because it was through Rafi that Lisa was able to understand David's career as an artist. David goes back to Rafi to apologize and offer to give her a child because that is what she wants the most. Rafi realizes how deep David's love must be for him to make such a sacrifice. Ultimately, they both realize that love is not enough to keep a relationship going, and they break up.

A year later, David and his friend are leaving a restaurant — the first restaurant where he and Rafi had a proper date. Going back to retrieve his forgotten hat, he spots Rafi but she does not see him; he gets his hat, rushes out the door, and hides. He defrosts the glass a bit to watch her, and she turns around and sees him. They share a smile before parting

Production

The role of Rafi was originally going to be played by Sandra Bullock. Bullock completed rehearsals with the Director and Greenberg, but pulled out just before filming began, because she wanted major script changes, and the director was not willing to change the script.

Bryan Greenberg's trip to New York to film this movie is documented as part of HBO's semi-reality series *Unscripted*.

Soundtrack

The soundtrack is a mix of different music genres such as jazz and pop. The composer of this soundtrack is Ryan Shore.

1. Ghostwriter (Remix) - Performed By RJD2
2. In A Sentimental Mood - Performed By Duke Ellington And John Coltrane
3. Peach Trees - Performed By Rufus Wainwright
4. Rafi And David - Composed By Ryan Shore
5. Fake French - Performed By Le Tigre
6. Isn't This A Lovely Day - Performed By Stacey Kent
7. Still Got Me - Performed By Daniel Merriweather
8. Shelter - Performed By Ray LaMontagne
9. Laylo - Performed By Debbie Nova
10. Try - Performed By Sidsel Endresen / Bugge Wesseltoft
11. I Wish You Love - Performed By Rachael Yamagata
12. Prime Suite - Composed By Ryan Shore

Reception

Critical response

Rotten Tomatoes gave the film a normalized average score of 49% based on 115 reviews.[1] Metacritic gave the film a weighted mean score of 58% based on 32 reviews[2]

Box office

The film opened at #3 at the U.S. box office, making $6,220,935 USD in its opening weekend, behind *The Legend of Zorro* and *Saw II*.[3]

External links

- Official website [4]
- *Prime* [5] at the Internet Movie Database
- *Prime* [6] at Allmovie
- Soundtrack at CDuniverse [7]

References

[1] *Prime* (http://www.rottentomatoes.com/m/prime/) at Rotten Tomatoes
[2] *Prime* (http://www.metacritic.com/film/titles/prime) at Metacritic
[3] http://www.the-numbers.com/charts/weekly/2005/20051028.php
[4] http://www.primemovie.net/
[5] http://www.imdb.com/title/tt0387514/
[6] http://www.allmovie.com/work/315164
[7] http://www.cduniverse.com/search/xx/music/pid/6976891/a/Prime.htm

A Prairie Home Companion (film)

A Prairie Home Companion	
Theatrical release poster	
Directed by	Robert Altman
Produced by	Robert Altman Fisher Stevens
Written by	Garrison Keillor
Starring	Garrison Keillor Woody Harrelson L. Q. Jones Tommy Lee Jones Kevin Kline Lindsay Lohan Virginia Madsen John C. Reilly Maya Rudolph Meryl Streep Lily Tomlin
Music by	Garrison Keillor
Cinematography	Ed Lachman
Distributed by	Picturehouse New Line Cinema
Release date(s)	June 9, 2006
Running time	106 minutes
Country	USA
Language	English
Budget	$10 million
Gross revenue	$25,978,442

A Prairie Home Companion is a 2006 ensemble comedy elegy directed by Robert Altman, and was his final film, released just five months before his death. It is a fictional representation of behind-the-scenes activities at the long-running public radio show of the same name.

Plot

A long-running live radio show is in danger of being canceled by new owners of the company that owns both the radio station and the theater from which the show is broadcast. The film takes place on the night of the show's last performance. The show has two visitors: an angel calling herself Asphodel (Virginia Madsen) comes to comfort the people who work on the show and to escort one of them to the afterlife, while "the Axeman" (Tommy Lee Jones), a representative of the new owners, arrives to judge whether the show should be canceled. He makes it clear that the show is not what he considers modern popular programming, and though he too is escorted by the angel, the show is shut down anyway. In an epilogue at the end of the film the former cast members are reunited at Mickey's Diner. Their conversation pauses as they are joined by Asphodel, leaving the implication that she has arrived for another of their number.

Cast

- Garrison Keillor (the show's creator) as himself
- Meryl Streep and Lily Tomlin as Yolanda and Rhonda Johnson, who hail from Oshkosh, Wisconsin, the last two members of what was once a popular family country music act
- Lindsay Lohan as Lola Johnson, Yolanda's daughter, who writes poems about suicide
- Woody Harrelson and John C. Reilly as Keillor's radio characters Dusty and Lefty, the singing cowboys.
- Tommy Lee Jones as the Axeman, a businessman from Texas who has come to shut down the show
- Kevin Kline as Keillor's radio character Guy Noir, a film noir P.I. repurposed as the program's security director
- Virginia Madsen as the Dangerous Woman, "Asphodel", who may or may not be the Angel of Death (Asphodel is a flower, referenced in the poem "Demeter And Persephone" by Alfred Lord Tennyson and associated with death and Hades in Greek mythology)
- L. Q. Jones as Chuck Akers
- Tim Russell & Maya Rudolph as the stage manager and his assistant
- Robin & Linda Williams as themselves
- Tom Keith, as the Sound-Effects Guy
- Sue Scott, as the Make-Up Artist

Five of the stars (Keillor, Kline, Tomlin, Reilly, and Madsen) as well as the rest of the cast (except Scott, Streep and Lohan) are midwesterners. Three (Tommy Lee Jones, L. Q. Jones, and Harrelson) are from Texas, the state given rough treatment by the WLT cast and crew.

Production notes

To receive insurance for the shoot, Robert Altman had to hire Paul Thomas Anderson as a "backup" director to observe filming at all times and be prepared to take over for Altman in case of his incapacity.[1] [2] [3] . Principal photography for the film began on June 29, 2005, at the Fitzgerald Theater in St. Paul, Minnesota (the usual venue for the radio show). Filming ended on July 28, 2005. The film was the second major picture (after *North Country*, starring Charlize Theron and Harrelson) to be filmed in Minnesota in 2005.

Because the Fitzgerald is a rather small building, other stage theaters in the Minneapolis-St. Paul region had been considered as stand-ins. With some effort, the necessary film equipment was crammed into the structure. The basement was also used for sets due to lack of space. Set design had to make the show more visually interesting, and fake dressing rooms were used in the film (the movie's production designer noted that Keillor's actual dressing room is "about the size of a very, very small bathroom"). Mickey's Diner, a downtown St. Paul landmark, is also featured.

On November 1, 2005, the *Star Tribune* reported that an early screening in New York City for film distributors resulted in a heavy bidding war. Picturehouse bought the rights, and company president Bob Berney, "aiming to capitalize on the name recognition of the 31-year-old radio program, recommended that the title revert to *A Prairie Home Companion*. 'At the screening, Garrison said that to broaden the film's appeal, they were thinking about changing the name to *Savage Love*, so we may have an argument there,' Berney said."

Reception

Critics

A Prairie Home Companion opened the 2006 South by Southwest film festival on March 10, then premiered in St. Paul, on May 3, 2006, at the Fitzgerald Theater, which had projection and sound equipment specially brought in for that purpose. The film's stars arrived in ten horse-drawn carriages. Brian Williams of *NBC Nightly News* anchored his newscast from neighboring Minneapolis that night so that he would be able to attend.

The general reaction to the film by critics was favorable, and it garnered an 81% fresh rating at Rotten Tomatoes. Roger Ebert awarded the film four out of four stars, saying, "What a lovely film this is, so gentle and whimsical, so simple and profound"[4] , and later added the film to his "Great Movies" list.[5]

Michael Medved gave the film one and a half stars out of four, saying, "The entertainment value stands somewhere between thin and nonexistent" and "[it may be] the worst movie ever made that pooled the talents of four (count 'em - four!) Oscar winners"[6]

Desson Thomson from *The Washington Post* fell in between, saying in a review headlined "Honey, You Could Ask For More" (a reference to the theme song of the radio show and film) that while the movie had its strengths, it was weaker than it should have been[7] .

Awards

Meryl Streep won the Best Supporting Actress Award from the National Society of Film Critics for her role in this and *The Devil Wears Prada*; Altman was also posthumously nominated for an Independent Spirit Award for Best Director.

Box office

The film had a successful limited release in the States and grossed $20,338,609 domestically and $25,978,442 worldwide.

Home media

The DVD was released on October 10, 2006.

Special features

- deleted scenes
- behind-the-scenes documentary
- commentary by Altman and Kline

Soundtrack

A Prairie Home Companion Original Motion Picture Soundtrack was released on May 23, 2006, by New Line.

External links

- Official site [8]
- *A Prairie Home Companion* [9] at the Internet Movie Database
- *A Prairie Home Companion* [10] at Box Office Mojo

References

[1] Indie Wire (http://www.indiewire.com/ots/2006/02/daily_dispatch_3.html)

[2] Washington Post (http://www.washingtonpost.com/wp-dyn/content/article/2005/07/27/AR2005072702372_pf.html)

[3] New York Times (http://www.nytimes.com/2005/07/23/movies/MoviesFeatures/23prai.html?ex=1279771200&
     en=3fa151765fc0ec7f&ei=5090&partner=rssuserland&emc=rss)

[4] Chicago Sun-Times review by Roger Ebert (http://rogerebert.suntimes.com/apps/pbcs.dll/article?AID=/20060608/REVIEWS/
     60606001)

[5] Great Movies review by Roger Ebert (http://rogerebert.suntimes.com/apps/pbcs.dll/article?AID=/20081112/REVIEWS08/811129987/
     1004)

[6] Michael Medved's Movie Minute (http://www.michaelmedved.com/pg/jsp/eot/home.jsp)

[7] The Washington Post review by Desson Thomson (http://www.washingtonpost.com/wp-dyn/content/article/2006/06/08/
     AR2006060801841.html)

[8] http://www.aprairiehomecompanionmovie.com/

[9] http://www.imdb.com/title/tt0420087/

[10] http://www.boxofficemojo.com/movies/?id=prairiehomecompanion.htm

The Devil Wears Prada (film)

The Devil Wears Prada	
Theatrical release poster	
Directed by	David Frankel
Produced by	Wendy Finerman Karen Rosenfelt
Written by	Aline Brosh McKenna Novel Lauren Weisberger
Starring	Anne Hathaway Meryl Streep Emily Blunt Stanley Tucci Simon Baker Adrian Grenier
Music by	Theodore Shapiro
Cinematography	Florian Ballhaus
Editing by	Mark Livolsi
Distributed by	20th Century Fox
Release date(s)	June 30, 2006
Running time	109 minutes
Country	United States France
Language	English French
Budget	$35 million[1]
Gross revenue	$326,551,094[1]

The Devil Wears Prada is a 2006 comedy-drama film, a loose screen adaptation of Lauren Weisberger's 2003 novel of the same name. It stars Anne Hathaway as Andy Sachs, a recent college graduate who goes to New York City and gets a job as a co-assistant to powerful and demanding fashion magazine editor Miranda Priestly, played by Meryl Streep. Emily Blunt and Stanley Tucci co-star in support of the two leads, as catty co-assistant Emily Charlton, and critical yet supportive Art Director Nigel, respectively. Adrian Grenier, Simon Baker and Tracie Thoms play key supporting roles. Wendy Finerman produced and David Frankel directed; the film was distributed by 20th Century Fox.

Streep's performance drew rave reviews from critics and later earned her many award nominations, including her record-setting 14th Oscar bid, as well as the Golden Globe for Best Actress in a Comedy or Musical. Blunt also drew favorable notice and nominations, as did many of those involved in the film's production. While critical reaction to the film as a whole was more measured, it was well received by the public, becoming a surprise summer box-office hit following its June 30 North American release. The commercial success and critical praise for Streep's performance continued in foreign markets, with the film leading the international box office for most of October. The U.S. DVD release likewise was the top rental during December. Ultimately, it would gross over $300 million, mostly from its international run, and finish in 2006's top 20 both in the U.S. and overseas. It is also the second highest-grossing film in Streep's career (the first being *Mamma Mia!*) and the third highest in Hathaway's (the first two being *Alice in Wonderland* and *Get Smart*).

Although the movie is set in the fashion world, most designers and other fashion notables avoided appearing as themselves for fear of displeasing U.S. *Vogue* editor Anna Wintour, who is widely believed to have been the inspiration for Priestly. Many designers allowed their clothes and accessories to be used in the film, making it the most expensively-costumed film in history.[2] Wintour later overcame her initial skepticism,[3] saying she liked the film and Streep in particular.

Plot

Andrea "Andy" Sachs (Anne Hathaway) is an aspiring journalist fresh out of Northwestern University. Despite ridiculing the shallowness of the fashion industry, she lands the job "a million girls would kill for": junior personal assistant to Miranda Priestly (Meryl Streep), the icy editor-in-chief of *Runway* fashion magazine. Andy has to put up with Miranda's bizarre and humiliating treatment in hopes of getting a job as a reporter or writer somewhere else. At first, Andy fumbles with her job and fits in poorly with her catty coworkers, especially Miranda's senior assistant Emily Charlton (Emily Blunt).

During a dinner with her father who came to visit her in New York City, Miranda calls her: the airports in Florida where she is are all closed due to a hurricane but she needs to get home and orders Andy to get her home somehow. Andy tries every airline company there is, but none of them are flying out because of the weather. When Miranda does arrive back at the office she tells Andy she has disappointed her more than any other of her previous assistants.

Andy has a talk with *Runway*'s art director Nigel (Stanley Tucci), who gives a whole new perspective of Miranda, her work and fashion in general. Andy decides to change and gradually learns her responsibilities and begins to dress more stylishly. Slowly but surely, Andy begins to sacrifice her personal life to her career. Miranda notices the change in Andy and gives her a new task: delivering "The Book" (a mock-up of the next edition's feature spreads) to her Upper East Side townhome. However, Andy is tricked by Miranda's daughters into going upstairs, where she inadvertently walks in on Miranda and her husband arguing. Mortified, she drops the book and leaves.

Miranda punishes Andy by giving her an impossible task: securing the unpublished manuscript for the next book in the *Harry Potter* series for her twin daughters to read on the train. Andy is just about to quit when Christian Thompson, a famous writer and acquaintance of Andy's informs her he has gotten it for her. Andy delivers the copies to a stunned Miranda and keeps her job, much to her boyfriend's disappointment.

When Emily falls ill Miranda commands Andy to accompany the two of them to a charity benefit where the two masquerade as party goers when in reality they are reminding her important information about the people approaching her for a greeting. At the event, Andy saves Miranda from being embarrassed by Emily who had forgotten one of the names, meets Jacqueline Follet, the editor-in-chief of French *Runway* and Miranda's rival, turns down an offer to meet a big publisher from Christian, but all the while misses her boyfriend's birthday party.

One evening, while returning The Book, Miranda informs her that she needs "the best team possible" for her Paris trip, which means stepping over Emily. Andy hesitates, as Emily has been boasting about going to Paris for months, but Miranda tells her that if she declines it will send the message that she is not committed to her job or any future job at another publication. Andy has no choice but to accept. Miranda then tells Andy to be the bearer of bad news to Emily who, meanwhile, is hurrying back to the office after purchasing scarves from Hermes of Paris for Miranda. Just as Andy is about to tell her, Emily crosses at a "no cross" point and is hit by a taxi. Andy has a rough day confronting Emily about Paris and then at her friend Lily's art gallery, where she accepts a kiss on the cheek from Christian. Lily catches this and berates Andy, to then confront her boyfriend about the fact that she is going to Paris. He realizes that they no longer have anything in common, and they break up.

In Paris, Andy attends the shows and even meets designer Garavani Valentino, being introduced as "the new Emily". One night Andy comes into Miranda's suite only to find her in her bathrobe, undressed, and crying. While deciding on a seating chart, Miranda opens up saying that her husband is divorcing her, but that her biggest worry is for her daughters, who have lost yet another father figure. Later, Andy learns from Nigel that he has gotten a job as creative director at fashion designer James Holt's new company. Andy has dinner with Christian who figures out that she is single again. After a few glasses of wine she succumbs to Christian's charms and sleeps with him.

In his hotel room the next morning, while dressing, Andy finds out that *Runway* 's owner is planning to replace Miranda with Jacqueline Follet. Andy storms out to find Miranda and warn her. When Andy finally tells her, Miranda seems unfazed. At a luncheon in honor of James Holt, Miranda announces that Jacqueline will be the new creative director of James Holt's company much to the surprise of Andy and Nigel.

En route to another event, Miranda explains to a still-stunned Andy that she knew about the plan to get rid of her all along, but she found an alternative for Jacqueline and presented "the list" (a list of all the designers, stylists, company owners, and models that were "raised and nurtured" by Miranda and who have promised their loyalty to her whenever and should she ever leave *Runway*) to the owner of *Runway*, who realized that without those people, *Runway* would be doomed, was forced to reconsider. Miranda also says that she was pleased by Andy's display of loyalty and that she sees a great deal of herself in her. Andy says she could never do to anyone what Miranda did to Nigel. Miranda replies that she already did, stepping over Emily. Miranda tentatively comforts her, saying that those choices are necessary to live the life that she lives. At the event, Andy gets out of the car and simply walks away. When receiving a call from Miranda, she throws her phone into a fountain on the Place de la Concorde.

Back in New York, she meets her boyfriend for breakfast. He has accepted an offer to work as a sous-chef in a popular Boston restaurant. Andy is disappointed, but her hope is rejuvenated when he says they could work something out.

Andy goes to an interview for a newspaper job. The interviewer reveals that Miranda told him she was by far her biggest disappointment, but that if he did not hire her, he would be an idiot. Afterwards Andy sees Miranda getting into her car across the street. They exchange looks and Andy smiles at her, but Miranda acts as if the two are strangers. Once in the car, Miranda gives a soft smile before angrily telling her driver, "Go!".

Cast

- Anne Hathaway as Andrea "Andy" Sachs: a recent Northwestern University graduate and aspiring journalist who, despite no real knowledge of fashion, is hired as the junior personal assistant to the powerful and demanding editor of *Runway* magazine, Miranda Priestly.
- Meryl Streep as Miranda Priestly: The editor of *Runway*. Feared by her staff and many in the fashion world, and powerful enough that she can discard a $300,000 photo shoot with impunity and lead a designer to redo an entire collection with the pursing of her lips. Nevertheless, she cares a lot about her twin daughters.
- Emily Blunt as Emily Charlton: Miranda's haughty senior assistant, who tolerates her boss's rudeness and insults so that she may accompany her to Paris for Fall Fashion Week.
- Stanley Tucci as Nigel: Art director for *Runway* and the only person at the magazine Andrea feels she can trust, despite his sometimes cutting remarks about her wardrobe and weight.
- Simon Baker as Christian Thompson: An up-and-coming magazine writer Andrea grows increasingly attracted to, especially after his connections help her get the advance *Harry Potter* books Miranda requests for her daughters. He hints he could help her with her journalistic aspirations.
- Adrian Grenier as Nate Cooper: Andrea's boyfriend, a chef at a Manhattan restaurant who eventually breaks up with her due to the strain her job places on their relationship.
- Tracie Thoms as Lily: Andrea's close friend, who runs an art gallery.
- Rich Sommer as Doug: A college friend of Andrea, Nate and Lily who seems to work as a corporate research analyst.
- Daniel Sunjata as James Holt: An up-and-coming designer.
- David Marshall Grant as Richard Sachs, Andrea's father.
- Tibor Feldman as Irv Ravitz: The board chairman of Elias-Clark (fictional version of Conde-Nast), the company that publishes *Runway*.
- Gisele Bündchen as Serena: An editorial staffer at *Runway* and friend of Emily's.
- Alyssa Sutherland as Clacker: An editorial staffer at *Runway*.
- Ines Rivero as Clacker at elevator

Cameos

- Valentino Garavani
- Giancarlo Giammetti
- Carlos de Souza
- Charlene Shorto
- Bridget Hall
- Heidi Klum
- Maggie Grace
- Lauren Weisberger (uncredited) as the twins' nanny

Production

Director David Frankel and producer Wendy Finerman had originally read *The Devil Wears Prada* in book proposal form.[4] It would be Frankel's second theatrical feature. He, cinematographer Florian Ballhaus and costume designer Patricia Field, drew heavily on their experience in making *Sex and the City*.

Filming

Principal photography took place over 57 days in New York and Paris between October and December 2005.[5] The film's budget was $35 million.[1]

Hathaway between takes while shooting a scene in Midtown Manhattan

Ballhaus, at Finerman and Frankel's suggestion, composed as many shots as possible, whether interiors or exteriors, to at least partially take in busy New York street scenes in the background, to convey the excitement of working in a glamorous industry in New York. He also used a handheld camera during some of the busier meeting scenes in Miranda's office, to better convey the flow of action, and slow motion for Andrea's entrance into the office following her makeover. A few process shots were necessary, mainly to put exterior views behind windows on sets and in the Mercedes where Miranda and Andrea are having their climactic conversation.[5]

Acting

Streep made a conscious decision not to play the part as a direct impression of Wintour,[6] right down to not using an accent and making the character American rather than English ("I felt it was too restricting").[7] "I think she wanted people not to confuse the character of Miranda Priestly with Anna Wintour at all," said Frankel. "And that's why early on in the process she decided on a very different look for her and a different approach to the character."[4] The "that's all,"[8] "please bore someone else ..."[9] catch phrases; her coat-tossing on Andrea's desk[10] and discarded steak lunch[11] are retained from the novel. Streep prepared by reading a book by Wintour protegé Liz Tilberis and the memos of *Vogue* editor Diana Vreeland. She lost enough weight during shooting that the clothes had to be taken in.[6]

Hathaway prepared for the part by volunteering for a week as an assistant at an auction house; Frankel said she was "terrified" before starting her first scene with Streep. The older actress began her working relationship with Hathaway by saying first "I think you're perfect for the role and I'm so happy we're going to be working on this together" then warning her that was the last nice thing she would say.[12] Streep applied this philosophy to everyone else on set as well, keeping her distance from the cast and crewmembers unless it was necessary to discuss something with her.[5]

She also suggested the editorial meeting scene, which does not advance the plot but shows Miranda at work without Andrea present.[13] It was also her idea that Miranda not wear makeup in the scene where she opens up to Andrea and worries about the effect on her daughters of her divorce becoming public knowledge.[4]

Costuming

Frankel, who had worked with Patricia Field, before on his feature-film debut, *Miami Rhapsody* as well as *Sex and the City*, knew that what the cast wore would be of utmost importance in a movie set in the fashion industry. "My approach was to hire her and then leave the room," he joked later.[14]

While none appeared onscreen, designers were very helpful to Field. Her $100,000 budget for the film's costumes was supplemented by help from friends from throughout the industry. Ultimately, she believes, at least $1 million worth of clothing was used in the film, making it one of the most expensively costumed movies in cinema history.[2] The single priciest item was a $100,000 Fred Leighton necklace on Streep.[15]

Chanel asked to dress Hathaway for the film, and Dolce & Gabbana and Calvin Klein helped Field as well. Although Field avoids making Streep look like Wintour, she dresses her in generous helpings of Prada. (By Field's own estimate, 40% of the shoes on Streep's feet are Prada.) Field added that much of the audience would not be familiar with Wintour's look and that "Meryl looks nothing like Anna, so even if I wanted to copy Anna, I couldn't."[2] But, like Wintour and her *Vogue* predecessor Diana Vreeland, the two realized that Miranda needed a signature look, which was provided primarily by the white wig and forelock she wore as well as the clothes the two spent much time poring over look-books for.[4] Field said she avoided prevailing fashion trends for Miranda during production in favor of a more timeless look based on Donna Karan archives and pieces by Michaele Vollbracht for Bill Blass,[16] a look she describes as "rich-lady clothes."[2] She didn't want people to easily recognize what Miranda was wearing.[17]

Emily Blunt in the appearance Field created for her character.

She contrasted Andrea and Emily by giving Andrea a "textbook" sense of style, without much risk-taking, that would suggest clothing a fashion magazine would have on hand for shoots.[2] Much of her high-fashion wardrobe is, indeed, Chanel, with some Calvin Klein thrown in for good measure.[17] Blunt, on the other hand was "so on the edge she's almost falling off."[18] For her, Field chose pieces by Vivienne Westwood and Rick Owens, to suggest a taste for funkier, more "underground" clothing.[17] After the film's release, some of the looks Field chose became popular, to the filmmakers' amusement.[13] [19]

Tucci praised Field's skill in putting ensembles together that were not only stylish but helped him develop his character:

> She just sort of sits there with her cigarette and her hair, and she would pull stuff — these very disparate elements — and put them together into this ensemble, and you'd go, "Come on, Pat, you can't wear that with that." She'd say, "Eh, just try it on." So you'd put it on, and not only did it work, but it works on so many different levels — and it allows you to figure out who the guy is. Those outfits achieve exactly what I was trying to achieve. There's flamboyance, there's real risk-taking, but when I walk into the room, it's not flashy. It's actually very subtle. You look at it and you go, "That shirt, that tie, that jacket, that vest? What?" But it works.[20]

He found one Dries van Noten tie he wore during the film to his liking and kept it.[20]

Production design

After touring some offices of real fashion magazines, Jess Gonchor gave the *Runway* offices a clean, white look meant to suggest a makeup compact[5] ("the chaste beiges and whites of impervious authority," Denby called it[21]). Miranda's office bears some strong similarities to the real office of Anna Wintour, down to an octagonal mirror on the wall, photographs and a floral arrangement on the desk[22] (a similarity so marked Wintour had her office redecorated after the movie[2]). The magazine itself is very similar to *Vogue*, and one of the covers on the wall of the office, showing three models, is a direct homage to the August 2004 cover of that magazine.[23]

Miranda Priestly's office design in film, showing its strong resemblance to that of Anna Wintour

She even chose separate computer wallpaper to highlight different aspects of Blunt's and Hathaway's character: Paris's Arc de Triomphe on Blunt's suggests her aspirations to accompany Miranda to the shows there, while the floral image on Andy's suggests the natural, unassuming qualities she displays at the outset of her tenure with the magazine. For the photo of Andrea with her parents, Hathaway posed with her own mother and David Marshall Grant.[5] One of the purported Harry Potter manuscripts was later sold at auction for $586 on eBay, along with various clothing used in the film, to benefit Dress for Success, a charity which provides business clothing to help women transition into the workforce.[24]

Products

Aside from the clothing and accessories, some other well-known brands are conspicuous in the film.

- Apple computers are used in the *Runway* offices, consistent with many real publishing companies.
- Bottles of Italian San Pellegrino mineral water are seen in the *Runway* offices.
- Miranda drinks coffee from a nearby Starbucks.
- Andrea uses a Danger Hiptop 2 (or a T-Mobile Sidekick 2) mobile phone, and Miranda a Motorola RAZR V3 in silver, same as Nigel's.
- The two are frequently driven around in Lincoln Town Cars and Mercedes-Benz S-Class S550 (without Vehicle registration plate) sedans.

Locations

New York

- The News Corporation building on Sixth Avenue was used for the exteriors and lobby of Elias-Clark's headquarters.
- The *Runway* offices are partially corridors in the neighboring Fox building and partially sets.[5]
- The Elias-Clark cafeteria is the one at the Reuters office in Manhattan.[5]
- Nate and Andy's apartment is on the Lower East Side.[19]
- The restaurant Nate works at (and where Andrea, Doug and Lily eat dinner on occasion) is in TriBeCa.[19]
- The Smith and Wollensky and its kitchen were used.[5]
- The Calvin Klein showroom is used in the deleted scenes.[25]

The McGraw-Hill Building, home to Elias-Clark in the film

- Holt's studio is a loft used by an actual designer.[19]
- The American Museum of Natural History was used for the exterior of the museum benefit, while the lobby of one of the Foley Square courthouses is used for the interior.[5]

- The Priestly townhouse is on the Upper East Side and belongs to a friend of Finerman's. It had to be dressed on short notice after another one could not be used.[19]
- The Amtrak train the twins are taking is going up the Hudson River at Haverstraw Bay.
- Streep exits her limousine, supposedly in Paris, at 77th Street and Central Park West.
- The *New York Mirror* newsroom where Andrea gets hired at the end of the film is that of the *New York Sun*.[5]

Paris

The crew was in Paris for only two days, and used only exteriors. Streep did not make the trip.[4]

- The fountain Andy throws her phone into is on the Place de la Concorde.
- All the hotel interiors are actually the St. Regis in Manhattan. The fashion shows were filmed on a soundstage in Queens. Likewise, Christian's hotel is the Times Square W Hotel[5]

Post-production

Editing

Mark Livolsi realized, as McKenna had on the other end, that the film worked best when it focused on the Andrea-Miranda storyline. Accordingly, he cut a number of primarily transitional scenes, such as Andrea's job interview and the *Runway* staff's trip to Holt's studio. He also took out a scene early on where Miranda complimented Andrea. Upon reviewing them for the DVD, Frankel admitted he hadn't even seen them before, since Livolsi didn't include them in any prints he sent to the director.[25]

Frankel praised Livolsi for making the film's four key montages — the opening credits, Miranda's coat-tossing, Andrea's makeover and the Paris introduction — work. The third was particularly challenging as it uses passing cars and other obstructions to cover Hathaway's changes of outfit. Some scenes were also created in the editing room, such as the reception at the museum, where Livolsi wove B-roll footage in to keep the action flowing.[5]

Music

Composer Theodore Shapiro relied heavily on guitar and percussion, with the backing of a full orchestra, to capture a contemporary urban sound. He ultimately wrote 35 minutes of music for the film, which were performed and recorded by the Hollywood Studio Symphony, conducted by Pete Anthony.[26] His work was balanced with songs by U2 ("City of Blinding Lights," Miranda and Andrea in Paris), Madonna ("Vogue" & "Jump," Andrea's fashion montage & her first day on the job, respectively), KT Tunstall ("Suddenly I See," female montage during opening credits), Alanis Morissette ("Crazy," Central Park photo shoot), Bitter:Sweet ("Our Remains," Andrea picks up James Holt's sketches for Miranda; Bittersweet Faith, Lily's art show), Azure Ray ("Sleep," following the breakdown of her relationship with Nate), Jamiroquai ("Seven Days In Sunny June," Andrea and Christian meet at James Holt's party) among others. Frankel had wanted to use "City of Blinding Lights" in the film since he had used it as a soundtrack to a video montage of Paris scenes he had put together after scouting locations there.[5] Likewise, Field had advocated just as strongly for "Vogue."[17]

The soundtrack album was released on July 11 by Warner Music. It includes all the songs mentioned above (except Madonna's "Jump") as well as a suite of Shapiro's themes. Among the tracks not included is "Suddenly I See," which disappointed many fans.[27] It became popular as a result of the film although the single did not crack the U.S. Top Forty. It nonetheless became a popular radio hit.[28]

Pre-release and marketing

Two decisions by 20th Century Fox's marketing department that were meant to be preliminary wound up being integral to promoting the film. The first was the creation of the red stiletto heel ending in a pitchfork as the film's teaser poster.[29] It was so successful and effective, becoming almost "iconic" (in Finerman's words), that it was used for the actual release poster as well. It became a brand, and was eventually used on every medium related to the film — the tie-in reprinting of the novel and the soundtrack and DVD covers as well.[4]

The studio also put together a trailer of scenes and images strictly from the first three minutes of the film, in which Andrea meets Miranda for the first time, to be used at previews and film festivals until they could create a more standard trailer drawing from the whole film. But, again, this proved so effective with early audiences it was retained as the main trailer, since it created anticipation for the rest of the film without giving anything away.[4]

Reception

The film did surprisingly well[30] with audiences both inside and outside the U.S. Critics gave a fairly positive reaction to the film as a whole. Streep's performance drew universal acclaim, with some going as far as saying it was the only reason to see the film.

Critical response

Metacritic reported the film had an average score of 62%, based on 40 reviews.[31] The film holds a 75% fresh rating on Rotten Tomatoes based on 184 reviews.[32]

Initial reviews of the film focused primarily on Streep's performance, praising her for making an extremely unsympathetic character far more complex than she had been in the novel. "With her silver hair and pale skin, her whispery diction as perfect as her posture, Ms. Streep's

The stars of *The Devil Wears Prada* at the Venice premiere

Miranda inspires both terror and a measure of awe," wrote A. O. Scott in *The New York Times*. "No longer simply the incarnation of evil, she is now a vision of aristocratic, purposeful and surprisingly human grace."[33] Kyle Smith agreed at the *New York Post*: "The snaky Streep wisely chooses not to imitate *Vogue* editrix Anna Wintour, the inspiration for the book, but creates her own surprisingly believable character."[34] "Wintour should be flattered by Streep's portrayal," agreed Jack Mathews in the *Daily News*.[35]

David Edelstein, in *New York* magazine, criticized the film as "thin", but praised Streep for her "fabulous minimalist performance."[36] J. Hoberman, Edelstein's onetime colleague at *The Village Voice*, called the movie an improvement on the book and said Streep was "the scariest, most nuanced, funniest movie villainess since Tilda Swinton's nazified White Witch [in 2005's *The Chronicles of Narnia: The Lion, the Witch and the Wardrobe*]."[37]

Blunt, too, earned some favorable notice. "[She] has many of the movie's best lines and steals nearly every scene she's in," wrote Clifford Pugh in the *Houston Chronicle*.[38] Other reviewers and fans concurred.[39] [40]

Roger Ebert gave the movie "thumbs down,"[41] while Richard Roeper gave it a "thumbs up."[42]

While all critics were in agreement about Streep and Blunt, they pointed to other weaknesses, particularly in the story. Reviewers familiar with Weisberger's novel assented to her judgement that McKenna's script greatly improved upon it.[21] [33] A rare exception was Angela Baldassare at MSN Canada, who felt the film needed more of the nastiness others had told her was abundant in the novel.[43]

David Denby summed up this response in his *New Yorker* review: "*The Devil Wears Prada* tells a familiar story, and it never goes much below the surface of what it has to tell. Still, what a surface!"[21]

Reactions to Hathaway's performance were not as unanimous as for many of her costars. Denby said "she suggests, with no more than a panicky sidelong glance, what Weisberger takes pages to describe."[21] On the other hand, to Baldassare, she "barely carrie[d] the load."[43]

Amid the generally positive reception for the film, there were two criticisms apart from aesthetics. Some journalists familiar with the fashion world thought its portrayal unrealistic, and some gay viewers took issue with how the film presented Nigel.

Depiction of fashion industry

Some media outlets allowed their present or former fashion reporters to weigh in on how realistic the movie was. Their responses varied widely.

Booth Moore at *Los Angeles Times* chided Field for creating a "fine fashion fantasy with little to do with reality," a world that reflects what outsiders think fashion is like rather than what the industry actually is. Unlike the movie, in her experience fashionistas were less likely to wear makeup and more likely to value edgier dressing styles (that would not include toe rings).[44] "If they want a documentary, they can watch the History Channel," retorted Field.[45] Another newspaper fashion writer, Hadley Freeman of *The Guardian*, likewise complained the film was awash in the sexism and clichés that, to her, beset movies about fashion in general.[46]

Charla Krupp, the executive editor of SHOP, Inc., says "It's the first film I've seen that got it right ... [It] has the nuances of the politics and the tension better than any film — and the backstabbing and sucking-up."[15] Joanna Coles, the editor of the U.S. edition of *Marie Claire*, agreed:

> The film brilliantly skewers a particular kind of young woman who lives, breathes, thinks fashion above all else ... those young women who are prepared to die rather than go without the latest Muse bag from Yves Saint Laurent that costs three times their monthly salary. It's also accurate in its understanding of the relationship between the editor-in-chief and the assistant.[15]

Ginia Bellefante, former fashion reporter for *The New York Times*, also agreed, calling it "easily the truest portrayal of fashion culture since *Unzipped*" and giving it credit for depicting the way fashion had changed in the early 21st century.[47] Her colleague Ruth La Ferla found a different opinion from industry insiders after a special preview screening. Most found the fashion in the movie too safe and the beauty too overstated, more in tune with the 1980s than the 2000s. "My job is to present an entertainment, a world people can visit and take a little trip," responded Field.[45]

Nigel's homosexuality

Stanley Tucci told the gay magazine *Out* that he played the part with no doubt whatsoever that the character was gay.[20] While many viewers, gay and straight, shared the assumption, nothing in the film directly suggests his sexual orientation other than a brief glance he makes at an attractive man.[48] In the novel, he, and the other male *Runway* staffers are very out, often described as flamboyant,[49] freely discussing their sex lives,[50] and sometimes checking each other out.[51]

There is none of this in the film. Instead, Nigel tells Andrea that, as a child, he told his family he was attending soccer practice when he was really taking sewing lessons, and read *Runway* under the covers of his bed at night with a flashlight. Finerman also says that during his first scene in the film, his visit to Andrea's hotel room in Paris to celebrate his imminent promotion, they had not yet decided how "extravagant" he would be.[19] The film also gives no indication that he is involved in any male/female marriage or relationship with a woman. No other male staffer or editor has a significant part and indeed there is no reference to homosexuality at all. Jeffy and James, two of the gay men in the novel, were eliminated. One viewer, David Poland, pointed out this aspect of the film on his blog, *The Hot Button*, but noted it was part of a general desexualization that led him to call the movie *No Sex in the City*.[52] On the other hand, a gay viewer who blogs about gay content in movies as Queer Beacon, found Tucci's portrayal refreshingly free of overdone stereotypes,[53] while another gay blogger expressed his displeasure that a movie about an industry well-known for its openly gay men seemed so determined to avoid the subject.[54] Controversy notwithstanding, readers of Gay.com voted the film the best of 2006.[55] William Maltese, from AfterElton.com, called it "refreshing that the jokes in *Devil* do not come at Nigel's expense or because of his sexuality."[56] It is also mentioned that Nigel is key for Andy's transformation from ugly-duck-to-swan that propels her into the second half of the film.

Queer Beacon also wondered if Doug might be gay, since he is more aware of Miranda's importance to fashion than Andrea; also, later, when Lily takes him from Andrea at the gallery to introduce him to "someone he might find interesting," she doesn't specify that person's gender.[53] Sommer wrote that Doug was not written to be gay and was merely based on a friend of McKenna's.[57]

Commercial

On its opening weekend, the film was on 2,847 screens. It grossed $27 million, second only to the much bigger-budget *Superman Returns*, and added $13 million more during the first week. This success led Fox to add 35 more screens the next week, the widest domestic distribution the film enjoyed. Although it was never any week's top-grossing film, it remained in the top 10 through July. Its theatrical run continued through December 10, shortly before the DVD release.[58]

It had a very successful run in theaters, making nearly $125 million domestically and over $325 million worldwide,[1] a career high for Meryl Streep, until *Mamma Mia* was released in 2008 and surpassed it.

Anna Wintour, on whom Miranda is supposedly based, was at first skeptical of the film but later came to appreciate it.

Anna Wintour

Anna Wintour attended the film's New York premiere, wearing Prada. Her friend Barbara Amiel reported that she said shortly afterward that the movie would go straight to DVD.[59] But in an interview with Barbara Walters that aired the day the DVD was released, she called the film "really entertaining" and said she appreciated the "decisive" nature of Streep's portrayal. "Anything that makes fashion entertaining and glamorous and interesting is wonderful for our industry. So I was 100 percent behind it."[3] Streep said Wintour was "probably more upset by the book than the film."[60]

"Curse" on placed products

A couple of weeks after the film's release, Reuters reported a striking phenomenon: *All* of the publicly traded companies that made products featured in the film had seen their share prices fall in that time. Analysts attributed the fall to the effect of rising gas prices on the economy, which led many consumers to cut back their purchases of luxury brands, rather than anything associated with the film.[61]

International

Weisberger's novel had been translated into 37 different languages, giving the movie a strong potential foreign audience. It would ultimately deliver 60 percent of the film's gross.

The Devil Wears Prada topped the charts on its first major European release weekend on October 9, after a strong September Oceania and Latin America opening. It would be the highest-grossing film that weekend in Britain, Spain and Russia, taking in $41.5 million overall.[62] Continued strong weekends as it opened across the rest of Europe helped it remain atop the overseas charts for the rest of the month.[63] [64] [65] By the end of the year only its Chinese opening remained; it was released there on February 28, 2007.

Most reviews from the international press echoed the domestic response, heaping praise on Streep and the other actors, but calling the whole film "predictable."[66] *The Guardian*'s Peter Bradshaw, who found the film "moderately entertaining," took Blunt to task, calling her a "real disappointment ... strained and awkward."[67] In *The Independent*, Anthony Quinn said Streep "may just have given us a classic here" and concluded that the film as a whole was "as snappy and juicy as fresh bubblegum."[68]

In most markets the title remained unchanged; either the English was used or a translation into the local language. The only exceptions were Argentina, Ecuador, Mexico and Venezuela, where it was *El diablo que viste Prada* and *El diablo se viste à la moda*. In Poland, the title was *Diabel ubiera się u Prady* which roughly means "The Devil Dresses in Prada" rather than "The Devil Wears Prada." In Turkey, the title was "Şeytan Marka Giyer," roughly translated as "The Devil Wears Brand-Names." In Romania, the title was "Diavolul se îmbracă de la Prada," which roughly means "The Devil Dresses itself from Prada", the same construction being found in the French title, "Le Diable s'habille en Prada". The Japanese version is titled "プラダを着た悪魔", which translates as "The devil who wore Prada".

Awards and nominations

Three months after the film's North American release (October 2006), Frankel and Weisberger jointly accepted the first Quill *Variety* Blockbuster Book to Film Award. A committee of staffers at the magazine made the nominations and chose the award winner. Editor Peter Bart praised both works.

> The Devil Wears Prada' is an energetically directed, perfect-fit of a film that has surprised some in the industry with its box-office legs. It has delighted the country, much as did Lauren Weisberger's book, which is still going strong on several national bestseller lists[69]

The film was honored by the National Board of Review as one of the year's ten best.[70] The American Film Institute gave the film similar recognition.[71]

The film received ample attention from the Hollywood Foreign Press Association when its Golden Globe Award nominations were announced on December 14, 2006. The film itself was in the running for Best Picture (Comedy/Musical) and Supporting Actress (for Blunt). Streep later won the Globe for Best Actress (Musical/Comedy).[72]

On January 4, 2007, her fellow members of the Screen Actors Guild nominated Streep for Best Actress as well.[73] Four days later, at the National Society of Film Critics awards, Streep won Best Supporting Actress for her work both in *Devil* and *A Prairie Home Companion*.[74] McKenna earned a nomination from the Writers Guild of America Award for Best Adapted Screenplay on January 11, 2007.[75]

The following day, the British Academy of Film and Television Arts announced its 2006 nominations; Blunt, Field, McKenna and Streep were all among the nominees, as were makeup artist and hairstylists Nicki Ledermann and Angel de Angelis.[76]

On January 23, 2007 Streep received her 14th Academy Award nomination for Best Actress, lengthening her record from 13 for most nominations by any actor male or female. Field received a Costume Design nomination as well.[77] Neither won, but Blunt and Hathaway presented the last mentioned award, amusing the audience by slipping into their characters for a few lines, nervously asking which of them had gotten Streep her cappucino. Streep played along with a stern expression before smiling.[78]

Proposed Television Series

The success of the film lead to a proposed, but unrealised, American dramedy series that was in contention to air for the 2007-08 television season on Fox. It was to be produced by Fox Television Studios.

The series was to be based on the book and 2006 film (which was produced by 20th Century Fox), but with the premise adjusted for the confines of a traditional half-hour or one-hour dramedy with a single camera set-up. Fox TV president Angela Shapiro-Mathes told *Variety*: "The TV series will not be exactly like the movie or the book. The reason you loved the book and the reason you loved the movie was these were characters you really cared about in a world you wanted to learn more about. You can't read that book and not feel that the two characters are ones that you want to keep following. It's something you can get really passionate about."[79] The project never got to the pilot stage, and was shelved.

Home media

The DVD has, in addition to the film, the following extras:[30]

- Audio commentary from Frankel, editor Mark Livolsi, Field, screenwriter Aline Brosh McKenna, producer Wendy Finerman and cinematographer Florian Ballhaus.
- A five-minute blooper reel featuring, among other shots, unintentional pratfalls by Hathaway due to the high stiletto heels she had to wear. It also includes gag shots such as a chubby crewmember in loose-fitting clothing walking along the runway at the fashion show, and Streep announcing "I have some nude photographs to show you" at the Paris brunch scene.[80] Unlike most blooper reels, it is not a collection of sequential takes but rather a fast-paced montage set to music from the film with many backstage shots and a split screenshot allowing the viewer to compare the actual shot with the blooper. The many shots of actors touching their noses are, Rich Sommer says, a game played to assign blame for ruined takes.[81]
- Five featurettes
    - "Trip to the Big Screen," a 12-minute look at the film's pre-production, discussing the changes made from the novel, how Frankel was chosen to direct and other issues.
    - "NYC and Fashion," a look at the real New York fashion scene and how it is portrayed in the film.
    - "Fashion Visionary Patricia Field," a profile of the film's costume designer.
    - "Getting Valentino," covering how the designer was persuaded to appear as himself in the film.
    - "Boss From Hell," a short segment on difficult, nightmarish superiors like Priestly.
- Fifteen deleted scenes, with commentary from Frankel and Livolsi available (see below).
- The theatrical trailer, and promotional spots for the soundtrack album and other releases.

Closed captions in French and Spanish are also available. The DVD is available in both full screen and widescreen versions. Pictures of the cast and the tagline "Hell on Heels" were added to the red-heel image for the cover. It was released in the UK on February 5, 2007.

A Blu-ray Disc of the film was released simultaneuously with the DVD. The featurettes were dropped and replaced with a subtitle pop-up trivia track that can be watched by itself or along with the audio commentary.[82]

Reception

Immediately upon its December 12 release, it became the top rental in the USA. It held that spot through the end of the year, adding another $26.5 million to the film's grosses.[83] The following week it made its debut on the DVD sales charts in third position.[84]

Deleted scenes

Among the deleted scenes are some that added more background information to the story, with commentary available by the editor and director. Most were deleted by Livolsi in favor of keeping the plot focused on the conflict between Miranda and Andrea, often without consulting Frankel.[25]

Frankel generally approved of his editor's choices, but differed on one scene, showing Andrea on her errand to the Calvin Klein showroom. He felt that scene showed Andrea's job was about more than running personal errands for Miranda.[25]

See also

The September Issue; a 2009 documentary film which follows Anna Wintour prior to the release of the September 2007 *Vogue* issue.

Works cited

- Weisberger, Lauren; *The Devil Wears Prada,* Broadway Books, New York 2003, ISBN 0-7679-1476-7

External links

- Official website [85]
- *The Devil Wears Prada* [86] at Allmovie
- DVD site [87]
- *The Devil Wears Prada* [88] at the Internet Movie Database
- The Devil Wears Prada soundtrack [89] questions, answers and other music information
- On location photos on [[Flickr [90]]]
- Anne Hathaway interview [91] at stv.tv
- Rich Sommer's blog posts on the movie [92] (includes full gag reel).
- See where the outfits in the movie came from [93]

References

[1] The Devil Wears Prada (http://www.boxofficemojo.com/movies/?id=devilwearsprada.htm) at boxofficemojo.com, retrieved September 15, 2006.

[2] Whitworth, Melissa; June 9, 2006; " The Devil has all the best costumes (http://www.telegraph.co.uk/fashion/main.jhtml?xml=/fashion/2006/09/06/efpatricia06.xml)"; *The Daily Telegraph*; retrieved January 10, 2007.

[3] Walters, Barbara; December 12, 2006; Anna Wintour: Always in Vogue (http://abcnews.go.com/2020/story?id=2716887&page=3); "The 10 Most Fascinating People of 2006"; retrieved from abcnews.go.com December 18, 2006.

[4] Grove, Martin A. *The Hollywood Reporter*. " Oscar-Worthy 'Devil Wears Prada' Most Enjoyable Film in Long Time: 'The Hollywood Reporter' (http://web.archive.org/web/20060708134342/http://www.thebookstandard.com/bookstandard/news/hollywood/article_display.jsp?vnu_content_id=1002763479)." June 28, 2006; retrieved July 4, 2008

[5] Frankel, David (2006). Commentary track on *The Devil Wears Prada* [DVD]. USA: 20th Century Fox.

[6] January 31, 2007; Exclusive Interview: Meryl Streep (http://web.archive.org/web/20070830012928/http://www.who.com/who/magazine/article/0,19636,7401070219-1583696,00.html); *Who*; retrieved July 4, 2008. "I wanted the freedom to make this person up"

[7] Davies, Hugh; September 9, 2006; " Meryl Streep plays the Devil her own way (http://www.telegraph.co.uk/news/main.jhtml?xml=/news/2006/09/08/wvenice08.xml)"; *The Daily Telegraph*; retrieved January 10, 2007.

[8] Weisberger, 80.

[9] Weisberger, 204.

[10] Weisberger, 201.

[11] *Ibid.*, 150-51.

[12] Hill, Amelia; October 8, 2006; " The secret of success? Kindness (http://observer.guardian.co.uk/focus/story/0,,1890311,00.html)"; *The Observer*; retrieved January 10, 2007.

[13] McKenna, Aline Brosh (2006). Commentary track on *The Devil Wears Prada* [DVD]. USA: 20th Century Fox.

[14] Frankel, David. (2006). *"NYC and Fashion"* on *The Devil Wears Prada.* [DVD]. USA: 20th Century Fox.

[15] June 25, 2006; " Meet the acid queen of New York fashion (http://film.guardian.co.uk/features/featurepages/0,,1806322,00.html)"; *The Observer*; retrieved January 10, 2007.

[16] French, Serena; June 21, 2006; "The $1 Million Wardrobe"; *The New York Post*, 41-43

[17] Field, Patricia (2006). Commentary track on *The Devil Wears Prada* [DVD]. USA: 20th Century Fox. [18] Field, Patricia. (2006). *"NYC and Fashion" on The Devil Wears Prada*. [DVD]. USA: 20th Century Fox. [19] Finerman, Wendy. (2006). Commentary track on *The Devil Wears Prada* [DVD]. USA: 20th Century Fox.

[20] Lamphier, Jason; " Playing Devil's Advocate (http://www.out.com/detail.asp?id=18884)"; *Out*; retrieved January 9, 2007.

[21] Denby, David; July 3, 2006; " Dressed to Kill (http://www.newyorker.com/critics/cinema/articles/060710crci_cinema)"; *The New Yorker*; retrieved January 7, 2007

[22] See photos here (http://www.oficinadeestilo.com.br/blog/wp-content/office.jpg)

[23] Trivia for The Devil Wears Prada (http://www.imdb.com/title/tt0458352/trivia), retrieved from imdb.com December 24, 2006.

[24] "DEVIL WEARS PRADA Hero Faux "Harry Potter Book 7"!" (http://web.archive.org/web/20060820064047/http://cgi.ebay.com/ws/eBayISAPI.dll?ViewItem&item=200003242289). Archived from the original (http://cgi.ebay.com/ws/eBayISAPI.dll?ViewItem&item=200003242289#ebayphotohosting) on 2006-08-20. .; retrieved from ebay.com January 18, 2007.

[25] Frankel, David and Livolsi, Mark; commentary on deleted scenes on *The Devil Wears Prada* [DVD]. USA: 20th Century Fox.

[26] Goldwasser, Dan; May 3, 2006; Theodore Shapiro scores The Devil Wears Prada (http://www.soundtrack.net/news/article/?id=756); soundtrack.net; retrieved September 21, 2006.

[27] Customer reviews, as of December 12, 2006; *The Devil Wears Prada* (http://www.amazon.com/Devil-Wears-Prada-Original-Soundtrack/dp/B000FZESR6) soundtrack; amazon.com; retrieved December 18, 2006.

[28] "KT Tunstall: Artist Chart History" (http://web.archive.org/web/20070312040122/http://www.billboard.com/bbcom/retrieve_chart_history.do?model.vnuArtistId=646480&model.vnuAlbumId=761102). *Billboard*. Archived from the original (http://www.billboard.com/bbcom/retrieve_chart_history.do?model.vnuArtistId=646480&model.vnuAlbumId=761102) on March 12, 2007. . Retrieved July 23, 2006.

[29] Both the opening credit sequence and the clappers seen in the blooper reel use the same all-lower case Bodoni type for the title as the cover of the novel.

[30] DVD review: *The Devil Wears Prada* (http://www.currentfilm.com/dvdreviews8/devilwearspradadvd.html),currentfilm.com, retrieved December 9, 2006.

[31] "The Devil Wears Prada : Reviews" (http://www.metacritic.com/film/titles/devilwearsprada). *Metacritic*.Amazon.com. . Retrieved 2008-02-21.

[32] *The Devil Wears Prada* (http://www.rottentomatoes.com/m/the_devil_wears_prada/) at Rotten Tomatoes Flixster

[33] Scott, A.O.; June 30, 2006; " In 'The Devil Wears Prada,' Meryl Streep Plays the Terror of the Fashion World (http://movies.nytimes.com/2006/06/30/movies/30devi.html)"; *The New York Times*, retrieved June 30, 2006

[34] Smith, Kyle; June 30, 2006; Guy at the movies (http://www.moviecrazed.com/guymovies/crixdevprada.html) *The New York Post*; retrieved May 26, 2009

[35] Mathews, Jack; June 30, 2006; " She's devilicious: Streep a delight as infernal fashion diva in 'Prada' (http://www.nydailynews.com/entertainment/2006/06/30/2006-06-30_shes_devilicious_streep_a_delight_as_inf.html)"; The *New York Daily News*;retrieved June 30, 2006

[36] Edelstein, David; June 30, 2006; Review of *The Devil Wears Prada* (http://nymag.com/movies/listings/rv_52489.htm);*New York*; retrieved June 30, 2006.

[37] Hoberman, J.; June 27, 2006; Myths American (http://www.villagevoice.com/film/0626,hoberman,73669,20.html);*The Village Voice*; retrieved June 30, 2006.

[38] Pugh, Clifford; June 30, 2006; " More about runaway egos than runway ensembles (http://www.chron.com/disp/story.mpl/ent/movies/reviews/3965896.html)"; *Houston Chronicle*; retrieved December 24, 2006.

[39] Elliott, Michael; undated; A Movie Parable: The Devil Wears Prada (http://www.christiancritic.com/mov2006/devprada.asp); christiancritic.com; retrieved December 24, 2006. Archived (http://web.archive.org/web/20061126002104/http://www.christiancritic.com/mov2006/devprada.asp) November 26, 2006 at the Wayback Machine.

[40] Commentators on post by Slezak, Michael; August 11, 2006 *et seq.*; Who's your favorite summer-movie scene stealer? (http://popwatch.ew.com/popwatch/2006/08/whos_your_favor_1.html) popwatch; retrieved from ew.com December 24, 2006.

[41] Ebert, Roger; June 30, 2006; " The Devil Wears Prada (http://rogerebert.suntimes.com/apps/pbcs.dll/article?AID=/20060629/REVIEWS/60620007/1023)";*Chicago Sun-Times*; retrieved December 19, 2006.

[42] Ebert & Roeper, *The Devil Wears Prada* (http://tvplex.go.com/buenavista/ebertandroeper/mp3/060703-devil_wears_prada.mp3), retrieved December 19, 2006.

[43]   Baldassare, Angela; undated; " The Devil Wears Predictability (http://entertainment.sympatico.msn.ca/movies/articles/1375850. armx)"; sympatico.msn.ca; retrieved January 7, 2007, Archived (http://web.archive.org/web/20070614182736/http://entertainment. sympatico.msn.ca/movies/articles/1375850.armx) June 14, 2007 at the Wayback Machine.

[44]   Moore, Booth; June 30, 2006; "This fashion world exists only in the movies"; *Los Angeles Times*; quoted in Elsworth, Catherine; July 4, 2006; The Devil Makes a Fashion Faux Pas (http://blogs.telegraph.co.uk/foreign/catherineelsworth/july06/fashionfauxpas.htm) *The Daily Telegraph*; retrieved from telegraph.co.uk December 22, 2006.

[45]   La Ferla, Ruth; June 29, 2006; " The Duds of 'The Devil Wears Prada' (http://www.nytimes.com/2006/06/29/fashion/thursdaystyles/ 29PRADA.html?ex=1309233600&en=b6c00dd73e0b62e9&ei=5090&partner=rssuserland&emc=rss)"; *The New York Times*; retrieved January 18, 2007.

[46]   Freeman, Hadley; September 6, 2006; Prada and prejudice (http://www.guardian.co.uk/commentisfree/2006/sep/06/film.comment); *The Guardian*; retrieved January 10, 2007.

[47]   Bellefante, Ginia; June 18, 2006; " In 'The Devil Wears Prada,' It's Not Couture, It's Business (With Accessories) (http://www.nytimes. com/2006/06/18/movies/18bell.html?ex=1169010000&en=b66a0a85a204be9f&ei=5070)"; *The New York Times*; retrieved January 15, 2007.

[48]   June 30, 2006; Review: The Devil Wears Prada (http://www.screenit.com/movies/2006/the_devil_wears_prada.html);screenit.com; retrieved December 15, 2006.

[49]   Weisberger, 41.

[50]   Weisberger, 172.

[51]   Weisberger, 219-220.

[52]   Poland, Michael; June 23, 2006; blog entry for June 23, 2006 (http://www.thehotbutton.com/today/hot.button/2006_thb/060623_fri. html); The Hot Button; retrieved January 15, 2007.

[53]   July 3, 2006; " The Devil Wears Prada (http://queerbeacon.typepad.com/queer_beacon/2006/07/the_devil_wears.html)"; retrieved January 15, 2007.

[54]   July 6, 2006; " Just Don't Say the Word 'Gay' (http://ezculture.com/index.php/2006/07/06/flicks-just-dont-say-the-word-gay/)"; retrieved from ezculture.com January 15, 2007.

[55]   December 28, 2006; Winners: Gay.com Gay Vote Best of 2006! (http://www.gay.com/news/roundups/package.html?sernum=2964); retrieved January 16, 2007.

[56]   Maltese, William; July 3, 2006; The Devil Wears Prada, and Wears It Very Well Indeed (http://www.afterelton.com/archive/elton/ movies/2006/7/prada.html); AfterElton.com; retrieved May 18, 2008.

[57]   Sommer, Rich; July 10, 2006; " Poor, misunderstood Doug (http://richsommer.vox.com/library/post/poor-misunderstood-doug.html)"; retrieved from richsommer.vox.com on January 15, 2007.

[58]   The Devil Wears Prada (2006) - Weekend box office (http://www.boxofficemojo.com/movies/?page=weekend&id=devilwearsprada. htm), retrieved from boxofficemojo.com January 8, 2007.

[59]   Amiel, Barbara; July 2, 2006; " The 'Devil' I know (http://www.telegraph.co.uk/arts/main.jhtml?xml=/arts/2006/07/02/svdevil02. xml)"; *The Daily Telegraph*; retrieved January 10, 2007.

[60]   Brockes, Emma; September 23, 2006; " The devil in Ms Streep (http://film.guardian.co.uk/interview/interviewpages/0,,1879049,00. html)"; *The Guardian*; retrieved January 10, 2007.

[61]   Bhattarai, Abha; July 16, 2006; " Curse of the Devil Wears Prada (http://www.luxuryinstitute.com/doclib/doclib_popup. cgi?file=123-cb396e7bab9b8c0bcc24cde6e1e57d94.pdf)"; Reuters; retrieved January 17, 2007, from luxuryinstitute.com in .PDF format printed from *The Washington Post*.

[62]   Bresnan, Conor; October 9, 2006; " Around the World Roundup: 'Prada' Prances to the Top (http://www.boxofficemojo.com/news/ ?id=2173&p=.htm)"; boxofficemojo.com; retrieved January 8, 2007.

[63]   Bresnan, Conor; October 16, 2006; " Around the World Roundup: 'Prada' Parade Continues (http://www.boxofficemojo.com/news/ ?id=2180&p=.htm); boxofficemojo.com; retrieved January 8, 2007.

[64]   Bresnan, Conor; October 23, 2006; " Around the World Roundup: 'Prada' Struts to Third Victory (http://www.boxofficemojo.com/news/ ?id=2188&p=.htm)"; boxofficemojo.com; retrieved January 8, 2007.

[65]   Bresnan, Conor; October 30, 2006; " Around the World Roundup: 'Prada' Still in Vogue (http://www.boxofficemojo.com/news/ ?id=2192&p=.htm)"; boxofficemojo.com; retrieved January 8, 2007.

[66]   French, Philip; October 8, 2006; The Devil Wears Prada (http://film.guardian.co.uk/News_Story/Critic_Review/ Observer_Film_of_the_week/0,,1891091,00.html); *The Observer*; retrieved January 10, 2007.

[67]   Bradshaw, Peter; October 6, 2006; The Devil Wears Prada (http://arts.guardian.co.uk/filmandmusic/story/0,,1888063,00.html); *The Guardian*; retrieved January 10, 2007.

[68]   Quinn, Anthony; October 6, 2006; " Claws out, dressed to kill (http://web.archive.org/web/20061108015222/http://enjoyment. independent.co.uk/film/reviews/article1808686.ece)"; *The Independent; retrieved July 4, 2008.*

[69]   The Quills Literacy Foundation (2006-09-26). "The Quill Awards Announce The Devil Wears Prada as First Recipient of Its Variety Blockbuster Book to Film Award" (http://www.randomhouse.com/features/devilwearsprada/quills.html). Press release. . Retrieved 2006-12-16.

[70]   National Board of Review; Awards for 2006 (http://www.nbrmp.org/awards/); retrieved December 19, 2006.

[71]   American Film Institute; AFI Awards 2006 (http://www.afi.com/tvevents/afiawards06/default.aspx), retrieved December 19, 2006.

[72]   Hollywood Foreign Press Association; January 16, 2007; HFPA — Nominations and Winners (http://www.hfpa.org/nominations/index. html); retrieved January 16, 2007.

[73]   Screen Actors Guild; January 4, 2007; SAG Awards Official website (http://www.sagawards.org/PR_070104), retrieved from sagawards.org January 4, 2007.

[74]   Kilday, Gregg; January 8, 2007; National Society picks 'Pan' as best pic (http://www.hollywoodreporter.com/hr/content_display/film/ news/e3i5b2bddf1415bc8d7073596f319df0d11?imw=Y); *Hollywood Reporter*; retrieved January 10, 2007.

[75]   Writers Guild of America Award, 2007 WGA Award nominations (http://www.wga.org/awards/awardssub.aspx?id=1516); retrieved January 11, 2007.

[76]   British Academy of Film and Television Arts; January 12, 2007; LATEST WINNERS & NOMINEES (http://web.archive.org/web/ 20070820074034/http://www.bafta.org/site/page287.html); retrieved July 4, 2008.

[77]   Academy of Motion Picture Arts and Sciences, January 23, 2007; Nominations List: 79th Annual Academy Awards (http://www.oscars. org/79academyawards/noms.html), retrieved January 23, 2007. Archived (http://web.archive.org/web/20070123171029/http://www. oscars.org/79academyawards/noms.html) January 23, 2007 at the Wayback Machine.

[78]   Dehnhart, Andy; February 26, 2007; Oscar's best moments weren't in the script (http://www.msnbc.msn.com/id/17339214/); *MSNBC*; retrieved February 26, 2007.

[79]   "Variety" (October 11, 2006); subscrpition req. (http://www.variety.com/index.asp?layout=upsell_article&articleID=VR1117951748& categoryID=14&cs=1)

[80]   Blooper reel. (2006). *The Devil Wears Prada* [DVD]. USA: 20th Century Fox.

[81]   Sommer, Rich; January 3, 2007; " Fun (http://richsommer.vox.com/library/post/fun.html)"; retrieved January 16, 2007.

[82]   Bracke, Peter M.; December 11, 2006; " Blu-Ray Review: The Devil Wears Prada (http://bluray.highdefdigest.com/devilwearsprada. html)"; highdefdigest.com; retrieved January 18, 2007.

[83]   The Devil Wears Prada (2006) - DVD/Home Video rentals (http://www.boxofficemojo.com/movies/?page=homevideo& id=devilwearsprada.htm); retrieved from boxofficemojo.com January 8, 2007.

[84]   The Digital Entertainment Group; DVD Sales Charts (http://www.digitalentertainmentinfo.com/TitleSearch/titles.cfm); retrieved from digitalentertainment.info January 8, 2007.

[85]   http://www.devilwearsprada.com

[86]   http://www.allmovie.com/work/336015

[87]   http://www.thedevilwearspradadvd.com/

[88]   http://www.imdb.com/title/tt0458352/

[89]   http://www.soundtrackinfo.com/ost.asp?soundtrack=5656

[90]   http://www.flickr.com/photos/73516598@N00/tags/thedevilwearsprada/

[91]   http://www.stv.tv/out/showArticle.jsp?source=opencms&articleId=/out/hotnow/films/ Anne_Hathaway_-_The_Devil_Wears_Prada_In

[92]   http://richsommer.vox.com/library/posts/tags/devil+wears+prada/

[93]   http://www.celebritystyleguide.com/?op=component&sid=35&cid=196/

The Ant Bully (film)

The Ant Bully	
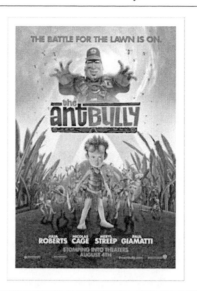	
Directed by	John A. Davis
Produced by	Tom Hanks Gary Goetzman John A. Davis
Written by	John A. Davis Book: John Nickle
Starring	Zach Tyler Eisen Julia Roberts Nicolas Cage Meryl Streep Paul Giamatti Regina King Bruce Campbell Lily Tomlin
Music by	John Debney
Cinematography	Ken Mitchroney
Editing by	Jon Price
Studio	Legendary Pictures DNA Productions Playtone
Distributed by	Warner Bros.
Release date(s)	July 28, 2006
Running time	89 minutes
Country	United States
Language	English
Budget	$50,000,000
Gross revenue	$55,181,129

The Ant Bully is a 2006 computer-animated film based on the 1999 children's book and produced by Tom Hanks and Gary Goetzman's Playtone, John Davis and Keith Alcorn's DNA Productions and directed by the aforementioned Davis. Released in movie theatres on July 28, 2006 by Warner Bros. and Legendary Pictures, it is based on a book by John Nickle and features the voices of Nicolas Cage, Julia Roberts, Meryl Streep, Allison Mack, Paul Giamatti and Ricardo Montalbán (in his final film role). Concurrently with the general release, the film was offered in big screen IMAX 3D, the format also used with *The Polar Express.*

Plot

The story is about a lonely 10-year-old, Lucas Nickle (Zach Tyler Eisen). His parents, who fail to understand him, go to Puerto Vallarta, leaving him with his older sister and his Grandmother, who obsesses over aliens. Tormented by a local bully, Lucas attacks an anthill with a squirt gun. This terrifies the ants. One ant, an eccentric wizard named Zoc (Nicolas Cage), tries to fight back. His girlfriend, a nurse ant named Hova (Julia Roberts), attempts to communicate with Lucas. She is almost crushed but is rescued by Zoc. The leaders of the colony decide to use a potion to shrink Lucas down to ant size.

Meanwhile, the local exterminator, Stan Beals (Paul Giamatti), convinces Lucas to sign a contract to kill vermin. Later, Zoc and a small troop of ants pour the potion into his ear. Lucas wakes up and discovers that he is now tiny. He is carried to the anthill into a world of giant caves, caterpillars and ants. Zoc insists that Lucas should be studied then eaten, but he is overruled by the Queen (Meryl Streep). She sentences Lucas to hard labor. Hova volunteers to train Lucas, much to Zoc's mortification. Hova and Lucas both learn about the differences between ants and humans. But when she forces him to forage for jelly beans with Kreela (Regina King) and Fugax (Bruce Campbell) Lucas is unsuccessful. The ants are attacked by wasps. Lucas finds a discarded firecracker and uses it to scare away the wasps. This earns him the admiration of all the ants – except Zoc.

Lucas is introduced to honeydew, the feces of caterpillars. He is shown a painting which depicts the Great Ant Mother and the evil "Cloud-Breather", an exterminator. Lucas is told that the Great Ant Mother will return and shower the ants with honeydew, while the Cloud-breather will spell destruction for all of them. He and his friends go back the house, where he tries to cancel the contract but dials for pizza instead. Then Lucas' sister comes home and they are forced into hiding until dark. When Zoc finds out that Lucas put Hova in possible danger, he accuses Lucas of further treachery and tells him that he should find another wizard because there is no way that he will give Lucas the potion to turn him back again. Lucas runs away, frightened, and Hova becomes angry with Zoc. But when Lucas is swallowed by a frog, Zoc frees him. Afterwards Zoc and Lucas discuss their differences. Zoc explains that ants work for the benefit of the colony. Lucas states that most humans work for personal gain. Zoc is confused as to how anything gets accomplished in Lucas' world.

They enlist the aid of the wasps; at first, the wasps want to eat Lucas, but hearing that their nest is destroyed by Beals, they agree to help. During the battle with the exterminator, Lucas saves the lives of Hova and an injured wasp. Both the ants and wasps were no match against pesticide, but as he is about to exterminate the ant hill, a beetle and glowworm manage to bite Beal. Lucas injects him with a shrinking potion. He runs away using a tricycle. The queen then pronounces Lucas an ant in honor of his heroic actions. Zoc gives him the antidote. Lucas grows back to normal size and finally stands up to the bully who runs away. Lucas then showers the colony with jelly beans as a farewell gift.

Cast

- Zach Tyler Eisen as Lucas Nickle, a boy whose family has moved into a new neighborhood where he gets tortured by a bully. He in turn attacks an ant hill to channel his anger, at the cost of being shrunk to ant size by the rebelling ant colony. He serves as the protagonist in the film.
- Nicolas Cage as Zoc, a wizard ant who wishes to use his magic to go the greater good for the colony. Despite his good intentions, he harbours a hatred against Lucas for attacking the ant hill until he realizes that Lucas isn't what he thought to be. He serves as the deuteragonist in the film.
- Julia Roberts as Hova, a worker ant who is assigned to teach Lucas about the ways of the ant and the first ant to see that there is goodness inside him.
- Regina King as Kreela
- Bruce Campbell as Fugax
- Paul Giamatti as Stan Beals, a local exterminator who convinces Lucas into signing a contract to exterminate all the pests around Lucas' house. He is believed to be known as the 'Cloud-Breather' who kills insects, and serves as the primary antagonist in the film.
- Meryl Streep as The Queen Ant
- Cheri Oteri as Doreen Nickle, Lucas' mother.
- Creagen Dow as Mullet Boy, the local neighborhood bully who likes to torture Lucas, as well as calling him 'Pucas'. Other than torturing Lucas, Mullet Boy also likes to torture his members of his gang. He serves as the secondary antagonist in the film.
- Larry Miller as Fred Nickle, Lucas' father.
- Clive Robertson as Wasp
- Lily Tomlin as Grandma (Mommo)
- Jake T. Austin as Nicky
- Don Frye as Soldier Ant
- Ricardo Montalban as The Head of Council
- Allison Mack as Tiffany Nickle, Lucas' older sister.
- Rob Paulsen as Beetle
- Tyler James Williams as Blue Teammate #1
- Jaishon Fisher as Blue Teammate #2
- Frank Welker as Spindle / Frog / Caterpillar
- Tom Kenny as Drone Ant
- Zack Shada as Blonde Boy (uncredited)
- Benjamin Bryan as Kid (uncredited)
- Jordan Orr as Ant (uncredited)

Development

Hanks originally conceived the idea for an animated film adaptation after reading the book with his child. He then sent a copy of the book to Davis because of Davis' work on the computer-animated film *Jimmy Neutron: Boy Genius*.[1] Davis came up with a potential take on the story within a few days. "To be honest, when I first looked at it, I thought Oh, why does it have to be ants again?" said Davis. "But the more I thought about it, I said, So what? It's got as much to do with *The Incredible Shrinking Man* as it does the other bug movies. It's a completely different story."[2] Also, Hanks agreed that the story could be expanded considerably (the original book being around only 2,000 words). Alcorn had a similar initial reaction to the project as Davis did. "My first thought," recalled Alcorn, "was, 'not another ant movie.' But looking at the actual story, this was really about a little boy and how he learns about the world by having to live beneath the surface."[3] Davis states that he felt like a something of a hypocrite when, while he was working on the script, carpenter ants infested his house and he called an exterminator.[4]

Technical information

The movie was rendered on DNA Productions' 1400-CPU render farm, managed by the open source Sun Grid Engine job scheduler. The nodes started out with Fedora Core 2 Linux with a modern 2.6.x kernel, but the new AMD Opteron nodes are running Fedora Core 4. Most of the applications are commercial, including Maya, Houdini, Massive and the Pixar RenderMan.[5]

IMAX 3D

Along with the theatrical release of *The Ant Bully*, there was an IMAX 3D version presented in only some of the IMAX theaters. The others continued to run the 3D version of *Superman Returns*. The special IMAX 3D version was remastered in 3D with IMAX DMR. Critics within the 3D motion picture community have given the film high marks, as unlike *Superman Returns*, the entire film is projected in 3D stereo. The process to turn a pure animation film into 3D is much simpler than converting a film having live actors.

Release

Box office

The Ant Bully closed on November 16, 2006, with $28 million in North America and a total of $55 million worldwide. The estimated production budget was $50 million.[6] Considering that studios receive just over half of the final gross, this is viewed as a box office disappointment, for *Monster House* and *Barnyard* both sold far more. The 3D version did considerably better per screen in its few playdates, though this is due partially to the higher admission prices of IMAX theaters.

Reception

The film garnered a 63% positive rating on Rotten Tomatoes. Tom Long of the Detroit News wrote that "there's a sweet simplicity and humility to this film." Ruthe Stein of *The San Francisco Chronicle* wrote that "the brilliance of *The Ant Bully* is in the crafty way it delves into the minds of ants as they plot to save themselves from extermination... Davis creates a marvelously labyrinthine society for them, right below the surface of a bland suburb." Lisa Schwarzbaum of *Entertainment Weekly* liked Roberts and Cage in their roles, and referred to Streep's queen ant as "excellently magisterial." She also wrote that "the kind of life lessons that usually gum up the fun go down as easily as jelly beans in *The Ant Bully*."[7] However, Jeffrey E. McCants of the Minneapolis *Star Tribune* wrote that "the film's heavy-handed lessons turn it from a fun romp through a cartoonish insect world to a predictable and preachy snoozefest". Lou Lumenick of the *New York Post* called the film "generic" and wrote that "adults will be less than enchanted by its preachiness, talkiness and Communist Party-line political views". Bill Muller of *The Arizona Republic* wrote that "*The Ant Bully*, in trying to match *Antz* or *A Bug's Life*, just digs itself into a big hole".[8] Jack Mathews of the New York *Daily News* was positive about the film's lack of pop culture references and thought that the film does not "talk down" to children. Additionally, he noted that "adults may be amused (or maybe not) by the Christian parallel in the ants' religion."[9]

Ratings

This film was rated PG by the MPAA for some mild rude humor and action.

Video game

Games publisher Midway released *The Ant Bully*, the official video game tie-in to the film on GameCube, PlayStation 2, PC, Wii and Game Boy Advance on July 24, 2006. The game was developed by the Montreal Studio Artificial Mind and Movement (A2M).

Soundtrack

The soundtrack's music score was composed and conducted by John Debney and there are no songs in this film. The entire movie score was released by Varèse Sarabande.

External links

- Official website [10]
- *The Ant Bully* [11] at the Internet Movie Database
- *The Ant Bully* [12] at Allmovie
- *The Ant Bully* [13] at Rotten Tomatoes
- *The Ant Bully* [14] at Box Office Mojo

References

[1] Comingsoon.net, (http://www.comingsoon.net/news/movienews.php?id=15686), Hanks and Davis on the Ant Bully, July 27, 2006

[2] Jenny Donelan, Computer Graphics World, September 2002, Volume 29 Number 9, pages 24–26

[3] John Cawley, Animation World Magazine, (http://mag.awn.com/index.php?article_no=2956), July 28, 2006

[4] Kotek, Elliot V. (2006). "John A. Davis: Ant Bully's Architect" (http://www.movingpicturesmagazine.com/features/themedarticle/johnadavis_antbully). Moving Pictures Magazine. . Retrieved 2008-11-24.

[5] "Making movies with Grid Engine" (http://gridengine.info/pages/profile-DNA-Productions)

[6] "Weekend Box Office Actuals (U.S.) Aug 4 - 6 weekend" (http://movies.yahoo.com/mv/boxoffice/weekend/2006/08/06)

[7] Entertainment Weekly, July 26, 2006, (http://www.ew.com/ew/article/0,,1219235,00.html)

[8] Azcentral.com, (http://www.azcentral.com/ent/movies/articles/0728antbully0728.html),accessed March 25, 2006

[9] Rotten Tomatoes, Top Critic Reviews, (http://www.rottentomatoes.com/m/ant_bully/?critic=creamcrop#mo), accessed March 25, 2008

[10] http://www.theantbully.com/

[11] http://www.imdb.com/title/tt0429589/

[12] http://www.allmovie.com/work/332269

[13] http://www.rottentomatoes.com/m/ant_bully/

[14] http://www.boxofficemojo.com/movies/?id=antbully.htm

Dark Matter (film)

Dark Matter	
Theatrical release poster	
Directed by	Chen Shi-zheng
Produced by	Janet Yang Mary Salter Andrea Miller
Written by	Billy Shebar
Starring	Liu Ye Aidan Quinn Meryl Streep
Release date(s)	2007 Sundance Film Festival April, 2008
Running time	90 min
Country	United States
Language	English

Dark Matter (simplified Chinese: 暗 物 质) is the first feature film by opera director Chen Shi-zheng, starring Liu Ye, Aidan Quinn and Meryl Streep. It won the Alfred P. Sloan Prize at the 2007 Sundance Film Festival.

Liu Ye plays a young scientist whose rising star must confront the dark forces of politics, ego, and cultural insensitivity. The film is based on true events.

Plot summary

The film is loosely inspired by the true story of Gang Lu, a Chinese physics graduate student who killed four faculty members and one student at the University of Iowa, although it has substantial differences in plot and character motivation. The film stars Liu Xing (Liu Ye) as a humble but brilliant Chinese student who arrives at Valley State University and makes a bumpy transition into American life with the help of Joanna Silver (Meryl Streep), a wealthy university patron who takes a liking to the young student. Xing joins a select cosmology group under the direction of his hero, the famous cosmologist Professor Jacob Reiser (Aidan Quinn). The group is working to create a model of the origins of the universe, based on Reiser's theory. Xing's enormous talent leads him quickly to become Reiser's protégé, and it seems that only hard work stands between him and a bright future in science. But Xing is obsessed with the study of dark matter, an unseen substance that he believes shapes the universe, and a theory that conflicts with the Reiser model. When Xing begins to make scientific breakthroughs of his own, he begins to encounter unexpected obstacles. Not being able to assimiliate, understand, or react appropriately to defend himself from the academic politics, he blames his mentors, and goes on a killing spree.

Soundtrack

No official soundtrack has been released. Here is a list of songs and production music featured in the film according to the end credits[1] .

- From 00:00:24 to 00:02:17, the song "Nostalgia" is used when Joanna Silver is playing Tai chi chuan and Liu Xing is waiting to see Professor Jacob Reiser. It is performed by the Beijing Angelic Choir. It is Track 13 from the choir's album "Praying" released by Wind Music. The name of this song should rather be known as "Going Home." It is based on Antonín Dvořák's Symphony No. 9 in E minor 'From The New World', Op. 95 - II. Largo.

- From 00:03:46 to 00:04:44, a lute version of the said music "Going Home" is used when Liu Xing finishes the meeting with Professor Jacob Reiser and is greeted by his secretary. It ends after Liu Xing enters the Cosmology Research Group and sits down putting a floppy into the computer. It is unknown who performs the music.

- From 00:05:07 to 00:05:25, the music "Square Wheels" is played when Liu Xing leaves the campus and goes back to his apartment. It is written by Simon Stewart and published by De Wolfe Music (ASCAP), known as American Society of Composers, Authors and Publishers.

- From 00:05:59 to 00:06:34, the music "Gettin' it On" is played when a porn movie is airing after Liu Xing's roommate manages to hook up the antenna. The music is said to be an 80's porn theme with sax, flutes & synth. "Funky" as advertised. It is written by Richard Boisson and published by ZFC Music (ASCAP), under license from FirstCom Music.

- From 00:08:36 to 00:09:00, Johann Sebastian Bach's "Brandenburg concertos#Brandenburg Concerto No. 5 in D major, BWV 1050" is used when Joanna Silver ignites her car and drives the students to a cowboy town. It is performed by Concerto Italiano & Rinaldo Alessandrini.

- From 00:09:39 to 00:10:01, a production music called "High Noon" is used when Liu Xing is ready to enter a "duet" with three other Chinese students dressed in cowboy costume. It is provided by APM Music LLC.

- From 00:10:05 to 00:10:08, the very beginning of the production music "Hot Desert" is used when the Chinese cowboys prepare to pull out their guns to duet. It is written by Tim Souster and published by Hudson Music (ASCAP), under License from De Wolfe Music.

- From 00:10:10 to 00:10:22, another western-styled music is played when Liu Xing and the other Chinese cowboys start to shoot at the other. The name of this music is not yet known.

- From 00:11:28 to 00:12:13, instrumentals of Bryan Bowers' version of "Red River Valley" is heard when Liu Xing is doing his studies and printing out his discovery. It is under license from Flying Fish / Rounder Records.

- From 00:15:33 to 00:16:06, Beijing Angelic Choir's "Old Black Joe" is used when Liu Xing is taking time off and having fun with his roommates. It is Track 3 from the choir's album "Praying" under license from Wind Music.

- From 00:18:43 to 00:19:42, the first movement of Wolfgang Amadeus Mozart's "Symphony No. 29 in A Major K. 201" is performed by the Unique Tracks Radio Orchestra when Liu Xing finishes the toast and explains dark matter to Joanna Silver.

- From 00:20:27 to 00:21:17, "Guantanamera" is performed by Joseíto Fernández when Liu Xing is having fun with his roommates and Liu Xing proposes a toast to himself, saying he is going to successfully tackle the dark matter issue and marry a white American girl.

- From 00:21:21 to 00:23:43, some disco-styled music is heard when Liu Xing goes into Beehive Tearoom and tries to hit on the tea lady. The name of this music is not yet known.
- From 00:26:56 to 00:27:30, Giacomo Puccini's "Tosca, Act III, 'E lucevan le stelle'" is performed by Jussi Björling when Professor Reiser says Liu Xing can always challenge him. It ends after Liu Xing and Joanna Silver leave Reiser's house in a car.
- From 00:33:23 to 00:33:43, the very beginning of the song "Bird Gehrl" is heard when Liu Xing is contemplating on the campus. It is composed by Antony Hegarty and performed by Antony and the Johnsons. It is Track 10 from the album "I'm a Bird Now."
- From 00:35:28 to 00:36:52, the production music titled "Shenandoah" under license from 5 Alarm Music is used when Liu Xing is reading on campus. The music ends when Liu Xing confronts with his colleague Feng Gang/Lawrence.
- From 00:45:53 to 00:46:15, some unknown production music is used when Liu Xing comes up with the idea how to tackle the dark matter issue and rushes to school to share his breakthrough with Professor Reiser.
- From 00:48:16 to 00:49:10, Beijing Angelic Choir's "Beautiful Dreamer" is used when Liu Xing walks in a wide-open field. It is Track 7 from the choir's album "Beautiful Dreamer" released by Wind Music.
- From 00:49:50 to 00:51:10, "La Rejouissance" under license from Cavendish Music / Non Stop Music can slightly be heard when Joanna Silver takes Liu Xing to a clothing store to check out a shirt for his dissertation presentation.
- From 00:52:14 to 00:52:45, VooDoo & Serano's "Cold Blood" is heard when Liu Xing awaits to give his dissertation presentation while his roommates are holding a party to congratulate his wouldbe ascension to PhD. It is written by Reinhard Raith and Andreas Litterscheid.
- From 00:54:50 to 00:55:16, "Cold Blood" is heard again when Liu Xing's dissertation presentation is rebuked.
- From 00:58:37 to 01:00:45, the song "Soft Black Stars" is heard when Liu Xing contemplates about his future and goes to the tea lady to express his feelings towards her and gets rejected. It is composed by David Tibet and performed by Antony and the Johnsons from the single "I Fell in Love with a Dead Boy."
- From 01:05:12 to 01:08:15, Johann Sebastian Bach's "Cantata #82, 'Ich habe genug'" is heard when Liu Xing goes to Joanna Silver's house to sell her skin care products. It is performed by Emmanuel Music Orchestra and conducted by Craig Smith, featuring Lorraine Hunt Lieberson.
- From 01:11:54 to 01:14:27, Beijing Angelic Choir's "Long Long Ago" is used when Liu Xing leaves Joanna Silver's house, failing to sell her the skin care products. He then writes a check bearing his savings over the years to his parents. It is Track 13 from the choir's album "Praying" released by Wind Music.
- From 01:14:57 to 01:19:48, Beijing Angelic Choir's "Serenade" is used when Liu Xing goes to Feng Gang/Lawrence's presentation, killing four people. It is Track 13 from the choir's album "Wild Roses" released by Wind Music. The music itself is originally composed by Franz Schubert.
- Through out the end credits, "This Land is Your Land" is used. It is written by Woody Guthrie and performed by Sharon Jones. The song is published by Ludlow Music.

So far, four pieces of music listed in the end credits cannot be identified. They could have been used in the said unidenfiable interval between 00:10:10 to 00:10:22 and 00:21:21 to 00:23:43. They are known as:

- "Hombre" written by John Leach and published by Hudson Music (ASCAP); under license from De Wolfe Music
- "Cappuccino" under license from 5 Alarm Music
- "Deep Thought" under license from 5 Alarm Music
- "From the Bench", the production music by Lazy Bones Records.

Release

This film's general US release date, originally set for April of 2007, was pushed back over a year because its plot line of an Asian student involved in a mass shooting on a US college campus too closely resembled the Virginia Tech massacre.[2] It was finally released in the US market in April of 2008.

Critical reception

Critics gave the film generally negative to mixed reviews. As of April 11, 2008, the review aggregator Rotten Tomatoes reported that 32% of critics gave the film positive reviews, based on 19 reviews.[3] Metacritic reported the film had an average score of 49 out of 100, based on 7 reviews.[4]

See also

- List of American films of 2007
- Gang Lu

External links

- Official site [5]
- *Dark Matter* [6] at the Internet Movie Database
- *Dark Matter* [7] at Rotten Tomatoes
- *Dark Matter* [8] at Metacritic
- *Dark Matter* [9] at Box Office Mojo
- *Dark Matter* [10] at Allmovie
- *Dark Matter* [11] at the 25th San Francisco International Asian American Film Festival
- *Dark Matter* [12] at sundance.org
- Dark Matter [13] Review by Orville Schell from *The New York Review of Books*

References

[1] "Dark Matter (2008) Cast & Credits - Music" (http://movies.yahoo.com/movie/1809721362/cast). *Dark Matter*. . Retrieved 2008-07-13.

[2] msnbc.msn.com, Streep film delayed because of campus shooting, updated 5:37 p.m. ET, Fri., Feb. 15, 2008 (http://www.msnbc.msn.com/id/23189744/)

[3] "Dark Matter Movie Reviews, Pictures - Rotten Tomatoes" (http://www.rottentomatoes.com/m/dark_matter/). Rotten Tomatoes. . Retrieved 2008-04-11.

[4] "Dark Matter (2008): Reviews" (http://www.metacritic.com/film/titles/darkmatter). Metacritic. . Retrieved 2008-04-11.

[5] http://www.darkmatterthefilm.com/

[6] http://www.imdb.com/title/tt0416675/

[7] http://www.rottentomatoes.com/m/dark_matter/

[8] http://www.metacritic.com/film/titles/darkmatter

[9] http://www.boxofficemojo.com/movies/?id=darkmatter.htm

[10] http://www.allmovie.com/work/316636

[11] http://www.asianamericanfilmfestival.org/2007/films-events/film-detail/?i=23

[12] http://festival.sundance.org/filmguide/popup.aspx?film=7541

[13] http://www.nybooks.com/articles/21715

Evening (film)

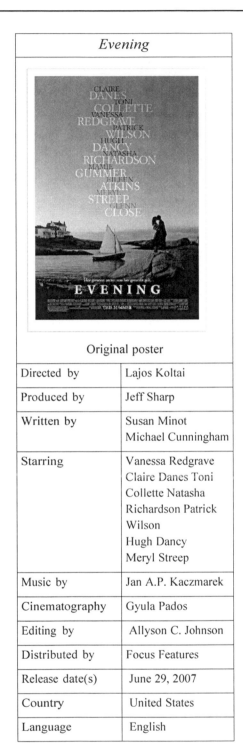

Evening	
Original poster	
Directed by	Lajos Koltai
Produced by	Jeff Sharp
Written by	Susan Minot Michael Cunningham
Starring	Vanessa Redgrave Claire Danes Toni Collette Natasha Richardson Patrick Wilson Hugh Dancy Meryl Streep
Music by	Jan A.P. Kaczmarek
Cinematography	Gyula Pados
Editing by	Allyson C. Johnson
Distributed by	Focus Features
Release date(s)	June 29, 2007
Country	United States
Language	English

Evening is a 2007 American drama film directed by Lajos Koltai. The screenplay by Susan Minot and Michael Cunningham is based on the 1998 novel of the same name by Susan Minot.

Plot

The film alternates between two time periods, the 1950s and the present, in which a dying Ann Grant Lord reflects on her past. Her confusing comments about people she never mentioned before leave her daughters, reserved Constance and restless Nina, wondering if their mother is delusional.

As a young woman in her early twenties, cabaret singer Ann arrives at the spacious Newport, Rhode Island, home of her best friend Lila Wittenborn, who is on the verge of getting married. Lila's brother (and Ann's college friend) Buddy introduces her to Harris Arden, the son of a former family servant. Buddy tells Ann his sister always has adored Harris, and expresses his concern that she's marrying another man out of a sense of duty rather than love. Inebriated, Buddy passes out, and as Ann and Harris chat they find themselves bonding.

On Lila's wedding day, she confesses to Ann she confronted Harris with her feelings for him and he rebuffed her, so she goes along with the ceremony as planned. At the reception, at Lila's request, Ann sings a song and is joined on stage by Harris. Afterwards Buddy, drunk again, confronts the two about their growing closeness and kisses Harris. As Lila prepares to depart with her new husband, Ann offers to take the bride away with her, but Lila refuses and leaves for her honeymoon.

Buddy admits to Ann he's had a crush on Harris since his childhood, though he also claims not to be "that way" - he denies that this would be okay as Ann assures him. He then changes the subject, confessing he has loved Ann ever since their college days, offering as proof a note she once sent him he has kept in his pocket ever since. Ann later expresses her anger at him for repressing his sexual orientation by building her up as his true love. She and Harris slip off to his secret hideaway, where the two make love.

Buddy, in search of the couple, stumbles into the road and is hit by a car. His friends find him, but too late to save his life. The following morning, Ann and Harris, oblivious to what transpired the night before, jokingly consider sailing away, but at the Wittenborn house they hear the tragic news.

In the present day, Lila arrives at Ann's bedside to comfort her and reminisce. Ann recalls a day when she ran into Harris in the street in New York City. By then she had one daughter and was on the verge of moving to Los Angeles, and he was married with a son. He intimated he still loved her before the two exchanged cordial goodbyes.

As Lila leaves, she tells Nina about Harris and reassures her that her mother did not make any mistakes in her life. Nina sits with Ann, who encourages her daughter to have a happy life. Nina finally musters up the courage to tell her boyfriend Luc she is pregnant with their child. An ecstatic Luc proudly announces the news to Constance and promises he always will be there for Nina. Their joy is interrupted by Ann's nurse, who urges the women to rush to their mother's bedside to bid her farewell.

Production notes

The original screenplay, as was the novel, was set in Maine, but according to the commentary on the DVD release of the film, director Lajos Koltai was so taken with the Newport house found by his location scouts he opted to change the setting. Tiverton and Providence, Rhode Island, Greenwich Village, and the Upper West Side of Manhattan also were used for external scenes.

The song "Time After Time" Ann sings for Lila at the wedding was written in 1947 by Sammy Cahn and Jule Styne. The song "I See the Moon" she later sings to her daughters is based on a traditional nursery rhyme.

The film is markedly different from the book, which was much darker and nihlistic. Whereas the film presents a love story between Harris and Ann, the book portrayed Harris as a callous womanizer with whom Ann became obsessed. A significant portion of the book is dedicated to telling the stories of Ann's three doomed marriages, each of which failed, in part, because of Ann's destructive infatuation with the absent Harris. Harris himself is presented as an enigmatic and unsympathetic character who carries on multiple affairs during the course of the wedding night, intent on returning home to marry his fiancee.

The film grossed $12,406,646 in the US and $478,928 in foreign markets for a total worldwide box office of $12,885,574.[1]

Principal cast

The 1950s

- Claire Danes ..... Ann Grant
- Mamie Gummer ..... Lila Wittenborn
- Patrick Wilson ..... Harris Arden
- Hugh Dancy ..... Buddy Wittenborn
- Glenn Close ..... Mrs. Wittenborn
- Barry Bostwick ..... Mr. Wittenborn

The Present

- Vanessa Redgrave ..... Ann Grant Lord
- Toni Collette ..... Nina Mars
- Natasha Richardson ..... Constance Haverford
- Meryl Streep ..... Lila Wittenborn Ross
- Ebon Moss-Bachrach..... Luc
- Eileen Atkins ..... Mrs. Brown, the Night Nurse

Additional production credits

- Production Design ..... Caroline Hanania
- Art Direction ..... Jordan Jacobs
- Set Decoration ..... Catherine Davis
- Costume Design ..... Ann Roth

Critical reception

Manohla Dargis of the *New York Times* said, "Stuffed with actors of variable talent, burdened with false, labored dialogue and distinguished by a florid visual style better suited to fairy tales and greeting cards, this miscalculation underlines what can happen when certain literary works meet the bottom line of the movies. It also proves that not every book deserves its own film."[2]

In the *San Francisco Chronicle*, Mick LaSalle observed, "The film arrives at a pessimistic and almost nihilistic view of life as something not very important - and then invites us to take strength and comfort in the notion. It's not what you'd expect, and it's certainly not the typical message. It might be the most interesting thing about the picture."[3]

Peter Travers of *Rolling Stone* rated the film 2½ out of a possible four stars and commented, "the actors . . . provide flashes of brilliance. Hugh Dancy scores as the plot's catalyst for tragedy. And Claire Danes is stellar as the young Ann . . . [Mamie] Gummer proves her talent is her own in a star-is-born performance that signals an exceptional career ahead."[4]

In the *St. Petersburg Times*, Steve Persall graded the film C and added, "Strong performances and an author's weak backbone make *Evening* a curious mistake . . . [it] is memorable only for lovely period designs and for casting mothers and daughters to ensure better continuity."[5]

Justin Chang of *Variety* said, "The more immediate problem with this ambitious, elliptical film is Koltai and editor Allyson C. Johnson's difficulty in establishing a narrative rhythm, as the back-and-forth shifts in time that seemed delicately free-associative on the page are rendered with considerably less grace onscreen. In ways reminiscent of Stephen Daldry's film of *The Hours*, the telling connections between past and present feel calculated rather than authentically illuminating."[6]

In *Time*, Richard Schickel said the film "represents perhaps the greatest diva round-up in modern movie history . . . Wow, you might think, how bad can *that* be? To which one responds, after two lugubrious hours in their company, really awful. Rarely have so many gifted women labored so tastefully to bring forth such a wee, lockjawed mouse . . . . This may in part because it was Michael Cunningham, author of the book *The Hours*, another stupefying exercise in unspoken angst, who was hired to punch up the script Susan Minot was trying to make out of her novel. They share screenplay credit for *Evening*, but even in the press kit you can sense her loathing for his work. He's sort of Henry James without the cojones and definitely the most constipated sensibility the literary community has lately been in awe of. But I suspect that the director, Lajos Koltai, a Hungarian, has even more to do with the film's inertness."[7]

Lisa Schwarzbaum of Entertainment Weekly rated Evening as the 2nd worst movie of 2007.[8]

See also

- List of American films of 2007

External links

- *Evening (film)* [9] at the Internet Movie Database

References

[1] *Evening* at *The Numbers* (http://www.the-numbers.com/movies/2007/EVNIN.php)

[2] *New York Times* review (http://movies.nytimes.com/2007/06/29/movies/29even.html)

[3] *San Francisco Chronicle* review (http://www.sfgate.com/cgi-bin/article.cgi?f=/c/a/2007/06/29/DDG2MQN4IE1.DTL)

[4] *Rolling Stone* review (http://www.rollingstone.com/reviews/movie/11781196/review/15040100/evening)

[5] *St. Petersburg Times* review (http://www.sptimes.com/2007/06/28/Movies/You_ve_read_the_book_.shtml)

[6] *Variety* review (http://www.variety.com/review/VE1117933970.html?categoryid=31&cs=1)

[7] *Time* review (http://www.time.com/time/arts/article/0,8599,1638792,00.html)

[8] (http://www.ew.com/ew/gallery/0,,20162677_20164091_20167446_3,00.html)

[9] http://www.imdb.com/title/tt0765447/

Rendition (film)

For the British 2007 film starring Andy Serkis see Extraordinary Rendition (film)

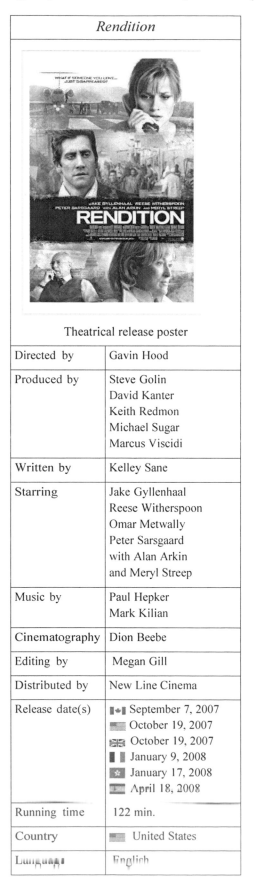

Rendition	
Theatrical release poster	
Directed by	Gavin Hood
Produced by	Steve Golin David Kanter Keith Redmon Michael Sugar Marcus Viscidi
Written by	Kelley Sane
Starring	Jake Gyllenhaal Reese Witherspoon Omar Metwally Peter Sarsgaard with Alan Arkin and Meryl Streep
Music by	Paul Hepker Mark Kilian
Cinematography	Dion Beebe
Editing by	Megan Gill
Distributed by	New Line Cinema
Release date(s)	September 7, 2007 October 19, 2007 October 19, 2007 January 9, 2008 January 17, 2008 April 18, 2008
Running time	122 min.
Country	United States
Language	English

Gross revenue	$27,038,732 (Worldwide)

Rendition is a 2007 drama film directed by Gavin Hood and starring Reese Witherspoon, Meryl Streep, Peter Sarsgaard, Alan Arkin, Jake Gyllenhaal, and Omar Metwally. It centers on the controversial CIA practice of extraordinary rendition, and is based on the true story of Khalid El-Masri who was mistaken for Khalid al-Masri. The movie also has similarities to the case of Maher Arar.

Synopsis

CIA analyst Douglas Freeman (Jake Gyllenhaal) is briefing a newly arrived CIA agent in a square in an unnamed country in North Africa (filmed in Marrakech) when a suicide attack kills the latter and eighteen other people. The target was a high ranking police official, Abasi Fawal (Yigal Naor), who is in liaison with the United States and whose tasks include conducting interrogations, and even overseeing the application of techniques amounting to torture. Fawal escapes unscathed.

Egyptian-born Anwar El-Ibrahimi (Omar Metwally), a chemical engineer who lives in Chicago with his pregnant wife Isabella (Reese Witherspoon), their young son and his mother, is linked to a violent organization by telephone records indicating that known terrorist Rashid placed several calls to Anwar's cell phone. While returning to the United States from a conference in South Africa, he is detained by American officials and sent to a secret detention facility near the location of the suicide attack depicted earlier, where he is interrogated and tortured. Isabella is not informed and all records of him being on the flight from South Africa are erased, although records remain of him boarding the plane at Cape Town Airport and making a purchase enroute.

For lack of more experienced staff, Freeman is assigned the task of observing the interrogation of Anwar, whose interrogator is Fawal himself. After Freeman briefly questions Anwar himself, he is convinced of Anwar's innocence. However, his boss, Corrine Whitman (Meryl Streep), insists that the detention continue, justifying such treatments as necessary to save thousands from becoming victims of terrorism.

Growing worried, Isabella travels to Washington DC, where she meets up with an old friend, Alan Smith (Peter Sarsgaard), who now works as an aide to Senator Hawkins (Alan Arkin), and pleads with him to find out what has happened to her husband. Initially, she is informed that there had been a mistake in South Africa and Anwar was not on the flight, but Isabella presents Anwar's credit card record, which shows that Anwar had purchased something in the in-flight duty free shop, thus confirming that he was on the flight. Smith slowly pieces together details of Anwar's detention. He is unable to convince the senator, nor Corrine Whitman, who had ordered the rendition, to give proper details of the detention, nor to release him. After the senator advises him to let it go, as he is currently fighting to have a bill passed in Congress and it is not the right time to start debating an extraordinary rendition, Smith advises Isabella to get a very good lawyer he knows on the case, but she refuses. Upon hearing the confrontation from her office, his sympathetic secretary quietly tips Isabella off on when Whitman will be next in the office. The next day, Isabella confronts Whitman, but Whitman pretends not to know anything and avoids her questions. Frustrated, Isabella storms out of the office, only to go into labour in the hallway.

Eventually, Anwar confesses to have advised Rashid on how to make more powerful bombs, and to have been promised $40,000 in return. Freeman, suspicious that it is a false confession, asks Anwar where the money is and Anwar's response is that it was supposed to be delivered to him in South Africa, but the courier failed to show up. Freeman's suspicions are confirmed when he has the names Anwar gives traced by Interpol and draws a blank. He then Googles the names and finds out that they are the names of the Egyptian football team from the year Anwar left Egypt. He also expresses doubt as to whether Anwar would be willing to put his life, family and job in danger for $40,000 when he earns $200,000 a year in his job. He quotes Shakespeare's *The Merchant of Venice* in a discussion with the minister of the interior on the value of intelligence gathered through torture:

> I fear you speak upon the rack
>
> Where men enforced do speak anything.

Without the consent of his superiors, and not caring what happens to him, Freeman gets a warrant for Anwar's release and sends him back to America via a clandestine ship to Spain. When Lee Mayers, his immediate boss, calls him to tell him to give Anwar back to Abasi Fawal, he simply hangs up. Angered by the injustice Anwar has suffered, Freeman then leaks the details of Anwar's detention to the American press, to the horror of Whitman and Senator Hawkins.

Another story line is shown in parallel. Abasi's daughter Fatima (Zineb Oukach) has run away from home with her boyfriend Khalid (Moa Khouas). Fatima sees a picture of Khalid's brother, but he does not tell her what has happened to him. Abasi is told that Khalid's brother was an inmate at his prison and later died. Fatima is unaware that Khalid is a member of a terrorist group until his friends are arrested at a planned march and he leads her to the terrorist group's base. Near the end of the movie, Fatima discovers a notebook that contains pictures of Khalid and his brother together, showing that they were extremely close, as well as a picture of the two brandishing AK-47s, then some pictures of a grief-stricken Khalid standing over his brother's corpse, some pictures of her father and finally a statement saying that Khalid is doing a deed in revenge for his brother's death. Realizing that Khalid's brother met his death at the hands of her father and that Khalid is about to assassinate him, she runs off. It is then revealed that this second story took place before the suicide attack (From the briefing with the CIA agent in the beginning we know that the first story took place AFTER the suicide attack). At the town square Fatima begs him not to do it, arguing that the target is her father. After removing the pin of his detonator he hesitates, and is therefore killed by the organizers of the attack. As a result he releases the handle of the detonator, and the bomb explodes, killing Fatima also. In the present, Abasi rushes to Khalid's apartment and discovers his grandmother, who is stricken with grief over the loss of both her grandchildren and Fatima. Abasi then realises that his daughter died trying to protect him and is filled with grief himself.

The record of a phone call supposedly made by Rashid to Anwar is not explained in the film. However, earlier it was mentioned that phones are sometimes passed on from one person to another (the DVD extras explain that there was a subplot dropped from the film that elaborated on this concept). Yet despite this reasonable doubt the CIA officials refused to release him. It turned out that in South Africa, while Anwar's phone was off, there had been a call to it from an unknown person.

Cast

- Jake Gyllenhaal - Douglas Freeman
- Omar Metwally - Anwar El-Ibrahimi
- Reese Witherspoon - Isabella Fields El-Ibrahimi
- Aramis Knight - Jeremy El-Ibrahimi
- Rosie Malek-Yonan - Nuru El-Ibrahimi
- Moa Khouas - Khalid El-Emin
- Zineb Oukach - Fatima Fawal
- Yigal Naor - Abasi Fawal
- J. K. Simmons - Lee Mayers
- Meryl Streep - Corrine Whitman
- Bob Gunton - Lars Whitman
- Raymonde Amsalem - Layla Fawal
- Simon Abkarian - Said Abdel Aziz
- Wendy Phillips - Samantha
- Peter Sarsgaard - Alan Smith
- Christian Martin - Senator Lewis' Aide
- Alan Arkin - Senator Hawkins

Reception

Reviews for *Rendition* were mixed. At Rotten Tomatoes, it achieved a 47% Tomatometer from 146 reviews. And based on 34 reviews, the film averaged a score of 55 at Metacritic.[1] Roger Ebert awarded the film four stars out of four, saying that, "*Rendition* is valuable and rare. As I wrote from Toronto: 'It is a movie about the theory and practice of two things: torture and personal responsibility. And it is wise about what is right, and what is wrong.'"[2] In contrast, Peter Travers of *Rolling Stone* applauded the cast, but noted that the film was a "bust as a persuasive drama".[3] Travers declared the film the year's Worst Anti-War Film on his list of the Worst Movies of 2007.[4]

External links

- Official website [5]
- Official trailer [6]
- *Rendition* [7] at the Internet Movie Database
- *Rendition* [8] at Rotten Tomatoes
- *Rendition* [9] at Metacritic
- *Rendition* [10] at Box Office Mojo
- *Rendition* [11] at Allmovie

References

[1]   "Rendition (2007): Reviews" (http://www.metacritic.com/film/titles/rendition?q–Rendition). . Retrieved October 20, 2007.

[2]   "::rogerebert.com:: Reviews:: Rendition (xhtml)" (http://rogerebert.suntimes.com/apps/pbcs.dll/article?AID=/20071018/REVIEWS/ 710180307). . Retrieved October 20, 2007.

[3]   "Rendition: Review: Rolling Stone" (http://www.rollingstone.com/reviews/movie/14216810/review/16970903/rendition). . Retrieved October 20, 2007.

[4]   Travers, Peter, (December 19, 2007) "Peter Travers' Best and Worst Movies of 2007" (http://www.rollingstone.com/news/story/ 17686508/peter_travers_best_and_worst_movies_of_2007/19) *Rolling Stone*. Retrieved 2007-12-20

[5]   http://www.renditionmovie.com/

[6]   http://www.renditionmovie.com/trailer.html

[7]   http://www.imdb.com/title/tt0804522/

[8]   http://www.rottentomatoes.com/m/rendition/

[9]   http://www.metacritic.com/film/titles/rendition

[10] http://www.boxofficemojo.com/movies/?id=rendition.htm

[11] http://www.allmovie.com/work/375406

Lions for Lambs

Lions for Lambs	
	Lions for Lambs poster
Directed by	Robert Redford
Produced by	Robert Redford Matthew Michael Carnahan Tracy Falco Andrew Hauptman
Written by	Matthew Michael Carnahan
Starring	Robert Redford Meryl Streep Tom Cruise Michael Peña Derek Luke Andrew Garfield Peter Berg
Music by	Mark Isham
Cinematography	Philippe Rousselot
Editing by	Joe Hutshing
Studio	United Artists Cruise/Wagner Productions Andell Entertainment Brat Na Pont Productions Wildwood Enterprises
Distributed by	MGM
Release date(s)	Hong Kong: November 8, 2007 United States: November 9, 2007
Running time	88 minutes
Country	United States

Language	English
Budget	USD$35 million[1]
Gross revenue	$63 million[2]

Lions for Lambs is a 2007 American drama film about the connection between a platoon of United States soldiers in Afghanistan, a U.S. senator, a reporter, and a California college professor. It stars Tom Cruise, Meryl Streep, and Robert Redford. It was the first Cruise/Wagner Productions film since the company joined with United Artists subsequent to Cruise's falling out with Paramount Pictures in 2006.[3]

With a title that alludes to incompetent leaders sending brave soldiers into the slaughter of battle, the film takes aim at the U.S. government's prosecution of the wars in the Middle East, showing three different simultaneous stories: a senator who launches a new military strategy and details it to a journalist on the edge of a mental breakdown, two soldiers involved in said operation, and their college professor trying to re-engage a promising student. The film was written by Matthew Michael Carnahan, and directed by Redford. It was released in North America on Friday, November 9, 2007, to negative reviews and disappointing box office receipts.

Plot

Two determined students at a West Coast university, Arian (Derek Luke) and Ernest (Michael Peña), at the urging of their idealistic professor, Dr. Malley (Redford), attempt to do something important with their lives. They make the bold decision to enlist in the army to fight in Afghanistan after graduating from college.

Dr. Malley also attempts to reach talented and privileged, but disaffected, student Todd Hayes (Andrew Garfield) who is not at all like Arian and Ernest. He is naturally bright, comes from a privileged background, but has apparently slipped into apathy upon being disillusioned at the present state of affairs. Now he devotes most of his time to his girlfriend and to his role as president of his fraternity. Malley tests him by offering a choice between a respectable grade of 'B' in the class with no additional work required, or a final opportunity to re-engage with the material of the class and "do something."

Meanwhile, in Washington, D.C., a charismatic Republican presidential hopeful, Senator Jasper Irving (Cruise), has invited liberal TV journalist Janine Roth (Streep) to his office to announce a new war strategy in Afghanistan: the use of small units to seize strategic positions in the mountains ("forward operating points") before the Taliban can occupy them. The senator hopes that Roth's positive coverage will help convince the public that the plan is sound.

Roth has her doubts and arrogantly assumes she is being asked to become an instrument of government propaganda. Near the end of the film, lacking conclusive facts, she still confronts her commercially-minded boss for selling out. Ultimately Irving's version of the story is run without the critical interaction and paranoid re-interpretation Roth wanted to see. It is not clear whether Roth gave in and toed the company policy or if she quit her job.

A helicopter carrying Arian and Ernest is hit by Taliban soldiers. Ernest falls out and Arian jumps after him. Ernest's leg is badly wounded and he suffers a compound fracture, rendering him immobile as the Taliban arrive. After a drawn-out gunfight, the U.S. soldiers run out of ammunition. Rather than getting captured, Arian helps Ernest stand up, facing the enemies and turning their empty weapons against them, an action which prompts the Taliban to kill them. The unit commanders attempt a rescue of the downed soldiers, sending A-10 Warthogs, but the weather, time and distance interfere.

Hayes is then seen watching television with a friend. A reporter is discussing a singer's private life, while below runs a strip announcing Senator Irving's new military plan for Afghanistan. He suddenly falls quiet, contemplating the choices his teacher had left him with.

Selected cast

Actor	Role
Robert Redford	Professor Stephen Malley
Meryl Streep	Janine Roth
Tom Cruise	Senator Jasper Irving (R-IL)
Michael Peña	Ernest Rodriguez
Derek Luke	Arian Finch
Andrew Garfield	Todd Hayes
Peter Berg	Lt. Col. Falco

Production

Matthew Michael Carnahan was inspired to write the script when, while channel surfing trying to find a USC Trojans football game, he saw a news report about a Humvee that had flipped into an Iraqi river, drowning about five U.S. soldiers. Carnahan considered it an awful way to die, and "couldn't get past it fast enough", considering he was too indifferent, "talking so much and not doing a damn thing",[4] and "the same hypocrite that I so can't stand in our country, the kind of people that will flip right past the news to get to *Access Hollywood*".[5] He first considered turning it into a stage play, but the military scenes, in particular the helicopter ones, made him turn it into a film screenplay.[6] The character of Todd Hayes was inspired by Carnahan himself during college.[6]

When Robert Redford read the script, he got very interested, considering it smart as opposed to Hollywood's many "straight-out entertainment" projects, and also tricky due to the three stories "that seem to be disparate but are connected and have to come together in a vortex at the end", and that needed to be represented in a way the movie "wouldn't be categorized as a lefty film".[7] Redford considered that the movie's focus was for audiences "to be entertained in a way that made them think."[5]

The name of the film is derived from a remark made by a German officer during World War I, comparing British soldiers' bravery with the calculated criminality of their commanders.[8] While several reviewers in the UK have criticized the film for misquoting the commonly used phrase of "lions led by donkeys",[9] [10] [11] in an article on the origin of the title, Brian Dimuccio and Dino Vindeni wrote for *The Times*:

> One such composition included the observation, 'Nowhere have I seen such Lions led by such Lambs.' While the exact provenance of this quotation has been lost to history, most experts agree it was written during the Battle of the Somme, one of the bloodiest clashes in modern warfare. While some military archivists credit the author as an anonymous infantryman, others argue that the source was none other than General Max von Gallwitz, Supreme Commander of the German forces. In either case, it is generally accepted to be a derivation of Alexander the Great's proclamation, 'I am never afraid of an army of Lions led into battle by a Lamb. I fear more the army of Lambs who have a Lion to lead them.'[12]

Though *Lions for Lambs* was the first United Artists venture since Cruise and Paula Wagner attained control, executives billed the film as a "Robert Redford vehicle."[13] Filming began on January 29, 2007,[14] and Redford considered the movie "the tightest schedule I've ever worked with," with barely a year between announcement and release.[5]

Promotion

Lions for Lambs is the first film under Cruise's and Wagner's new venture with film studio United Artists.[15] *MSNBC* reported that Cruise was worried about how the film would perform, because of how the film industry would view him based on its success or failure at the box office.[15]

Critical reception

Lions for Lambs received generally negative to mixed reviews from critics. As of July 8, 2008 on the review aggregator Rotten Tomatoes, the film has received a "rotten" rating of 28%, based on 168 reviews.[16] On Metacritic, the film had an average score of 47 out of 100, based on 36 reviews.[17]

Film critic Roger Ebert gave it two and a half stars, noting that at the beginning of the film the viewer is "under the delusion that it's going somewhere." As the film progresses, Ebert wrote that interest is lost, noting, "When we begin to suspect it's going in circles, our interest flags."[18] Matt Pais of the *Chicago Tribune* also gave the film two and a half stars, and wrote in summation: "Redford and Streep give it their all, but Cruise is Cruise, and the go-nowhere "Lions" is more of an imitation of life than a reflection on it."[19] A *USA Today* review gave the film two and a half stars as well, in a negative review titled: "As entertainment, 'Lions' whimpers rather than roars."[20] Reviewer Claudia Puig commented, "Though characters make some strong points, the film feels preachy and falls flat as entertainment."[20] The *New York Post* gave the film one and a half stars, and did not recommend it, writing: "...if you want to be bored by pompous-assery, 'Meet the Press' is free."[21] *The Guardian* was more critical, giving the film only one star, and calling it, "...a muddled and pompous film about America's war on terror."[22]

Derek Elley of *Variety* wrote that though the film was "star-heavy", it felt like "the movie equivalent of an Off Broadway play," and "uses a lot of words to say nothing new."[23] *The New York Times* also mentioned the amount of dialogue in the film, writing: "It's a long conversation, more soporific than Socratic, and brimming with parental chiding, generational conflict and invocations of Vietnam," and the *Los Angeles Times* described the lecturing in the film as "dull and self-satisfied."[24] [25] The subtitle of the review in the *Los Angeles Times* was: "As a matter of policy, 'Lions for Lambs' doesn't play."[25] In a review entitled "Political drama feels more like a lecture" in *The Boston Globe*, Wesley Morris wrote: "It does not feel good to report that a movie with Robert Redford, Meryl Streep, and Tom Cruise makes the eyelids droop. But that's what "Lions for Lambs" does."[26] Writing in the *Seattle Post-Intelligencer*, reviewer William Arnold wrote positively of the segments of the film involving Robert Redford's character.[27] Arnold wrote of Redford's character: "His character, who hopes to save America one slacker at a time, rings true; and his real-life conviction and his fears for democracy come through."[27] Amy Biancolli of the *Houston Chronicle* highlighted Redford's direction of the film, commenting that it was not his best film, but it was "his bravest."[28] Ray Bennett of *The Hollywood Reporter* described *Lions for Lambs* as "...a well-made movie that offers no answers but raises many important questions."[29]

Box office results

The film took in USD$6.7 million in its opening weekend and debuted at the number four spot.[30] This was one of Cruise's worst wide opener box office takes since *The Color of Money*, and Cathering Elsworth of *The Daily Telegraph* wrote that this result "puts it on course to be Cruise's lowest-grossing movie of all time."[30] [31] The film also opened poorly in Europe, with *Variety* reporting: "Savage reviews dealt the talky political drama a big blow."[32] In the United Kingdom, *Lions for Lambs* took in $1.4 million and opened in sixth place.[32] The film debuted at the number six spot in Germany, and number five in Brazil.[33] Overall, the film pulled in a total of $10.3 million in markets in its opening weekend outside the United States, and *Reuters* noted "Tom Cruise's "Lambs" got slaughtered at the worldwide box office."[13] By January 14, 2008, the film's domestic returns were just under $15 million.[34]

MSNBC reported that Cruise was concerned about the opening weekend results, and quoted a source: "Tom wanted to really hit a home run with his first United Artists movie. It was more about how the industry was going to view him than the movie going public that Tom was worried about."[35] In response to the opening weekend results, a representative at United Artists stated: "We performed right at the pre-weekend predictions and are glad to have done that. Given the modest production and marketing budgets we do not need to be a blockbuster hit. Everyone at United Artists are very proud of the film and could not have had a more perfect filmmaker to have made our first film."[36]

International experts said that the film did not attract its core audience, and that the box office results were due to a failure of the film to cross over to the general public.[33] On November 28, 2007, *The Wall Street Journal* reported that "Lions for Lambs has performed so poorly that it may not make back its $35 million investment."[37] On December 3, 2007, the *New York Post* reported that the film was "assessed to blow as much as $25 mil," and a report in *Variety* made the same assessment.[38] [39] Multiple sources have referred to the film as a "Box office bomb", including the *San Francisco Chronicle*,[40] *U.S. News & World Report*,[41] *Orlando Sentinel*,[42] the *New York Post*,[39] and *New York Magazine*.[43] *New York Magazine* called the film "a critical flop and a box-office bomb," and a report by NewsMax Media characterized it among "miserable box-office flops."[43] [44] An article in *The Daily Telegraph* discussed the film among a "slew of new movies" that "have flopped at the box office."[31] The *Associated Press* called the film a "box-office clunker."[45] The film ultimately grossed $63 million worldwide, which included $15 million for its domestic gross and $48 million internationally.[2]

See also

- Lions led by donkeys
- War on Terrorism
- Operation Red Wing

External links

- *Lions for Lambs* Official website [46]
- *Lions for Lambs* [47] at TomCruise.com
- *Lions for Lambs* [48] at the Internet Movie Database
- *Lions for Lambs* [49] at Rotten Tomatoes
- *Lions for Lambs* [50] at Metacritic
- *Lions for Lambs* [51] at Box Office Mojo
- *Lions for Lambs* [52] at Allmovie

References

[1]   Vivarelli, Nick (October 23, 2007). "'Lions' star roars at Rome: Cruise leaves it to Redford to lash out" (http://www.variety.com/article/ VR1117974560.html?categoryId=19&cs=1). *Variety*. . Retrieved 2007-11-10.

[2]   "Lions for Lambs (2007)" (http://www.boxofficemojo.com/movies/?id=lionsforlambs.htm). Box Office Mojo. . Retrieved 2008-11-28.

[3]   Hayes, Dade (October 21, 2007). "Cruise rolls out 'Lions for Lambs': Film puts stars on frontlines of political debate" (http://www.variety. com/article/VR1117974448.html?categoryId=1064&cs=1). *Variety*. . Retrieved 2007-11-10.

[4]   Horn, John (2007-11-04). "Sick of doing nothing" (http://articles.latimes.com/2007/nov/04/entertainment/ca-carnahan4). *Los Angeles Times*. . Retrieved 2008-11-28.

[5]   Halbfinger, David M. (September 9, 2007). "Mr. Sundance Goes Back to Washington" (http://www.nytimes.com/2007/09/09/movies/ moviesspecial/09halb.html). *The New York Times*. . Retrieved 2008-11-28.

[6]   Summers, J. Ryan (2008-11-08). "Matthew Michael Carnahan Explains Lions for Lambs Agenda" (http://www.rottentomatoes.com/m/ lions_for_lambs/news/1687458/matthew_michael_carnahan_explains_lions_for_lambs_agenda). Rotten Tomatoes. . Retrieved 2008-11-28.

[7]   Corliss, Richard (2007-11-02). "The Lions Roar" (http://www.time.com/time/magazine/article/0,9171,1680133,00.html). Time. . Retrieved 2008-11-28.

[8]   Lynch, Donal; Padraic McKiernan, Constance Harris, Madeleine Keane (November 11, 2007). "Trouble with their lions" (http://www. independent.ie/entertainment/film-cinema/trouble-with-their-lions-1216662.html). *Irish Independent*. . Retrieved 2007-11-11.

[9]   Tookey, Christopher (November 13, 2007). "Redford's anti-war lecture Lions For Lambs is missing in action" (http://www.dailymail.co. uk/pages/live/articles/showbiz/reviews.html?in_article_id=492601&in_page_id=1924). Daily Mail. . Retrieved 2007-11-14.

[10] Bradshaw, Peter (November 9, 2007). "Lions for Lambs" (http://film.guardian.co.uk/News_Story/Critic_Review/Guardian_review/ 0,,2207478,00.html). London: The Guardian. . Retrieved 2007-11-14.

[11] Lister, David (November 10, 2007). "The Week in Arts: Redford's sheepish response" (http://comment.independent.co.uk/columnists/ david_lister/article3146426.ece). London: The Independent. . Retrieved 2007-11-14.

[12] DiMuccio, Brian; Dino Vindeni (October 16, 2007). "What's the significance of the title 'Lions for Lambs'?" (http://entertainment. timesonline.co.uk/tol/arts_and_entertainment/film/london_film_festival/article2672737.ece). London: Times. . Retrieved 2007-11-13.

[13] Staff; The Hollywood Reporter (November 13, 2007). "Cruise film "Lions" a lamb at foreign box office" (http://www.reuters.com/article/ filmNews/idUSN1351463420071114). *Reuters* (Reuters/Hollywood Reporter). . Retrieved 2007-11-14.

[14] Metro-Goldwyn-Mayer Studios (February 21, 2007). "United Artists' "Lions for Lambs" to Be Released Worldwide by MGM" (http:// www.mgm.com/news/pr8.php). Press release. . Retrieved 2007-11-10.

[15] Hazlett, Courtney (November 8, 2007). "Tom Cruise 'extremely worried' about 'Lions'". *MSNBC*.

[16] "Lions for Lambs - Rotten Tomatoes" (http://www.rottentomatoes.com/m/lions_for_lambs/). Rotten Tomatoes. . Retrieved 2008-07-08.

[17] "Lions for Lambs (2007): Reviews" (http://www.metacritic.com/film/titles/lionsforlambs). Metacritic. . Retrieved 2008-07-08.

[18] Ebert, Rogert (November 8, 2007). "Lions for Lambs" (http://rogerebert.suntimes.com/apps/pbcs.dll/article?AID=/20071108/ REVIEWS/711080303).*Chicago Sun-Times*. . Retrieved 2007-11-09.

[19] Pais, Matt (November 7, 2007). "Lions for Lambs: Finally, someone is having a basic conversation about American foreign policy!" (http:// chicago.metromix.com/movies/movie_review/lions-for-lambs/247669/content). *Chicago Tribune*: pp. Metromix Chicago Movies. . Retrieved 2007-11-10.

[20] Puig, Claudia (November 9, 2007). "As entertainment, 'Lions' whimpers rather than roars" (http://www.usatoday.com/life/movies/ reviews/2007-11-08-lions-for-lambs_N.htm). *USA Today* (USA TODAY, a division of Gannett Co. Inc.). . Retrieved 2007-11-10.

[21] Smith, Kyle (November 9, 2007). "Sheep Shots" (http://www.nypost.com/seven/11092007/entertainment/movies/sheep_shots_663602. htm). *New York Post* (NYP Holdings, Inc.). . Retrieved 2007-11-10.

[22] Bradshaw, Peter (November 9, 2007). "Reviews: Lions for Lambs" (http://film.guardian.co.uk/News_Story/Critic_Review/ Guardian_review/0,,2207478,00.html). *The Guardian* (London). . Retrieved 2007-11-10.

[23] Elley, Derek (October 22, 2007). "Lions for Lambs Review" (http://www.variety.com/review/VE1117935172.html?categoryid=31& cs=1). *Variety*. . Retrieved 2007-11-10.

[24] Dargis, Manohla (November 9, 2007). "Movie Review: Lions for Lambs". *The New York Times* (The New York Times Company).

[25] Chocano, Carina (November 9, 2007). "MOVIE REVIEW, 'Lions for Lambs': As a matter of policy, 'Lions for Lambs' doesn't play". *Los Angeles Times*.

[26] Morris, Wesley (November 9, 2007). "Lions for Lambs Movie Review: Political drama feels more like a lecture" (http://www.boston. com/movies/display?display=movie&id=10207). *The Boston Globe*. . Retrieved 2007-11-09.

[27] Arnold, William (November 8, 2007). "Disjointed plots butcher the powerful potential in 'Lions for Lambs'" (http://seattlepi.nwsource. com/movies/338861_lions09q.html). *Seattle Post-Intelligencer* (HearstNewspapers). . Retrieved 2007-11-15.

[28] Biancolli, Amy (November 8, 2007). "Not Redford's best, but his bravest" (http://www.chron.com/disp/story.mpl/ent/movies/reviews/ 5254940.html). *Houston Chronicle*. . Retrieved 2007-11-15.

[29] Bennett, Ray (October 23, 2007). "Bottom Line: An honest but a bit dry attempt at a serious discussion on the merits of current U.S. military strategies." (http://www.hollywoodreporter.com/hr/film/reviews/article_display.jsp?&rid=10088). *The Hollywood Reporter*. . Retrieved 2007-11-15.

[30] Rich, Joshua (November 11, 2007). "Box Office Report:*Bee Movie*: Swarm Alert! Jerry Seinfeld's animated comedy flew into first place on its second weekend, *Fred Claus* performed way under expectations, and the latest Cruise missile misfired" (http://www.ew.com/ew/article/ 0,,20159596,00.html). *Entertainment Weekly* (Entertainment Weekly and Time Inc.). .

[31] Elsworth, Cathering (November 12, 2007). "Hollywood misreads response to war on terror: Hollywood has misjudged the public's appetite for films about Iraq and the war on terror, Cathering Elsworth says, as a slew of new movies have flopped at the box office." (http://www. telegraph.co.uk/arts/main.jhtml?xml=/arts/2007/11/12/bflions112.xml). *The Daily Telegraph* (London:Telegraph Media Group Limited). . Retrieved 2007-12-03.

[32] Thomas, Archie (November 13, 2007). "'Lions' meek after Euro mauling: Fox pic finds solace in Spanish returns". *Variety* (Reed Elsevier Inc.).

[33] Hollinger, Hy; Leo Cendrowicz, Mark Russell (November 13, 2007). "'Lions' a lamb in overseas bow: Two films from India dominate weekend int'l box office" (http://www.hollywoodreporter.com/hr/content_display/film/news/e3i1c7f5ec28ee21fcb3e7eeebf9b8e61cc). *The Hollywood Reporter* (Nielsen Business Media, Inc.). . Retrieved 2007-11-14.

[34] Ryan, Joal (January 14, 2008). "Driving Mr. Nicholson and Mr. Freeman" (http://www.eonline.com/news/article/index. jsp?uuid=298e1145-eaab-4d71-a874-81fdddbe1a6e&entry=index). *E! Online: News* (E! Entertainment Television, Inc). . Retrieved 2008-01-19.

[35] Staff (November 13, 2007). "Cruise concerned about 'flop' movie" (http://breakingnews.iol.ie/entertainment/story.asp?j=237428506& p=z374z9zyz). *Ireland Online* (Thomas Crosbie Media). . Retrieved 2007-12-03.

[36] Hazlett, Courtney (November 12, 2007). "Tom Cruise's disappointing weekend" (http://www.msnbc.msn.com/id/21567559/). *MSNBC*: pp. The Scoop. . Retrieved 2007-11-14.

[37] "Hollywood Bombs" (http://online.wsj.com/article/SB119621011146905938.html?mod=googlenews_wsj). The Wall Street Journal. November 28, 2007. pp. A22. . Retrieved 2007-11-29.

[38] Degrandpre, Andrew (Army Times) (December 24, 2007). "Today's war films miss the target at box office" (http://www.indystar.com/apps/pbcs.dll/article?AID=/20071224/LIVING/712240328/1007/LIVING). *The Indianapolis Star* (Gannett Co. Inc.). . Retrieved 2008-01-19.

[39] Adams, Cindy (December 3, 2007). "He's Not Known For Watching His Tongue" (http://www.nypost.com/seven/12032007/gossip/cindy/hes_not_known_for_watching_his_tongue_369173.htm). *New York Post* (NYP Holdings, Inc.). . Retrieved 2007-12-03.

[40] Garofoli, Joe (November 23, 2007). "War Is a Box Office Bomb" (http://www.sfgate.com/c/acrobat/2007/11/23/Chronicle.11-23-2007.ALL.A.1.MainNews.5star-dot.pdf). *San Francisco Chronicle*. . Retrieved 2007-12-03.

[41] Tolson, Jay (November 16, 2007). "War: the Box Office Bomb: Americans shun new films" (http://www.usnews.com/articles/news/national/2007/11/16/war-movies-are-box-office-bombs-despite-superstar-casts.html). *U.S. News & World Report* (U.S. News & World Report, L.P. (Alternate site (http://www.cbsnews.com/stories/2007/11/19/usnews/whispers/main3522889.shtml), *CBS News*)). . Retrieved 2007-12-03.

[42] Staff (January 17, 2008). "Is Tom Cruise REALLY Toast...this time?" (http://blogs.orlandosentinel.com/entertainment_movies_blog/2008/01/is-tom-cruise-t.html). *Orlando Sentinel*. . Retrieved 2008-01-19.

[43] Kois, Dan; Lane Brown (November 16, 2007). "Oscar Futures: A Big Week for 'The Diving Bell and the Butterfly'" (http://nymag.com/daily/entertainment/2007/11/oscar_futures_a_big_week_for.html). *New York Magazine* (New York Magazine Holdings LLC.). . Retrieved 2007-12-03.

[44] Hirsen, James (November 27, 2007). "Another Anti-war Flick Bombs at the Box-Office" (http://www.newsmax.com/hirsen/Susan_Sarandon/2007/11/27/52556.html). *Newsmax.com* (NewsMax Media). . Retrieved 2007-12-03.

[45] Staff (January 3, 2008). "Survey: Depp Remains No. 1 at Box Office" (http://ap.google.com/article/ALeqM5gznmp9UudV_wcxNY3J5Eh2f3N1EAD8TUKKK80). *Associated Press*. . Retrieved 2008-01-19.

[46] http://www.mgm.com/sites/lionsforlambs/

[47] http://www.tomcruise.com/tom-cruise-lions-for-lambs-movie.html

[48] http://www.imdb.com/title/tt0891527/

[49] http://www.rottentomatoes.com/m/lions_for_lambs/

[50] http://www.metacritic.com/film/titles/lionsforlambs?part=rss

[51] http://www.boxofficemojo.com/movies/?id=LionsforLambs.htm

[52] http://www.allmovie.com/work/380101

Mamma Mia! (film)

Mamma Mia!	
 Promotional poster	
Directed by	Phyllida Lloyd
Produced by	Phyllida Lloyd Judy Cramer Benny Andersson Björn Ulvaeus Tom Hanks Rita Wilson
Written by	Catherine Johnson
Starring	Meryl Streep Amanda Seyfried Pierce Brosnan Colin Firth Stellan Skarsgård Dominic Cooper Julie Walters Christine Baranski
Music by	Benny Andersson (score) Benny Andersson Björn Ulvaeus Stig Anderson (songs) Original Music by ABBA
Cinematography	Haris Zambarloukos
Editing by	Lesley Walker
Studio	Playtone
Distributed by	Universal Pictures
Release date(s)	June 30, 2008 (United Kingdom) July 18, 2008 (United States)
Running time	110 minutes

Country	United States United Kingdom
Language	English
Budget	$52 million
Gross revenue	$609,841,637[1]

Mamma Mia!, promoted as *Mamma Mia! The Movie*, is a 2008 musical/romantic comedy film adapted from the 1999 West End musical of the same name, based on the songs of successful pop group ABBA, with additional music composed by ABBA member Benny Andersson. Distributed by Universal Pictures in partnership with Tom Hanks' and Rita Wilson's Playtone and Littlestar,[2] it became the highest-grossing film musical of all time breaking the 30-year-old record of Grease. The title originates from ABBA's 1975 chart-topper "Mamma Mia". Meryl Streep heads the cast, playing the role of single mother Donna Sheridan. Pierce Brosnan, Colin Firth, and Stellan Skarsgård play the three possible fathers to Donna's daughter, Sophie (Amanda Seyfried).

Plot

On a Greek island called Kalokairi, 20-year-old bride-to-be Sophie Sheridan (Amanda Seyfried) posts three wedding invitations ("I Have a Dream") to three different men. From across the globe, the men set off for the wedding.

Sophie's two bridesmaids arrive and she reveals that she found her mother's diary and learned she has three possible dads: New York-based Irish architect Sam Carmichael (Pierce Brosnan), Swedish adventurer and writer Bill Andersson (Stellan Skarsgård), and British banker Harry Bright (Colin Firth). She invited them without telling her mother, believing that after she spends time with them she will know who her father is ("Honey, Honey").

Villa owner Donna Sheridan (Meryl Streep) is ecstatic to reunite with her former Donna and the Dynamos bandmates, wisecracking author Rosie (Julie Walters) and wealthy multiple divorcée Tanya (Christine Baranski), and reveals her bafflement at her daughter's desire to get married. Donna shows the villa, rumored to be built on the legendary fountain of Aphrodite, and explains her precarious finances to Rosie and Tanya ("Money, Money, Money").

The three men arrive, and Sophie smuggles them to their room and explains that she, not her mother, sent the invitations. She begs them to hide so Donna will have a surprise at the wedding: seeing the old friends of whom she "so often" favorably speaks. They overhear Donna working (humming "Fernando") and swear to Sophie they won't reveal her secret.

Donna spies them and is dumbfounded to find herself facing three former lovers she could never forget ("Mamma Mia"), and is adamant that they leave. She confides in Tanya and Rosie ("Chiquitita") a secret she has kept from everyone — she is uncertain which of the three men is Sophie's father. Tanya and Rosie rally her spirits by getting Donna to dance with the female staff and islanders ("Dancing Queen").

Sophie finds the men aboard Bill's yacht, and they sail around Kalokairi ("Our Last Summer") and tell stories of Donna as a carefree girl. Sophie musters up the courage to speak with her fiancé Sky (Dominic Cooper) about her ploy, but loses her nerve. Sky and Sophie sing to each other ("Lay All Your Love on Me"), but are interrupted when Sky is kidnapped for his bachelor party.

At Sophie's bachelorette party, Donna, Tanya, and Rosie perform as Donna and The Dynamos ("Super Trouper"). Sophie is delighted to see her mother rock out, but becomes nervous when the festivities are interrupted by the arrival of Sam, Bill and Harry. She decides to get each of her three prospective dads alone to talk.

While her girlfriends dance with the men ("Gimme! Gimme! Gimme! (A Man After Midnight)"), Sophie learns from Bill that Donna received the money to invest in her villa from his great aunt Sofia. Sophie guesses she must be her namesake and Bill is her father. She asks him to give her away and to keep their secret from Donna until the wedding.

Sophie's happiness is short-lived as Sam and Harry each tell her they must be her dad and will give her away ("Voulez-Vous"). A shocked Sophie can't tell them the truth and, overwhelmed by the consequences of her actions, faints.

In the morning, Rosie and Tanya reassure Donna they will take care of the men. On Bill's boat, Bill and Harry are about to confide in each other, but are interrupted by Rosie.

Donna confronts Sophie in the courtyard, believing Sophie wants the wedding stopped. Sophie says that all she wants is to avoid her mother's mistakes and storms off. An upset Donna is accosted by Sam, concerned about Sophie getting married so young. Donna confronts him and both realize they still have feelings for each other ("SOS").

Down on the beach, Tanya and young Pepper (Philip Michael) continue their flirtations from the previous night ("Does Your Mother Know").

Sophie comes clean to Sky and asks for his help. He reacts angrily to his fiancée's deception and Sophie turns to her mother for support. As Donna helps her daughter dress for the wedding, their rift is healed and Donna reminisces about Sophie's childhood and how quickly she's grown ("Slipping Through My Fingers"). Sophie asks Donna to give her away. As the bridal party walks to the chapel, Sam intercepts Donna and begs her to talk. She reveals the pain she felt over losing him ("The Winner Takes It All").

During the wedding, Donna tells Sophie that her father is present but he could be any of the three candidates, whom Sophie admits to inviting. Sam reveals that although he left to get married, he didn't go through with it and returned, only to find Donna with another man, so he married his former fiancée (and later divorced her). Harry confesses that Donna was the first (and last) woman he loved. The three men concur that they would be happy to be one-third of a father for Sophie. She tells Sky that they should postpone their wedding and travel the world as they have always wanted. Sam suddenly proposes to Donna ("I Do, I Do, I Do, I Do, I Do"). She accepts and they are married.

At the wedding reception, Sam sings to Donna ("When All Is Said and Done"), which prompts Rosie to make a play for Bill ("Take a Chance on Me"). All the couples present proclaim their love ("Mamma Mia" reprise), as their raucous dancing causes the ground to crack and erupt with water from the fountain of Aphrodite. Sophie and Sky bid farewell to Kalokairi and sail away ("I Have a Dream" reprise).

During the principal credits, Donna, Tanya, and Rosie reprise "Dancing Queen", followed by "Waterloo" with the rest of the cast. Finally, Amanda Seyfried sings "Thank You for the Music" over the end credits.

Cast

- Meryl Streep as Donna Sheridan: Sophie's mother, owner of the hotel Villa Donna, and wife of Sam at the end. She is also Rosie and Tanya's friend.[3]
- Amanda Seyfried as Sophie Sheridan: Donna's daughter and Sky's fiancée.[4]
- Pierce Brosnan as Sam Carmichael: Sophie's possible father, husband to Donna, and an Irish architect.[5]
- Julie Walters as Rosie Mulligan: One of Donna's former bandmates in Donna and the Dynamos. an unmarried fun-loving author.
- Christine Baranski as Tanya Wilkinson: Donna's other former bandmate. Divorced three times and rich.
- Colin Firth as Harry Bright: Sophie's possible father and an English banker. Based on "Our Last Summer", which he sings at one point.
- Stellan Skarsgård as Bill Anderson: Sophie's possible father, a Swedish sailor and travel writer.
- Dominic Cooper as Sky: Sophie's fiancé, designing a website for the hotel.
- Enzo Squillino as Gregoris: One of Donna Sheridan's employees.
- Philip Michael as Pepper: Sky's best man who likes Tanya. He is also a bartender.
- Ashley Lilley as Ali: Close friend of Sophie and her bridesmaid.

- Rachel McDowall as Lisa: Close friend of Sophie and her bridesmaid.
- Niall Buggy as Father Alex: Priest who marries Sam and Donna
- Benny Andersson as Piano Player
- Björn Ulvaeus as a Greek god
- Rita Wilson as a Greek goddess

Musical numbers

The following songs are included in the film, of which 17 are on the soundtrack album:

1. "I Have a Dream" - Sophie
2. "Honey, Honey" - Sophie, Ali, and Lisa
3. "Money, Money, Money" - Donna, Tanya, Rosie, and Greek Chorus
4. "Mamma Mia" - Donna, Sophie, Ali, Lisa, and Greek Chorus
5. "Chiquitita" - Rosie, Tanya, and Donna
6. "Dancing Queen" - Tanya, Rosie, Donna, Greek Chorus, and Company
7. "Our Last Summer" - Harry, Bill, Sam, Sophie, and Donna
8. "Lay All Your Love on Me" - Sky, Sophie, Sky's Bachelor party friends.
9. "Super Trouper" - Donna, Tanya, and Rosie
10. "Gimme! Gimme! Gimme! (A Man After Midnight)" - Sophie, Donna, Tanya, Rosie, Ali, Lisa and Greek Chorus
11. "The Name of the Game" - Sophie (deleted scene)
12. "Voulez-Vous " - Donna, Sam, Tanya, Rosie, Harry, Bill, Sky, Ali, Lisa, and Pepper
13. "SOS" - Sam, Donna, and Greek Chorus
14. "Does Your Mother Know" - Tanya, Pepper, Guys, and Girls
15. "Slipping Through My Fingers" - Donna and Sophie
16. "The Winner Takes It All" - Donna
17. "I Do, I Do, I Do, I Do, I Do" - Sam, Donna, and Company
18. "When All Is Said and Done" - Sam, Donna, and Company
19. "Take a Chance on Me" - Rosie, Bill, Tanya, Pepper, and Harry
20. "Mamma Mia!" (Reprise) - Company
21. "I Have a Dream" (Reprise) - Sophie
22. "Dancing Queen" (Reprise) - Donna, Rosie, and Tanya
23. "Waterloo" - Donna, Rosie, Tanya, Sam, Bill, Harry, Sky, and Sophie
24. "Thank You for the Music" - Sophie

Production

Most of the filming was done on the small Greek island of Skopelos (during August/September 2007),[6] and the seaside hamlet of Damouchari in the Pelion area of Greece. On Skopelos, Kastani beach on the south west coast was the film's main location site.[6] The producers built a beach bar and jetty along the beach, but removed them both when they left.[6]

The part of the film where Pierce Brosnan's character, Sam, leaves his New York office to go to the Greek Island was actually filmed at the iconic Lloyds Building on Lime Street in the City of London. He dashes down the escalators and through the porte-cochere, where yellow cabs and actors representing New York mounted police were used for authenticity.[7]

The "*Fernando*" Bill Anderson's beautiful yacht (actually a ketch) in the movie was the *Tai-Mo-Shan* built in 1934 by H. S. Rouse at the Hong Kong and Whampoa dockyards.[8] [9]

Actress Meryl Streep had taken opera singing lessons as a child, and as an adult, she had previously sung in several movies, including *Postcards from the Edge*, *Silkwood*, *Death Becomes Her*, and *A Prairie Home Companion*.[10]

Release

Anni-Frid Lyngstad and Agnetha Fältskog joined Björn Ulvaeus and Benny Andersson at the Swedish premiere of the film, held at the Rival Theatre in Mariatorget, Stockholm, owned by Andersson, on July 4, 2008. It was the first time all four members of ABBA had been photographed together since 1986.[11]

ABBA appeared together with the film's cast in 2008.

Reception

Mamma Mia! received mixed reviews from critics. *Rotten Tomatoes* reported that 53% of critics gave the film positive reviews based upon a sample of 168 reviews, with an average rating of 5.5/10.[12] *The Times* gave it four stars out of five,[13] as did Channel 4 which said it had "all the swing and sparkle of sequined bell-bottoms."[14] BBC Radio 5 Live's film critic Mark Kermode delivered an all-singing, all-dancing review, describing the experience as 'the closest you get to see A-List actors doing drunken karaoke'.[15] *The Guardian* was more negative, giving it one star, stating that the film gave the reviewer a "need to vomit"[16], while Bob Chipman of *Escape to the Movies* said it was "so base, so shallow and so hinged on meaningless spectacle, it's amazing it wasn't made for men".[17] *The Daily Telegraph* stated that it was enjoyable but poorly put together ("Finding the film a total shambles was sort of a shame, but I have a sneaking suspicion I'll go to see it again anyway."),[18] whereas *Empire* said it was "cute, clean, camp fun, full of sunshine and toe tappers."[19]

The casting of actors not noted for their singing abilities led to some mixed reviews. *Variety* stated that "some stars, especially the bouncy and rejuvenated Streep, seem better suited for musical comedy than others, including Brosnan and Skarsgård."[20] Brosnan, especially, was savaged by many critics: his singing was compared to "a water buffalo" (*New York Magazine*),[21] "a donkey braying" (*The Philadelphia Inquirer*)[22] and "a wounded raccoon" (*The Miami Herald*),[23] and Matt Brunson of *Creative Loafing Charlotte* said he "looks physically pained choking out the lyrics, as if he's being subjected to a prostate exam just outside of the camera's eye."[24]

Box office

As of April 6, 2009, *Mamma Mia!* has grossed a worldwide total of $602,609,487 and is the fifth highest grossing film of 2008[1] as well as being the 50th highest grossing film of all time.[25] As of October 26, 2008, it became the highest-grossing movie musical of all time worldwide.[25] It is also the most successful British-made film of all time,[26] [27] [28] as well as being the highest grossing film of all time at the UK box office, eclipsing the record previously held by *Titanic* on the December 16, 2008, some 20 weeks after the film's original release, until Avatar broke the record. This is not adjusted for inflation.[29]

It is the third highest-grossing film of 2008 internationally (i.e., outside North America) with an international total of $458,479,424 and the thirteenth highest gross of 2008 in North America (the US and Canada) with $144,130,063.

In the United Kingdom, *Mamma Mia!* has grossed £69,166,087 as of January 23, 2009, and is the second highest grossing film of all time at the UK box office.[30] The film opened at #1 in the U.K, taking £6,594,058 on 496 screens. It managed to hold onto the top spot for 2 weeks, narrowly keeping Pixar's *WALL-E* from reaching #1 in its second week.

When released on July 3 in Greece, the film grossed $1,602,646 in its opening weekend, ranking #1 at the Greek box office.[31]

The film made $9,627,000 in its opening day in the United States and Canada, and $27,605,376 in its opening weekend, ranking #2 at the box office, behind *The Dark Knight*.[32] At the time, it made *Mamma Mia!* the record-holder for the highest grossing opening weekend for a movie musical, surpassing *Hairspray*'s box office record in 2007.

Awards and nominations

Year	Award	Category	Winner/Nominee	Result
2009	BAFTA Awards	Best Music	Benny Andersson and Björn Ulvaeus	Nominated
		Outstanding British Film	Universal Pictures	Nominated
	Costume Designer Guild Awards	Excellence in Costume Design for Film - Contemporary	Ann Roth	Nominated
	Eddie Awards	Best Edited Feature Film (Comedy or Musical)	Lesley Walker	Nominated
	Empire Awards	Best Soundtrack	Benny Andersson and Björn Ulvaeus	Won
	Golden Globe Awards	Best Motion Picture - Comedy or Musical	Universal Pictures	Nominated
		Best Performance by an Actress in a Motion Picture - Comedy or Musical	Meryl Streep	Nominated
	Golden Reel Awards (Motion Picture Sound Editors)	Best Sound Editing - Music in a Musical Feature Film	Nick Adams	Won
	Grammy Awards	Best Compilation Soundtrack Album for a Motion Picture, Television or Other Visual Media	Various Artists	Nominated
	Irish Film and Television Awards	Best International Actress	Meryl Streep	Won
	MTV Movie Awards	Breakthrough Performance Female	Amanda Seyfried	Nominated
2008	National Movie Awards	Best Musical	Universal Pictures	Won
		Best Performance - Female	Meryl Streep	Won
		Best Performance - Male	Pierce Brosnan	Nominated
			Colin Firth	Nominated

2009	People's Choice Awards	Favorite Song from a Soundtrack	Meryl Streep for the song "*Mamma Mia*"	Won
		Favorite Cast	Meryl Streep, Amanda Seyfried, Pierce Brosnan, Colin Firth, Julie Walters, Stellan Skarsgård, Christine Baranski, Dominic Cooper, Ashley Lilley and Rachel McDowall	Nominated
		Favorite Movie Comedy	Universal Pictures	Nominated
	Raspberry Awards	Worst Supporting Actor	Pierce Brosnan	Won
	Rembrandt Awards	Best Female Actress	Meryl Streep	Won
		Best International Actress		Won
		Best International Film	Phyllida Lloyd	Won
2008	Satellite Awards	Best Actress in a Motion Picture, Comedy or Musical	Meryl Streep	Nominated

Sequel

Because of *Mamma Mia!'s* financial success, Hollywood studio chief David Linde, the co-chairman of Universal Studios told *The Daily Mail* that it would take a while, but there could be a sequel. He stated that he would be delighted if Judy Craymer, Catherine Johnson, Phyllida Lloyd, Benny Andersson, and Björn Ulvaeus agreed to the project, noting that there are still plenty of ABBA songs to use.[33]

DVD and Blu-ray Disc release

Mamma Mia! was released in Australia and New Zealand on DVD on November 6, 2008, and was released on Blu-ray on December 3. It was released on both DVD and Blu-ray in the UK and Norway on November 24 and November 26 respectively. It was released in US on December 16.

On November 24, *Mamma Mia!* became the fastest-selling DVD of all time in the UK, according to Official UK Charts Company figures. It sold 1,669,084 copies on its first day of release, breaking the previous record (held by *Titanic*) by 560,000 copies. By the end of 2008, The Official UK Charts Company declared it had become the biggest selling DVD ever in the UK, with one in every four households owning a copy (over 5 million copies sold).[34] The record was previously held by *Pirates of the Caribbean: The Curse of the Black Pearl* with sales of 4.7 million copies.

On November 26, 2008, *Mamma Mia!* became the best-selling DVD in Finland, by selling 110,000 copies and is the first DVD to earn a platinum award in that country.

In the United States the DVD made over $30 million on its first day of release.[35] To date it has sold 6,318,582 units in the US.

By December 31, 2008, *Mamma Mia!* had become the best-selling DVD of all time in Sweden with 545,000 copies sold.[36]

The DVD was released as a single-disc edition and a two-disc special edition.

On December 15, 2009, the *Mamma Mia! The Gimme! Gimme! Gimme! More Gift Set* was released. The set includes the 2-disc special edition with bonus soundtrack and 32-page collective booklet.

There is a 2-disc Ultimate Party Edition available in Hong Kong that includes all the 2-disc features with the *30 Rock* episode "Mamma Mia!".

Single-disc features

- Sing-along
- "The Name of the Game" deleted musical number
- Audio commentary with director Phyllida Lloyd

The single-disc DVD released in Sweden on 26 November contains all of the following:

- Sing-along
- "The Name of the Game" deleted musical number
- Deleted scenes
- Outtakes
- *The Making of Mamma Mia!* featurette
- Anatomy of a Musical Number: "Lay All Your Love on Me"
- *Becoming a Singer* featurette
- *A look inside Mamma Mia!* featurette
- "Gimme! Gimme! Gimme!" music video
- Björn Ulvaeus cameo
- Audio commentary with director Phyllida Lloyd
- German and English audio
- Subtitles in English, German, Danish, Dutch, Finnish, Norwegian and Swedish

Two-disc special edition

The widescreen single-disc includes a bonus disc which includes:

- Limited time only digital copy
- Deleted scenes
- Outtakes
- *The Making of Mamma Mia!* featurette
- Anatomy of a Musical Number: "Lay All Your Love on Me"
- *Becoming a Singer* featurette
- Behind the scenes with Amanda
- *On Location in Greece* featurette
- *A Look Inside Mamma Mia!* featurette
- "Gimme! Gimme! Gimme!" music video
- Björn Ulvaeus cameo

Blu-ray exclusives

- Universal Pictures' U-Control[37]
- Behind the Hits (details and trivia of the music while the musical performance plays)
- Picture-in-picture (access to cast and crew interviews and behind the scene while the movie plays)

Comic Relief Satire

The BBC's 2009 Red Nose Day special for Comic Relief featured a 10-minute satire of *Mamma Mia*. The short starred Jennifer Saunders and her long-time collaborators, Dawn French and Joanna Lumley as Donna, Rosie and Tanya, respectively. Sienna Miller appeared as Sophie. While the opening credits listed Saunders and French's characters as Meryl Streep and Julie Walters, rather than the character names, Lumley's portrayal of Tanya was described in dialogue and the opening credits as "Patsy" whom she played opposite Saunders in *Absolutely Fabulous*. Christine Baranski's booming, oompy "Maryanne" on *Cybill* had been often compared to Patsy. The three possible fathers appear only momentarilly in a spoof of their introduction to Sophie: Phillip Glenister is dressed and credited as Pierce Brosnan but references Colin Firth's joking reference to Brosnan by saying "I'm Bond," while Alan Carr is credited as Colin Firth and introduces himself, "I'm Darcy," referencing his parts in both *Pride and Prejudice* and the two Bridget Jones films, and a swede is credited as "the Swede". A recurring theme is awkward transitions into the songs.[38]

External links

- Official website [39]
- *Mamma Mia!* [40] at the Internet Movie Database
- *Mamma Mia!* [41] at Allmovie
- *Mamma Mia!* [42] at Box Office Mojo
- *Mamma Mia!* [43] at Rotten Tomatoes
- *Mamma Mia!* [44] at Metacritic
- *Mamma Mia!* production notes [45]

References

[1] "Mamma Mia! (2008)" (http://www.boxofficemojo.com/movies/?id=mammamia.htm). Box Office Mojo. . Retrieved 2009-02-05.

[2] "Mamma Mia! (2008) - Company Credits" (http://www.imdb.com/title/tt0795421/companycredits).*IMDb.com*. . Retrieved 2008-04-05.

[3] Gans, Andrew (2007-01-11). "Playbill News: Meryl Streep to Star in Mamma Mia! Film" (http://www.playbill.com/news/article/104803.html). *Playbill*. . Retrieved 2008-03-09.

[4] "Amanda Seyfried" (http://www.imdb.com/name/nm1086543/). Imdb.com. . Retrieved 2009-01-17.

[5] "Brosnan set for Abba show movie" (http://news.bbc.co.uk/1/hi/entertainment/6428471.stm). *BBC*. 2007-03-07. . Retrieved 2008-03-09.

[6] Mansfield, Paul (2008-07-15). "Mamma Mia! - Unfazed by the fuss in Skopelos" (http://www.telegraph.co.uk/travel/artsandculture/2229868/Mamma-Mia---Unfazed-by-the-fuss-in-Skopelos.html). London: The Telegraph. . Retrieved May 12, 2010.

[7] description of London locations (http://flamin.filmlondon.org.uk/content.asp?CategoryID=1078&ArticleID=1826),accessed 28 August 2009.

[8] "45' Teak Ketch 1933. Yacht for sale from classic yacht broker in Poole" (http://www.sandemanyachtcompany.co.uk/details/?id=233). *Sandeman Yacht brokerage Poole*. Sandeman Yacht Company. . Retrieved 2009-09-28.

[9] "Tai-Mo-Shan" (http://www.coburgbrokers.com/tai.html). *Coburg Yacht Brokers website*. Coburg Yacht Brokers. . Retrieved 2009-09-28.

[10] Hiscock, John (2008-07-04). "Meryl Streep the singing and dancing queen" (http://www.telegraph.co.uk/arts/main.jhtml?xml=/arts/2008/07/04/bfmeryl104.xml). London: The Telegraph. . Retrieved May 12, 2010.

[11] Sandra Wejbro (2008-07-04). "ABBA återförenades på röda mattan (Swedish)" (http://www.aftonbladet.se/nojesliv/film/article2836959.ab). Aftonbladet. . Retrieved 2008-07-06.

[12] "Mamma Mia! Reviews" (http://rottentomatoes.com/m/mamma_mia/). *Rotten Tomatoes*. Rotten Tomatoes. . Retrieved 2008-07-18.

[13] Times Online (http://entertainment.timesonline.co.uk/tol/arts_and_entertainment/film/article4245117.ece)

[14] Channel 4 review (http://www.channel4.com/film/reviews/film.jsp?id=167267.)

[15] BBC 5 Live Kermode and Mayo Film Review (http://www.youtube.com/watch?v=61UolzFTVPI)

[16] Guardian Review (http://www.guardian.co.uk/culture/2008/jul/10/film.reviews)

[17] (http://www.youtube.com/watch?v=CSKFjUDEyuM)

[18] Telegraph review (http://www.telegraph.co.uk/arts/main.jhtml?xml=/arts/2008/07/11/bfmamma111.xml)

[19] Empire review (http://uk.rottentomatoes.com/m/mamma_mia/)

[20] Variety Review (http://www.variety.com/VE1117937623.html)

[21] New York Magazine, New York Movies (http://nymag.com/movies/reviews/48514/index1.html)

[22] Philadelphia Inquirer Movie Review, July 18, 2008 (http://www.philly.com/inquirer/columnists/carrie_rickey/20080718__Mamma_Mia__here_we_go_again_-_this_time_on_screen.html)

[23] Miami Herald Movies, July 18, 2008 (http://www.miamiherald.com/1058/story/607314.html)

[24] Charlotte Film Reviews, July 23, 2008 (http://charlotte.creativeloafing.com/gyrobase/out_of_tune/Content?oid=336031)

[25] Box Office Mojo - All Time Worldwide Box Office (http://www.boxofficemojo.com/alltime/world/)

[26] (http://www.abbasite.com/infocus/index.php?ret=/infocus/index.php&flash=yes)Official Abba website

[27] Digital Spy (http://www.digitalspy.co.uk/movies/a134069/mamma-mia-is-uks-biggest-ever-movie.html)

[28] The Telegraph Online (http://www.telegraph.co.uk/news/newstopics/celebritynews/3283481/Mamma-Mia-becomes-highest-grossing-British-film.html)

[29] "Mamma Mia! beats UK cinema record" (http://news.bbc.co.uk/1/hi/entertainment/7785345.stm). http://news.bbc.co.uk/1/hi/entertainment/default.stm. December 16, 2008. . Retrieved 2008-12-16.

[30] "UK all time top grossing films" (http://www.25thframe.co.uk/chartspagetemplate.php?source=ukboxoffice).25thframe.co.uk. . Retrieved 2008-12-24.

[31] "Greece Box Office Index" (http://www.boxofficemojo.com/intl/greece/). Box Office Mojo. June 10, 2008. . Retrieved 2008-06-10.

[32] "Box Office Mojo" (http://www.boxofficemojo.com/movies/?id=mammamia.htm). Box Office Mojo. July 19, 2008. . Retrieved 2008-07-19.

[33] "Baz Bamigboye on a possible Mamma Mia sequel, Kate Winslet, Leonardo DiCaprio and much more" (http://www.dailymail.co.uk/tvshowbiz/article-1078332/Baz-Bamigboye-possible-Mamma-Mia-sequel-Kate-Winslet-Leonardo-DiCaprio-more.html).Mail Online. 2008-10-17. . Retrieved 2010-01-17.

[34] Hollywood Reporter - Mamma Mia now biggest selling DVD in UK history (http://www.hollywoodreporter.com/hr/content_display/news/e3i17e8d113d82a5300a568d1520c7ee9ac)

[35] MAMMA MIA! DVD Takes In 30 Million In First Day Of Sales (http://www.broadwayworld.com/article/MAMMA_MIA_DVD_Takes_In_30_Million_In_First_Day_Of_Sales_20081217)

[36] http://nyhetskanalen.se/1.799701/2009/01/09/mamma_mia_slog_dvd_rekord

[37] "Updated: Mamma Mia! Offers a Blu-ray First, Details Announced | HDR TheHDRoom" (http://www.thehdroom.com/news/Updated_Mamma_Mia_Offers_a_Blu-ray_First_Details_Announced/3561). Thehdroom.com. 2008-10-29. . Retrieved 2009-01-17.

[38] (http://www.youtube.com/watch?v=dq-FX1ced8g)

[39] http://www.mammamiamovie.com/

[40] http://www.imdb.com/title/tt0795421/

[41] http://www.allmovie.com/work/385390

[42] http://www.boxofficemojo.com/movies/?id=mammamia.htm

[43] http://www.rottentomatoes.com/m/mamma_mia/

[44] http://www.metacritic.com/film/titles/mammamia

[45] http://madeinatlantis.com/movies_central/2008/mamma_mia_production_details.htm

Doubt (2008 film)

Doubt	
US Theatrical release poster	
Directed by	John Patrick Shanley
Produced by	Scott Rudin
Written by	John Patrick Shanley
Starring	Meryl Streep Philip Seymour Hoffman Amy Adams Viola Davis
Music by	Howard Shore
Cinematography	Roger Deakins
Editing by	Dylan Tichenor
Distributed by	Miramax Films
Release date(s)	October 30, 2008 (AFI Fest) December 12, 2008 (limited) December 25, 2008 (wide)
Running time	104 min.
Country	United States
Language	English
Budget	$20 million
Gross revenue	$37,309,677[1]

Doubt is a 2008 film adaptation of John Patrick Shanley's Pulitzer Prize winning fictional stage play *Doubt: A Parable*. Written and directed by Shanley and produced by Scott Rudin, the film stars Meryl Streep, Philip Seymour Hoffman, Amy Adams, and Viola Davis, who were all nominated for Oscars at the 81st Academy Awards. It premiered on October 30, 2008 at the AFI Fest before being distributed by Miramax Films in limited release on

December 12, 2008 and in a wide release on Christmas Day.

Plot

Set in 1964 at a Catholic church in the Bronx, New York, the film opens with Father Flynn (Philip Seymour Hoffman) giving a sermon on the nature of doubt, noting that, like faith, it can be a unifying force. The next evening, Sister Aloysius (Meryl Streep), the strict principal of the attached school, discusses the sermon with her fellow nuns, the Sisters of Charity of New York. She asks if anyone has observed unusual behavior to give Father Flynn cause for preaching about doubt, and instructs them to keep their eyes open for any such behavior.

Sister James (Amy Adams), a young and naïve teacher, observes the closeness between Father Flynn and Donald Miller, the school's only black student and an altar boy. One day during class, Sister James receives a call in her class asking for Donald Miller to meet Father Flynn in the rectory. When he returns, Donald is distraught and Sister James notices the smell of alcohol on his breath. Later, while her students are learning a dance, she sees Father Flynn placing a white shirt in Donald's locker. On guard for unusual behavior, Sister James reveals her suspicions to Sister Aloysius.

Under the pretext of discussing problems with the school's Christmas play, Sisters Aloysius and James confront Father Flynn with their suspicions that his relationship with Donald may be inappropriate. Several times Father Flynn asks them to leave the matter alone as a private issue between the boy and himself but Sister Aloysius persists. Father Flynn then reveals that Donald had been caught drinking altar wine and that he had promised Donald not to tell anyone about the incident, and to allow Donald to remain an altar boy. Having now been forced to break that promise and reveal the truth, he will need to dismiss Donald as an altar boy. Father Flynn tells Sister Aloysius that he is displeased in the way she handled this.

Initially, Sister James is relieved and convinced of Father Flynn's innocence, but Sister Aloysius' belief that he has behaved inappropriately with the boy is unshakable. Sister James later confronts Father Flynn about the shirt she saw him leaving in Donald's locker, having not revealed this detail to Sister Aloysius. They discuss his relationship with the boy. Father Flynn reveals a reasonable explanation for the situation and Sister James' doubts are assuaged.

Sister Aloysius sends for Donald Miller's mother to reveal her suspicions. Mrs. Miller (Viola Davis) shocks Sister Aloysius by stating that she should not pursue the matter further and that he only has to last until the end of the school year before he goes on to attend high school. She also hints at Donald's homosexuality and reveals that his father is physically abusive, suggesting that the abuse is on that account. She begs Sister Aloysius to drop the matter, and rationalizes Donald's relationship with Father Flynn to protect him from his father, and because his chances of going to a better high school would increase after finishing from a prestigious church school.

Despite having no evidence and no support from Donald's mother, Sister Aloysius in their final showdown demands that Father Flynn tell the truth or she will go to his superiors. Father Flynn repeats that there is no illicit relationship, but Sister Aloysius says she knows that he has a history of problems, having moved to three different parishes in five years. She tells him that she has contacted a nun at one of his prior churches (she refuses to say whom) and that this nun corroborated her suspicions. Father Flynn is furious that she has contacted a nun rather than the church's pastor; the latter being the proper church protocol. Sister Aloysius demands that he resign. Unable to stand up to her willingness to destroy his reputation, he succumbs to her demands.

Following his final sermon, the nuns sit together in the church garden. Sister Aloysius tells Sister James that although Father Flynn has left his position as assistant pastor at their church, he has been made pastor at a different church and its parochial school, in effect, a promotion. She goes on to reveal that she lied about speaking to a nun at Father Flynn's former church, and thus never found hard evidence against him. Repeating a line from earlier in the film, Sister Aloysius says that "in the pursuit of wrongdoing, one steps away from God."

Sister Aloysius concludes that one also pays a price in pursuing wrongdoing. She breaks down in tears and reveals to Sister James "I have such doubts."

Cast

- Meryl Streep as Sister Aloysius Beauvier
- Philip Seymour Hoffman as Father Brendan Flynn
- Amy Adams as Sister James
- Viola Davis as Mrs. Miller
- Joseph Foster as Donald Miller
- Alice Drummond as Sister Veronica
- Paulie Litt as Tommy Conroy

Production

Production began on December 1, 2007.[2] The film, which centers on a Bronx Catholic school, was filmed in various areas of the Bronx, including Parkchester, St. Anthony's Catholic School, and the College of Mount Saint Vincent, as well as Bedford-Stuyvesant, Brooklyn.[3] The "garden" exterior scenes were shot at the historic Episcopal Church St. Luke in the Fields on Hudson Street in New York's Greenwich Village. The associated St. Luke's School was also heavily featured.

Reception

Based on 203 reviews collected by Rotten Tomatoes, the film has a 77% approval rating. The site reported in a consensus that "*Doubt* succeeds on the strength of its top-notch cast, who successfully guide the film through the occasional narrative lull."[4] Another review aggregator, Metacritic, gave the film a 68/100 approval rating based on 36 reviews.[5] Critic Manohla Dargis of *The New York Times* concluded that "the air is thick with paranoia in 'Doubt,' but nowhere as thick, juicy, sustained or sustaining as Meryl Streep's performance."[6]

Viola Davis' performance drew her critical raves. Salon magazine declared that Davis' character Mrs. Miller was acted with "a near-miraculous level of believability ... Davis, in her small, one-scene role, is incredibly moving - I can barely remember a Davis performance where I haven't been moved ... [she] plays her character, an anxious, hardworking woman who's just trying to hold her life and family together, by holding everything close. She's not a fountain of emotion, dispensing broad expression or movement; instead, she keeps it all inside and lets us in."[7]

NPR called Davis' acting in the movie "the film's most wrenching performance ... the other [actors] argue strenuously and occasionally even eloquently, to ever-diminishing effect; Davis speaks plainly and quietly, and leaves [no] doubt that the moral high ground is a treacherous place to occupy in the real world."[8]

Roger Ebert, who thought Davis' performance worthy of an Academy award, gave the film four stars, his highest rating, and praised its "exact and merciless writing, powerful performances and timeless relevance. It causes us to start thinking with the first shot," he continued, "and we never stop."[9]

Top ten lists

The film appeared on many critics' top ten lists of the best films of 2008.[10]

- 2nd – James Berardinelli, ReelViews[10]
- 2nd – Joe Neumaier, *New York Daily News*[10]
- 8th – Kyle Smith, *New York Post*[10]
- 8th – Peter Travers, *Rolling Stone*[10]
- 9th – David Edelstein, *New York* magazine[10]
- 10th – Michael Rechtshaffen, *The Hollywood Reporter*[10]
- 10th – Shawn Levy, *The Oregonian*[10]

Awards

Doubt received five Academy Awards nominations on January 22, 2009, for its four lead actors and for Shanley's script.

Awards			
Award	Category	Recipient(s)	Outcome
Academy Awards	Best Actress	Meryl Streep	Nominated
	Best Supporting Actor	Philip Seymour Hoffman	Nominated
	Best Supporting Actress	Amy Adams	Nominated
	Best Supporting Actress	Viola Davis	Nominated
	Best Adapted Screenplay	John Patrick Shanley	Nominated
BAFTA Awards	Best Leading Actress	Meryl Streep	Nominated
	Best Supporting Actor	Philip Seymour Hoffman	Nominated
	Best Supporting Actress	Amy Adams	Nominated
Chicago Film Critics Association Awards	Best Actress	Meryl Streep	Nominated
	Best Supporting Actor	Philip Seymour Hoffman	Nominated
	Best Supporting Actress	Amy Adams	Nominated
	Best Supporting Actress	Viola Davis	Nominated
	Best Adapted Screenplay	John Patrick Shanley	Nominated
Critics' Choice Awards	Best Picture		Nominated
	Best Actress	Meryl Streep	Won
	Best Supporting Actor	Philip Seymour Hoffman	Nominated
	Best Supporting Actress	Viola Davis	Nominated
	Best Acting Ensemble		Nominated
	Best Writer	John Patrick Shanley	Nominated
Dallas-Fort Worth Film Critics Association Awards	Best Supporting Actress	Viola Davis	Won
Detroit Film Critics Society Awards	Best Actress	Meryl Streep	Nominated
	Best Supporting Actress	Amy Adams	Nominated
Golden Globe Awards	Best Performance by an Actress in a Motion Picture – Drama	Meryl Streep	Nominated
	Best Performance by an Actor in a Supporting Role in a Motion Picture	Philip Seymour Hoffman	Nominated
	Best Performance by an Actress in a Supporting Role in a Motion Picture	Amy Adams	Nominated
	Best Performance by an Actress in a Supporting Role in a Motion Picture	Viola Davis	Nominated
	Best Screenplay – Motion Picture	John Patrick Shanley	Nominated
Houston Film Critics Society Awards	Best Supporting Actress	Viola Davis	Won
	Best Cast		Won

National Board of Review Awards	Breakthrough Performance by an Actress	Viola Davis	Won
	Best Cast		Won
Palm Springs International Film Festival	Spotlight Award	Amy Adams	Won
Phoenix Film Critics Society Awards	Best Actress	Meryl Streep	Won
Satellite Awards	Best Actress in a Motion Picture – Drama	Meryl Streep	Nominated
	Best Actor in a Supporting Role	Philip Seymour Hoffman	Nominated
	Best Actress in a Supporting Role	Viola Davis	Nominated
	Best Screenplay – Adapted	John Patrick Shanley	Nominated
Screen Actors Guild Awards	Outstanding Performance by a Female Actor in a Leading Role	Meryl Streep	Won
	Outstanding Performance by a Male Actor in a Supporting Role	Philip Seymour Hoffman	Nominated
	Outstanding Performance by a Female Actor in a Supporting Role	Amy Adams	Nominated
	Outstanding Performance by a Female Actor in a Supporting Role	Viola Davis	Nominated
	Outstanding Performance by a Cast in a Motion Picture		Nominated
St. Louis Gateway Film Critics Association Awards	Best Supporting Actress	Amy Adams	Nominated
	Best Supporting Actress	Viola Davis	Won
Washington D.C. Area Film Critics Association Awards	Best Actress	Meryl Streep	Won
	Best Cast		Won

External links

- Official site [11]
- Times online, "John Patrick Shanley's Doubt: in the church of poisoned minds" [12]
- *Doubt* [13] at the Internet Movie Database
- *Doubt* [14] at Rotten Tomatoes
- "Trailers" [15]. Apple: Miramax.

References

[1] "Doubt" (http://www.boxofficemojo.com/movies/?id=doubt.htm). *Box Office Mojo*. 4 January 2009. . Retrieved 4 January 2009.

[2] Pincus-Roth, Zachary (19 April 2007). "Meryl Streep and Philip Seymour Hoffman to Star in Doubt Film" (http://www.playbill.com/news/article/107473.html). *Playbill*. . Retrieved 7 February 2008.

[3] "The benefit of the 'Doubt'" (http://www.nydailynews.com/entertainment/galleries/the_benefit_of_the_doubt/the_benefit_of_the_doubt.html). *Daily News (New York)*. 5 February, 2008. . Retrieved 7 February 2008.

[4] "Doubt - Movie Reviews" (http://www.rottentomatoes.com/m/doubt). Rotten Tomatoes. 30 December 2008. . Retrieved 30 December 2008.

[5] "Doubt (2008):Reviews" (http://www.metacritic.com/film/titles/doubt). *Metacritic*. 30 December 2008. . Retrieved 30 December 2008.

[6] *The New York Times* Movie Review of Doubt, Dec 12, 2008 (http://movies.nytimes.com/2008/12/12/movies/12doub.html?partner=Rotten Tomatoes&ei=5083)

[7] Madden, Mike (2008-12-12). "Stephanie Zacharek" (http://www.salon.com/ent/movies/review/2008/12/12/doubt/index.html). Salon.com. . Retrieved 2010-04-27.

[8] "Viola Davis Tackles Fear, Shines In 'Doubt'" (http://www.npr.org/templates/story/story.php?storyId=98088645).NPR. 2008-12-10. . Retrieved 2010-04-27.

[9] Ebert review (http://rogerebert.suntimes.com/apps/pbcs.dll/article?AID=/20081210/REVIEWS/812109991)

[10] "Metacritic: 2008 Film Critic Top Ten Lists" (http://www.metacritic.com/film/awards/2008/toptens.shtml).Metacritic. . Retrieved
      January 11, 2009.

[11] http://www.doubt-themovie.com/

[12] http://entertainment.timesonline.co.uk/tol/arts_and_entertainment/film/article5561304.ece

[13] http://www.imdb.com/title/tt0918927/

[14] http://www.rottentomatoes.com/m/doubt/

[15] http://www.apple.com/trailers/miramax/doubt/

Julie & Julia

Julie & Julia	
Theatrical release poster	
Directed by	Nora Ephron
Produced by	Nora Ephron Laurence Mark Eric Steel Amy Robinson
Written by	Nora Ephron Screenplay Julie Powell Book
Starring	Meryl Streep Amy Adams Stanley Tucci Chris Messina Linda Emond
Music by	Alexandre Desplat
Cinematography	Stephen Goldblatt
Editing by	Richard Marks
Distributed by	Columbia Pictures
Release date(s)	August 7, 2009
Running time	123 minutes
Country	United States
Language	English
Budget	$40 million
Gross revenue	$129,538,392 [1]

Julie & Julia is a 2009 American comedy-drama film written and directed by Nora Ephron. The film depicts events in the life of chef Julia Child in the early years in her culinary career, contrasting her life with Julie Powell, who aspires to cook all 524 recipes from Child's cookbook during a single year, a challenge she described on her popular blog that would make her a published author.

Ephron's screenplay is adapted from two books: *My Life in France*, Child's autobiography, written with Alex Prud'homme, and a memoir by Julie Powell. In August 2002, Powell started documenting online her daily experiences cooking each of the 524 recipes in Child's *Mastering the Art of French Cooking*, and she later began reworking that blog, The Julie/Julia Project.[2] Both of these books were written and published in the same time frame of 2004 to 2006. The film is the first major motion picture based on a blog.[3]

Ephron began filming *Julie & Julia* in March 2008. Meryl Streep portrays Julia Child, and Amy Adams appears as Julie Powell. The film officially premiered on July 30, 2009, at the Ziegfeld Theatre in New York City and opened throughout North America on August 7, 2009.[4] Meryl Streep and Amy Adams previously starred together in the critically acclaimed film *Doubt*. *Julie & Julia* also reunited Streep with Stanley Tucci, who previously shared the screen in the 2006 box office smash *The Devil Wears Prada*.

Plot

In 2002, Julie Powell (Amy Adams) is a young writer trapped in a rather unpleasant job at the Lower Manhattan Development Corporation's call center, where she answers telephone calls from victims of the September 11 attacks, as well as members of the general public calling to complain about the LMDC's controversial plans for rebuilding the World Trade Center. To enliven her dreary life, she attempts to cook every recipe in Julia Child's cookbook, *Mastering the Art of French Cooking*, which was published in 1961, and writes a blog to document her progress.

Woven into her story is the story of Julia Child's time in Paris, in the 1950s, in which she learns about French cooking. The plot structure carefully highlights similarities in the challenges encountered by both Julie and Julia. Both women get much support from their husbands, although at one point Powell's husband is fed up with her excessive devotion to her hobby and leaves her for a few days.

Eventually, Julie's blog is highlighted in a story published in the *New York Times*, after which her project finally begins to receive the attention of journalists, literary agents, and publishers, as well as a dismissive response from Child herself. After Julia's book is initially rejected by Houghton Mifflin, it is eventually accepted and published by Alfred A. Knopf. The last scene shows Julia Child receiving a first print of her cookbook and celebrating the event with her husband.

Cast

- Meryl Streep as Julia Child
- Amy Adams as Julie Powell
- Stanley Tucci as Paul Child, Julia Child's husband
- Chris Messina as Eric Powell, Julie Powell's husband[5]
- Linda Emond as Simone Beck ("Simca"), with whom Julia wrote *Mastering the Art of French Cooking*
- Helen Carey as Louisette Bertholle, co-author of *Mastering the Art of French Cooking*
- Jane Lynch as Dorothy McWilliams, Julia Child's sister[6]
- Mary Lynn Rajskub as Sarah, Powell's best friend[7]
- Joan Juliet Buck as Madame Bassart
- Vanessa Ferlito as Cassie, one of Julie's friends
- Casey Wilson as Regina, one of Julie's friends
- Jillian Bach as Annabelle, one of Julie's friends
- Mary Kay Place as the voice of Julie's Mom

Reception

Critical reaction

The film has received generally positive reviews from critics.[8] Rotten Tomatoes reported that 75% of critics gave positive reviews based on 155 reviews with an average score of 6.7/10 with a "Certified Fresh" rating. [9] Another review aggregator, Metacritic, which assigns a normalized rating out of 100 top reviews from mainstream critics, gave it an average score of 65%, based on 32 reviews. [8] Meryl Streep has been widely praised for her performance as Julia Child. Movie critic A.O. Scott of The New York Times affirmed that "By now this actress [Streep] has exhausted every superlative that exists and to suggest that she has outdone herself is only to say that she's done it again. Her performance goes beyond physical imitation, though she has the rounded shoulders and the fluting voice down perfectly."[10] Reviewer Peter Travers wrote in Rolling Stone that "Meryl Streep — at her brilliant, beguiling best — is the spice that does the trick for the yummy Julie & Julia."[11] Similarly, Stephanie Zacharek of Salon magazine concluded that "Streep isn't playing Julia Child here, but something both more elusive and more truthful — she's playing our idea of Julia Child."[12]

Los Angeles Times critic Kenneth Turan commented, "[Julie & Julia] does it right. A consummate entertainment that echoes the rhythms and attitudes of classic Hollywood, it's a satisfying throwback to those old-fashioned movie fantasies where impossible dreams do come true. And, in this case, it really happened. Twice."[13] *The A.V. Club* gave the film a C, explaining, "Julie & Julia is two movies in one. That's one more movie than it needs to be."[14] *Entertainment Weekly* gave it a B+.[15] The review by Slate was also positive.[16]

Box office

On its opening weekend, the film opened #2 behind *G.I. Joe: The Rise of Cobra* with $20.1 million. [17] As of February 6, 2010, the film has made $118,610,261 worldwide, surpassing its $40 million budget.[18]

Awards and Nominations

Awards and Nominations			
Award	Category	Nominee	Result
Academy Awards[19]	Best Actress	Meryl Streep	Nominated
BAFTA Awards[20]	Best Actress	Meryl Streep	Nominated
Boston Society of Film Critics Awards[21]	Best Actress	Meryl Streep	Won
Broadcast Film Critics Association Awards[22]	Best Actress	Meryl Streep	Won (tied with Sandra Bullock)
Chicago Film Critics Association Awards[23]	Best Actress	Meryl Streep	Nominated
Detroit Film Critics Society Awards[24]	Best Actress	Meryl Streep	Nominated
EDA Awards[25]	Best Actress	Meryl Streep	Nominated
Golden Globe Awards[26]	Best Actress – Motion Picture Musical or Comedy	Meryl Streep	Won
	Best Motion Picture – Musical or Comedy	Film	Nominated

Houston Film Critics Society Awards	Best Actress	Meryl Streep	Nominated
Kansas City Film Critics Circle Awards[27]	Best Actress	Meryl Streep	Won
London Film Critics' Circle Awards[28]	Best Actress	Meryl Streep	Won
New York Film Critics Circle Awards[29]	Best Actress	Meryl Streep	Won
New York Film Critics Online Awards[30]	Best Actress	Meryl Streep	Won
North Texas Film Critics Association Awards[31]	Best Actress	Meryl Streep	Won
Oklahoma Film Critics Circle Awards[32]	Best Actress	Meryl Streep	Won
Phoenix Film Critics Society Awards[33]	Best Actress	Meryl Streep	Won
San Diego Film Critics Society Awards	Best Actress	Meryl Streep	Nominated
San Francisco Film Critics Circle Awards[34]	Best Actress	Meryl Streep	Won
Satellite Awards[35]	Best Actress – Motion Picture Musical or Comedy	Meryl Streep	Won
	Best Film – Musical or Comedy	Film	Nominated
	Best Adapted Screenplay	Nora Ephron	Nominated
Screen Actors Guild Awards[36]	Best Actress	Meryl Streep	Nominated
Southeastern Film Critics Association Awards[37]	Best Actress	Meryl Streep	Won
St. Louis Gateway Film Critics Association Awards	Best Actress	Meryl Streep	Nominated
Toronto Film Critics Association Awards[38]	Best Actress	Meryl Streep	Nominated
Washington DC Area Film Critics Association Awards[39]	Best Actress	Meryl Streep	Nominated

Home release

Julie & Julia was released on DVD and Blu-ray on December 8, 2009.

External links

- Official website [40]
- *Julie & Julia* [41] at the Internet Movie Database
- *Julie & Julia* [42] at Allmovie
- *Julie & Julia* [43] at Box Office Mojo
- *Julie & Julia* [44] at Rotten Tomatoes
- *Julie & Julia* [45] at Metacritic
- Original blog [46]

References

[1] http://www.boxofficemojo.com/movies/?id=julieandjulia.htm

[2] The Julie/Julia Project (http://blogs.salon.com/0001399/2002/08/25.html)

[3] *Philadelphia Weekly* (http://www.philadelphiaweekly.com/screen/Six-Films-Inspired-By-Items-on-the-Internets.html)

[4] "Tweetin' Streep" (http://www.zagat.com/Blog/Detail.aspx?SNP=NB&SCID=34&BLGID=22599). *Zagat.com*. July 30,, 2009. .

[5] "Chris Messina Joins Julie & Julia" (http://www.comingsoon.net/news/movienews.php?id=40198).2007-12-13. . Retrieved 2008-06-18.

[6] Bryon Perry (2008-03-05). "Jane Lynch" (http://www.variety.com/article/VR1117981898.html?categoryid=28&cs=1). *Variety*. . Retrieved 2008-06-18.

[7] "24's Rajskub Cooks Up Role in Julie and Julia" (http://community.tvguide.com/blog-entry/TVGuide-Editors-Blog/Movie-News/24s-Mary-Lynn/800036860). . Retrieved 2008-06-19.

[8] "Julie & Julia (2009): Reviews" (http://www.metacritic.com/film/titles/julieandjulia). Metacritic. . Retrieved 2009-08-09.

[9] "Julie & Julia Movie Reviews, Pictures" (http://www.rottentomatoes.com/m/julie_and_julia/). *IGN Entertainment*. Rotten Tomatoes. . Retrieved 2009-08-09.

[10] A.O. Scott, The New York Times: Two for te Stove, movie review of Julie & Julia. Aug 7, 2009. (http://movies.nytimes.com/2009/08/07/movies/07julie.html?ref=movies)

[11] Peter Travers, Rolling Stone: Movie Review of Julie & Julia. Aug 6, 2009. (http://www.rollingstone.com/reviews/movie/21376803/review/29554759/julie__julia)

[12] Stephanie Zacharek, Salon: Movie review of Julie & Julia. Aug 7, 2009. (http://www.salon.com/ent/movies/review/2009/08/07/julie_julia_review/index.html)

[13] LA Times review (http://www.latimes.com/entertainment/news/reviews/movies/la-et-julie-julia7-2009aug07,0,1724703.story), August 12, 2009

[14] A.V. Club review (http://www.avclub.com/articles/julie-julia,31381/),August 12, 2009

[15] EW review (http://www.ew.com/ew/article/0,,20296109,00.html), August 12, 2004

[16] Slate review (http://www.slate.com/id/2224414/), August 12, 2009

[17] "'G.I. Joe' commands box office with $56.2M debut" (http://news.yahoo.com/s/ap/20090809/ap_on_en_mo/us_box_office). Yahoo! News. . Retrieved 2009-08-09.

[18] "Julie & Julia (2009)" (http://www.boxofficemojo.com/movies/?id=julieandjulia.htm). *Box Office Mojo*. . Retrieved February 6, 2010.

[19] Gans, Andrew (2010-2-02). "Academy Award Nominations Announced Feb. 2; "Nine" Receives Four Noms" (http://www.playbill.com/news/article/136504-Academy-Award-Nominations-Announced-Feb-2-Nine-Receives-Four-Noms). *Playbill.com*. . Retrieved 2010-2-21. [20] Karger, Dave (2010-1-21). "'Avatar,' 'An Education,' 'Hurt Locker' dominate BAFTA nominations work = [[Entertainment Weekly (http://oscar-watch.ew.com/2010/01/21/avatar-an-education-hurt-locker-dominate-bafta-nominations/)]"]. . Retrieved 2010-1-21.

[21] Verniere, James (2009-12-14). "Meryl Streep, Mo'nique pick up Boston Film Critics' nods" (http://www.bostonherald.com/track/inside_track/view/20091214meryl_streep_monique_pick_op_boston_film_critics_nods/srvc=home&position=also).*Boston Herald*. . Retrieved 2010-1-3.

[22] "THE 15th CRITICS' CHOICE AWARDS NOMINEES" (http://www.bfca.org/ccawards/2009.php).BFCA. . Retrieved 2010-1-3.

[23] ""The Hurt Locker" Takes Top Honours" (http://www.chicagofilmcritics.org/). Chicago Film Critics Association. 2009-12-21. . Retrieved 2010-1-3.

[24] Tabouring, Frank (2009-12-18). "Detroit Film Critics Society Awards 2009" (http://www.us.imdb.com/news/ni1316302/). *IMDb*. . Retrieved 2010-1-3.

[25] "T2009 EDA Awards Nominees" (http://awfj.org/eda-awards/2009-eda-awards-nominees/). [Alliance of Women Film Journalists]. . Retrieved 2010-1-5.

[26] "Nominations & Winners" (http://www.goldenglobes.org/nominations/). HFPA. . Retrieved 2010-1-3.

[27] "Kansas City Film Critics Circle Homepage" (http://www.kcfcc.org/). Kansas City Film Critics Circle. . Retrieved 2010-1-5.

[28] "Film" (http://criticscircle.org.uk/film/). LFCC. . Retrieved 2010-1-12.

[29] "Best Actress Awards" (http://nyfcc.com/awards.php?cat=3). New York Film Critics. . Retrieved 2010-1-3.

[30] "NEW YORK FILM CRITICS ONLINE AWARDS FOR 2009" (http://www.azreporter.com/news/index.php?itemid=782). Arizona
      Reporter. . Retrieved 2010-1-5.

[31] "North Texas Film Critics Association announces results of member voting for best of 2009". Pegasus News.

[32] "Oklahoma Film Critics Circle Names "The Hurt Locker" Best Movie of 2009" (http://ofccircle.org/post/295663561/
      oklahoma-film-critics-circle-names-the-hurt-locker). OFCC. . Retrieved 2010-1-3.

[33] "DLocal Film Society Announces Awards" (http://www.kpho.com/entertainment/22025993/detail.html). *KPHO Entertainment News*.
      2009-12-22. . Retrieved 2010-1-3.

[34] "2009 SAN FRANCISCO FILM CRITICS CIRCLE AWARDS" (http://sffcc.org/2009awards.html). SFFCC. 2009-12-14. . Retrieved
      2010-1-3.

[35] "2009 14th Annual SATELLITE AWARDS™" (http://www.pressacademy.com/satawards/awards2009.shtml). *International Press
      Academy*. 2009. . Retrieved 2010-1-3.

[36] Nominations Announced for the 16th Annual Screen Actors Guild Awards® (http://www.sag.org/press-releases/december-17-2009/
      nominations-announced-16th-annual-screen-actors-guild-awardsÂ®)

[37] "Awards". SFFCC. 2009.

[38] "Toronto Film Critics Association Awards 2009" (http://torontofilmcritics.com/blog/2009/12/16/
      toronto-film-critics-association-awards-2009/). . Retrieved 2010-1-5.

[39] "Our Awards: 2009" (http://www.dcfilmcritics.com/awards/index.htm). *WAFCA*.2009-12-7. . Retrieved 2010-1-3.

[40] http://www.julieandjulia.com/

[41] http://www.imdb.com/title/tt1135503/

[42] http://www.allmovie.com/work/423340

[43] http://www.boxofficemojo.com/movies/?id=julieandjulia.htm

[44] http://www.rottentomatoes.com/m/julie_and_julia/

[45] http://www.metacritic.com/film/titles/julieandjulia

[46] http://blogs.salon.com/0001399/

Fantastic Mr. Fox (film)

Fantastic Mr. Fox	
Theatrical poster	
Directed by	Wes Anderson
Produced by	Wes Anderson Scott Rudin Allison Abbate Steven M. Rales

Written by	Wes Anderson Noah Baumbach (screenplay) Roald Dahl (book)
Starring	George Clooney Meryl Streep Jason Schwartzman Bill Murray Michael Gambon Jarvis Cocker Owen Wilson Willem Dafoe Helen McCrory
Music by	Alexandre Desplat
Cinematography	Tristan Oliver
Editing by	Andrew Weisblum
Studio	20th Century Fox Animation Indian Paintbrush Regency Enterprises American Empirical Pictures
Distributed by	20th Century Fox
Release date(s)	November 25, 2009
Running time	87 minutes
Country	United States United Kingdom
Language	English
Budget	$40 million[1]
Gross revenue	$46,293,911[1]

Fantastic Mr. Fox is a 2009 stop-motion animated film based on the Roald Dahl children's novel of the same name. Released in the autumn of 2009, it was produced by Regency Enterprises and Indian Paintbrush, and features the voices of George Clooney, Meryl Streep, Jason Schwartzman, and Bill Murray. It is the first animated film directed by Wes Anderson, and the first stop-motion animated film to be distributed by 20th Century Fox, also the first film by Anderson not to be rated R by the MPAA. Development on the project began in 2004 as collaboration between Anderson and Henry Selick (who worked with Anderson on the 2004 film *The Life Aquatic with Steve Zissou*) under Revolution Studios. In 2006 Revolution folded, Selick left to direct *Coraline*, and work on the film moved to 20th Century Fox. Production began in London in 2007.

Plot

While raiding a squab farm, Mr. Fox (George Clooney) and his wife Felicity (Meryl Streep) trigger a fox trap and become caged. Felicity reveals to Fox that she is pregnant and pleads with him to find a safer job should they escape.

Two years later, the Foxes and their sullen son Ash (Jason Schwartzman), are living in a hole. Fox, now a newspaper columnist, decides to move the family into a better home and buys one in the base of a tree, ignoring the warnings of his lawyer Badger (Bill Murray). The tree is located very close to the enormous facilities run by farmers Walter Boggis, Nathan Bunce, and Franklin Bean (Michael Gambon). Soon after the Foxes move in, Felicity's nephew Kristofferson (Eric Chase Anderson) comes to live with them, as his father has become very ill. Ash finds this situation intolerable considering his soft-spoken cousin is apparently superior to him in every possible aspect and seemingly everyone, including his own father, is charmed by Kristofferson at Ash's expense.

Fox and the opossum building superintendent, Kylie (Wallace Wolodarsky), make plans to steal various types of produce and poultry from the three farms, one by one. After all three heists are a success, the farmers decide to camp out near the Fox family's tree and kill Fox. When he emerges, the farmers open fire, only managing to shoot off his tail before he retreats back into his home. The farmers then attempt to dig Fox out, first by hand and then with three excavators. After tearing the hill site of the tree into a massive crater, the farmers discover that the Foxes have dug an escape tunnel deep underground.

Reasoning that the Foxes will eventually have to surface in search of food and water, the farmers lie in wait at the tunnel mouth. Underground, Fox encounters Badger and many of the other local animal residents whose homes have also been destroyed. As the animals begin to fear starvation, Fox leads a digging expedition to the three nearby farms, robbing them clean of Boggis' chickens, Bunce's ducks and geese, and Bean's turkeys, apples, and alcoholic cider. While the other animals feast, Ash and Kristofferson, beginning to reconcile after Kristofferson defended his cousin from a bully, return to Bean's farm, intending to reclaim Fox's tail, only to find that Bean has taken to wearing it as a necktie. When they are interrupted by the arrival of Bean's wife, Ash escapes but Kristofferson is captured.

After discovering that Fox has stolen all of their produce, the farmers decide to flood the animals' tunnel network by pumping it full of cider. The animals are forced to retreat into the sewers, and Fox learns that the farmers plan to use Kristofferson as bait to lure him into an ambush. They are soon confronted by Rat (Willem Dafoe), Bean's security guard. After a struggle with Fox that leaves him mortally wounded, Rat divulges Kristofferson's location.

Fox sends a message to the farmers, asking for a meeting in a town near the sewer hub wherein he will surrender in exchange for Kristofferson's freedom. The farmers set up an ambush, but Fox and the others anticipate it and launch a counterattack. Fox, Ash, and Kylie escape the scene at the town and slip into Bean's farm. In the operation, a much matured Ash frees Kristofferson and later deeply impresses his father and the gang by braving enemy fire to release a rabid beagle loose to keep the farmers at bay while the group escapes back to the sewers. The group manage to grab Fox's tail from Bean as they flee the compound.

The animals become accustomed to living in the sewers, and Ash and Kristofferson have completely settled their differences and have become good friends, sharing meditation time together among other activities. Fox, now taking to wearing his tail as an pin-on, leads them to a drain opening that is built into the floor of a large supermarket, which is shown to the viewing audience to be owned by the three farmers. Celebrating their abundant new food source and the news that Felicity is pregnant again, the animals dance in the aisles.

Cast

- George Clooney as Mr. Fox[2]
- Meryl Streep[3] as Mrs. Felicity Fox[4] (Cate Blanchett was prearranged to voice Mrs. Fox but she left the role for undisclosed reasons)[5]
- Jason Schwartzman[2] as Ash Fox
- Eric Chase Anderson as Kristofferson Silverfox
- Wallace Wolodarsky as Kylie Sven Opossum
- Bill Murray as Clive Badger[6]
- Willem Dafoe as Rat
- Owen Wilson as Coach Skip
- Michael Gambon as Franklin Bean
- Robin Hurlstone as Walter Boggis
- Hugo Guinness as Nathan Bunce
- Helen McCrory as Mrs. Bean
- Jarvis Cocker as Petey

Production

Joe Roth and Revolution Studios bought the film rights to *Fantastic Mr Fox* in 2004. Wes Anderson signed on as director with Henry Selick, who worked with Anderson on *The Life Aquatic with Steve Zissou*, as animation director. Anderson stated that he signed on because Roald Dahl was one of his heroes.[7] The story the novel covers would amount to the second act of the film. Anderson added new scenes to serve for the film's beginning and end.[8] The new scenes precede Mr. Fox's plan to steal from the three farmers and follow the farmers' bulldozing of the hill, beginning with the flooding of the tunnel. Selick left the project to work on the Neil Gaiman story *Coraline* in early 2006.[9] Mark Gustafson [10] is his replacement.[11] 20th Century Fox became the project's home in October 2006 after Revolution folded.[12]

In September 2007, Anderson announced voice work would begin.[2] The director chose to record the voices outside rather than in a studio: "We went out in a forest, [..] went in an attic, [and] went in a stable. We went underground for some things. There was a great spontaneity in the recordings because of that."[11] He said of the production design, "We want to use real trees and real sand, but it's all miniature."[2] Great Missenden, where Roald Dahl lived, has a major influence on the film's look.[7] The film mixes several forms of animation but consists primarily of stop motion.[12] Animation took place in London,[11] on stage C at 3 Mills Studio,[13] with Anderson directing the crew, many of whom animated Tim Burton's *Corpse Bride*.[14] Selick, who kept in contact with Anderson, said the director would act out scenes while in Paris and send them to the animators via iPhone.[15]

Fantastic Mr. Fox is Regency Enterprises' first completely animated film.

Soundtrack

Fantastic Mr. Fox	
Soundtrack by various artists	
Released	November 3, 2009
Genre	Film score Rock
Length	43:41
Label	ABKCO
Professional reviews	
• Allmusic	link [16]
Wes Anderson film soundtrack chronology	
The Darjeeling Limited (2007)	*Fantastic Mr. Fox* (2009)

The score for the film was composed by Alexandre Desplat. Jarvis Cocker commented that he wrote "three, four" songs for the film, one of which was included on the soundtrack.[17] The soundtrack also contains a selection of songs by The Beach Boys, The Bobby Fuller Four, Burl Ives, Georges Delerue, The Rolling Stones, and other artists. A soundtrack album for the film was released on November 3, 2009. It contains the following tracks:[18]

No.	Title	Artist	Length
1.	"American Empirical Pictures"	Alexandre Desplat	0:15
2.	"The Ballad of Davy Crockett" (from *Davy Crockett, King of the Wild Frontier*)	The Wellingtons	1:40
3.	"Mr. Fox in the Fields"	Alexandre Desplat	1:03
4.	"Heroes and Villains"	The Beach Boys	3:37
5.	"Fooba Wooba John"	Burl Ives	1:07
6.	"Boggis, Bunce, and Bean"	Alexandre Desplat	0:51
7.	"Jimmy Squirrel and Co."	Alexandre Desplat	0:46
8.	"Love" (from *Robin Hood*)	Nancy Adams	1:49
9.	"Buckeye Jim"	Burl Ives	1:19
10.	"High-speed French Train"	Alexandre Desplat	1:26
11.	"Whack-bat Majorette"	Alexandre Desplat	2:57
12.	"The Grey Goose"	Burl Ives	2:49
13.	"Bean's Secret Cider Cellar"	Alexandre Desplat	2:07
14.	"Une Petite Île" (from *Two English Girls*)	Georges Delerue	1:36
15.	"Street Fighting Man"	The Rolling Stones	3:15
16.	"Fantastic Mr Fox AKA Petey's Song"	Jarvis Cocker	1:21
17.	"Night and Day"	Art Tatum	1:28
18.	"Kristofferson's theme"	Alexandre Desplat	1:36
19.	"Just Another Dead Rat in a Garbage Pail (behind a Chinese Restaurant)"	Alexandre Desplat	2:34
20.	"Le Grand Choral" (from *Day for Night*)	Georges Delerue	2:24
21.	"Great Harrowsford Square"	Alexandre Desplat	3:21
22.	"Stunt Expo 2004"	Alexandre Desplat	2:28
23.	"Canis Lupus"	Alexandre Desplat	1:16
24.	"Ol' Man River"	The Beach Boys	1:18
25.	"Let Her Dance"	The Bobby Fuller Four	2:32

Release

The film had its world premiere as the opening film of the 53rd edition of the London Film Festival on October 14, 2009.[19] It went on general UK release on October 23, 2009, distributed by 20th Century Fox. A limited US release of the film began on November 13, 2009, followed by a nationwide release on November 25, 2009. As of January 28, 2010 the film has made $20,226,767 in the United States.

The film was released on DVD and Blu-Ray on March 23, 2010.[20]

Reception

Fantastic Mr. Fox has received positive reviews from a vast majority of critics,[21] with the film currently having a 93% 'Certified Fresh' rating on Rotten Tomatoes based on 197 reviews, becoming the second highest-rated animation film in 2009 in the site, behind *Up*.[22] Also, it has an 83 "universal acclaim" average review score from review aggregator Metacritic, which includes positive reviews from publications such as *Rolling Stone* and *The New York Times*.[23]

However, despite its critical success, it didn't gain a huge audience (although the film managed to gross slightly above the $40,000,000 budget). The film grossed $21,002,919 in the U.S., and $25,000,000 worldwide, making a total of $46,002,919 as of May 2010.

Awards

The film was nominated for Best Animated Feature and Best Original Score at the 82nd Academy Awards. The film has also nominated for the 2010 Critics Choice Awards for Best Animated Feature,[24] and the film was also nominated for The 2010 Golden Globe Award for Best Animated Feature Film[25] , but ultimately lost all the nominations to *Up*.

On January 14, 2010, the National Board of Review awarded Anderson a Special Filmmaking Achievement award[26] . After giving his acceptance speech, the audio of the speech was used in a short animation of Anderson's character (Weasel) giving the speech, animated by Payton Curtis, a key stop-motion animator on the film.[27]

External links

- Official website [28]
- *Fantastic Mr. Fox* [29] at the Internet Movie Database
- *Fantastic Mr. Fox* [30] at Rotten Tomatoes
- *Fantastic Mr. Fox* [31] at Allmovie
- George Clooney, Bill Murray and Wes Anderson Interview for *Fantastic Mr. Fox* [32]

References

[1] "Fantastic Mr. Fox (2009)" (http://www.boxofficemojo.com/movies/?id=fantasticmrfox.htm). *Box Office Mojo*. . Retrieved 28 January 2010.

[2] Josh Horowitz (September 26, 2007). "Wes Anderson Enlists Bill Murray For 'The Fantastic Mr. Fox'" (http://moviesblog.mtv.com/2007/09/26/wes-anderson-enlists-bill-murray-for-the-fantastic-mr-fox). *MTV Movies Blog*. . Retrieved September 26, 2007.

[3] Michael Fleming (August 6, 2008). "Streep in deep with Meyers" (http://www.variety.com/article/VR1117990178.html?categoryid=13&cs=1). *Variety*. . Retrieved August 8, 2008.

[4] "Meryl Streep voicing a role in Wes Anderson's 'Fantastic Mr. Fox'" (http://news-briefs.ew.com/2009/05/meryl-streep-vo.html). *Entertainment Weekly*. May 6, 2009. . Retrieved May 6, 2009.

[5] "EXCL: 1st Mr. Fox pic!" (http://www.joblo.com/excl-1st-mr-fox-pic). *JoBlo.com*. July 10, 2009. . Retrieved July 11, 2009.

[6] Max Evry (October 9, 2008). "Talking to City of Ember Mayor Bill Murray" (http://www.comingsoon.net/news/movienews.php?id=49375). *ComingSoon.net*. . Retrieved October 9, 2008.

[7] Gritten, David (November 17, 2007). "The Darjeeling Limited: Who needs a film set in LA when you have a speeding train in India?" (http://www.telegraph.co.uk/arts/main.jhtml?xml=/arts/2007/11/17/bfwes.xml). *The Telegraph* (London). . Retrieved November 22, 2007.

[8] "Selick Crazy For Fox" (http://www.scifi.com/scifiwire/art-main.html?2004-12/15/13.00.film). *Sci Fi Wire*. December 15, 2004. . Retrieved November 22, 2007.

[9] "Selick no longer at work on The Fantastic Mr. Fox" (http://www.aintitcool.com/display.cgi?id=22929). *Ain't It Cool News*. February 15, 2006. . Retrieved July 11, 2006.

[10] http://www.imdb.com/name/nm0348993/

[11] Joe Utichi (November 22, 2007). "Interview: Wes Anderson talks Darjeeling Limited and Mr. Fox" (http://www.rottentomatoes.com/m/darjeeling_limited/news/1691098/). *Rotten Tomatoes*. . Retrieved November 22, 2007.

[12] Michael Fleming (October 25, 2006). "Fox catches Dahl's Fox" (http://www.variety.com/article/VR1117952669.html?categoryid=1050&cs=1&query=Fantastic+Mr+Fox). *Variety*. . Retrieved February 25, 2007.

[13] "Who Are the Animators on Fantastic Mr. Fox?" (http://lineboil.com/2010/01/who-animated-fantastic-mr-fox/).*Lineboil*. January 12, 2010. . Retrieved January 17, 2010.

[14] Edward Douglas (February 2, 2009). "Henry Selick on Making Coraline" (http://www.comingsoon.net/news/movienews.php?id=51902). *ComingSoon.net*. . Retrieved February 2, 2009.

[15] Steve Prokopy (February 2, 2009). "Capone Talks with CORALINE Director and Wizard Master Henry Selick!!!" (http://www.aintitcool.com/node/39977). *Ain't It Cool News*. . Retrieved February 2, 2009.

[16] http://allmusic.com/cg/amg.dll?p=amg&sql=10:fbfrxzqald6e

[17] Brent DiCrescenzo (July 17, 2008). "From the UK to the Magic Kingdom" (http://www.timeout.com/chicago/articles/music/39791/from-the-uk-to-the-magic-kingdom). *Time Out*. . Retrieved August 8, 2008.

[18] http://www.slashfilm.com/2009/09/21/fantastic-mr-fox-soundtrack-listing/

[19] Ben Child (July 28, 2009). "Fantastic Mr Fox to open London Film Festival=[[The Guardian (http://www.guardian.co.uk/film/2009/jul/28/fantastic-mr-fox-open-london-film-festival)]"]. . Retrieved July 28, 2009.

[20] http://www.amazon.com/gp/product/B001QOGYBI/

[21] "Picture-book classic mixes the familiar and the stylish with imaginative results" (http://alibi.com/index.php?story=29931&scn=film). *Weekly Alibi*. .

[22] "Fantastic Mr. Fox" (http://au.rottentomatoes.com/m/1197696-fantastic_mr_fox/). Rotten Tomatoes. . Retrieved January 12, 2010.

[23] "Fantastic Mr. Fox" (http://www.metacritic.com/film/titles/fantasticmrfox).Metacritic. . Retrieved 2010-01-12.

[24] "15th Annual Critics Choice Award Nominees" (http://screencrave.com/2009-12-14/15th-annual-critics-choice-award-nominees/). ScreenCrave. . Retrieved December 14, 2009.

[25] "Nominations and Winners" (http://www.goldenglobes.org/nominations/). Hollywood Foreign Press Assoc.. . Retrieved December 15, 2009.

[26] "National Board of Review: Special Filmmaking Achievement award list" (http://www.nbrmp.org/awards/awards.cfm?award=Special Filmmaking Achievement). National Board of Review. . Retrieved January 17, 2010.

[27] http://www.youtube.com/watch?v=FTMSJ_qDC6o

[28] http://www.fantasticmrfoxmovie.com/

[29] http://www.imdb.com/title/tt0432283/

[30] http://www.rottentomatoes.com/m/1197696-fantastic_mr_fox/

[31] http://www.allmovie.com/work/378039

[32] http://www.flicksandbits.com/?p=42

It's Complicated (film)

It's Complicated	
Theatrical poster	
Directed by	Nancy Meyers
Produced by	Nancy Meyers Scott Rudin
Written by	Nancy Meyers
Starring	Meryl Streep Steve Martin Alec Baldwin
Music by	Heitor Pereira Hans Zimmer
Cinematography	John Toll
Editing by	Joe Hutshing David Moritz
Studio	Relativity Media
Distributed by	Universal Pictures
Release date(s)	December 25, 2009
Running time	121 minutes
Country	United States
Language	English
Budget	$85 million[1] [2]
Gross revenue	$219,069,702 (worldwide) [3]

It's Complicated is a 2009 American romantic comedy film written and directed by Nancy Meyers, starring Meryl Streep, Steve Martin and Alec Baldwin.[4] [5] [6] [7]

Plot

Jane (Meryl Streep) is a self-reliant divorcée who owns a successful bakery in Santa Barbara, California. After 10 years of separation and three grown children, she finally achieves a good relationship with her ex-husband Jake (Alec Baldwin), a successful attorney who has remarried the much-younger Agness (Lake Bell).

Jane and Jake attend their son Luke's college graduation in New York. A dinner together develops into an affair, making Jane "the other woman". Part of Jane knows it is wrong, since Jake and Agness are still married and trying to have a baby; the other part of Jane relishes being "the other woman" and continues the affair with Jake in Santa Barbara. Jake is just enjoying the clandestine sex and doesn't show much interest in Jane's growth as a person. He however feels nostalgic for the family life he once had with Jane, particularly her cooking, and being close with his children, and wonders if he should be growing old with Jane rather than starting a new family in late middle-age with Agness. While Agness has Jake scheduled for regular sessions at the fertility clinic, Jake secretly administers sperm control pills, and leaves one day to meet Jane for lunch.

Jake and Jane's children know nothing of their parents' affair, although Harley (John Krasinski), who is engaged to their daughter Lauren, spots them in a hotel and keeps silent. Agness knows nothing, as Jake still has sex with her on demand; her five-year-old son Pedro suspects something when Jake makes phone calls from the bathroom.

Complicating matters is Adam (Steve Martin), an architect hired to remodel Jane's home, who is himself healing from a divorce of his own, and who has begun to fall in love with Jane. He spends time getting to know her as a person. On the night of Luke's graduation party, Jane invites Adam to the party, but is high when he picks her up because she has smoked a joint that Jake had given her earlier. Later, at the party, Adam also smokes the joint and becomes high as well. Jake becomes jealous observing them, but with some cajoling by Jane, he gets high as well. Harley confronts Jake and Jane, stressed from keeping their secret, and eventually agrees to smoke some pot as well. Agness then observes Jake and Jane dancing together, and becomes suspicious of their renewed closeness.

When they leave, Adam asks if they could have something to eat so Jane takes him to her bakery-restaurant and offers to make him anything; he asks for a chocolate croissant, which they make from scratch laughing and having fun. This takes hours, and they enjoy the time together. As her architect, he shows great sensitivity in listening to her needs and vision for her remodeled kitchen and bedroom.

Jake leaves Agness, who kicks him out of their house as he confesses that he's still in love with Jane, who rebuffs his gesture. Eventually via webcam under embarrassing circumstances, Adam learns Jane is still seeing Jake. Adam knows his boundaries and tells Jane he cannot continue seeing her as this triangle will only lead to heartbreak. Her kids also find out, and they are not happy about Mom and Dad getting together again, as they are still recovering from the divorce ten years ago. Jane tells them she is not getting back with their dad, who then drives off in his Porsche while the children go to Harley and Lauren's house. Jane soon reconciles with the kids, citing that she wanted to do this for herself, which they sympathize. When she returns home, Jake awaits her to talk, and the two end their affair on amicable terms.

The film ends with Adam returning to Jane's house to work on her addition and before the credits roll Jane and Adam are seen laughing while walking into her house.

Cast

- Meryl Streep as Jane Adler
- Alec Baldwin as Jake Adler
- Steve Martin as Adam Schaffer
- John Krasinski as Harley
- Lake Bell as Agness Adler
- Mary Kay Place as Joanne
- Rita Wilson as Trisha
- Alexandra Wentworth as Diane
- Hunter Parrish as Luke Adler
- Zoe Kazan as Gabby Adler
- Caitlin Fitzgerald as Lauren Adler
- James Patrick Stuart as Dr. Moss
- Blanchard Ryan as Annalise
- Michael Rivera as Eddie
- Robert Curtis Brown as Peter
- Peter Mackenzie as Dr. Alan
- Rosalie Ward as Alex

Production

In May 2008, Nancy Meyers agreed to a project for Universal Studios that she would write and direct, to be co-produced with Scott Rudin.[8] The project was referred to as *The Untitled Nancy Meyers Project* during its inception and early production. Establishing commitments from the principals began in 2008, with Meryl Streep and Alec Baldwin entering discussions in August,[4] [6] and Steve Martin joining the cast in October.[5] Casting continued through 2009, with Zoe Kazan, Lake Bell, and Hunter Parrish joining in January,[9] John Krasinski in February,[10] Rita Wilson in March,[11] and Caitlin Fitzgerald in June.[12]

The sets were easy to design. Most scenes take place in the protagonist's home and interior courtyard, and as such the architectural details had to be fastidiously worked out, but the rooms were kept bare to reflect the character's functional tastes and limited budget. There are relatively few decorations, just "a bunch of thrift-store things haphazardly thrown together", in the words of production designer Jon Hutman. The building itself is a traditional 1920s Spanish-ranch-style adobe-mud house which "epitomised the Santa Barbara area."[13]

Filming commenced in New York City in April 2009,[14] and completed in August 2009.[15] *It's Complicated* was released on December 25, 2009.[16] [17]

Reception

Critics

The film has received generally mixed reviews. Review aggregate Rotten Tomatoes reports that 57% of critics have given the film a positive review based on 161 reviews, with an average score of 5.8/10. The critical consensus is: *Despite fine work by an appealing cast, It's Complicated is predictable romantic comedy fare, going for broad laughs instead of subtlety and nuance.*[18] Another review aggregator, Metacritic, which assigns a weighted average score from 1 to 100 based on reviews from mainstream critics, gave the film an average score of 57% based on 30 reviews.[19]

Box office

The film took #4 in its opening weekend behind *Avatar*, *Sherlock Holmes*, and *Alvin and the Chipmunks: The Squeakquel* with $22,100,820. It currently has a total gross of $112,927,070 in North America and a total of $214,727,200 worldwide.[3]

Awards and nominations

Awards			
Award	Category	Recipient(s)	Outcome
Broadcast Film Critics Association Awards	Best Comedy Film	Film	Nominated
Golden Globe Awards[20]	Best Actress – Motion Picture Musical or Comedy	Meryl Streep	Nominated
	Best Motion Picture - Musical or Comedy	Nancy Meyers	Nominated
	Best Screenplay	Nancy Meyers	Nominated
National Board of Review Awards	Best Cast	Alec Baldwin, Meryl Streep and Steve Martin	Won
Satellite Awards	Best Film – Musical or Comedy	Film	Nominated
BAFTA Awards	Best Supporting Actor	Alec Baldwin	Nominated

Home media

It's Complicated became available on DVD and Blu-ray Tuesday, April 27, 2010.[21]

External links

- Official website [22]
- *It's Complicated* [23] at the Internet Movie Database
- *It's Complicated* [24] at Box Office Mojo

References

[1] Abramowitz, Rachel (September 12, 2009). "Meryl Streep's got legs" (http://articles.latimes.com/2009/sep/12/entertainment/ et-streep12?pg=3). *Los Angeles Times*. . Retrieved January 6, 2010. "With the exception of "It's Complicated", with a budget of $75 million [...]"

[2] Fritz, Ben (December 28, 2009). "Holiday box-office take is highest in recent history" (http://www.latimes.com/business/ la-fi-ct-boxoffice28-2009dec28,0,1741915.story). *Los Angeles Times*. . Retrieved January 3, 2010. "[...] "It's Complicated", which stars Meryl Streep, wasn't particularly impressive given its budget of about $85 million."

[3] "It's Complicated (2009)" (http://www.boxofficemojo.com/movies/?id=itscomplicated.htm). *Box Office Mojo*.. Retrieved April 29, 2010.

[4] Fleming, Michael (August 5, 2008). "Streep in deep with Meyers" (http://www.variety.com/article/VR1117990178.html?categoryid=13& cs=1). *Variety*. . Retrieved 2009-08-23.

[5] Fleming, Michael (October 13, 2008). "Steve Martin joins Nancy Meyers film" (http://www.variety.com/article/VR1117993916 html?categoryid=1238&cs=1). *Variety*. . Retrieved 2009-08-23.

[6] Fleming, Michael (August 14, 2008). "Baldwin flirts with romantic comedy" (http://www.variety.com/article/VR1117990582. html?categoryid=13&cs=1&query=Alec+Baldwin+++Nancy+Meyers). *Variety*. . Retrieved 2009-08-23.

[7] Labrecque, Jeff (August 7, 2009). "Meryl Streep on the prowl in 'Its Complicated" trailer" (http://popwatch.ew.com/2009/08/07/ meryl-streep-on-the-prowl-in-its-complicated-trailer/). *Entertainment Weekly*. . Retrieved August 23, 2009.

[8]   Fleming, Michael (May 7, 2008). "Universal woos next Meyers movie" (http://www.variety.com/article/VR1117985259. html?categoryid=13&cs=1&query=Nancy+Meyers). *Variety*. . Retrieved 2009-08-23.

[9]   Fleming, Michael (January 21, 2009). "Meyers casts Kazan, Bell, Parrish" (http://www.variety.com/article/VR1117998906. html?categoryid=1236&cs=1&query=Alec+Baldwin+++Nancy+Meyers). *Variety*. . Retrieved 2009-08-23.

[10] Goldberg, Matt (February 10, 2009). "John Krasinski Boards Untitled Nancy Meyers Project" (http://www.collider.com/entertainment/ news/article.asp?aid=10869&tcid=1). Collider. . Retrieved 2009-08-23.

[11] Kemp, Stuart (March 20, 2009). "Wilson in demand" (http://www.independent.co.uk/arts-entertainment/films/features/ screen-talk-losers-club-could-be-big-winner-1649267.html). *The Independent*. . Retrieved 2009-08-23.

[12] Kroll, Justin (June 7, 2009). "Players" (http://www.variety.com/article/VR1118004643.html?categoryId=28&cs=1). *Variety*. .

[13] Harrison, Penny (2010-01-09). "Home movies". *Herald Sun*: p. Home magazine, pp. 16–17.

[14] "Films recently shot in New York" (http://www.variety.com/article/VR1118002677.html?categoryid=3602&cs=1&query=Alec+ Baldwin+++Nancy+Meyers). *Variety*. April 21, 2009. . Retrieved 2009-08-23.

[15] Reuters, Thomas (August 14, 2009). "Still the love interest" (http://www.screenindia.com/news/still-the-love-interest/500706/). *Screen*. . Retrieved 2009-08-23.

[16] Goldstein, Patrick (August 17, 2009). "Universal takes a public spanking for its movie flops" (http://latimesblogs.latimes.com/ the_big_picture/2009/08/universal-takes-a-public-spanking-for-its-movie-flops-.html). *Los Angeles Times*. . Retrieved 2009-08-23.

[17] "Universal Pictures' Fall/Holiday 2009 Sneak Preview!" (http://www.movieweb.com/news/NELfbMPLCfEnPN).*Movieweb*. August 13, 2009. . Retrieved 2009-08-23.

[18] "It's Complicated Movie Reviews, Pictures" (http://www.rottentomatoes.com/m/1208806-its_complicated/). *Rotten Tomatoes*. *IGN Entertainment*. . Retrieved June 11, 2010.

[19] "It's Complicated (2009): Reviews" (http://www.metacritic.com/film/titles/itscomplicated). *Metacritic*. CNET Networks. . Retrieved February 11, 2010.

[20] "Nominations and Winners" (http://www.goldenglobes.org/nominations/). *Hollywood Foreign Press Association*.December 15, 2009. . Retrieved 2009-12-15.

[21] "NBC Universal Store" (http://www.nbcuniversalstore.com/detail.php?p=258092). .

[22] http://www.itscomplicatedmovie.com/

[23] http://www.imdb.com/title/tt1230414/

[24] http://www.boxofficemojo.com/movies/?id=itscomplicated.htm

Bart's Girlfriend

The Simpsons episode	
"Bart's Girlfriend"	
Episode no.	110
Prod. code	2F04
Orig. airdate	November 6, 1994
Show runner(s)	David Mirkin
Written by	John Collier
Directed by	Susie Dietter
Chalkboard	"I will not send lard through the mail."[1]
Couch gag	Five pairs of eyes float in the air, before being reunited with the Simpsons.
Guest star(s)	Meryl Streep as Jessica Lovejoy[1]
DVD commentary	Matt Groening David Mirkin Jonathan Collier Julie Kavner Susie Dietter David Silverman

"Bart's Girlfriend" is the seventh television episode of *The Simpsons*' sixth season. It originally aired on the Fox network in the United States on November 6, 1994. The plot of the episode follows the secret romance of Bart and Jessica Lovejoy, Reverend Lovejoy's daughter. Bart tries to end the romance when he discovers that, behind her innocent facade, she is an even bigger troublemaker than he is. Jessica then steals the money from the collection plate, leaving Bart to take the blame and Lisa to expose the truth.

The episode was written by Jonathan Collier, and directed by Susie Dietter. Former *The Simpsons*' show runner David Mirkin originally came up with the idea of Bart having a girlfriend that was more evil than him. Meryl Streep guest stars in the episode as Jessica Lovejoy. It features cultural references to films such as *Planet of the Apes* and *The Silence of the Lambs*. Since airing, the episode has received many positive reviews from fans and television critics, and *Entertainment Weekly* named Meryl Streep's role as one of the best guest appearances on *The Simpsons*.

Plot

Bart falls in love with Reverend Lovejoy's daughter, Jessica. However, when he approaches her, she ignores him. The next Sunday, Bart decides to attend Sunday school to try to convince Jessica that he is a good person, but she still ignores him. Frustrated, Bart goes to the park to play a prank on Groundskeeper Willie, and is punished with detention. Jessica approaches him to express sympathy and asks him to dinner with her family.

During a formal dinner with the Lovejoys, Bart's crude mannerisms and language cause him to get banned from ever seeing Jessica again. However, Jessica realizes that Bart is a bad boy and tells Bart that she likes him. They begin secretly dating and causing mischief through the town. Bart quickly realizes that Jessica is even more badly behaved than he, and at the next church service, he tries to make her see the error of her ways. Although she seems to agree, Jessica immediately steals from the church collection plate before forcing it back upon the hapless Bart. The congregation mistakenly believes that Bart took the money when they see him with the empty plate. Although Homer assumes Bart is guilty, Marge is willing to hear him out, but Bart claims he does not know who did it.

Upon finding out the truth, Lisa is determined not to allow her brother to take blame for something he did not do, and she tells the church congregation that Jessica is the guilty person. The townspeople then search Jessica's room, where the money is found under her bed, and Jessica admits she did it to gain attention. She is punished by being forced to scrub the church steps, and Bart receives an apology from the congregation at Marge's insistence. Later, Bart approaches Jessica at church and tells her what he has learned, to which Jessica responds that she has learned that she can make boys do whatever she wants. Bart then agrees to finish Jessica's chores as she runs off with another boyfriend. However, as soon as she leaves, he snickers about how bad a job he is going to do on the steps to get back at her.

Production

"Bart's Girlfriend" was written by Jonathan Collier and directed by Susie Dietter.[2] David Mirkin, who was show runner at the time, originally had the idea of Bart having a girlfriend that was more evil than him.[3] Mirkin gave the idea to Collier to write it with the help of the show's executive producer, James L. Brooks. Collier said later that he thought it was a case of Brooks coming up with good ideas and him "giggling insequentially".[4] The idea for the ending of the episode was to have none of the characters learn anything from the experience.[3]

Meryl Streep guest starred in the episode as Jessica Lovejoy.

Matt Groening, the creator of *The Simpsons*, felt that Jessica Lovejoy was hard to draw in his own style but at the same time make her attractive.[5] Julie Kavner, who provides the voice of Marge Simpson on the show, was particularly impressed by the eyes.[6] Jessica was made the Reverend's daughter to give the impression that she was good at first and then to show that she was rebelling against the righteousness of her family.[4] In the scene where Bart talks to Jessica outside her house, her baton playing was in the script but the exact choreography was not. Dietter liked its incorporation because it gave Jessica something else, other than Bart, to pay attention to. This was also done in the final scene when Jessica scrubs the church steps and plays with the scrub brush.[7]

Academy Award winning actress Meryl Streep was called in to do the voice of Jessica.[6] Nancy Cartwright, who provides the voice of Bart Simpson on the show, was a huge fan of Streep and she assumed that Streep would record her lines individually, but all of their recordings were done together.[8] Streep showed up alone with no entourage at the Village Recorder in West Los Angeles at 2:30 P.M., where she recorded her parts with Cartwright.[8] Streep was continually doing many different versions of her lines.[8] Mirkin felt she was easy to work with because she was versatile and keen to do a lot of different things, and as Mirkin expressed it, "easily evil".[3] Cartwright said in an interview with *The Pantagraph* that she really wanted Streep's autograph, but was afraid to ask for it.[9] After the recording session, Streep tapped Cartwright on the shoulder, and said her kids were big *The Simpsons* fans and that she would be in "big trouble" if she did not get Cartwright's autograph.[9]

In a take off of John Travolta in the 1983 film *Staying Alive*, Bart struts down a street in Springfield after he is invited to dinner at the Lovejoys, just as Travolta strutted through Times Square to the same tune.[3] That joke was written by Jace Richdale, who was the co-executive producer of *The Simpsons* at the time.[3] When Homer is musing over Bart's first date, he begins to sing "Sunrise, Sunset" from *Fiddler on the Roof*, before moving on to "Cat's in the Cradle", and then "Yes, We Have No Bananas". He then begins to weep due to the people in the song having no bananas. The joke was reportedly very expensive for the writers to put in because they had to pay thousands of dollars for the rights to use the songs on the show.[4]

"Bart's Girlfriend" originally aired on the Fox network in the United States on November 6, 1994.[1] The episode was selected for release in a 2001 video collection of selected episodes titled: *The Simpsons – Love, Springfield Style.*[10] Other episodes included in the collection set were "It's A Mad, Mad, Mad, Mad Marge", "The Two Mrs Nahasapeemapetilons", and "I'm with Cupid".[10] The episode was included in *The Simpsons* season 6 DVD set, which was released on August 16, 2005, as *The Simpsons – The Complete Sixth Season.*[11]

Cultural references

In the beginning of the episode, the parents chase the children in a cornfield to eventually round them up for church, which parodies a similar scene from the 1968 film *Planet of the Apes*, where the humans are rounded up by apes.[3] After Bart is accused of stealing from the church collection plate, he is forced to wear a straitjacket in church, which is a reference to Hannibal Lecter's straitjacket in *The Silence of the Lambs.*[1] "Misirlou", the theme song of the 1994 film *Pulp Fiction*, plays during Bart and Jessica's date.[2] Bart calls Jessica "smart, beautiful and a liar..." and then claims she's "...so much better than that *Sarah, plain and tall*". The scene then cuts to a shot of a plain and tall girl named Sarah that overhears Bart and begins to cry.[7] The Lovejoy family has a replica of Leonardo Da Vinci's painting *The Last Supper* hanging on the wall in their dining room.[1] The sign on the Springfield Church marquee reads: "Evil Women in History: From Jezebel to Janet Reno".[1]

Reception

In its original American broadcast, "Bart's Girlfriend" finished 53rd in the ratings for the week of October 31 to November 6, 1994, with a Nielsen rating of 9.6.[12] The episode was the third highest rated show on the Fox network that week, beaten only by *Beverly Hills, 90210*, and *Married... With Children.*[12]

Since airing, the episode has received many positive reviews from fans and television critics. Warren Martyn and Adrian Wood, the authors of the book *I Can't Believe It's a Bigger and Better Updated Unofficial Simpsons Guide*, said: "Poor Bart gets picked on very cruelly by Jessica in a cleverly drawn study of pre-pubescent love. We're very fond of the scene in which Bart leaps out of the window at the church, after which Homer cries: He's heading for the window!"[1] Colin Jacobson at DVD Movie Guide said in a review of the sixth season DVD: "We don't often

David Mirkin named "Bart's Girlfriend" and "Homer the Great" his favorites of the season.

see Bart in a sympathetic light, so shows like this one are fun. "Girlfriend" reminds me of Season Four's "New Kid on the Block" since it also featured Bart in love, though the programs differ since here the girl reciprocates. Streep does nicely as the bad kid and we get many fine moments in this memorable program."[13] TV Squad's Adam Finley said: "Homer and Marge remained in the background for most of this episode, with Bart and Lisa becoming the main focus. Earlier episodes seemed to focus more on the dynamics between the two siblings, and it's always a nice change of pace when the show examines their love for one another as opposed to constant rivalries. Lisa really wants to help Bart in this episode, and it's actually quite touching."[14]

In a 2008 article, *Entertainment Weekly* named Meryl Streep's role as Jessica Lovejoy as one of the sixteen best guest appearances on *The Simpsons.*[15] *Total Film*'s Nathan Ditum ranked Streep's performance as the fifth best guest appearance in the show's history, commenting that she is "the perfect mix of beguiling and devilish as Reverend Lovejoy's rebellious daughter."[16] David Mirkin told the *Daily News of Los Angeles* that "Bart's Girlfriend" and "Homer the Great" are his favorite episodes of the season.[17] Mirkin liked the scene where Bart is punched by Nelson at the playground because Bart takes a while to recover, which made the scene more realistic.[2] Nancy Cartwright told the *Chicago Tribune* that this episode, and "Lisa's Substitute" from season two, are her two favorite *The Simpsons* episodes.[18]

External links

- "Bart's Girlfriend" [19] at The Simpsons.com
- "Bart's Girlfriend" [20] episode capsule at The Simpsons Archive
- "Bart's Girlfriend" [21] at TV.com
- "Bart's Girlfriend" [22] at the Internet Movie Database

References

[1]   Richmond, Ray; Antonia Coffman (1997). *The Simpsons: A Complete Guide to our Favorite Family*. Harper Collins Publishers. p. 156. ISBN 0-00-638898-1.

[2]   Martyn, Warren; Wood, Adrian (2000). "Bart's Girlfriend" (http://www.bbc.co.uk/cult/simpsons/episodeguide/season6/page7.shtml). BBC. . Retrieved 2008-08-02.

[3]   Mirkin, David. (2005). *The Simpsons The Complete Sixth Season DVD commentary for the episode "Bart's Girlfriend"*. [DVD]. 20th Century Fox.

[4]   Collier, Jonathan. (2005). *The Simpsons The Complete Sixth Season DVD commentary for the episode "Bart's Girlfriend"*. [DVD]. 20th Century Fox.

[5]   Groening, Matt. (2005). *The Simpsons The Complete Sixth Season DVD commentary for the episode "Bart's Girlfriend"*. [DVD]. 20th Century Fox.

[6]   Kavner, Julie. (2005). *The Simpsons The Complete Sixth Season DVD commentary for the episode "Bart's Girlfriend"*. [DVD]. 20th Century Fox.

[7]   Dietter, Susie. (2005). *The Simpsons The Complete Sixth Season DVD commentary for the episode "Bart's Girlfriend"*. [DVD]. 20th Century Fox.

[8]   Cartwright, Nancy (2000). *My Life as a 10-Year-Old Boy*. New York City: Hyperion. pp. 185–194. ISBN 0-7868-8600-5.

[9]   Woulfe, Sharon (November 3, 2001). "Ay caramba! Animated actress live at IWU - Bart's voice a real character Stories shared about popular ' Simpsons ' show". *The Pantagraph* (Pantagraph Publishing Co).

[10]   "The Simpsons – Love, Springfield Style (VHS)" (http://www.amazon.co.uk/Simpsons-Love-Springfield-Style/dp/B00005J9PL). Amazon.com. . Retrieved 2008-11-14.

[11]   "The Simpsons - The Complete Sixth Season". *The Simpsons* (20th Century Fox). August 16, 2005.

[12]   "What we watch, what we don't...". *Austin American-Statesman*. November 13, 1994. p. 36. Retrieved on October 17, 2008.

[13]   Jacobson, Colin (2003). "The Simpsons: The Complete Sixth Season (1994)" (http://www.dvdmg.com/simpsonsseasonsix.shtml). DVD Movie Guide. . Retrieved 2008-10-08.

[14]   Adam Finley (2006-08-10). "The Simpsons: Bart's Girlfriend" (http://www.tvsquad.com/2006/07/13/the-simpsons-barts-girlfriend/). *TV Squad*. . Retrieved 2008-10-01.

[15]   "16 great 'Simpsons' guest stars" (http://www.ew.com/ew/article/0,,20049408,00.html). Entertainment Weekly. 2008-05-11. . Retrieved 2008-05-11.

[16]   Ditum, Nathan (March 29, 2009). "The 20 Best Simpsons Movie-Star Guest Spots" (http://www.totalfilm.com/features/the-20-best-simpsons-movie-star-guest-spots). *Total Film*. . Retrieved 2009-08-02.

[17]   Lowman, Rob (August 16, 2005). "DVD - Reviews Of New Releases". Daily News of Los Angeles. p. U4.

[18]   Funk, Tim (September 18, 1995). "Is she fed up doing Bart Simpson's voice? No way, man!". *Chicago Tribune*: p. 5.

[19]   http://www.thesimpsons.com/episode_guide/0607.htm

[20]   http://www.snpp.com/episodes/2F04.html

[21]   http://www.tv.com/the-simpsons/barts-girlfriend/episode/1395/summary.html

[22]   http://www.imdb.com/title/tt0701065/

List of King of the Hill episodes

This is a list of episodes of the Fox animated television series *King of the Hill*. The series was originally broadcast from January 12, 1997 to September 13, 2009.

Seasons

Season	# of Episodes	Originally aired	Prod. line	DVD releases
1	12	1997	4Exx	R1: July 1, 2003 R2: March 13, 2006 R4: March 15, 2006
2	23	1997 – 1998	5Exx	R1: November 11, 2003 R2: March 13, 2006 R4: May 23, 2006
3	25	1998 – 1999	3ABExx	R1: December 28, 2004 R2: August 28, 2006 R4: September 26, 2006
4	24	1999 – 2000	4ABExx	R1: May 3, 2005 R2: January 15, 2007 R4: June 20, 2007
5	20	2000 – 2001	5ABExx	R1: November 22, 2005 R2: February 26, 2007 R4: April 23, 2008
6	22	2001 – 2002	6ABExx	R1: May 2, 2006
7	23	2002 – 2003	7ABExx	--
8	22	2003 – 2004	8ABExx	--
9	15	2004 – 2005	9ABExx	--
10	15	2005 – 2006	AABExx	--
11	12	2007	BABExx	--
12	22	2007 – 2008	CABExx	--
13	24	2008 – 2009	DABExx	--

Episodes

- № = Overall episode number
- # = Episode number within the season
- Code = Production code

Pilots: 1995-1996

#	Title	Original air date	Code
Pilot	"Original Pilot"	September 24, 1995	3E01
This is the Original Pilot Episode of King of the Hill Short			
Pilot	"Last Short"	December 29, 1996	3E02
This is the Original Last Episode of King of the Hill Short			

Season 1: 1997

№	#	Title	Directed by	Written by	Original air date	Code
1	1	"Pilot"	Wes Archer	Mike Judge & Greg Daniels	January 12, 1997	4E01
When a baseball hits Bobby in the eye during a baseball game, the resulting black eye and Hank's short temper (from dealing with a teenaged Mega-Lo-Mart clerk) cause a social worker to suspect Hank of child abuse. Meanwhile, Hank's friends, conspiracy nut Dale Gribble, down-and-out Army barber Bill Dauterive, and womanizer Jeff Boomhauer, try to fix Hank's truck.						
2	2	"Square Peg"	Gary McCarver	Joe Stillman	January 19, 1997	4E02
Peggy is mortified and tongue-tied when she finds out she has been chosen to teach the middle school's sexual education class.						
3	3	"The Order of the Straight Arrow"	Klay Hall	Cheryl Holliday	February 2, 1997	4E03
Hank, Bill, Dale, and Boomhauer take Bobby and his friends on an Order of the Straight Arrow camping trip where the men send the boys on a snipe hunt...and Bobby ends up killing a whooping crane. Meanwhile, Peggy sneaks out to buy special shoes for her large feet.						
4	4	"Hank's Got the Willies"	Monte Young	Johnny Hardwick	February 9, 1997	4E05
Hank is worried that Bobby doesn't have a role model in life--and things get worse when Bobby accidentally hits Hank's idol, Willie Nelson (voiced by Nelson himself) with a golf club during a day on the green. Rated TV-PG-DL.						
5	5	"Luanne's Saga"	Patty Shinagawa	Paul Lieberstein	February 16, 1997	4E04
Buckley breaks up with Luanne. Hank's promise to find Luanne a new boyfriend (guest-voiced by Mando Navarro) in forty-eight hours backfires when Luanne hooks up with Boomhauer. Also with Chuck Mangione, as a guest voice.						
6	6	"Hank's Unmentionable Problem"	Adam Kuhlman	Mike Judge & Greg Daniels	February 23, 1997	4E07
Hank's ongoing constipation causes great concern for Peggy and, much to Hank's embarrassment, everyone else in Arlen.						
7	7	"Westie Side Story"	Brian Sheesley	Jonathan Aibel & Glenn Berger	March 3, 1997	4E06
Hank's attempt to be neighborly with the new Laotian family next door is sorely tested after his neighbor treats him rudely, and even more so when he's convinced his neighbor served him hamburgers made from dog meat. Rated TV-PG-DL.						
8	8	"Shins of the Father"	Martin Archer	Alan R. Cohen & Alan Freedman	March 23, 1997	4E08

Hank's brash, sexist father, Cotton Hill, crashes Bobby's 12th birthday party--and stays over the Hill's house, which doesn't sit well with Peggy when Cotton's misogyny begins rubbing off on Bobby. Rated TV-PG-DLV.

| 9 | 9 | "Peggy the Boggle Champ" | Chuck Sheetz | Jonathan Aibel & Glenn Berger | April 13, 1997 | 4E09 |

Hank's promise to coach Peggy at the Texas State Boggle Championship is jeopardized when his buddies try to lure him away to the Ninth Annual Dallas Mower Expo. Meanwhile, Bobby and Luanne freak out when they leave a condensation ring on the new coffee table. Rated TV-PG-L.

| 10 | 10 | "Keeping Up With Our Joneses" | John Rice | Jonathan Collier & Joe Stillman | April 27, 1997 | 4E10 |

When Hank catches Bobby smoking a cigarette, he punishes him by forcing him to smoke an entire carton. The plan backfires when Bobby begins, while Hank and Peggy resume, an addiction to tobacco. Rated TV-PG-L.

| 11 | 11 | "King of the Ant Hill" | Gary McCarver | Johnny Hardwick & Paul Lieberstein | May 4, 1997 | 4E13 |

After telling Dale never to spray insecticide on his lawn again, Hank's expensive new lawn becomes mysteriously infested with fire ants. Rated TV-PG-L.

| 12 | 12 | "Plastic White Female" | Jeff Myers | David Zuckerman | May 11, 1997 | 4E11 |

Bobby is invited to his first boy/girl party, and Peggy is horrified when she discovers him playing Spin the Bottle with one of Luanne's plastic beautician school heads. Rated TV-PG-DL.

Season 2: 1997-1998

№	#	Title	Directed by	Written by	Original air date	Code
13	1	"How to Fire a Rifle Without Really Trying"	Adam Kuhlman	Paul Lieberstein	September 21, 1997	5E10

When Bobby displays a talent for target shooting, Hank signs up for a father–son fun shoot competition — only to discover a buried childhood memory is still sadly affecting his aim.

| 14 | 2 | "Texas City Twister" | Jeff Myers | Cheryl Holliday | October 12, 1997 | 5E02 |

Hank must save Peggy and Luanne from a tornado after he regrets not showing remorse for throwing Luanne out of the house and moving her back to the trailer that she moved out of after her mother tried to kill her father. Rated TV-PG-DL.

| 15 | 3 | "The Arrow Head" | Klay Hall | Jonathan Aibel & Glenn Berger | October 19, 1997 | 5E04 |

Peggy's excitement over finding Indian artifacts in the front yard distresses Hank when a condescending university professor tricks Peggy into letting him dig in the Hills' yard. Rated TV-PG-DL.

| 16 | 4 | "Hilloween" | John Rice | David Zuckerman | October 26, 1997 | 5E06 |

Hank goes to war with a litigious Evangelical Christian woman bent on banning Halloween and indoctrinating the kids by inviting them to a hell house. Rated TV-PG-DL.

| 17 | 5 | "Jumpin' Crack Bass" | Gary McCarver | Alan R. Cohen & Alan Freedman | November 2, 1997 | 5E03 |

Hank finds himself facing possible jail time after mistakenly buying crack cocaine to use as fish bait. Rated TV-PG-DL.

| 18 | 6 | "Husky Bobby" | Martin Archer | Jonathan Collier | November 9, 1997 | 5E05 |

Hank is determined to save his son from humiliation after Bobby decides to model for a husky boy clothing line. Rated TV-PG-DL.

| 19 | 7 | "The Man Who Shot Cane Skretteberg" | Monte Young | Johnny Hardwick | November 16, 1997 | 5E07 |

Hank, Boomhauer, Bill and Dale face off in a paintball war against the teenage members of a garage band (guest-voiced by the members of Green Day).

20	8	"The Son That Got Away"	Tricia Garcia	Jim Dauterive	November 23, 1997	5E08

Bobby, Connie and Joseph run away to "The Caves", where "half of Arlen's unplanned pregnancies begin," after each of them gets in trouble at school for disrupting class. Rated TV-PG-DL.

21	9	"The Company Man"	Klay Hall	Jim Dauterive	December 7, 1997	4E12

When a new housing development is in need of a propane supplier, Buck instructs Hank to show the owner, an obnoxious Northerner who acts like a Southerner, a good time. Rated TV-PG-DLSV.
NOTE: This episode is included on the *King of the Hill* complete first season DVD set due to its production code.

22	10	"Bobby Slam"	Chris Moeller	Gina Fattore	December 14, 1997	5E01

Hank is delighted when Bobby announces he's joining the school wrestling team, but Peggy is mortified when she learns her son must first wrestle Connie in order to make the team. Rated TV-PG-L.

23	11	"The Unbearable Blindness of Laying"	Cyndi Tang Loveland	Paul Lieberstein	December 21, 1997	5E09

In this first Christmas episode, Hank is psychologically shocked into blindness after accidentally catching a glimpse of his mother and her new boyfriend having sex on Hank's kitchen table.

24	12	"Meet the Manger Babies"	Jeff Myers	Jonathan Aibel & Glenn Berger	January 11, 1998	5E12

Hank faces a dilemma of Biblical proportions when Luanne asks him to portray God in a live TV broadcast of her Christian puppet show, which is scheduled to occur during Hank's beloved Super Bowl party.

25	13	"Snow Job"	Adam Kuhlman	Cheryl Holliday and Alan R. Cohen & Alan Freedman and Jim Dauterive	January 18, 1998	5E11

During a snow storm, a shaken and confused Hank becomes disillusioned about his life and career after discovering that his boss doesn't use a propane stove in his house and doesn't share Hank's passion for propane.

26	14	"I Remember Mono"	Wes Archer	Paul Lieberstein	March 1, 1998	5E13

While updating files at Arlen High School, Peggy learns that Hank's two-week absence from classes during their high school days was due to mononucleosis, not a back injury, and is crushed that the story of how they met in high school is now a sham. Rated TV-PG-DL.

27	15	"Three Days of the Kahndo"	Lauren MacMullan	John Altsculer & Dave Krinsky	March 8, 1998	5E15

Kahn's misreading of an advertisement for a Mexican time share results in him, Hank, and Dale getting trapped in Mexico. Rated TV-PG-DL.

28	16	"Traffic Jam"	Klay Hall	Johnny Hardwick	March 15, 1998	5E14

When Hank and Kahn collide with each other, they are both forced to attend traffic school courses taught by a raunchy black comedian (voiced by Chris Rock), who begins mentoring Bobby in the art of stand-up. Rated TV-PG-DL.
NOTE: Originally, Buddha Sack's name was "Busta Nut", but FOX censors objected. The name was then changed to Busta Sack, but was also objected by FOX censors.

29	17	"Hank's Dirty Laundry"	Shaun Cashman	Jonathan Aibel & Glenn Berger	March 22, 1998	5E16

While purchasing a new dryer, Hank discovers that his credit is bad, thanks to a video store clerk who accuses Hank of renting a porno film and never returning it.

30	18	"The Final Shinsult"	Jack Dyer	Alan R. Cohen & Alan Freedland	April 12, 1998	5E17

After losing his driver's license, Cotton moves in with Dale and plots to steal Antonio López de Santa Anna's wooden leg to use as a bargaining chip with the DMV. Rated TV-PG-DL.

31	19	"Leanne's Saga"	Tricia Garcia	David Zuckerman	April 19, 1998	5E18

Luanne's alcoholic mother is released from prison and starts dating Bill, who she begins to abuse. Rated TV-PG-DLSV.

32	20	"Junkie Business"	Cyndi Tang Loveland	Jim Dauterive	April 26, 1998	5E19
Strickland Propane's new employee (who Hank hired because he preferred a man over the qualified woman who applied) turns out to be a drug addict who uses a legal trick that frees him from responsibility on the job and from being fired. Rated TV-PG-LS.							
33	21	"Life in the Fast Lane, Bobby's Saga"	Adam Kuhlman	John Altshuler & Dave Krinsky	May 3, 1998	5E21
Bobby gets a job at the Arlen race track, where he discovers that his boss is a mildly retarded sociopath (played by David Herman). Hank does not empathize with Bobby's horror stories until he witnesses the mistreatment firsthand. Meanwhile, Boomhauer is given the chance to drive the pace car in an upcoming race. Seven-time NASCAR Winston Cup Series champion Dale Earnhardt guest appears in the episode.							
34	22	"Peggy's Turtle Song"	Jeff Myers	Brent Forrester	May 10, 1998	5E22
When Bobby is misdiagnosed with attention deficit disorder (after eating too much sugary cereal and disrupting class), Peggy quits her job as a substitute teacher and becomes a stay-at-home mom. Rated TV-PG-DL.							
35	23	"Propane Boom (Part 1)"	Gary McCarver	Norm Hiscock	May 17, 1998	5E23
Part one of two. Strickland Propane closes its doors after Mega-Lo-Mart begins selling propane for cheap, leaving Hank out of a job — and into one that he despises.							

Season 3: 1998-1999

№	#	Title	Directed by	Written by	Original air date	Code
36	1	"Death of a Propane Salesman (Part 2)"	Lauren MacMullan	Alan R. Cohen & Alan Freedman	October 4, 1998	5E24
Conclusion. The aftermath of the propane explosion from part one leaves Hank suffering from post-traumatic stress disorder around propane, a now bald Luanne repressing her grief for Buckley (who was the only casualty in the propane explosion) by becoming a Sinéad O'Connor-esque activist, and Bobby worried about death.							
37	2	"And They Call It Bobby Love"	Cyndi Tang Loveland	Norm Hiscock	October 11, 1998	3ABE01
Bobby falls in love with a 14-year old classmate (guest-voiced by Sarah Michelle Gellar), but soon learns that love hurts when the girl confesses that she only wants a platonic friend. Meanwhile, Hank, Dale, Bill, and Boomhauer become attached to a couch that was thrown out in the Hills' yard.							
38	3	"Peggy's Headache"	Chris Moeller	Joe Stillman	October 18, 1998	5E20
Peggy gets hired to write for the *Arlen Bystander*, but the stress of a new career leads her to get treated by John Redcorn--and she soon discovers that John Redcorn had an affair with Nancy and is Joseph's biological father. Rated TV-PG-DL.							
39	4	"Pregnant Paws"	Chris Moeller	Jonathan Aibel & Glenn Berger	October 25, 1998	3ABE02
While Hank is busy trying to breed Ladybird, Dale decides to add a little excitement to his life by enrolling in a 4-hour bounty hunter training course.							
40	5	"Next of Shin"	Jeff Myers	Alan R. Cohen & Alan Freedland	November 1, 1998	3ABE05
After Hank learns his sperm count is low, his mood worsens when Cotton shows up boasting that his new wife Didi is pregnant.							
41	6	"Peggy's Pageant Fever"	Tricia Garcia	Norm Hiscock	November 8, 1998	3ABE07
Peggy enters the Mrs. Heimlich County Beauty pageant in hopes of winning a truck, but quickly discovers that she is not fit to compete with the other contestants.							
42	7	"Nine Pretty Darn Angry Men"	Shaun Cashman	Jim Dauterive	November 15, 1998	3ABE08

While shopping at the mall on the Friday after Thanksgiving, Hank, Dale, Bill, Kahn, and Boomhauer are invited to be part of a focus group for a new mower (with Cotton as an uninvited guest), Luanne goes ice skating to forget about Buckley, and Peggy falls asleep at a shoe repair shop after tearing her loafer.						
43	8	"Good Hill Hunting"	Klay Hall	Joe Stillman	December 6, 1998	3ABE04
Hank takes Bobby hunting in order to initiate him into the mysteries of manhood. However, everything goes wrong when Hank discovers that it is too late for him to get a hunting license.						
44	9	"Pretty, Pretty Dresses"	Dominic Polcino	Paul Lieberstein	December 20, 1998	3ABE10
In this second Christmas episode, Bill becomes more depressed than usual. Hank, Dale, and Boomhauer decide to watch Bill so he doesn't commit suicide, but when Hank yells at him for being a burden, Bill's depression turns into delusion when he begins dressing in drag and impersonating his estranged wife, Lenore.						
45	10	"A Firefighting We Will Go"	Cyndi Tang Loveland	Alan R. Cohen & Alan Freedland	January 10, 1999	3ABE11
In a *Rashomon*-style story, Hank, Dale, Bill, and Boomhauer tell their own versions of their day as firefighters after getting arrested for burning the firehouse to the ground. Meanwhile, Peggy pulls a groin muscle and Bobby helps her recover.						
46	11	"To Spank with Love"	Adam Kuhlman	David Zuckerman	January 17, 1999	3ABE03
Peggy gains a reputation as an abusive disciplinarian when she spanks Dooley for humiliating her during class.						
47	12	"Three Coaches and a Bobby"	Chris Moeller	Johnny Hardwick	January 24, 1999	3ABE12
Hank gets his former football coach to take on guidance of Bobby's football team, but the plan falls apart when Bobby joins the soccer team headed by a politically correct coach (voiced by Will Ferrell). Meanwhile, Hank realizes that his former coach is a lot more erratic than he remembers.						
48	13	"De-Kahnstructing Henry"	Klay Hall	Paul Lieberstein	February 7, 1999	3ABE14
Hank accidentally gets Kahn fired after revealing one of Kahn's top secret plans for his company. Kahn eventually abandons his family, leaving Hank to fix the mess.						
49	14	"The Wedding of Bobby Hill"	Jack Dyer	Jonathan Collier	February 14, 1999	3ABE09
To teach Bobby and Luanne a lesson in playing pranks, Hank orders Bobby to marry Luanne after Bobby takes her birth control pills.						
50	15	"Sleight of Hank"	Jeff Myers	Jonathan Aibel & Glenn Berger	March 7, 1999	3ABE15
Peggy is chosen to be a magician's assistant, but angers Hank when she won't tell him the secret behind one of his tricks.						
51	16	"Jon Vitti Presents: 'Return to La Grunta'"	Gary McCarver	Jon Vitti	March 14, 1999	3ABE06
Luanne gets a job as a drink girl at a resort called "La Grunta", where she's being sexually harassed by the golfers. Meanwhile, Hank goes to La Grunta to swim with the dolphins--and gets molested by one of them.						
52	17	"Escape from Party Island"	Gary McCarver	Jonathan Collier	March 21, 1999	3ABE16
Hank reluctantly drives his mom and her friends to Port Aransas to shop for glass miniatures, but things get even worse when Hank and the rude old women are trapped on the island by college-age spring break revelers.						
53	18	"Love Hurts and So Does Art"	Adam Kuhlman	John Altshuler & Dave Krinsky	March 28, 1999	3ABE13
An X-ray of Hank's colon from "Hank's Unmentionable Problem" winds up as the main attraction in an art museum. Meanwhile, Bobby is diagnosed with gout after eating chicken livers at a new deli.						
54	19	"Hank's Cowboy Movie"	Shaun Cashman	Jim Dauterive	April 4, 1999	3ABE18
Hurt by Bobby's negative views of his hometown, Hank tries to get the Dallas Cowboys to move their training camp from Wichita Falls to Arlen. However, his promotion video for Arlen is ruined by his wife's and his friends' incompetence.						
55	20	"Dog Dale Afternoon"	Tricia Garcia	Jon Vitti	April 11, 1999	3ABE17

After Dale annoys his friends by gloating over his new mower, he goes insane when they steal it as part of a prank.						
56	21	"Revenge of the Lutefisk"	Jack Dyer	Jonathan Aibel & Glenn Berger	April 18, 1999	3ABE19
Bobby accidentally burns down his church after getting sick from eating lutefisk, but Cotton gets blamed for it due to his sexist attitude towards the church accepting a female pastor.						
57	22	"Death and Texas"	Wes Archer	John Altshuler & Dave Krinsky	April 25, 1999	3ABE20
Peggy visits a convict who tricks her into thinking he was a former student and uses her as a cocaine mule.						
58	23	"Wings of the Dope"	Cyndi Tang Loveland	Johnny Hardwick	May 2, 1999	3ABE21
Hank Hill gets a trampoline for his yard, where Luanne begins seeing the spirit of her dead boyfriend, Buckley, who tries to guide her to do something better with her life than attend beauty school.						
59	24	"Take Me out of the Ball Game"	Chris Moeller	Alan R. Cohen & Alan Freedland	May 9, 1999	3ABE22
Hank is picked to coach the company's softball team, spurring friction between Peggy and Hank.						
60	25	"As Old as the Hills"	Adam Kuhlman	Norm Hiscock	May 16, 1999	3ABE23
Part one of two. Fearing that they may be getting too old to be cool, Hank and Peggy spend their anniversary sky-diving, which comes to an end when Peggy's parachute malfunctions and she crashes onto a field. Meanwhile, Bobby struggles with taking his pregnant step-grandmother Didi to the hospital when her water breaks.						

Season 4: 1999-2000

№	#	Title	Directed by	Written by	Original air date	Code
61	1	"Peggy Hill: The Decline and Fall"	Klay Hall	Paul Lieberstein	September 26, 1999	3ABE24
Conclusion. Peggy struggles to regain her strength following her skydiving accident. Meanwhile, Bobby delivers Cotton's son (which Cotton names "Good Hank") but gets overwhelmed when neither Cotton or Didi embrace new parenthood.						
62	2	"Cotton's Plot"	Anthony Lioi	Jonathan Aibel & Glenn Berger	October 3, 1999	4ABE01
Cotton takes over Peggy's physical therapy in exchange for help getting a burial plot in the Texas State cemetery, but Peggy discovers a discrepancy about Cotton's service in the Army during World War II.						
63	3	"Bills Are Made to Be Broken"	Jeff Myers	John Altschuler & Dave Krinsky	October 24, 1999	4ABE02
Bill's high school football record is broken unfairly and he tries to get back on the field to set things right.						
64	4	"Little Horrors of Shop"	Adam Kuhlman	Kit Boss	October 31, 1999	4ABE03
Buck Strickland insists that Hank take two weeks off from Strickland Propane, where Hank begins teaching wood shop at Tom Landry Middle School. However, Hank gets in trouble for violating the school's zero-tolerance policy on weapons when he asks his students to bring in tools from home.						
65	5	"Aisle 8A"	Allan Jacobsen	Garland Testa	November 7, 1999	4ABE04
Kahn and Minh go to Hawaii for Kahn's job and asks Hank to take care of Connie, who's excited that she'll be staying with Bobby, but becomes emotional and mean-spirited when she gets her first period, leaving an extremely uncomfortable Hank to both deal with the unstable Connie and have to explain "the birds and the bees" to his son, Bobby (who doesn't know why Connie is so emotional).						
66	6	"A Beer Can Named Desire"	Chuck Austen & Chris Moeller	Jim Dauterive	November 14, 1999	4ABE05
Hank wins an Alamo Beer contest for a chance to win a million dollars by throwing a football through a one-foot hole in a giant Alamo Beer can, while Bill visits his extended Cajun relatives in Louisiana.						

67	7	"Happy Hank's Giving"	Martin Archer	Alan R. Cohen & Alan Freedland	November 21, 1999	4ABE08

The Hills plan to fly to Montana, but are stranded with their neighbors at the airport by a snowstorm. Amanda Mealing guest stars.

68	8	"Not in My Back-hoe"	Shaun Cashman	Paul Lieberstein	November 28, 1999	4ABE06

Drew Carey guest stars as a man who befriends Hank Hill after the two discover that they are very much alike. Meanwhile, Bill and Dale steal Hank's backhoe and take it to a pet cemetery, with disastrous results.

69	9	"To Kill a Ladybird"	Wes Archer	Norm Hiscock	December 12, 1999	4ABE07

Dale and Ladybird may have contracted rabies from a raccoon Bobby befriended.

70	10	"Hillennium"	Tricia Garcia	Johnny Hardwick	December 19, 1999	4ABE10

As Christmas approaches, Hank gets irritated over everyone panicking about the supposed technological apocalypse that will happen on January 1st, 2000 due to the Y2K computer virus -- but soon finds himself trying to safeguard his family after a propane shortage.

71	11	"Old Glory"	Gary McCarver	Norm Hiscock	January 9, 2000	4ABE09

Peggy writes a school essay for Bobby, and they both catch fire for it by a vengeful English teacher who accuses them of plagiarism. Meanwhile, Hank and his friends try to get rid of an oversized American flag.

72	12	"Rodeo Days"	Cyndi Tang Loveland	Jon Vitti	January 16, 2000	4ABE11

Bobby becomes a rodeo clown, much to Hank and Peggy's dismay.

73	13	"Hanky Panky (Part 1)"	Jeff Myers	Jim Dauterive	February 6, 2000	4ABE13

Part one of two. When Buck Strickland and his wife Miz Liz separate, and Buck dumps his secretary/mistress Debbie Grund, Hank ends up getting seduced by Miz Liz--and Debbie Grund ends up dead and in the Dumpster behind Sugarfoots'.

74	14	"High Anxiety (Part 2)"	Adam Kuhlman	Alan R. Cohen & Alan Freedland	February 13, 2000	4ABE14

Conclusion. Peggy is put in charge of Sugarfoots'--with disastrous results, while Hank unwittingly tries marijuana and becomes a suspect in the murder of Debbie Grund.

75	15	"Naked Ambition"	Anthony Lioi	Jonathan Aibel & Glenn Berger	February 20, 2000	4ABE12

Bobby accidentally sees Luanne naked. When Joseph hears the story, his imagination runs wild and he wants to see her nude too.

76	16	"Movin' On Up"	Klay Hall	Garland Testa	February 27, 2000	4ABE16

Luanne moves out of Hank's den and into her own house--with three deadbeat roommates who aggravate her.

77	17	"Bill of Sales"	Dominic Polcino	Paul Lieberstein	March 12, 2000	4ABE15

Peggy and Bill become salesmen for a pyramid scheme, but Bill's unrequited love for Peggy gets in the way of business.

78	18	"Won't You Pimai Neighbor?"	Boowhan Lim & Kyounghee Lim	John Altschuler & Dave Krinsky	March 19, 2000	4ABE18

Bobby undergoes tests to find out if he is the reincarnation of the Buddhist Lama Sanglug, much to Hank's discomfort.

79	19	"Hank's Bad Hair Day"	Gary McCarver	Jon Vitti	April 9, 2000	4ABE19

Hank gets a haircut on base from Bill, and puts Bill out of the job after lodging a complaint to the government about a $900 bill for the tonsorial procedure.

80	20	"Meet the Propaniacs"	Shaun Cashman	Kit Boss	April 16, 2000	4ABE17

While working for Hank during the summer at Strickland Propane (instead of going to an acting camp), Bobby, some Strickland co-workers, Dale, and Luanne form a sketch comedy troupe calle The Propaniacs.

81	21	"Nancy's Boys"	Tricia Garcia	Jonathan Aibel & Glenn Berger	April 30, 2000	4ABE20

Nancy breaks off her adulterous affair with John Redcorn after going on a date with Dale and falling in love with him all over again.

82	22	"Flush with Power"	Allan Jacobsen	Alex Gregory & Peter Huyck	May 7, 2000	4ABE22
Arlen's City Council forces Hank to install low-flow toilets against his wishes when a drought hits town. Hank's anger leads him to join the local zoning board, which he discovers is rife with corruption.						
83	23	"Transnational Amusements Presents: Peggy's Magic Sex Feet"	Cyndi Tang Loveland	Jonathan Collier	May 14, 2000	4ABE21
After admitting her real shoe size during a night of bowling, Peggy feels ashamed of her big feet -- until a man makes Peggy an Internet star on a foot fetish website.						
84	24	"Peggy's Fan Fair"	Jeff Myers	Alan R. Cohen & Alan Freedland	May 21, 2000	4ABE23
While attending a Nashville music festival with Hank and the guys, Peggy claims that Randy Travis stole lyrics from a song she wrote years ago.						

Season 5: 2000-2001

№	#	Title	Directed by	Written by	Original air date	Code
85	1	"The Perils of Polling"	Boohwan Lim & Kyounghee Lim	Jim Dauterive	October 1, 2000	5ABE02
When Hank takes Luanne to an election fair, Hank meets George W. Bush and shakes his hand, only to discover that Bush's handshake is weak, making Hank have second doubts about voting for him. Meanwhile, Luanne becomes infatuated with Communist candidate Robert Parigi. Rated TV-PG-DL.						
86	2	"The Buck Stops Here"	Michael Dante DiMartino	Norm Hiscock	November 5, 2000	5ABE01
Bobby becomes a golf caddy for Buck Strickland, who takes him along for the ride on a gambling junket. Hank and Peggy are disturbed when Buck's habits rub off on Bobby. Brad Renfro guest stars. Rated TV-PG-DL.						
87	3	"I Don't Want to Wait for Our Lives to Be Over..."	Adam Kuhlman	Paul Lieberstein	November 12, 2000	4ABE24
With Bobby's 13th birthday approaching, Joseph comes back from summer vacation having grown six inches. Bobby is upset that everyone still treats him like a little kid, and Joseph is being driven crazy by the onset of puberty. Meanwhile, Hank tries to build coffins for himself and Peggy.						
88	4	"Spin the Choice"	Allan Jacobsen	Paul Lieberstein	November 19, 2000	5ABE05
Despite Hank's promise to let him carve the turkey this year, Bobby boycotts Thanksgiving after talking with John Redcorn about the shameful history behind it. Meanwhile, Peggy creates a pointless new game called "Spin the Choice" when everyone gets sick of playing Boggle with her every year.						
89	5	"Peggy Makes the Big Leagues"	Dominic Polcino	Johnny Hardwick	November 26, 2000	5ABE04
Peggy substitute-teaches at Arlen High School, but arouses the enmity of nearly all (including Hank and her fellow teachers) when she flunks the school's unacademic football star (guest voiced by Brendan Fraser).						
90	6	"When Cotton Comes Marching Home"	Tricia Garcia	Alan R. Cohen & Alan Freedland	December 3, 2000	5ABE03
Cotton moves to the VFW, and wants to march in the Veterans Day parade, but his boss will not let him have the time off from his degrading restroom attendant job.						
91	7	"What Makes Bobby Run?"	Cyndi Tang Loveland	Alex Gregory & Peter Huyck	December 10, 2000	5ABE07
When Bobby becomes the school mascot, the "Landry Longhorn," he is deemed a coward after he runs away from a traditional half-time beating by the opposing team's band.						

92	8	"Twas the Nut Before Christmas"	Jeff Myers	John Altschuler & Dave Krinsky	December 17, 2000	5ABE08
In the third Christmas episode, Bill's holiday loneliness leads to him opening a "Christmas village" in his yard, but things get out of hand when he takes on a twenty-something petty criminal as a surrogate son.						
93	9	"Chasing Bobby"	Anthony Lioi	Garland Testa	January 21, 2001	5ABE10
Peggy takes Hank to see a tearjerking movie about a father and son's relationship, and mistakes Hank's crying as evidence that he doesn't spend enough time with Bobby, but Hank is actually upset about his truck breaking down.						
94	10	"Yankee Hankee"	Adam Kuhlman	Kit Boss	February 4, 2001	5ABE06
Hank deals with the utter shock of discovering that he was born in a women's bathroom at Yankee Stadium in New York City, while Cotton and his cronies hatch a hare-brained scheme to assassinate Castro.						
95	11	"Hank and the Great Glass Elevator"	Gary McCarver	Jonathan Collier	February 11, 2001	5ABE12
Hank moons the former Governor of Texas, Ann Richards, and Bill enters into a relationship with her.						
96	12	"Now Who's the Dummy?"	Dominic Polcino	Johnny Hardwick	February 18, 2001	5ABE14
Bobby acquires a ventriloquist's dummy named Chip Block, which dredges up childhood anxieties for Dale. Meanwhile, Hank becomes overly attached to Chip due to the dummy's "knowledge" of sports.						
97	13	"Ho Yeah!"	Tricia Garcia	Alex Gregory & Peter Huyck	February 25, 2001	5ABE15
Tammi (guest voiced by Renee Zellweger), a prostitute from "The OKC" (Oklahoma City, Oklahoma) hires on at Strickland Propane, moves in with the Hills, and encourages Peggy to add spice to her own life. Things heat up when Tammi's ex-pimp Alabaster Jones (guest voiced by Snoop Dogg) comes to Arlen and mistakes Hank for a pimp trying to steal Tammi away from him. NOTE: On FOX, this episode was rated TV-14 for offensive language (L), making it the first *King of the Hill* episode not to carry a TV-PG rating. On Cartoon Network, this episode is rated TV-PG for suggestive dialogue (D) and offensive language (L).						
98	14	"The Exterminator"	Shaun Cashman	Dean Young	March 4, 2001	5ABE09
Dale is forced to quit the exterminating business after learning that the cumulative effect of on-the-job exposure to poisons may kill him before he turns 50 years old, so he accepts a position at an adhesives company called "Stik Tek" (formerly Stik Co), where his job is firing other employees.						
99	15	"Luanne Virgin 2.0"	Adam Kuhlman	Kit Boss	March 11, 2001	5ABE16
When Luanne reveals to Hank that she's no longer a virgin (after her latest boyfriend breaks up with her), Hank puts Luanne in the church's "born-again virgin" program, where Luanne meets a sexually insecure man (guest-voiced by Owen Wilson) and Peggy confesses that she had sex with a man (who turned out to be a homosexual) before she met Hank.						
100	16	"Hank's Choice"	Boohwan Lim & Kyounghee Lim	Jon Vitti	April 1, 2001	5ABE11
When it turns out that Bobby is allergic to Ladybird, he ends up living in Ladybird's luxurious new doghouse while Ladybird continues living in the household. The arrangement is enjoyed by all parties until Hank and Peggy discover that their neighbors are mocking them as a result.						
101	17	"It's Not Easy Being Green"	Jeff Myers	John Altschuler & Dave Krinsky	April 8, 2001	5ABE18
When the quarry is going to be drained for a landfill, Hank must pretend he is interested in environmental issues in order to keep a secret from Boomhauer.						
102	18	"The Trouble with Gribbles"	Shaun Cashman	Jim Dauterive	April 22, 2001	5ABE19
When Nancy turns 40, the television station replaces her with Luanne, who is much younger. This leads to Nancy telling Dale that she wants a facelift. Dale plans to pay for it by filing suit against the makers of his favorite brand, Manitoba Cigarettes ("Manitoba is the brand to smoke, you'll enjoy it toke for toke..."), claiming that second-hand smoke has made his Nancy unattractive. This results in Dale being both counter-sued and estranged from Nancy.						
103	19	"Hank's Back Story"	Cyndi Tang Loveland	Alan R. Cohen & Alan Freedland	May 6, 2001	5ABE17

Hank finds out his back problems are caused by "diminished gluteal syndrome" (a condition that has worn down Hank's butt and has put pressure on his spine), and attempts to come to terms with wearing a prosthetic posterior while preparing to compete in a lawn-mower race.

104	20	"Kidney Boy and Hamster Girl: A Love Story"	Gary McCarver	Garland Testa	May 13, 2001	5ABE22

Bobby pretends to be a high school student with a kidney disorder that stunted his growth, and helps the student body win a radio station contest, with No Doubt performing at the high school prom as the prize.

Season 6: 2001-2002

№	#	Title	Directed by	Written by	Original air date	Code
105	1	"Bobby Goes Nuts"	Tricia Garcia	Norm Hiscock	November 11, 2001	5ABE24

After getting attacked at a slumber party by Chane Wassonasong, Hank lets Bobby sign up for a boxing class at the YMCA, but Bobby ends up taking a women's self-defense course where Bobby is taught to attack his aggressors by kicking them in the groin. This results in him kicking Hank in the groin.

106	2	"Soldier of Misfortune"	Anthony Lioi	J.B. Cook	December 9, 2001	6ABE02

Dale is running for re-election as the Arlen Gun Club president, but his chances seem to be shot when he accidentally discharges his gun. To give Dale his confidence back, Hank pretends to be "Mr. Big," answers Dale's ad in *Soldier of Fortune* magazine, and assigns Dale to pick up a briefcase. But Dale bungles the job, and nearly gets his friends killed by his opponent at the Gun Club.
Gary Busey guest stars.

107	3	"Lupe's Revenge"	Allan Jacobsen	Dean Young	December 16, 2001	5ABE13

Peggy takes the school Spanish club on a field trip to Mexico, and ends up in trouble for kidnapping a Mexican girl named Lupe thanks to Peggy's horrible comprehension of the Spanish language. Meanwhile, Hank finds himself the object of a female cop's affections, who keeps pulling him over for various reasons, in order to spend time with him.

108	4	"The Father, the Son, and J.C."	Tricia Garcia & Cyndi Tang Loveland	Etan Cohen & Dean Young	December 20, 2001	6ABE04

While Hank is building a Habitat for Humanity house for Buck Strickland, Buck promotes him to manager of Strickland Propane. In the excitement of the moment, Hank emotes and declares, "I love you" to Mr. Strickland. Because of this, Cotton Hill is angry with Hank. Peggy's attempts to bring father and sons together only throws gasoline onto the fire. They get into an altercation, which must be solved by former U.S. President Jimmy Carter.

109	5	"Father of the Bribe"	Cyndi Tang Loveland	Dean Young	February 3, 2002	6ABE06

Kahn tries to bribe Bobby to break up with Connie. Connie and Bobby decide to pretend to break up so they can get the money. When a schoolteacher thinks Connie may be depressed after Connie writes a note that reads "I'm so bored, I could kill myself" (which was a response to a dull lecture), her parents try to push her and Bobby back together. After endless double dates with the parents, they become tired of each other, and decide to break up, to Kahn's horror. Meanwhile, Dale hosts a pirated radio show.

110	6	"I'm With Cupid"	Cyndi Tang Loveland	John Altschuler & Dave Krinsky	February 10, 2002	6ABE09

Following the events from the previous episode, Bobby seems fine in regards to his breakup with Connie and the upcoming Valentine's Day. However when he is left home alone while Peggy and Hank go out, Bill depresses Bobby by suggesting that Bobby blew his only shot at true love. Hank then asks Boomhauer to give Bobby advice on how to deal with women.

111	7	"Torch Song Hillogy"	Anthony Lioi	Emily Spivey	February 17, 2002	6ABE12

Peggy nominates Bobby to carry the 2002 Winter Olympic Torch through Arlen, but it's Hank who wins the honor — and bungles it.

112	8	"Joust Like a Woman"	Dominic Polcino	Garland Testa	February 24, 2002	6ABE03

Peggy works as a cleaning wench at a Renaissance Faire, where her boss (Alan Rickman) refuses to give his female workers equal pay and benefits.

113	9	"The Bluegrass Is Always Greener"	Tricia Garcia	Norm Hiscock	December 15, 2002	6ABE14
Connie and the guys form a bluegrass band and head to Branson, Missouri, against Kahn's wishes. NOTE: Vince Gill provides Boomhauer's singing voice. Also, Charlie Daniels and Yakov Smirnoff makes guest appearances.						
114	10	"The Substitute Spanish Prisoner"	Boowhan Lim & Kyounghee Lim	Etan Cohen	March 3, 2002	5ABE21
After handing back tests to her class, Peggy is dumbfounded when Dooley asks her to explain the answer to a question. To restore her self-confidence, Peggy takes an internet IQ test and discovers she's a genius, but discovers that the IQ test is a scam when she blows Hank's retirement fund on a diploma. Jeff Goldblum guest stars.						
115	11	"Unfortunate Son"	Anthony Lioi	Alex Gregory & Peter Huyck	March 10, 2002	5ABE20
Cotton's VFW is in dire straits as members are dying and the veterans are behind on their propane bill, so the VFW move to Hank's house.						
116	12	"Are You There God? It's Me, Margaret Hill"	Gary McCarver	Silvert Glarum & Michael Jamin	March 17, 2002	6ABE07
Peggy must pretend she is a nun after she gets a job at a Catholic school.						
117	13	"Tankin' It to the Streets"	Monte Young	Alan R. Cohen & Alan Freedland	March 24, 2002	6ABE10
After Bill finds out the Army performed a secret medical experiment called "Operation Infinite Walrus" on him, he gets drunk and steals a tank, leaving his friends to try and save him from life in prison. Meanwhile, Peggy and Bobby try to win a free ice cream sundae at the Mega Lo Mart.						
118	14	"Of Mice and Little Green Men"	Shaun Cashman	Silvert Glarum & Michael Jamin	April 7, 2002	6ABE08
When Hank and Dale find they have more in common with each others' sons than their own, Dale comes to the conclusion that Joseph is actually the offspring of an alien.						
119	15	"A Man Without a Country Club"	Boowhan Lim & Kyounghee Lim	Kit Boss	April 14, 2002	6ABE11
Hank is asked to join the exclusive all-Asian Nine Rivers Country Club as a token white male, enraging a highly envious Kahn.						
120	16	"Beer and Loathing"	Dominic Polcino	Etan Cohen	April 14, 2002	6ABE13
Peggy lands a job at Alamo Beer, which is a dream come true for Hank... until the new batch of beer makes everyone sick.						
121	17	"Fun with Jane and Jane"	Adam Kuhlman	Garland Testa	April 21, 2002	6ABE15
Luanne and Peggy unwittingly join a cult disguised as a college sorority. Meanwhile, Hank and his buddies try to find a place for Buck Strickland's emus.						
122	18	"My Own Private Rodeo"	Cyndi Tang Loveland	Alex Gregory & Peter Huyck	April 28, 2002	6ABE16
Dale and Nancy renew their wedding vows, and Nancy invites Dale's gay dad, who Dale hates for supposedly hitting on Nancy, to the ceremony.						
123	19	"Sug Night"	Adam Kuhlman	Alex Gregory & Peter Huyck	May 5, 2002	6ABE05
Hank freaks out when he has a dream where he's grilling naked -- with Dale's wife, Nancy.						
124	20	"Dang Ol' Love"	Gary McCarver	Dean Young	May 5, 2002	6ABE17
Boomhauer falls in love with a woman who wanted only a one-night stand, which crushes Boomhauer now that he feels like the many women he's seduced in the past.						
125	21	"Returning Japanese"	Allan Jacobsen & Anthony Lioi	Kit Boss & Etan Cohen	May 12, 2002	6ABE20
Part one of two. Cotton wants to return to Japan to apologize to the widow of a soldier he killed, and Peggy arranges to bring the family along. Hank is shocked to discover that Cotton actually had an affair with the widow and fathered another son.						

126	22	"Returning Japanese II"	Klay Hall	Alex Gregory & Peter Huyck	May 12, 2002	6ABE21

Conclusion. When Junichiro renounces his Hill ancestry, Cotton declares his own personal war on Japan by spitting in the Japanese emperor's face.

Season 7: 2002-2003

№	#	Title	Directed by	Written by	Original air date	Code
127	1	"Get Your Freak Off"	Tricia Garcia	Garland Testa	November 3, 2002	7ABE01

Hank takes Bobby and his friends to a music concert but is dismayed to see Bobby and a friend dancing inappropriately to boy band music, so he tries to make Bobby's adolescence more wholesome. Meanwhile Peggy, Nancy and Minh discuss who is the best-looking out of Hank, Dale, Boomhauer, Kahn, Bill and John Redcorn.

| 128 | 3 | "The Fat and the Furious" | Allan Jacobsen | Alex Gregory & Peter Huyck | November 10, 2002 | 7ABE03 |

Bill becomes a competitive eater after downing Hank's entire platter of hot dogs during a barbecue, but his dreams are soon crushed when Dale (who thinks competitive eating is degrading) beats him.
Guest stars include: Jeff Garlin, Pamela Anderson, and Kid Rock.

| 129 | 3 | "Bad Girls, Bad Girls, Whatcha Gonna Do" | Boowhan Lim & Kyounghee Lim | Kell Cahoon & Tom Saunders | November 17, 2002 | 6ABE19 |

Connie's criminal cousin, Tid Pau (voiced by Lucy Liu), becomes Bobby's science project partner and makes him an unwitting accomplice in creating a drug lab.
NOTE: In the original airing, Tid Pau calls Bobby a "pigfucker" (with "fucker" bleeped out). In all reruns, the word was changed to "pig farmer".

| 130 | 4 | "Goodbye Normal Jeans" | Boowhan Lim & Kyounghee Lim | Kit Boss | November 24, 2002 | 6ABE01 |

Peggy becomes jealous of Bobby when he uses his Home Ec class cooking skills in the Hill kitchen.

| 131 | 5 | "Dances with Dogs" | Anthony Lioi | Norm Hiscock | December 1, 2002 | 7ABE02 |

Bobby and Hank use Ladybird to compete in a dog dancing contest. Meanwhile, Bill is tricked into buying an ill-tempered Rottweiler from an animal shelter.
Scott Hamilton guest stars.

| 132 | 6 | "The Son Also Roses" | Dominic Polcino | Dan Sterling | December 8, 2002 | 6ABE22 |

Bobby becomes a rose grower and recruits the help of two cannabis cultivators to help him win a contest.

| 133 | 7 | "The Texas Skilsaw Massacre" | Shaun Cashman | Alan R. Cohen & Alan Freedland | December 15, 2002 | 6ABE18 |

The Hills are forced to live in Dale's house after Dale digs a tunnel underneath the Hill's kitchen, and the inspector declares the Hill house uninhabitable until the necessary repairs are done. Things get worse when Hank is sentenced to take anger management classes after accidentally cutting Dale's finger off with a skilsaw.

| 134 | 8 | "Full Metal Dust Jacket" | Adam Kuhlman | Dan McGrath | January 5, 2003 | 7ABE04 |

Peggy takes over the lease of a bookstore, but when the bookstore's business plummets, she allows Dale and his gun group to sell firearms at the store.

| 135 | 9 | "Pigmalion" | Dominic Polcino | Jonathan Collier | January 12, 2003 | 5ABE23 |

Luanne becomes involved with the psychotic owner of a pork processing plant who wants Luanne to be just like the woman on the company logo.
NOTE: This was originally supposed to air as a season six episode (even though it has a season 5 production code), but was pulled, presumably for its violent, disturbing content.

| 136 | 10 | "Megalo Dale" | Cyndi Tang Loveland | J.B. Cook | January 12, 2003 | 7ABE05 |

Dale is hired to exterminate at the Mega Lo Mart, but it turns out the "pest" is Chuck Mangione, the Mega Lo Mart spokesman.

137	11	"Boxing Luanne"	Michael Dante DiMartino	Dean Young	February 2, 2003	7ABE07
To prove to men that she's more than just a pretty face and a sexy body, Luanne becomes a boxer, but soon learns that the boxing she's been doing is foxy boxing, and that every fight she's won has been fixed.							
138	12	"Vision Quest"	Dominic Polcino	Etan Cohen	February 9, 2003	7ABE09
John Redcorn is worried about how Dale is raising Joseph so he gets Hank to take Joseph on a "vision quest," but Dale is the one who gets a vision and mistakenly believes that he's an American Indian.							
139	13	"Queasy Rider"	Wes Archer	Kit Boss	February 16, 2003	7ABE10
Hank and Peggy try to fix their strained marriage by buying a motorcycle and immersing themselves in the biker lifestyle.							
140	14	"Board Games"	Boowhan Lim & Kyounghee Lim	Silvert Glarum & Michael Jamin	March 2, 2003	7ABE08
Peggy, Nancy, and Minh run for school board against each other after Tom Landry Middle School cuts all after-school programs out of the budget.							
141	15	"An Officer and a Gentle Boy"	Gary McCarver	Dan Sterling	March 9, 2003	7ABE06
Hank sends Bobby to Cotton's old military academy, where Cotton tries to break the boy's spirit.							
142	16	"The Miseducation of Bobby Hill"	Tricia Garcia	Tim Croston & Chip Hall	March 16, 2003	7ABE11
Bobby becomes a salesman at Strickland Propane and uses unethical tactics from Joe Jack to sell more grills. Meanwhile, Dale gets a weather balloon and tests it out on Bill, who ends up flying away.							
143	17	"The Good Buck"	Allan Jacobsen	Alex Gregory & Peter Huyck	March 30, 2003	7ABE13
Buck becomes a born-again Christian (courtesy of Luanne) after his wife divorces him, but Hank is worried that Buck only wants Luanne for sex. Meanwhile, Bobby hides out from his track coach and makes friends with two old ladies at Hotel Arlen's restaurant during tea time. NOTE: On FOX, this episode was rated TV-G (making it one of two *King of the Hill* episodes that don't have the TV-PG rating ["Ho Yeah", originally rated TV-14, is the other]). On Cartoon Network, the episode is rated TV-PG for suggestive dialogue (D).							
144	18	"I Never Promised You an Organic Garden"	Adam Kuhlman	Tony Gama-Lobo & Rebecca May	April 13, 2003	7ABE14
Peggy takes over the organic garden at the school, but she is caught using pesticides on the garden.							
145	19	"Be True to Your Fool"	Anthony Lioi	Dan McGrath	April 27, 2003	7ABE12
When Hank gets his head shaved (after Bill gives Hank, Dale, and Boomhauer lice), he discovers a tattoo in the back of his head he got as a teenager during a drunken night out. Meanwhile, Bill makes friends with a bullpen of prisoners at the county jail.							
146	20	"Racist Dawg"	Michael Dante DiMartino	Kit Boss	May 4, 2003	7ABE17
Hank hires an African-American repairman (guest-voiced by Bernie Mac), whom Ladybird attacks, prompting the town to think that Hank and his dog are racists.							
147	21	"Night and Deity"	Gary McCarver	Garland Testa	May 11, 2003	7ABE16
After Bill attracts pigeons to the alley, Dale must work with an attractive female exterminator, who makes Nancy jealous.							
148	22	"Maid in Arlen"	Boohwan Lim & Kyounghee Lim	Dan Sterling	May 18, 2003	7ABE18
Bill and Laoma, Kahn's mother, enter into a romantic relationship that Kahn works overtime to sabotage.							
149	23	"The Witches of East Arlen"	Matt Engstrom	Silvert Glarum & Michael Jamin	May 18, 2003	7ABE20
Bobby gets involved with a group of post-adolescent geeks who are into tarot cards and witchcraft. David Cross guest stars.							

Season 8: 2003-2004

№	#	Title	Directed by	Written by	Original air date	Code
150	1	"Patch Boomhauer"	Anthony Lioi	J.B. Cook	November 2, 2003	8ABE01
Boomhauer's brother, Patch (voiced by Brad Pitt), is getting married to a woman Boomhauer has always been in love with, opening old wounds between the two.						
151	2	"Reborn to Be Wild"	Dominic Polcino	Tony Gama-Lobo & Rebecca May	November 9, 2003	8ABE02
Fearing that Bobby is succumbing to bad influences, Hank makes him join a local church youth group. Bobby discovers that the group consists of cool punks (guest voiced by the band members of Sum 41[1]), including their tattooed pastor, i.e. "Pastor K", who worship God through skateboarding and rock. Hank approves of Bobby's newfound interest in religion, but disapproves of the way the group treats Christianity as a fad. Meanwhile, Hank's friends (and Kahn) start a club called "The Last Meal Club", where they come up with what meals they would like to eat before they die.						
152	3	"New Cowboy on the Block"	Cyndi Tang Loveland	Dean Young	November 16, 2003	7ABE15
A washed-up former Dallas Cowboys player moves into the neighborhood, and no one, not even Hank, can admit that he's a jerk--until the player starts harassing Hank.						
153	4	"The Incredible Hank"	Wes Archer	Dan Sterling	November 23, 2003	8ABE04
Hank takes Bobby to the doctor to get him some testosterone supplements to boost his energy, but Hank becomes the one who sorely needs a testosterone boost. Meanwhile, Bobby faces his fear of showering after gym class.						
154	5	"Flirting with the Master"	Anthony Lioi	Norm Hiscock	December 7, 2003	7ABE22
The actor who plays TV's "Monsignor Martinez" invites Peggy to Mexico City to tutor his children for an English language exam. Meanwhile, Luanne takes on Peggy's duties at home.						
155	6	"After the Mold Rush"	Dominic Polcino	Kit Boss	December 14, 2003	7ABE19
When Hank's house sustains minor water damage, a man from the insurance company sets out to get rich by determining that the Hill household is infested with mold.						
156	7	"Livin' on Reds, Vitamin C and Propane"	John Rice	Dan McGrath	December 21, 2003	8ABE05
Hank needs to take some antique furniture to his mother in Arizona, so he rents an 18-wheeler and takes Bobby on a road trip (with Dale, Bill and Boomhauer stowing away). Meanwhile, Peggy and Luanne try to write a Christmas novelty song.						
157	8	"Rich Hank, Poor Hank"	Tricia Garcia	Etan Cohen	January 4, 2004	7ABE21
Bobby thinks Hank is secretly a rich miser after hearing Peggy talking about Hank's new $1000 bonus, and Bobby steals Hank's emergency credit card to go on a shopping spree.						
158	9	"Ceci N'Est Pas Une King of the Hill"	Tricia Garcia	Etan Cohen	January 25, 2004	8ABE03
When Hank asks Peggy to design an art piece for Strickland Propane, she creates the "Probot," a statue made out of propane tanks. Her sculpture is rejected by the city board, but picked up by an art dealer from Dallas. Unfortunately, Peggy finds out that the dealer presents her to the public as an uneducated hillbilly. Meanwhile, Dale starts wearing a suit of armor and uses his newfound invincibility to insult people without consequences. The episode won an Annie Award for writing.[2]						
159	10	"That's What She Said"	Cyndi Tang Loveland	Silvert Glarum & Michael Jamin	February 8, 2004	8ABE06
A new employee named Rich (voiced by Ben Stiller) becomes popular around Strickland Propane for telling lewd jokes, but Hank thinks this is a breach of sexual harassment laws.						

160	11	"My Hair Lady"	Allan Jacobsen	Wyatt Cenac	February 15, 2004	8ABE09

Luanne and Bill both get jobs at the hippest hair salon in Arlen called "Hottyz." But in order to keep his job, Bill must pretend to be a homosexual. Meanwhile, Hank's elderly barber has a hard time staying in business.

161	12	"Phish and Wild Life"	Matt Engstrom	Greg Cohen	February 22, 2004	8ABE10

Hank takes Bobby and the guys on a fishing trip, where they vow to eat only what they catch. A very hungry Bobby befriends the campers next to them, who are a group of hippies. After they feed him half of a hamburger bun, Bobby starts to eat with them. The hippies run out of their supply, and come to Bobby for repayment.

162	13	"Cheer Factor"	Boohwan Lim & Kyounghee Lim	Christy Stratton	March 7, 2004	8ABE07

Peggy volunteers to help with the school cheerleading squad, in order to get them to learn some cheers to motivate the football team. Up until now, the squad is only concerned with winning the dance competitions and trophies from other schools. When Peggy gets the crowds behind the team, the school principal replaces the current coach with Peggy....who takes it too far.

163	14	"Dale Be Not Proud"	Anthony Lioi	Jonathan Collier	March 14, 2004	8ABE11

When NHRA driver John Force needs an organ transplant, Dale is the only one who can save him. Hank encourages Dale to ignore his fear of hospitals and give up his kidney to save Force. Dale reluctantly agrees, but only if Hank takes his place being Dale for the day, a task that consists of outlandish duties.

164	15	"Après Hank, le Deluge"	Gary McCarver	Kit Boss	March 21, 2004	8ABE08

When flood threatens the town, the Arlenites gather in the communal shelter: the Tom Landry gym. Meantime, the kids go wild in the yearbook office, Peggy regresses, and Dale schemes to build an ark to float his family to safety.

165	16	"DaleTech"	Dominic Polcino	J.B. Cook	March 28, 2004	8ABE12

Dale starts a security company called "DaleTech", but his business is threatened by Cotton, who has become a new local auxiliary police officer.

166	17	"How I Learned to Stop Worrying and Love the Alamo"	Brian Sheesley	Christy Stratton	April 18, 2004	8ABE14

Hank tries to teach Bobby about the Alamo after discovering that the new history textbooks in school contain revisionist history. Meanwhile, Peggy and Luanne mail out a paper cut-out boy named Flat Stanley to be passed around America.

167	18	"Girl, You'll Be a Giant Soon"	Cyndi Tang Loveland	Dan McGrath	April 25, 2004	8ABE16

Luanne tries to help Hank protest against a grilling contest when it's revealed that the contest doesn't allow propane grills. Meanwhile, Peggy tries to visit a house where a famous murder took place, but the real estate agent is only letting in potential buyers.

168	19	"Stressed for Success"	Tricia Garcia	Tony Gama-Lobo & Rebecca May	May 2, 2004	8ABE13

Bobby joins the school's Quiz Bowl team because of his extensive knowledge of pop culture, but he becomes stressed out by the pressure.

169	20	"Hank's Back (AKA The Unbearable Lightness of Being Hank)"	Robin Brigstocke	Aron Abrams & Gregory Thompson	May 9, 2004	8ABE15

When Hank suffers a back injury at work and none of his doctors can fix it, he tries the healing powers of Yoga. At first, he finds it a little too wacky, but thanks to the help of Yogi Victor (Johnny Depp), he realizes that it actually works, but Hank's insurance company uses this to prove that Hank is taking unfair advantage of his workman's comp. Meanwhile, Peggy fights to keep the old Pink & White market open. Angela Bloomfield guest stars.

170	21	"The Redneck on Rainey Street"	Gary McCarver	Jim Dauterive	May 16, 2004	8ABE17

Connie is turned down for admission to a prestigious summer school after filling its quota of Asian kids. Realizing that working hard and overachieving will never help them get ahead in life, Kahn and Minh decide to give up and live like beer-drinking, El Camino-driving rednecks, which nearly drive them to homelessness when they stop making payments on their house. Bob Hoskins guest stars.

171	22	"Talking Shop"	Anthony Lioi	Garland Testa	May 23, 2004	8ABE20

Despite Hank's wishes for Bobby to take auto shop, Bobby takes peer counseling so he can give advice to vulnerable teenage girls. Meanwhile, Hank finds a wrecked car for Bobby to fix.

NOTE: Guest stars include: Alyson Hannigan, Laura Prepon, and Lindsay Lohan.

Season 9: 2004-2005

№	#	Title	Directed by	Written by	Original air date	Code
172	1	"A Rover Runs Through It"	Tricia Garcia	Dan Sterling	November 7, 2004	8ABE22

The Hills travel to Montana to visit Peggy's mother. There, they find out the family is losing the ranch to Henry Winkler because of high property taxes.

| 173 | 2 | "Ms. Wakefield" | Allan Jacobsen | J.B. Cook | December 19, 2004 | 9ABE05 |

When an elderly stranger, Ms. Wakefield (Marion Ross), visits the Hill residence during Christmas, Hank is thrilled to show her his house since it was also her childhood home. However, when Ms. Wakefield announces that she wants to die in their house, Hank and Peggy want nothing more than for her to leave, despite her bothersome insistence.

| 174 | 3 | "Death Buys a Timeshare" | Boohwan Lim & Kyounghee Lim | Etan Cohen | January 16, 2005 | 8ABE18 |

Cotton inherits $10,000 from the will of his friend Topsy, and goes to Mexico, with Bill in tow, to buy a timeshare. Feeling lonely after the death of his friend, Cotton gets suckered in by tales of the timeshare development's owner, O'Kelly, and decides to buy — even though Americans cannot own land in Mexico. Meanwhile, Peggy, Bobby and Dale search for a pool to swim in.

| 175 | 4 | "Yard, She Blows!" | Allan Jacobsen | Silvert Glarum & Michael Jamin | January 23, 2005 | 8ABE19 |

Peggy is jealous that Hank always gets complimented on his yard, so she starts a garden in the front yard. When that doesn't work she puts Winklebottom the garden gnome in their front yard, which drives Hank nuts.

| 176 | 5 | "Dale to the Chief" | Anthony Lioi | Garland Testa | May 22, 2005 | 9ABE02 |

When Dale reads Joseph the Warren Commission Report, he discovers that the U.S. government could be right about who assassinated John F. Kennedy and turns his government-hating, right-wing mania into insufferable, flag-waving patriotism. Meanwhile, Hank discovers a mistake on his driver's license and is sent through a boatload of red tape in order to fix it.

| 177 | 6 | "The Petriot Act" | Robin Brigstocke | Christy Stratton | February 13, 2005 | 9ABE06 |

When Hank agrees to take in a soldier's pet, he gets Duke, a vicious, mean-spirited cat, against Hank's wishes. Hank takes Duke to visit Dr. Leslie, a veterinarian who runs a battery of tests and presents Hank with a bill for several thousand dollars.

| 178 | 7 | "Enrique-cilable Differences" | Dominic Polcino | Greg Cohen | February 20, 2005 | 9ABE12 |

Hank's co-worker Enrique is having marital problems, and starts spending all his time with Hank. Meanwhile, Bobby tries to unblock the Fox network from the Hills' TV.

| 179 | 8 | "Mutual of Omabwah" | Dominic Polcino | Tony Gama-Lobo & Rebecca May | March 6, 2005 | 9ABE03 |

When Hank forgets to mail his insurance payment, Hank and Bobby must protect themselves from any accidents until their insurance can be re-activated in 36 hours. Meanwhile, Dale decides to raise bees, Bill and Boomhauer discover the joys of deep-frying, and Peggy and Luanne get stuck at a rest stop when Hank won't let them drive uninsured.

| 180 | 9 | "Care-Takin' Care of Business" | Cyndi Tang Loveland | Dan McGrath | March 13, 2005 | 9ABE01 |

When the Tom Landry Middle School football team has to forfeit a game due to poor field maintenance when the caretaker goes senile, the booster club resolves to replace the school's elderly groundskeeper, Smitty, and Hank resolves to help him keep his job by secretly doing upkeep on the field. Meanwhile, Luanne starts dating a redneck named Lucky (first seen in "The Redneck on Rainey Street"), much to Peggy's dismay.

| 181 | 10 | "Arlen City Bomber" | Boohwan Lim & Kyounghee Lim | Jonathan Collier | March 27, 2005 | 9ABE07 |

To pay off her credit card debts, Luanne signs up to be a roller derby girl. Peggy gets in on it too and uses borrowed money to make improvements on the team, sinking both Luanne and Peggy deeper into debt.						
182	11	"Redcorn Gambles with His Future"	Matt Engstrom	Etan Cohen	April 10, 2005	9ABE09
Hank is in charge of organizing the Strickland Family Fun Day. Meanwhile, John Redcorn and his band "Big Mountain Fudgecake" are having trouble finding a venue to play their music. Acting on Hank's advice, John Redcorn uses his land to open a casino so his band can have a place to play.						
183	12	"Smoking and the Bandit"	Cyndi Tang Loveland	Dan McGrath	April 17, 2005	9ABE10
When Arlen bans smoking in all restaurants and bars, Dale becomes the "Smoking Bandit" to impress Joseph.						
184	13	"Gone with the Windstorm"	Yvette Kaplan	Wyatt Cenac	May 1, 2005	9ABE08
When Channel 84 hires a new meteorologist, Irv Bennett, Nancy and her less-than-accurate weather reports are left out in the cold. Meanwhile, Bobby tries to fight back against a bully who constantly scares him at school.						
185	14	"Bobby on Track"	Tricia Garcia	Aron Abrams & Gregory Thompson	May 8, 2005	9ABE13
Upset with Bobby's habit of giving up what he starts (after Bobby doesn't complete the miles needed to run for a charity race), Hank puts Bobby on the school's track team, but soon learns that the coach only wants Bobby so he can push the other team members to do better.						
186	15	"It Ain't Over 'til the Fat Neighbor Sings"	Julius Wu	Etan Cohen	May 15, 2005	9ABE19
Bill joins an all-male chorus (based on the Dallas-based men's chorus the Vocal Majority) who end up using Bill and forcing him to blow off his appointment to cut the general's hair at the Army base. Meanwhile, Peggy and Bobby get caught up in a game of Pong.						

Season 10: 2005-2006

The majority of episodes in this season are leftover episodes from the 8ABE and 9ABE production line. The AABE production line (much like *The Simpsons'* 3G production line for seasons eight and nine) is a short-lived line and only lasts for five episodes (four airing this season and the fifth airing as a leftover episode next season).

№	#	Title	Directed by	Written by	Original air date	Code
187	1	"Hank's on Board"	Allan Jacobsen	Silvert Glarum & Michael Jamin	October 16, 2005	9ABE14
Hank fears he is being shunned when his friends go on a vacation without him.						
188	2	"Bystand Me"	Dominic Polcino	Kit Boss	October 6, 2005	8ABE21
When the *Arlen Bystander* newspaper gets a new editor, Peggy gets a job writing a household hints column (even though Peggy doesn't know any household hints). Meanwhile, Hank makes Bobby get a paper route.						
189	3	"Bill's House"	Robin Brigstocke	Tony Gama-Lobo & Rebecca May	November 13, 2005	9ABE15
Bill turns his house into a rehabilitation center for alcoholics.						
190	4	"Harlottown"	Tricia Garcia	Aron Abrams & Gregory Thompson	November 20, 2005	9ABE04
Peggy and Hank protest when Arlen's city manager wants to open a Museum of Prostitution and host the Adult Video Awards.						
191	5	"Portrait of the Artist as a Young Clown"	Anthony Lioi	Christy Stratton & Garland Testa	December 4, 2005	9ABE16
Bobby goes to clown college and becomes a classical clown, but he discovers his new act isn't funny.						
192	6	"Orange You Sad I Did Say Banana?"	Adam Kuhlman	Dan Sterling	December 11, 2005	9ABE11

Upon being told that he is too Americanized and called a "banana" (the Asian equivalent to an Oreo [a black person who acts white]), Kahn vows to return to his Laotian roots.						
193	7	"You Gotta Believe (In Moderation)"	Yvette Caplan	Kit Boss	December 18, 2005	9ABE17
Hank invites a softball team to compete against his own team of misfits, to raise money to save Tom Landry Middle School's baseball team.						
194	8	"Business Is Picking Up"	Matt Engrstrom	Dan Sterling	March 19, 2006	9ABE18
Hank tries to get Bobby interested in working as a propane salesman during Tom Landry Middle School's Career Day, but Bobby shadows a young, handsome man (Knoxville) who makes his living picking up animal (and human) waste. Guest Voice Star: Johnny Knoxville						
195	9	"The Year of Washing Dangerously"	Cyndi Tang Loveland & Ken Wong	J.B. Cook	March 26, 2006	9ABE20
Kahn buys the local car wash as part of a plan to get rich, and Hank finds himself working for his disrespectful, money-obsessed neighbor when Buck takes a stake in the business as well.						
196	10	"Hank Fixes Everything"	Ronald Rubio	Kit Boss	April 2, 2006	9ABE21
Buck Strickland hires the guys from the reality show *American Chopper* to perform at Strickland Propane in order to win a price war with Thatherton Fuels, then gets into a price fixing conspiracy with the other propane companies in Arlen.						
197	11	"Church Hopping"	Robin Brigstocke	Jim Dauterive	April 9, 2006	9ABE22
When the Hill family finds out that their pew of many years has been given away to another family at church they abandon their staid Methodist church and come about to worship at a new megachurch.						
198	12	"24 Hour Propane People"	Robin Brigstocke	Aron Abrams & Gregory Thompson	April 23, 2006	AABE01
When Buck gets banned from his favorite strip club, he refocuses on making Strickland Propane a "fun" place to work, which sits well with everyone but Hank.						
199	13	"The Texas Panhandler"	Ronald Rubio & Ken Wong	Tony Gama-Lobo & Rebecca May	April 30, 2006	AABE02
Instead of getting a real job, Bobby and Joseph discover that they can make more money, and look cooler, by hanging out on street corners and begging for money.						
200	14	"Hank's Bully"	Kyounghee Lim	J.B. Cook	May 7, 2006	AABE03
A young boy, Caleb, starts following Hank around, making fun of him and generally annoying him. Meanwhile, Dale and Peggy enter a taxidermy competition.						
201	15	"Edu-macating Lucky"	Adam Kuhlman	Silvert Glarum & Michael Jamin	May 14, 2006	AABE04
Lucky asks Peggy to help him get his GED in the hopes of improving his chances of marrying Luanne. Peggy agrees to help him study for the test, but is torn between her wish to help him and her wish to keep him away from her niece.						

Season 11: 2007

№	#	Title	Directed by	Written by	Original air date	Code
202	1	"The Peggy Horror Picture Show"	Kyounghee Lim	Christy Stratton	January 28, 2007	BABE02
		Peggy, feeling a bit unfeminine because of her masculine clothes and size-16 feet, befriends Carolyn, who views Peggy as the epitome of womanhood. Hank is thrilled that Peggy finally has someone else to talk to about her girl problems, but discovers that Carolyn is a drag queen who thinks Peggy is one too.				
203	2	"serPUNt"	Robin Brigstocke	Greg Cohen	March 11, 2007	BABE01
		When a python Lucky gives to Bobby as a gift gets into the toilet, Hank calls Animal Control. But instead of taking care of the problem, they make the city believe that the problem is worse than it is in order to get higher salaries, causing panic.				
204	3	"Blood and Sauce"	Tricia Garcia	Dan McGrath	March 18, 2007	BABE03
		Bill calls a reunion of all the Dauterives due to feeling lonely. After amassing a giant barbecue it's found out that Gilbert, his cousin, is the only other Dauterive.Due to such good tasting food, people want to buy the recipe, however Gilbert won't let Bill whore out the Dauterive family.				
205	4	"Luanne Gets Lucky"	Ken Wong	Jonathan Collier	March 25, 2007	BABE04
		Lucky neglects Luanne when he becomes obsessed with retrieving a walnut stump his grandfather found, so Luanne accepts a 15-year-old's invitation to the senior prom.				
206	5	"Hank Gets Dusted"	Michael Loya	Kit Boss	April 1, 2007	BABE05
		Hank is devastated when Cotton's Cadillac is given to Hank's cousin Dusty (voice of ZZ Top's Dusty Hill), but when Dusty and his bandmates show up at Hank's house to play practical jokes for a reality show taping, it's more than Hank can bear.				
207	6	"Glen Peggy Glen Ross"	Tony Kluck	Jim Dauterive	April 8, 2007	BABE06
		Peggy is fired from *The Arlen Bystander* and begins a new career as a real estate agent. Meanwhile, after Dale buys a set of titanium golf clubs at a police auction, he gives the clubs to Hank, who doesn't want them after learning they were used as a murder weapon.				
208	7	"The Passion of Dauterive"	Anthony Chun	Tony Gama-Lobo & Rebecca May	April 15, 2007	BABE07
		Bill searches for meaning in his life after surviving a roof collapse, leading to a relationship with Reverend Stroup.				
209	8	"Grand Theft Arlen"	Ronahld Rubio	Sanjay Shah	April 22, 2007	BABE08
		Hank protests against a new school program that lets failing gym students play video games--and becomes addicted to a *Grand Theft Auto*-style video game centered on propane and featuring Hank as the protagonist. Meanwhile, Bobby trains for the Presidential Physical Fitness Test.				
210	9	"Peggy's Gone to Pots"	Robin Brigstocke	Paul Corrigan & Brad Walsh	May 6, 2007	BABE09
		Peggy tries to reach the pinnacle of real estate success by selling houses in the exclusive neighborhood of Arlen Heights, but she winds up selling kitchen supplies for a scam company. Meanwhile, Rusty Shackleford, the man whose identity Dale often uses, pays a visit to Dale.				
211	10	"Hair Today, Gone Tomorrow"	Kyounghee Lim	Christy Stratton	May 13, 2007	BABE10
		Nancy turns to her mother (voiced by Rue McClanahan) for help when the stress of home life and unresolved feelings for John Redcorn cause her to lose her hair. Meanwhile, Dale takes a ride with Kahn's delinquent nephew in a souped-up racecar during the vernal equinox and thinks he's traveled through time.				
212	11	"Bill, Bulk and the Body Buddies"	Tricia Garcia	Blake McCormick	May 20, 2007	BABE11
		Bill meets a body builder named Dirk who agrees to help him train for an upcoming Army physical, but when Bill starts working out with Dirk and his two meat head buddies, Bill develops a bad attitude and alienates his former friends.				
213	12	"Lucky's Wedding Suit"	Julius Wu	Jim Dauterive	May 20, 2007	AABE05

When Lucky wants to give Luanne the expensive wedding that she desires, he sues Dale with a frivolous lawsuit after having an accident on the job. Rated TV-PG-L

NOTE: This episode was originally scheduled to be *King of the Hill*'s final episode (explaining why the AABE production line is so short and why this episode contained many secondary characters). [3]

Season 12: 2007-2008

№	#	Title	Directed by	Written by	Original air date	Code
214	1	"Suite Smells of Excess"	Michael Loya	Dave Schiff	September 23, 2007	BABE13
When the guys take Bobby to a University of Texas football game their hijinks land them in a VIP box suite, where Hank is mistaken for a former player of the opposing Nebraska Cornhuskers, and is asked to call a crucial play for the team.						
215	2	"Bobby Rae"	Ken Wong	Tim Croston & Chip Hall	October 7, 2007	BABE12
Bobby feigns interest in activism when he goes after the heart of a real student activist, who protests the installation of soda machines in the school (and the funds from said soda machines being used to pay for the teachers' vacation).						
216	3	"The Powder Puff Boys"	Ronald Rubio	Christy Stratton	October 14, 2007	BABE16
Hank encourages Bobby to be a part of the school's Powder Puff team (a team where boys dress in drag and impersonate female cheerleaders). However, the boys learn that Peggy and the PTA are trying to put a stop to the tradition.						
217	4	"Four Wave Intersection"	Anthony Chun	Judah Miller & Murray Miller	October 21, 2007	BABE15
Arlen is hit by a heat wave and Hank takes the kids to the water park. Unfortunately, they have to tangle with a group of surfer bullies to enjoy the "Endless Wave." Meanwhile, Boomhauer, who is usually cool, winds up embarrassing himself, and Bill becomes known as the famous "Heat-Waver" when he begins to stand on the side of the highway and wave to motorists.						
218	5	"Death Picks Cotton"	Tony Kluck	Judah Miller & Murray Miller	November 11, 2007	BABE14
While at a Japanese restaurant, Cotton suffers a war flashback and ends up getting hospitalized after falling on the grill, where Peggy learns that Cotton may not have long to live. [4]						
219	6	"Raise the Steaks"	Robin Brigstocke	Paul Corrigan & Brad Walsh	November 18, 2007	BABE17
After buying tough, unsavory steaks at the Mega-Lo-Mart, Hank, at Appleseed's suggestion, visits the town co-op in search of better meat. After falling in love with the delicious organic food, Hank becomes a co-op volunteer and co-owner.						
220	7	"Tears of an Inflatable Clown"	Tricia Garcia	Erin Ehrlich	November 25, 2007	BABE19
Bobby convinces the student council to put on a carnival, and he's put in charge of it, but a dour so-called "diversity expert" comes to school and nearly puts the kibosh on Bobby's plan by making everything politically correct. Meanwhile, Dale, Bill and Boomhauer try to get a reluctant Lucky to the hospital when he injures himself.						
221	8	"The Minh Who Knew Too Much"	Kyounghee Lim	Dan McGrath	December 9, 2007	BABE18
Minh joins the Arlen Gun Club to learn skeet shooting, a skill she hopes will make an exclusive country club want her and Kahn as members. Meanwhile, Hank tries to solve the mystery of who's been discarding trash in his trash cans.						
222	9	"Dream Weaver"	Ken Wong	Jennifer Barrow	December 16, 2007	BABE20
Nancy wants Dale to get a new job since he's not making any money, so he and Hank go on a "vocation vacation" to learn basket weaving. Meanwhile Peggy, Kahn and Bill try to achieve Internet stardom by creating a wacky viral video.						
223	10	"Doggone Crazy"	Michael Loya	Dave Schiff	February 3, 2008	CABE01
The Hill's dog, Ladybird, goes on a rampage, breaking things all over the house and later biting Hank's hand. After Ladybird is put on a list of vicious dogs, the veterinarian suggests that Hank takes her to a dog spiritualist.						

224	11	"Trans-Fascism"	Kyounghee Lim	Paul Corrigan & Brad Walsh	February 10, 2008	CABE02
When the Arlen City Council bans the sale of foods containing trans fats, Sugarfoot's Restaurant goes out of business. Hank, who feels the ban is an infringement on freedom, encourages Strickland to fix things. Strickland's solution to the problem is to sell his delicious, trans-fatty foods on a lunch truck so he can evade the law.						
225	12	"Untitled Blake McCormic Project"	Ken Wong	Blake McCormick	February 17, 2008	CABE03
Bill becomes involved with a single mother, Charlene, who once had an affair with John Redcorn, and, like Nancy Gribble, has a half-Native American child who, like Joseph Gribble, is oblivious to her biological father's identity.						
226	13	"The Accidental Terrorist"	Robin Brigstocke	Tim Croston & Chip Hall	March 2, 2008	CABE04
Hank finds out his car salesman has been tricking him into paying more than he should when purchasing a car, and gets tangled in a botched plan cooked up by two college-aged activists.						
227	14	"Lady and Gentrification"	Anthony Chun	Judah Miller & Murray Miller	March 9, 2008	CABE05
Peggy inadvertently ruins Enrique's life when she sells a house in Enrique's neighborhood to a hipster (who invites his hipster (voiced by Dax Shepard) friends over to live in the same neighborhood). Meanwhile, Hank is asked to speak at Enrique's daughter's Quinceaños celebration.						
228	15	"Behind Closed Doors"	Tony Kluck	Christy Stratton	March 16, 2008	CABE06
Tom Landry Middle School holds an emergency community meeting when a child goes missing in Arlen. Relationship expert Stephens Davies is invited to speak at the meeting and makes an example of Peggy by questioning her parenting skills, prompting Peggy to become stricter in her parenting						
229	16	"Pour Some Sugar on Kahn"	Tricia Garcia	Sanjay Shah	March 30, 2008	CABE07
Kahn's father-in-law, General Gum, visits the Souphanousinphone family. The General gives Kahn a hard time and makes him feel like a failure. Kahn becomes depressed until he stumbles upon a Laotian karaoke bar where he becomes a star singing "The Morning After".						
230	17	"Six Characters in Search of a House"	Ronald Rubio	Erin Ehrlich	April 6, 2008	CABE08
Peggy, a passionate realtor, finds a great home listing that she must sell within two weeks. One catch, though, the home is currently occupied by the strangest family in Arlen. Peggy doesn't feel they are visually appealing enough to get the home sold in time, so she decides to bring in a "Hollywood" family to sell the home.						
231	18	"The Courtship of Joseph's Father"	Michael Loya	Tony Gama-Lobo & Rebecca May	April 13, 2008	CABE09
Joseph becomes the Star quarterback at Tom Landry Middle School, and gives the school hope that they'll actually win this year. A wealthy prep school offers Joseph to play for their school instead. Joseph wants to stay at Landry, but Dale wants him to take the cash offering. Dale realizes that his family doesn't fit in the upper-class lifestyle and tries to raise money to pay back the school's exclusive contract.						
232	19	"Strangeness On a Train"	Kyounghee Lim	Jim Dauterive	April 27, 2008	CABE10
Depressed over her botched birthday parties, Peggy schedules a 1970s-style murder mystery party on a train, but when Dale ruins the surprise, thanks to Luanne's discovery of what her role is, a new mystery crops up -- after Hank and Peg have sex in the train bathroom.						
233	20	"Cops and Robert"	Ken Wong	Dave Schiff	May 4, 2008	CABE11
When Hank accidentally steals another man's wallet (thinking that the man pickpocketed him), the man begins exacting his revenge on Hank. Meanwhile, Bobby gets sentenced to spend the day with the school security guard after being framed for throwing a soda can at him and Dale attempts to get a job at a Hooters-esque restaurant called "Bazooms" by citing sexual discrimination if he's not hired. Paul Sorvino guest stars.						
234	21	"It Came From the Garage"	Robin Brigstocke	Blake McCormick	May 11, 2008	CABE12
Hank and Bobby get in some father/son bonding time when Hank dumps the old team of Dale, Bill and Boomhauer to help Bobby in a boat-building competition. During the building process, Hank gets spooked by bats that invade the construction garage, forcing Bobby to do the building all alone.						

| 235 | 22 | "Life: A Loser's Manual" | Anthony Chun | Dan McGrath | May 18, 2008 | CABE13 |

Luanne's long lost father and Peggy's brother, Hoyt (voiced by Johnny Knoxville), returns to Arlen after being incarcerated for years (it had been assumed that he worked on an oil rig). With nowhere to go, he turns to his daughter and sister for guidance and a little bit of dough. When Peggy denies him, he decides to take matters into his own hands and robs a restaurant for cash. Meanwhile, Luanne's husband, Lucky, turns to Hank for some insight on how to become a better father.

Season 13: 2008-2009

Beginning with the episode "Lucky See, Monkey Do," *King of the Hill* is now shown in 720p high-definition. This is also the final season of *King of the Hill*.

№	#	Title	Directed by	Written by	Original air date	Code
236	1	"Dia-BILL-ic Shock"	Ronald Rubio	Sanjay Shah	September 28, 2008	CABE16

Bill, unwilling to change his sugary eating habits, is diagnosed with diabetes by a mean-spirited doctor who tells him that he is going to lose his legs. After deciding to use a wheelchair (which he really doesn't need), he is befriended by a rugby player named Thunder, who teaches him how to be independent, but their friendship is strained when Thunder realizes Bill isn't really disabled.

| 237 | 2 | "Earthly Girls are Easy" | Matt Engstrom | Paul Corrigan & Brad Walsh | October 5, 2008 | CABE17 |

A local paper plans to run a story about Strickland Propane illegally dumping old propane tanks into the river. Hank suggests the company go green, and when the ladies of Arlen hear of the eco-efforts made by the company, Dale decides to help out Strickland with their carbon off-sets to garner the attention of the girls. To impress the ladies, Mr. Strickland organizes an earth benefit concert that goes wrong.

| 238 | 3 | "Square-Footed Monster" | Kyounghee Lim | Jerry Collins | October 19, 2008 | CABE18 |

After Hank and the guys fix up the recently deceased Dotty Dwyer's house, Dotty's nephew sells the house to Ted Wassonasong. But when Ted has construction workers tear down the home to make way for a "McMansion", the Hill family and the rest of the neighborhood visit the City Council to protest the construction.

| 239 | 4 | "Lost in MySpace" | Tony Kluck | Judah Miller & Murray Miller | November 2, 2008 | CABE14 |

To boost business, Strickland Propane creates a MySpace page despite Hank's bad feelings about the idea. Mr. Strickland gives Donna full responsibility over the page, but she fills it with personal information about the employees, leading to conflicts throughout the office. Meanwhile, Dale rents a pig to hunt truffles, loses it, and has to borrow Ladybird in order to track it down.

| 240 | 5 | "No Bobby Left Behind" | Tricia Garcia | Tim Croston & Chip Hall | November 9, 2008 | CABE15 |

To raise the school's grade point average due to the No Child Left Behind program, Bobby and Joseph are assigned as "special needs" students, which irks Hank.

| 241 | 6 | "A Bill Full of Dollars" | Steve Robertston | Dan McGrath | November 16, 2008 | CABE19 |

After losing money in the stock market, Peggy, Minh and Dale decide to study Bill, "an average man", in order to improve their odds.

| 242 | 7 | "Straight as an Arrow" | Robin Brigstocke | Tony Gama-Lobo & Rebecca May | November 30, 2008 | CABE20 |

When Bobby decides to become a member of the Order of the Straight Arrow (even though it was established that Bobby is already a member according to the season one episode "Order of the Straight Arrow"), Hank decides to get involved as well, but when he bumps heads with the Arrowmaster, who happens to be a new resident of Arlen, this stirs up trouble with Peggy, who has volunteered to serve as the Welcome Wagon representative for the town.

| 243 | 8 | "Lucky See, Monkey Do" | Kyounghee Lim | Paul Corrigan & Brad Walsh | February 8, 2009 | DABE01 |

When Peggy plans a baby shower for Luanne, Lucky invites his sister Myrna and her children to the party. Myrna has conflicting parenting information to give Luanne, and is described by Peggy as a "modern mother". After a scuffle between Myrna and Peggy on where to birth the baby, Luanne decides to do it "her way" and take Peggy's advice about going to the hospital to give birth. Meanwhile, Bill goes to Arizona to find a woman who he is attracted to after speaking with her at his favorite fast-food restaurant.

NOTE: This was the first episode of the series to air in 720p High Definition.

244	9	"What Happens at the National Propane Gas Convention in Memphis Stays at the National Propane Gas Convention in Memphis"	Ronald Rubio	Jim Dauterive	February 15, 2009	DABE02

When Buck Strickland is invited to the National Propane Gas Convention as the newest inductee into the Propane Hall of Flame, he asks Hank to accompany him. Although Hank is honored, he quickly realizes his primary responsibility will be babysitting Buck and preventing him from getting into trouble. Hank's job is made that much more difficult when Buck meets his illegitimate son Ray Roy (guest voice Diedrich Bader) at the convention and stays out late carousing with him.

245	10	"Master of Puppets"	Tony Kluck	Blake McCormick	March 1, 2009	DABE03

When Hank and Peggy forget to pick up Bobby at the mall, Bobby begins using emotional blackmail to get them to do whatever he wants. Meanwhile, Dale emulates *Survivorguy* (a parody of Survivorman) by camping out in the backyard.

246	11	"Bwah My Nose"	Jeff Myers	Judah Miller & Murray Miller	March 8, 2009	DABE04

During a football game practice for an upcoming rematch, Bill breaks Hank's nose. After trying to live with the injury, Hank reluctantly gets plastic surgery... and becomes hung up on his looks.

247	12	"Uncool Customer"	Tricia Garcia	Christy Stratton	March 15, 2009	DABE05

After Peggy finds out that she is not cool, she befriends one of Arlen's most glamorous and coolest moms in an effort to learn how to be cool. Bobby finds himself enchanted by her daughter. Hank finds a restaurant that sells delicious meatloaf sandwiches, but cannot get used to its seating arrangements.

248	13	"Nancy Does Dallas"	Michael Loya	Tony Gama-Lobo & Rebecca May	March 22, 2009	DABE06

Nancy moves to Dallas after landing a job as a reporter for a metropolitan news station and back-stabs her way to the top. Meanwhile, Dale conducts a hare-brained experiment by turning the house into an igloo.

249	14	"Born Again on the Fourth of July"	Ken Wong	Erin Ehrlich	April 19, 2009	DABE07

Hank gets involved in a neighborhood war over 4th of July decorations, and Bobby discovers that his apathy over neighborhood pride is what's tearing the neighborhood apart.

250	15	"Serves Me Right for Giving General George S. Patton the Bathroom Key"	Steve Robertson	Tim Croston & Chip Hall	April 26, 2009	DABE08

Hank receives a special delivery of his recently deceased father's personal belongings, including a list of bizarre final requests -- one of which calls for Hank to flush Cotton's ashes in the toilet of a bar once used by General George S. Patton. Meanwhile, Dale and Bill bicker over an empty beer can Dale discarded in Bill's yard and won't pick up.

251	16	"Bad News Bill"	Ronald Rubio	Dave Schiff	May 3, 2009	DABE10

When Hank tries to be realistic about Bobby's below-average baseball abilities, he is vilified by Bobby's over-enthusiastic Little League coach, who only wants to set Bobby up for disappointment. Meanwhile, Bill is hired as the head of the baseball field's snack counter.

252	17	"Manger Baby Einstein"	Kyounghee Lim	Sanjay Shah	May 10, 2009	DABE09

While adjusting to her new career and life as a mom, Luanne resurrects her Manger Baby puppets and, with help from John Redcorn, starts a series of direct-to-DVD educational shows, but risks selling out when the franchise grows stale and other entertainers line up to take her place. Final appearance of John Redcorn.

253	18	"Uh-oh, Canada"	Tony Kluck	Jerry Collins	May 17, 2009	DABE11
When Boomhauer decides to house-swap with the Huskins, a Canadian family, for the duration of the summer, Hank and the Rainey St. regulars find themselves putting up with the neighbors from hell. Meanwhile, Boomhauer romances a Quebecer. Mira Sorvino guest stars. Buck Strickland makes his final appearance in this episode.						
254	19	"The Boy Can't Help It"	Jeff Myers	Dan McGrath	September 13, 2009	DABE12
Bobby becomes quite the ladies' man when several girls in his class consider him a potential date for the Homecoming dance, but Hank is worried that Bobby is being used. Meanwhile, Hank and the guys try to put together the ultimate homeless person's shopping cart.						
255	20	"To Sirloin with Love"	Kyounghee Lim	Jim Dauterive, Tony Gama-Lobo, Rebecca May & Christy Stratton	September 13, 2009	DABE17
In the series finale, Hank discovers that Bobby has a talent for inspecting and distinguishing cuts of meat, and puts Bobby on a meat-inspecting team run by Heimlich County's community college. This episode reveals that Boomhauer has a job as a Texas ranger. The episode ends with Bobby and Hank grilling; everyone in their neighborhood comes to their house to eat, and the final shot of the series is a view of the Arlen Water Tower. The post-credits line is also the famous "yep" scene, the first dialogue of the series.						

Syndication: 2010

20th Century Fox Television initially ordered 13 DABE[3] production episodes, but decided to keep the show in production for four additional episodes (DABE14-DABE17). However, the network only aired the last of those four episodes (13 total for that production season), and confirmed it would not air the remaining four unaired episodes (DABE13-DABE16) in prime time, opting instead for syndication. These episodes premiered between May 3 and May 6, 2010 on local stations. They also premiered on Cartoon Network's Adult Swim between May 17 and May 20, 2010, followed by the series finale (DABE17) on May 21, 2010.

№	Title	Original syndication air date	Original Adult Swim air date	Code
256	"The Honeymooners"	May 3, 2010	May 17, 2010	DABE13
Hank is shocked when his mother announces she is marrying a man she has only known for a few weeks. Soon after, the newlyweds celebrate by purchasing an RV and heading to Hank's. When Hank's mom and new stepfather have a heated argument, she takes off with the RV and Hank is left to rescue his mother once again.				
257	"Bill Gathers Moss"	May 4, 2010	May 18, 2010	DABE14
Bill decides to take in roommates, and Hank fears it will lead to disaster. Meanwhile, Bobby and Joseph go ghost hunting at their school.				
258	"When Joseph Met Lori, and Made Out with Her in the Janitor's Closet"	May 5, 2010	May 19, 2010	DABE15
After getting into an argument with Joseph about the girl he has been dating, Dale attempts to give Joseph the "sex talk" but fails to, and takes a test claiming he has "dementia" leading to him joining a mental home, but then realizes he has to get out before Joseph and Lori go "all the way".				
259	"Just Another Manic Kahn-Day"	May 6, 2010	May 20, 2010	DABE16
Kahn's bouts of manic depression threaten to derail Hank's plan to build a tricked-out barbecue grill for an upcoming Strickland event. Meanwhile, Bobby tries to figure out why his parents and other adults think a "Raymond J. Johnson, Jr." comedy record is funny.				

References

[1] ""King of the Hill" Reborn to Be Wild (2003)" (http://www.imdb.com/title/tt0620295/). . Retrieved 2009-11-03.

[2] http://annieawards.org/32ndwinners.html

[3] "King of the Hill Originals still on Tap for next Season" (http://www.thefutoncritic.com/news.aspx?id=8068).*thefutoncritic.com.* April 30, 2009. . Retrieved 2009-04-30.

[4] tv.com; "Death Picks Cotton" (http://www.tv.com/king-of-the-hill/death-picks-cotton/episode/1145274/summary.html)

... First Do No Harm

...First Do No Harm	
Directed by	Jim Abrahams
Produced by	Jim Abrahams
Written by	Ann Beckett
Starring	Meryl Streep Fred Ward Seth Adkins Allison Janney Margo Martindale Oni Faida Lampley Leo Burmester Tom Butler Mairon Bennett Michael Yarmush Millicent Kelly Diana Belshaw
Music by	Hummie Mann
Cinematography	Pierre Letarte
Editing by	Terry Stokes
Distributed by	Walt Disney Video
Release date(s)	16 February 1997
Running time	94 min.
Language	English

...First Do No Harm is a 1997 television film, directed by Jim Abrahams, about a boy whose severe epilepsy, unresponsive to medications with terrible side effects, is controlled by the ketogenic diet. Aspects of the story mirror Abrahams' own experience with his son Charlie.

Plot

The film tells a story in the life of a Midwestern family, the Reimullers. Lori (played by Meryl Streep) is the mother of three children and the wife of Dave (Fred Ward), a truck driver. The family are presented as happy, normal and comfortable financially: they have just bought a horse and are planning a holiday to Hawaii. Then the youngest son, Robbie (Seth Adkins), has a sudden unexplained fall at school. A short while later, he has another unprovoked fall while playing with his brother, and is seen having a convulsive seizure. Robbie is taken to the hospital where a number of procedures are performed: a CT scan, a lumbar puncture, an electroencephalogram (EEG) and blood tests. No cause is found but the two falls are regarded as epileptic seizures and the child diagnosed with epilepsy.

Robbie is started on phenobarbital, an old anticonvulsant drug with well known side effects including cognitive impairment and behavior problems. The latter cause the child to run berserk through the house, leading to injury. Lori urgently phones the physician to request a change of medication. It is changed to phenytoin (Dilantin) but the dose of phenobarbital must be tapered slowly, causing frustration. Later, the drug carbamazepine (Tegretol) is added.

Meanwhile, the Reimullers discover that their health insurance is invalid and their treatment is transferred from private to county hospital. In an attempt to pay the medical bills, Dave takes on more dangerous truck loads and works long hours. Family tensions reach a head when the children realize the holiday is not going to happen and a foreclosure notice is posted on the house.

Robbie's epilepsy gets worse and he develops a serious rash known as Stevens-Johnson syndrome as a side effect of the medication. He is admitted to hospital where his padded cot is designed to prevent him escaping. The parents fear he may become a "vegetable" and are losing hope. At one point, Robbie goes into status epilepticus (a continuous convulsive seizure that must be stopped as a medical emergency). Increasing doses of diazepam (Valium) are given intravenously to no effect. Eventually, paraldehyde is given rectally. This drug is described has having possibly fatal side effects and is seen dramatically melting a plastic cup (a glass syringe is required).

The neurologist in charge of Robbie's care, Dr. Melanie Abbasac (Allison Janney), has poor bedside manner and paints a bleak picture. Abbasac wants the Reimullers to consider surgery and start the necessary investigative procedures to see if this is an option. These involve removing the top of the skull and inserting electrodes on the surface of the brain to achieve a more accurate location of any seizure focus than normal scalp EEG electrodes. The Reimullers see surgery as a dangerous last resort and want to know if anything else can be done.

Lori begins to research epilepsy at the library. After many hours, she comes across the ketogenic diet in a well-regarded textbook on epilepsy. However, their doctor dismisses the diet as having only anecdotal evidence of its effectiveness. After initially refusing to consider the diet, she appears to relent but sets impossible hurdles in the way: the Reimullers must find a way to transport their son to Johns Hopkins Hospital in Baltimore, Maryland with continual medical support—something they cannot afford.

That evening, Lori attempts to abduct her son from the hospital and, despite the risk, fly with him to an appointment she has made with Dr Freeman at Johns Hopkins. However, she is stopped by hospital security at the exit to the hospital. A sympathetic nurse warns Lori that she could lose custody of her son if a court decides she is putting her son's health at risk.

Dave makes contact with an old family friend who once practiced as a physician and is still licensed. This doctor and the sympathetic nurse agree to accompany Lori and Robbie on the trip to Baltimore. During the flight, Robbie has a prolonged convulsive seizure, which causes some concern to the pilot and crew.

When they arrive at Johns Hopkins, it becomes apparent that Lori has deceived her friends as her appointment (for the previous week) was not rescheduled and there are no places on the ketogenic diet program. After much pleading, Dr Freeman agrees to take Robbie on as an outpatient. Lori and Robbie stay at a convent in Baltimore.

The diet is briefly explained by Millicent Kelly (played by herself) a dietitian who has helped run the ketogenic diet program since the 1940s. Robbie's seizures begin to improve during the initial fast that is used to kick-start the diet. Despite the very high-fat nature of the diet, Robbie accepts the food and rapidly improves. His seizures are eliminated and his mental faculties are restored. The film ends with Robbie riding the family horse at a parade through town. Closing credits claim Robbie continued the diet for a couple of years and has remained seizure- and drug-free ever since.

Background

The director and producer, Jim Abrahams, was inspired to make the film as a result of his own experiences with his son Charlie. Charlie developed a very serious seizure condition that proved intractable despite several medications and surgery. His cognitive decline was described by Abrahams as "a fate worse than death". He came across the diet in a book on childhood epilepsy by Dr John Freeman, director of the Pediatric Epilepsy Center at Johns Hopkins Hospital. Charlie was started on the diet and rapidly became seizure free. In addition, medications were tapered and his mental development restored. Abrahams was outraged that nobody had informed him of the diet. He created the Charlie Foundation to promote the diet and funded research studies to demonstrate its effectiveness.

Although the film plot has parallels with the Abrahams' story, the character of Robbie is a composite one and the family circumstances are fictional. Several minor characters in the film are played by people who have been on the ketogenic diet and had their epilepsy "cured" as a result. The dietitian Millicent Kelly plays herself. Charlie Abrahams appears as a young boy playing with Robbie in the hospital, whose mother quickly removes him when she discovers Robbie has epilepsy—as though it were an infectious disease.

Commenting on the film, Dr John Freeman said "The movie was based on a true story and we see this story often, but not everyone is cured by the diet and not everyone goes home to ride in a parade." He later noted that the film had "fueled a grass-roots effort for more research on the diet."

The ketogenic diet was developed by Russel Wilder at the Mayo Clinic in 1921. The diet aims to reproduce some of the metabolic changes seen during fasting, which had been shown to be effective in treating epilepsy but obviously not sustainable. Although initially popular in all age groups, the diet was largely replaced by effective anticonvulsant medications beginning with phenytoin in 1938. It remained a treatment of last resort in children with intractable seizures. Since the film was produced, the diet has seen a dramatic revival with numerous published research studies and it is now in use at 75 epilepsy centers in 45 countries.

The film was first aired on CityTV and ABC for public viewing on 16 February 1997. It is available on DVD from retailers and directly from the Charlie Foundation. Meryl Streep's performance was nominated for an Emmy, a Golden Globe and in the Satellite Awards in the category Best Actress in a TV Film. Writer Ann Beckett was nominated for the Humanitas Prize (90 minute category). Seth Adkins won a Young Artist Award for his performance as Robbie.

References

- Jim Abrahams (2003). "Things I Wish They Had Told Us: A Parent's Perspective on Childhood Epilepsy" [1]. The Charlie Foundation. Retrieved 2008-03-30.
- John Freeman (2003). "Talk with John Freeman: Tending the Flame" [2]. *Brainwaves* 16 (2). Retrieved 2008-03-30.
- Denise Mann (2000-07-06). "Movie First Do No Harm Boosts Popularity of Diet for Epileptic Children". WebMD Medical News.
- Venita Jay (April 1997). "...first do no harm" [3]. Epilepsy Ontario 'Sharing' News. Retrieved 2008-03-30.
- Kathleen Fackelmann (1999-01-12). "Recognizing a 'miracle' The high-fat ketogenic diet can ease seizures in epileptic children" [4]. USA Today. Retrieved 2010-07-23.
- Freeman JM, Kossoff EH, Hartman AL (March 2007). "The ketogenic diet: one decade later" [5]. *Pediatrics* 119 (3): 535–43. doi:10.1542/peds.2006-2447. PMID 17332207.

See also

• Never events

External links

• *...First Do No Harm* [6] at the Internet Movie Database
• *...First Do No Harm* [7] at Allmovie
• The Charlie Foundation [8] A US charity and information resource, set up by Jim Abrahams.

References

[1] http://www.charliefoundation.org/noframes/whoweare/essay.php
[2] http://www.hopkinsneuro.org/epilepsy/research.cfm?research=A_Talk_with_John_Freeman.htm
[3] http://www.epilepsyontario.org/client/EO/EOWeb.nsf/web/First+Do+No+Harm+(Movie)
[4] http://www.charliefoundation.org/articles/
     usa-today-reports-%E2%80%98miracle%E2%80%99-diet-treat-children-epilepsy%E2%80%93-11999
[5] http://pediatrics.aappublications.org/cgi/content/full/119/3/535
[6] http://www.imdb.com/title/tt0118526/
[7] http://www.allmovie.com/work/205822
[8] http://www.charliefoundation.org/frames/index.php

Angels in America (miniseries)

	Angels in America
	 DVD cover for *Angels in America*
Approx. run time	352 min.
Genre	Miniseries
Written by	Tony Kushner
Directed by	Mike Nichols
Produced by	Celia D. Costas
Starring	Al Pacino Meryl Streep Patrick Wilson Emma Thompson Mary-Louise Parker Jeffrey Wright Justin Kirk
Editing by	John Bloom Antonia Van Drimmelen
Music by	Thomas Newman
Cinematography	Stephen Goldblatt
Country	United States Canada
Language	English Hebrew Aramaic Yiddish
Original channel	HBO
Original run	December 7, 2003 – December 14, 2003
No. of episodes	6 chapters

Angels in America is a 2003 HBO miniseries adapted from the Pulitzer Prize winning play of the same name by Tony Kushner. Kushner adapted his original text for the screen, and Mike Nichols directed. Set in 1985, the film has at its core the story of two couples whose relationships dissolve amidst the backdrop of Reagan era politics, the spreading AIDS epidemic and a rapidly changing social and political climate.[1]

HBO broadcast the film in various formats: two three hour chunks that correspond to "Millennium Approaches" and "Perestroika," as well as six one-hour "chapters" that roughly correspond to an act or two of each of these plays; the first three chapters ("Bad News", "In Vitro" and "The Messenger") were initially broadcast on December 7, 2003 to international acclaim, with the final three chapters ("Stop Moving!", "Beyond Nelly" and "Heaven, I'm in Heaven") following.

Angels in America was the most watched made-for-cable movie in 2003, garnering much critical acclaim and multiple Golden Globe and Emmy nominations. In 2006, *Seattle Times* listed the series amongst "Best of the filmed AIDS portrayals" on the occasion of the 25th anniversary of AIDS.[2]

Plot

It's 1985: Ronald Reagan is in the White House and Death swings the quiet scythe of AIDS across the nation. In Manhattan, Prior Walter tells Lou, his lover of four years, he's ill; Lou, unable to handle it, leaves him. As disease and loneliness ravage Prior, guilt invades Lou. Joe Pitt, an attorney who is Mormon and Republican, is pushed by right-wing fixer Roy Cohn toward a job at the United States Department of Justice. Both Pitt and Cohn are in the closet: Pitt out of shame and religious turmoil, Cohn to preserve his power and access. Pitt's wife Harper is strung out on Valium, causing her to hallucinate constantly, and she longs to escape from her sexless marriage. An angel commands Prior to be a prophet. Pitt's mother and Belize, a close friend, help Prior choose. Joe leaves his wife and goes to live with Lou, but the relationship doesn't work out.

Roy gets diagnosed with AIDS early on, and as his life comes to a close he is haunted by Ethel Rosenberg, as he was instrumental in her conviction as a Communist spy and execution years ago. As the film continues, these lost souls come together to create bonds of love, loss, and loneliness and in the end discover forgiveness and overcome abandonment.[3] [4]

Cast

- Al Pacino as Roy Cohn
- Meryl Streep as Hannah Pitt / Ethel Rosenberg / The Rabbi / The Angel Australia
- Patrick Wilson as Joe Pitt / the Antarctic Eskimo
- Mary-Louise Parker as Harper Pitt
- Emma Thompson as Nurse Emily / the Homeless Woman / The Angel America
- Justin Kirk as Prior Walter / Leatherman in the Park
- Jeffrey Wright as Mr. Lies / Belize / Homeless Man / The Angel Europa
- Ben Shenkman as Louis Ironson / The Angel Oceania
- James Cromwell as Henry, Roy's Doctor

Soundtrack

The soundtrack of the series by Thomas Newman was nominated for Grammy Award for Best Score Soundtrack Album for a Motion Picture, Television or Other Visual Media.

Production

Executive producer of the series, Cary Brokaw worked for over ten years to bring the 1991 stage production to television, having first read it in 1989, before its first production. In 1993, Al Pacino committed to playing the role of Roy Cohn. In the meantime, a number of directors, including Robert Altman, were part of the project. Altman worked on the project in 1993 and 1994, before budget constraints forced him to move out, as few studios could risk producing two successive 150 minute movies at the cost of $40 million. Subsequently, Kushner tried squeezing the play into a feature film, at which he eventually failed, realizing there was "literally too much plot," and settling for the TV miniseries format. While Kushner continued adapting the play until the late 1990s, HBO Films stepped in as producer, allocating a budget of $60 million.[5]

Bethesda Fountain at the Bethesda Terrace in New York City's Central Park, where many scenes were shot

Below Bethesda Terrace, Central Park, where final scene was shot

Canopus of Hadrian's Villa, where the heaven sequence was shot

Brokaw gave Mike Nichols the script while he was working with him on *Wit* (2001) starring Emma Thompson, who also co-adapted the play of the same title. The principal cast, including Meryl Streep, Al Pacino and Emma Thompson, having recently worked with Nichols, was immediately assembled by him. Jeffrey Wright was the only original cast member to appear in the film version, and had won the 1994 Tony Award for Best Performance by a Featured Actor for his stage performance.[6] The shooting started in May 2002, and after a 137-day schedule, ended in January 2003. Filming was done primarily at Kaufman Astoria Studios, New York City, with important scenes at

Bethesda Fountain, Central Park, Manhattan. The heaven sequence was shot at Hadrian's Villa, the Roman archaeological complex at Tivoli, Italy, dating early 2nd century.

Special effects in the series were by Richard Edlund (Star Wars trilogy), who created the two important Angel visitation sequences, as well as the opening sequence wherein the angel at the Bethesda Fountain opens its eyes in the end, signifying her "coming to life."[5]

Critical reception

The *New York Times* wrote that "Mike Nichols's television version is a work of art in itself."[7] According to a *Boston Globe* review, "director Mike Nichols, and a magnificent cast led by Meryl Streep have pulled a spellbinding and revelatory TV movie out of the Tony- and Pulitzer Prize-winning work" and that he "managed to make "Angels in America" thrive onscreen..." [8]

Awards and nominations

Golden Globe Awards

- Best Miniseries or Made for TV Movie
- Best Actor in a Miniseries or TV Movie (Al Pacino)
- Best Actress in a Miniseries or TV Movie (Meryl Streep)
- Best Supporting Actor in a Series, Miniseries, or Movie (Jeffrey Wright)
- Best Supporting Actress in a Series, Miniseries, or Movie (Mary-Louise Parker)

Emmy Awards

In 2004, *Angels in America* broke the record previously held by *Roots* for the most Emmys awarded to a program in a single year by winning 11 awards from 21 nominations. The record was broken four years later by *John Adams*.

Won

- Outstanding Miniseries
- Outstanding Directing for a Miniseries, Movie or a Dramatic Special (*Mike Nichols*)
- Outstanding Lead Actor – Miniseries or a Movie (*Al Pacino*)
- Outstanding Lead Actress – Miniseries or a Movie (*Meryl Streep)*
- Outstanding Supporting Actor – Miniseries or a Movie (*Jeffrey Wright*)
- Outstanding Supporting Actress - Miniseries or a Movie (*Mary-Louise Parker*)
- Outstanding Casting for a Miniseries, Movie or a Special
- Outstanding Art Direction for a Miniseries, Movie or a Special (Part I & II)
- Outstanding Makeup for a Miniseries, Movie or a Special (Non-Prosthetic)
- Outstanding Single-Camera Sound Mixing for a Miniseries or a Movie
- Outstanding Writing for a Miniseries, Movie or a Dramatic Special (*Tony Kushner*) [9]

Nominated

- Outstanding Lead Actress – Miniseries or a Movie
  - (*Emma Thompson*)
- Outstanding Supporting Actor – Miniseries or a Movie
  - (*Patrick Wilson*)
  - (*Ben Shenkman*)
  - (*Justin Kirk*)
- Outstanding Main Title Design
- Outstanding Special Visual Effects - Miniseries or a Movie

- Outstanding Single-Camera Picture Editing for a Miniseries, Movie or a Special
- Outstanding Cinematography for a Miniseries or Movie
- Outstanding Costumes for a Miniseries, Movie or a Special
- Outstanding Hairstyling for a Miniseries, Movie or a Special

Other

Broadcast Film Critics

- Best Picture Made for Television

Directors Guild of America (DGA)

- Outstanding Directorial Achievement in Movies for Television (Mike Nichols)

GLAAD Media Awards

- Best Miniseries or Film Made for TV
- Best Score Soundtrack Album for a Motion Picture, Television or Other Visual Media (Thomas Newman)

National Board of Review

- Best Film Made for Cable TV

Producers Guild of America (PGA)

- Producer of the Year Award in Longform (Mike Nichols, Cary Brokaw, Celia D. Costas and Michael Haley)

Satellite Awards

- Best Actress - Miniseries or Film Made for TV (Meryl Streep)
- Best Miniseries
- Best Supporting Actor - (Mini)Series or Film Made for TV (Justin Kirk)
- Best Actor - Miniseries or TV Film (Al Pacino)
- Best Supporting Actor - (Mini)Series or Film Made for TV(Patrick Wilson)
- Best Supporting Actor - (Mini)Series or Film Made for TV (Jeffrey Wright)
- Best Supporting Actress - (Mini)Series or Film Made for TV (Mary-Louise Parker)
- Best Supporting Actress - (Mini)Series or Film Made for TV (Emma Thompson)

Screen Actors Guild (SAG)

- Best Actor in a Miniseries or Television Movie: Al Pacino (won)
- Best Actress in a Miniseries or Television Movie : Meryl Streep (won)
- Best Actor - Miniseries or Film Made for TV (Justin Kirk)
- Best Actor - Miniseries or Film Made for TV (Jeffrey Wright)
- Best Actress - Miniseries or Film Made for TV (Mary-Louise Parker)
- Best Actress - Miniseries or Film Made for TV (Emma Thompson)

External links

- Official website [10]
- *Angels in America* [11] at the Internet Movie Database
- *Angels in America* [12] at Rotten Tomatoes
- Winged Victory: [13] New York Television Review
- The Lector Effect: [14] A *Slate Magazine* review arguing that the miniseries "gets Kushner wrong".

References

[1] Angels in America:Overview (http://movies.nytimes.com/movie/299769/Angels-in-America/overview) New York Times

[2] An AIDS anniversary: 25 years in the arts (http://seattletimes.nwsource.com/html/entertainment/2003079432_filmaids25.html) Seattle
     Times, June 25, 2006.

[3] Part one (http://www.film4.com/reviews/2003/angels-in-america-part-one) Film4

[4] Part two (http://www.film4.com/reviews/2003/angels-in-america-part-two)Film4.

[5] Edgerton, Gary Richard; Jeffrey P. Jones (2008). "10. Angels in America" (http://books.google.co.in/books?id=odSAPSA1JFEC&
     pg=PA135&dq=Angels+in+America+2003&cd=1#v=onepage&q=Angels in America 2003&f=false).*The essential HBO reader.*
     University Press of Kentucky. p. 136. ISBN 0813124522. .

[6] Trivia (http://www.imdb.com/title/tt0318997/trivia) IMDB

[7] Critics Choice:Movies (http://query.nytimes.com/gst/fullpage.html?res=9A07EFDB1E3EF934A25757C0A9639C8B63) by Anita Gates,
     New York Times, April 17, 2005.

[8] TELEVISION REVIEW: HBO infuses `Angels' with new life Nichols, cast triumph in inspiring production (http://www.boston.com/ae/
     tv/articles/2003/12/05/hbo_infuses_angels_with_new_life/) By Matthew Gilbert, Boston Globe Staff, 12/5/2003.

[9] Awards (http://www.imdb.com/title/tt0318997/awards) IMDB

[10] http://www.hbo.com/films/angelsinamerica

[11] http://www.imdb.com/title/tt0318997/

[12] http://www.rottentomatoes.com/m/angels_in_america/

[13] http://nymag.com/nymetro/arts/tv/reviews/n_9578/

[14] http://www.slate.com/id/2092434/

One act plays by Tennessee Williams

One-act plays by Tennessee Williams is a list of the one-act plays written by American playwright Tennessee Williams.

1930s

Beauty Is the Word

Beauty Is the Word is Tennessee Williams' first play. The 12-page one-act was written in 1930 while Williams was a freshman at University of Missouri in Columbia, Missouri and submitted to a contest run by the school's Dramatic Arts Club.[1] *Beauty* was staged in competition and became the first freshman play ever to be selected for citation (it was awarded honorable mention); the college paper noted that it was "a play with an original and constructive idea, but the handling is too didactic and the dialog often too moralistic.".[1] The play tells the story of a South Pacific missionary, Abelard, and his wife, Mabel, and "both endorses the minister's life and corrects his tendency to Victorian prudery."[1]

Why Do You Smoke So Much, Lily?

Why Do You Smoke So Much, Lily? was written in February 1935. In it, Lily, a frustrated chain-smoking young woman, is hounded by her mother. After being discovered in the papers left to the University of the South in Sewanee, Tennessee, "Lily" was first produced by the Chattanooga Theatre Centre (Chattanooga, TN) as part of the Fellowship of Southern Writers' Conference on Southern Literature, a biennial event hosted by the Arts and Education Council of Chattanooga.

Cairo! Shanghai! Bombay!

Cairo, Shanghai, Bombay! was Williams first produced play. He wrote it in 1935 while he was staying in the Midtown, Memphis home of his grandparents. It was first performed July 12, 1935 by the *Garden Players* community theater in Memphis, Tennessee.[2] Regarding this production, Williams wrote, "The laughter ... enchanted me. Then and there the theatre and I found each other for better and for worse. I know it's the only thing that saved my life."[3]

The Magic Tower

The Magic Tower was written quickly by Williams in April 1936 in order to meet the deadline for a one-act play contest sponsored by the Webster Groves Theatre Guild in St. Louis, Missouri.[4] Williams won first place and *The Magic Tower* was performed by the Guild on October 13, 1936 to positive reviews.[5] The play tells the story of a young artist and his ex-actress wife living in a slum that they refer to as their "magic tower," following them as their optimism gradually fades.

Summer at the Lake

Written in 1937 under the title *Escape, Summer at the Lake* was unproduced until November 11, 2004, when it opened at the New York City Center in a collection of rarely-seen Williams one-acts titled *Five by Tenn*.[6] The autobiographical play tells the story of Donald Fenway, a sensitive teenager who feels trapped by his self-absorbed Southern mother and his shoe-company executive father, who wants him to abandon his plans for college and find a menial job. The play was interpreted by several critics as "an early snapshot" of the characters and themes that later appeared in Williams' breakthrough 1944 play *The Glass Menagerie*, which also focused on a combative mother and a dreamy son left fatherless.[6][7]

The Palooka

The Palooka is a 1937 one act about an old has-been boxer. The characters are The Palooka (Galveston Joe), The Kid and The Trainer. The Kid is nervous about his first fight, and The Palooka relieves the Kid's anxiety by telling about the fictional life he wanted to lead after he retired as Galveston Joe. Its world premiere was presented by the Chattanooga Theatre Centre (Chattanooga, TN) as part of the Fellowship of Southern Writers' Southern Writers Conference in 2000, and was later performed on October 2, 2003, by the Hartford Stage Company in Hartford, Connecticut.

The Fat Man's Wife

The Fat Man's Wife was written by Williams in 1938 but remained unproduced until November 11, 2004, when it opened at the New York City Center in a collection of rarely-seen Williams one-acts titled *Five by Tenn*.[6] The play tells the story of Vera Cartwright, a sophisticated Manhattan society lady who is forced to choose between her boorish husband, a theatrical producer, and a young playwright who has become her admirer. *The Fat Man's Wife* received the sharpest criticism of any of the five exhumed plays; in *The New Yorker*, John Lahr called it a "heterosexual fantasy awash with false emotion and bad writing,"[7] and *The New York Times* noted that "Williams is obviously attempting to write in a style entirely alien to him, trying on a faux-urbane manner that fits him like a rented tuxedo in the wrong size."[6]

Adam and Eve on a Ferry

Adam and Eve on a Ferry was written in 1939. It contains three characters: D.H. Lawrence, his wife Frieda, and a female visitor named Ariadne. Ariadne comes seeking D.H. Lawrence because she had a run-in on a boat with a man, and wants romance and sex advice from Lawrence. The setting is described as "The sun porch of a villa in the Alps Maritimes." The only things mentioned on the stage are numerous potted plants, two wicker chairs, and "a banner bearing the woven figure of a phoenix in a nest of flames." Ariadne is described as plain and "spinsterish looking," and she wears a hat, while Lawrence sports a "gold satin dressing robe with a lavender shawl."

1940s

The Parade, or Approaching the End of a Summer

The Parade, or Approaching the End of a Summer is a short autobiographical play that was written in 1941. *The Parade* is set on the wharfs of Provincetown, Massachusetts, and tells the story of a young playwright named Don dealing with his unrequited homosexual love for another man. The situations and characters in the play were "clearly drawn from a very autobiographical foundation,"[8] with Don's dilemma reflecting a relationship Williams had in Provincetown with "his actual lover for [one] summer, Kip Kiernan."[9] *The Parade* was written after a fight with Kiernan, and Williams reflected in 1962 that "[the version of Kip in that play] is very, in fact completely different from Kip as he was. When someone hurts us deeply, we no longer see them at all clearly. Not until time has put them back in focus."[10] That year, Williams retitled and expanded *The Parade* into a full-length play that was produced in 1981 as *Something Cloudy, Something Clear*.[9] [10] *The Parade* was not performed until 2006, when it opened on October 1 in Provincetown as part of the First Annual Provincetown Tennessee Williams Festival by Shakespeare on the Cape. Original cast members: Ben Griessmeyer, Vanessa Caye, Elliot Eustis, Megan Bartle, David Landon. Co-Directed by Jef Hall-Flavin and Eric Powell Holm.

The Long Goodbye

The Long Goodbye is a 1940 one act that deals with the male main character's memories of his life from when his family consisted of four people through his father leaving the family, his mother's death, and his sister's fall from grace. The scheme of the play consists of the main character moving out of the apartment he grew up in while experiencing extreme flashbacks of both terrible and glorious moments in his past.

Auto Da Fé

Auto Da Fé was written in 1941.

The Lady of Larkspur Lotion

The Lady of Larkspur Lotion was written in 1941. It depicts the conflict between a dreamy, delusional heroine (à la Blanche DuBois in *A Streetcar Named Desire*) and her brusque, practical landlady, who wants to kick her out of her apartment.

At Liberty

At Liberty was written in 1941 and tells the story of a once-successful actress who retreats to her childhood home in Mississippi, with fantasies of resuscitating her career.

Portrait of a Madonna

In January 1941, Williams completed a one act play centering around "a deranged spinster living in poverty and with her memories of a former lover."[11] Variously titled *Port Mad* and *The Leafless Block*, he revised the play in 1944 and renamed it *Portrait of a Madonna*.[11] After seeing Jessica Tandy's performance in a 1947 West Coast production of *Madonna*, Williams decided to cast her in the original production of *A Streetcar Named Desire*. He later wrote, "It was instantly apparent to me that Jessica was Blanche [DuBois]."[12]

Moony's Kid Don't Cry

Moony's Kid Don't Cry originated as an eight-page melodrama titled *Hot Milk at Three in the Morning*, which Williams wrote in 1930 at the University of Missouri.[1] *Hot Milk* was produced at MU in 1932, and was revised and titled *Moony's Kid Don't Cry* in 1941, when it was published in Margaret Mayorga's *Best One Act Plays of 1940*.[13] It was the first of Williams' plays to be published. In both versions of the play, a poor young married couple get into an argument over their child and, eventually, their relationship.

The Strangest Kind of Romance

The Strangest Kind of Romance was written in 1942.

The Purification

The Purification is the only verse play Tennessee Williams wrote; Williams recalled that it was written in the summer of 1940, although his biographer Lyle Leverich thought it more likely written in spring 1942. It was published in 1944 in the anthology *New Directions 1944* under the title *Dos Ranchos, or the Purification* (in later publications, this was shortened to *The Purification*). Set on a ranch in the mid-1800s, the play deals with an incestuous brother/sister relationship and a murder trail.[14] *The Purification* had its New York debut off-Broadway at the Theatre de Lys on December 8, 1959.

Ten Blocks on the Camino Real

Ten Blocks on the Camino Real is a one-act play that was written in early 1946 and published in Williams' 1948 play collection *American Blues*; in 1952, the playwright expanded it into a full-length play, *Camino Real*.[15] Williams directs the reader to use the Anglicized pronunciation "Cá-mino Réal"

This Property Is Condemned

This one-act play was written in 1946. In 1966, the play was expanded into the film of the same name, which starred Natalie Wood and Robert Redford.

27 Wagons Full of Cotton

27 Wagons Full of Cotton is a 1946 one-act that Williams referred to as "a Mississippi Delta comedy." In it, Jake, a middle-aged, shady cotton gin owner burns down the mill of Silva Vicarro, a rival in the cotton business. His rival, who knows what happened but cannot prove it, seeks revenge by seducing Jake's young, frail, delicate wife, Flora. Elia Kazan's controversial 1956 movie *Baby Doll* was based on this play. Incidentally, the play's title is written as a line of trochaic pentameter (e.g. TWENty SEVen WAGons FULL of COTTon).

The Last of My Solid Gold Watches

The Last of My Solid Gold Watches was written in 1946, and centers around a Mississippi shoe salesman named Charlie Colton "whose time has passed and who pathetically echoes himself"; Williams is thought to have drawn on aspects of his father, a traveling salesman, in his portrait of Colton.[16]

Hello from Bertha

Hello from Bertha is a 1946 one act, about the dramatic life and death of a prostitute in a low-class bordello. It is very strong and very poetic as Bertha imagines events and allusions to her last moments. There are three characters in the play: Lena, a young prostitute who listens to Bertha, and Goldie the old lady of the house who wants to evict Bertha.

Lord Byron's Love Letter

Written in 1946, *Lord Byron's Love Letter* takes place in New Orleans in the late 1800s during Mardi Gras. A Spinster and an Old Woman advertise that they have one of Lord Byron's love letters (written to her grandmother). A Matron stops by to look at it and drags her partially inebriated Husband along. As the spinster reads from her grandmother's diary, it becomes apparent that the grandmother and the old woman are one and the same. According to the two women, the grandmother met Lord Byron in Greece, shortly before his death, and they had a summer filled with romance. After he died, the grandmother retired from the world and remained in complete seclusion as an honor to his memory (this does not prevent her from commenting on the spinster's every action). The Matron and her Husband aren't permitted to read the letter, only to look at it from a distance.

1950s

I Rise in Flame, Cried the Phoenix

I Rise in Flame, Cried the Phoenix presents a fictionalized version of the death of English writer D. H. Lawrence on the French Riveria; Lawrence was one of Williams' chief literary influences.[17] The play was completed in 1941, but was not published until 1951, when New Directions Publishers released it in a limited edition.[18]

Talk to Me Like the Rain and Let Me Listen

Talk to Me Like the Rain and Let Me Listen was written in 1953.

The Dark Room

The Dark Room was written in 1956.

The Case of the Crushed Petunias

The Case of the Crushed Petunias was written in 1956 and is the story of Dorothy Simple, a woman trapped in her job at a prim and proper shop in Massachusetts. Her complacent existence is interrupted by a visit from a tall man who works for LIFE Inc. who, she discovers, trampled her petunias the night before. With offers of poetry and packets of seeds, he helps her break free from her dreary life.

A Perfect Analysis Given by a Parrot

A Perfect Analysis Given by a Parrot was written in 1958.

Suddenly, Last Summer

Suddenly, Last Summer was written in 1958, and debuted as part of a double bill of one-act plays written by Williams titled *Garden District*. (The other one-act play was *Something Unspoken*.) *Garden District* premiered Off-Broadway at the York Playhouse on January 7, 1958.

Something Unspoken

Something Unspoken was written in 1958, and debuted as part of a double bill of one-act plays written by Williams titled *Garden District*. (The other one-act was *Suddenly, Last Summer*.) *Garden District* premiered Off-Broadway at the York Playhouse on January 7, 1958. The title *Garden District* is a misnomer, because while *Suddenly, Last Summer* takes place in the Garden District of New Orleans, *Something Unspoken* takes place in Meridian, Louisiana.

And Tell Sad Stories of the Deaths of Queens . . .

And Tell Sad Stories of the Deaths of Queens . . . (A Play in Two Scenes) was initially written in 1957 and worked on as late as 1962. It was published in 2005 by New Directions in *Mister Paradise and Other One-Act Plays* (NDP1007). A slightly different version was first published in *Political Stages: Plays That Shaped a Century* (Applause Theatre & Cinema Books, 2002). The play concerns the private life of "Candy" Delaney, a successful interior decorator and landlord who is also a transvestite. It was first performed by the Shakespeare Theatre Company on April 22, 2004 at the Kennedy Center in Washington, D.C.

1960s

The Mutilated

The Mutilated was written in 1966, and debuted as part of a double-bill of one act plays written by Williams titled *Slapstick Tragedy* (the other one act was *The Gnädiges Fräulein*.) *Slapstick Tragedy* premiered on Broadway at the Longacre Theatre on February 22, 1966.

The Gnädiges Fräulein

The Gnädiges Fräulein was written in 1966, and debuted as part of a double-bill of one act plays written by Williams titled *Slapstick Tragedy* (the other one act was *The Mutilated*.) *Slapstick Tragedy* premiered on Broadway at the Longacre Theatre on February 22, 1966.

Now the Cats with Jewelled Claws

Now the Cats with Jewelled Claws was written in 1969. Set in the anteroom of Hell, it was described by Williams biographer Donald Spoto as "gruesome....a tale of madness, depravity and death."[19]

1970s

I Can't Imagine Tomorrow

I Can't Imagine Tomorrow was a two-character play written for television, broadcast with *Talk To Me Like The Rain And Let Me Listen* under the collective title "Dragon Country" on WNET-TV in 1970. Kim Stanley plays a lonely but spirited spinster being courted by a pathologically shy teacher, played by William Redfield. "Dragon Country" is available on DVD as part of the Broadway Theatre Archive.

The Frosted Glass Coffin

Written in 1970, *The Frosted Glass Coffin* follows a group of retirees living at a hotel in Miami, Florida. In his memoirs, Williams wrote that he believed the "rather depressing" work to be "one of [his] best short plays."[20]

The Demolition Downtown

The Demolition Downtown was written in 1976.

Kirche, Küche und Kinder

Kirche, Küche und Kinder was written in 1979. The title translates as "Church, Kitchen and Children" and is a reference to a well-known German slogan. It was first performed by The Jean Cocteau Repertory Company as a work-in-progress in September, 1979 at the Bouwerie Lane Theatre in New York City where it ran in repertory until January, 1980. The play is subtitled *(An Outrage for the Stage)*. It was published in 2008 by New Directions in *The Traveling Companion & Other Plays* (NDP1106).

Lifeboat Drill

Lifeboat Drill was written in 1979.

1980s one acts

The Chalky White Substance

The Chalky White Substance was written in 1980. It was originally published in Issue 66 of *Antaeus (magazine)* in 1991. It was first performed by the Running Sun Theater Company on May 3, 1996 at the Center Stage in New York City on a double-bill with *The Traveling Companion*, collectively entitled *Williams' Guignol*. The play is dedicated to author *James Purdy*.

This Is Peaceable Kingdom or Good Luck God

This Is Peaceable Kingdom or Good Luck God was written in 1980.

Steps Must be Gentle

Steps Must be Gentle was written in 1980.

The One Exception

The One Exception was written in 1983. It was originally published in *The Tennessee Williams Annual Review*, Volume 3, in 2000. It was first performed on October 2, 2003 by the Hartford Stage Company of Hartford, Connecticut.

One act publication history

- *27 Wagons Full of Cotton* (New Directions Publishers, February 1946, first edition; NDP217)
  - Collects *27 Wagons Full of Cotton*; *The Lady of Larkspur Lotion*; *The Last of My Solid Gold Watches*; *Portrait of a Madonna*; *Auto Da Fé*; *Lord Byron's Love Letter*; *This Property Is Condemned*; *The Long Goodbye*; *At Liberty*; *Moony's Kid Don't Cry*; *The Strangest Kind of Romance*; *Hello from Bertha*; and *The Purification*.
- *American Blues: Five Short Plays* (Dramatists Play Service, 1948)
  - Collects *The Dark Room*; *Ten Blocks on the Camino Real*; *The Case of the Crushed Petunias*; *The Unsatisfactory Supper*; and *Moony's Kid Don't Cry*.
- *Dragon Country: A Book of Plays* (New Directions Publishers, 1970; NDP287)
  - Collects (along with the full-length play *In the Bar of a Tokyo Hotel*) *I Rise in Flame, Cried the Phoenix*; *The Mutilated*; *I Can't Imagine Tomorrow*; *Confessional*; *The Frosted Glass Coffin*; *The Gnädiges Fräulein*; and *A Perfect Analysis Given by a Parrot*.
- *Tennessee Williams, Plays 1937-1955* (Library of America, 2000; #119)
  - Collects (along with his full-length plays) *27 Wagons Full of Cotton*; *The Lady of Larkspur Lotion*; *The Last of My Solid Gold Watches*; *Portrait of a Madonna*; *Auto Da Fé*; *Lord Byron's Love Letter*; *This Property Is Condemned*; *Talk to Me Like the Rain and Let Me Listen*; and *Something Unspoken*.
- *Tennessee Williams, Plays 1957-1980* (Library of America, 2000; #120)
  - Collects (along with his full-length plays) *Suddenly, Last Summer* and *The Mutilated*.
- *Mister Paradise and Other One-Act Plays* (New Directions Publishers, 2005; NDP1007)
  - Collects *These Are the Stairs You Got to Watch*; *Mister Paradise*; *The Palooka*; *Escape*; *Why Do You Smoke So Much, Lily?*; *Summer at the Lake*; *The Big Game*; *The Pink Bedroom*; *The Fat Man's Wife*; *Thank You*

Kind Spirit; *The Municipal Abattoir*; *Adam and Eve on a Ferry*; and *And Tell Sad Stories of the Deaths of Queens*.

- *The Traveling Companion & Other Plays* (New Directions Publishers, 2008; NDP1106)
  - Collects (along with the full-length play *Will Mr. Merriwether Return from Memphis?*) *The Chalky White Substance*; *The Day on Which a Man Dies*; *A Cavalier for Milady*; *The Pronoun "I"*; *The Remarkable Rooming-House of Mme. LeMonde*; *Kirche, Küche, Kinder*; *Green Eyes*; *The Parade*; *The One Exception*; *Sunburst*; and *The Traveling Companion*.
- *Camino Real* (New Directions Publishers, 2008; NDP1122)
  - Collects (along with the full-length play *Camino Real*) *Ten Blocks on the Camino Real*.
- *Sweet Bird of Youth* (New Directions Publishers, 2008; NDP1123)
  - Collects (along with the full-length play *Sweet Bird of Youth*) *The Enemy: Time*.

References

- Leverich, Lyle (1995). *Tom: The Unknown Tennessee Williams*. New York: Crown. ISBN 0-393-31663-7.
- Spoto, Donald (1985). *The Kindness of Strangers: The Life of Tennessee Williams*. Boston: Little Brown. ISBN 0-306-80805-6.
- Williams, Tennessee (1975). *Memoirs*. New York City: New Directions. ISBN 08112-1669-1.
- Williams, Tennessee (2000). *Plays 1937-1955*. New York: Library of America. ISBN 1-883011-86-8.

References

[1] Spoto (1985). p. 33.

[2] Kimberly Richard and Christina Rossini. Theatre Three, Inc. The Education Zone. Author Biography — Tennessee Williams. (http://www.theatre3dallas.com/education/sg0607_1.pdf) (Thomas Lanier Williams III). 2006.

[3] Tennessee State Historical Marker 2 May 2008. (http://www.waymarking.com/waymarks/WM3PX5)

[4] Leverich (1995). p. 167.

[5] Leverich (1995). p. 185.

[6] Isherwood, Charles (2004-11-12). "Rhinestones Are Next Door to Glass" (http://theater2.nytimes.com/2004/11/12/theater/reviews/12five.html?ex=1180497600&en=c1c23c3e3d8fe4e4&ei=5070). The New York Times. . Retrieved 2007-05-28.

[7] Lahr, John (2004-11-22). "Soul Sketches" (http://www.newyorker.com/archive/2004/11/22/041122crth_theatre). The New Yorker. . Retrieved 2007-05-28.

[8] Sanderson, Jordan, and Raymond W. Wachter. "Something Cloudy, Something Clear" (http://www.litencyc.com/php/sworks.php?rec=true&UID=16712) (fee required), Literary Encyclopedia, 2005-03-03. Retrieved on 2007-05-30.

[9] Fritscher, Jack (2001-09-20). "We All Live on Half of Something" (http://www.jackfritscher.com/PDF/TennWilliams/NY Art Theatre-Williams.pdf) (reprint). Playbill. . Retrieved 2007-05-30.

[10] Leverich (1995). p. 364.

[11] Spoto (1985). p. 87.

[12] Williams (1975). p. 132.

[13] Spoto (1985). p. 89.

[14] Leverich (1995). p. 447.

[15] Williams (2000.) p. 1033-1034.

[16] Leverich (1995.) p. 488.

[17] Williams (2000.) p. 288.

[18] Williams (2000.) p. 1030.

[19] Spoto (1985). p. 353.

[20] Williams (1975). p. 150.

A Memory of Two Mondays

A Memory of Two Mondays is a one-act play by Arthur Miller.

Based on Miller's own experiences, the play focuses on a group of desperate workers earning their livings in a Brooklyn automobile parts warehouse during the Great Depression of the 1930s--a time of 25 percent unemployment in the United States. Concentrating more on character than plot, it explores the dreams of a young man yearning for a college education in the midst of people stumbling through the workday in a haze of hopelessness and despondency. Three of the characters in the story are provided very severe alcohol problems.

Paired with the original one-act version of *A View from the Bridge*, the first Broadway production, directed by Martin Ritt, opened on September 29, 1955 at the Coronet Theatre, where it ran for 149 performances. The cast included Van Heflin, J. Carrol Naish, Jack Warden, Eileen Heckart, and Richard Davalos, who won the Theatre World Award for his performance.

In 1959, Miller adapted the play for an ITV broadcast starring Alan Bates [1].

Miller adapted the play for a 1971 television movie directed by Paul Bogart. The cast included George Grizzard, Barnard Hughes, Estelle Parsons, Catherine Burns, Jerry Stiller, J. D. Cannon, Harvey Keitel, Tony Lo Bianco, Kristoffer Tabori, Dick Van Patten, and Jack Warden.

After seven previews, a Broadway revival directed by Arvin Brown opened on January 26, 1976 at the Playhouse Theatre where, paired this time with *27 Wagons Full of Cotton* by Tennessee Williams, it ran for 67 performances. The cast included Thomas Hulce, John Lithgow, Tony Musante, Meryl Streep, and Joe Grifasi.

1976 awards and nominations

- Tony Award for Best Featured Actress in a Play (Streep, nominee)
- Theatre World Award (Streep, winner)
- Drama Desk Award for Outstanding Actress in a Play (Streep, nominee)
- Drama Desk Award for Outstanding Featured Actor in a Play (Leonardo Cimino and Roy Poole, nominees)
- Drama Desk Award for Outstanding Featured Actress in a Play (Alice Drummond, nominee)
- Drama Desk Award for Outstanding Director of a Play (nominee)
- Drama Desk Award for Outstanding Costume Design (nominee)
- Drama Desk Award for Outstanding Lighting Design (nominee)
- Drama Desk Award for Outstanding Set Design (nominee)
- Drama Desk Award for Outstanding Revival (nominee)

External links

- 1955 production at the Internet Theatre Database [2]
- 1976 production at the Internet Theatre Database listing [3]
- Internet Movie Database listing [4]

References

[1] http://www.alanbates.com/abarchive/tv/memory.html
[2] http://www.ibdb.com/production.asp?ID=2527
[3] http://www.ibdb.com/production.asp?ID=3787
[4] http://www.imdb.com/title/tt0211511/

The Cherry Orchard

The Cherry Orchard (Вишнёвый сад or *Vishniovy sad* in Russian) is Russian playwright Anton Chekhov's last play. It premiered at the Moscow Art Theatre 17 January 1904 in a production directed by Constantin Stanislavski. Chekhov intended this play as a comedy and it does contain some elements of farce; however, Stanislavski insisted on directing the play as a tragedy. Since this initial production, directors have had to contend with the dual nature of this play.

Bust of Anton Chekhov at Badenweiler, Germany

The play concerns an aristocratic Russian woman and her family as they return to the family's estate (which includes a large and well-known cherry orchard) just before it is auctioned to pay the mortgage. While presented with options to save the estate, the family essentially does nothing and the play ends with the estate being sold to the son of a former serf, and the family leaving to the sound of the cherry orchard being cut down. The story presents themes of cultural futility — both the futility of the aristocracy to maintain its status and the futility of the bourgeoisie to find meaning in its newfound materialism. In reflecting the socio-economic forces at work in Russia at the turn of the 20th century, including the rise of the middle class after the abolition of serfdom in the mid-19th century and the sinking of the aristocracy, the play reflects forces at work around the globe in that period.

Since the first production at the Moscow Art Theatre, this play has been translated into many languages and produced around the world, becoming a classic work of dramatic literature. Some of the major directors in the West have directed this play, each interpreting the work differently. Some of these directors include Charles Laughton, Peter Brook, Andrei Serban, Eva Le Gallienne, Jean-Louis Barrault, Tyrone Guthrie and Giorgio Strehler.

The play's influence has also been widely felt in dramatic works by many including Eugene O'Neill, George Bernard Shaw and Arthur Miller.

Background

There were several experiences in Chekhov's own life that are said to have directly inspired his writing of *The Cherry Orchard*. When Chekhov was sixteen, his mother went into debt after having been cheated by some builders she had hired to construct a small house. A former lodger, Gabriel Selivanov, offered to help her financially, but in turn secretly bought the house for himself. At approximately the same time, his childhood home in Taganrog was sold to pay off its mortgage. These financial and domestic upheavals imprinted themselves on his memory greatly and would reappear in the action of *The Cherry Orchard*.

Later in his life, living on a country estate outside Moscow, Chekhov developed an interest in gardening and planted his own cherry orchard. After relocating to Yalta due to his poor health, Chekhov was devastated to learn that the buyer of his former estate had cut down most of the orchard. Returning on one trip to his childhood haunts in Taganrog, he was further horrified by the devastating effects of industrial deforestation. It was in those woodlands and the forests of his holidays in Ukraine that he had first nurtured his ecological passion (this passion is reflected in the character of Dr. Astrov, whose love of the forests is his only peace, in his earlier play *Uncle Vanya*.). A lovely and locally famous cherry orchard stood on the farm of family friends where he spent childhood vacations, and in his early short story "Steppe", Chekhov depicts a young boy crossing the Ukraine amidst fields of cherry blossoms. Finally, the first inklings of the genesis for the play that would be his last came in a terse notebook entry of 1897:

"cherry orchard". Today, Chekhov's Yalta garden survives alongside *The Cherry Orchard* as a monument to a man whose feeling for trees equaled his feeling for theatre. Indeed, trees are often unspoken, symbolic heroes and victims of his stories and plays; so much so that Chekhov is often singled out as Europe's first ecological author.

Chekhov wrote *The Cherry Orchard* during the course of several years, alternating between periods of lighthearted giddiness and despondent frustration which he considered as bordering upon sloth (in a letter he wrote, "Every sentence I write strikes me as good for nothing.") Throughout this time he was also further inhibited by his chronic tuberculosis. Guarded by nature, Chekhov seemed overly secretive about all facets of the work, including even the title. As late as the Summer of 1902 he still had not shared anything about the play with anyone in his immediate family or the Art Theatre. It was only to comfort his wife Olga Knipper, who was recovering from a miscarriage, that he finally let her in on the play's title, whispering it to her despite the fact that the two were alone. Chekhov was apparently delighted with the very sound of the title, and enjoyed the same sense of triumph months later when he finally revealed it to Stanislavski. By October 1903 the play was finished and sent to the Moscow Art Theater. Three weeks later Chekhov arrived at rehearsals in what would be a vain attempt to curb all the "weepiness" from the play which Stanislavski had developed. The author apparently also snickered when, during rehearsals, the word "orchard" was substituted with the more practical "plantation", feeling he had perfectly and symbolically captured the impracticality of an entire way of life.

Although critics at the time were divided in their response to the play, the debut of *The Cherry Orchard* by the Moscow Art Theater on January 17, 1904 (Chekhov's birthday) was a resounding theatrical success and the play was almost immediately presented in many of the important provincial cities. This success was not confined only to Russia, as the play was soon seen abroad with great acclaim as well. Shortly after the play's debut, Chekhov departed for Germany due to his worsening health, and by July 1904 he would be dead.

Synopsis

Act I

Act I opens in the early morning hours of a day in May in the nursery of Madame Ranevskaya's ancestral estate somewhere in the provinces of Russia just after the turn of the 20th Century. Lyubov Andreyevna Ranevskaya returns to her country house with her 17-year old daughter Anya and her German governess Charlotta Ivanovna, as well as her valet, Yasha, from Paris where they have been living for the past five years. The trio is met by Varya, Mme. Ranevskaya's adopted daughter who has overseen the estate in her absence; Yermolai Alexeevich Lopakhin, a local merchant and family friend; Leonid Andreevich Gayev, Mme. Ranevskaya's brother; as well as members of the household staff including Dunyasha, the chambermaid who behaves like a refined lady; Semyon Yepikhodov a clumsy clerk in the Ranevskaya household who has proposed to Dunyasha; and the aged footman, Firs, who was once a serf to the Ranevskaya family and who, after the emancipation of the serfs in 1861, remained in their service for lack of a better opportunity for work. Dunyasha becomes smitten with the cultured Yasha, who steals a kiss from her while the two are alone.

Mme. Ranevskaya is reminded that the estate will be auctioned in August to pay the estate's mortgage. Lopakhin offers a plan to save the estate if only she will allow part of it to be developed into summer cottages. However, this will incur the destruction of the famous cherry orchard which Mme. Ranevskaya states is nationally known. It is clear that the orchard has become to her a symbol of her youth and childhood. Other solutions to the debt are also proposed but nothing is resolved and the conversation is diverted to other topics. While Ranevskaya enjoys the view of the orchard as day breaks, she is surprised by Petya Trofimov, a young student who acted as tutor to Ranevskaya's son, Grisha. We learn that Grisha drowned five years prior to the beginning of the play, and that this was a contributing factor to Ranevskaya's fleeing Russia and her home. Ranevskaya is grief-stricken at the reminder of this tragedy, despite Trofimov's insistence on seeing her upon her return (much to the consternation of Varya.)

After Ranevskaya retires for the evening, Anya confesses to Varya that their mother is heavily in debt and their uncle Gayev suggests sending Anya to Yaroslavl where their great aunt lives in the hopes that she will lend them the money to save the estate. Gayev also reminds Varya that Lophakhin is a wealthy man and has always been enamoured of her, and that a marriage with him would ensure the family's survival. They all go to bed with a renewed hope that the estate will be saved and the cherry orchard preserved. Trofimov stares after the departing Anya and mutters "My sunshine, my spring" in adoration.

Act II

Act II opens on a road bordering the cherry orchard in mid-summer. The estate is still in jeopardy but the family seems more concerned with courtships. Yasha and Yepikhodov are each attempting to attract the attentions of Dunyasha. The young Anya has fallen in love with Trofimov, infuriating Varya, who herself has become the subject of rumours that she will be engaged to Lopakhin. Lopakhin tries to steer the conversation towards the business of the estate but Mme. Ranevskaya reveals the sad truth about her finances and her relationship with a man in Paris who cruelly took advantage of her money and feelings. The old footman Firs speaks of the past on the estate before the emancipation of the serfs. The sound of a Jewish band is heard in the distance and Ranevskaya decides to hold a party and invite them to play. When Trofimov appears, Lopakhin teases the boy for his being a perpetual student and Trofimov espouses his philosophy of work and useful purpose to the delight and humour of everyone around. During their conversations, a dishevelled vagrant passes by and begs for money; Ranevskaya thoughtlessly gives him all of her money, despite the protestations of Varya. Shaken by the disturbance, the family departs for dinner, with Lopakhin futilely insisting that the cherry orchard be sold to pay down the debt. Anya stays behind to talk with Trofimov, who disapproves of Varya's constant hawk-like eyes, reassuring Anya that they are "above love". To impress Trofimov and win his affection, Anya vows to leave the past behind her and start a new life. The two depart for the river as Varya calls scoldingly in the background.

Act III

Several months have passed, and the evening of Ranevskaya's party has come. Offstage the musicians play as the family and their guests drink, carouse, and entertain themselves. It is also the day of the auction for the estate and the cherry orchard; Gayev has received a paltry amount of money from his and Ranevskaya's stingy aunt in Yaroslavl, and the family members, despite the general merriment about them, are both anxious and distracted while they wait for word of their fates. Varya worries about paying the musicians and scolds their neighbour Pischik for drinking, Dunyasha for dancing and Yepikhodov for playing billiards. Charlotta entertains the group by performing several magic tricks. Ranevskaya scolds Trofimov for his constant teasing of Varya, whom he refers to as "Madame Lopakhin". She then urges Varya to marry Lopakhin, but Varya demurs, reminding her that it is Lopakhin's duty to ask for her hand in marriage, not the other way around. She says that if she had money she would move as far away from him as possible. Left alone with Ranevskaya, Trofimov insists that she finally face the truth that the house and the cherry orchard will be sold at auction. Ranevskaya shows him a telegram she has received from Paris and reveals that her former lover is ill again and has begged for her to return to his aid. She also reveals that she is seriously considering joining him, despite his cruel behaviour to her in the past. Trofimov is stunned at this news and the two argue about the nature of love and their respective experiences. Trofimov leaves in a huff but offstage falls down the stairs and is carried in by the others. Ranevskaya laughs and forgives him for his folly and the two quickly reconcile. Anya enters declaring a rumour that the cherry orchard has been sold. Lopakhin arrives with Gayev, both of whom are exhausted from the trip and the day's events. Gayev is distant, virtually catatonic and goes to bed without saying a word of the outcome of the auction. When Ranevskaya asks who bought the estate, Lopakhin reveals that he himself is the purchaser and intends to attack the orchard with his axe. Varya, enraged, hurls the keys to the estate on the floor, and Lopakhin, half-drunk and smug, tells how he outbid everyone and gleefully (and angrily) celebrates his victory. Ranevskaya, distraught, clings to Anya, who tries to calm her and reassure her that the future will be better now that the cherry orchard has been sold.

Act IV

It is several weeks later, once again in the nursery (as in Act I), only this time the room is being packed and taken apart as the family prepares to leave the estate forever. Lopakhin arrives with champagne as a going-away present but Ranevskaya snubs him - despite his best intentions for the family he loves, she views him as a destroyer of her youth and happiness. Trofimov enters in search of his galoshes, and he and Lopakhin exchange opposing world views. Anya enters and reprimands Lopakhin for ordering his workers to begin chopping down the cherry orchard while the family is still in the house. Lopakhin apologizes and rushes out to stop them for the time being in the hopes that he will be somehow reconciled with them. Anya also inquires about Firs' health and Yasha informs her that he has been taken to a hospital that morning. Dunyasha enters and begs Yasha for some sort of affectionate parting; Yasha for his part wants nothing to do with her or life in Russia, as he hungers to return to Paris and to live in style. Charlotta enters, lost and in a daze, and insists that the family find her a new position. Gayev and Ranevskaya return to say goodbye to the room where they grew up and spent their childhood. Gayev gaily announces that he has a job at the local bank, and Ranevskaya reveals that she is indeed returning to Paris to be with her former lover. She also scolds Lopakhin for not yet asking Varya to marry him. Lopakhin concedes to do so, and the rest withdraw to give the two some privacy. When Varya enters (knowing that he will propose to her), Lopakhin and she converse about the weather and various mundane subjects, both trying to find a way to reveal their feelings. One of the workers calls for Lopakhin and he exits hastily without asking Varya to marry him. Varya is devastated and Ranevskaya comforts her when she returns. The family and their servants all gather to say their respective goodbyes to the estate and the cherry orchard, one by one departing for their new lives. Ranevskaya tearfully bids her old life goodbye and leaves as the house is shut up forever. In the darkness Firs wanders into the room and discovers that they have left without him and boarded him inside the abandoned house to die. He lies down on the couch and resigns himself to his fate (apparently dying on the spot), as offstage we hear the axes as they cut down the cherry orchard.

Themes

One of the main themes of the play is the effect social change has on people. The emancipation of the serfs on 19 February 1861 by Alexander II allowed former serfs to gain wealth and status while some aristocrats were becoming impoverished, unable to tend their estates without the cheap labor of slavery. The effect of these reforms was still being felt when Chekhov was writing forty years after the mass emancipation.[1]

Chekhov originally intended the play as a comedy (indeed, the title page of the work refers to it as such), and in letters noted that it is, in places, almost farcical[2] . When he saw the original Moscow Art Theatre production directed by Constantin Stanislavski, he was horrified to find that the director had moulded the play into a tragedy. Ever since that time, productions have had to struggle with this dual nature of the play (and of Chekhov's works in general.)

Ranevskaya's failure to address problems facing her estate and family mean that she eventually loses almost everything and her fate can be seen as a criticism of those people who are unwilling to adapt to the new Russia. Her petulant refusal to accept the truth of her past, in both life and love, is her downfall throughout the play. She ultimately runs between her life in Paris and in Russia (she arrives from Paris at the start of the play and returns there afterwards). She is a woman who lives in an illusion of the past (often reliving memories about her son's death, etc.). The speeches by the student Trofimov, attacking intellectuals were later seen as early manifestations of Bolshevik ideas and his lines were often censored by the Tsarist officials. Cherry trees themselves are often seen as symbols of sadness or regret at the passing away of a certain situation or of the times in general.

The theme of identity, and the subversion of expectations of such, is one that can be seen in The Cherry Orchard; indeed, the cast itself can be divided up into three distinct parts: the Gayev family (Ranevskaya, Gayev, Anya and Varya), family friends (Lopakhin, Pishchik and Trofimov), and the "servant class" (Firs, Yasha, Dunyasha, Charlotta and Yepikhodov), the irony being that some of them clearly act out of place - think of Varya, the adopted daughter of an aristocrat, alternatively being a housekeeper; Trofimov the thinking student, being thrown out of university, Yasha considering himself part of the Parisian cultural élite; and both the Ranevskayas and Pishchik running low on money while Lopakhin, born a peasant, is practically a millionaire.

While the Marxist view of the play is more prevalent, an alternative view is that *The Cherry Orchard* was Chekhov's tribute to himself. Many of the characters in the play hearken back to his earlier works and are based on people he knew in his own life. It should also be noted that his boyhood house was bought and torn down by a wealthy man that his mother had considered a friend. The breaking guitar string in acts 2 and 4 herald back to his earliest works. Finally the classic "loaded gun" that appears in many of Chekhov's plays appears here, but this is his only play in which a gun is shown but not fired.

Production history

The play opened on January 17, 1904, the playwright's birthday, at the Moscow Art Theatre under the direction of legendary actor/director Constantin Stanislavski. During rehearsals, the entire structure of Act Two was re-written (to include the passer-by and the twang from the string dying away to empathise the audience with the mining disaster of the time). Famously contrary to Chekhov's wishes, Stanislavski's version was, by and large, a tragedy. Chekhov disliked the Stanislavski production intensely, concluding that Stanislavski had "ruined" his play, which was in turn under-rehearsed (the Moscow Arts Theatre only rehearsing it for six months, unlike the common practise to rehearse for 18 months, or even more). In one of many letters on the subject, Chekhov would complain, "Anya, I fear, should not have any sort of tearful tone ... Not once does my Ania cry, nowhere do I speak of a tearful tone, in the second act there are tears in their eyes, but the tone is happy, lively. Why did you speak in your telegram about so many tears in my play? Where are they? ... Often you will find the words "through tears," but I am describing only the expression on their faces, not tears. And in the second act there is no graveyard."[3]

The modest and newly-urbanized audiences attending pre-revolutionary performances at S. V. Panin's People's House in Saint Petersburg reportedly cheered as the cherry orchard was felled onstage.[4]

The playwright's wife Olga Knipper played Madame Ranevskaya in the original Moscow Art Theatre production, as well as in the 300th production of the play by the theatre in 1943.

A 1934 production at the Sadler's Wells Theatre in London directed by Tyrone Guthrie and translated by Hubert Butler was among the first English-language productions of the play.

The Cherry Orchard memorabilia at the Chekhov Gymnasium literary museum.

A television version featuring Helen Hayes as Ranevskaya, E.G. Marshall as Lophakin and Susan Strasberg as Anya, directed by Daniel Petrie, was broadcast as part of the *Play of the Week* television series in 1959.

Royal Shakespeare Company/BBC TV, black and white, Peggy Ashcroft plays Ranevskaya, John Gielgud Gaev, Judi Dench Anya, Ian Holm Trofimov, Dorothy Tutin Varya, production by Michel Saint-Denis, directed by Michael Elliott, 1962, released on DVD by BBC Worldwide Ltd 2009.

A production starring Irene Worth as Ranevskaya, Raul Julia as Lopakhin, Mary Beth Hurt as Anya and Meryl Streep as Dunyasha, directed by Andrei Şerban and featuring Tony Award-winning costumes and set by Santo Loquasto, opened at the Lincoln Center for the Performing Arts in 1977.

A production directed by Peter Hall, translated by Michael Frayn (*Noises Off*) and starring Dorothy Tutin as Ranevskaya, Albert Finney as Lopakhin, Ben Kingsley as Trofimov and Ralph Richardson as Firs, appeared at the Royal National Theatre in London in 1978 to nearly universal acclaim. A minimalist production directed by Peter

Gill opened at the Riverside Studios in London at virtually the same time, to good reviews.

In 1981, renowned director Peter Brook mounted a production in French with an international cast including Brook's wife Natasha Parry as Ranevskaya, Niels Arestrup as Lophakin and Michael Piccoli as Gayev. The production was remounted at the Brooklyn Academy of Music in 1988 after tours through Africa and the Middle East.

Also in 1981, the BBC produced a version for English television by Trevor Griffiths from a translation by Helen Rappaport and directed by Richard Eyre. Instead of her 1962 BBC role as daughter Anya, Judi Dench here played the mother Ranevskaya to Bill Paterson's Lopakhin, Anton Lesser as Trofimov, Frederick Treves as Gaev, Anna Massey as Charlotte, and a 24-year-old Timothy Spall as Yepikhodov.

A film version starring Charlotte Rampling as Ranevskaya, Alan Bates, Owen Teale as Lophakin, Melanie Lynskey as Dunyasha and Gerard Butler as Yasha, directed by Michael Cacoyannis, appeared in 1999.

The Steppenwolf Theatre Company performed a version that was translated by Associate Artistic Director Curt Columbus and directed by ensemble member Tina Landau. The play premiered on November 4, 2004 and ran until March 5, 2005 at the Downstairs Theatre, Chicago, Illinois, USA. Appearing in the performance were Robert Breuler, Francis Guinan, Amy Morton, Yasen Peyankov, Rondi Reed, Anne Adams, Guy Adkins, Chaon Cross, Leonard Kraft, Julian Martinez, Ned Noyes, Elizabeth Rich, Ben Viccellio, and Chris Yonan

The Atlantic Theatre Company in 2005 mounted a new adaptation of *The Cherry Orchard* by the acclaimed Tom Donaghy, where much more of the comedy was present as the playwright had originally intended.

A new production of the play starring Annette Bening as Ranevskaya and Alfred Molina as Lophakin, translated by Martin Sherman (*Bent*) and directed by Sean Mathias (*Indiscretions*) opened at the Mark Taper Forum in Los Angeles in February 2006.

The Huntington Theatre Company[5] at Boston University produced a version in January 2007 using Richard Nelson's translation, directed by Nicholas Martin with Kate Burton as Madame Ranevskaya, Joyce Van Patten as Charlotta Ivanova, and Dick Latessa as Firs.

Jonathan Miller directed the play in March-April 2007 at the Crucible Theatre, Sheffield, England. The play represents Miller's return to the British stage after nearly a decade away[6] and stars Joanna Lumley as Ranevskaya.

Libby Appel adapted and directed the play in 2007 for her farewell season as artistic director of the Oregon Shakespeare Festival. The new translation, based on an original literal translation by Allison Horsley, is considered to be "strongly Americanized".

A version of the play was performed as the opening production on the Chichester Festival Theatre Stage during the 2008 summer season with a star-studded cast including Dame Diana Rigg, Frank Finlay, Natalie Cassidy, Jemma Redgrave and Maureen Lipman.

In 2009, a new version of the play by Tom Stoppard was performed as the first production of The Bridge Project, a partnership between North American and U.K. theaters. Sam Mendes directed the production with a cast including Simon Russell Beale, Sinéad Cusack, Richard Easton, Rebecca Hall and Ethan Hawke.

A brand new adaptation of the play was produced by Blackeyed Theatre [7] in spring 2009 as a UK tour, with a cast of four.

In September 2009, a new adaptation of the play by Stuart Paterson was produced at the Dundee Repertory Theatre with guest director Vladimir Bouchler.

A new translation of the play in Punjabi was performed in September 2009 by the students of Theatre Art Department of Punjabi University, Patiala, India.

A version of the play in Afrikaans was performed in late September 2009 by students of the Department of Drama at the University of Cape Town, South Africa.

A new adaption was commissioned by the Brighton Festival and performed by the dreamthinkspeak group. [8] They renovated the old co-op home-store on the London Road using the whole store as a stage. They renamed it Before I

Sleep and said it was inspired by the original play. It received positive reviews from both The Guardian[9] and The Independent[10] newspapers. It was funded by Arts Council England, National Lottery and a long list of other Brighton and Hove based businesses.

In April 2010 at the Royal Lyceum Theatre in Edinburgh the Scottish playwright John Byrne staged a new version of the play as a Scottish 'social comedy' under its original title.

In pop culture

- In Robert De Niro's film *The Good Shepherd*, a performance of the play is attended by a CIA agent, portrayed by Matt Damon.
- *Monty Python's Flying Circus* included a sketch on their record *Another Monty Python Record* which involved a production of the play performed entirely by Gumbies. One gets his head stuck in a cupboard, and the others behave in a similar manner, yelling "hello!" at each other and destroying the set.
- The play is somewhat obliquely referenced in *The Fifth Elephant* by Terry Pratchett. A minor subplot in the novel centers around an extended Chekhov joke in which three sisters are living together in a small dacha surrounded by a cherry orchard (one of the sisters longs for an axe). They end up assisting Commander Samuel Vimes, by providing him with "the gloomy and purposeless trousers of Uncle Vanya".
- The plot of Gabriele Salvatores's *Turnè* revolves around a company that performs *The Cherry Orchard* in various theatres in Italy.
- In *Being John Malkovich* a portion of the play is read by John Malkovich.
- In *The Simpsons* episode "The Regina Monologues", the play is used as a sly dig at Joe Millionaire, where star Evan Marriott admits he does not have a cherry orchard, much like in the show where he admits he was not a millionaire.
- In J.D. Salinger's short story "Franny and Zooey", Zooey reads from a letter his elder brother Buddy wrote to him years prior. Buddy laments in the letter that nobody has yet staged a production of *The Cherry Orchard* that matches "word for word" Chekhov's brilliance.
- The New York comedy group, Improv Everywhere, had an imposter pretending to be Anton Chekhov, give a speech and reading of *The Cherry Orchard* at New York's central Barnes and Noble bookstore.
- *The Fever*, starring Vanessa Redgrave, features a scene in which the main character attends the play, although the end of the play is all that's shown.
- In *Some Like It Hot* Marylin Monroe's character suggests that she perform a monologue from *The Cherry Orchard* but the idea is quickly dismissed by her manager.
- In *The Royal Tenenbaums*, Margot Tenenbaum is seen reading the *The Cherry Orchard* in an early scene.
- In one episode (Show No. 7001) of the American version of *Whose Line Is It Anyway?* in the introduction for the game Greatest Hits, series regular Colin Mochrie announces "Hi. We'll be right back to Jerry Van Dyke, Jerry Vale, Jerry Lewis, and Jerry the cartoon mouse in Anton Chekhov's *The Jerry Orchard* in just a second."

References

[1] A general overview of these themes, among others, can be found in: Jean-Pierre Barricelli, ed., *Chekhov's Great Plays: A Critical Anthology* (New York, 1981), Richard Peace, *Chekhov: A Study of the Four Major Plays* (New Haven, 1983), Donald Rayfield, *Understanding Chekhov: A Critical Study of Chekhov's Prose and Drama* (Madison, 1999).

[2] Hirst, David L. *Tragicomedy: Variations of melodrama: Chekhov and Shaw.* London: Routledge, 1984, 83

[3] Gregory Stroud, *Retrospective Revolution: A History of Time and Memory in Urban Russia, 1903-1923* (Urbana-Champaign, 2006), 63-4.

[4] Richard Stites, *Revolutionary Dreams: Utopian Vision and Experimental Life in the Russian Revolution* (New York, 1989), 63.

[5] Huntington Theatre Company (http://web.archive.org/web/20071227030833/http://www.bu.edu/cfa/theatre/huntington.htm)

[6] *The Cherry Orchard*, reviewed by Lynne Barber (http://enjoyment.independent.co.uk/theatre/reviews/article2381515.ece) in *The Independent* on 22 March 2007. (Retrieved 30 March 2007) (#4)

[7] http://www.blackeyedtheatre.co.uk

[8] http://www.dreamthinkspeak.com/sleep.htm

[9] http://www.guardian.co.uk/stage/2010/may/07/before-i-sleep-review

[10] http://www.independent.co.uk/arts-entertainment/theatre-dance/reviews/
before-i-sleep-old-coop-building-brightonbreurydice-maria-young-vic-londonbrmacbeth-globe-london-1968908.html

Books

- Chekhov, Anton. *The Cherry Orchard*, translated by David Magarshack. *Modern and Contemporary Drama* edited by Miriam Gilbert, Carl H. Klaus and Bradford S. Field, Jr. New York: St. Martin's Press, 1994. ISBN 0-312-09077-3

External links

- Full text of *The Cherry Orchard* (http://ilibrary.ru/text/472/) (Russian)

- Project Gutenberg eText (http://www.gutenberg.org/etext/7986), English translations of several Chekhov plays, including *The Cherry Orchard*

- A public domain version of the play (http://www.ibiblio.org/eldritch/ac/chorch.htm) (English translation)

- A discussion of the OSF adaptation (http://www.aislesay.com/SF-OREGON-2007-1.html)

- *The Cherry Orchard* (http://www.shmoop.com/cherry-orchard/) *study guide, themes, quotes, teacher resources*

The Taming of the Shrew

The Taming of the Shrew is a comedy by William Shakespeare, believed to have been written between 1590 and 1594. It was published in 1623.

The play begins with a framing device, often referred to as the Induction, in which a drunken tinker named Sly is tricked into thinking he is a nobleman by a mischievous Lord. The Lord has a play performed for Sly's amusement, set in Padua with a primary and sub-plot.

The main plot depicts the courtship of Petruchio, a gentleman of Verona, and Katherina, the headstrong, obdurate shrew. Initially, Katherina is an unwilling participant in the relationship, but Petruchio tempers her with various psychological torments — the "taming"

Petruchio (Kevin Black) and Kate (Emily Jordan) from a Carmel Shake-speare Festival production of *The Taming of the Shrew* at the outdoor Forest Theater in Carmel, CA., Oct, 2003.

— until she is an obedient bride. The sub-plot features a competition between the suitors of Katherina's more tractable sister, Bianca.

The play's apparent misogynistic elements have become the subject of considerable controversy, particularly among modern audiences and readers. It has nevertheless been adapted numerous times for stage, screen, opera, and musical theatre; perhaps the most famous adaptations being Cole Porter's *Kiss Me, Kate* and the film *10 Things I Hate About You*.

Characters

- Katherina (Kate) Minola – the "shrew" of the title
- Bianca – sister of Katherina; the ingénue
- Baptista Minola – father of Katherina and Bianca
- Petruchio – suitor of Katherina
- Gremio – elderly suitor of Bianca
- Lucentio – suitor of Bianca
- Hortensio – suitor of Bianca and friend to Petruchio
- Grumio – servant of Petruchio
- Tranio – servant of Lucentio
- Biondello – servant of Lucentio
- Vincentio – father of Lucentio
- A Widow
- A Pedant
- A Haberdasher
- A Tailor

- Curtis
- Nathaniel
- Joseph
- Peter
- An Officer
- Servants

Characters appearing in the Induction:

- Christopher Sly – a drunken tinker
- A Lord
- Bartholomew – A page
- Hostess of an alehouse
- Huntsman of the Lord
- Players
- Servingmen
- Messenger

Synopsis

The Shrew Katherina by Edward Robert Hughes (1898)

Prior to the first act, an induction frames the play as a "kind of history" played in front of a befuddled drunkard named Christopher Sly who is tricked into believing that he is a lord.

In the play performed for Sly, the "Shrew" is Katherina Minola, the eldest daughter of Baptista Minola, a Lord in Padua. Katherina's temper is notorious and it is thought no man would ever wish to marry her. On the other hand, two men – Hortensio and Gremio – are eager to marry her younger sister Bianca. However, Baptista has sworn not to allow his younger daughter to marry before Katherina is wed, much to the despair of her suitors, who agree that they will work together to marry off Katherina so that they will be free to compete for Bianca.

The plot becomes more complex when Lucentio, who has recently come to Padua to attend the famous university there, sees Bianca and instantly falls in love with her.

Lucentio overhears Baptista announce that he is on the lookout for tutors for his daughters, so he has his servant Tranio pretend to be him while he disguises himself as Cambio, a Latin tutor, so that he can woo Bianca.

In the meantime Petruchio arrives in Padua, accompanied by his witty servant, Grumio. Petruchio tells his old friend Hortensio that he has come to seek his fortune "farther than at home/Where small experience grows" (1.2.50-51). Hearing this, Hortensio seizes the opportunity to recruit Petruchio as a suitor for Katherina, and to present him (Hortensio) to Baptista as Litio, a music tutor. Thus, Lucentio

C.R. Leslie's illustration of Act 4, Scene 3 from the *Illustrated London News*, Nov. 3, 1886

and Hortensio, pretending to be teachers, attempt to woo Bianca behind her father's back.

Petruchio, to counter Katherina's shrewish nature, woos her with reverse psychology, pretending that every harsh thing she says or does is kind and gentle. Katherina allows herself to become engaged to Petruchio, and they are married in a farcical ceremony during which (amongst other things) he strikes the priest, and then takes her home against her will. Once there, he begins the "taming" of his new wife, using more reverse psychology. She is refused food and clothing because nothing – according to Petruchio – is good enough for her. Finally, Katherina catches on to Petruchio's game of spoof, and when they are on a journey to the house of her father, Baptista, she wittily agrees with Petruchio that the sun is the moon, and proclaims that "if you please to call it a rush-candle,/Henceforth I vow it shall be so for me" (4.5.14-15).

Meanwhile Bianca elopes with Lucentio, and Hortensio is persuaded by Tranio that Bianca is not worthy of his attentions. Hortensio marries a rich widow, and so in the final scene of the play there are three newly married couples at Baptista's banquet. Because of the general opinion that Petruchio is married to a shrew, a quarrel breaks out about whose wife is the most obedient. Petruchio proposes a wager whereby each will send a servant to call for their wives, and whichever comes most obediently will have won the wager for her husband. Katherina is the only one of the three who comes, winning the wager for Petruchio. At the end of the play, after the other two wives have been hauled into the room by Katherina, she gives a speech on the subject of why wives should always obey their husbands, and tells them that their husbands ask only "love, fair looks and true obedience" (5.2.153). The play ends with Baptista, Hortensio and Lucentio marvelling at Petruchio's taming of the shrew.

Sources

Although there is no direct literary source for the Induction, the tale of a tinker being duped into thinking he is a lord is a universal one found in many literary traditions. For example, a similar tale is recorded in *Arabian Nights* where Harun al-Rashid plays the same trick on a man he finds sleeping in an alley, and in *De Rebus Burgundicis* by the Dutch historian Pontus de Heuiter, where the trick is performed by Philip the Good, i.e. Philip III, Duke of Burgundy. *Arabian Nights* was not translated into English until the mid 18th century, although Shakespeare could have known it by word of mouth. He could also have known the Philip III story as, although *De Rebus* wasn't translated into French until 1600, and into English until 1607, there is evidence the Philip III story existed in a jest book (now lost) by Richard Edwardes, written in 1570, which Shakespeare certainly could have known.[1]

Something similar is the case with regard to the Petruchio/Katherina story. The basic elements of the narrative are present in the 14th-century Castilian tale by Don Juan Manuel of the "young man who married a very strong and fiery woman".[2] Again however, there is no evidence that Shakespeare directly used this text during the composition of *The Shrew*. Indeed, as with the Induction plot, the story of a headstrong woman tamed by a man was a universal and well known one, found in numerous traditions. For example, according to *The Canterbury Tales* by Geoffrey Chaucer, Noah's wife was just such an individual (""Hastow nought herd", quod Nicholas, "also/The sorwe of Noë with his felaschippe/That he had or he gat his wyf to schipe""; *The Miller's Tale*, l.352-354). Historically another such woman is Xanthippe, Socrates' wife, who is mentioned by Petruchio himself. Such characters also occur throughout medieval literature, in popular farces both before and during Shakespeare's life, and in folklore.

In 1959, J.W. Shroeder conjectured that the literary source for the Petruchio/Katherina story could have been William Caxton's translation of the Queen Vastis story from *Book of the Knight of La Tour Landry*.[3] A more detailed argument was put forward in 1964 by Richard Hosley, who suggested that the main source could have been the anonymous ballad *A Merry Jest of a Shrewde and Curste Wyfe, Lapped in Morrell's Skin, for Her Good Behavyour*.[4] The ballad tells the story of a headstrong woman who is frustrated because her father seems to love her sister more than her. Due to her obstinacy, the father marries her to a man who vows to tame her, despite her objections. The man takes her to his house, and begins the taming. Ultimately, the couple return to the father's house, where she lectures her sister on the merits of being an obedient wife. However, the 'taming' in this version is much more physical than in Shakespeare; the shrew is beaten with birch rods until she bleeds, and is also wrapped in the flesh of a plough horse (the Morrell of the title) which was killed specially for the occasion.[5] However, due to the lack of verbal parallels usually found when Shakespeare used a specific source, most critics do not accept either Shroeder or Hosley's arguments.

The general feeling amongst twentieth century critics is that Shakespeare most likely adapted the popular tradition, fashioning it to fit his own story. A major factor in the dominance of this theory is the work of Jan Harold Brunvand. In 1966, Brunvand argued that the main source for the play was not literary, but instead the oral folktale tradition. Specifically, Brunvand argued that the Petruchio/Katherina story represents a subtype of Type 901 ('Shrew-taming Complex') in the Aarne-Thompson classification system. Brunvand discovered 383 oral examples of Type 901 spread over all of Europe, whereas he could find only 35 literary examples, leading him to the conclusion that if Shakespeare took this story from anywhere, he most likely took it from the oral tradition.[6] Most contemporary critics accept Brunvand's findings.

Unlike the Induction and the main plot however, there *is* a recognised source for Shakespeare's sub-plot, first suggested by Alfred Tolman in 1890;[7] Ludovico Ariosto's *I Suppositi* (1551), which Shakespeare used either directly or through George Gascoigne's English prose translation *Supposes* (performed in 1566, printed in 1573).[8] In *I Suppositi*, Erostrato (the equivalent of Lucentio) falls in love with Polynesta (Bianca), daughter of Damon (Baptista). Erostrato disguises himself as Dulipo (Tranio), a servant, whilst the real servant Dulipo pretends to be Erostrato. Having done this, Erostrato is hired as a tutor for Polynesta. Meanwhile, Dulipo pretends to formally woo Polynesta so as to frustrate the wooing of the aged Cleander (Gremio). Dulipo outbids Cleander, but he promises far more than he can deliver, so he and Erostrato dupe a travelling pedant into pretending to be Erostrato's father, Philogano (Vincentio), and to guarantee the dower. However, Polynesta is found to be pregnant with Erostrato's child, but everyone thinks it is Dulipo's, and Damon has Dulipo imprisoned. Soon after, the real Philogano arrives, and all comes to a head. Erostrato reveals himself, and begs clemency for Dulipo. At this point, Damon realises that Polynesta truly is in love with Erostrato, and so forgives the subterfuge. Having been released from jail, Dulipo then discovers that he is Cleander's long lost son. There is no counterpart to Hortensio in the original story, although an important character named Pasiphilo has no counterpart in Shakespeare's adaptation.

An additional minor source could have been *Mostellaria* by Plautus, from which Shakespeare probably took the names of Tranio and Grumio.

Date and text

The play's date of composition and genesis cannot be easily discerned, due to its uncertain relationship with another Elizabethan play with an almost identical plot but different wording and character names, entitled *A Pleasant Conceited Historie, called the taming of a Shrew*, which is often theorised to be either a reported text of a performance of *The Shrew*, a source for *The Shrew*, or an early draft (possibly reported) of *The Shrew*.[9] *A Shrew* was entered on the Stationers' Register on May 2, 1594, suggesting that whatever the relationship between the two plays, *The Shrew* was most likely written somewhere between 1590 and 1594.[10]

Some critics have attempted to narrow this date down however, with many positing a date of 1591/1592. For example, in his 1982 edition of the play for the *Oxford Shakespeare*, H.J. Oliver suggests 1592. According to the title page of *A Shrew*, the play had been performed recently by Pembroke's Men. When the London theatres were closed on 23 June 1592 due to an outbreak of plague, Pembroke's Men went on a regional tour to Bath and Ludlow. The tour was a financial failure, and the company returned to London on September 28, financially ruined. Over the course of the next three years,

First Folio (1623) title page facsimile

four plays with their name on the title page were published; Christopher Marlowe's *Edward II* (published in quarto in July 1593), and Shakespeare's *Titus Andronicus* (published in quarto in 1594), *The True Tragedy of Richard Duke of York* (published in octavo in 1595) and *The Taming of a Shrew* (published in quarto in May, 1594). Oliver concludes that these four plays were reported texts sold by members of Pembroke's Men who were broke after the failed tour. As such, if they began their tour in June 1592, and one accepts that *A Shrew* is a reported version of *The Shrew*, the assumption is that *The Shrew* must have been in their possession when they began their tour, as they didn't perform it upon returning to London in September, nor would they have taken possession of any new material at that time or during the tour itself. As such, Oliver believes, *The Shrew* must have been written prior to June 1592, most likely in early 1592, and it was one of the performances during the Bath/Ludlow tour which gave rise to *A Shrew*.[11]

A similar theory is suggested by Ann Thompson, who also supports the reported text theory, in her 1984 edition of the play for the *Cambridge Shakespeare*. She too focuses on the closure of the theatres on 23 June 1592, arguing, like Oliver, that the play must have been written prior to June 1592 for it to have given rise to *A Shrew*. She argues that a stage direction in *A Shrew* seems to indicate a part to be played by the minor actor Simon Jewell, who died in August 1592. This places the date of composition of *A Shrew* as prior to August 1592, and if *The Shrew* gave rise to *A Shrew*, it suggests that *The Shrew* must have been written at least several months prior to that, probably in late 1591/early 1592. Thompson also detects a reference to *The Shrew* in Anthony Chute's *Beawtie Dishonour'd written under the title of Shores Wife* (1592). She suggests that the line, "He calls his *Kate* and she must come and kiss him" references *The Shrew*, as *A Shrew* contains no kissing scenes, which supports her argument for a date of composition in late 1591/early 1592. She also cites verbal similarities between both *Shrew* plays and the anonymous play *A Knack to Know a Knave* (*c*1592), which was first performed at The Rose on 10 June 1592. She argues that if *Knack* borrows from both *The Shrew* and *A Shrew*, it means *The Shrew* must have been on stage by mid-June 1592 at the latest, and again suggests a date of composition of somewhere in late 1591/early 1592.[12] Stephen Roy Miller in his 1998 edition of *A Shrew* for the *Cambridge Shakespeare* agrees with the Oliver/Thompson date of late 1591/early 1592, as he too believes *The Shrew* preceded *A Shrew* (although he rejects the reported text theory in favour of an adaptation/rewrite theory).[13]

The 1594 quarto was published under the full title *A Pleasant Conceited Historie, called the taming of a Shrew*, printed by Peter Short for the bookseller Cuthbert Burbie. It was republished in 1596 (again by Short for Burbie), and again in 1607 (by Valentine Simmes for Nicholas Ling). *The Shrew* was not published until the First Folio of 1623. The only quarto version of *The Shrew* was printed by William Stansby for the bookseller John Smethwick in 1631 as *A Wittie and Pleasant comedie called The Taming of the Shrew*. This quarto text was based on the 1623 folio text.[14] W.W. Greg has shown that for the purposes of copyright, *A Shrew* and *The Shrew* were treated as the same text, i.e. the ownership of one constituted the ownership of the other, and when Smethwick purchased the rights from Ling in 1609, which enabled him to print the play in the *First Folio* in 1623, he was actually purchasing the rights for *A Shrew*, not *The Shrew*.[15]

Analysis and criticism

Critical history

The Taming of the Shrew has been the subject of much analytical and critical controversy, often relating to a feminist view of the play in general, and Katherina's final speech in particular, as offensively misogynistic and patriarchal. Others have defended the play by highlighting the (frequently unstaged) Induction as evidence that the play's sentiments are not meant to be taken at face value, that the entire play is, in fact, a farce. Despite this argument being hundreds of years old, however, no critical consensus has been reached as to the true intentions of the play. This issue however, represents only one of the many critical disagreements brought up by the play.

Authorship and *The Taming of a Shrew*

One of the most fundamental debates regarding the play is the issue of authorship. The existence of *A Shrew*, which appeared in 1594, has led to an examination of authenticity regarding *The Shrew*. As Karl P. Wentersdorf points out, *A Shrew* and *The Shrew* have "similar plot lines and parallel though differently named characters."[16] As such, there are five main theories as to the relationship between *The Shrew* and *A Shrew*:

1. The two plays are unrelated other than the fact that they are both based on another play which is now lost. This is the so-called *Ur-Shrew* theory (in reference to *Ur-Hamlet*).[17]
2. *A Shrew* is a reconstructed version of *The Shrew*; i.e. a bad quarto of *The Shrew*, an attempt by actors to reconstruct the original play from memory and sell it.[18]
3. Shakespeare used the previously-existing *A Shrew*, which he did not write, as a source for *The Shrew*.[19]
4. Both versions were legitimately written by Shakespeare himself; i.e. *A Shrew* is an earlier draft of *The Shrew*.[20]
5. *A Shrew* is an adaptation of *The Shrew* by someone other than Shakespeare.[21]

Although the exact relationship between *The Shrew* and *A Shrew* remains uncertain, and without complete critical consensus, there is a tentative agreement amongst many critics that *The Shrew* is the original, and *A Shrew* is derived from it in some way. The main reason for assuming *The Shrew* came first is "those passages in *A Shrew* [...] that make sense only if one knows the *The Shrew* version from which they must have been derived;"[22] i.e. parts of *A Shrew* simply don't make sense without recourse to *The Shrew*.

The debate regarding the relationship between the two plays began in 1725, when Alexander Pope incorporated extracts from *A Shrew* into *The Shrew* in his edition of Shakespeare's works. Pope added the Sly framework to *The Shrew*, and this practice remained the norm amongst editors until Edmond Malone removed all extracts from *A Shrew* and returned to the strict 1623 text in his edition of the plays in 1792. At this time, it was primarily felt that *A Shrew* was a non-Shakespearean source play for *The Shrew*, and hence to include extracts from *A Shrew* in the body of *The Shrew* was to graft extraneous material onto the play which the playwright did not write.

This theory prevailed until 1850, when, in a series of articles for the magazine *Notes and Queries*, Samuel Hickson compared the texts of *The Shrew* and *A Shrew*, concluding that *The Shrew* was the original, and *A Shrew* was derived from it, not the other way around. Hickson chose seven passages that are similar in both plays and analysed them to conclude that *A Shrew* was dependent on *The Shrew*, although he was unsure exactly how *The Shrew* gave rise to *A Shrew*.[23] In 1926, building on Hickson's research, Peter Alexander suggested the bad quarto theory. He based his argument on three main pieces of evidence:

1. There is clear evidence that *A Shrew* was dependent for meaning upon *The Shrew*.
2. The subplot in *The Shrew* is closer to the source *I Suppositi* than in *A Shrew*.
3. New material in the subplot not found in *I Suppositi* is incoherent in *A Shrew* but coherent in *The Shrew*.

Alexander argued this evidence suggested that the direction of change was from *The Shrew* to *A Shrew*, i.e. *A Shrew* was derived from *The Shrew* and hence must be a bad quarto.[24] In their 1928 edition of the play for the *New Shakespeare*, Arthur Quiller-Couch and John Dover Wilson wholeheartedly supported Alexander's theory, which has remained popular ever since.

However, not everyone agreed with Alexander. For example, in 1930, E.K. Chambers rejected Alexander's theory and reasserted the source theory.[25] Similarly, in 1938, Leo Kirschbaum also rejected Alexander's claim. Although Kirschbaum agreed with the bad quarto theory in general, he didn't believe *A Shrew* qualified as a bad quarto. He argued that *A Shrew* was simply too different from *The Shrew* to come under the bad quarto banner, unlike Alexander's other examples of bad quartos *The First part of the Contention betwixt the two famous Houses of Yorke and Lancaster* and *The True Tragedy of Richard Duke of Yorke*.[26] Stephen Roy Miller supports Kirschbaum's opinion, pointing out that "the relation of the early quarto to the Folio text is unlike other early quartos because the texts vary much more in plotting and dialogue."[27] Character names are changed, plot points are altered (Kate has two sisters for example, not one), the play is set in Athens instead of Padua, Sly continues to comment on events throughout the play, and entire speeches are completely different. Thus from other plays are also found in *A Shrew*, especially from Marlowe's *Tamburlaine*), all of which suggests that the author/reporter of *A Shrew* thought he (or she) was working on something different to Shakespeare's play, not simply transcribing it. As Miller points out, "underpinning the notion of a 'Shakespearean bad quarto' is the assumption that the motive of whoever compiled that text was to produce, differentially, a verbal replica of what appeared on stage,"[28] and both Kirschbaum and Miller argue that *A Shrew* does not fulfil this rubric.

Alexander's theory continued to be challenged as the years went on. In 1942, building on the work of Charles Knight, R.A. Houk developed what came to be dubbed the *Ur-Shrew* theory. In 1943, in a controversial argument, G.I. Duthie combined Alexander's bad quarto theory with Houk's *Ur-Shrew* theory. Duthie argued that *A Shrew* was a memorial reconstruction of *Ur-Shrew*, a now lost play upon which Shakespeare's *The Shrew* was based; "*A Shrew* is substantially a memorially constructed text and is dependent upon an early *Shrew* play, now lost. *The Shrew* is a reworking of this lost play".[29] Duthie argued that the time-scheme of *A Shrew* shows that it was a garbled version of something which probably made more sense in an original form, and that Shakespeare reorganised the plot when composing *The Shrew* so as to make more chronological sense. Although Duthie's argument wasn't fully accepted at the time, it has been gaining increased support in the late twentieth century.

In the light of Duthie's theory, in 1958, J.W. Shroeder attempted to revive the source theory by disproving both Hickson and Alexander's bad quarto theory and Houk and Duthie's *Ur-Shrew* theory. Shroeder's argument (which rests on the hypothesis that *The Shrew* was not written until at least 1597) was based on an analysis of parallel passages (some of which had been used by Hickson to argue the bad quarto theory) and chronological problems within both plays to show that there was no need for an *Ur-Shrew* theory or a bad quarto theory, when a source theory could address all the problems raised by comparing the two plays.[30] Shroeder's argument, however, was never fully accepted.

Subsequently, in 1964, Richard Hosley, in his edition of the play for the *Pelican Shakespeare* challenged the theories of Hickson, Alexander, Houk, Duthie and Shroeder, and suggested an early draft theory. Hosley's argument was based on the relative complexity of *A Shrew* when compared to contemporaneous plays. If *A Shrew* was *not* an early draft (i.e. not by Shakespeare), we would have "to assume around 1593 the existence of a dramatist other than Shakespeare who was capable of devising a three-part structure more impressive that the structure of any extant play by Lyly, Peele, Greene, Marlow, or Kyd."[31] In this sense, Shakespeare must have written *A Shrew*, and as it is decidedly inferior to *The Shrew*, it follows that it is an early draft of the later play.

Alexander himself returned to the debate in 1969, once again re-presenting his bad quarto theory in light of the many objections raised in the preceding forty years. In particular, Alexander concentrated on the various complications and inconsistencies in the subplot of *A Shrew*, which had been used by Houk and Duthie as evidence for an *Ur-Shrew*, to argue that the reporter of *A Shrew* attempted to recreate the complex subplot from *The Shrew* but got muddled and imported ideas and lines for other plays, especially Marlow. For much of the remainder of the twentieth century, Alexander's views remained predominant.[32]

After little further discussion of the issue in the 1970s, the 1980s saw the publication of three scholarly editions of *The Shrew*, all of which re-addressed the question in light of the by now general acceptance of Alexander's theory; Brian Morris' 1981 edition for the *Arden Shakespeare*, H.J. Oliver's 1982 edition for the *Oxford Shakespeare* and Ann Thompson's 1984 edition for the *New Cambridge Shakespeare*. Morris summarised the issue at that time by pointing out, "Unless new, external evidence comes to light, the relationship between *The Shrew* and *A Shrew* can never be decided beyond a peradventure. It will always be a balance of probabilities, shifting as new arguments and opinions are added to the scales. Nevertheless, in the present century, the movement has unquestionably been towards an acceptance of the Bad Quarto theory, and this can now be accepted as at least the current orthodoxy."[33]. Thompson wholeheartedly supported the bad quarto theory, but both Morris and Oliver were less sure, arguing instead for a combination of the bad quarto theory and the early draft theory.

Other critics have also spoken on this issue. Championing the bad quarto theory, Ann Barton says, *A Shrew* is "now generally believed to be either a pirated and inaccurate version of Shakespeare's comedy or else a "bad quarto" of a different play, now lost, which also served Shakespeare as a source."[10] Leah S. Marcus, whilst discussing the prevailing bad quarto theory, suggests that *A Shrew* is not a transcription of a performance of *The Shrew*, but is in fact an earlier version of *The Shrew*; that is to say, Shakespeare himself authored both works. However, she notes that many critics have rejected the idea of *A Shrew* being a work of Shakespeare's, subscribing instead to the bad quarto theory. She states that the reason for this, apart from the many differences in the text, and some extremely sloppy writing in *A Shrew*, is "because it identifies the acting company with an audience of lowlifes like Sly".[34] Marcus writes that this is seen by editors as out of character for Shakespeare and is therefore an indication that he did not write *A Shrew*. Wentersdorf also discusses the idea that Shakespeare penned both plays, and that *A Shrew* may have been either an early version of *The Shrew* written before it, or an abridged version written after it. Both theories would explain the differences between the two versions. Wentersdorf admits, though, that his theory is based primarily on speculation, and there is no real way of knowing for certain why Sly disappeared from *The Shrew*.[35] Others, such as Mikhail M. Morozov, have maintained that Shakespeare may not have been entirely original in his writing of the play (whether *The Shrew* or *A Shrew*), suggesting that the ideas found in the story were those of another author.[36] Kenneth Muir, for his part, believes that Shakespeare had a *laissez-faire* attitude to borrowing content from other authors in general, and he cites *The Shrew* as an instance of this.[37]

One of the most extensive examinations of the question came in 1998 in Stephen Roy Miller's edition of *A Shrew* for the *Cambridge Shakespeare*. Miller argues that *A Shrew* is indeed derived from *The Shrew*, but it is neither a bad quarto nor an early draft. Instead, it is an adaptation by someone other than Shakespeare. Miller argues that Alexander's suggestion in 1969 that the reporter became confused, and introduced elements from other plays is unlikely, and instead suggests an adapter at work (whom he refers to as the 'compiler'), writing in the romantic comedy tradition; "the most economic explanation of indebtedness is that whoever compiled *A Shrew* borrowed the lines from Shakespeare's *The Shrew*, or a version of it, and adapted them."[38] Part of Miller's evidence relates to Gremio, who has no counterpart in *A Shrew*. In *The Shrew*, after the wedding, Gremio expressed doubts as to whether or not Petruchio will be able to tame Katherina. In *A Shrew*, these lines are extended and split between Polidor and Phylema. As Gremio *does* have a counterpart in *I Suppositi*, Miller concludes that "to argue the priority of *A Shrew* in this case would mean arguing that Shakespeare took the negative hints from the speeches of Polidor and Phylema and gave them to a character he resurrected from *Supposes*. This is a less economical argument than to suggest that the compiler of *A Shrew*, dismissing Gremio, simply shared his doubts among the characters available."[39] Miller argues that there is even evidence in the play of what the compiler felt he was doing, working within a specific literary tradition; "as with his partial change of character names, the compiler seems to wish to produce dialogue much like his models, but not the same. For him, adaptation includes exact quotation, imitation and incorporation of his own additions. This seems to define his personal style, and his aim seems to be to produce his own version, presumably intended that it should be tuned more towards the popular era than *The Shrew*."[40]

As had Alexander, Houk, Duthie and Shroeder, Miller argues that the subplot in *A Shrew* and *The Shrew* holds the key to the debate, as it is here where the two plays differ most. Miller points out that the subplot in *The Shrew* is based on "the classical style of Latin comedy with an intricate plot involving deception, often kept in motion by a comic servant." The subplot in *A Shrew* however, which features an extra sister and addresses the issue of marrying above and below one's class, "has many elements more associated with the romantic style of comedy popular in London in the 1590s."[41] Miller cites plays such as Robert Greene's *Friar Bacon and Friar Bungay* and *Fair Em* as evidence of the popularity of such plays. He points to the fact that in *The Shrew*, there is only eleven lines of romance between Tranio and Bianca, but in *A Shrew*, there is an entire scene between Kate's two sisters and their lovers. This, he argues, is evidence of an adaptation rather than a faulty report; "while it is difficult to know the motivation of the adapter, we can reckon that from his point of view an early staging of *The Shrew* might have revealed an overly wrought play from a writer trying to establish himself but challenging too far the current ideas of popular comedy. *The Shrew* is long and complicated. It has three plots, the subplots being in the swift Latin or Italianate style with several disguises. Its language is at first stuffed with difficult Italian quotations, but its dialogue must often sound plain when compared to Marlowe's thunder or Greene's romance, the mouth filling lines and images that on other afternoon were drawing crowds. An adapter might well have seen his role as that of a 'play doctor' improving *The Shrew* – while cutting it – by stuffing it with the sort of material currently in demand in popular romantic comedies."[42] Miller goes on to summarise his theory; "he appears to have wished to make the play shorter, more of a romantic comedy full of wooing and glamorous rhetoric, and to add more obvious, broad comedy."[43] As such, Miller rejects the bad quarto theory, the early draft theory, the *Ur-Shrew* theory *and* the source theory in favour of his own adaptation theory.

Hortensio problem

Another aspect of the authorship question concerns the character of Hortensio. Building on the work of John Dover Wilson,[44] W.W. Greg[45] and Brian Morris[46] , H.J. Oliver argues that the version of the play in the 1623 First Folio was most likely taken not from a prompt book, or a transcript, but from the author's own foul papers (probably with some annotations by the book keeper), which he argues bear signs of edits, primarily related to Hortensio.[47] This is significant because some critics argue that in an original version of the play, now lost, Hortensio was *not* a suitor to Bianca, but simply an old friend of Petruchio (this is a modification of the *Ur-Shrew* theory, which instead of arguing that a play by someone other than Shakespeare served as a source, argues that an earlier draft by Shakespeare once existed). When Shakespeare rewrote the play so that Hortensio became a suitor in disguise (as Litio), many of Hortensio's original lines were either omitted or given to Tranio (disguised as Lucentio).

This theory was first suggested by P.A. Daniel in his 1879 book *A Time Analysis of the Plots of Shakespeare's Plays*, and subsequently elaborated upon by E.A.J. Honigmann in 1954. Daniel and Honigmann cite Act 2, Scene 1, where Hortensio is omitted from the scene where Tranio (as Lucentio) and Gremio bid for Bianca, despite the fact that everyone knows Hortensio is also a suitor. Daniel argues that Hortensio's absence suggests that Shakespeare forgot to change this part of the play after making Hortensio a suitor in a later draft. Another such omission is found in Act 3, Scene 1, where Lucentio, disguised as Cambio, tells Bianca that "we might beguile the old Pantalowne", saying nothing of Hortensio's attempts to woo her, and implying his only rival is Gremio. Additionally, in Act 3, Scene 2, Tranio is briefly presented as an old friend of Petruchio, who knows his mannerisms and explains his tardiness prior to the wedding, a role which, up until now, had been performed by Hortensio. Daniel argues that this is suggestive of the theory that some of Hortensio's original lines were transferred to Tranio because Hortensio was now occupied elsewhere in disguise as Litio. Another problem occurs in Act 4, Scene 3, where Hortensio tells Vincentio that Lucentio has married Bianca. However, as far as Hortensio should be concerned, Lucentio has denounced Bianca (in Act 4, Scene 2, Tranio (disguised as Lucentio) agreed with Hortensio that neither of them would pursue Bianca, because she obviously loved Cambio), and as such, his knowledge of the marriage of who he supposes to be Lucentio and Bianca makes no sense, and again seems to suggest some careless editing on Shakespeare's part. Daniel and Honigmann believe that an original version of the play existed in which Hortensio was simply a friend of Petruchio's, and had no involvement in the Bianca subplot, but wishing to complicate things, Shakespeare rewrote the play, expanding Hortensio's role, but not fully correcting everything to fit the presence of a new suitor.

The reason this is important is because it is theorised by supporters of the bad quarto theory that it is the original version of *The Shrew* upon which *A Shrew* was based; not the version which appears in the 1623 Folio. As Oliver argues, "*A Shrew* is a report of an earlier, Shakespearian, form of *The Shrew* in which Hortensio was not disguised as Litio."[48] As such, this theory is something of a combination of the *Ur-Shrew* theory, the early draft theory *and* the bad quarto theory; *A Shrew* is a bad quarto of an early draft of *The Shrew*, and this early draft also performs the role traditionally assigned to *Ur-Shrew*. Oliver suggests that when Pembroke's Men left London in June 1592, they had in their possession a now lost version of the play. Upon returning to London, they published *A Shrew* in 1594, some time after which Shakespeare rewrote his original play. This means that in the early 1590s there were at least three versions of the same play in circulation: Shakespeare's original *The Shrew*, Shakespeare's edited *The Shrew*, and *A Shrew*.

In 1943, Duthie did hint at this possibility. Based upon the fact that all of the verbal parallels come in relation to the Induction and the main plot, none in relation to the subplot, he concluded that *Ur-Shrew* could in fact be an earlier version of *The Shrew*, of which *A Shrew* is a reported text. Duthie's arguments were never fully accepted however. As such, critics have tended to look on the relationship between the two plays as an either-or situation; *A Shrew* is *either* a reported text *or* an early draft. Recently however, the possibility that a text could be both has shown to be critically viable. For example, in his 2003 *Oxford Shakespeare* edition of *Henry VI, Part 2*, Roger Warren makes the same argument for *The First Part of the Contention*. Similarly, in relation to *The True Tragedy of Richard Duke of York*, Randall Martin reaches the same conclusion in his 2001 *Oxford Shakespeare* edition of *Henry VI, Part 3*. This lends support to the theory that *A Shrew* could be both a reported text and an early draft. As Stephen Roy Miller argues in his 1998 edition of *A Shrew* (although he does so in support of his adaptation theory), "the differences between the texts are substantial and coherent enough to establish that there was deliberate revision in producing one text out of the other; hence *A Shrew* is not merely a poor report (or 'bad quarto') of *The Shrew*."[27]

Controversy

The history of the analysis of *The Taming of the Shrew* is saturated with controversy almost from its inception, something Stevie Davies summarises when she writes, response to *The Shrew* "is dominated by feelings of unease and embarrassment, accompanied by the desire to prove that Shakespeare cannot have meant what he seems to be saying; and that therefore he cannot really be saying it."[49] The play *seems* to be a harshly misogynistic celebration of patriarchy and female submission, and as such, it has generated heated debates about its 'true' meaning.

The misogynistic side of Petruchio (Kevin Black), appearing in his "wedding outfit", in the 2003 Carmel Shake-speare Festival production

Some critics argue that even in Shakespeare's own day, the play was controversial. Oliver, for example, believes that Shakespeare created the Induction so as the audience wouldn't react badly to the inherent misogyny in the Petruchio/Katherina story; he was in effect defending himself against charges of sexism. Dana Aspinall also suggests that an Elizabethan audience would have been similarly taken aback by the play's harsh, misogynistic language; "Since its first appearance, some time between 1588 and 1594, *Shrew* has elicited a panoply of heartily supportive, ethically uneasy, or altogether disgusted responses to its rough-and-tumble treatment of the 'taming' of the 'curst shrew' Katherina, and obviously, of all potentially unruly wives."[50] She further explains that "arranged marriages began to give way to newer, more romantically informed experiments," and thus people's views on women's' position in society, and their relationships with men, were in the process of shifting at the time of the play, so audiences may not have been as predisposed to enjoy the harsh treatment of Katherina as is often thought.[51]

Evidence of at least some initial societal discomfort with *The Shrew* is found in a contemporary, alternate ending which has Christopher Sly being "[thrashed] by his wife for dreaming here tonight" at the end of the play, suggesting that there was a market for an audience who were comfortable with the women 'winning'.[52] More evidence is found in the fact that John Fletcher, a contemporary of Shakespeare, felt the need to respond to the play with one of his own. He wrote *The Woman's Prize, or The Tamer Tamed* as a quasi-sequel to *The Shrew*, telling the story of Petruchio's remarriage after Katherina's death. In a mirror of the original, his new wife attempts (successfully) to tame Petruchio – thus the tamer becomes the tamed. Although Fletcher's sequel is often downplayed as merely a farcical mockery of *The Shrew*, some critics acknowledge the more serious implications of such a reaction. Linda

Boose, for example, writes, "Fletcher's response may in itself reflect the kind of discomfort that *Shrew* has characteristically provoked in men and why its many revisions since 1594 have repeatedly contrived ways of softening the edges."[53]

As women achieved a more equal social status due to the feminist movements of the twentieth century, reactions to the play changed, with society's new and progressive views on gender impacting upon the critical approach to *The Shrew*; "In short, Kate's taming was no longer as funny as it had been for some readers and spectators; her domination became, in George Bernard Shaw's words 'altogether disgusting to modern sensibility'."[54]

However, this is by no means the prevailing opinion on the play. Director Conall Morrison for example, writing in 2008, argues that "I find it gobsmacking that some people see the play as misogynistic. I believe that it is a moral tale. I believe that it is saying – 'do not be like this' and 'do not do this.' 'These people are objectionable.' By the time you get to the last scene all of the men – including her father are saying – it's amazing how you crushed that person. It's amazing how you lobotomised her. And they're betting on the women as though they are dogs in a race or horses. It's reduced to that. And it's all about money and the level of power. Have you managed to crush Katharina or for Hortensio and Lucentio? Will you be able to control Bianca and the widow? Will you similarly be able to control your proto-shrews? It is so self-evidently repellent that I don't believe for a second that Shakespeare is espousing this. And I don't believe for a second that the man who would be interested in Benedict and Cleopatra and Romeo and Juliet and all these strong lovers would have some misogynist aberration. It's very obviously a satire on this male behaviour and a cautionary tale [...] That's not how he views women and relationships, as demonstrated by the rest of the plays. This is him investigating misogyny, exploring it and animating it and obviously damning it because none of the men come out smelling of roses. When the chips are down they all default to power positions and self-protection and status and the one woman who was a challenge to them, with all with her wit and intellect, they are all gleeful and relieved to see crushed. It's interesting that we can't watch the play because the gender and fault line is still so strong in terms of women's awareness or a liberal going audience, their guilt. We are so quick to rush and judge the play rather than say this is what's really going on."[55]

Induction

A vital component of the misogynistic argument is the Induction, and
its purpose within the larger framework of the play. Critics have
argued about the 'meaning' of the Induction for many years, and
according to Oliver, "it has become orthodoxy to claim to find in the
Induction the same 'theme' as is to be found in both the Bianca and the
Katherine-Petruchio plots of the main play, and to take it for granted
that identity of theme is a merit and 'justifies' the introduction of
Sly."[47] For example, Geoffrey Bullough argues that the three plots
"are all linked in idea because all contain discussion of the relations of
the sexes in marriage."[56] Oliver disagrees with this assessment
however, arguing that "the Sly Induction does not so much announce
the theme of the enclosed stories as establish their *tone*."[57]

This point becomes important in terms of determining the seriousness
of Katherina's final speech. Oliver argues that the Induction is used to
remove the audience from the world of the enclosed plot – to place the
ontological sphere of the Sly story on the same level of reality as the
audience, and to place the ontological sphere of the
Katherina/Petruchio story on a different level of reality, where it will
seem less real, more distant from the reality of the viewing public.
This, he argues, is done so as to ensure the audience does not take the
play literally, that it sees it as a farce; "The drunken tinker may be

H.C. Selous' illustration of Sly and the Hostess in
the Induction; from *The Plays of William
Shakespeare: The Comedies*, edited by Charles
Cowden Clarke and Mary Cowden Clarke (1830)

believed in as one believes in any realistically presented character; but we cannot 'believe' in something that is not
even mildly interesting to him. The play within the play has been presented only after all the preliminaries have
encouraged us to take it as a farce [...] the main purpose of the Induction was to set the tone for the play within the
play – in particular, to present the story of Kate and her sister as none-too-serious comedy put on to divert a drunken
tinker."[58] If one accepts this theory, then the Induction becomes vital to interpretation, as it serves to undermine any
questions of the seriousness of Katherina's closing sentiments. As such, if the Induction is left out of a production of
the play (as it almost always is), a fundamental part of the inherent structure of the whole has been removed. If one
agrees with Oliver, not only does the Induction prove that Katherina's speech is not to be taken seriously, it removes
even the need to ask the question of its seriousness in the first place. In this sense then, the Induction has a vital role
to play in the controversy of the play, especially as it relates to misogyny, as, if Oliver's argument is accepted, it
serves to undercut any charges of misogyny before they can even be formulated – the play is a farce, and that is all it
is, it is not to be taken seriously by the audience, so questions of seriousness simply don't come into play.

Language

Language is not simply a carrier of meaning in the play, but is itself a major theme. Katherina is described as a shrew
because of her sharp tongue and harsh language to those around her, often causing offence. For example,

> Iwis it is not halfway to her heart.
> But if it were, doubt not her care should be
> To comb your noodle with a three-legged stool,
> And paint your face and use you like a fool.

(1.1.61–65)

Petruchio, for his part, attempts to tame her – and thus her language – with rhetoric that specifically undermines her
tempestuous nature;

Say that she rail, why then I'll tell her plain

She sings as sweetly as a nightingale.

Say that she frown, I'll say that she looks as clear

As morning roses newly washed with dew.

Say she be mute and will not speak a word,

Then I'll commend her volubility

And say she uttereth piercing eloquence.

If she do bid me pack, I'll give her thanks,

As though she bid me stay by her a week.

If she deny to wed, I'll crave the day

When I shall ask the banns, and when be marri'd.

(2.1.169–179)

Here Petruchio is specifically attacking the very function of Katherina's language, vowing that no matter what she says, he will purposely misinterpret it, thus undermining the very basis of the linguistic sign, and disrupting the relationship between signifier and signified.

Apart from undermining her language, Petruchio also uses language to objectify her. This is perhaps seen most clearly in Act 3, Scene 2, where Petruchio explains to all present that Katherina is now literally his property:

I will be master of what is mine own.

She is my goods, my chattels, she is my house,

My household stuff, my field, my barn,

My horse, my ox, my ass, my any thing.

(ll.231-234)

Tita French Baumlin also discusses Petruchio's objectification of Katherina, emphasizing the role of his rhetoric in his taming machinations, and using his puns on her name as an example. By referring to Katherina as a "cake" and a "cat" (2.1.185–195), he objectifies her in a more subtle manner than the above quotation.[59] A further notable aspect of Petruchio's taming rhetoric is the repeated comparison of Katherina to animals. In particular, Petruchio is prone to comparing her to a hawk (2.1.8 and 4.1.188–211), often adhering to an overarching hunting metaphor ("My falcon now is sharp and passing empty,/And till she stoop she must not be full-gorged"). Katherina, however, appropriates this method herself, leading to a trading of insults rife with animal imagery, such as in Act 2, Scene 1 (l.194ff.), where she compares Petruchio to a turtle and a crab.

Language itself has thus become a battleground, with Petruchio seemingly emerging as the victor. The final blow is dealt towards the end of the play, in Act 4, Scene 5, when Katherina is made to switch the words *moon* and *sun*, and she acknowledges that she will agree with whatever Petruchio says no matter how absurd:

> And be it the moon, or sun, or what you please;
> And if you please to call it a rush-candle,
> Henceforth I vow it shall be so for me
>
> ...
>
> Sun it is not, when you say it is not,
> And the moon changes even as your mind:
> What you will have it named, even that it is,
> And so it shall be so for Katherine.

(ll.12-15; ll.19-22)

From this point, Katherina's language drastically changes from her earlier vernacular; instead of defying Petruchio and his words, she has apparently succumbed to his rhetoric and accepted that she will use *his* language instead of her own – both Katherina and her language have, seemingly, been tamed.

Petruchio's rhetoric is not reserved solely for Katherina, however. By denying that she is a shrew to others, such as to Baptista in Act 2, Scene 1 (ll.290–298), he effectively changes her reputation. The Katherina of the past (her reputation) is changed as well as the Katherina of the present (her actual self). Katherina's reputation as a shrew is a result of her language and the public perception of her, and Petruchio uses rhetoric to change both.

Julius Caesar Ibbetson's illustration of Act 4, Scene 5 from *The Boydell Shakespeare Prints* (1803)

The important role of language however, is not confined to Petruchio and Katherina. For example, Joel Fineman suggests that the play draws a distinction between male and female language, and further subcategorises the latter into good and bad, epitomised by Bianca and Katherina respectively.[60] Language is also important in relation to the Induction. Here, Sly speaks in prose until he begins to accept his new role as lord, then switching into blank verse and adopting the royal 'we'. Language is also important in relation to Tranio and Lucentio, who appear on stage speaking a highly artificial style of blank verse full of classical and mythological allusions and elaborate metaphors and similes, thus immediately setting them aside from the more straightforward language of the Induction, and alerting the audience to the fact that we are now in an entirely different *milieu*. Another important use of language occurs in relation to the Pedant. When he is speaking as himself, his dialogue has a strong metre, but when he impersonates Vincentio, the metre suddenly begins to limp, thus suggesting he is having difficulty playing this new role. It is examples such as this which illustrate that subtle modulations in a character's speech can in fact have profound implications for that character.

Themes

Female submissiveness

In productions of the play, it is often a director's interpretation of Katherina's final speech that defines the tone of the entire production, such is the importance of this speech and what it says, or implies, about female submission. Many critics have taken the final scene literally, such as G.I. Duthie, who argues that "what Shakespeare emphasises here is the foolishness of trying to destroy order."[61] In a modern society, with relatively egalitarian perspectives on gender, the staging of Shakespeare's original text thus presents a moral dilemma. Two methods are most commonly employed when attempting to perform *The Shrew* while still remaining faithful to the text. The first is to emphasise the play's farcical elements, such as Sly and the metatheatrical nature of the Katherina/Petruchio play, thus suggesting that what happens is not to be taken in any way seriously. The second strategy is to steep the play "in irony, such as Columbia Pictures' 1929 *Taming of the Shrew* where Kate winks as she advocates a woman's submission to her husband."[54]

Critically, four distinct theories have emerged as regards interpretation of the final speech;

"WHAT IS YOUR WILL, SIR, THAT YOU SEND FOR ME?"

Arthur Rackham illustration of Act 5, Scene 2 from *Tales from Shakespeare*, edited by Charles Lamb and Mary Lamb (1890)

1. Katherina's speech is sincere and Petruchio has successfully tamed her (this is how it is presented in the 1983 *BBC Shakespeare* adaptation for example).

2. Katerina's speech is sincere, not because Petruchio has "tamed" her, but because she's come to see that they're well-matched in temperament (this is how it is presented in the 1967 Franco Zeffirelli adaptation).

3. Katherina's speech is ironic, she is not being sincere in her statements, but sarcastic, pretending to have been tamed when in reality, she has completely duped Petruchio.

4. Katherina's speech cannot be taken seriously due to the farcical nature of what has preceded it (this theory emphasises the importance of the Induction).

5. Katherina's speech both satirises gender roles, and also emphasises the social need for wives to be obedient to their husbands.

If one accepts the theory that the speech is sincere, then the final scene must be interpreted literally. As such, the final speech appears to indicate that Katherina willingly accepts her newly submissive role and both comments upon and agrees with the social and physical differences between a husband and wife, emphasising that the role of a wife is to support and obey a husband in all things. Phyllis Rackin, for example, argues that the speech is an emphasis of contemporary Elizabethan social norms. Rackin also sees the language of the speech as politically and sociologically rationalizing the submission of wives to husbands.[62] Some critics believe that as the speech (and, of course, the play) was written by a man, performed by a man, and viewed by a predominantly male audience, what is represented in the speech is the patriarchal ideal of female compliance. Some even view the language of the speech as a completely sincere change of heart; John C. Bean writes that Katherina has been "liberated into the bonds of love" and highlights the speech's mentions of women's warmth and beauty rather than their stereotypical sinfulness.[63]

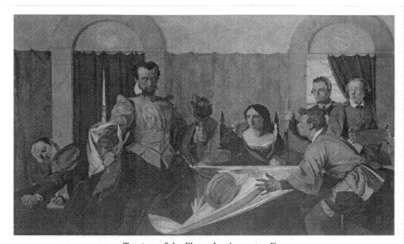

Taming of the Shrew by Augustus Egg

On the other hand, some critics detect irony at play in the final speech. They view the physical description of women as evidence of a more farcical intention when considered alongside both the historical context of the Elizabethan theatre in which female characters are always played by prepubescent boys, and the Induction in which Sly is attracted to the Lord's page disguised as his wife; thus Shakespeare is satirizing gender roles. Harold Bloom, for example, reads Katherina's final speech as ironic, proposing that she is explaining that in reality women control men by appearing to obey them.

The fourth school of thought, that the play is a farce, is based upon attributing a great deal of importance to the Induction. Oliver, for example, argues that in the speech, there is no clear evidence of either seriousness or irony, but instead "this lecture by Kate on the wife's duty to submit is the only fitting climax *to the farce* – and for that very reason it cannot logically be taken seriously, orthodox though the views expressed may be [...] attempting to take the last scene as a continuation of the realistic portrayal of character leads some modern producers to have it played as a kind of private joke between Petruchio and Kate – or even have Petruchio imply that by now he is thoroughly ashamed of himself. It does not, cannot, work. The play has changed key: it has modulated back from something like realistic social comedy to the other, 'broader' kind of entertainment that was foretold by the Induction."[64]

The fifth theory claims that the speech simultaneously belittles women while also explaining the essential and central place of women in relationship with men. The play manages to both lampoon chauvinistic behaviour while simultaneously reaffirming its social validity; it celebrates the quick wit and fiery spirit of its heroine even while revelling in her humiliation.

Nevertheless, despite the formulation of these theories, and others, there is little critical consensus as to the inherent 'meaning' behind Katherina's speech.

Gender relations

One thing that critics do seem to agree on is that gender relations are a hugely important part of the play. Emily Detmer, for example, explains that "rebellious women" were a point of concern for men during the late 16th and early 17th century and thus the presentation of the issue of gender relations, and therefore domestic violence, comes as little surprise.[65] Petruchio's treatment of Katherina may well have the effect of making the domination of one's wife seem tolerable, as long as physical force is not used.[66] The psychological cruelty may be intended to be seen as a more civil way to dominate one's wife, though to a modern audience at least it is viewed as an equally oppressive form of physical abuse.[67]

In the sixteenth century it *was* permissible for men to beat their wives. Rebellious women were a concern for Englishmen because they posed a threat to the patriarchal model of a good household upon which Elizabethan society was built. Some see *The Shrew* as novel because, although it does promote male dominance, it does not condone violence towards women *per se*; the "play's attitude was characteristically Elizabethan and was expressed more humanly by Shakespeare than by some of his sources."[68] However, although

'Williams' cartoon from Caricature Magazine, "Tameing a Shrew; or, Petruchio's Patent Family Bedstead, Gags & Thumscrews" (1815)

Petruchio never strikes Katherina, he does threaten to and he also uses other tactics to physically tame her and thus exert his superiority. Many critics, including Detmer, see this as a modern view on perpetuating male authority and "legitimizing domination as long as it is not physical."[69] George Bernard Shaw was of a similar mind, condemning the play in a letter to *Pall Mall Gazette* as "one vile insult to womanhood and manhood from the first word to the last."[70]

Although Petruchio is not characterised as a violent man, he still embodies the subjugation and objectification of women during the 16th century as manifested in many stories of this nature; "The object of the tale was simply to put the shrew to work, to restore her (frequently through some gruesome form of punishment) to her proper productive place within the household economy".[71] Other critics, such as Natasha Korda, believe that even though Petruchio does not use force to tame Katherina, his actions are still an endorsement of patriarchy; Petruchio makes Katherina his property. Two examples present themselves while Katherina and Petruchio are courting. First, Petruchio offers to marry Katherina and save her from an impending spinsterhood because she has a large dowry. In Elizabethan society, a woman of age was expected to become a wife. Second, Katherina is objectified when they are first introduced; Petruchio wishes to physically judge Katherina and asks her to walk for his observation. Subsequently, he announces that he is pleased with her "princely gait" and that she has passed the 'test'. Indeed, the objectification of Katherina isn't only carried out by Petruchio. For example, Tranio refers to her as "a commodity" (2.1.330).

Male perception of women is also addressed albeit through a comedic situation in the Induction, as the Lord explains to his serving man how to act like a woman:

> With soft low tongue and lowly courtesy
> And say, 'What is't your honour will command
> Wherein your lady and your humble wife
> May show her duty and make known her love?
> And then, with kind embranchments, tempting kisses,
> And with declining head into his bosom,
> Bid him shed tears, as being overjoyed

To see her noble lord restored to health,

Who for this seven years hast esteem'ed him

No better than a poor and loathsome beggar.

And if the boy have not a woman's gift

To rain a shower of commanded tears...

(Induction I.110–21)

This represents the Lord's view of how a woman ought to behave; she should be courteous, humble, loyal, and obedient. He also believes that females are emotional – crying is a "woman's gift". The Induction thus acts as suitable preparation for Katherina's character and her disgust for such stereotyping as well as her rebellion against Elizabethan society's gender values.

Cruelty

Some critics, such as Marvin Bennet Krims, believe that cruelty permeates the entire play, including the Induction, and is therefore a major theme. The Sly frame, with the Lord's spiteful practical joke, is seen to prepare the audience for a play willing to treat cruelty as a comedic matter. A modern audience may find the cruel actions of the main characters comical, but should they consider the situation in reality, they would very likely be appalled. While Katherina displays physical cruelty on stage – in the tying together of her sister's hands, the beating of Hortensio with his lute, and the striking of Petruchio – Petruchio utilises cruelty as a psychological weapon; he purposely misunderstands, dismisses, and humiliates Katherina, while all the time attempting to project his own wishes onto her. Krims believes such treatment makes Katherina's final speech seem a forced camouflage of pain as well as a final humiliation. He believes that cruelty is a more important theme than the more often debated controversy surrounding gender, as the play portrays a broad representation of human cruelty rather than merely cruelty between the sexes.[72]

Money

The theme of money is mentioned numerous times throughout the play, but is especially noticeable in the early stages of the story. Of particular importance is not so much money *per se*, but the motivation money can give to men. For example, when speaking of whether or not someone may ever want to marry Katherina, Hortensio says "Though it pass your patience and mine to endure her loud alarums, why man, there be good fellows in the world, and a man could light on them, would take her with all faults and money enough" (1.1.125–128). Later, Petruchio confirms that Hortensio was right in this assertion;

John Drew as Petruchio

If thou know

one rich enough to be Petruchio's wife-

As wealth is burden of my wooing dance-

Be she as foul as was Florentius' love,

As old as Sibyl, and as curst and shrewd

As Socrates' Xanthippe, or a worse,

She moves me not.

(1.2.65–71)

Grumio is even more explicit a few lines later; "Why give him gold enough and marry him to a puppet or an aglet baby, or an old trot with ne're a tooth in her head, though she have as many diseases as two and fifty horses.

Why, nothing comes amiss, so money comes withal" (1.2.77–80). Furthermore, Petruchio is urged on in his wooing of Katherina by Gremio, Tranio (as Lucentio) and Hortensio, all of whom vow to pay him if he wins her, on top of Baptista's sizable dowry ("After my death, the one half of my lands, and in possession, twenty thousand crowns"). Later, Petruchio corrects Baptista when he speculates that love is all-important;

BAPTISTA
When the special thing is well obtained,
That is, her love; for that is all in all.
PETRUCHIO
Why that is nothing.

(2.1.27–29)

Similarly, Gremio and Tranio literally bid for Bianca. As Baptista says, "'Tis deeds must win the prize, and he of both/That can assure my daughter greatest dower/Shall have my Bianca's love" (2.1.344–346).

Petruchio's decision to marry is based almost wholly on his desire to accrue money; he vows to marry Katherina knowing next to nothing about her, other than the fact that she is a shrew and comes with a sizable dowry. As such, Katherina's dowry is enough to convince Petruchio to marry her; similarly Tranio's (as Lucentio) dower is enough to convince Baptista that Bianca should marry him. Marriage is treated like a business transaction, something which involves great sums of money 'behind the scenes', and is often looked on as a father selling a "commodity" to a suitor. Lucentio and Bianca are the only characters in the play who seem motivated by genuine love, yet even they are only given permission to marry after Vincentio confirms that his family is rich.

Performance

The earliest known performance of the play is recorded in Philip Henslowe's *Diary* on June 13, 1594, as *The Tamynge of A Shrowe* at the Newington Butts Theatre. This could have been either *A Shrew* or *The Shrew*, but as the Admiral's Men and the Lord Chamberlain's Men were sharing the theatre at the time, and as such Shakespeare himself would have been there, scholars tend to assume that it was *The Shrew*. The canonical Shakespearean version was definitely performed at court before King Charles I and Queen Henrietta Maria on November 26, 1633, where it was described as being "liked".[73]

Ada Rehan as Katherine in Augustin Daly's production of *The Taming of the Shrew*, 1887

That the play was successful in Shakespeare's day is evidenced by the existence of *The Woman's Prize, or The Tamer Tamed*, John Fletcher's pseudo-sequel, perhaps written around 1611. Additionally, the title page of the 1631 quarto states that the play had been acted by the King's Men both at the Globe and Blackfriars, and as the King's Men had only began performing at Blackfriars since 1610, it suggests that the play was still popular enough to be performed at least sixteen years after its debut.[74]

In the later half of the 17th century however, performances of *The Taming of the Shrew* greatly decreased compared to many of Shakespeare's other plays, and when performed the play was often an adaptation of Shakespeare's original. In the 18th century, however, there was a revival of the original text. According to Aspinall, "as the 18th century demanded a greater realism and a more authentic Shakespeare, both on stage and in print, a newfound admiration for Petruchio accumulated rapidly."[75]

After over 200 years of adaptations, Shakespeare's original text returned to the stage in 1844 in a Benjamin Webster production, under the direction of J.R. Planché, with Louisa Cranstoun Nisbett as Katherina.[76] In this production, the Induction was included in full, with Sly remaining at the front of the stage after Act 1, Scene 1, and slowly falling asleep over the course of the play. At the end, as the final curtain falls, the Lord's attendants came and carried Sly off-stage.[77] Major productions then took place in 1847 and 1856, both directed by Samuel Phelps. Phelps left Sly on stage until the end of Act 1, having him carried off between Acts. However, although the play did use Shakespeare's original text, Phelps cut much of Katherina's final speech in both productions.

In the United States, Shakespeare's original play returned to the stage in 1887, under the direction of Augustin Daly, with Ada Rehan as Katherina. This production was hugely successful and ran for over 120 performances. However, as with Phelps, whilst the play again used Shakespeare's text, changes were made. Specifically, Daly reorganised Act 4 so that Act 4, Scene 2 comes before Act 4, Scene 1, and Act 4, Scene 4 precedes Act 4, Scene 3. Some of Katherina's final speech was also cut.[78]

"Actor Aleksandr Pavlovich Lensky in the role of Petruchio in *The Taming of the Shrew*" (1883) by Ivan Kramskoi

Lily Brayton was a noted Katherina in the Edwardian era, playing the part in a number of productions, sometimes opposite her husband Oscar Asche, and in the 1907 Oxford University Dramatic Society production opposite Gervais Rentoul. In 1913, Martin Harvey staged a major production at the Prince of Wales Theatre, as did William Bridges Adams in 1919, where the Induction was completely omitted. In 1923, Max Reinhardt included the Induction and concentrated on the farcical nature of the play, presenting it as a type of *Commedia dell'arte*. Barry Jackson also kept the Induction in his 1928 production at the Royal Court Theatre. In 1931, Harcourt Williams used the conclusion of *A Shrew* (in which, after the Petruchio/Katherina story is finished, the Lord returns the now sleeping Sly to the inn where he was found, and who, upon waking up, announces he has had a dream in which he has learned how to tame his own wife). The longest running Broadway production was the 1935 Theatre Guild adaptation with husband and wife Alfred Lunt (who also directed) and Lynn Fontanne, which ran for 129 performances. Presented as a rollicking farce involving circus animals, dwarfs, acrobats and clowns, the production also toured the United States after its run on Broadway. According to some reports, *Kiss Me Kate*, a 1953 filmic adaptation of the Cole Porter musical *Kiss Me, Kate* was inspired by the backstage antics of Lunt and Fontanne, who continually fought both on and off stage, but who always reconciled, both on and off stage.[79]

Notable later 20th century productions include the Hilton Edwards' 1959 production at the Gate Theatre in Dublin, starring Milo O'Shea and Anna Manahan; John Barton's 1960 Royal Shakespeare Company (RSC) production at the Royal Shakespeare Theatre, starring Peter O'Toole and Peggy Ashcroft, and which included both the complete Induction and the epilogue from *A Shrew*; Maurice Daniels's 1961 RSC production at the Aldwych Theatre, starring Derek Godfrey and Vanessa Redgrave; Trevor Nunn's 1969 RSC production also at the Aldwych, starring Michael Williams and Janet Suzman; Clifford Williams' 1973 RSC production at the Royal Shakespeare Theatre, starring Alan Bates and Susan Fleetwood; William Ball's 1976 *Commedia dell'arte*-style production at the American Conservatory Theater; William Leach's 1978 production at the Delacorte Theater, starring Raúl Juliá and Meryl Streep; Barry Kyle's 1982 RSC production at the Barbican Centre, starring Alun Armstrong and Sinéad Cusack; Toby Robertson's 1986 production at the Clwyd Theatr Cymru, starring Timothy Dalton and Vanessa Redgrave; Jonathan Miller's 1987 RSC production at the Barbican, starring Brian Cox and Fiona Shaw; A.J. Antoon's 1990

production at the New York Shakespeare Festival, starring Morgan Freeman and Tracey Ullman, which was set in the old west; Bill Alexander's 1992 RSC production at the Barbican, starring Anton Lesser and Amanda Harris, in which the Induction was rewritten in modern language, and the play-within-the-play featured actors carrying scripts and continually forgetting lines; Delia Taylor's 1999 production at the Clark Street Playhouse, which featured an all female cast, with Diane Manning as Petruchio and Elizabeth Perotti as Katherina; Phyllida Lloyd's 2003 production at the Globe, again with an all female cast, starring Janet McTeer as Petruchio and Kathryn Hunter as Katherina; Gregory Doran's 2003 RSC production at the Royal Shakespeare Theatre, where the play was presented with Fletcher's *The Tamer Tamed* as a two-part piece, with Jasper Britton and Alexandra Gilbreath (playing both Katherina in *The Shrew* and Maria (Petruchio's second wife) in *The Tamer Tamed*); Edward Hall's 2006 Propeller Company production at the Courtyard Theatre, featuring an all-male cast, with Dugald Bruce Lockhart as Petruchio and Simon Scardifield as Katherina; and Conall Morrison's 2008 RSC production at the Royal Shakespeare Theatre, starring Stephen Boxer and Michelle Gomez. Morrison's production included the Induction, but in an unusual way. Stephen Boxer played both Sly and Petruchio, however, the Lord of the play was changed to a Lady, and both she and Katherina were played by Michelle Gomez. The play was then presented as a "*Big Brother* type social experiment"[80] , in which the Lady plays Katherina and allows Sly (as Petruchio) to dominate where the action goes, all the while attempting to gauge how the male mind works under a given set of circumstances.

Two especially well known productions are Michael Bogdanov's 1978 RSC production at the Aldwych, starring Jonathan Pryce and Paola Dionisotti and Gale Edwards's 1995 RSC production at the Royal Shakespeare Theatre, starring Michael Siberry and Josie Lawrence. In the Bogdanov modern dress production, after the house lights go down, nothing happens on stage for a moment. Then, a commotion rises from within the audience. The house lights go on, and a member of the audience (Pryce) is seen to be in altercation with an usherette. After pushing the usherette to the ground, the man then clambered onto the stage, and began to smash parts of the set before being restrained by actors and theatre staff, striped and thrown into a bath. The subsequent play is then presented as his dream, with Pryce doubling as Petruchio. At several performances of the play, audience members were duped into thinking the fight between the man and the usherette was real, and several times, other audience members attempted to intervene in the conflict.[81]

In Edwards' production, the play opens with a woman (Lawrence) dressed in rags trying to get her drunk husband (Siberry) to come home. He refuses, and falls asleep outside the tavern. His wife leaves, whereupon the Lord and the hunting party enter. The 'play within the play' is then presented as Sly's dream, and as such, the main plot is set in a surreal landscape, with Siberry and Lawrence doubling as Petruchio and Katherina. The Shakespeare text is cut at the end of Katherina's speech (which is not delivered seriously, and by which time Petruchio has become bowed with shame). At this point, the play returns back to the Induction setting. Sly has been deeply moved by his dream, and the play ends with him condemning the subjugation of women and embracing his wife.[82]

Petruchio (Michael Siberry) and Grumio (Robin Nedwell) arrive for Petruchio's wedding in Gale Edward's 1995 RSC production at the Royal Shakespeare Theatre

Adaptations

Plays

The first known adaptation of *The Taming of the Shrew* was entitled *The Woman's Prize, or The Tamer Tamed*, a sequel and reply written by John Fletcher around 1611. In Fletcher's play, the recently-widowed Petruchio is remarried to a bride who "tames" him with the help of her friends, driving him from his house and refusing to consummate their marriage until he promises to respect her and endeavours to satisfy her. When the two plays were revived together in 1633, Fletcher's play proved more popular than Shakespeare's. This is evidenced by the fact that on November 28, Fletcher's play was performed for King Charles I and Queen Henrietta Maria. Two nights previously, the Shakespearian text had been performed and was "liked," but Fletcher's was "very well liked."[74]

In the 1660s, *The Shrew* was adapted by John Lacy, an actor for Thomas Killigrew's King's Company, to make it better match with Fletcher's sequel.[83] Originally performed under the title *The Taming of a Shrew*, it was published in 1698 as *Sauny the Scot: or, The Taming of the Shrew: A Comedy*. This version somewhat inconsistently anglicised the character names and recast the play in prose. Most significantly, Lacy expanded the part of Grumio into the title role Sauny (who speaks in a heavy Scottish brogue), which he played himself. Sauny is an irreverent, cynical companion to Petruchio, comically terrified of his master's new bride. Lucentio becomes Winlove, who has travelled from Warwickshire to London to study. Baptista becomes Lord Beaufoy. Petruchio is much more vicious in this version, threatening to whip Katherina if she doesn't marry him, then telling everyone she is dead, and tying her to a bier. The play ends with her thoroughly tamed, and with a dance. The Induction was also removed. Lacy's work premiered at the Theatre Royal, Drury Lane in 1667. Samuel Pepys saw Lacy's adaptation on April 9, 1667 and again on November 1, enjoying it on both occasions. The play was popular enough that it was still being performed as late as 1732, when it was staged at Goodman's Fields Theatre.[84]

Another adaptation was Christopher Bullock's *Cobbler of Preston*, which was staged at Lincoln's Inn Fields in 1715, and which concentrated on the Induction and omitted entirely the Petruchio/Katherina story.

Marie Thérèse Kemble as Catharine in David Garrick's *Catharine and Petruchio*

The most successful adaptation was David Garrick's *Catharine and Petruchio,* which was introduced in 1754 and dominated the stage for almost two centuries, with Shakespeare's play not returning until 1844 in England and 1887 in the United States, although Garrick's version was still being performed as late as 1879, when Herbert Beerbohm Tree staged it. In Garrick's version, the subplot is entirely omitted, Bianca is married to Hortensio when the play opens. Consequently, it is not a full length play, and was often performed with Garrick's shorter version of *The Winter's Tale.* Much of Shakespeare's dialogue is reproduced verbatim. Much of the plot is also similar; Petruchio vows to marry Catharine before he has even seen her, she smashes a lute over the music tutor's head, Baptista fears no one will ever want to marry her; the wedding scene is identical, as is the scene where Grumio teases her with food; the haberdasher and tailor scene is very similar; the sun and moon conversation, and the introduction of Vincentio are both taken from Shakespeare. At the end, however, there is no wager. Catharine makes her speech to Bianca, and Petruchio tells her,

> Kiss me Kate, and since thou art become
> So prudent, kind, and dutiful a Wife,

Petruchio here shall doff the lordly Husband;
An honest Mark, which I throw off with Pleasure.
Far hence all Rudeness, Wilfulness, and Noise,
And be our future Lives one gentle Stream
Of mutual Love, Compliance and Regard.

The play ends with Catharine stating that she is unworthy of Petruchio's love. Garrick's play was a huge success, and major productions took place in the United States in 1754 (with Hannah Pritchard as Catharine), in 1788 (with Sarah Siddons and John Philip Kemble), in 1810 (again with Kemble and his real life wife, Priscilla Hopkins Brereton), and in 1842 (with William Charles Macready as Petruchio).[85]

A more recent adaptation is Charles Marowitz' acclaimed 1975 production *The Shrew,* which was performed at The Studio in the Sydney Opera House. Refashioned as a gothic tale, the adaptation removed all the comedy, and instead concentrated on examining the themes of sadism and brain washing. Petruchio was played by Stuart Campbell as a savage and vicious misogynist, who rapes and beats Katherina (Elaine Hudson), ultimately driving her mad. At the end of the play, as Katherina delivers her speech, she does so as if she has learned it, without any emotion or inflection. In this version, the happy ending of Shakespeare's play thus takes on a disturbing irony. Due to the extreme nature of the performance, the play divided critics, but those who did enjoy it celebrated it as a genuinely original and relevant treatment of a difficult Shakespeare text.[86]

Another recent adaptation came in 2008, when Laurentian University professor Dr. Ian Maclennan wrote *The Squaddies Shrew.* In this version, the play is set within an army barracks, performed by 6 males as soldiers or "Squaddies", with the cast playing the roles of multiple characters throughout the play.[87]

Opera

The earliest operatic adaptation of the play was James Worsdale's ballad opera *A Cure for a Scold*, which was performed at Drury Lane in 1735, and was itself an adaptation of Lacy's *Sauny the Scot*. Lucentio becomes Gainlove, Petruchio is Manly, Katherina becomes Margaret (nicknamed Peg) and Baptista is Sir William Worthy. At the end, there is no wager. Instead, Peg pretends she is dying, and as Petruchio runs for a doctor, Peg reveals that she is fine, and that she has been tamed.

In 1795 the Spanish composer Vicente Martín y Soler wrote *La capricciosa corretta*, with libretto by Lorenzo Da Ponte, partly adapted from the play. It was first performed in London.

Another operatic version came in 1828, when Frederic Reynolds adapted Garrick's *Catherine and Petruchio*. Starring Henry Irving and Ellen Terry, the play was staged at Drury Lane, but it was not successful, and closed after only a few performances.[88]

In 1874, Hermann Goetz created *Der Widerspänstigen Zähmung*, a comic opera first performed at the National Theatre Mannheim in Germany. The libretto was by Joseph Widmann and Goetz, and the opera featured Eduard Schlosser as Petruchio (baritone) and Ottilie Ottiker as Katherina (soprano).

In 1927, Ermanno Wolf-Ferrari wrote a verismo opera called *Sly, or The Legend of the Sleeper Awoken*, based on the prologue of the play, with a libretto by Giovacchino Forzano. First performed at La Scala in Milan, the opera starred Aureliano Pertile as Sly (tenor) and Mercedes Llopart as Dolly (soprano).

In 1953, Vittorio Giannini adapted the play into an opera buffa, with a libretto by Giannini and Dorothy Fee.

Musicals

The earliest musical adaptation of the play was Charles Johnson's *Cobbler of Preston* (1716), which was performed at Drury Lane, and which concentrated on the Induction, omitting entirely the Petruchio/Katherina story.

The most famous musical adaptation is Cole Porter's *Kiss Me, Kate* (1948). Porter wrote the music and lyrics. The book was written by Samuel and Bella Spewack. The musical opened on Broadway at the New Century Theatre, where it ran for nineteen months before transferring to the Shubert Theatre and running for a total of 1,077 performances. Directed by John C. Wilson with choreography by Hanya Holm, it starred Alfred Drake and Patricia Morison. As well as being a box office hit, the musical was also a critical success, winning five Tony Awards including Best Musical, Best Original Score and Best Author. Since its debut, it has been revived twice: in 1999 at the Martin Beck Theatre on Broadway (which won five Tony Awards including Best Revival of a Musical), and in 2007 at the Teatro delle Celebrazioni in Bologna, Italy. Both the original Broadway production and the 1999 revival also played the West End: at the Coliseum Theatre (1951) and at the Victoria Palace Theatre (2001).

Another musical adaptation is the ballet by John Cranko (1969), which played at Staatstheater Stuttgart. Performed by the Stuttgart Ballet, with music by the Stuttgart Radio Symphony Orchestra, it was directed by Bernard Kontarsky, and starred Richard Cragun and Marcia Haydee.

Film

The Taming of the Shrew has been adapted for cinema many times. The earliest known adaptation is the eleven minute 1908 silent version directed by D.W. Griffith and starring Arthur V. Johnson and Florence Lawrence. The next production was the twelve minute 1911 silent version directed by F.R. Benson, and starring Benson himself and his wife Constance Benson. A filmed extract from Benson's Shakespeare Memorial Theatre production, the film presented a short pantomime version of the play, with pieces of Shakespeare's original text used as intertitles throughout.[89] This film is now believed lost. Another silent version made in 1911 was the French production *La mégère apprivoisée*, directed by Henri Desfontaines and starring Romauld Joubé and Cécile Didier. A 1913 Italian version, *La bisbetica domata*, was directed by Arrigo Frusta and starred Eleuterio Rodolfi and Gigetta Morano (*La bisbetica domata* was also the name under which the 1967 Franco Zeffirelli version would be released in Italy).

Another adaptation took place in 1915. The scene where Petruchio and Katherina first meet was shot using a primitive sound process known as Voxograph, where the actors spoke the complete text during filming. Then, when the film was played at the theatre, "the same actors, one at each side of the screen but unseen, repeated the words in what was supposed to be synchronisation. It was expected that the operator, after rehearsal, would be able to project the film so that picture and voice would jibe."[90]

The first American cinematic adaptation of the play was the 1915 film *The Iron Strain* (released in the UK in 1917 under the title *The Modern Taming of the Shrew*).[91] Written by C. Gardner Sullivan and directed by Reginald Barker, the film tells of the love affair between high society girl Octavia van Ness (Enid Markey) and the loutish Chuck Hemingway (Dustin Farnum). Octavia lives in New York with her grandfather (Charles K. French), a retired mining entrepreneur, but fearing that she is not getting enough real life experience, he sends her to Alaska. There she meets Hemingway, a man unconcerned with social niceties. She instantly dislikes him, but he decides he is going to woo her, simply because it seems impossible he would be able to do so. Octavia believes Hemingway is her social inferior and will not have anything to do with him. But with the grandfather's blessing, Hemingway kidnaps and forcibly marries Octavia. They maintain a chaste relationship with Octavia reluctantly keeping house for Hemingway, until he becomes attracted to cabaret star Kitty Molloy (Louise Glaum). Octavia finds herself becoming jealous and realises that she loved him all along. She successfully woos him away from Kitty, and at the end of the film, it is revealed that he is actually a wealthy prospector and very much of her class. The film features no intertitles from the play text, although it is credited as being based on Shakespeare's play.

Another loose silent American adaptation came in 1919, under the title *Impossible Catherine*. Written by Frank S. Beresford and directed by John B. O'Brien, the film tells the story of John Henry Jackson (William B. Davidson) and Catherine Kimberly (Virginia Pearson). Catherine is the daughter of a wealthy banker but she is much too wild for him to control. At a Yale University dinner, she meets Jackson, who, having just read *The Taming of the Shrew*, decides that he can tame her. Imprisoning her on his airplane, she eventually agrees to marry him, and which point he abducts her and takes her to a remote log cabin where he imposes domestic duties on her. Distraught at her situation, Catherine hires a local man to attack Jackson so she can escape, but the man is a friend of Jackson's and instead he starts to beat Catherine. At this point, Jackson comes to her aid, and is wounded when saving her. Upon realising he put himself at risk for her, Catherine realises she has fallen in love with him, and they happily return to the cabin together.

The next significant film version was the twenty-two minute silent version made in 1923. Directed by Edwin J. Collins, adapted by Eliot Stannard, and starring Lauderdale Maitland and Dacia Deane, it was one of a series of forty minute adaptations of classic texts released under the banner *Gems of Literature*.[92]

The first sound version on film is the sixty-eight minute 1929 adaptation starring Mary Pickford and Douglas Fairbanks, with "additional dialogue by Sam Taylor" (who also directed). This version was originally shot as a silent film, with all the dialogue and sound effects added at a later stage.[93] This version of the film is primarily known for how Pickford delivers Katherina's last speech. As she moves though the litany of reasons why a woman should obey her husband, she faces the camera and winks toward Bianca (Dorothea Jordan), unseen by Petruchio. Bianca smiles in silent communication with Katherina, thus acknowledging that Katherina has not been tamed at all.

The 1967 film adaptation directed by Franco Zeffirelli and starring Elizabeth Taylor and Richard Burton is the most widely seen version of the play. This version omits the Induction, and heavily cuts the Bianca subplot, spending much more time with Petruchio and Katherina. Dialogue is cut from every scene of the play, and lines are moved from one scene to another throughout. Some dialogue is also changed (for example, Katherina's "Is it your will to make a stale of me amongst these mates?" is changed to "Is it your will to make a whore of me amongst these mates?"). The bidding scene from Act 2, Scene 1 is almost entirely absent, as is the whole of Act 3, Scene 1.

Elizabeth Taylor and Richard Burton in the 1967 Franco Zeffirelli adaptation

The next significant film version of the play was in 2004, when Roberto Lione wrote and directed an animated version of the play called *Kate-La bisbetica domata*. Featuring the voices of Neri Marcorè and Daniela Cavallini, the film used standard animation techniques, as well as stop motion and crude crayon drawings. In the film, Petruchio is ruined by gambling and plans to get out of debt by marrying a rich woman – Kate, the daughter of a successful industrialist (Carlo Reali). Kate however is a fiercely independent woman and doesn't tolerate any kind of masculine posturing. Nevertheless, she agrees to court Petruchio as she is curious to see how things turn out. After a stormy courtship (which makes up the majority of the film), Kate finally decides to marry Petruchio. However, prior to their wedding, she has to protect him from the Mafia boss, Don Sarago (Pino Amendola), to whom he owes money. Upon her successful completion of this task, Petruchio realises that he has found a good woman, and he vows to be obedient to her for the rest of their lives.

There have been many international adaptations of the play throughout the 20th century. For example, the 1942 Italian adaptation *La bisbetica domata*, directed by Ferdinando Maria Poggioli; the 1943 Hungarian adaptation *Makacs Kata* [94], directed by Viktor Bánky; the 1956 Spanish adaptation *La fiercilla domada*, directed by Antonio Román; the 1961 Russian adaptation *Ukroshchenie stroptivoy*, directed by Sergei Kolosov; the 1962 Egyptian adaptation *Ah min hawaa*, directed by Fatin Abdel Wahab; and the 1980 Italian comedy *Il Bisbetico Domato* [95], directed by Franco Castellano and Giuseppe Moccia.

Other film versions (which are loose adaptations as opposed to straight translations from stage to screen) include: the 1933 *You Made Me Love You* [96], written by Frank Launder and directed by Monty Banks; the 1938 *Second Best Bed* [97], written by Ben Travers and directed by Tom Walls; the 1963 western *McLintock!*, written by James Edward Grant, directed by Andrew McLaglen and starring John Wayne and Maureen O'Hara; the 1999 teen movie *10 Things I Hate About You*, written by Kirsten Smith and Karen McCullah Lutz, directed by Gil Junger and starring Julia Stiles as Kat Stratford (Katherina) and Heath Ledger as Patrick Verona (Petruchio); and the 2003 comedy *Deliver Us from Eva*, written by James Iver Mattson and B.E. Brauner and directed by Gary Hardwick.

Television

The earliest screening of the play is often thought to have been broadcast on BBC 1 in 1939, directed by Dallas Bower and starring Austin Trevor and Margaretta Scott. However, this was an adaptation of Garrick's *Catherine and Petruchio*, not Shakespeare's original text.

The first television performance of the Shakespearean text was broadcast in the United States on CBS in 1950 as part of the *Westinghouse Studio One* series. A heavily edited sixty minute performance, written by Worthington Miner and directed by Paul Nickell, it starred Charlton Heston and Lisa Kirk. A BBC 1 adaptation was screened in 1952 as part of the *BBC Sunday-Night Theatre* series, directed by Desmond Davis and starring Stanley Baker and Margaret Johnston. In 1956, another American adaptation aired as part of NBC's *Hallmark Hall of Fame* series. Adapted by Agnes Nixon and directed by George Schaefer, starring Maurice Evans (who also produced) and Lilli Palmer. This particular adaptation was heavily influenced by the *commedia dell'arte* tradition, with a bare stage featuring clowns carrying props as required, whilst the first meeting of Katherina and Petruchio takes plays in a boxing ring. Also in America in 1976, PBS broadcast a videotaped version of William Ball's 1976 stage production for their *Great Performances* series starring Marc Singer and Fredi Olster. This production was also set against a *commedia dell'arte* backdrop. In 1982, CBC broadcast Peter Dews's production from the Stratford Shakespeare Festival in Ontario. Directed for television by Norman Campbell, it starred Len Cariou and Sharry Flett.

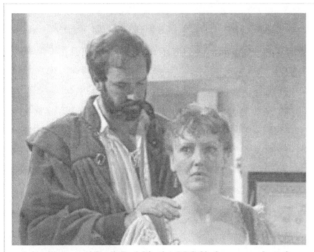

John Cleese and Sarah Badel in the *BBC Shakespeare* adaptation

In 1980, the BBC produced a version of the play for their *BBC Shakespeare* series, directed by Jonathan Miller and starring John Cleese and Sarah Badel. In this adaptation, the induction and all subsequent references to Sly are absent, but apart from that, it is almost word-for-word the 1623 First Folio text. Minor differences include; the omission of Tranio's "Well said, master. Mum, and gaze your fill" (1.1.74) and Gremio's "A proper stripling and an amorous" (1.2.141). Additionally, much of the conversation between Grumio and Curtis at the start of Act 4, Scene 1 is absent, as is the brief conversation between Biondello and Lucentio which opens Act 5, Scene 1. Perhaps most significantly, Act 5, Scene 2 ends differently to the play. The last line spoken is Petruchio's "We three are married, but you two are sped;" thus omitting Petruchio's comment to Lucentio "'Twas I won the wager, though you hit the white,/And being a winner, God give you good night," as well as Hortensio's line, "Now go thy ways, thou has tamed a curst shrew," and Lucentio's closing statement, "'Tis a wonder, by your leave, she will be tamed so." Additionally, Petruchio and Katherina do not leave the banquet prior to the end of the play, but remain, and engage in a song with all present.

In 1982, the play inaugurated the Channel 4 series *Shakespeare Lives!* [98], where it was used as the basis of a two-part National Theatre workshop run by Michael Bogdanov, and starring Daniel Massey and Suzanne Bertish. The main theme of the workshop was whether or not the play demeans women, or simply depicts how they are demeaned.

In 1986, the television series *Moonlighting* produced an episode entitled "Atomic Shakespeare", written by Ron Osborn and Jeff Reno (with a writing credit for William 'Budd' Shakespeare), and directed by Will Mackenzie. The episode recast the show's main characters in a self-referential comedic parody of *The Taming of the Shrew*. The episode opens with a boy who is annoyed that he has to read *The Shrew* for his homework, rather than watching his favourite programme, *Moonlighting* itself. He goes to his room and begins reading, and the episode then takes place in his mind as he imagines the members of the cast of *Moonlighting* in an adaptation of the play itself (Bruce Willis plays Petruchio, Cybill Shepherd plays Katherina).

In 1994, the *Shakespeare: The Animated Tales* series screened a version of the play which adapted the end of *A Shrew* to round out the Induction, but it also added a new element. After Sly announces he now knows how to tame a shrew, he proudly walks back into the tavern to confront the hostess, but almost immediately, he is flung back out, in exactly the same way as the episode began. Directed by Aida Ziablikova and adapted from Shakespeare by Leon Garfield, it was voiced by Nigel Le Vaillant and Amanda Root.

The 2000 Brazilian soap opera *O Cravo e a Rosa* was also based on the play (this title means "The Carnation and the Rose" and comes from a children's song about a couple of engaged flowers who had a serious "fight" – which, in Portuguese, may mean either an awful argument or some physical confrontation).

In 2002, the television series *One on One* produced an episode entitled "Tame me, I'm a Shrew". Written by Kenny Buford and directed by Dana De Vally Piazza the episode depicts the main character, Breanna (Kyla Pratt) getting the leading part in a school performance of *The Taming Of The Shrew*. Upon finding Shakespeare's language difficult and out of date however, she decides to liven it up into a rap version. However, she allows her ego to get the better of her, and unconsciously attempts to take over the production from the director, who ultimately fires her, and hires her best friend for the role instead.

In 2005, BBC One broadcast an adaptation for the *ShakespeaRe-Told* series, written by Sally Wainwright and directed by Dave Richards, which set the story in modern-day Britain, with Katherine (played by Shirley Henderson) as an abrasive career politician who is told she must find a husband as a public relations exercise. Meanwhile, her sister Bianca (Jaime Murray) has fallen in love with Lucentio (Santiago Cabrera) and wants to marry him, but Bianca's manager (Simon Chandler) has fallen in love with her and he wants to marry her. As such, to put him off, Bianca announces that she will not marry until her sister is married (as she believes Katherine will never marry). As such, the manager arranges a meeting between his friend Petruchio (Rufus Sewell) and Katherine. The manager bets Petruchio that he will not be able to woo Katherine, so, determined to prove him wrong, Petruchio sets out to win her over. Their courtship goes well until he shows up at the wedding drunk...and dressed as a woman, starting their marriage out tempestuously. Katherine's climactic speech is triggered when Bianca is surprised and annoyed that Lucentio refuses to sign a pre-nuptial agreement. This version still has Katherine stating it is a woman's duty to love and obey her husband, but with the requirement that he do precisely the same for her.

In 2009, ABC Family adapted the play for a new television situation comedy entitled *10 Things I Hate About You*, stretching out and modernizing the plot of the 1999 film. It starred Lindsey Shaw as Kat Stratford, Meaghan Jette Martin as Bianca Stratford, Larry Miller as Dr. Walter Stratford (reprising his role from the film) and Ethan Peck as Patrick Verona. 10 episodes were produced for the first season. A second season of 10 episodes aired in March 2010.

There have also been numerous international adaptations over the years. For example, the 1961 French adaptation *La mégère approvoisée*, directed by Pierre Badel, which aired on TF1; the 1971 Polish adaptation *Poskromienie Zlosnicy*, directed by Zygmunt Hubner, which aired on TVP1; the 1974 German adaptation *Der widerspenstigen zähmung*, directed by Otto Schenk, which aired on Das Erste; the 1975 Dutch adaptation *De getemde feeks*, directed by Robert Lussac and Senne Rouffaer, which aired on KRO; another Dutch production, from 1990, under the same name, directed by Berend Boudewijn and Dirk Tanghe, which also aired on KRO; and the 1993 Polish adaptation *Poskromienie zlosnicy*, directed by Jerzy Stuhr and Stanislaw Zajaczkowski, which aired on TVP1.

Radio

The play has been adapted for radio many times, especially in the early 20th century.[99] In 1924, extracts were broadcast on BBC Radio 1, performed by the Cardiff Station Repertory Company as the eight episode of a series of programs showcasing Shakespeare's plays, entitled *Shakespeare Night*. Extracts were also broadcast in 1925 as part of *Shakespeare: Scene and Story*, with William Charles Macready and Edna Godfrey-Turner, and in 1926 as part of *Shakespeare's Heroines*, with Edmund Willard and Madge Titheradge. In 1927, a forty-three minute truncated version of the play written by Dulcima Glasby was broadcast on Radio 1, with Barbara Couper and Ian Fleming. Another Glasby adaptation aired in 1932 on BBC National Programme, this time running eighty-five minutes, and again starring Couper. Petruchio was played by Francis James. In 1935, a Peter Creswell adaptation aired on National Programme, under the title *The Witty and pleasant conceited Comedy called The Taming of the Shrew*, starring Godfrey Tearle and Mary Hinton. Another Creswell adaptation aired on BBC Home Service in 1941, again with Tearle, and with Katherina played by Fay Compton. In 1947, BBC Light Programme aired an episode of their *Theatre Programme* which featured an analysis of the play by Ralph Richardson and scenes recorded from John Burrell's Edinburgh Festival production starring Trevor Howard and Patricia Burke. In 1954, a full-length version of the play aired on BBC Home Service, directed and adapted for radio by Peter Watts, and starring Joseph O'Connor and Mary Wimbush. BBC Radio 4 aired another full length broadcast in 1973 as part of their *Monday Night Theatre* series, directed by Ian Cotterell and starring Paul Daneman and Fenella Fielding. In 1989, BBC Radio 3 aired an adaptation of the play directed by Jeremy Mortimer and starring Bob Peck and Cheryl Campbell. In 2000, Radio 4 aired another full-length production as part of their *Shakespeare for the New Millennium* series, directed by Melanie Harris and starring Gerard McSorley and Ruth Mitchell.

In America, the first major radio production was in 1937 on NBC Radio, when John Barrymore adapted the play into a forty-five minute piece, starring Barrymore himself and Elaine Barrie. Another 1937 adaptation was a sixty minute piece by Gilbert Seldes, with Edward G. Robinson and Frieda Inescort, which aired on CBS Radio. In 1940, a thirty minute musical version of the play written by Joseph Gottlieb and Irvin Graham aired on CBS as part of their *Columbia Workshop* series, with Carleton Young and Nan Sunderland. In 1941, NBC Blue aired a sixty minute adaptation of the play as part of their *Great Plays* series, written by Ranald MacDougall and directed by Charles Warburton, starring Herbert Rudley and Grace Coppin. ABC Radio aired an adaptation in 1949, directed by Homer Fickett and starring Burgess Meredith and Joyce Redman. In 1953, NBC broadcast an adaptation of the play by Philip Hanson, based on William Dawkins' production for the Oregon Shakespeare Festival. Directed by Andrew C. Love, the cast list has been lost, but it is known that George Peppard appeared in the play, probably as Petruchio, although that cannot be categorically determined. In 1960, NBC Red aired a sixty minute version adapted by Carl Ritchie from Robert Loper's stage production for the Oregon Shakespeare Festival, starring Gerard Larson and Ann Hackney.

References

Notes

All references to *The Taming of the Shrew*, unless otherwise specified, are taken from the Oxford Shakespeare (Oliver, 1982), which is based on the 1623 First Folio. Under this referencing system, 1.2.51 means Act 1, Scene 2, line 51.

[1] Thompson (1984: 10)

[2] Juan Manuel, *Libro de los ejemplos del conde Lucanor y de Patronio, Exemplo XXXVº – De lo que contesçió a un mançebo que casó con una muger muy fuerte et muy brava*.

[3] Shroeder (1959: 252)

[4] Hosley (1964: 289–308)

[5] Complete Text of *A Merry Jest* (http://ebooks.gutenberg.us/Renascence_Editions/jest.html)

[6] Brunvand (1966: 345-359)

[7] Tolman (1890: 201-278)

[8] Halliday (1964: 181, 483)

[9] See Morris (1981: 12-50), Oliver (1982: 22–34), and Miller (1998: 1-58). (From this point forward, *The Taming of a Shrew* will be referred to as *A Shrew*; *The Taming of the Shrew* as *The Shrew*)

[10] Evans (1974: 106)

[11] Oliver (1982: 31–33)

[12] Thompson (1984: 4-9)

[13] Miller (1998: 31-34)

[14] Oliver (1982: 14)

[15] See W.W. Greg *The Shakespeare First Folio* (1955) and Morris (1981: 13)

[16] Wentersdorf (1978: 202)

[17]   See esp. Houk (1942: 1009-1038) and Duthie (1943: 337–356). See also Morris (1981: 16-24) and Oliver (1982: 24)

[18]   See esp. Hickson (1850: 345-347), Alexander (1926) and Alexander (1969: 111-116). See also Morris (1981: 14-16) and Oliver (1982: 31-33)

[19]   See esp. Shroeder (1958: 424-442). See also Morris (1981: 24-26) and Evans (1974: 104-107)

[20]   See Duthie (1943: 337–356) and Oliver (1982: 28-34)

[21]   See Miller (1998: 1-58)

[22]   Oliver (1982: 19)

[23]   Hickson (1850: 345-347)

[24]   Alexander (1926)

[25]   Chambers (1930: 372)

[26]   Kirschbaum (1938: 43)

[27]   Miller (1998: ix)

[28]   Miller (1998: 6)

[29]   Duthie (1943: 356)

[30]   Shroeder (1958: 424-442)

[31]   Hosley (1964: 302)

[32]   The complex arguments of Hickson, Alexander, Chambers, Kirschbaum, Houk, Duthie, Shroeder and Hosley are summarised in detail in Morris (1981: 12-50) and in Miller (1998: 1-58)

[33]   Morris (1981: 45)

[34]   Marcus (1991: 172)

[35]   Wentersdorf (1978: 214)

[36]   Makaryk (1982: 286)

[37]   Muir (2005: 28)

[38]   Miller (1998: 10)

[39]   Miller (1991: 26-27)

[40]   Miller (1998: 27)

[41]   Miller (1998: 9)

[42]   Miller (1998: 12)

[43]   Miller (1998: 28)

[44]   *The New Shakespeare (1955)*

[45]   *The Shakespeare First Folio* (1955)

[46]   *The Arden Shakespeare, Second Series* (1981)

[47]   Oliver (1982: 3–9)

[48]   Oliver (1982: 27)

[49]   Davies (1995: 26)

[50]   Aspinall (2001: 3)

[51]   Aspinall (2001: 12)

[52]   Bate & Rasmussen (2007: 527)

[53]   Boose (1991: 179)

[54]   Aspinall (2001: 30)

[55]   RSC downloads: Conall Morrison on directing *The Taming of the Shrew* (http://www.rsc.org.uk/downloads/pdfs/Conall_Morrison_QA.pdf) (link no longer active)

[56]   Bullough (1975: 58)

[57]   Oliver (1982: 39)

[58]   Oliver (1982: 40–42)

[59]   Baumlin (1989: 237–257)

[60]   Fineman (2004: 399–416)

[61]   Duthie (1951: 59)

[62]   Rackin (2005)

[63]   Bean (1980: 65–78)

[64]   Oliver (1982: 57)

[65]   Detmer (1997: 273)

[66]   Detmer (1997: 247)

[67]   Detmer (1997: 275)

[68]   West (1974: 65)

[69]   Detmer (1997: 274)

[70]   The letter, dated June 8, 1888, is reproduced in full in Archibald Henderson, *George Bernard Shaw: His Life and Works, a Critical Biography* (Montana: Kessinger, 2004), 196

[71]   Detmer (1997: 110)

[72] Krims (2006: 51–59)

[73] Bawcutt (1996: 185)

[74] Oliver (1982: 64)

[75] Aspinall (2001: 26)

[76] Halliday (1964: 483–84)

[77] Oliver (1982:70)

[78] Oliver (1982: 71)

[79] 'Performance History', RSC Online Play Guide (http://www.rsc.org.uk/tame/about/performance.html)(2003) (link no longer active)

[80] RSC 'Exploring Shakespeare', Play Guide (http://www.rsc.org.uk/explore/multimedia/transcripts/tam_0804_01_transcript.pdf) (link
no longer active) [81]
     Miller (1998: 52)

[82] Miller (1998: 53–55)

[83] Dobson (1995: 23)

[84] Oliver (1982: 66)

[85] All information regarding *Catharine and Petruchio* is taken from Oliver (1982: 67–70)

[86] Thompson (2003: 24)

[87] Laurentian University English Department (http://www.laurentian.ca/Laurentian/Home/Departments/Thorneloe+University/Theatre+
     Arts/Events/2008-02-04+Squaddies+Shrew.htm?Laurentian_Lang=en-CA)

[88] Oliver (1982: 70)

[89] Michael Brooke, 'ScreenOnline: *The Taming of the Shrew* On Screen' (http://www.screenonline.org.uk/tv/id/564739/index.html)

[90] Robert Hamilton Ball. *Shakespeare on Silent Film: A Strange Eventful History* (London: George Allen & Unwin, 1968), 359

[91] *British Universities Film & Video Council* (http://bufvc.ac.uk/shakespeare/index.php/title/AV68593)

[92] Michael Brooke, 'ScreenOnline: *The Taming of the Shrew* (1923)' (http://www.screenonline.org.uk/film/id/1054406/index.html)

[93] Kenneth S. Rothwell, 'The Age of Sound' (2002) (http://internetshakespeare.uvic.ca/Theater/spotlight/2005-10/filmintro3.html)

[94] http://www.imdb.com/title/tt0134807/

[95] http://www.imdb.com/title/tt0080439

[96] http://www.imdb.com/title/tt0024794/

[97] http://www.imdb.com/title/tt0140539/

[98] http://www.imdb.com/title/tt0446637/

[99] Unless otherwise noted, all information in this section comes from the *British Universities Film and Video Council* (http://bufvc.ac.uk/
     shakespeare/search.php?q=&date_start=&date_end=&title_format=&play=30&sort=date_asc&page_size=50)

Editions of *The Taming of the Shrew*

- Bate, Jonathan and Rasmussen, Eric (eds.) *The RSC Shakespeare: The Complete Works* (London: Macmillan, 2007)

- Bond, R. Warwick (ed.) *The Taming of the Shrew* (The Arden Shakespeare, 1st Series; London: Arden, 1904)

- Evans, G. Blakemore (ed.) *The Riverside Shakespeare* (Boston: Houghton Mifflin, 1974; 2nd edn., 1997)

- Greenblatt, Stephen; Cohen, Walter; Howard, Jean E. and Maus, Katharine Eisaman (eds.) *The Norton Shakespeare: Based on the Oxford Shakespeare* (London: Norton, 1997; 2nd edn. 2008)

- Heilman, Robert B. (ed.) *The Taming of the Shrew* (Signet Classic Shakespeare; New York: Signet, 1966; revised edition, 1986; 2nd revised edition 1999)

- Hibbard, G.R. (ed.) *The Taming of the Shrew* (The New Penguin Shakespeare; London: Penguin, 1968; revised edition 1995)

- Hodgdon, Barbara (ed.) *The Taming of the Shrew* (The Arden Shakespeare, 3rd Series; London: Arden, 2010)

- Hosley, Richard (ed.) *The Taming of the Shrew* (The Pelican Shakespeare; London, Penguin, 1964; revised edition 1978)

- Kidnie, Margaret Jane (ed.) *The Taming of the Shrew* (The New Penguin Shakespeare, 2nd edition; London: Penguin, 2006)

- Oliver, H.J. (ed.) *The Taming of the Shrew* (The Oxford Shakespeare: Oxford: Oxford University Press, 1982)

- Miller, Stephen Roy (ed.) *The Taming of a Shrew: The 1594 Quarto* (The New Cambridge Shakespeare; Cambridge: Cambridge University Press, 1998)

- Morris, Brian (ed.) *The Taming of the Shrew* (The Arden Shakespeare, 2nd Series; London: Arden, 1981)

- Orgel, Stephen (ed.) *The Taming of the Shrew* (The Pelican Shakespeare, 2nd edition; London, Penguin, 2000)

- Quiller-Couch, Arthur and Wilson, John Dover (eds.) *The Taming of the Shrew* (The New Shakespeare; Cambridge: Cambridge University Press, 1928; 2nd edn. edited by only Dover Wilson, 1953)
- Thompson, Ann (ed.) *The Taming of the Shrew* (The New Cambridge Shakespeare; Cambridge: Cambridge University Press, 1984; 2nd edn. 2003)
- Wells, Stanley; Taylor, Gary; Jowett, John and Montgomery, William (eds.) *The Oxford Shakespeare: The Complete Works* (Oxford: Oxford University Press, 1986; 2nd edn., 2005)
- Werstine, Paul and Mowat, Barbara A. (eds.) *The Taming of the Shrew* (Folger Shakespeare Library; Washington: Simon & Schuster, 2004)

Secondary Sources

- Addison-Roberts, Jeanne. "Horses and Hermaphrodites: Metamorphoses in *The Taming of the Shrew*", *Shakespeare Quarterly*, 34:2 (Summer, 1983), 159–171
- Alexander, Peter. "*The Taming of the Shrew*", *The Times Literary Supplement*, (16 September 1926)
- ———. "The Original Ending of *The Taming of the Shrew*", *Shakespeare Quarterly*, 20:1 (Spring 1969), 111-116
- Aspinall. Dana E. (ed.) *The Taming of the Shrew: Critical Essays* (London: Routledge, 2001)
- Bawcutt, N.S. (ed.) *The Control and Censorship of Caroline Drama: The Records of Sir Henry Herbert, Master of the Revels, 1623–73* (Oxford: Clarendon Press, 1996)
- Baumlin, Tita French. "Petruchio the Sophist and Language as Creation in *The Taming of the Shrew*", *Studies in English Literature, 1500–1900*, 29:2 (Summer, 1989), 237–257
- Bean, John C. "Comic Structure and the Humanizing of Kate in *The Taming of the Shrew*", in Carolyn Ruth Swift Lenz, Gayle Greene and Carol Thomas Neely (editors), *The Woman's Part: Feminist Criticism of Shakespeare* (Illinois: University of Illinois Press, 1980), 65–78
- Boose, Linda E. "Scolding Brides and Bridling Scolds: Taming the Woman's Unruly Member", *Shakespeare Quarterly*, 42:2 (Summer, 1991), 179–213
- Brunvand, J.H. "The Folktale Origin of *The Taming of the Shrew*", *Shakespeare Quarterly*, 17:4 (Winter, 1966), 345–359
- Bullough, Geoffrey. *Narrative and Dramatic Sources of Shakespeare (Volume 1): Early Comedies, Poems, Romeo and Juliet* (Columbia: Columbia University Press, 1957)
- Chambers, E.K. *William Shakespeare: A Study of Facts and Problems, Volume 1* (Oxford: Clarendon Press, 1930)
- Daniel, P.A. *A Time Analysis of the Plots of Shakespeare's Plays* (London: New Shakspere Society, 1879)
- DeRose, David J. and Kolin, Phillip C. "Shakespeare and Feminist Criticism: An Annotated Bibliography and Commentary", *TDR*, 37:2 (Summer, 1993), 178–181
- Dessen, Alan C. "The Tamings of the Shrews" in M.J. Collins (editor), *Shakespeare's Sweet Thunder: Essays on the Early Comedies* (Newark: Associated University Presses, 1997), 35–49
- Detmer, Emily. "Civilizing Subordination: Domestic Violence and the *Taming of the Shrew*", *Shakespeare Quarterly*, 48:3 (Fall, 1997), 273–294
- Dobson, Michael S. *The Making of the National Poet: Shakespeare, Adaptation and Authorship, 1660–1769* (Oxford, Oxford University Press, 1995)
- Dusinberre, Juliet. *Shakespeare and the Nature of Women* (London: Macmillan, 1996)
- Duthie, G.I. "*The Taming of a Shrew* and *The Taming of the Shrew*", *Review of English Studies*, 19 (1943), 337–356
- ———. *Shakespeare* (London: Hutchinson, 1951)
- Fineman, Joel. "The Turn of a Shrew", in Russ McDonald (editor), *Shakespeare: An Anthology of Criticism and Theory, 1945–2000* (Oxford: Blackwell, 2004), 399–416
- Foakes. R.A. and Rickert R.T. (eds.) *Henslowe's Diary* (Cambridge: Cambridge University Press, 1961; 2nd edn. edited by only Foakes, 2002)
- Green, Stanley. *The World of Musical Comedy* (San Diego: Da Capo Press, 1974; 4th edn. 1980)

- Halliday, F.E. *A Shakespeare Companion, 1564–1964* (Baltimore: Penguin, 1964)
- Heilman, Robert B. "*The Taming* Untamed: or, the Return of The Shrew", *Modern Language Quarterly*, 27:2 (Summer, 1966), 147–161
- Helms, Lorraine. "Playing the Woman's Part: Feminist Criticism and Shakespearean Performance", *Theatre Journal*, 41:2 (May, 1989), 190–200
- Hickson, Samuel. "*The Taming of the Shrew*", *Notes & Queries*, 22:2, (Summer, 1850), 345-347 (republished in its entirety in Morris (1981), 299-303)
- Hodgdon, Barbara. "Katherina Bound; Or, Play(K)ating the Strictures of Everyday Life", *PMLA*, 107:3 (May, 1992), 538–553
- Honigmann, E.A.J. "Shakespeare's Lost Source-Plays", *Modern Language Review*, 49:1 (Spring, 1954), 293-307
- Hosley, Richard. "Was there a Dramatic Epilogue to *The Taming of the Shrew?*", *Studies in English Literature, 1500–1900*, 1:1 (Spring, 1961),17–34
- ———. "Sources and Analogues of *The Taming of the Shrew*", *Huntington Library Quarterly*, 27:3 (Fall, 1964), 289–308
- Houk, R.A. "The Evolution of *The Taming of the Shrew*", *PMLA*, 57:4 (Winter, 1942), 1009–1038
- Kahn, Coppélia. "*The Taming of the Shrew*: Shakespeare's Mirror of Marriage", *Modern Language Studies*, 5:1 (Spring, 1975), 88–102
- Kirschbaum, Leo. "A Census of Bad Quartos", *Review of English Studies*, 14 (1938), 20-43
- Korda, Natasha. "Household Kates: Domesticating Commodities in the *Taming of the Shrew*." *Shakespeare Quarterly*, 47:2 (Summer, 1996), 109–131
- Krims, Marvin Bennet. *The Mind According to Shakespeare: Psychoanalysis in the Bard's Writing* (London: Praeger, 2006)
- Lenz, Carolyn Ruth Swift. "The Woman's Part: Feminist Criticism of Shakespeare", *South Atlantic Review*, 46:2 (May, 1981), 119–122
- Makaryk, Irene R. "Soviet Views of Shakespeare's Comedies", *Shakespeare Studies*, 15 (1982), 281–313
- Marcus, Leah S. "Levelling Shakespeare: Local Customs and Local Texts", *Shakespeare Quarterly*, 42:2 (Summer, 1991), 168–178
- ———. *Unediting the Renaissance: Shakespeare, Marlow, Milton* (London: Routledge, 1996)
- Marowitz, Charles. *The Marowitz Shakespeare* (London: Marion Boyers, 1978)
- Mincoff, Marco. "The Dating of *The Taming of the Shrew*", *English Studies*, 54:4 (Winter, 1973), 454–565
- Moore, W.H. "An Allusion in 1593 to *The Taming of the Shrew?*", *Shakespeare Quarterly*, 15:1 (Spring, 1964), 55–60
- Morozov, Mikhail M. *Shakespeare on the Soviet Stage* (London: Open Library, 1947)
- Muir, Kenneth. *The Sources of Shakespeare's Plays* (London: Routledge, 1977; rpt 2005)
- Onions, C.T. *A Shakespeare Glossary* (Oxford: Oxford University Press, 1953; 2nd edn. edited by Robert D. Eagleson, 1986)
- Orlin, Lena Cowen. "The Performance of Things in *The Taming of the Shrew*", *The Yearbook of English Studies*, 23 (1993), 167–188
- Rackin, Phyllis. *Shakespeare and Women* (Oxford: Oxford University Press, 2005)
- Rebhorn, Wayne A. "Petruchio's "Rope Tricks": *The Taming of the Shrew* and the Renaissance Discourse of Rhetoric", *Modern Philology*, 92:3 (Fall, 1995), 294–327
- Rutter, Carol. *Clamorous Voices, Shakespeare's Women Today with Sinead Cusack, Paola Dionisotti, Fiona Shaw, Juliet Stevenson and Harriet Walter (London: The Woman's Press, 1988)*
- ———. "Kate, Bianca, Ruth and Sarah: Playing the Woman's Part in *The Taming of the Shrew*" in M.J. Collins (editor), *Shakespeare's Sweet Thunder: Essays on the Early Comedies* (Newark: Associated University Presses, 1997), 176–215

- Schneider, Gary. "The Public, the Private, and the Shaming of the Shrew", *Studies in English Literature, 1500–1900*, 42:2 (Spring, 2002), 235–258
- Shapiro, Michael. "Framing the Taming: Metatheatrical Awareness of Female Impersonation in *The Taming of the Shrew*", *The Yearbook of English Studies*, 23 (1993), 143–166
- Shroeder, J.W. "*The Taming of a Shrew* and *The Taming of the Shrew*: A Case Reopened", *Journal of English and Germanic Philology*, 57:4 (October, 1958), 424–442
- ———. "A New analogue and possible sources for *The Taming of the Shrew*", *Shakespeare Quarterly*, 10:2 (Summer, 1959), 251–255
- Speaight, Robert. *Shakespeare on the Stage: An Illustrated History of Shakespearian Performance* (London: Collins, 1973)
- Tillyard. E.M.W. *Shakespeare's Early Comedies* (London: The Athlone Press, 1965; rpt. 1992)
- Tolman, Alfred. "Shakespeare's Part in *The Taming of the Shrew*, *PMLA*, 5:2 (March, 1890), 201–278
- Wentersdorf, Karl P. "The Authenticity of *The Taming of the Shrew*", *Shakespeare Quarterly*, 5:1 (Spring, 1954), 11–32
- ———. "The Original Ending of *The Taming of the Shrew*: A Reconsideration", *Studies in English Literature, 1500–1900* 18:2 (Summer, 1978), 201–215
- Wells, Stanley; Taylor, Gary; Jowett, John and Montgomery, William. *William Shakespeare: A Textual Companion* (Oxford: Oxford University Press, 1987)
- Williams, Gordon. *A Glossary of Shakespeare's Sexual Language* (London: The Athlone Press, 1997)

External links

- *The Taming of the Shrew* Navigator (http://shakespeare-navigators.com/shrew/index.html) – includes searchable text with notes, line numbers and scene summaries.
- *The Taming of the Shrew* (http://www.gutenberg.org/dirs/etext00/0ws1010.txt) – plain vanilla text from Project Gutenberg.
- *The Taming of the Shrew* (http://www.shakespeare-literature.com/The_Taming_of_the_Shrew/index.html) – searchable, indexed e-text.
- *The Taming of the Shrew* (http://www.maximumedge.com/shakespeare/taming.htm) – scene-indexed, searchable version of the play.
- *The Taming of the Shrew* (http://www.nalanda.nitc.ac.in/resources/english/etext-project/william_shakespeare/the_taming_of_the_shrew/) – HTML version, with original First Folio spelling.
- *The Taming of the Shrew* Home Page (http://internetshakespeare.uvic.ca/Library/plays/Shr.html) at *Internet Shakespeare Editions* (http://internetshakespeare.uvic.ca/index.html).
- *The Taming of the Shrew* (http://shakespeare.emory.edu/illustrated_playdisplay.cfm?playid=27) at *Shakespeare Illustrated* (http://shakespeare.emory.edu/illustrated_index.cfm).
- Important Quotations from *The Taming of the Shrew* Analysed by Medha Patel-Schwarz (http://www.medhasnotes.com/TamingoftheShrew.html).
- The Textual Problem of *The Taming of the Shrew* (http://www.shakessays.info/The Taming of the Shrew and the Taming of a Shrew.htm).
- "Petruchio's Horse: Equine and Household Mismanagement in *The Taming of the Shrew*", by Peter F. Heaney; *Early Modern Literary Studies* 4:1 (May, 1998), 1–12 (http://extra.shu.ac.uk/emls/04-1/heanshak.html).
- ""Caparisoned like the horse": Tongue and Tail in Shakespeare's *The Taming of the Shrew*", by LaRue Love Sloan; *Early Modern Literary Studies*, 10:2 (September, 2004), 1–24 (http://extra.shu.ac.uk/emls/10-2/sloacapa.htm).
- *The Taming of the Shrew* (http://www.imdb.com/title/tt0061407/) at the Internet Movie Database (Franco Zeffirelli Version).

- *The Taming of the Shrew* (http://www.imdb.com/title/tt0081597/) at the Internet Movie Database (*BBC Television Shakespeare* Version).

The Seagull

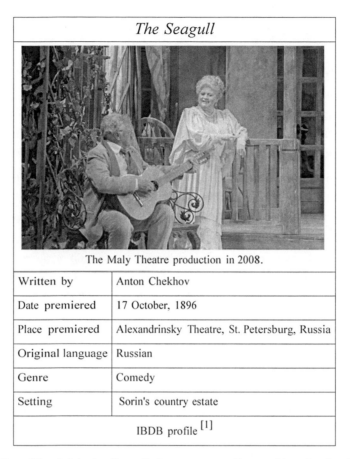

The Seagull	
The Maly Theatre production in 2008.	
Written by	Anton Chekhov
Date premiered	17 October, 1896
Place premiered	Alexandrinsky Theatre, St. Petersburg, Russia
Original language	Russian
Genre	Comedy
Setting	Sorin's country estate
IBDB profile [1]	

The Seagull (Russian: Чайка, *Chayka*) is the first of what are generally considered to be the four major plays by the Russian dramatist Anton Chekhov. *The Seagull* was written in 1895 and first produced in 1896. It dramatises the romantic and artistic conflicts between four characters: the ingenue Nina, the fading actress Irina Arkadina, her son the symbolist playwright Konstantin Treplyov, and the famous middlebrow story writer Trigorin.

As with the rest of Chekhov's full-length plays, *The Seagull* relies upon an ensemble cast of diverse, fully-developed characters. In contrast to the melodrama of the mainstream theatre of the 19th century, lurid actions (such as Konstantin's suicide attempts) are not shown onstage. Characters tend to speak in ways that skirt around issues rather than addressing them directly, a dramatic practice known as subtext.[2]

The opening night of the first production was a famous failure. Vera Komissarzhevskaya, playing Nina, was so intimidated by the hostility of the audience that she lost her voice.[3] Chekhov left the audience and spent the last two acts behind the scenes. When supporters wrote to him that the production later became a success, he assumed that they were merely trying to be kind.[3] When Constantin Stanislavski, the seminal Russian theatre practitioner of the time, directed it in 1898 for his Moscow Art Theatre, the play was a triumph. Stanislavski's production of *The Seagull* became "one of the greatest events in the history of Russian theatre and one of the greatest new developments in the history of world drama."[4]

Writing

After his purchase of the Milikhovo farm in 1892, Chekhov had built in the middle of a cherry orchard a lodge consisting of three rooms, one containing a bed and another a writing table. In spring, when the cherries were in blossom, it was pleasant to live in this lodge, but in winter it was so buried in the snow that pathways had to be cut to it through drifts as high as a man. Chekhov eventually moved in and in a letter written in October 1895 wrote:

> I am writing a play which I shall probably not finish before the end of November. I am writing it not without pleasure, though I swear fearfully at the conventions of the stage. It's a comedy, there are three women's parts, six men's, four acts, landscapes (view over a lake); a great deal of conversation about literature, little action, tons of love.[5]

Thus he acknowledged a departure from traditional dramatic action. This departure would become a critical hallmark of the Chekhovian theater. Chekhov's statement also reflects his view of the play as comedy, a viewpoint he would maintain towards all his plays. After the play's disastrous opening night his friend Aleksey Suvorin chided him as being "womanish" and accused him of being in "a funk." Chekhov vigorously denied this, stating:

> Why this libel? After the performance I had supper at Romanov's. On my word of honour. Then I went to bed, slept soundly, and next day went home without uttering a sound of complaint. If I had been in a funk I should have run from editor to editor and actor to actor, should have nervously entreated them to be considerate, should nervously have inserted useless corrections and should have spent two or three weeks in Petersburg fussing over my *Seagull,* in excitement, in a cold perspiration, in lamentation.... I acted as coldly and reasonably as a man who has made an offer, received a refusal, and has nothing left but to go. Yes, my vanity was stung, but you know it was not a bolt from the blue; I was expecting a failure, and was prepared for it, as I warned you with perfect sincerity beforehand.

And a month later:

> I thought that if I had written and put on the stage a play so obviously brimming over with monstrous defects, I had lost all instinct and that, therefore, my machinery must have gone wrong for good.

The eventual success of the play, both in the remainder of its first run and in the subsequent staging by the Moscow Art Theatre under Stanislavski, would encourage Chekhov to remain a playwright and lead to the overwhelming success of his next endeavor *Uncle Vanya*, and indeed to the rest of his dramatic oeuvre.

Characters

- Irina Nikolayevna Arkadina - an actress.
- Konstantin Gavrilovich Treplyov - Irina's son, a playwright.
- Peter Sorin - Irina's brother.
- Nina Mikhailovna Zarechnaya - the daughter of a rich landowner.
- Ilya Afanasyevich Shamrayev - a retired lieutenant and the manager of Sorin's estate.
- Polina Andryevna - Ilya's wife.
- Masha - Ilya and Polina's daughter.
- Boris Alexeyevich Trigorin - a well known novelist.
- Yevgeny Sergeyevich Dorn - a doctor.

Chekhov reads *The Seagull* with the Moscow Art Theatre company. Chekhov reads (centre), Stanislavski (to the left of him) and Meyerhold (seated far right) listen.

- Semyon Semyonovich Medvedenko - a teacher.
- Yakov - a hired workman.
- Cook - a worker on Sorin's estate.
- Maid - a worker on Sorin's estate.
- Watchman - a worker on Sorin's estate; he carries a warning stick at night.

Plot synopsis

Act I

The play takes place on a country estate owned by Sorin, a former government employee with failing health. He is the brother of the famous actress Arkadina, who has just arrived at the estate with her lover, Trigorin, for a brief vacation. In Act I, the people staying at Sorin's estate gather to see an unconventional play that Arkadina's son Konstantin has written and directed. The play-within-a-play stars Nina, a young girl who lives on a neighboring estate, as the "soul of the world." The play is his latest attempt at creating a new theatrical form, and resembles a dense symbolist work. Arkadina laughs at the play, finding it ridiculous and incomprehensible, while Konstantin storms off in disgrace. Act I also sets up the play's many romantic triangles. The schoolteacher Medvedenko loves Masha, the daughter of the estate's steward. Masha, in turn, is in love with Konstantin, who is in love with Nina. When Masha tells the kindly old doctor Dorn about her longing, he helplessly blames the moon and the lake for making everybody feel romantic.

Act II

Act II takes place in the afternoon outside of the estate, a few days later. After reminiscing about happier times, Arkadina engages the house steward Shamrayev in a heated argument and decides to leave immediately. Nina lingers behind after the group leaves, and Konstantin shows up to give her a seagull that he has shot. Nina is confused and horrified at the gift. Konstantin sees Trigorin approaching, and leaves in a jealous fit. Nina asks Trigorin to tell her about the writer's life. He replies that it is not an easy one. Nina says that she knows the life of an actress is not easy either, but she wants more than anything to be one. Trigorin sees the seagull that Konstantin has shot and muses on how he could use it as a subject for a short story: "A young girl lives all her life on the shore of a lake. She loves the lake, like a seagull, and she's happy and free, like a seagull. But a man arrives by chance, and when he sees her, he destroys her, out of sheer boredom. Like this seagull." Arkadina calls for Trigorin and he leaves as she tells him that she has changed her mind, and they will not be leaving immediately. Nina lingers behind, enthralled with Trigorin's celebrity and modesty, and she gushes, "My dream!"

Act III

Act III takes place inside the estate, on the day when Arkadina and Trigorin have decided to depart. Between acts Konstantin attempted suicide by shooting himself in the head, but the bullet only grazed his skull. He spends the majority of Act III with his scalp heavily bandaged. Nina finds Trigorin eating breakfast and presents him with a medallion that proclaims her devotion to him using a line from one of Trigorin's own books: "If you ever need my life, come and take it." She retreats after begging for one last chance to see Trigorin before he leaves. Arkadina appears, followed by Sorin, whose health has continued to deteriorate. Trigorin leaves to continue packing. There is a brief argument between Arkadina and Sorin, after which Sorin collapses in grief. He is helped off by Medvedenko. Konstantin enters and asks his mother to change his bandage. As she is doing this, Konstantin disparages Trigorin and there is another argument. When Trigorin reenters, Konstantin leaves in tears. Trigorin asks Arkadina if they can stay at the estate. She flatters and cajoles him until he agrees to return to Moscow. After she has left, Nina comes to say her final goodbye to Trigorin and to inform him that she is running away to become an actress, against her parents' wishes. They kiss passionately and make plans to meet again in Moscow.

Act IV

Act IV takes place during the winter two years later, in the drawing room that has been converted to Konstantin's study. Masha has finally accepted Medvedenko's marriage proposal, and they have a child together, though Masha still nurses an unrequited love for Konstantin. Various characters discuss what has happened in the two years that have passed: Nina and Trigorin lived together in Moscow for a time until he abandoned her and went back to Arkadina. Nina never achieved any real success as an actress, and is currently on a tour of the provinces with a small theatre group. Konstantin has had some short stories published, but is increasingly depressed. Sorin's health is failing, and the people at the estate have telegraphed for Arkadina to come for his final days. Most of the play's characters go to the drawing room to play a game of bingo. Konstantin does not join them, and spends this time working on a manuscript at his desk. After the group leaves to eat dinner, Konstantin hears someone at the back door. He is surprised to find Nina, whom he invites inside. Nina tells Konstantin about her life over the last two years. She starts to compare herself to the seagull that Konstantin killed in Act II, then rejects that and says "I am an actress." She tells him that she was forced to tour with a second-rate theatre company after the death of the child she had with Trigorin, but she seems to have a newfound confidence. Konstantin pleads with her to stay, but she is in such disarray that his pleading means nothing. She embraces Konstantin, and leaves. Despondent, Konstantin spends two minutes silently tearing up his manuscripts before leaving the study. The group reenters and returns to the bingo game. There is a sudden gunshot from off-stage, and Dorn goes to investigate. He returns and takes Trigorin aside. Dorn tells Trigorin to somehow get Arkadina away, for Konstantin has just killed himself.[6]

Performance history

Premiere in St. Petersburg

The first night of *The Seagull* on 17 October 1896 at the Alexandrinsky Theatre in Petersburg was a disaster, booed by the audience. The hostile audience intimidated Vera Komissarzhevskaya, who some considered the best actor in Russia and who, according to Chekhov, had moved people to tears as Nina in rehearsal, and she lost her voice.[3] The next day, Chekhov, who had taken refuge backstage for the last two acts, announced to Suvorin that he was finished with writing plays.[7] When supporters assured him that later performances were more successful, Chekhov assumed they were just being kind. *The Seagull* impressed the playwright and friend of Chekhov Vladimir Nemirovich-Danchenko, however, who said Chekhov should have won the Griboyedov prize that year for *The Seagull* instead of himself.[8]

The Moscow Art Theatre production

Nemirovich overcame Chekhov's refusal to allow the play to appear in Moscow and convinced Stanislavski to direct the play for their innovative and newly-founded Moscow Art Theatre in 1898.[10] Stanislavski prepared a detailed directorial score, which indicated when the actors should "wipe away dribble, blow their noses, smack their lips, wipe away sweat, or clean their teeth and nails with matchsticks", as well as organising a tight control of the overall *mise en scène*.[11] This approach was intended to facilitate the unified expression of the inner action that Stanislavski perceived to be hidden beneath the surface of the play in its subtext.[12] Stanislavski's directorial score was published in 1938.[13]

Stanislavski played Trigorin, while Vsevolod Meyerhold—the future director and practitioner who Stanislavski on his death-bed declared to be "my sole heir in the theatre"—played Konstantin and Olga Knipper (Chekhov's future wife) played Arkadina.[14] The production opened on 17 December 1898 with a sense of crisis in the air in the theatre; most of the actors were mildly self-tranquilised with Valerian drops.[15] In a letter to Chekhov, one audience member described how:

Studio portrait of Stanislavski as Trigorin from the 1898 Moscow Art Theatre production.[9]

> In the first act something special started, if you can so describe a mood of excitement in the audience that seemed to grow and grow. Most people walked through the auditorium and corridors with strange faces, looking as if it were their birthday and, indeed, (dear God I'm not joking) it was perfectly possible to go up to some completely strange woman and say: "What a play? Eh?"[16]

Nemirovich described the applause, which came after a prolonged silence, as bursting from the audience like a dam breaking.[17] The production received unanimous praise from the press.[17]

It was not until 1 May 1899 that Chekhov saw the production, in a performance without sets but in make-up and costumes at the Paradiz Theatre.[18] He praised the production but was less keen on Stanislavski's own performance; he objected to the "soft, weak-willed tone" in his interpretation (shared by Nemirovich) of Trigorin and entreated Nemirovich to "put some spunk into him or something".[19] He proposed that the play be published with Stanislavski's score of the production's *mise en scène*.[20] Chekhov's collaboration with Stanislavski proved crucial to the creative development of both men. Stanislavski's attention to psychological realism and ensemble playing coaxed the buried subtleties from the play and revived Chekhov's interest in writing for the stage. Chekhov's unwillingness to explain or expand on the script forced Stanislavski to dig beneath the surface of the text in ways that were new in theatre.[21] The Moscow Art Theatre to this day bears the seagull as its emblem to commemorate the historic production that gave it its identity.[22]

Recent productions

Uta Hagen made her Broadway debut as Nina, at the age of 18, in a production with Alfred Lunt and Lynn Fontanne in 1938 at the Shubert Theatre.

In November 1992, a Broadway staging directed by Marshall W. Mason opened at Lyceum Theatre, New York. The production starred Tyne Daly as Arkadina, Ethan Hawke as Treplyov, Jon Voight as Trigorin, and Laura Linney as Nina.

The Joseph Papp Public Theater presented Chekhov's play as part of the New York Shakespeare Festival summer season in Central Park from July 25, 2001 to August 26, 2001. The production, directed by Mike Nichols, starred Meryl Streep as Arkadina, Christopher Walken as Sorin, Philip Seymour Hoffman as Treplyov, John Goodman as Shamrayev, Marcia Gay Harden as Masha, Kevin Kline as Trigorin, Debra Monk as Polina, Stephen Spinella as Medvedenko, and Natalie Portman as Nina.

In early 2007, the Royal Court Theatre staged a production of *The Seagull* starring Kristin Scott Thomas as Arkadina, Mackenzie Crook as Treplyov and Carey Mulligan as Nina. It also featured Chiwetel Ejiofor and Art Malik. The production was directed by Ian Rickson, and received great reviews, including *The Metro Newspaper* calling it "practically perfect". It ran from January 18 to March 17, and Scott Thomas won an Olivier Award for her performance.

A more recent production was that of The Royal Shakespeare Company, which did an international tour before coming into residence at the West End's New London Theatre until 12 January 2008, starring William Gaunt, Ian McKellen (who alternated with William Gaunt in the role of Sorin, as he also played the title role in *King Lear*), Richard Goulding as Treplyov, Frances Barber as Arkadina, Jonathan Hyde as Dorn, Monica Dolan as Masha, and Romola Garai as Nina. Garai in particular received rave reviews, *The Independent* calling her a "woman on the edge of stardom"[23] , and *This Is London* calling her "superlative", and stating that the play was "distinguished by the illuminating, psychological insights of Miss Garai's performance."[24] Despite the grim plot, the play was written as a comedy and is preceded by the legend: "A comedy in four acts". It played in repertory with *King Lear*.

The Classic Stage Company in New York City revived the work on March 13, 2008, in a production of Paul Schmidt's translation directed by Viacheslav Dolgachev. This production was notable for the casting of Dianne Wiest in the role of Arkadina, and Alan Cumming as Trigorin.

On September 16, 2008 the Walter Kerr Theatre on Broadway began previews of Ian Rickson's production of *The Seagull* with Kristin Scott Thomas reprising her role as Arkadina. The cast also includes Peter Sarsgaard as Trigorin, Mackenzie Crook as Konstantin, Art Malik as Dorn, Carey Mulligan as Nina, Zoe Kazan as Masha, and Ann Dowd as Polina.[25]

A new film adaptation is in the works.[26] It will be reuniting cast members from the Broadway revival, including Thomas, Crook, and Mulligan, with Rickson directing. Shooting is scheduled to begin in May 2010.

Robert Falls will be directing a production at Goodman Theatre in the fall of 2010. [27]

Analysis and criticism

The play has an intertextual relationship with Shakespeare's *Hamlet*. Arkadina and Treplyov quote lines from it before the play-within-a-play in the first act (and this device is itself used in *Hamlet*). There are many allusions to Shakespearean plot details as well. For instance, Treplyov seeks to win his mother back from the usurping older man Trigorin much as Hamlet tries to win Queen Gertrude back from his uncle Claudius.

Translating The Seagull

The Seagull was first translated into English for a performance at the Royalty Theatre, Glasgow, in November 1909.[28] Since that time, there have been numerous translations of the text—from 1998 to 2004 alone there were 25 published versions.[28] In the introduction of his own version, Tom Stoppard wrote: "You can't have too many English Seagulls: at the intersection of all of them, the Russian one will be forever elusive."[29] However, some early translations of The Seagull have come under criticism from modern Russian scholars. The Marian Fell translation, in particular, has been criticized for its elementary mistakes and total ignorance of Russian life and culture.[28] [30] Renowned translator and author of the book *The Oxford Guide to Literature in English Translation* Peter France wrote of Chekhov's multiple adaptations:

> Proliferation and confusion of translation reign in the plays. Throughout the history of Chekhov on the British and American stages we see a version translated, adapted, cobbled together for each new major production, very often by a theatre director with no knowledge of the original, working from a crib prepared by a Russian with no knowledge of the stage.[31]

Notable Translations

Translator	Year	Publisher	Notes
George Calderon	1909	Glasgow Repertory Theatre	This is the first known English translation of The Seagull. This translation premiered at the Royalty Theatre, Glasgow on November 2, 1909, also directed by Calderon.[32]
Marian Fell	1912	Charles Scribner's Sons	First published English language translation of The Seagull in the United States, performed at the Bandbox Theatre on Broadway by the Washington Square Players in 1916.[33] Complete text from Project Gutenberg here [34].
Constance Garnett	1923	Bantam Books	Performed on Broadway at the Civic Repertory Theatre in 1929,[35] directed by Eva Le Gallienne.
Stark Young	1939	Charles Scribner's Sons	Used in the 1938 Broadway production starring Uta Hagen as Nina,[36] as well as the 1975 movie directed by John Desmond.[37]
Elisaveta Fen	1954	Penguin Classics	Along with Constance Garnett's translation, this is one of the most widely read translations of "The Seagull."[38]
David Magarshack	1956	Hill and Wang	Commissioned for the 1956 West End production at the Saville Theatre, directed by Michael Macowan, and starring Diana Wynyard, Lyndon Brook, and Hugh Williams.[39]
Moura Budberg	1968	Sidney Lumet Productions	Commissioned and used for the 1968 movie directed by Sidney Lumet.[40]
Tennessee Williams	1981	New Directions Publishers	Williams' "free adaptation" is titled The Notebook of Trigorin. First produced at the Vancouver Playhouse in 1981, the United States premier occurred at the Cincinnati Playhouse in 1996, starring Lynn Redgrave as Madame Arkadina. Williams was still revising the script when he died in 1983.[41]
Tania Alexander & Charles Sturridge	1985	Applause Books	Commissioned and used for the 1985 Oxford Playhouse production directed by Charles Sturridge and Vanessa Redgrave.

Michael Frayn	1988	Methuen Publishing	Translated Nina's famous line "I am a seagull," to "I am *the* seagull," as in the seagull in Trigorin's story. This was justified by Frayn, in part, because of the non-existence of indefinite or definite articles in the Russian language.[42]
Pam Gems	1991	Nick Hern Books	
David French	1992	Talonbooks	Used in the 1992 Broadway production by the National Actors Theatre at the Lyceum Theatre, directed by Marshall W. Mason and featuring Tyne Daly, Ethan Hawke, Laura Linney, and Jon Voight.[43]
Paul Schmidt	1997	Harper Perennial	Used in the 2008 off Broadway production at the Classic Stage Company, starring Diane Wiest, Alan Cumming, and Kelli Garner.[44]
Tom Stoppard	1997	Faber and Faber	Premiered at the Old Vic theater in London on April 28, 1997. Its United States premiere in July 2001 in New York City drew crowds who sometimes waited 15 hours for tickets.[45]
Peter Gill	2000	Oberon Books	
Peter Carson	2002	Penguin Classics	
Christopher Hampton	2007	Faber and Faber	Used in the Royal Court Theatre's 2008 production of The Seagull at the Walter Kerr Theatre, directed by Ian Rickson and featuring Peter Sarsgaard, Kristin Scott Thomas, Mackenzie Crook and Carey Mulligan.[46]

Adaptations

The American playwright Tennessee Williams adapted the play as *The Notebook of Trigorin*, which premiered in 1981. That year, Thomas Kilroy's adaptation, *The Seagull* also premiered at the Royal Court Theatre in London. The Canadian playwright Daniel MacIvor wrote an adaptation called *His Greatness*. Patrick Marmion's *Pieta* is a contemporary re-imagagining of the play.

It was made into a ballet by John Neumeier on his Hamburg Ballet company in June 2002.[47]

Emily Mann wrote and directed an adaptation called *A Seagull in the Hamptons*. The play premiered at the McCarter Theatre May 2008.[48]

Sources

- Allen, David. 2001. *Performing Chekhov*. London: Routledge. ISBN 0415189347.
- Balukhaty, Sergei Dimitrievich, ed. *'The Seagull' Produced By Stanislavsky*. Trans. David Magarshack. London: Denis Dobson. New York : Theatre Arts Books.
- Benedetti, Jean. 1989. *Stanislavski: An Introduction*. Revised edition. Original edition published in 1982. London: Methuen. ISBN 0-413-50030-6.
- ---. 1999. *Stanislavski: His Life and Art*. Revised edition. Original edition published in 1988. London: Methuen. ISBN 0-413-52520-1.
- Braun, Edward. 1982. "Stanislavsky and Chekhov". *The Director and the Stage: From Naturalism to Grotowski*. London: Methuen. p. 59-76. ISBN 0-413-46300-1.
- Chekhov, Anton. 1920. *Letters of Anton Chekhov to His Family and Friends with Biographical Sketch*. Trans. Constance Garnett. New York: Macmillan. Full text available online at Gutenberg [49]
- Gilman, Richard. 1997. *Chekhov's Plays: An Opening into Eternity*. New York: Yale University Press. ISBN 0-300-07256-2
- Miles, Patrick. 1993. *Chekhov on the British Stage*. London: Cambridge University Press. ISBN 0-521-38467-2

- Rudnitsky, Konstantin. 1981. *Meyerhold the Director*. Trans. George Petrov. Ed. Sydney Schultze. Revised translation of *Rezhisser Meierkhol'd*. Moscow: Academy of Sciences, 1969. ISBN 0-88233-313-5.
- Worrall, Nick. 1996. *The Moscow Art Theatre*. Theatre Production Studies ser. London and NY: Routledge. ISBN 0-415-05598-9.

External links

- *The Sea-Gull* [50] at Project Gutenberg
- Full text of *The Seagull* in the original Russian [51]
- Cast List of 2007/8 RSC Production [52]
- Geography of Regret [53] *The New Yorker* review of the current Ian Rickson revival.
- Free audiobook [54] from LibriVox [55]

References

[1] http://www.ibdb.com/show.asp?id=7804

[2] Benedetti (1989, 26).

[3] Chekhov (1920); Letter to A. F. Koni, 11 November 1896. Available online at Project Gutenberg (http://www.gutenberg.org/etext/6408).

[4] Rudnitsky (1981, 8).

[5] Chekhov (1920).

[6] Gilman (1997, 98-99).

[7] Chekhov (1920). Letter to Suvorin, 18 October 1896. Available online at Project Gutenberg (http://www.gutenberg.org/etext/6408).

[8] Benedetti (1989, 16) and (1999, 59, 74).

[9] "Elegantly coiffured, clad in evening dress, mournfully contemplating the middle distance with pencil and notepad, suggests someone more intent on resurrecting the dead seagull in deathless prose than plotting the casual seduction of the ardent female by his side." - Worrall (1996, 107).

[10] Benedetti (1999, 73) and (1989, 25).

[11] Worrall (1996, 109) and Braun (1981, 62-63).

[12] Braun (1981, 62-63).

[13] Benedetti (1999, 79). For an English translation of Stanislavski's score, see Balukhaty (1952).

[14] Braun (1982, 62) and Benedetti (1999, 79-81).

[15] Benedetti (1999, 85, 386).

[16] Quoted by Benedetti (1999, 86).

[17] Benedetti (199, 86).

[18] Benedetti (1999, 89).

[19] Benedetti (1999, 89-90) and Worrall (1996, 108).

[20] Benedetti (1999, 90).

[21] Chekhov and the Art Theatre, in Stanislavski's words, were united in a common desire "to achieve artistic simplicity and truth on the stage"; Allen (2003, 11).

[22] Braun (1981, 62, 64).

[23] "Romola Garai: A woman on the edge of stardom" (http://www.independent.co.uk/news/people/romola-garai-a-woman-on-the-edge-of-stardom-440326.html). *The Independent* (London). 2007-03-15. . Retrieved 2010-05-25.

[24] The fall of a high-flying bird| Theatre | This is London (http://www.thisislondon.co.uk/theatre/show-23377371-details/The Seagull/showReview.do?reviewId=23423456)

[25] http://www.seagulltheplay.com/

[26] "Royal Court's Seagull flies to big screen" (http://www.guardian.co.uk/stage/2009/sep/04/kristin-scott-thomas-mackenzie-crook-seagull-chekhov). *The Guardian* (London). 2009-09-04. . Retrieved 2010-05-25.

[27] http://www3.timeoutny.com/chicago/blog/out-and-about/2010/02/goodmans-2010%E2%80%9311-season-zimmerman-falls-taylor-bradshaw-ruhl/

[28] Henry, Peter (2008-03). "Chekhov in English" (http://www.basees.org.uk/down/Chekhov_Bibliography.pdf)(PDF). *British Association for Slavonic and East European Studies*: 3. . Retrieved 2009-04-06.

[29] Stoppard, Tom (2001-08). *The Seagull*. Faber & Faber. ISBN 978-0571192700.

[30] Byrne, Terry (2008-07-04). "For 'Seagull,' director dove into translation" (http://www.boston.com/ae/theater_arts/articles/2008/07/04/for_seagull_director_dove_into_translation/). *The Boston Globe* (The New York Times Company). . Retrieved 2009-04-06.

[31] France, Peter (2000-02-24). *The Oxford Guide to Literature in English Translation*. Oxford University Press. pp. 600. ISBN 978-0-19-818359-4.

[32] Tracy, Robert (Spring, 1960). "A Cexov Anniversary" (http://www.jstor.org/stable/304054). *The Slavic and East European Journal* 4 (1): 25. doi:10.2307/304054. . Retrieved 2009-03-22.

[33] "1916 production of The Seagull at IBDb" (http://www.ibdb.com/production.php?id=7749). *Internet Broadway Database*. . Retrieved 2008-09-30.

[34] http://www.gutenberg.org/files/1754/1754-h/1754-h.htm

[35] "Civic Repertory Theatre at IBDb" (http://www.ibdb.com/person.php?id=20184). *Internet Broadway Database*. . Retrieved 2008-09-30.

[36] "1938 production of The Seagull at IBDb" (http://www.ibdb.com/production.php?id=7945). *Internet Broadway Database*. . Retrieved 2008-09-30.

[37] "The Seagull at IMDb" (http://www.imdb.com/title/tt0215164/). *The Internet Movie Database*.. Retrieved 2008-09-30.

[38] Kirsch, Adam (1997-07). "Chekhov in American" (http://www.theatlantic.com/issues/97jul/chekhov.htm). *The Atlantic Monthly* (Atlantic Monthly Group). . Retrieved 2009-02-08.

[39] Miles (1993, 242)

[40] "The Sea Gull at IMDb" (http://www.imdb.com/title/tt0063569/). *The Internet Movie Database*.. Retrieved 2008-09-30.

[41] Klein, Alvin (2001-01-28). "THEATER REVIEW; Start With Chekhov; Add Lots of Williams" (http://theater2.nytimes.com/mem/theater/treview.html?pagewanted=print&res=9407E1D8173FF93BA15752C0A9679C8B63). *The New York Times* (The New York Times Company). . Retrieved 2009-03-22.

[42] Callow, Simon (2008-05-24). "The play's the thing" (http://www.guardian.co.uk/books/2008/may/24/stage). *The Guardian* (London: Guardian Media Group). . Retrieved 2009-03-22.

[43] "1992 Production of The Seagull at IBDb" (http://www.ibdb.com/production.php?id=4698). *Internet Broadway Database*. The Broadway League. . Retrieved 2009-02-08.

[44] Cino, Maggie (2008-03-08). "The Seagull" (http://www.nytheatre.com/nytheatre/showpage.php?t=seag5711). *nytheater.com*. . Retrieved 2009-01-06.

[45] "Press Release: CSC Studio Series Features Anton Chekhov's The Seagull in New Stoppard Translation" (http://www.cinstages.com/article.asp?CinstagenewsID=2118). *Cinstages.com*. 2008-12-19. . Retrieved 2009-03-22.

[46] "2008 Production of The Seagull at IBDb" (http://www.ibdb.com/production.php?id=480037). *Internet Broadway Database*. The Broadway League. . Retrieved 2009-02-08.

[47] biography of John Neumeier on Hamburg Ballet website (http://www.hamburgballett.de/e/neumeier.htm)

[48] http://www.mccarter.org/ticketoffice/eventdetail.aspx?page_id=7&event_id=3325

[49] http://www.gutenberg.org/etext/6408

[50] http://www.gutenberg.org/etext/1754

[51] http://ilibrary.ru/text/971/

[52] http://www.rsc.org.uk/onstage/plays/4656.aspx

[53] http://www.newyorker.com/arts/critics/theatre/2008/10/13/081013crth_theatre_lahr

[54] http://librivox.org/the-seagull-by-anton-chekhov-trans-fell/

[55] http://librivox.org

Mother Courage and Her Children

Mother Courage and Her Children (German: *Mutter Courage und ihre Kinder*) is a play written in 1939 by the German dramatist and poet Bertolt Brecht (1898–1956) with significant contributions from Margarete Steffin.[2] After four very important theatrical productions in Switzerland and Germany from 1941 to 1952—the last three supervised and/or directed by Brecht—the play was filmed several years after Brecht's death in 1959/1960 with Brecht's widow and leading actress, Helene Weigel.[3]

Mother Courage is considered by some to be the greatest play of the 20th century, and perhaps also the greatest anti-war play of all time.[4]

Context

Mother Courage is one of nine plays that Brecht wrote in an attempt to counter the rise of Fascism and Nazism. Written largely in response to the invasion of Poland (1939) by the German armies of Adolf Hitler, Brecht

Mother Courage and Her Children, with Therese Giehse in the title role, with Erni Wilhemi, Hans Christian Blech, and Karl Lieffen, at the Munich Kammerspiele, directed by Bertolt Brecht, Munich, 1950. Photo shows the famous cart Mother Courage pulls through the Thirty Years War, here on a revolving stage, designed by Theo Otto.[1]

wrote *Mother Courage* in what writers call a "white heat"—in a little over a month.[5] As leading Brecht scholars Ralph Manheim and John Willett wrote:

> *Mother Courage*, with its theme of the devastating effects of a European war and the blindness of anyone hoping to profit by it, is said to have been written in a month; judging by the almost complete absence of drafts or any other evidence of preliminary studies, it must have been an exceptionally direct piece of inspiration.[6]

> "'Brecht's genius was to mix humor in the great tragedies '- not always, but as a contrast."
>
> Therese Giehse, 1968.[7]

Following Brecht's own principles for political drama, the play is not set in modern times but during the Thirty Years' War of 1618–1648. It follows the fortunes of Anna Fierling, nicknamed "Mother Courage", a wily canteen woman with the Swedish Army who is determined to make her living from the war. Over the course of the play, she loses all three of her children, Swiss Cheese, Eilif, and Kattrin, to the same war from which she sought to profit.

Overview

The name of the central character, Mother Courage, is drawn from the picaresque writings of the seventeenth-century German writer, Grimmelshausen, whose central character in the early short novel, *The Runagate Courage*,[8] also struggles and connives her way through the Thirty Years' War in Germany and Poland, but otherwise the story is mostly Brecht's, in collaboration with Steffin.

The action of the play takes place over the course of 12 years (1624 to 1636), represented in 12 scenes. Some give a sense of Courage's career without being given enough time to develop sentimental feelings and empathize with any of the characters. Meanwhile, Mother Courage is not depicted as a noble character – here the Brechtian epic theatre sets itself apart from the ancient Greek tragedies in which the heroes are far above the average. With the same alienating effect, the ending of Brecht's play does not arouse our desire to imitate the main character, Mother Courage.

Mother Courage is among Brecht's most famous plays, and has been considered by some to be the greatest play of the 20th century.[9] His work attempts to show the dreadfulness of war and the idea that virtues are not rewarded in corrupt times. He used an epic structure so that the audience focuses on the issues being displayed rather than getting involved with the characters and emotions. Epic plays are of a very distinct genre and are typical of Brecht; a strong case could be made that he invented the form.[10]

Mother Courage as Epic Theatre

Mother Courage is an example of Brecht's concepts of Epic Theatre and *Verfremdungseffekt* or "estrangement effect". *Verfremdungseffekt* is achieved through the use of placards which reveal the events of each scene, juxtaposition, actors changing characters and costume on stage, the use of narration, simple props and scenery. For instance, a single tree would be used to convey a whole forest, and the stage is usually flooded with bright white light whether it's a winter's night or a summer's day. Several songs, interspersed throughout the play, are used to underscore the themes of the play, while making the audience think about what the playwright is saying.

Roles

- Mother Courage (also known as "Canteen Anna")
- Kattrin, (Catherine) *her mute daughter*
- Eilif, *her oldest son*
- Swiss Cheese, (also mentioned as Feyos) *her youngest son*
- Recruiting Officer
- Sergeant
- Cook
- Swedish Commander
- Chaplain
- Ordinance Officer

- Yvette Pottier
- Man with the Bandage
- Another Sergeant
- Old Colonel
- Clerk
- Young Soldier
- Older Soldier
- Peasant
- Peasant Woman
- Young Man
- Old Woman
- Another Peasant
- Another Peasant Woman
- Young Peasant
- Lieutenant
- Voice

Synopsis

The play is set in the 1600s in Europe during the Thirty Years' War. The Recruiting Officer and Sergeant are introduced, both complaining about the difficulty of recruiting soldiers to the war. A canteen woman named Mother Courage enters pulling a cart that she uses to trade with soldiers and make profits from the war. She has three children, Eilif, Kattrin, and Swiss Cheese. The sergeant negotiates a deal with Mother Courage while Eilif is led off by the recruiting officer. One of her children is now gone.

Two years from then, Mother Courage argues with a Protestant General's cook over a capon, or chicken. At the same time, Eilif is congratulated by the General for killing peasants and slaughtering their cattle. Eilif and his mother sing "The Song of the Girl and the Soldier." Mother Courage scolds her son for taking risks that could have got him killed and slaps him across the face.

Three years later, Swiss Cheese works as an army paymaster. The camp prostitute, Yvette Pottier, sings "The Fraternization Song." Mother Courage uses this song to warn Kattrin about involving herself with soldiers. Before the Catholic troops arrive, the Cook and Chaplain bring a message from Eilif. Swiss Cheese hides the regiment's paybox. Mother Courage & co. hurriedly switch their insignia from Protestant to Catholic. Swiss Cheese is captured by the Catholics while attempting to return the paybox to his General. Mother Courage deals her cart to get money to try and barter with the soldiers to free her son. Swiss Cheese is shot anyway. To acknowledge the body could be fatal, so Mother Courage does not acknowledge it and it is thrown into a pit.

Later, Mother Courage waits outside of the General's tent in order to register a complaint and sings the "Song of Great Capitulation" to a young soldier waiting for the General as well. The soldier is angry that he has not been paid and also wishes to complain. The song persuades the soldier that complaining would be unwise, and Mother Courage (reaching the same conclusion) decides she also does not want to complain.

When Catholic General Tilly's funeral approaches, Mother Courage discusses with the Chaplain about whether the war will continue. The Chaplain then suggests to Mother Courage that she marry him, but she rejects his proposal. Mother Courage curses the war because she finds Kattrin disfigured after collecting more merchandise.

At some point about here Mother Courage is again following the Protestant army.

Two peasants wake Mother Courage up and try to sell merchandise to her while they find out that peace has broken out. The Cook appears and creates an argument between Mother Courage and the Chaplain. Mother Courage departs for the town while Eilif enters, dragged in by soldiers. Eilif is executed for killing peasants but his mother never finds out. When the war begins again, the Cook and Mother Courage start their own business.

The seventeenth year of the war marks a point where there is no food and no supplies. The Cook inherits an inn in Utrecht and suggests to Mother Courage that she operate it with him, but he refuses to harbour Kattrin. It is a very small inn. Mother Courage will not leave her daughter and they part ways with the Cook. Mother Courage and Kattrin pull the wagon by themselves.

The Catholic army attacks the small Protestant town of Halle while Mother Courage is away from town, trading. Kattrin is woken up by a search party that is taking peasants as guides. Kattrin fetches a drum from the cart, climbs onto the roof, and beats it in an attempt to awake the townspeople. Though the soldiers shoot Kattrin, she succeeds in waking up the town.

Early in the morning, Mother Courage sings to her daughter's corpse, has the peasants bury her and hitches herself to the cart. The cart rolls lighter now because there are no more children and very little merchandise left.

Performances

The play was originally produced in Zürich at the Schauspielhaus, produced by Leopold Lindtberg in 1941. Music was written by Paul Dessau. The musicians were placed in view of the audience so that they could be seen, one of Brecht's many techniques in Epic Theatre. Therese Giehse, (a well-known actress at the time) took the title role.

The second production of *Mother Courage* took place in then East Berlin in 1949, with Brecht's (second) wife Helene Weigel, his main actress and later also director, as Mother Courage. This production would highly influence the formation of Brecht's company, the Berliner Ensemble, which would provide him a venue to direct many of his plays. Brecht died directing *Galileo* for the Ensemble. Brecht revised the play for this production in reaction to the reviews of the Zürich production, which empathized with the "heart-rending vitality of all maternal creatures." Even so, he wrote that the Berlin audience failed to see Mother Courage's crimes and participation in the war and focused on her suffering instead.[11]

The next production (and second production in Germany), was directed by Brecht at the Munich Kammerspiele in 1950, with the original Mother Courage, Therese Giehse, with a set designed by Theo Otto (see photo, above.)

In Spanish, was premiered in 1954 in Buenos Aires with Alejandra Boero and in 1958 Montevideo with China Zorrilla.

In 1955, Joan Littlewood's Theatre Workshop gave the play its London première, with Littlewood performing the title role. In 1995/6, Diana Rigg was awarded an Evening Standard Theatre Award for her performance as *Mother Courage*, directed by Jonathan Kent, at the Royal National Theatre.

From August to September 2006, *Mother Courage and Her Children* was produced by the Public Theatre in New York City with a new translation by playwright Tony Kushner (*Angels in America*). This production included new music by composer Jeanine Tesori (*Caroline, or Change*) and was directed by George C. Wolfe. Meryl Streep played "Mother Courage" with a supporting cast that included Kevin Kline and Austin Pendleton. This rare production of *Mother Courage and Her Children* was free to the public and played to full houses at the Public Theatre's Delacorte Theatre in Central Park. It ran for four weeks.

This same Tony Kushner translation was performed in a new production at London's Royal National Theatre between September and December 2009, with Fiona Shaw in the title role, directed by Deborah Warner and with new songs performed live by Duke Special.

Popular culture

In the Tony Award-winning musical Urinetown, the character of Penelope Pennywise is roughly based on Mother Courage.

The rock band My Chemical Romance created the character "Mother War" for their third album *The Black Parade*. The song a highly conceptual work on the nature of modern life. Mother War's song, "Mama" is influenced by themes from Mother Courage and Her Children, including the effect of war on personal morals.

Mother Courage also has similarities to the popular musical, Fiddler on the Roof; in both stories, a parent has three children he/she sees taken from him/her by outside forces; in both stories the central character ends by dragging his/her cart on as the final curtain falls. And both productions made use of a massive revolving stage. As Matthew Gurewitsch wrote in *The New York Sun,* "Deep down, Mother Courage has a lot in common with Tevye the Milkman in *Fiddler on the Roof.* Like him, she's a mother hen helpless to protect the brood."[12]

Mother Courage was the inspiration for Lynn Nottage's Pulitzer winning play *Ruined*.[13]

English versions

- 1941 - H. R. Hays (translation) for New Directions Publishers
- 1955 - Eric Bentley (translation) for Doubleday/Garden City
- 1965 - Eric Bentley (translation) and W. H. Auden (songs translation) for the Royal National Theatre, London
- 1972 - Ralph Manheim (translation) for Random House/Pantheon Books
- 1980 - John Willett (translation) for Methuen Publishing
- 1980 - Ntozake Shange (adaptation) for New York Shakespeare Festival New York
- 1984 - Hanif Kureishi (adaptation) and Sue Davies (songs translation) for the Barbican Arts Centre, London (Samuel French Ltd.)
- 1995 - David Hare (adaptation) for the Royal National Theatre, London (A & C Black, 1996)
- 2000 - Lee Hall (adaptation) and Jan-Willem van Den Bosch (translation) for Yvonne Arnaud Theatre, England (Methuen Drama, 2003)
- 2001 - Joe O'Byrne (translation) for Vesuvius Theatre Company, Dublin (unpublished)
- 2006 - Michael Hofmann (adaptation) and John Willett (songs translation) for the English Touring Theatre (A & C Black, 2006)
- 2006 - Tony Kushner (adaptation) for The Public Theater, New York City, published in the form used in the 2009 Royal National Theatre production.

References

Sources consulted (main article)

Sources consulted (English versions list)

- University of Wisconsin Digital Collections, *Brecht's Works in English: A Bibliography*, online database [14].
- Doollee the Playwrights Database of Modern Plays, "Adaptations/Translations of Plays by Bertolt Brecht", online list [15].
- Doollee the Playwrights Database of Modern Plays,

"Ntozake Shange - complete guide to the Playwright and Plays".

- The International Brecht Society, "Brecht in English Translation", online list [16].
- The Bertolt Brecht Forum, "Bertolt Brecht in English", online tabular list [17].

Endnotes

[1] Therese Giehse had performed the first Mother Courage in Zürich, Switzerland, in 1941; this photo is from her second appearance in that role in 1950.

[2] *Brecht Chronik*, Werner Hecht, editor. (Suhrkamp Verlag, 1998), p. 566.

[3]   *Mutter Courage und ihre Kinder*. (DEFA-Film 1959/60), after the production by Bertolt Brecht and Erich Engel at the Berliner Ensemble, with Helene Weigel, Angelika Hurwicz, Ekkehard Schall, Heinz Schubert, Ernst Busch; directed by Peter Palitzsch and Manfred Wekwerth; with music by Paul Dessau.

[4]   Oskar Eustis, Program Note for the New York Shakespeare Festival production of *Mother Courage and Her Children* with Meryl Streep, August, 2006. See also Brett D. Johnson, "Review of *Mother Courage and Her Children*". *Theatre Journal*, Volume 59, Number 2, May 2007, pp. 281–282, in which Johnson writes: "Although numerous theatrical artists and scholars may share artistic director Oskar Eustis's opinion that Brecht's masterpiece is the greatest play of the twentieth century, productions of *Mother Courage* remain a rarity in contemporary American theatre."

[5]   Klaus Volker. *Brecht Chronicle*. (Seabury Press, 1975). P. 92.

[6]   "Introduction," *Bertolt Brecht: Collected Plays*, vol. 5. (Vintage Books, 1972) p. xi

[7]   Therese Giehse interview with W. Stuart McDowell, 1968, in "Acting Brecht: The Munich Years," *The Brecht Sourcebook*, Carol Martin, Henry Bial, editors (Routledge, 2000) p. 71.

[8]   Online text (German original). (http://gutenberg.spiegel.de/grimmels/courasch/Druckversion_courasch.htm)

[9]   Oscar Eustis (Artistic Director of the New York Shakespeare Festival), Program Note for N.Y.S.F. production of *Mother Courage and Her Children* with Meryl Streep, August, 2006.

[10]   Bertolt Brecht. "Brecht on Theatre", Edited by John Willett. Page 121.

[11]   For information in English on the revisions to the play, see John Willet and Ralph Manheim, eds. *Brecht, Collected Plays: Five (Life of Galileo, Mother Courage and Her Children)*, Metheuen, 1980: 271, 324-5.

[12]   Matthew Gurewitsch. *The New York Sun*, August 22, 2006.

[13]   Iqbal, Nosheen (20 April 2010). "Lynn Nottage: a bar, a brothel and Brecht" (http://www.guardian.co.uk/stage/2010/apr/20/lynn-nottage-ruined). *The Guardian*. . Retrieved 26 April 2010.

[14]   http://digicoll.library.wisc.edu/BrechtGuide/

[15]   http://www.doollee.com/PlaywrightsB/brecht-bertolt.html

[16]   http://german.lss.wisc.edu/brecht/english.html

[17]   http://members.tripod.com/~go20ccm/bine03021999.html

See also

- Mother Courage, the character upon whom the play was based

Article Sources and Contributors

Meryl Streep *Source*: http://en.wikipedia.org/w/index.php?oldid=381019404 *Contributors*: *drew, 15lsoucy, 17Drew, 3finger, @pple, AKR619, Absinthe88, Ace Bryan, Actryan, Adi827, Ahoerstemeier, Ajh16, Ajw786, Aka042, Al-Andalus, Alan smithee, Alansohn, Alaric Deschain, AlbertSM, Alexd18, Alexius08, Alfredosolis, All Hallow's Wraith, Alsandro, Altone, Amalthea, Ameliorate!, And1987, Andland, Andres, Andrewglasson, Andrewire, Andrewsthistle, Angel caboodle, Angelic-alyssa, AngelofMusic07, Aphasia83, Aquila89, Arbero, Arguepower22, Arniep, Arnobarnard, Artstrek, Aspects, Astuishin, AtheWeatherman, Atif.t2, Avono, Awroutsdfgvbajvbasdughasdgb, BD2412, Bahar101, Bakerccm, Basco, BaseballDetective, Bash, Belovedfreak, Ben-Zin, Bencherlite, Beneteau0262, Benjiboi, Bgoldberg86, Bgtgwazi, BigDunc, Bigjimr, Bigweeboy, Biiru, BirdDogg34, Black Falcon, Blacwainwright, Blake-, Blue387, Bmerrell, Bobblewik, Bogdangiusca, Bostonboi28, Bovineboy2008, Branddobbe, Brandinian, Braza258, BreeVandeKamp, Briaboru, Brian Honne, Brian1979, Briantw, C777, COLOisCOOL, CUSENZA Mario, Can't sleep, clown will eat me, Candice, CanisRufus, Cantus, CardinalDan, Carmen22, Catgut, Cathiepops, Cburnett, Charlie White, CharlotteWebb, Charmeryl, Cheezyie, Chensiyuan, Chenzw, Cherrydrops13, Chick Bowen, Chickster1996, Chris Rocen, Chris the speller, Cjwright79, Ckatz, Classicfilms, Cmichael, Colin, Collard, Colonies Chris, Comelloyellow, Commander Shepard, CommonsDelinker, Confiteordeo, Conrail6370, Cosprings, Cpl Syx, CrankyEditrix, CrazyLegsKC, Crboyer, Creepy Crawler, Cremepuff222, Crumbsucker, Crystal Clear x3, Cynthia B., D10, D6, DO'Neil, DStoykov, Daniel Case, Dave6, Daydream believer2, Dbtfz, Deanb, Deathphoenix, Decrypt3, Designquest10, Diloretojazz, Discospinster, Djbj16, Djistus, Donmike10, Doradus, Dougher, Dougie WII, Doulos Christos, Downtown dan seattle, Downtownstar, Dr. Blofeld, DracoLunaMalfoy, Drakehottie, Duncancumming, Dysepsion, Dysprosia, Eagle Owl, Eastlaw, Edmundolee, Edwy, Ejfetters, Elbablo, Elon.rutberg, Emerson7, Emloo, Emoll, Empoor, Enauspeaker, English Bobby, Enosfam, Epbr123, Ericxpenner, Ernst-Günther Baade, Eva in wonderland, Everyking, Excuseme99, ExistingLight, Fang Aili, Fastily, Fbv65edel, Filmmaven, Films addicted, Flabergas, ForDorothy, Fram, FrankBelushi, Fraortiz, FreplySpang, Frostlion, Fuzheado, Fvasconcellos, Gadig, Gareth E Kegg, Garion96, Gauravl146, Gcm, Geniac, GetThePapersGetThePapers, Ghostwords, Ginnina, Ginsengbomb, Giraffelady, Girl2k, Gmosaki, Gogo Dodo, Goldie777, Good Olfactory, GoodNewsShesDead2012, Goodgirl, Googlemonsterwtf, Gouldog, Gr8lyknow, Grafen, Graham87, GregorB, Grenouille vert, Guat6, Guillermo Ugarte, Gurudatt, HJ Mitchell, HOT L Baltimore, Hadal, Hano4kin, HarveyDent1234, Hippo43, Hmains, Hobbesy3, Hongooi, Hotwiki, Hydrogen Iodide, Hzecher48, I-10, I.am.lost, IW.HG, Ianblair23, In Defense of the Artist, Indisciplined, Infrogmation, IronGargoyle, Ixfd64, J.D., J.delanoy, JDoorjam, JGKlein, JJstroker, JNW, JSpung, JYOuyang, JYi, Jack Cox, Jack Merridew, Jack O'Lantern, JackO'Lantern, JackofOz, Jake Wartenberg, Janemajas, Janjones, Janzzy, Jaranda, Jason song, Jasonqueue, Jaxico, Jaxsonjo, Jay-W, Jaydec, Jczekai, JeCaB, JeanColumbia, Jeandré du Toit, Jeanenawhitney, Jeffpw, Jeremy221, Jeromealden 85, Jessica A R H, Jet0425, Jgold03, Jhsounds, Jklamo, Jodie-Rock-Chick., Joey80, John Cardinal, Jon Kay, Jonyandrhe, Joseph A. Spadaro, Jusdafax, Jusjih, Just a name, Justme89, Jweed, Jxw13, Jzummak, Jóna Þórunn, KF, Kaktus999, Kanags, Kane5187, Kaneshirojj, Katalaveno, Kayaker, Keithjoshua319, Kevphenry, Kgrad, King Pickle, Kittybrewster, Klinean, Koavf, KosMetfan, Krich, Kyliecrazy12, LaVidaLoca, Ladida, Ladygaga223, Lata, Lathrop1885, Lauren, Laurynxo, Leafyplant, Leahbookworm, LeaveSleaves, Lectonar, Leociu, Leuliett, Levineps, Lhademmor, Lights, LindsayH, Lipothymia, LiteraryMaven, Little Savage, Littlealii, LostLeviathan, Louklou, Ludivine, Luk, Luke4545, Luna Santin, Lx 121, MBJ1994, MIP, Madr1000, Majicwand, Malcolmxl5, Mallanox, Maneisis, Mango Lassi, Manuel Trujillo Berges, Mark Foskey, Marketing Comms, Martarius, Marylynn 03, Mastorrent, Matt Deres, Matt Fanning, Mattbr, Maverick maquis, Maxim, Mcilroga, Meegs, Meeso, MegX, Mensurs, Mezforprez, MichaelCaricofe, Mike 7, Mike Rosoft, Mike309, Mintleaf, Misterkillboy, Mkirshner, Moncrief, Mooveeguy, Movieguru2006, Moyda, MrConstantin, MrDolomite, Mrblondnyc, Ms.Cb.Er.Rock, Mschlindwein, Mswake, Mufka, Mushroom, Musical Linguist, Mwilk59, Mydnight, Myrockstar, Mórtas is Dóchas, N5iln, NAD 0108, Natalie Erin, Natalie's Aunt, NawlinWiki, Neilymon, NekoDaemon, NewInn, NickBurns, Night Time, Ninjawarriordex, Noah Salzman, Nonoisense, Nymf, Nyxaus, Oanabay04, Obi777, Oda Mari, Ohnoitsjamie, Ohthelameness, Olivier, Omgshdude, OnBeyondZebrax, Onorem, Operabones, Orbicle, Otto85, Ozgod, Pablo X, PacificBoy, Paine Ellsworth, Pandion auk, Pantaallou, Papasan1, Pardy, Parishan, Pascal.Tesson, PatadyBag, Patchyreynolds, Patrick, Paul A, Paulo Brasil, Pawebster, PeaceNT, Peer Gynt, Pegship, PhantomS, Pharillon, Phillip Andrae Pipes, Phoenix Hacker, Piano non troppo, Pickle23, Piledhigheranddeeper, Portillo, Postcard Cathy, Preaky, PrimroseGuy, Promking, Punchbunny, Purplephlogiston, Qqqqqq, Quadzilla99, RJASE1, RainbowOfLight, Raudys, Ravenscroft32, Razorflame, Rdcarter, Reader781, RealityBoy, Rebecca-louise97, RedWolf, Redeagle688, Remember, Remember the dot, Reorion, RevelationDirect, Rfsilveira, Rgoodermote, Rharris587, Riana, Ribonucleic, Richard Arthur Norton (1958-), Richard Keatinge, RickK, Rito Revollto, Rito Revolto, RobbieNomi, Robertb-dc, Rockpocket, Rodhullandemu, Rogerd, Ron whisky, Ronaldomundo, Ronhjones, Rossrs, Route 82, Rpeh, Rror, Rs09985, Rui789, Runningfridgesrule, Russell McBride, RyanGerbil10, Ryulong, SDS, SFTVLGUY2, SGGH, SP-KP, Saaws, Sam Hocevar, SamuelM555, Sara's Song, Sarahjane10784, Sb1990, Sbo, Schweiwikist, Scott Enos, ScottDavis, ScottyBoy900Q, Seanvolk, Seaphoto, SebRovera, Seidenstud, Sgeureka, Shadowjams, Shaynelp, ShelfSkewed, Shenme, Shimjuan, Shreevatsa, Shshshsh, Shufengbai, Signalhead, Sjö, Skier Dude, Sky678trax, Sky83, Sladey4077, Slarre, Sleepyjuly, Slp, Snake 086, Snigbrook, Snovember, Sopoforic, Spearhead, Spellcast, StarbuckDude, Steevo714, Stepford, Stephenb, SteveCrook, Stevenscollege, Stinna, Stonnman, Stormie, Stuart Drewer, Stymphal, Sunray, Supernova028, Supertigerman, Swango, TFBCT1, TJ Spyke, TRBP, Tabercil, Tabletop, Tangsyde, Tarheelz123, Teiladnam, Tgies, The JPS, The Man in Question, The Thing That Should Not Be, The wub, The-G-Unit-Boss, Theonlyone1234, Thereaderandmerylstreep, Thesavagenorwegian, Thief12, Thingg, ThinkBlue, Thismightbezach, Thunderwing, Thuresson, Tide rolls, Tills, Time420, Titocavalera, Titoxd, Tjwells, Tlbracken, Tobias denton, Tom harrison, Tombadevil, Tone, Tony Sidaway, TonyW, Toolazy21, Tqmartini, Trekphiler, Treybien, Trickzakky, Trusilver, Truthanado, Tryggvia, Tubesurfer, Tuesdaytumble, Turgidson, TutterMouse, Tvoz, Twix1875, Ulric1313, Ume, Uncle Milty, Unika542, Unscented, Urcolors, Va396053, Vasif', Versus22, VeryVerily, Vesperholly, Viridae, Vontafeijos, Voodoo4936, Vulturell, W Tanoto, Wafry, Walgert, Ward3001, Wellsjc, Welshleprechaun, Whkoh, Who, Wik, WikiDan61, WikiPikiUser, Wikiauthor6, Wikiklrsc, Wildhartlivie, Will Beback, Willking1979, Wimt, WojPob, Wompa99, Woohookitty, Wool Mintons, Written92, X--BAH, Xevior, Xlaughalot08, Yakofujimato, Yamla, YggDrasil, Yinzland, Yllosubmarine, Yokes14, ZimZalaBim, Zoe, Zoicon5, Zutopiaa, Zzyzx11, 1547 anonymous edits

List of awards and nominations received by Meryl Streep *Source*:http://en.wikipedia.org/w/index.php?oldid=377361553 *Contributors*: After Midnight, Alecsdaniel, Ben Ram, CactusWriter, Charlie White, Cnbrb, Colin, Dabomb87, Dimody, EmmyWinner, Graham87, JamesAM, Joseph A. Spadaro, Kai81, Koavf, Lacp hp93, Ladida, Mmxx, MrDolomite, NWill, Operabones, Otto4711, Ozgod, Pdcook, RayOfLight, Scott Enos, ShelfSkewed, Spinerod, TenPoundHammer, Theydiskox, Thomas Blomberg, UnitedStatesian, YeLLeY511, 94 anonymous edits

Julia (1977 film) *Source*: http://en.wikipedia.org/w/index.php?oldid=380814451 *Contributors*: *drew, Aibdescalzo, AlbertSM, Ameliorate!, Bobet, Carbuncle, Cburnett, Cherubino, Cop 663, Cybercobra, Daniel Case, David Gerard, Discospinster, ExpressingYourself, Fierce Beaver, Foofbun, Fuhghettaboutit, Hazel75, Hnsampat, Iain99, Ilario, IronGargoyle, JHMM13, Jerzy, Jhsounds, John K, Johnbod, LGagnon, Lady Aleena, Loul, MachoCarioca, Mca2001, MovieNut14, Msw1002, Nice poa, Orbicle, Pathfinder general, Phbasketball6, Quentin X, Retired username, Someone else, Sreejithk2000, Supernumerary, Ted Wilkes, ThatsGoodTelevision, TheMadBaron, Thismightbezach, Treybien, Varlaam, Zoe, 62 anonymous edits

The Deer Hunter *Source*: http://en.wikipedia.org/w/index.php?oldid=380991355 *Contributors*: 21655, 2T, ABoerma, AEMoreira042281, Abelson, Adam78, Adraeus, Adrian 1001, Ahoerstemeier, Ahseaton, Aim Here, Airproofing, Al Fecund, Albrozdude, Alexander Iwaschkin, Aliotra, Alleborgo, Altzinn, Ameliorate!, Andrzejbanas, Angel caboodle, Apple1976, AppleJuggler, Aramko, Arataman 79, ArielGold, Ashley Pomeroy, Asidemes, Athene cunicularia, Atlanticwriter, Attilios, BD2412, Baconpatroller, Badagnani, Barfoos, Baxelson, Bdve, Bigjimr, Billitch, Bobo192, Bramabull201, Btreen, Bysmuth, Caknuck, Cburnett, CelticJobber, Chainclaw, Charles F. Xavier, Chris Bainbridge, ChrisGriswold, Chrisjie, ChuckyDarko, Cinemaretro, Ckatz, Ckenney5, Clancy60, CodeMonk, Conqueror100, Crazyeye343, Cronosmantas, DArcyFD, DHN, Dabilharo, Daniel Case, DaveJB, Daveswagon, David Gerard, Dcabrilo, Ddlfan, Discographer, Discospinster, Dmitri Lytov, Doczilla, Donmike10, DoubleCross, Download, Dr. Blofeld, Drewcifer3000, Drmies, DulcetTone, DurotarLord, Dutzi, Ed Fitzgerald, Edlitz36, Edward, Eggsaladbob, Ekki01, Erik, FMAFan1990, Favonian, Fenderguy68, Fk-, FlipmodePlaya, Flyboy03191, Folding Chair, Forbsey, Fortdj33, Freikorp, Fuhghettaboutit, Funkyvoltron, Furrykef, G8bluSti, Gamaliel, Gig.panas, Gilliam, Girolamo Savonarola, GoingBatty, Goustien, Havardj, Henry Flower, Hilldog, Hillock65, Hiphats, Hit bull, win steak, Horatio325, Hurrah for vomit, IDarreni, ILikeThings, Ikonologist, Irishguy, IronGargoyle, J.D., JMMuller, JackalsIII, JackofOz, Jacopo, Jason One, Java13690, Jbarta, Jennavecia, Jennica, Jienum, Jim Jackson, Jiy, Joegeiger61, Joey80, John, John Riemann Soong, John Williams Fan, Jonny5244, Jordancelticsfan, Junehealy, Jureff, Jzummak, Kakun, Kbdank71, Keilana, Khaosjr, Kitty Davis, Knowledgebycoop, Konczewski, Kont Dracula, Koyaanis Qatsi, Kukini, Kusma, LGagnon, LLBBooks, Lampica, Lawikitejana, Le Anh-Huy, Levelistchampion, Lfh, Liane1950, LilHelpa, Lion for truth, Longlivefolkmusic, Lugnuts, MADaboutforests, MCDRLx, MONGO, MachoCarioca, Mackcat, Magnet For Knowledge, Mallfox68, Malo, Mariavb, MarnetteD, Marychan41, Matlefebvre20, Matsumuraseito, Matthew Platts, Mensurs, Mild Bill Hiccup, Mintrick, Mjkeliher, Mrblondnyc, MwNNrules, NWill, Natesway78, Ndteegarden, Neek, Nehrams2020, NorthernThunder, Notaninja, Nreive, Olivier, Otto4711, Oxymoron83, PDTantisocial, PaZuZu, Pais, Parallel33, Parrot of Doom, Parsar, Paul Stansifer, Paulinho28, Pearle, Pegship, Peter G Werner, Phbasketball6, Philosophistry, Phyland, Picapica, Pinktulip, Piriczki, Plutonium27, Preisler, Q8-falcon, RBBrittain, Radar123, RandomCritic, Rangek, RattleandHum, Rbmoore, RepublicanJacobite, RevRagnarok, Rich Farmbrough, Rjwilmsi, Rmenard, RobNS, Robertkelly50, Rpravak, Rudowsky, RyanDaniel, SDJ, SGGH, SHODAN, Salgueiro, Sam, Savidan, Scooteristi, Scorpion0422, Scythre, Seamanrob, Sfahey, Sgeureka, Shakesphere17, Sharkface217, Shervinafshar, SilkTork, Sir Buzz Killington, Sir Tobek, SlamDiego, Smyth, Spellmaster, Steve C. Litchfeld., Steveprutz, Stillstudying, Sureworksforme, Svick, Swellman, Sydfrog, Szumyk, TJ Spyke, TallulahBelle, Tangotango, Tatiana.larina, Tatrgel, Tdogg241, Tempshill, Terrypin, ThatGuamGuy, The Glow Pt. 2, The Singing Badger, The monkeyhate, TheLastAmigo, TheMadBaron, TheOnlyOne12, Thepangelinanpost, Theradu123, Timc, Tommyt, Tool2Die4, Torourkeus, Treybien, Triddle, Ttc817, Tucu Mann, Typhoon966, Tzahy, Ukzombie, Userafw, Ustye, Uucp, Verkhovensky, Vladimir Skala, Waldir, Who, Wikispork, Wildhartlivie, Willerror, Wolfer68, Wool Mintons, Wwestarwars, Yaf, Yamla, Yekrats, Yoshi Canopus, Zeerfszeerfs, ZeroJanvier, Zoe, Zone46, Zorastrus, Zzyzx11, 550 anonymous edits

Manhattan (film) *Source*: http://en.wikipedia.org/w/index.php?oldid=378596780 *Contributors*: APOCOLYPSE7, Adraeus, Alai, All Hallow's Wraith, Anshuk, ArglebargleIV, Asparagus, Astorknlam, B. Phillips, BONKEROO, Badzebra, Barrettmagic, Chris Bainbridge, Cop 663, Count Ringworm, Crumbsucker, Daniel Case, Davers, David Gerard, Dfmock, Dr. Blofeld, Easchiff, Ehmjay, Eighty8keys2life, Emc2, Erik, Father McKenzie, FightTheDarkness, FilmFemme, Froglars the frog, GHcool, Gamaliel, Garion96, Gjones0316, Good Olfactory, Grafen, Hu Totya, IronGargoyle, ItsTheClimb17, J.D., JAF1970, JackalsIII, Jahsonic, Jajhill, JamesAM, Jeremy706, Jerry FM, John of Reading, John254, Jordgubbe, Jpbowen, Juranas, Jzummak, Kbdank71, Kieranthompson, Koyaanis Qatsi, Lach Graham, Lady Aleena, Lampford, Levineps, Lugnuts, MAG1, MJBurrage, MachoCarioca, Mallanox, Mantanmoreland, MarnetteD, Mathew5000, Modemac, Morgan Wick, Morval, Moshe Constantine Hassan Al-Silverburg, Mporch, Mrblondnyc, NorthernThunder, NotACow, Orioane, Ortzinator, Patrick, Pblair44, Pearle, Phaeton23, Philip Cross, Portia327, Purslane, PyotrPetr1, Quiddity, Raliugar, Rhobite, Rich Farmbrough, Saculeramacal13, Sanfranman59, Scooby7292, ScottyBoy900Q, Siroxo, SteinbDJ, Steven Walling, Sugar Bear, THEN WHO WAS PHONE?, TallulahBelle, Tangcameo, Teodor605, The Anome, The JPS, Thismightbezach, TonyW, Treybien, Truthiness Jones, Turkeyphant, Utergar, Wikiwatcher1, WillSloan, Woohookitty, Zoe, 59 anonymous edits

The Seduction of Joe Tynan Source: http://en.wikipedia.org/w/index.php?oldid=373198577 Contributors: Andrzejbanas, Bovineboy2008, Davidbspalding, Donfbreed, Dravecky, Frecklefoot, IronGargoyle, Lugnuts, Luigibob, Orbicle, TheMovieBuff, Trumpetrep, Zoicon5, 2 anonymous edits

Kramer vs. Kramer Source: http://en.wikipedia.org/w/index.php?oldid=380244577 Contributors: *drew, 17Drew, AdamSmithee, Alcyrty, Amakuru, Ameliorate!, Amphytrite, Andycjp, Aryan song, Bantosh, Bladeofgrass, Bovineboy2008, Breckinridge, Brycee, Burglekutt, Bzuk, CapDac, Catgut, Cattus, Cburnett, Christianster45, Classicfilms, Cotoco, DJZK, Daniel Case, David Gerard, Davstin2002, Dead3y3, DerHexer, Donreed, Dr. Blofeld, EchetusXe, Edlitz36, EoGuy, Erik, Erika1042, ExpressingYourself, FightTheDarkness, Fighting for Justice, Fleebo, Fromgermany, GHcool, Garion96, Gp 1980, Gyrofrog, Heaven's Wrath, IronGargoyle, IrrTJMc, J Milburn, JGKlein, JHMM13, Jack Merridew, JavierMC, Joey80, Jonathan.s.kt, Jordancelticsfan, Jr2280, Jzummak, Kchishol1970, Kidlittle, Kollision, Koyaanis Qatsi, Ksnow, LFlippyl, LGagnon, Lacrimosus, Lady Aleena, Levineps, Liftarn, Luckyluke, Lugnuts, MachoCarioca, Mallanox, Marktreut, Martarius, Master Deusoma, Matlefebvre20, Maximus Rex, Mca2001, Mdb1370, Mike Payne, NWill, NapoliRoma, Nehrams2020, Ngchikit, OldSkoolGeek, Ozzykhan, Phbasketball6, Philip Trueman, Philthy Liar, Pink Bull, ProhibitOnions, Quixoto, RBBrittain, Rfc1394, RobJ1981, Routedge, Rrburke, Rungbachduong, Savidan, Shawnyboy13, Shshshsh, Skier Dude, Snowmanradio, Stormfin, SuperNova, Svencb, TJ Spyke, Tad Lincoln, Terrek, ThatGuamGuy, TheRedPenOfDoom, Thefourdotelipsis, Thismightbezach, Torrianne, Treybien, UZiBLASTER7, Uucp, Valermos, Vector Potential, VectorisPotential, Vipinhari, Vrenator, Wiki fanatic, Wikipeterproject, Wildhartlivie, Wildtornado, Yashveer r, Yestyest2000, Zepheus, Zoe, Zzyzx11, Александър, 191 anonymous edits

The French Lieutenant's Woman (film) Source: http://en.wikipedia.org/w/index.php?oldid=379921642 Contributors: AN(Ger), AdamSmithee, Andycjp, Berks105, Blanche of King's Lynn, Brian1979, Cgingold, DMChatterton, Daniel Case, Garion96, Hapleworth, Indisciplined, IronGargoyle, JSBVLA, JayHenry, Karin127, Liquidsnake, Lugnuts, MrDarcy, Orbicle, Pegship, Rodhullandemu, Ron whisky, Sreejithk2000, Tassedethe, TheMovieBuff, Thismightbezach, TonyW, Treybien, Yashveer r, Yorkshiresky, Zugy, 20 anonymous edits

Still of the Night (film) Source: http://en.wikipedia.org/w/index.php?oldid=374402130 Contributors: Abdowiki, Andrzejbanas, Aphasia83, Bovineboy2008, Cbradshaw, Elendil's Heir, IronGargoyle, J.D., JimboV1, Lugnuts, Skier Dude, Thefourdotelipsis, 6 anonymous edits

Sophie's Choice (film) Source: http://en.wikipedia.org/w/index.php?oldid=378125420 Contributors: 17Drew, Aff123a, Altone, Andycjp, Angel2001, AniMate, Antti29, Arsene, B$boy, Barticus88, Blueclare, Bovineboy2008, Caiaffa, Crainquebille, Crzycheetah, Daniel Case, David Gerard, Derbent 5000, Discospinster, Dogah, Dudeman5685, Durwoodie, Dutzi, EamonnPKeane, Easchiff, Ed Poor, Emoll, Exir Kamalabadi, Films addicted, Fothergill Volkensniff IV, Freshh, Fuhghettaboutit, GFlohr, Garion96, Hede2000, Hiphats, Hmains, IronGargoyle, ItsTheClimb17, Jauerback, Jeepday, Jmfossil, Joseph A. Spadaro, Jzummak, KJRehberg, Kbdank71, Kelly Martin, Kjudson16, Kransky, Litalex, Miss Dark, Mollywiki, Nice poa, NorthernThunder, Oneangrydwarf, Orbicle, Pegship, Persian Poet Gal, Pion, Prestonmcconkie, Qwertqwertqwert 1, Rahgsu, Ridgewoodian, Rklawton, Rlevse, Rodrigogomesonetwo, Schrandit, Sgeureka, Shaneymike, Srikeit, Symphony Girl, Tad Lincoln, TakuyaMurata, Teapot37, The monkeyhate, TheSPY, Timbouctou, Tkreuz, Tomdobb, Treybien, Twas Now, Ulric1313, Varlaam, WAS 4.250, Whoville, Wildhartlivie, Wålberg, גואנא, 118 anonymous edits

Silkwood Source: http://en.wikipedia.org/w/index.php?oldid=376464708 Contributors: Andrzejbanas, Bobet, Cburnett, CharlotteWebb, Daniel Case, Darkness2005, Erik9, Films addicted, Fuhghettaboutit, Gabrielkat, GregorB, Irishguy, IronGargoyle, Jeffman52001, Jeodesic, Jfitts, JonathanDP81, Kchishol1970, Kerowyn, LGagnon, Lachaume, Levineps, LimoWreck, LiteraryMaven, MegX, Megan1967, Minamoto, NickLee808, Otto4711, Phil Boswell, Reginald Perrin, Sottolacqua, Teleomatic, Treybien, Trilemma, User2004, Zoe, 31 anonymous edits

Falling in Love (film) Source: http://en.wikipedia.org/w/index.php?oldid=379777904 Contributors: Hagerman, Ionutzmovie, Ka ga, Lugnuts, Mchan2008, Mrblondnyc, Nehrams2020, Saberwyn, SammoHunk, Sreejithk2000, Teatreez, TheMovieBuff, Tvoz, Ume, Wisekwai, Wool Mintons, 10 anonymous edits

Plenty (film) Source: http://en.wikipedia.org/w/index.php?oldid=373589536 Contributors: *drew, AndrewHowse, Andrewire, Beardo, Bobet, CapitalLetterBeginning, D6, Daniel Case, ExpressingYourself, Grandpafootsoldier, GregorB, Hmains, IronGargoyle, JackofOz, KF, Lee M, Lord Cornwallis, Mydnight, Philip Cross, Pigsonthewing, Tamariki, TheMovieBuff, Yarnover, Zombie433, 8 anonymous edits

Out of Africa (film) Source: http://en.wikipedia.org/w/index.php?oldid=379367409 Contributors: *drew, 2T, AlbertSM, Alca Impenne, Ameliorate!, AndrewHowse, Andrzejbanas, Aranel, Azucar, Batman Jr., Big Bird, Birdienest81, Bletch, Bluemoose, Bob K31416, Bobblewik, Brion VIBBER, Bzuk, Calroscow, Captain Crawdad, Cattona, Cburnett, ChrisG, ChrisLoosley, Coelacan, Daniel Case, Darkness2005, David Gerard, David Levy, Delldot, Dpwkbw, Drbuzzard, Dreiundvierzig, Drolldurham, Easchiff, EchetusXe, Ed Fitzgerald, Edward, Elwinator, Enr1x, Estrose, Ezeu, Feudonym, FordPrefect42, Fuhghettaboutit, Gamaliel, Gaudio, Gousteiron, Gridge, Grstain, Harryboyles, Hegria66, IP4240207xx, IronGargoyle, JackofOz, Jaiwills, Jed, Jelins, Joey80, Johnbod, Jojocool117, Judgesurreal777, Julius Sahara, Jzummak, K1Bond007, Kbdank71, Ketiltrout, Klow, KnightRider, LGagnon, Levineps, Lugnuts, M samadi, MachoCarioca, Mallanox, Matlefebvre20, Matt Crypto, Meadow68, Michael Hardy, Mischa83, Mschlindwein, Muntuwandi, NWill, OlofE, Orbicle, Pegship, Phbasketball6, Plch, PurrfectPeach, Ruud Koot, Savidan, Sherool, Smaines, Snowmanradio, Stevenscollege, Supernumerary, Taiichi, Tassedethe, Tejblum, ThatGuamGuy, The Unknown Muncher, TheGerm, TheLastAmigo, TheMadBaron, Thismightbezach, Treybien, Twthmoses, UZiBLASTER7, Vlad, Whbjr, WhisperToMe, Wikid77, Wikipus, Xevior, Zyxoas, Zzyzx11, 101 anonymous edits

Heartburn (film) Source: http://en.wikipedia.org/w/index.php?oldid=347131889 Contributors: Angelo Somaschini, Baumi, Booshakla, BrownHairedGirl, Catamorphism, CharlotteWebb, Daniel Case, David Gerard, Flata, Fromgermany, Fuhghettaboutit, Greenchica, Grstain, Hede2000, Ianblair23, Irishguy, IronGargoyle, Jurinac, LiteraryMaven, Longhair, Mallanox, MarnetteD, Melly42, Mfolozi, Mishler77, Rirave, Sebesta, Treybien, Troy34, Ume, WBardwin, Wildhartlivie, 16 anonymous edits

Ironweed (film) Source: http://en.wikipedia.org/w/index.php?oldid=366360357 Contributors: AN(Ger), Andrewire, AttoRenato, Bearian, Bunker by, Cesarm, Daniel Case, David Gerard, Dycedarg, George415, Irishguy, IronGargoyle, Ironweed, Jansch, Jjpancake, Jonay81687, Ken Gallager, Khaosjr, Ling.Nut, Lugnuts, Luigibob, MachoCarioca, Max rspct, Parktravelling, Pethan, Rapido, Roberteldred, Ron whisky, Ronaldomundo, Sander Moholi, Thefourdotelipsis, Treybien, 29 anonymous edits

A Cry in the Dark Source: http://en.wikipedia.org/w/index.php?oldid=379747911 Contributors: Angmering, Anthony Appleyard, Armeisen, Bignoter, Bobak, Briantw, Bzuk, Canek, CapitalLetterBeginning, Cburnett, Clarkk, Daniel Case, Demomoke, Dl2000, DonQuixote, Eregli bob, Erik, Erik9, Ewen, FMAFan1990, Feydey, Films addicted, Gabbe, Grandpafootsoldier, GregorB, HaroldPGuy, Irishguy, IronGargoyle, JackofOz, Jeffpw, JimDunning, Kckoch, Kwah-LeBaire, Longhair, Lugnuts, Mattinbgn, Mattisgoo, Meredyth, MithrandirAgain, Mliss4816, MovieMadness, Musical Linguist, Nehrams2020, Nightscream, Orbicle, Otrfan, PFHLai, Pegship, Plasticspork, Rich Farmbrough, Ron whisky, ST47, Sophruhig Vita@comcast.net, Squids and Chips, Steve, T3hllama, TheMovieBuff, Tony1, Treybien, Ty11good, Wafry, Wisekwai, 36 anonymous edits

She-Devil (film) Source: http://en.wikipedia.org/w/index.php?oldid=378131607 Contributors: Agtaz, Anturiaethwr, BD2412, Bhoywunda88, Btobw, Cleanupbabe, Colonies Chris, Daibhid C, Daniel Case, David Gerard, DepressedPer, E-Kartoffel, Easchiff, EoGuy, Faradayplank, Films addicted, Fratrep, Frongle, Homeworlds, Ilana, IronGargoyle, Kollision, Lindy43, Lugnuts, McJeff, MegTheGem, Mendaliv, Mro, Pedant 666, Pegship, Pethan, RedRollerskate, Samuella, Sawznhamrs, ShelfSkewed, Soccer5525, Station1, Tassedethe, Tauroneo v2, TreoBoy680, USN1977, Vikasztrenz, Wikid77, Woohookitty, Zoltarpanaflex, зейпал, 45 anonymous edits

Postcards from the Edge (film) Source: http://en.wikipedia.org/w/index.php?oldid=378453992 Contributors: Bender235, Chaosdruid, Darkness2005, Ekabhishek, Levineps, LiteraryMaven, N-HH, Revery, Sanwood, ShelfSkewed, TenPoundHammer, Treybien, 5 anonymous edits

Defending Your Life Source: http://en.wikipedia.org/w/index.php?oldid=369383267 Contributors: Andrzejbanas, Avalyn, Benscripps, CJMylentz, Clarityfiend, D6, David Gerard, EagleFan, Earendilmm, Erik9, Everything counts, Fairsing, Flopsy Mopsy and Cottonmouth, FrankRizzo2006, Frschoonover, Funky Monkey, I AM THE MAN IN NYS, Lolliapaulina51, MJD86, Mahjong705, Mallanox, Michig, Nightscream, Noirish, PrimeHunter, Quackslikeaduck, Quentin X, SamSock, See918, Shawn in Montreal, SilverDrake11, Sohollywood, Supernumerary, Tabletop, Tim1965, WOSlinker, Zoltarpanaflex, 40 anonymous edits

Death Becomes Her Source: http://en.wikipedia.org/w/index.php?oldid=379634670 Contributors: 159753, 6afraidof7, 9ign, Aminto, Andrzejbanas, Angel caboodle, AngelofMusic07, Ashish20, Avalyn, Barneca, Bdesham, Big Bird, BlessedPsycho, Boredalot, BruceMajors, Bubba287, Chris the speller, Citizenjamesford, Crunkier21, CyberSkull, DNewhall, Daedalus969, DaliJim, Darkness2005, David Gerard, Deathawk, Discospinster, Djfspence, Dmlandfair, Dollvalley, Dominic Hardstaff, DrSamba, Drippingmintleaves, DropDeadGorgias, Easchiff, Easterbradford, EmiOfBrie, Frecklefoot, Freikorp, Freshh, GMc, Garion96, Grandpafootsoldier, Hobbesy3, HoneyBee, Hourton Cladwell, Hullabaloo Wolfowitz, I c u trippin, IW.HG, Inspector 34, Irk, Islander, Jamesbanesmith, Jason Palpatine, Jeff Muscato, Jogers, John K, Johnlongbond, Joho777, Jojhutton, Jryfle, Lots42, Manadarax, Marktreut, Meegs, Micione, Minefal, Mistamagic28, Morshem, Motor, Nehrams2020, NeilN, Olağan Şüpheli, PBP, Passive, PhantomS, Phbasketball6, Puckly, QuasyBoy, Rivertown, Rossumcapek, Sawblade5, SergioGeorgini, Shakirfan, Slawojarek, Slicing, Soetermans, Sottolacqua, Sreejithk2000, Sugar Bear, SunnyParadigm, Supernumerary, Sweetalker79, TMC1982, Tassedethe, Template namespace initialisation script, TestPilot, Tfine80, ThomasO1989, Tony Sidaway, Tony1, Tough Little Ship, Treybien, Trovatore, Tzartzam, USN1977, Valermos, Veelmeet, VicGeorge2K7, Violetriga, Wjrb, Wonderboy72, Xezbeth, Yaksar, Yopohari, ZeroJanvier, Zoe, Zoltarpanaflex, Zombie433, 183 anonymous edits

The House of the Spirits (film) Source: http://en.wikipedia.org/w/index.php?oldid=379960147 Contributors: AN(Ger), Attilios, Bart133, Binksternet, Caiaffa, CanisRufus, Cecilia.fariasf, Daniel Case, Darkness2005, Donmike10, El Slameron, Emiellaiendiay, Esp rus, Evenfiel, Eztigma, Films addicted, Goplat, Grandpafootsoldier, GregorB, Grm wnr, Insanephantom, IronGargoyle, Isaac Sanolnacov, Jay-W, Katyciai, Kerowyn, Lady Aleena, Lmnbk, Maitch, Man pl, Mild Bill Hiccup, Mnemosine, Mona, MrPanyGoff, Nadavspi, Nehrams2020, Niteowlneils, Reedy, Richard Arthur Norton (1958-), Rjwilmsi, SISLEY, Smetanahue, Spiel, Sreejithk2000, Steam5, Tabletop, Taestell, Tavilis, TheMadBaron, Twthmoses, Wiki-uk, Wool Mintons, Xezbeth, 76 anonymous edits

The River Wild *Source*: http://en.wikipedia.org/w/index.php?oldid=380525340 *Contributors*: Alembic, All Hallow's Wraith, Amire80, Andrzejbanas, Angel caboodle, Bensin, CanadianCaesar, Cherry blossom tree, Colonies Chris, Crotchety Old Man, Darkness2005, David Gerard, Donteatyellowsnow, DoubleCross, Dr. Blofeld, Dreamafter, Easchiff, EncMstr, Gaius Cornelius, Hitm1, Imagineanewworld, Irishguy, Jeepday, Jgpete74, Jmorgan, Levineps, LogicallyCreative, Lots42, Lugnuts, Lukeowens, Martarius, Paul Barlow, Pitamakan, Reimelt, Runt, Schizodelight, Shenme, TFunk, Tabletop, Tea&magpies, Thecheesykid, Thorpe, Vegaswikian, Victor Lopes, WereSpielChequers, 60 anonymous edits

The Bridges of Madison County (film) *Source*: http://en.wikipedia.org/w/index.php?oldid=380257377 *Contributors*: 66richardson, Abc10, Absinthe88, Anshuk, Antti29, Ar-ras, BillMaddock, Black Falcon, Bovineboy2008, Cybercobra, Dabackgammonator, Daniel Case, Darkness2005, David Gerard, Debresser, Del91, Dr. Blofeld, FrankRizzo2006, Gökhan, IronGargoyle, Jajhill, Java13690, KConWiki, Lady Aleena, Lavarock1234, Levineps, Mollywiki, NWill, Notpietru, Orbicle, Paul A, Pegship, Quentin X, RattleandHum, RepublicanJacobite, RicJac, Russellhome, S h i v a (Visnu), SISLEY, Smyth, Spinerod, Taestell, Urashimataro, Yaroslav Blanter, Yoho2001, 39 anonymous edits

Before and After (film) *Source*: http://en.wikipedia.org/w/index.php?oldid=357349347 *Contributors*: AN(Ger), Academic Challenger, Andrzejbanas, ApolloBoy, David Gerard, Freshh, Hoverfish, Lugnuts, MZMcBride, Nehrams2020, Pegship, Quentin X, Qworty, Radiojon, RicJac, Rich Farmbrough, Ryangibsonstewart, ShelfSkewed, SilkTork, Skier Dude, Stinna, TheMovieBuff, Treybien, Zandarx, 9 anonymous edits

Marvin's Room (film) *Source*: http://en.wikipedia.org/w/index.php?oldid=377349396 *Contributors*: AN(Ger), Astorknlam, Azucar, Bencey, Bovineboy2008, Catamorphism, Cburnett, Dan56, David Petrarca, Easchiff, Egghead06, Ekabhishek, Emerson7, Erik, Garion96, Garynine, Grandpafootsoldier, High Heels on Wet Pavement, Hullaballoo Wolfowitz, IronGargoyle, Jeannie's Glowball, Levineps, Lugnuts, MartinVillafuerte85, Mlaffs, Moriori, Nick Levine, Pohick2, SnapSnap, TheLastAmigo, Thryduulf, Tregoweth, Treybien, Wknight94, Xezbeth, Zoe, 20 anonymous edits

Dancing at Lughnasa (film) *Source*: http://en.wikipedia.org/w/index.php?oldid=379771303 *Contributors*: After Midnight, Andrewire, Another Believer, Aspects, DeWaine, Dravecky, Emerson7, Garynine, Judas2610, Lugnuts, Nandt1, Ruthyruth, TheMovieBuff, Treybien, 11 anonymous edits

One True Thing *Source*: http://en.wikipedia.org/w/index.php?oldid=373660224 *Contributors*: Andycjp, Anna678, Bovineboy2008, Carlaclaws, Cburnett, Commander Shepard, DavidRF, Dreamer.se, EllertMichael, Enderminh, Gabefarkas, Gtrmp, IronGargoyle, Kerowyn, Krobinson95, Leroyinc, Lugnuts, Maneisis, Mcornelius, Nono64, Quentin X, Rjwilmsi, Shadowhillway, Sohollywood, Stormie, Swimdb, TheMovieBuff, Trevor GH5, Treybien, Walker9010, WebHamster, Zoe, 36 anonymous edits

Music of the Heart *Source*: http://en.wikipedia.org/w/index.php?oldid=380471974 *Contributors*: AlbertSM, Andrewire, Antodav2007, BigrTex, Blackbone 5000, Blt1984, Bylandl, Catamorphism, CatherineMunro, Cburnett, Charlie White, Citizenjamesford, Crystallina, D6, Darwinek, Debresser, Edward, Fallout boy, Grandpafootsoldier, Iroc24, JamieS93, Jlover, Jwad, Kate, Klaus Baudelaire256, MakeRocketGoNow, McSly, MegX, Milton Stanley, Mlf107, NYDCSP, Niteowlneils, Oxymoron83, Pathoschild, Peytonbland, Prashanthns, RicJac, Robert Fraser, Shoessss, Silent Tom, Sreejithk2000, Stevietheman, Suckstobeabum, Swimdb, Topbanana, Toussaint, Treybien, Wildhartlivie, Wolfling, Wool Mintons, 45 anonymous edits

A.I. Artificial Intelligence *Source*: http://en.wikipedia.org/w/index.php?oldid=380849797 *Contributors*: *Ria777*, 23skidoo, 2T, 2rusty22, AKR619, AaronW, AceTracer, Ahoerstemeier, Ajm81, Alectrona, Alientraveller, AlistairMcMillan, All Hallow's Wraith, Allixpeeke, Ameliorate!, AmethystPhoenix, AndrewHowse, Andrzejbanas, Angel caboodle, Angr, Anthony Appleyard, Artihcus022, Asbestos, AskFranz, Asmallwhitecube, Astronaut, Avaloan, Avantgame, Balsa10, Batmanand, Blackjanedavey, Blt33, Bobblehead, Bobo192, Bovineboy2008, Boxclocke, Bryan Derksen, Bulgaroctonus, Burpelson AFB, Burschik, CannedLizard, Caspian, Cesarm, Chad44, Chaosdruid, Chaoticfluffy, CharlesFosterKane123, ChesterG, ChrisiPK, Christian75, Chuq, Closedmouth, Cmelsted, Cocoaguy, Codrdan, Colds7ream, Collard, ContiAWB, CoolKatt number 99999, Crumbsucker, Curps, Cvindustries, Damiens.rf, Dan4142, Dan8700, DanielCD, Dante Alighieri, Dark hyena, Darkness2005, David Gerard, Deletros, DirkvdM, Discospinster, Djfspence, Dlrohrer2003, DmcReif, Dom Kaos, Doradus, Dr. Blofeld, DrBob, Drake Clawfang, Druff, Dss1bond, Dumoren, Duncan5qwerty, Earle Martin, Ecthelion83, Editor510, Elfguy, Ellsworth, Emuzesto, Erik Zachte, Erik9, ErinM, Erp Erpington, Evans1982, Ewlyahoocom, FMAFan1990, Fabulous Creature, FaithLehaneTheVampireSlayer, Fallout boy, Fighting for Justice, Films addicted, Francisco Valverde, FrankRizzo2006, Frecklefoot, Fred Bradstadt, Freedomlinux, Freshh, Gabbe, Gaheris, Gangster Octopus, Garion96, Gatherton, Gbraad, Getana, Ghirlandajo, Gogo Dodo, Gorm, Goustien, Grandpafootsoldier, Grant65, Grognard3, Gtrmp, Happy Evil Dude, Harac, Harnad, Hede2000, Heilemann, Hermitage17, HighEnergyProtons, Hiphats, Home Row Keysplurge, Horkana, Husond, IKato, Imagechaos, Impaciente, Islandboy99, Ithinkhelikesit, J.J., JB82, JForget, Jafetdexter, James Emtage, Jamesontai, JasonAQuest, Jclemens, Jedi Master Fort, Jeff Muscato, Jetforme, Jguad1, Jiawen, Jmax-, JoeLeydon, JoeLoeb, John-107, Johners, Jolivetti, Judgesurreal777, Judson, JustPhil, Jwk3, Karynannestuckey, Kbdank71, Kea, KeithJonsn, Kieranthompson, Kingoomieiii, Koavf, Kody9100, Kona1611, Konczewski, Korath, Kosmopolis, Kosunen, Ktalon, Kubrick 908, Kylelovesyou, Ladiesman925, Lastorset, LilHelpa, Logical Gentleman, MacGyverMagic, MachoCarioca, Magnius, Malickfan86, Mallanox, Manuel Anastácio, Marco.rambaldi, MarnetteD, Martarius, MartinDK, Matteh, Matty j, Maximus Rex, McNoddy, Melvalevis, Menchi, Metlin, Michael Devore, Michaelbusch, Mighty Antar, Mika1h, Mikeo, Millahnna, Miranda, Mirror Vax, Mista-X, Mitaphane, Mjb, Mjparry716, Mjrmtg, Mjwilso7, Mnealon, Modi mode, Mrmewe, Mrwojo, Muchosucko, Mysdaao, N5iln, NAHID, NXK, Nabokov, Navstar, Norm mit, Norminator, Nv8200p, Olivier, Orangemike, Orpheus Machina, Oscarthecat, P0lyglut, PR Hero, Pag293, Pantologywhore, Passive, Patrick, Paul A, Pb30, Pd THOR, Pedist, Pedro cunha, Pegship, Pejman47, Peter Greenwell, Phazer1980, Pingveno, Pipedreamergrey, Plasticspork, Poketape, Ppntori, ProhibitOnions, Prtyjedi, Quadraxis, Quadzilla99, R'n'B, Raabscuttle, RadicalBender, Ramo0031, Rapscallion, Reball01, ReyBrujo, Rjwilmsi, Rlee0001, RobyWayne, Rojomoke, Rsrikanth05, Rtkat3, RyanGFilm, Rydra Wong, S Luke, SCPM08, SMC, ST47, Salamurai, Sarahmcphee, Saudade7, Sağlamcı, Schewek, ScottyBoy900Q, Shenme, Shimgray, Sin-man, SiobhanHansa, Sirveaux, Siurekrek, Sj, Sm8900, Smartsmith, Soc8675309, Softlavender, SonicNirvana, SpaceFlight89, Splash, Spookfish, Staecker, Stephenchou0722, Stoshmaster, Str1977, Sverdrup, TCorp, THINMAN, Tabletop, TaerkastUA, Template namespace initialisation script, Tethet2Tethet, The JPS, The Singing Badger, The Transhumanist, The Wookieepedian, TheGreenwalker, TheGrza, TheLastAmigo, TheLordGLod, Thedarkestclear, Theoldanarchist, ThomasO1989, Thoreau 222, Tiger Trek, TinyMark, Tobit2, Todd unt, Tomdobb, Tommyt, Tony1, TonyW, Trcunning, Treybien, Tuncrypt, Typhoon966, Tyw7, TøM, UDScott, Ukt-zero, Unyoyega, VI, Vainqueur, Van helsing, Vikrant42, Viriditas, Vision3001, Voldemore, Vroomfondel, Waldir, Ward3001, WatchAndObserve, Wdfarmer, Wereon, Who, Wik, Wik4, Wildroot, Will4311, Wlmg, Xezbeth, Xklsv, Xylke, Year 2144, Yongxinge, Yorkshiresky, Yossarian, ZENDELBACH, Zafiroblue05, Zen56749, Zepperdude, ZeroJanvier, Zoe, Zoicon5, Zooterkin, Zzyzx11, צבי דניאל, 505 anonymous edits

Adaptation (film) *Source*: http://en.wikipedia.org/w/index.php?oldid=377084922 *Contributors*: *drew, 97198, A bit iffy, AEMoreira042281, AaronSw, AdamSmithee, Airproofing, Alca Impenne, Alientraveller, Almostfamous83, Amelia Hunt, Ams80, Andre Engels, Aphid360, Aremith, Arman88, Arteitle, Azucar, Bartsimpelus, Belovedfreak, Bergsten, BlackWingsOfDestiny, Bluxxie, Bobak, Bongwarrior, BookhouseBoy, Bruce Campbell, Bullettoothfilms, Cburnett, CelticJobber, CharlotteWebb, Chriswiki, Citicat, Colby Peterson, Comelloyellow, CryptoDerk, Cun, Custardninja, DJ Clayworth, Daa89563, Dalkaen, Daniel Case, Dantesque1, David Gerard, Dbenbenn, Donmike10, Dr. Blofeld, Drbreznjev, Duncancumming, Dyl, Ekabhishek, Erik, Exomnium, Fastily, FlorisGroen, Gabbe, Gary King, Girolamo Savonarola, Goatasaur, Gridge, Harej, Hemidemisemiquaver, Husky, Ike9898, Im.a.lumberjack, Intelligence3, Irishguy, IronGargoyle, ItsTheClimb17, J.J., Jabbathenut, Jeandré du Toit, Jenny Wong, JeremyCherfas, Jmax-, Jogers, Jonathan.s.kt, Joseph A. Spadaro, KConWiki, Kawaputra, Kingstowngalway, Konczewski, Korny O'Near, Kripkenstein, Kwiki, Lacrimosus, Lampman, Lenin and McCarthy, Liface, Loodog, Loona, Lord veritas, Losser00diction, LostLikeTearsInRain, Lpgeffen, Markhoney, Markhw42, MarnetteD, Matty j, MegX, Michael Hardy, Michael2926, Mullibok, Mydnight, NOLA504ever, NWill, Nervouswalking, Nkayesmith, Noirish, Pascal.Tesson, PatrickORiley, Peinwod, Pengo, Pethan, Plattopus, Polylerus, Quentin X, Qutezuce, RattleandHum, Rattusrattus, Rbb l181, Rich Farmbrough, Rjwilmsi, Robert Merkel, Salamurai, Sam, Sampi, Scrawlspacer, ScudLee, Sergay, Sethie, Shaken7, ShaleZero, Sharkface217, Shred, SilkTork, Sjorford, Skomorokh, Smooth0707, Soab015, Sohollywood, Somerset219, Sputnikstudios, SteveHFish, Stevertigo, Swern425, TRTX, Tangytoad, Tanlipkee, Tell-Tale Ghost, The Transhumanist, Thefourdotelipsis, Themta, Thomas Blomberg, Thornstrom, Thumperward, Tnxman307, Tony1, Torie, Treybien, Trickzakky, Troy 07, Tshase, Viriditas, WCityMike, Walkiped, Wildroot, WojPob, Woohookitty, Wtwhitejr, Zafiroblue05, 221 anonymous edits

The Hours (film) *Source*: http://en.wikipedia.org/w/index.php?oldid=380670807 *Contributors*: 17Drew, AKGhetto, Adammichael, Amynewyork4248, Andres, AndrewHowse, Andycjp, Angel caboodle, Anopheles, AriGold, Atemperman, BD2412, Belovedfreak, Bill shannon, Bob Castle, Bovineboy2008, Bzuk, COMPFUNK2, CactusWriter, Caiaffa, Caknuck, CastorOilRocks, CaveatLector, Chicagofan01, Classicfilms, Cloudedyellow, CoolKatt number 99999, DMacks, Daniel Case, Danny, Dante1707, Darrenhusted, Ddperk1980, Deb, Doczilla, Easchiff, Electric Storm89, Elynnia, Eric82oslo, Erik, FMAFan1990, Ferdinand Pienaar, Gammondog, Gargile, Geni, Geofjarvis, Gordenie, Gr8lyknow, Grandpafootsoldier, Gritchka, Grizzwald, Gzornenplatz, HMFS, Hapleworth, Hbdragon88, Heidi S, Irk, IronGargoyle, JHMM13, Jdforrester, Jessicapierce, Jiang, JohnOwens, Jonathan.s.kt, Jordancelticsfan, JulieADriver, JuneGloom07, Jwrosenzweig, Jzummak, KConWiki, KF, Kcam87, Kfgauss, Killing sparrows, Koavf, Kyliecrazy12, Laurascudder, LinkTiger, LiteraryMaven, Lohengrin1991, LostLikeTearsInRain, MARKELLOS, Maerk, Magiclite, MarnetteD, Matan yernberg, Maximus Rex, Melinda19, Mkoljone, Mustung, MythosEdddy, NWill, Nehrams2020, Nietzsche 2, Nihil novi, Ohthelameness, Otto4711, Oxymoron83, Parable1991, Paulinho28, Philip Cross, Pippin Wainwright, RJvH, RandomP, RattleandHum, Reorion, Rich Farmbrough, Rjwilmsi, Robin Stocker, SISLEY, ST47, Salur, ShelfSkewed, Skaterball00, Skudrafan1, StevenEdmondson, Stu21202, Supertigerman, Szumyk, TAnthony, Tassedethe, Tell-Tale Ghost, Tennjam, The Wrong Man, TheMovieBuff, Thesexualityofbereavement, Tjmayerinsf, Tpbradbury, Treybien, Tuesdaysarelovely, Varlaam, Veelmeet, Viewboard1, Wai Hong, Werldwayd, Wfeidt, WhisperToMe, Xezbeth, Xme, Yamla, Zwatkins, 191 anonymous edits

Stuck on You (film) *Source*: http://en.wikipedia.org/w/index.php?oldid=380416375 *Contributors*: *drew, 16@r, 25or6to4, 66richardson, 97198, Acalamari, All Hallow's Wraith, Almosthonest06, Amwestover, Andrzejbanas, Angr, Anthony Appleyard, Bacteria, Badagnani, BellyOption, BenOKZ, Bender235, Bjeversole, Bobet, CJMylentz, Chanlyn, David136a, Dofftoubab, Donmike10, Drplumm, Feudonym, FraDany, Goerlitz83, Grantsaylor1995, Hatch68, Horkana, Houldine, In Name And Blood, Irishpunktom, J.delanoy, Jc1033, Johnred32, Justme89, K10wnsta, Kekkomereq4, Lots42, Luckyact, Mallanox, Mandyvtz, Marilyn3238, Markdashark1212, Meg99, MegX, Michael.m.winters, MikeWazowski, Mr.Linderman, Nehrams2020, Nightscream, Northmeister, OS2Warp, Phalabi1963, Poppy, Postcard Cathy, Ppntori, Quentin X, Radosław10, RattleandHum, Redmanb11, SamisBond, Sergecross73, SiobhanHansa, Skateboardingtwinkie, Sonnyandcherfan, Suisui, Supernumerary, TBustah, Ted Wilkes, Ted87, TheBlazikenMaster, TheMovieBuff, Tinton5, Toddsschneider, Treybien, Vagrant, Veronica9, Violetriga, Vlad, Xezbeth, Zchris87v, Zer0431, Zomno, 133 anonymous edits

The Manchurian Candidate (2004 film) *Source*: http://en.wikipedia.org/w/index.php?oldid=380497926 *Contributors*: *drew, Absinthe88, AdamSmithee, AlbertSM, AnOrdinaryBoy, AndrewHowse, Andrewire, Andrzejbanas, Angelsy1, AstroZombieDC, Bhappydude, Bwithh, C777, CapitalR, Cardcapturs, Chowbok, Ckarraker, CyberSkull, D6, Daniel Case, Danielfolsom,

Darrenhusted, Daveswagon, David Gerard, Davodd, Debresser, Elvis1977, Erik, Freemarket, Fuhghettaboutit, Gabbe, Garion96, Gary King, Ginsengbomb, GregorB, Ground Zero, Hoplon, Iridescent, IronGargoyle, JE, James E. Clark, Jason One, Jeff Muscato, Jfruh, John K, K1Bond007, Kocio, Kollision, Kuralyov, LCpl, Lavenderbunny, Levineps, Lexor, Litalex, LtMuldoon, Master of the Orichalcos, Mgreason, Mrblondnyc, NatusRoma, Neutrality, NickelShoe, Noirish, Nsisim, Overand, P0p0, Pejorative.majeure, Pjt48, Poco a poco, QuasyBoy, RattleandHum, Rich Farmbrough, Sammyd487, Scarequotes, ScudLee, Sdalmonte, Sfoskett, Sjyglm, SlowJog, SpNeo, Ssilvers, Steinfeld7, Tabletop, Tanishh, Tassedethe, Tell-Tale Ghost, The Cake is a Lie, TheCoffee, Theoldanarchist, Tobelia, Tony Sidaway, Treybien, Troy34, Varlaam, Vulture19, WhisperToMe, Whkoh, Wwoods, Xezbeth, Yamla, ZeroJanvier, 163 anonymous edits

Lemony Snicket's A Series of Unfortunate Events *Source*:http://en.wikipedia.org/w/index.php?oldid=380207105 *Contributors*: 99ant99, Ableman, Acalamari, Aericanwizard, Aileza, Alakazam, Alientraveller, Almostfamous83, AlphaPhoenixDown, Andrei Iosifovich, Andrei55555, Andrewlp1991, Andrzejbanas, Angel caboodle, Anonymous from the 21th century, ApopkaATM, Ariasne, Art1991, AshTFrankFurter2, AskFranz, BD2412, Barticus88, Beaniegurl, Beemer69, Bibliomaniac15, Blakegripling ph, BlargDragon, Bobet, Bovineboy2008, BrianGriffin-FG, Broadway91, C Teng, CLW, Cabiria, Calabraxthis, Caldorwards4, Canadian-Bacon, CapitalSasha, Cbrown1023, Ccranium, Celestianpower, Cena404, Chanlyn, Chowbok, Chris 42, Chriscrutch, Cjdshaw, Clana4life55, Classic rocker, Clivestaples, CmaccompH89, Cmichael, Constantinelim, ContiAWB, CoolKatt number 99999, Crohnie, Crotchety Old Man, CyberGhostface, CyberSkull, DVD Smith, DaffyDuck619, Damnlikewhatever, Dan East, Darkknight13, Darklilac, David Gerard, Dbenbenn, Diego Grez, DiogenesNY, Discospinster, Dominic, Draktorn, Dreadpiratetif, Dylan Lake, Dyneslan, Electrumfan, Elfred, Elsbeth0, Emurphy42, Entegy, Erik, EronMain, Esse, Eurosong, FMAFan1990, Fairchiw, FastLizard4, Fastilysock, Fez2005, Floweramon, GeeJo, George Pelltier, GlobeGores, Gojira09, Granpuff, Gscshoyru, GuanoLad, Guat6, Happy Evil Dude, Harlot, Hede2000, HexaChord, Hooperbloob, Hu12, Hyenaste, Húrin, IKR1, IRP, Imperator3733, Inspiredefined, Ipod3196, Irishguy, J.J., J.J.Sagnella, JAD51287, JCO, JPG-GR, JackBarney, Jairo82798, Jamielynn cena, Jeppi, Jeremy Visser, Jguad1, Jhjackson97, Jisatsusha, Jklmcw, Jmac27@aol.com, John, JohnDBuell, Joseph Solis in Australia, Joshuadp, Jtomlin1uk, JustPhil, JustWong, JusticeMondeo, Jéské Couriano, KJS77, Kappa, Kariteh, Katy,Girl, Kbdank71, Kbolino, Kelapstick, Khaosjr, Khaosworks, Klaus Baudelaire256, KnowledgeOfSelf, Kribbeh, Kwertii, LGagnon, Largoplazo, Lee M, Leszek Jańczuk, Levineps, Liftarn, Limetolime, Liscobeck, Litalex, LittleDuude8, Livercheese, Luizalves, Lukebonjers, MCRGIRL, MSJapan, Mallanox, Mandy443, Marcus Brute, Marcus Qwertyus, Marshall, Matt Kurz, Mclay19, Mclovinst, Metta Bubble, Mike Rosoft, Mikedover, Mikeman4510, Mm40, Mr-susans, Mrmoocow, Mrseibert, N.samimi island, Ndboy, Neurillon, Nickolka, NikonMike, Nojo191, Notmicro, Nyvhek, ObtuseAngle, Oddmartian, Ohnoitsjamie, Olathe, Onepiece226, Pegship, Persian Poet Gal, Ph1.618, Phoenixrod, Pic Editor960, Piecraft, Ptubb, Quadratus, R. New, Rakez, Rangi, Redwolf24, Retodon8, Rex Imperator, RexNL, Rich Farmbrough, Richfife, Rje, Robert25, RoyBatty42, Ryddragyn, Ryulong, Saffran, Sanit, Scarian, ScotchMB, Seba5618, Shawn in Montreal, Sietse Snel, Slysplace, Smash, Snapboy300, Snicket master, Snowynight, Someguy1221, Sophiakorichi, SpNeo, SpaceCaptain, Splashmo, Sport woman, Squidward2602, Starkiller88, Stassats, Stellrmn, Stephenchou0722, Summerwind159, SunCreator, Sunil060902, SuperFlash101, SuperLuigi31, SuperPalpy, TL789, The Man in Question, The Shadow-Fighter, The Track Master, The Wrong Man, The wub, TheMadBaron, TheMovieBuff, TheRealFennShysa, Thief Lord, Timeineurope, Tony414, Tool2Die4, Tregoweth, Tsujigiri, Typhoon966, Typhoonchaser, Val42, Waltloc, Warrior princess15, Wik4, Wikidemon, Wildroot, Wklimon, XJDHDR, Xezbeth, Yamamoto Ichiro, ZeldaQueen, Zeldamaster3, Zepheus, Zetterberg40, 670 anonymous edits

Prime (film) *Source*: http://en.wikipedia.org/w/index.php?oldid=370495312 *Contributors*: *drew, AN(Ger), Abe Lincoln, Academic Challenger, All Hallow's Wraith, Aznph8playa2, BigFoot48, Bobet, Bovineboy2008, Brhaspati, Cbrown1023, Chocolateboy, Craklyn, Dalyup!, DavidHoag, Debresser, Denny, Did you know that I am a troll?, Emilyn, Erik, Filmmusicfan, Firsfron, Gabbe, Horkana, Invincible Ninja, IronGargoyle, JHunterJ, John Vandenberg, Kevin B12, Mephiston999, Msgj, Naniwako, NickBurns, Patrick, Prashanthns, Rlevse, Silentaria, Spaza-bozo, Suckstobeabum, TAnthony, 36 anonymous edits

A Prairie Home Companion (film) *Source*: http://en.wikipedia.org/w/index.php?oldid=376846700 *Contributors*: AdamBMorgan, Ahkond, All Hallow's Wraith, Alllexxxis, Andrewshungry, Andrzejbanas, Antonia1976, Arthur Smart, BD2412, BabuBhatt, Bellhalla, BenFrantzDale, Bown, Brian1979, CR85747, Cartoon Boy, CharlesCarroll, Chivista, Coemgenus, ConradPino, DannyZ, Darklilac, David Rush, DavidFarmbrough, DavidRF, Deamon138, Dhodges, Diberri, Diederich, Doctor Sunshine, Domingo Portales, EEMIV, Emurphy42, Eric444, Esprit15d, Extraordinary Machine, FMAFan1990, Falalalalalalalala29, Fbv65edel, Feeeshboy, Fountain09, Gaius Cornelius, Germanysmadhatter, Gridlock Joe, Guillermo Ugarte, Gurch, Horkana, Ianthegecko, Idp, Java13690, Jeffrey O. Gustafson, JnB987, Johnbod, KConWiki, Ka ga, Kaneshirojj, KathrynLybarger, Kayaker, LaVidaLoca, Leithp, LinkToddMcLovinMontana, Lmcelhiney, MPD01605, Masz, Mcsee, Mediaright, Melly42, Mooman95, MrTippet, Mtsangswom15, Mulad, Nehrams2020, Nyghtowl, Orangemike, Pakk77, Pantheonzeus, Patrick, Paul Klenk, Paul.Nord@valpo.edu, Pericles626, Peter Napkin Dance Party, Plastic editor, RadicalBender, RadioKirk, Ramanpotential, Repulsion, Rich Farmbrough, Richard Arthur Norton (1958-), Rje, Rockhopper10r, Rroser167, Santress, Schwerdf, Seinfreak37, Sgore, Sin-man, Smartiger, Spyderchan, Stan weller, Steam5, Stefanomione, Stwra, The Filmaker, TheMadBaron, Thwompson, Tnxman307, Treybien, UnitedStatesian, Val42, Ward3001, WikiJedits, WillC, Wisekwai, Yamla, Zoe, Zotdragon, 134 anonymous edits

The Devil Wears Prada (film) *Source*: http://en.wikipedia.org/w/index.php?oldid=380948216 *Contributors*: 97198, A.Beaz, AN(Ger), Aaron charles, AddDeWitt, Aefbafbabsgbgfb, Aekolman, Agfsdgagfdgsd, Alandeus, Alanm666, AlbertSM, Alice-san, Alwaysestatic, Andrzejbanas, Andycjp, Anish chaz, Annukii, AnonMoos, AnuSs, Apados, Apostrophe, Aquawarlock, Arbero, Arouet760, Astuishin, BYMAstudent, Bacchus87, Barticus88, Bearcat, Beetstra, Belle787, Bender235, Bennyp77, Bepp, BobiKav, Bobo192, Bohemian29, Bovineboy2008, BrunoLucio, Btphelps, CR85747, CTVampSlayer, Calliopejen, CanisRufus, Casliber, Cbrown1023, Ceeess, Cendar1212, Chris the speller, Circeus, Clancyolincy, Codrdan, ContiAWB, Covonia, Crimson-Radar, CyberSkull, Daniel Case, Danielba894, Danleary25, Danlev, Darimoma, DarkMissy, David Gerard, David Shankbone, DeC, Debresser, DirectRevelation, Dispenser, Dmadeo, Dr. Blofeld, Dr.alf, Dvd-junkie, Dycedarg, Eagle Owl, Ekabhishek, Emc2, Emurphy42, Engela15, Enpitsu, Enviroboy, Epbr123, Ericore, Erik, Everyking, Faithlessthewonderboy, FayssalF, Fbv65edel, Fladrif, Flixray, Gaceri, Garion96, Gasheadsteve, Geo16, Gold-Horn, Gordenie, Gridge, Guat6, Gwynand, H.U. Solder, Haoma, Harryboyles, Harthacnut, Heaven's Wrath, Hickoryhillster, Hippi ippi, Hkchan123, Hl, Hoary, Horkana, Hotwiki, IMLX, Ian Pitchford, Ibagli, IceUnshattered, Illinois2011, Iokseng, Ioscius, Iridescent, IronGargoyle, Iulus Ascanius, Jack O'Lantern, James Kemp, JamesAM, Jaranda, Jason.cinema, Jerome Charles Potts, John254, Joniscool98, Jpfagerback, Kaneshirojj, Katomin, Kberkely65, Keeves, Kevin, Klinean, Koavf, Kooliod, Lacrimosus, Laurinavicius, LeaveSleaves, Legolas2186, Levineps, LinDrug, Ling.Nut, Lossenelin, LovesMacs, Lowellian, M1ss1ontomars2k4, Mabalu, Madchester, Mahjong705, Marc-Olivier Pagé, Mark Michaelson, Master shepherd, Matthewedwards, Matty-chan, MegX, Mikeblas, Mjm46530690, Mlaffs, Monkbel, Morganiq, Myscrnnm, NJGW, NWill, Namflnamfl, Naphouse, NathanBeach, Nehrams2020, NeoThe1, Never Mystic, Nick Number, Nihon.ai, Notmicro, OH mAh gAwD, ObsessiveJoBroDisorder, Oscarthecat, PAWiki, Palfrey, Pascal.Tesson, Patrick.p.93, Pazuzu567, PeaceNT, Piano non troppo, Pogokidd, Polylerus, Ppk1980, Project.aspirants, Psantosj, Puppet125, Qrc2006, RBBrittain, RandomXYZb, Repulsion, Retroviseur, Rich Farmbrough, Richard Arthur Norton (1958-), Rjwilmsi, RobJ1981, Rrfayette, Ryan Reich, Samuel Pepys, SamuelM555, Sap123, Sb1990, Sdfisher, Serein (renamed because of SUL), Sharday17, Shauky, Simon12, Slartibartfass, Smalljim, Smallq, Soapfan06, Sohollywood, SpaceFlight89, SpuriousQ, Stanley011, Sterry2607, Suffieldlax24, TKD, Tabercil, Tabletop, Tad Lincoln, Taka76, Taranus, Tassedethe, Techman224, TenPoundHammer, Tertiary7, The 888th Avatar, The JPS, TheFilth, TheMovieBuff, Thedjatclubrock, Thefreakshow, Thepangelinanpost, Thirteen squared, Thiseye, Titoxd, Tommy2010, Tony1, Tpbradbury, Tregoweth, TreoBoy680, Treybien, Trickzakky, Troycrazy8, Tryptofeng, Tyler, Typhoon966, Uncle Milty, Underneath-it-All, Van der Hoorn, Varlaam, VeiledAbyss, Victoria nugroho, Voodoo4936, WCityMike, WLU, Ward3001, WhisperToMe, WiiKyle, Wknight94, Woohookitty, Wtmitchell, Wwoods, X96lee15, XoxSuagrMamix3, Yamanbaiia, Yamla, Youngandrestless, Zanimum, ZeldaQueen, Zscout370, Zuejay, 501 anonymous edits

The Ant Bully (film) *Source*: http://en.wikipedia.org/w/index.php?oldid=378560593 *Contributors*: Adrian J. Hunter, Alpha Ralpha Boulevard, Andromedabluesphere440, Andycjp, Anonymous from the 21st century, Another Believer, Art LaPella, Baa, Beatlesrclassic, Boleyn3, Candent shlimazel, Cartoon Boy, Christianster45, Crboyer, D.brodale, Das Baz, EchetusXe, Ecw.technoid.dweeb, Epbr123, Froztbyte, Fumitol, Gabrielkat, Grindor, Hannahcronin, Hekerui, ICarly fan 0246, Irishguy, JoshP129, Koavf, Lasius, Leostitan, Leoswiseman, Miquonranger03, Mjpresson, Moorglade, Mutt, Nymf, Od Mishehu, PMDrive1061, Parent Hoods Guy, RDBury, RainbowWerewolf, Ross92, SF007, Sepulwiki, SimonKSK, SoWhy, TMC1982, Tabletop, Tavix, The Thing That Should Not Be, Thingg, Twilightfan000, Vishnava, WadeSimMiser, Warreed, Websurfer246, Whoopee's Blues, 110 anonymous edits

Dark Matter (film) *Source*: http://en.wikipedia.org/w/index.php?oldid=379572526 *Contributors*: Ameliorate!, Anaisrand, Astorknlam, Bwithh, Colonies Chris, Erik9, GnuDoyng, GrahamHardy, Grandpafootsoldier, Ian Dalziel, IronGargoyle, Joel84932, Kolindigo, Maork, Nehrams2020, Pcopinion, Pixelface, Reader34, Seanvolk, ShortShadow, Singingdaisies, Skier Dude, SoWhy, SomeRandomFilmArticleEditor, Sreejithk2000, Staecker, Supermann, Tryptofeng, Winston365, Ynotswim, A, 26 anonymous edits

Evening (film) *Source*: http://en.wikipedia.org/w/index.php?oldid=369996415 *Contributors*: AN(Ger), Alofferman, Astorknlam, Beetstra, Bob Castle, Bovineboy2008, Cadillacread, CambridgeBayWeather, ConradKilroy, Courtens, Dahamsta7, David Shankbone, Dekimasu, Djbj16, Donmike10, Eino81, Ekabhishek, Erik, Erik9, FMAFan1990, Freiheit 89, Irishguy, IronGargoyle, Jlindauer, Kaijan, KrakatoaKatie, Maneisis, Mcgill lass, MoraSique, MovieMadness, Nehrams2020, Nixdorf, Patrick, Pcg13, Radosław10, Robertvan1, ShelfSkewed, SpecialOpsMedia, SpikeJones, Stormie, Tell-Tale Ghost, TrevorX, Viceone, Wetman, Wool Mintons, Yllosubmarine, 113 anonymous edits

Rendition (film) *Source*: http://en.wikipedia.org/w/index.php?oldid=373718073 *Contributors*: 3BluePenguins, A elalaily, AN(Ger), Acsicsek, AdamDeanHall, Alaric Deschain, All Hallow's Wraith, Anarsik, AnmaFinotera, Annoynmous, Arthur Warrington Thomas, Aximill, Badagnani, BandieraRossa, Barnabypage, Bendykst, Blizzardeagle, Bobo192, Bradley583, Briaboru, Cgingold, Ck lostsword, Cla68, Clpo13, David Gerard, Debresser, DeepFocus 1, Deiz, DepressedPer, Dh993, Dillard421, Djrobgordon, Dl2000, Donmike10, DoubleCross, Dsreyn, Epiphaniebloom, Erik, Esprit15d, FMAFan1990, Flyguy649, Gangle, Georgewilliamherbert, Grandpafootsoldier, GregorB, Grieferhate, JYi, Jak3m, Jcamtzf, Jerome Charles Potts, Jimworm, Jmrowland, Kaiser matias, Kross, Kuralyov, LilHelpa, LostLikeTearsInRain, LtMuldoon, Lugnuts, Luna Whistler, Maisnam, Malekhanif, Maneisis, Mathew5000, Melly42, Miracleworker5263, Mister BV, Mooncatcher, Mr link, Necrothesp, Patrick, Peregrine Fisher, Perspicacite, Philipashlock, Pixelface, Promking, Psychiker, RattleandHum, RobNS, Rodrigogomespaixao, Savidan, Series premiere (remake), Serkul, Skier Dude, Solidworksdesign, Somerut, Steve, Trcunning, Treybien, Trident13, Tripati, USAOwnz, Wiher, Wwestarwars, X--BAH, Yorkshiresky, Zayya, ZimZalaBim, 130 anonymous edits

Lions for Lambs *Source*: http://en.wikipedia.org/w/index.php?oldid=378347585 *Contributors*: 11Meredj, AN(Ger), AbbyKelleyite, Aboutaboutabout, Adrian Glamorgan, All Hallow's Wraith, Alwaysthrash 09, AmaraJV14, Ameliorate!, Andosmith, Android Mouse, Andrzejbanas, Apsorell, Arbon42, ArtichokesRule91, AuhsojSivart, Bovineboy2008, Brianbarney, Burke9077, CALEB B., Chris Bainbridge, Cirt, Confiteordeo, Dan100, Dan113, Danielba894, Darrenhusted, Donald McKinney, DoubleCross, Dreadstar, Erik, Feudonym, Firsfron, FrankRizzo2006, Gaius Cornelius, Garion96, Gregory j, Ground Zero, HarkenofAutumn, Harland1, Harold12, HurricaneJeanne, Icaros88, Igordebraga, Irishguy, JPLeonard, Jc-S0CO, Jdale1259, JimDunning, Kariteh, Kathryn rebecca42, Kieranthompson, Kookoo Star, KoshVorlon, LiquidOcelot24, Lox, Luatha, Madchester, Maneisis, Martinj63, Mdriver1981, Mentifisto, MisterHand, Mmcknight4, Mblandayr, Nardog, Nate Speed, Nehrams2020, Noebse, Passingtramp, Peter knight, Patrick, Pedist, Pixelface, Pocboc, Polylerus, RobMa189, RVJ, Radosław10, Rehnstar, Rich Farmbrough,

Ripounet, Robma, Rodrigogomespaixao, Romaioi, Ronhjones, SEWilco, Scarian, Searcher 1990, Shadowy Crafter, Simanos, Skew-t, Skier Dude, Smurrayinchester, SouthernNights, Steam5, Steve, SusanLesch, Tide rolls, TimothyChenAllen, Treybien, USS Noob Hunter, UpstateNYer, Walkiped, Whm2, WikiDon, Woohookitty, YUL89YYZ, 187 anonymous edits

Mamma Mia! (film) *Source*: http://en.wikipedia.org/w/index.php?oldid=380808905 *Contributors*: 19DrPepper91, 6afraidof7, AKeen, AMK1211, AN(Ger), Abtinb, Aegean57, Agustinaldo, Aktsu, Alexd18, Alientraveller, Alvareo, AlwaysUnderTheInfluence, Amadahugandkiss, Anabus, And1987, Andromeda, Andycjp, AnonEMouse, Arthur7171, AshTFrankFurter2, Aspects, Astorknlam, Avjoska, Banjo75, Barte, Barticus88, BassPlyr23, BellyOption, Bencey, Bewildebeast, BigTimeMovieLover, Boffinboy, Bovicuxyzt, Bovineboy2008, Braza258, Briaboru, Brideshead, Brighterorange, Brwest06, Bssc81, Bykergrove, C.Fred, CNash, CR85747, Cactusjump, Catgut, Cazzababy, Cburnett, Ceauntay59, Chris 42, ChrisDilke, Chrisboote, Cipkid292, Ckatz, Clark89, CombatShock, Commander Shepard, ContiAWB, Cornellrockey, Crossmr, Crotchety Old Man, Cyverius, D.kolesinski, DBlomgren, Danielåhskarlsson, Darrenhusted, David 5000, DavidK93, Deanb, Decltype, Dizagaox, Djbj16, Djdannyp, Doniago, DoubleCross, Dreadstar, Dt128, Dylancraigboyes, Dylbo25, E-Kartoffel, EchetusXe, Editorofthewiki, EganLA, Eight88, El Greco, El Pollo Diablo, Epbr123, Erik, Erikhansson1, ErinHowarth, Evenios, Excirial, ExpressingYourself, FClef, Faithlessthewonderboy, Falcon9x5, Farmer88, Fbv65edel, Fluteflute, Frankie816, Franklint, Funguy06, Garda40, Garion96, Gary King, Gausie jr, Gellar55, Gerardw, Gevorg89, Gilliam, Ginger.Russo, Gocyclonesgo, GregorB, Hahaha10253, Hbdragon88, Hbent, Headstrong 345, Horkana, Hroðulf, Huaiwei, Ilovetospoon, Inyesta, Iridescent, IronGargoyle, Isotope23, ItsTheClimb17, Izzak, J.delanoy, JForget, Jackol, Jacobsnchz, JamesAM, JamesMLane, Jamesmarkhetterley, Jammyjamminjar2, Jasonl1986, Jayneutral, JeanColumbia, Jedi Striker, Jerrying, Jezhotwells, Jezouie, JimDunning, JohnCD, JonasBrother1, Jordanceltics fan, JoshuaKuo, Jrnoel92, Jvd897, Kaffelars, Karina101, KathrynLybarger, Kbg80, KerryO77, Kherron, Kitch, Klassikal, Klknoles, Kookyunii, Korny O'Near, Kr2kol, LOL, Lawikitejana, LeaveSleaves, Leonidas23, Levineps, Lightmouse, LinkToddMcLovinMontana, Listor1989, Liujustin18, Luna909, Magicmat, Mammamiaitsannie, Manofthings, Manuel de Sousa, Marek69, MarizzaRojas, Markkolesinski, Marychan41, Mbakkel2, McGeddon, MearsMan, Mentifisto, Message From Xenu, Metstotop333, Mezaco, Michaelkourlas, Mickea, Micro101, Mikay, MileyDavidA, Milonica, Mississippi090909, Misterkillboy, Mr Stephen, Mr. Gustafson, Mrhalohunter24, MusicMaker5376, Mygerardromance, NBC Universal, Nakon, Naniwako, Nardog, Naur, Ndboy, Nemo24, Neurolysis, Nickwiki93, Noahvosen, Ntsimp, Nutter86, Nymf, Oanabay04, ObsessiveJoBroDisorder, Ohhcanada, Oreo Priest, OverThrone, OverlordQ, PL290, Pardy, Paste, Patrick, Paxsimius, Pb30, PhilKnight, Piano non troppo, Pierre cb, Pintosanchez, Plasticspork, Postdlf, Promking, Quentin X, R'n'B, R.braithwaite, RainbowOfLight, Raymondwinn, RazorICE, Redhead123, Redjedia, RegisPhalange, Reinthal, Riverwhich!, Rjwilmsi, Ron whisky, Rui789, Runefrost, SGBailey, Samuraihero1992, Sb1990, Scarian, Scjessey, Scohen707, Seaphoto, ShelfSkewed, SidneyH, Silent Tom, Simon's Double Trouble Lifetime, Skopelos-slim, Small5th, Smetanahue, Smooth0707, Smoth 007, Snowolf, Someguy1221, Sp4arkplug, Spidermedicine, Sportomanokin, Sposato, Starfish77, Stile4aly, Stuart1000, SummerPhD, SunCreator, Supershad3000, Swordsmankirby, TJ Spyke, Tabletop, Taifarious1, Talezassian, Tartarus, Tassedethe, Techwiz81, TenohHaruka, The 80s chick, The Anome, The Giant Puffin, Thehornet, Theleftorium, Themeparkfanatic, ThenaGrove, Theresa knott, Thirteen squared, ThuranX, Tinton5, Tnuriel, TobyJ, Tomasboij, TonyW, Tool2Die4, Toongenius, Toxicroak, TracyLinkEdnaVelmaPenny, Trafford09, Trailerspy, Treybien, Trotter, Truthanado, Tslocum, Tubby23, TubularWorld, Turdface123, Turzh, Unreal7, Usernamemehr, Utcursch, Vasil', Vauxhall1964, Veggiehead, Venatico, Versus22, Vicious 1990, VincenzoMc, W Tanoto, Websurfer246, Whysanitynet, WikiKatie4, Wikid77, Wikiklrsc, William Avery, Willking1979, Winchelsea, Wknight94, Wolfmann, Woohookitty, Wool Mintons, Writesiriusly, X--BAH, Yananding, Yorkshiresky, ZephyrWind, Zscout370, 梅 酒 , 1124 anonymous edits

Doubt (2008 film) *Source*: http://en.wikipedia.org/w/index.php?oldid=379734564 *Contributors*: 2D, A Nobody, ADM, Alansohn, AlbertSM, Alex43223, Alfvaen, American Eagle, And1987, Andrewire, Andrewsthistle, Anonymous Dissident, AyoubZubairi, Benatfleshofthestars, Bender235, Big Bird, Bkell, Blacwainwright, Butwhatdoiknow, Careful Cowboy, Causa sui, Cheappleasures, Cheddarjack, Christianster45, Cliff1911, Conti, Crotchety Old Man, CunningWizard, D15724C710N, Dabomb87, Davecrosby uk, Degenerate-Y, Djbj16, Doniago, Drdodge, DutchDevil, Ekabhishek, Emerson7, Endothermic, Erik, Erik Kennedy, Feclarid, Feelsstaa2, Feudonym, Fierce Beaver, Fountainhead82, Frisbeesandflipflops, Fritzpoll, GerardKennedy, Gilliam, Glane23, Glo145, GoneAwayNowAndRetired, Grandpafootsoldier, Ianrosenberg1, Immunize, Jacoplane, Jalexisonfiren, Jeff Muscato, JonBroxton, JzG, Koavf, Ladida, LeaveSleaves, Levineps, Litalex, Lucien leGrey, Mad Dingo704, Madhava 1947, Malcolmxl5, Marauding Monkey, Masalai, Massimo Macconi, Mikhailovich, Molotron, MovieFanAtic4Ever, Movieguru2006, NAHID, Nathankamal, Nike, NurseryRhyme, Oknazevad, Pakchooie, Panicpgh, Pastor Theo, Patrick, PeterKidd, Pixelface, Promking, PyroGamer, R'n'B, RashersTierney, ResignBen16, Rickterp, Roadnottaken, Robert Skyhawk, Rollingstone4, Ron whisky, Ron's Popcorn Reviews, Ruslik0, SHUSHHMEEx3, Sb1990, Schweiwikist, Schwnj, Skatemusiclife64, SkyWalker, Smith2006, Sreejithk2000, Steve, Stile4aly, Stratocracy, Strepon, TAnthony, The Thing That Should Not Be, Thingg, Timbouctou, Tony Sandel, Treybien, TubularWorld, Ultrawatchman, Unschool, Ward3001, Werldwayd, William Allen Simpson, Woohookitty, WurmWoode, 238 anonymous edits

Julie & Julia *Source*: http://en.wikipedia.org/w/index.php?oldid=380552230 *Contributors*: 007cupcakes, AcroX, Aldo samulo, All Hallow's Wraith, AnandaDaldal, And1987, Andrewire, AusJeb, Baseball Bugs, Big Bird, BillyPreset, Bjones, Bovineboy2008, Bssc, Bwv581, Ccacsmss, Centrino7, Chris Rocen, Christianster94, Coolcaesar, Crotchety Old Man, Dandywiki, David Rush, Debresser, Decltype, Delta foxtrot zulu 42, Djbj16, Donmike10, Doub95, Dylancraigboyes, Easchiff, Edifyyo, Espoo, Euro Mok, Evilhenny, Fierce Beaver, Flyguy33, FrankRizzo2006, Friendly person, Gellar55, Grandpafootsoldier, Healthpop, Hyju, JamieS93, Jeremy Butler, Jessica A R H, Jgreenbook, Julesd, Kchishol1970, Krakatoa, Kukini, Levineps, Mamoa, MariAna Mimi, McGeddon, Mdriver1981, Musicaldudepeter, Ophois, Patrick, Peppage, Pepso2, Quantpole, RayBirks, Richard Arthur Norton (1958-), Ronny corral, Rosestiles, SPHE, Sb1990, SchfiftyThree, Smartse, Smile4Chomsky, Smond359, Speedannayya, Spidey104, Starlemusique, TPIRFanSteve, Tagilbert, Tartarus21, The Master Puff, TheInformant09, TheMovieBuff, Thief12, Tinmanic, Toussaint, Treybien, Tuesdaytumble, Vertigo Acid, Wikipeterproject, Wool Mintons, Wwoods, Zombie433, Zulu foxtrot tango, 174 anonymous edits

Fantastic Mr. Fox (film) *Source*: http://en.wikipedia.org/w/index.php?oldid=379745821 *Contributors*: AEMoreira042281, AJCham, AaronRichard, Aasimpy, Abie the Fish Peddler, Abtinb, Aericanwizard, Ajax-and-Achilles, Alansohn, AlexLevyOne, Alientraveller, And1987, Andrzejbanas, Angel caboodle, AniMate, Anonymous from the 21st century, Antonrojo, Babyjazspanail, Benatfleshofthestars, Blackeagle, Bovineboy2008, Boxclocke, Bradley0110, Brain seltzer, CBM, CR85747, Cam486, Cartoon Boy, Cc0812, Ccs4ever, Chane 815, Cheddarjack, Christofurio, Ckatz, Conquistador2k6, Conti, Contributor777, Cooksey, CricketEater, CyberSkull, DCEdwards1966, Daedalus969, DaffyDuck619, Danceswithknifes2, Danucciguzman, Darkieboy236, Darkness2005, Darrenhusted, DatsMamaLuigi, Davewild, David Rush, DavidEGonzalez, Deor, Doctor Sunshine, Dogman15, Doman12, Doniago, Elliottsmith001, Emini4, Erik, Erik9, Esn, Esperant, EyeBuster, Fierce Beaver, Fintan264, Fishsticks64, Freshh, FriscoKnight, GAT27, Gkklein, Grandpafootsoldier, Greatrobo76, Harish, Heffajones, Henrytvwhiz, Hiphats, Horkana, Hyut7, IchWeigereMich, Intelligentsium, Irregulargalaxies, Iwasmadeforluvingya, J. Fanning, Jack334, JamesLucas, Jason.cinema, Jax MN, Jeremyadawson, Jerichochang97, Jikybebna, Joecab, Jules90, Karin127, Kchishol1970, KidzOnlyFan, King Rhyono, Klasky-Csupo, Koavf, Kocio, Kollision, Leonidas23, Leonopteryx, Lightrealm, Lordrsb, LucasRKOradiopictures1, LukeTheSpook, Luluxxx, Mabsal, Mariofan88, Masem, Maxbrown, Mclovinst, Meowjunywe, Mickey7474, Mike Teavee, MikeAllen, Misterwindupbird, Mthwaite, NO.47, Nappyrootslistener, Ndboy, Nips, Nlapierre, Otolemur crassicaudatus, PMDrive1061, Pacaman, Packinheat2u, Pegship, Planecrash111, Plmkoijnbhu12345, Pointer1, Poketape, RP9, Redmond Barry, RetroNickelodeonFan, RingtailedFox, Rjwilmsi, Sbpat21, Screech87, SfromHeaven, Sgt. R.K. Blue, ShadowRangerRIT, Silky Slim, Skppy1225, Skyler Kanegi, Slgrandson, Sloppy, Steven Walling, Sugar Bear, Supersmashbrawl, T. H. McAllister, TFunk, Tarnas, Tds247, Teafico, Tennis 52, The 80s chick, The Magnificent Clean-keeper, The Moving Finger Writes, The Rogue Penguin, The Thing That Should Not Be, The wub, TheInformant09, TheLH, TheStrayCat, TheValentineBros, Thebanjohype, Thechillinvillan, Thesoftbulletin82, Theworldstinks, Timeineurope, TimonandPumbaaFan, Tomm098, Tregoweth, Treybien, Trivialist, Trogga, Twilight Nightmare, Typhoon966, Ummit, Vanishdoom, Vapour, Varlaam, Versus22, Vgranucci, VofSteel, Wafulz, Warner Bros. Television, Whiner01, Wikidemon, Wildhartlivie, Wong1, 288 anonymous edits

It's Complicated (film) *Source*: http://en.wikipedia.org/w/index.php?oldid=380772366 *Contributors*: Adam Keller, All Hallow's Wraith, AndrewAllen15, Andycjp, Aquila89, Avij, Backslash Forwardslash, Benatfleshofthestars, Bencey, Bovineboy2008, C Teng, Christianster94, Colonies Chris, Corsair1944, Crotchety Old Man, Darev, Debresser, Donmike10, Doub95, Emeraldcityserendipity, EoGuy, Fierce Beaver, FrankRizzo2006, Gnowxilef, GreenBayPackersfan09, HM211980, Hypocrisyofcake, J1729, Jaydec, John K, Jpbowen, June w, Kollision, Levineps, Manhattan1626, Matty-chan, MichaelQSchmidt, MikeAllen, Mrschimpf, Nehrams2020, Ottre, Pharaway, Pmod, PrincessofLlyr, QuasyBoy, Quentin X, Raphael99, Rodmanfan91, Rodrigo-kun, Rorschach, Saa19952, Sam McPherson, Sjyglm, SkyWalker, Smond359, Somblsaldoms69, Subject name here, The Shadow-Fighter, TomCat4680, Typhoon966, Unika542, Woohookitty, Wool Mintons, YUL89YYZ, Муратик, 112 anonymous edits

Bart's Girlfriend *Source*: http://en.wikipedia.org/w/index.php?oldid=376008950 *Contributors*: A, Bignole, Bucs, CR85747, Cam486, Captain Infinity, Catrope, Chucat, Cncxbox, Cometstyles, Commander Keane, Ctjf83, DSZ444, Dave314159, Daverocks, David Gerard, DearPrudence, Denny, Dutzi, Edlitz36, Either way, Etincelles, Fingerknöchelkopf, GM11, Gaius Cornelius, Grahamdude, Gran2, Haoie, Irk, J.delanoy, JackSparrow Ninja, Jangelt, Jeff G., Jeydo, Jnelson09, Joeywhitesox00, Jonathan.Bruce, JonathanJosephsen, JustPhil, Jw21, KevinD Wilson, Kirrages, Krylonblue83, Lmcelhiney, Lugnuts, M Johnson, MMSH987, Maitch, Martarius, Marvin23vta, Mcstayinskool, Metalhead of the East, Michaelritchie200, Mithos64, Mm40, Mrzaius, Natalie Erin, New World Man, Ninington, Nymf, Optigan13, Pumpkingrrl, Registered user 92, Rich Farmbrough, Rjwilmsi, Rudjek, Scorpion0422, Shadow Blaze, ShelfSkewed, Silent Tom, Springfieldwiki, Spyroninja, SquarePeg, Srx, SteinbDJ, Stephen Bain, Theleftorium, Tim!, Treybien, UltimatePyro, WLU, WhiteDragon, Wile e2005, Wraithdart, Zone46, 109 anonymous edits

List of King of the Hill episodes *Source*: http://en.wikipedia.org/w/index.php?oldid=380406229 *Contributors*: 4twenty42o, 8mmfilm!, A, A.l.dang, After Midnight, Akskasdj, Alansohn, Anthony Appleyard, Astronaut, Athaenara, Auric, B. Wolterding, Badmachine, Bhirt, Blapazappa, Blester, Blester11, Bllasae, Booshakla, Brad, Brianomac, BurtonReingold, C-Son-L Sweaters, Captain Infinity, Cdumas, Chard513, Chicago119, ChicosBailBonds, Chrisnothb, Circeus, Cirt, Clq, Cosprings, Ctjf83, Cunners, Curtsurly, D-Rock, Danigro89, Dansham, DarkXWeather, Dave1185, David Gerard, Dnstest, DocDragon, Domim, Drunkasian, Drwarpmind, EagleOne, Edward130603, Ejay, Elagatis, Enigmatic2k3, Eoghan1234, Erechtheus, Erik-the-red, Everyoneandeveryone, FMAFan1990, Faethon Ghost, Fattydaniel, Felicity4711, Feudonym, Firsfron, Fishpaste8000, FlyingPenguins, FotoPhest, Fred Bradstadt, Gaius Cornelius, Garlic knots, Gh87, Gnbfd0, Gobonobo, Grande13, Grapesoda22, Gsn93, Guinea pig warrior, Hdonham, Hellevision123, Henryodell, Hoof Hearted, Hotdoglives, HouAstros1989, I am Paranoid, IDALGHAMTFPD, Imaginate, Inka 888, Ipstenu, JPG-GR, JRSiebz, Jabrona, Jack Merridew, Jako98146, Javert, Jay32183, JeffW, Jfcinternationalinc, Joekid, Johnnycobra, Joker3456, Jonh90, Josht152, Justin W Smith, KRRK, KafeEman, Kar98, Knownalias, Koavf, Korikitsune0, Kotare, Kramie, Kristen Eriksen, Lbm5007, Leland6914, LilHelpa, MJClapham, MOOOOOPS, Maddie!, Magsec4, Mapsax, Marioman12, Marskell, MatthewWilcox, Mick foley, Mild Bill Hiccup, Milton Stanley, Mobu69, Motley45, Mpc464, Mr.Grave, Mrf, Myfacesp5, NDynamite, NThomas, NapoleonD, Ndboy, Ned Scott, Neillavender, NeoAC, New World Man, Nick, NickBush24, NoD'ohnuts, Northwest, NuclearWarfare, Nwbeeman, Otto4711, PIZZZA, PYLrulz, Paul1337, Paulglor, PearlPop, Penbat, Philwelch, Phreaknrg, Pjedicke, Pointillist, Propower, QueenCake, Quentin X, R.A Huston, R7, RDVoDkA, Raiku Samiyaza, Rambo23, Rated 619 Superstar, Ratemonth, Redd Baron1, RetroNickelodeonFan, Rich Farmbrough, Rich012, Ridnik, Rigadoun, Ringerfan23, Rjanag, Rjwilmsi, Robina Fox, Ron2, Ruodyssey, Rutzy342, Ryoka7, Saberwolf116, Salavat, SchrutedIt08, ScottyWZ, Search4Lancer, Seresin, ShaunMacPherson, ShelfSkewed, Sillygostly, Simpsonic1111, Sk5893, Skier Dude, Skottiedawg, Slabba, Smiloid, SonPraises, Sposato, Stellrmn, Steveomania, Story V, Strongbad1982, Sujames, Supermanrulescom, SuzSides, Sweetfreek, T. Anthony, TBone777, TJ Spyke, TKD, TPIRFanSteve, Talladega87,

Tbhotch, Tcncv, Tdstom, Teletoonmaniac, TenPoundHammer, The Shadow-Fighter, The Thing That Should Not Be, TheClerksWell, TheDJ, TheHYPO, TheManThing, Thedemonhog, Theshroomhermit, Thiseye, Tkech, Tokufan, Tomgoes, TommyBoy, Tony1, Toolazy21, Toonmon2005, Topbanana, Tree Biting Conspiracy, Tv's emory, Underoathfan90, Valvicus, Van der Hoorn, Vblhe, Vianello, Vipinhari, VolatileChemical, Wackelpudding, Waggers, WarthogDemon, WaterJake, Wattlebird, Wean0r, Wikipedianinthehouse, Wolfrock, Woohookitty, Wrightaway, Wuffyz, XuxiRawe22, Zachary, Zone46, Zumbo, 926 anonymous edits

- First Do No Harm Source: http://en.wikipedia.org/w/index.php?oldid=292158414 Contributors: Australian Matt, Bachrach44, Belovedfreak, Catamorphism, Colin, DMCer, Dupont Circle, Flowerkiller1692, Koavf, Kusma, Lightmouse, MZMcBride, Mrblondnyc, OccamzRazor, ReyBrujo, Ron Ritzman, Sebwite, Stinna, Tassedethe, Thewinkone, Tim!, Tkynerd, Toughpigs, Wackymacs, Wavelength, WhatamIdoing, Wool Mintons, Xezbeth, 5 anonymous edits

Angels in America (miniseries) Source: http://en.wikipedia.org/w/index.php?oldid=263943355 Contributors: Adavidb, Ale flashero, AndrewHowse, Aphaia, Auntof6, AvatarMN, Bearcat, Bovineboy2008, Cardcapturs, Centrx, CharlotteWebb, Cnota, Donreed, Dravecky, Easchiff, Ekabhishek, Electric Storm89, Emerson7, Franko12, Grandia01, Ground Zero, Gth0824, ItsTheClimb17, J 1982, Jacrio, Jet0425, Jontts, Kevinsam, Koavf, Lalamore, Lampford, Litalex, Lordmarchmain, Mdiamante, Moonriver90, Mrblondnyc, Music2611, NWill, Phoebeheyman, Plasticspork, Rjwilmsi, Russeasby, Scooby7292, Tide rolls, Twas Now, Woohookitty, Yabancı, Yllosubmarine, 58 anonymous edits

One act plays by Tennessee Williams Source: http://en.wikipedia.org/w/index.php?oldid=282542121 Contributors: Andy M. Wang, Bebestbe, Belovedfreak, Calibansfolly, ChrisCork, DionysosProteus, DoubleBlue, Earbox, GoingBatty, Grey Wanderer, Gwguffey, Hobbesy3, Ida Shaw, Jokestress, Nmccracksublime, PlateBA, Robert1947, Ryanvill, SarekOfVulcan, TheRedPenOfDoom, Tjmayerinsf, WickerGuy, Witzonga, Zeamays, 50 anonymous edits

A Memory of Two Mondays Source: http://en.wikipedia.org/w/index.php?oldid=361725664 Contributors: Dantesque1, DionysosProteus, Eye.earth, Rich Farmbrough, SFTVLGUY2, Skier Dude, Tim!, 6 anonymous edits

The Cherry Orchard Source: http://en.wikipedia.org/w/index.php?oldid=380062372 Contributors: .mau., 66sankan, AG45, Academic Challenger, Al Clark, Alcmaeonid, Alexblainelayder, AmyChen, AndrewHowse, Antaeus Feldspar, Aquastor, Armchairslugger, Artoasis, AssegaiAli, Athaenara, Auntof6, Avono, Bamber gascoigne, Bennmorland, BilboBaggins182, BonsaiViking, Can't sleep, clown will eat me, Capitalistroadster, Cecropia, Cheesy Yeast, Chris the speller, Claridge, Colonies Chris, ConstantinetheGreat, Cprhodesact, Cryptic, Dannebrog Spy, David Gerard, DionysosProteus, Dsp13, Dthomsen8, Ernie and Bert fan, Fatal exception, Folantin, Frankie816, Gaius Cornelius, Ganymead, Ghirlandajo, Gonzalo84, Homonihilis, ISasha, IainStirling, In Defense of the Artist, IstvanWolf, JForget, JanSuchy, Japanese Searobin, Jengod, Jessline2006, Jogloran, John Thaxter, Johnleemk, Kanwarpreet90, Knavehearts, Latka, LilHelpa, Macphysto, Malcolma, Man vyi, Mandel, MegSimpson, MeltBanana, NBeale, Naniwako, Niteowlneils, OldakQuill, Paul A, Pdmeyer, Pixie2000, Pookiyama, RIPSAW1986, RayBirks, Rizzardi, Rjwilmsi, Sasquatch, Sbishop, Shandris, Shawfestival, Sjhalasz, Sjl0523, Someguy1221, Sophitus, Squiddy, Srittau, Staffwaterboy, StageStander, StanStepanic, Stuart Drewer, Teleomatic, Trapolator, Traxs7, Turgidson, Wayland, Whbrown, Wilybadger, Writtenright, Yumegusa, 281 anonymous edits

The Taming of the Shrew Source: http://en.wikipedia.org/w/index.php?oldid=380386142 Contributors: 12thNight, ALOHARONN, Absolutadam802, Achituv, Aitias, Ajraddatz, Alan smithee, Alansohn, AlbertSM, Alex S, AlexPlank, Anchoress, Andre Engels, Andreworkney, AndyJones, Andycjp, Animeangel722, AnonMoos, Anonymous Dissident, Antandrus, Art LaPella, Ashton1983, Atlant, B00P, Backslash Forwardslash, Balloonguy, Bantosh, Barbi6, Barney Jenkins, Bassbonerocks, Bearcat, Benjamin Mako Hill, Bernie Wadelheim, Bertaut, Billare, Bluepaladin, Bluesurfer42, Bobo192, Bonadea, Bridgecross, BrownHairedGirl, Browncoat101, Bruce1ee, CBorges, CCooke, CWii, Camembert, Can't sleep, clown will eat me, CardinalDan, Cate, Cattus, CelloDave, Charles Matthews, Chelsita maria, Cimon Avaro, Ckatz, Cleduc, Closedmouth, Coemgenus, Columcille, Comet Tuttle, Correogsk, Coughinink, Courcelles, Cowardly Lion, Craig Gustafson, Crouchbk, Cuckooman4, D, DGG, DMacks, Da monster under your bed, Daibhid C, Damicatz, Dark haillz, Darwinek, Dave L, Dbachmann, DeadEyeArrow, Declan Clam, Deep Shadow, Delldot, Demidivinity, Dfrg.msc, Discospinster, Doggieluver 101, Dondiboston, Dougg, Downstage right, Draggleduck, Dragonjorge, DrewSears, Dwayne, Eawonder, Ejg930, Ekellar, Error, Excirial, ExpressingYourself, Faradayplank, Favonian, Folantin, FredR, Frozenport, Fyyer, Gavri, Gettingtoit, Gillea2k8, Gimingham, Grandad, Hahreturns, Headbomb, HonoreDB, HowardW, Howcheng, Hslibrarygal, 11like2this, Ice Vision, Igodard, Iluvcole711, Imran1985, Iridescent, Itai, Ithashappenedbeforebutthereisnothingtocompareittonow, ItsLassieTime, Ivan Linares, J.delanoy, JaGa, Jegreeny, Jergen, Jhinman, Jinian, Jlittlet, JoanneB, Johnper, Joker99352, Jonemerson, JordeeBec, Joseph Solis in Australia, Josiah Rowe, Judithj1, KJS77, Kanonkas, Katalaveno, Kbdank71, Keith-264, Kelovy, Killing Vector, Kingpin13, La goutte de pluie, Lalaucafe, Lawrence King, Ld, Lightmouse, Lisa, LostBelmont, Lsaleh, Luk, Lumos3, Marek69, MarnetteD, Mattbr, Matthew Yeager, McSly, Mccaulay11, Mcorazao, Megan.rw1, Mentifisto, Midnightblueowl, Mikm, Mild Bill Hiccup, MisterHand, Mnd, Mojo lor, Morada1356, Mordechai4, Msariel, Muscleman r1, Museslave, Mysdaao, Nandesuka, NeilN, Neo-Jay, Nixeagle, Nocturnvs, NuclearWarfare, Old Moonraker, Opera hat, Orbicle, Pantherpuma, Paul A, Paul Barlow, Paweł ze Szczecina, Pcu123456789, Phgao, Philip Trueman, Pikiwyn, Pjweller, Puchiko, Quadell, QueenCake, Quuxplusone, RGCorris, Radioactivepoop, RainbowOfLight, Razorflame, Rewinn, Rideabike29, Ridernyc, Roadmr, Robertgreer, Roger Davies, Ronhjones, Rumping, Runewiki777, SYSS Mouse, SalvageTheSauce, Sango123, Schmloof, Scizor52, Scizor55, Scottandrewhutchins, Sephirothrr, Septemberfourth476, Seraphimblade, Shadowmaster13, Shamiyah, Shaun r3, Shirulashem, Shoemaker's Holiday, Shreevatsa, Smatprt, Soap, SolBasic, Someguy1221, Someone else, Spartan-James, Sprachpfleger, Starionwolf, Stephen, Stephenb, Steven Walling, Stratford490, Sverdrup, T.J.V., TFOWR, TMC1982, Taed, Tbone762, The Singing Badger, The Thing That Should Not Be, TheAznSensation, Thesavagenorwegian, Thomas Blomberg, Thumperward, Tjm123, ToKnow, Tominator 49, Tomisti, Tony Sidaway, Tregoweth, Trixi72, Tvfreak, Twooars, Ugajin, Underpuppy423, Valley2city, Valleywood, Venividiwplwiki, Versus22, VolatileChemical, Wayfarer1706, WereSpielChequers, Wereon, WhisperToMe, Wildhartlivie, William Avery, Wimt, Winstonsmith99, Wknight94, Woohookitty, Wrad, Wwefan981, XMNboy, Xlilstargirlx, Xover, Yamamoto Ichiro, Ylee, Yuriybrisk, ZooFari, Александър, 602 anonymous edits

The Seagull Source: http://en.wikipedia.org/w/index.php?oldid=375948863 Contributors: Alcmaeonid, Antaeus Feldspar, Apardoe, Artoasis, Benandorsqueaks, Brian Olsen, Charles Matthews, Cinemaniac86, ColorOfSuffering, Cturtle9, Danny, Darth Panda, David Gerard, Davidonline, Deb, Derekvanlessen, DionysosProteus, Drmies, Echinops, Excirial, ExpressingYourself, Figureskatingfan, Ganymead, Ghirlandajo, Goodmanintern, GregorB, Hammer Raccoon, Hedavid, In Defense of the Artist, Iridescent, IstvanWolf, James Crowley, Jan E. Schreiber, JanSuchy, Japanese Searobin, John of Reading, Joseph Solis in Australia, Kesla, Lynchboy, Maddog33, Malick78, Mani1, Meelar, Michael Bednarek, Michal Nebyla, MovieMadness, Netkinetic, Nivix, Paul A, Pennywisdom2099, Porqin, Qp10qp, RJHall, RandomP, RexNL, Robertgreer, Sam Hocevar, SidP, Smatprt, Someguy1221, StanStepanic, Stanislavsky, Starofwonder, Steven J. Anderson, Tabletop, Tacook47, Tassedethe, The Thing That Should Not Be, Thehipp, Timgreenwood, Travelbird, Wayland, Yossarian, Zoicon5, 100 anonymous edits

Mother Courage and Her Children Source: http://en.wikipedia.org/w/index.php?oldid=377178826 Contributors: Alien Girl Kinoko, Alpha 4615, Arcadian, Blahma, Bobo192, Bosmasije, Brooklyn-alvin, Camipco, Carinemily, Charles Matthews, Checktheemails, ChrisLeyland, Cleduc, Coffee, CommanderCool1654, Der Falke, DionysosProteus, Donreed, DropDeadGorgias, Feather Quill'89, Flewis, Ganymead, Glennwells, Gonzalo84, Ian Maxwell, InspectorTiger, Ipsherman, Jag123, Karl-Henner, Kbthompson, Kenneth M Burke, Kevin Forsyth, Kosmoshiva, Kwekubo, Ligulem, Litchick129, Lusanaherandraton, MER-C, MakeRocketGoNow, Marek69, Mau db, Mercury McKinnon, Mike Selinker, Murtasa, Nudve, Old Moonraker, Orinoco-w, Pauper Aristoteles, Pi zero, Pjmpjm, Ponyo, Rjwilmsi, Saaristo, Saluton, SeaPea, Sliggy, Sluzzelin, Sophitus, Spamguy, Sparafucil, Spitfire, Stevertigo, Tereneta, Theodolite, TomPurdue, Tomdobb, Tristan benedict, Tzavala, Victorianexplorer, Ville Siliämaa, Wayland, Weimar03, Wetman, 126 anonymous edits

Image Sources, Licenses and Contributors

File:Streep san sebastian 2008 2.jpg *Source*: http://en.wikipedia.org/w/index.php?title=File:Streep_san_sebastian_2008_2.jpg *License*: Creative Commons Attribution-Sharealike 3.0 *Contributors*: Andreas Tai

File:Meryl Streep 1989.jpg *Source*: http://en.wikipedia.org/w/index.php?title=File:Meryl_Streep_1989.jpg *License*: Creative Commons Attribution 2.0 *Contributors*: User:Wildhartlivie

File:Meryl Streep in St-Petersburg.jpg *Source*:http://en.wikipedia.org/w/index.php?title=File:Meryl_Streep_in_St-Petersburg.jpg *License*: Creative Commons Attribution-Sharealike 2.0 *Contributors*: Artem from St-Petersburg, russia

File:ABBA 2008 Av Daniel Åhs.jpg *Source*:http://en.wikipedia.org/w/index.php?title=File:ABBA_2008_Av_Daniel_Åhs.jpg *License*: Creative Commons Attribution 3.0 *Contributors*: User:Danielåhskarlsson

File:meryl streep harvard commencement 2010.JPG *Source*:http://en.wikipedia.org/w/index.php?title=File:Meryl_streep_harvard_commencement_2010.JPG *License*: GNU Free Documentation License *Contributors*: chensiyuan

Image:Merylstreep.jpg *Source*: http://en.wikipedia.org/w/index.php?title=File:Merylstreep.jpg *License*: Creative Commons Attribution 2.0 *Contributors*: Alan Light

File:Julia_imp.jpg *Source*: http://en.wikipedia.org/w/index.php?title=File:Julia_imp.jpg *License*: unknown *Contributors*: King of the North East, MachoCarioca

File:The Deer Hunter poster.jpg *Source*:http://en.wikipedia.org/w/index.php?title=File:The_Deer_Hunter_poster.jpg *License*: unknown *Contributors*: Dr. Blofeld, Erik, Lampica, Melesse, NWill, Nehrams2020, Skier Dude

File:Manhattan-poster01.jpg *Source*: http://en.wikipedia.org/w/index.php?title=File:Manhattan-poster01.jpg *License*: unknown *Contributors*: Cop 663, MachoCarioca

Image:woody allen manhattan.jpg *Source*: http://en.wikipedia.org/w/index.php?title=File:Woody_allen_manhattan.jpg *License*: unknown *Contributors*: Melesse, Morval, Nehrams2020, Skier Dude, Sugar Bear, The JPS, 1 anonymous edits

File:Seduction of Joe Tynan .jpeg *Source*: http://en.wikipedia.org/w/index.php?title=File:Seduction_of_Joe_Tynan_.jpeg *License*: unknown *Contributors*: Davidbspalding, Orbicle

File:Oscar posters 79.jpg *Source*: http://en.wikipedia.org/w/index.php?title=File:Oscar_posters_79.jpg *License*: unknown *Contributors*: MachoCarioca, Skier Dude

File:French lieutenants woman.jpeg *Source*:http://en.wikipedia.org/w/index.php?title=File:French_lieutenants_woman.jpeg *License*: unknown *Contributors*: Calmer Waters, Nehrams2020, Orbicle

File:Stillofnightposter.jpg *Source*: http://en.wikipedia.org/w/index.php?title=File:Stillofnightposter.jpg *License*: unknown *Contributors*: Aphasia83, J.D.

File:Sophie's Choice1.jpg *Source*: http://en.wikipedia.org/w/index.php?title=File:Sophie's_Choice1.jpg *License*: unknown *Contributors*: Calmer Waters, Derbent 5000, Nehrams2020, Sherool, Skier Dude

File:Silkwood_imp.jpg *Source*: http://en.wikipedia.org/w/index.php?title=File:Silkwood_imp.jpg *License*: Attribution *Contributors*: Films addicted, Grandpafootsoldier, Skier Dude, 1 anonymous edits

File:Falling in love movie poster.jpg *Source*:http://en.wikipedia.org/w/index.php?title=File:Falling_in_love_movie_poster.jpg *License*: unknown *Contributors*: Wisekwai

File:Plentyposter.jpg *Source*: http://en.wikipedia.org/w/index.php?title=File:Plentyposter.jpg *License*: Attribution *Contributors*: Grandpafootsoldier

File:Out of africa poster.jpg *Source*: http://en.wikipedia.org/w/index.php?title=File:Out_of_africa_poster.jpg *License*: unknown *Contributors*: Melesse, NWill, Nehrams2020, Project FMF, Skier Dude

File:HeartburnPoster.jpg *Source*: http://en.wikipedia.org/w/index.php?title=File:HeartburnPoster.jpg *License*: unknown *Contributors*: LiteraryMaven

File:Ironweed.jpg *Source*: http://en.wikipedia.org/w/index.php?title=File:Ironweed.jpg *License*: unknown *Contributors*: Blathnaid, Calmer Waters, MachoCarioca, Nehrams2020, Szyslak

File:Cry_in_the_dark_a_512.jpg *Source*: http://en.wikipedia.org/w/index.php?title=File:Cry_in_the_dark_a_512.jpg *License*: unknown *Contributors*: User:Briantw File:Shedevil.jpg *Source*:http://en.wikipedia.org/w/index.php?title=File:Shedevil.jpg *License*: Attribution *Contributors*: Films addicted, Grandpafootsoldier File:Postcards_from_the_edge.jpg *Source*:http://en.wikipedia.org/w/index.php?title=File:Postcards_from_the_edge.jpg *License*: unknown *Contributors*: Films addicted, ShelfSkewed, Skier Dude

File:Defending your life poster.jpg *Source*: http://en.wikipedia.org/w/index.php?title=File:Defending_your_life_poster.jpg *License*: unknown *Contributors*: Quentin X

File:Flag of the United States.svg *Source*:http://en.wikipedia.org/w/index.php?title=File:Flag_of_the_United_States.svg *License*: Public Domain *Contributors*: User:Dbenbenn, User:Indolences, User:Jacobolus, User:Technion, User:Zscout370

File:Death Becomes Her.jpg *Source*: http://en.wikipedia.org/w/index.php?title=File:Death_Becomes_Her.jpg *License*: unknown *Contributors*: Chrislk02, Grandpafootsoldier, Islander, Kbdank71, Nehrams2020, Passive, Quentin X

File:House_of_the_spirits_ver1.jpg *Source*: http://en.wikipedia.org/w/index.php?title=File:House_of_the_spirits_ver1.jpg *License*: unknown *Contributors*: Films addicted, Skier Dude

File:river_wild_movie_poster.jpg *Source*:http://en.wikipedia.org/w/index.php?title=File:River_wild_movie_poster.jpg *License*: unknown *Contributors*: Quentin X, Reimelt, Skier Dude

File:Kootenay valley.JPG *Source*:http://en.wikipedia.org/w/index.php?title=File:Kootenay_valley.JPG *License*: GNU Free Documentation License *Contributors*: User:Qyd

File:The Bridges Of Madison County.jpg *Source*:http://en.wikipedia.org/w/index.php?title=File:The_Bridges_Of_Madison_County.jpg *License*: Attribution *Contributors*: POV

File:Before and after poster.jpg *Source*:http://en.wikipedia.org/w/index.php?title=File:Before_and_after_poster.jpg *License*: unknown *Contributors*: Quentin X

File:Marvins room poster.jpg *Source*:http://en.wikipedia.org/w/index.php?title=File:Marvins_room_poster.jpg *License*: Attribution *Contributors*: User:Grandpafootsoldier

File:Dancing at Lughnasa (film).jpg *Source*:http://en.wikipedia.org/w/index.php?title=File:Dancing_at_Lughnasa_(film).jpg *License*: unknown *Contributors*: Emerson7

File:One true thing poster.jpg *Source*: http://en.wikipedia.org/w/index.php?title=File:One_true_thing_poster.jpg *License*: unknown *Contributors*: Quentin X

File:Music of the heart.jpg *Source*: http://en.wikipedia.org/w/index.php?title=File:Music_of_the_heart.jpg *License*: unknown *Contributors*: User:Grandpafootsoldier

File:AI Poster.jpg *Source*: http://en.wikipedia.org/w/index.php?title=File:AI_Poster.jpg *License*: unknown *Contributors*: Happy Evil Dude, Melesse, Nehrams2020, Skier Dude, Wildroot

File:Adaptation. film.jpg *Source*:http://en.wikipedia.org/w/index.php?title=File:Adaptation._film.jpg *License*: unknown *Contributors*: *drew, Project FMF, Skier Dude

Image:Doncage.jpg *Source*:http://en.wikipedia.org/w/index.php?title=File:Doncage.jpg *License*: Attribution *Contributors*: Wildroot

File:Hoursposter.jpg *Source*: http://en.wikipedia.org/w/index.php?title=File:Hoursposter.jpg *License*: Attribution *Contributors*: Grandpafootsoldier

File:Stuck on you ver2.jpg *Source*: http://en.wikipedia.org/w/index.php?title=File:Stuck_on_you_ver2.jpg *License*: unknown *Contributors*: Quentin X

File:The Manchurian Candidate poster.jpg *Source*:http://en.wikipedia.org/w/index.php?title=File:The_Manchurian_Candidate_poster.jpg *License*: unknown *Contributors*: MeekSaffron, PhilKnight, Tabor, Xezbeth

File:A Series Of Unfortunate Events poster.jpg *Source*:http://en.wikipedia.org/w/index.php?title=File:A_Series_Of_Unfortunate_Events_poster.jpg *License*: Attribution *Contributors*: Fuzzy510, Happy Evil Dude, JACK5555, Skier Dude, The Man in Question, Wildroot, 2 anonymous edits

File:ForcedMatte.jpg *Source*: http://en.wikipedia.org/w/index.php?title=File:ForcedMatte.jpg *License*: unknown *Contributors*: Wildroot

File:Primemovie.jpg *Source*: http://en.wikipedia.org/w/index.php?title=File:Primemovie.jpg *License*: unknown *Contributors*: Chocolateboy, Emilyn, Nehrams2020, Sfan00 IMG

File:Aphc_movieposter.jpg *Source*:http://en.wikipedia.org/w/index.php?title=File:Aphc_movieposter.jpg *License*: unknown *Contributors*: Drilnoth, Quentin X, Santress, Skier Dude

File:The Devil Wears Prada main onesheet.jpg *Source*:http://en.wikipedia.org/w/index.php?title=File:The_Devil_Wears_Prada_main_onesheet.jpg *License*: unknown *Contributors*: Daniel Case, MECU, Oden, Riana

Image:Anne Hathaway shooting DWP.jpg *Source*:http://en.wikipedia.org/w/index.php?title=File:Anne_Hathaway_shooting_DWP.jpg *License*: Creative Commons Attribution-Sharealike 2.0 *Contributors*: User:Daniel Case

Image:Emily Blunt in DWP.jpg *Source*: http://en.wikipedia.org/w/index.php?title=File:Emily_Blunt_in_DWP.jpg *License*: unknown *Contributors*: Cyrius, Daniel Case, Mangojuice, Melesse, Pd THOR

Image:Streep and Hathaway in DWP film.jpg *Source*:http://en.wikipedia.org/w/index.php?title=File:Streep_and_Hathaway_in_DWP_film.jpg *License*: unknown *Contributors*: Daniel Case, Eagle Owl

Image:McGraw-Hill Building Rock Center by David Shankbone.jpg *Source*:http://en.wikipedia.org/w/index.php?title=File:McGraw-Hill_Building_Rock_Center_by_David_Shankbone.jpg *License*: Creative Commons Attribution-Sharealike 2.5 *Contributors*: David Shankbone

Image:The devil wears Prada mod.jpg *Source*:http://en.wikipedia.org/w/index.php?title=File:The_devil_wears_Prada_mod.jpg *License*: Creative Commons Attribution 2.0 *Contributors*: User:Tabercil

License

LaVergne, TN USA
11 October 2011
200768LV00002BA/1/P

9 781742 444635